CLASSICAL MYTHOLOGY IN CONTEXT

CLASSICAL MYTHOLOGY IN CONTEXT

LISA MAURIZIO

Bates College

NEW YORK   OXFORD
OXFORD UNIVERSITY PRESS

Oxford University Press is a department of the University of Oxford.
It furthers the University's objective of excellence in research,
scholarship, and education by publishing worldwide.

Oxford   New York
Auckland   Cape Town   Dar es Salaam   Hong Kong   Karachi
Kuala Lumpur   Madrid   Melbourne   Mexico City   Nairobi
New Delhi   Shanghai   Taipei   Toronto

With offices in
Argentina   Austria   Brazil   Chile   Czech Republic   France   Greece
Guatemala   Hungary   Italy   Japan   Poland   Portugal   Singapore
South Korea   Switzerland   Thailand   Turkey   Ukraine   Vietnam

For titles covered by Section 112 of the US Higher Education
Opportunity Act, please visit www.oup.com/us/he for the
latest information about pricing and alternate formats.

Published by Oxford University Press
198 Madison Avenue, New York, New York 10016
http://www.oup.com

Library of Congress Cataloging-in-Publication Data

Maurizio, Lisa.
   Classical mythology in context / Lisa Maurizio, Bates College.
      pages cm
   ISBN 978-0-19-978283-3 (paperback : alkaline paper) 1. Mythology,
Greek. I. Title.
   BL783.M385 2016
   292.1'3--dc23
                                                     2015020910

Printing number: 9 8 7 6 5 4 3 2

Printed in the United States of America
on acid-free paper

BRIEF CONTENTS

CONTENTS

PREFACE

Classical Mythology in Context offers students an approach to understanding how Greek myths acquire meaning and significance in their historical, theoretical, comparative, and later artistic contexts. It integrates these four areas of inquiry into a dynamic, challenging, yet accessible format. *Classical Mythology in Context* is further distinguished by its inclusion of a robust selection of Greek sources, as well as Roman and Ancient Near Eastern texts, drawn from the acclaimed Oxford World's Classics and other authoritative translations.

A key challenge faced by teachers of introductory courses in classical mythology is deciding which myths students should study, and in what form. Most professors want students to encounter myths in their original form instead of through popularized versions or bowdlerized summaries. Yet it is sometimes difficult to choose between complete literary works, whose meanings often require substantial interpretation, and summaries that aim to distill the mythic content of such works. *Classical Mythology in Context* responds to this problem by seamlessly integrating authoritative translations of the most commonly taught texts in a classical mythology course.

Almost all scholars agree that the most relevant Greek literary sources for approaching classical mythology are the Homeric *Hymns*, Hesiod's *Theogony* and *Works and Days*, the Homeric epics, and Greek tragedies. *Classical Mythology in Context* includes *Theogony* and many of the Homeric *Hymns* in their entirety. It also features selections from the epics and tragedies chosen both to exemplify the themes discussed in the chapter and to allow students to thoughtfully apply the critical approaches proposed in each Theory section and extend their inquiry into the myth's resonance in modern and contemporary culture. These Greek sources, either thoughtfully excerpted or presented in their entirety, include the following:

Aeschylus, ***Prometheus Bound*** [Translated by James Scully and C. John Herington. *The Complete Aeschylus Volume II: Persians and Other Plays*. Peter Burian and Alan Shapiro, eds. Oxford University Press, 2009.]

Aeschylus, ***Eumenides*** [Aeschylus, *The Oresteia*. Translated by Alan Shapiro and Peter Burian. Oxford University Press, 2003.]

Euripides, ***Bacchae*** [Euripides, *Bacchae and Other Plays*. Translated by James Morwood. Oxford World's Classics. Oxford University Press, 2008.]

Euripides, ***Iphigenia among the Taurians*** [Euripides, *Bacchae and Other Plays*. Translated by James Morwood. Oxford World's Classics. Oxford University Press, 2008.]

Euripides, *Medea* [Euripides, *Medea and Other Plays*. Translated by James Morwood. Oxford World's Classics. Oxford University Press, 2008.]

Hesiod, *Theogony* [Hesiod, *Theogony and Works and Days*. Translated by M. L. West. Oxford World's Classics. Oxford University Press, 2008.]

Hesiod, *Works and Days* [Hesiod, *Theogony and Works and Days*. Translated by M. L. West. Oxford World's Classics. Oxford University Press, 2008.]

Homer, *The Iliad* [Homer, *The Iliad*. Translated by Barry B. Powell. Oxford University Press, 2014.]

Homer, *The Odyssey* [Homer, *The Odyssey*. Translated by Barry B. Powell. Oxford University Press, 2014.]

The Homeric Hymns [*The Homeric Hymns*. Translated by Michael Crudden. Oxford World's Classics. Oxford University Press, 2008.]:
- *Hymn 2: To Demeter*
- *Hymn 3: To Apollo*
- *Hymn 4: To Hermes*
- *Hymn 5: To Aphrodite*
- *Hymn 7: To Dionysos*
- *Hymn 27: To Artemis*

Plato, *Phaedrus* [Plato, *Phaedrus*. Translated by Robin Waterfield. Oxford World's Classics. Oxford University Press, 2009.]

Xenophon, *An Ephesian Tale* [Translated by Stephen M. Trzaskoma. *Two novels from Ancient Greece: Chariton's Callirhoe and Xenophon of Ephesos' An Ephesian Story: Anthia and Habrocomes*. Hackett Publishing Company, 2010.]

Roman sources include selections from or the entire works from the following list:

Catullus, "Attis" [Catullus, *The Complete Poems*. Translated by Guy Lee. Oxford World's Classics. Oxford University Press, 2008.]

Ovid, *Metamorphoses* [Ovid, *Metamorphoses*. Translated by A. D. Melville. Oxford World's Classics. Oxford University Press, 2008.]

Unknown, "The Acts of Paul and Thecla" [Translated by J. K. Elliott. *The Apocryphal Jesus: Legends of the Early Church*. J. K. Elliott, ed. Oxford University Press, 2008.]

Virgil, *Aeneid* [Virgil, *Aeneid*. Translated by Frederick Ahl. Oxford World's Classics. Oxford University Press, 2008.]

Ancient Near Eastern sources include selections from or the entire works from the following list:

"Cosmogonies at the Temple of Esna" [*Ancient Egyptian Science: A Source Book. Vol. 1, Part 2, Knowledge and Order.* Translated and edited by Marshall Clagett. American Philosophical Society, 1989.]

The Descent of Ishtar to the Underworld [*Myths from Mesopotamia: Creation, The Flood, Gilgamesh, and Others.* Translated by Stephanie Dalley. Oxford World's Classics. Oxford University Press, 2008.]

Epic of Gilgamesh [*Myths from Mesopotamia: Creation, The Flood, Gilgamesh, and Others.* Translated by Stephanie Dalley. Oxford World's Classics. Oxford University Press, 2008.]

Genesis [*The New Oxford Annotated Bible with Apocrypha.* New Revised Standard Version, 4th Edition. Oxford University Press, 2010.]

"The Hymn to Thoth" [*Ancient Egyptian Literature: The New Kingdom.* Translated and edited by Miriam Lichtheim. University of California Press, 2006.]

In the Desert by the Early Grass [*The Harps that Once . . . Sumerian Poetry in Translation.* Translated by Thorkild Jacobson. Yale University Press, 1997.]

APPROACH

Classical Mythology in Context allows students to directly encounter and explore ancient myths, whether they are told in words or images, and encourages students to understand myth in broader interpretative contexts. To this end, *Classical Mythology in Context* features:

- A sustained discussion of religious practices and sacred places that offers a key approach to the historical contextualization of Greek myths.
- An introduction to—and integration of—theoretical approaches to myth in each chapter, with paired chapters that demonstrate how theoretical approaches both enrich and complicate the ways in which myths and mythic figures can be understood.
- A thorough comparative approach that examines Greek myths alongside other myths from the Mediterranean basin and the Ancient Near East. Paired chapters introduce the people and cultures of Greece's neighboring regions.
- An approach to the reception of myths as interpretation and reflection in Western art, with an emphasis on contemporary culture.

ORGANIZATION AND STRUCTURE

Each chapter (with the exception of Chapter 1) coheres around one primary figure or topic. The modular structure of each chapter is built on the foundation of the four main components—or challenges—of a classical mythology course:

1. History
2. Theory
3. Comparison
4. Reception

Each of these sections aims to suggest interpretative questions about the myths under consideration, instead of simply providing all the facts about and various treatments of a particular myth or figure.

This modular structure provides teachers and students with two key benefits. First, the clear articulation of these sections indicates to students the various aspects and components of the study of myth. As students explore and then make distinctions among the different ways—historical, theoretical, comparative, and artistic—by which they can examine myths, they begin to discern the benefits and limitations of each approach. This encourages them to think critically about their own preferences.

Second, because each chapter's sections are discrete and clearly labeled, professors can easily survey their contents and select which sections to assign and in what order. For example, although the sections on theoretical questions and mythic reinventions are designed to deepen and inform students' understanding of the chapter's material, these sections can be either omitted or paired with material in other chapters. Although sections can be omitted, the appearance of these sections in each chapter nonetheless demonstrates that each type of approach is always possible and relevant to the understanding of every myth.

HISTORY

The "History" section of each chapter introduces fundamental historical and cultural concepts surrounding the chapter's main myth or topic. Over the course of several chapters, students will gradually build a comprehensive understanding of the historical context of Greek myths. For example, Chapter 2, "Creation," presents Greece's relationship to its neighbors in the Mediterranean in order to explore their respective creation myths, whereas Chapter 4, "Demeter and Hades," introduces the concept of mystery cults in contrast to civic religion in order to consider how both the Eleusinian Mysteries and the Homeric *Hymn to Demeter* address Greek understandings of (and anxieties about) mortality.

The narratives in the History sections are followed by substantial selections of literary sources from Greece as well as examples of visual art in different media and depictions of material evidence from Greece. Visual materials are judiciously selected to provide evidence of, for example, a god or goddess's attributes that are not evident in the literary sources.

THEORY

The second module in each chapter, "Theory," highlights a key theoretical approach to myths that might fruitfully be applied to the chapter's topic. Almost all of these sections contain a robust excerpt from the work of an influential scholar of myth, exposing students to the practices and rigors of literary scholarship and criticism. An introductory précis of the module's featured theory or theoretical school helps students to access the chosen reading with confidence and deploy the theoretical concepts therein to interpret myths.

Whereas the critical readings introduce students to the unique voice, style, and modes of argumentation of different scholars and also enrich their understanding of their own ideas, the readings are sufficiently thorough to allow for flexibility. Each theoretical section both complements and complicates the myths in the chapter in which it is placed, but its structure and content is flexible enough to allow instructors to assign it in a different chapter. Many chapters are "paired" in a way that allows for such enriching comparisons to be made, creating an opportunity for the kinds of scholarly conversations and inquiry in which classical scholars are engaged. Finally, general terms categorizing theory are presented and reinforced in these sections to help students organize these theories and compare them to one another.

COMPARISON

The third module, "Comparison," provides an introduction to literary and visual depictions of myths from the Mediterranean basin and the Ancient Near East. Comparative material allows students to frame a question about aspects or features of the Greek material they have encountered in the History section of the chapter. The objective of this module is to situate ancient Greece in broader geographical and linguistic contexts, raising questions of cultural diffusion and influence that might explain what is shared and what is unique in Greek myths. Emphasis is placed on the insights comparative material might shed on Greek myths and the avenues of inquiry such insights afford.

In some instances, parallel or related stories that may not have influenced Greek myths but nonetheless may point out an interesting aspect in the Greek material are featured. For example, Catullus's poem "Attis" (Chapter 9, "Dionysus") offers a fictional account of one man's experience of worshipping the goddess Cybele and joining a mystery cult. Each Comparison module introduces students to different pathways for understanding comparative mythology and along the way suggests the interconnections between Greece and its geographical and linguistic neighbors and forbears.

RECEPTION

The final module of each chapter, "Reception," provides a sustained examination of one specific myth or mythic theme through vivid—and occasionally provocative—examples of the visual and performing arts as well as poetry. Modern and contemporary artists, writers, playwrights, and filmmakers are featured. In this way, *Classical Mythology in Context* demonstrates to students that representations of classical mythology continue to resonate in surprising ways in the work of contemporary artists from diverse backgrounds working in many different media.

Classical Mythology in Context supports the way classical mythology courses are taught today. It features a generous selection of primary sources in authoritative translation; it incorporates the most recent scholarship by established classicists on how material culture is necessary to understanding religion and ritual; it moves important theoretical approaches to myth from the margins of consideration to the center of students' understanding; it encourages awareness of how Greece's place in the Mediterranean and its cultural connections to the Ancient Near East have contributed to the contours of its mythology and religion; and it provokes further thought and analysis through later reinventions of myth.

FEATURES

A study of classical myths should engage students' imagination. Yet classical myths can sometimes overwhelm students with unfamiliar names and unusual stories with many different and conflicting versions. The following features give students tools and resources to use when engaging with this sometimes difficult ancient material.

- **Compelling and relevant illustrations** The stories and characters of Greek and Ancient Near Eastern mythology are brought to life through a robust and thoughtful selection of images and artifacts. Every image is clearly referred to and discussed in the chapter text, deepening student engagement with both textual and visual resources. (All images are available as PowerPoint presentations; see "Additional Teaching and Learning Resources," below, for further information.)
- **Abundant maps** With the exception of Chapter 1, the History and Comparison sections of every chapter include maps that help students locate all sites in Greece as well as the Mediterranean basin world and in the Ancient Near East referred to in the chapter. In addition, the introduction to Part I includes a detailed map of the ancient Greek world.

- **Timeline** A detailed timeline for Greece, Rome, and the Ancient Near East helps students situate key works within their cultural and historical contexts. The timeline appears in the introduction to Part I.
- **"The Essentials"** With the exception of Chapter 1, each chapter in Part I begins with "The Essentials," a box that introduces students to the most essential information about a god or goddess, such as parentage, offspring, attributes, cult titles, rituals, and sanctuaries. In Part II, these boxes appear throughout the chapter at each point at which a new hero or heroine is introduced. These boxes help students preview a chapter's content as well as review the most important information about the main characters of Greek mythology.
- **"Before You Read"** Every primary source reading in the History and Comparison sections, and every critical reading in the Theory sections, is prefaced with a brief contextual overview followed by questions that encourage critical thinking about and engagement with the text. The questions are designed to facilitate comprehension and review, as well as prompt classroom discussion.
- **"Key Terms"** This carefully selected list at the end of each chapter helps students review and retain its most important points.
- **"For Further Exploration"** This brief, annotated bibliography at the end of each chapter provides a starting point for students who wish to learn more about the chapter's key figures, myths, and interpretations.
- **Select Bibliography** At the end of the book, a bibliography divided by chapter (and further divided by chapter section) emphasizes scholarly works that are both available and accessible to the general reader.
- **Combined glossary and index** The index includes a pronunciation key, the Greek form (where relevant), and a brief description of all figures, places, rituals, and similar things and concepts in the book.

ADDITIONAL TEACHING AND LEARNING RESOURCES

Classical Mythology in Context offers a complete suite of ancillaries for both instructors and students.

On the Ancillary Resource Center (http://oup-arc.com/) adopters can obtain access to the Instructor's Resource Manual, which provides lecture outlines, discussion questions, and suggested addiitonal sources for the History, Theory, Comparison, and Reception modules in each chapter, as well as a test bank of questions that can be used for assessment. PowerPoint-based slides of all of the photos, maps, and line art in the text are also available to adopters, as are lecture slides for each chapter.

For students, a comprehensive, open access companion website (www. oup.com/us/maurizio) offers quiz questions, flashcards, author videos, and links to YouTube videos.

Oxford University Press also provides discounted packaging for customers wishing to assign *Classical Mythology* with any **Oxford World's Classic** text (**www.oup.com/us/owc**). For more information, please contact your Oxford University Press sales representative at 1-800-445-9714.

A NOTE ON SPELLING

Most readers of literature and myths from ancient Greece are familiar with Latinized names of Greek words. "Achilles" is the great hero of Homer's *Iliad*, while Oedipus is protagonist of Sophocles' tragedy *Oedipus Rex*. Fewer readers have seen (and could easily pronounce) "Akhilleus" or "Oidipous." Yet, these two spellings replicate the Greek names of these heroes (᾿Αχιλλεύς and Οἰδίπους) more closely than their familiar Latin forms. The following list explains many of the differences between Greek words and their Latin and English forms.

Greek υ (upsilon) becomes y
Greek χ (chi) becomes ch
Greek κ (kappa) becomes c
Greek αι (alpha + iota) becomes ae or e
Greek ει (epsilon + iota) becomes ei or e
Greek ου (omicron + upsilon) becomes u
Greek οι (omicron + iota) becomes oe or i
Final ε or η (epsilon or eta) becomes a
Final ον (omicron + nu) becomes um
Final ος (omicron + sigma) becomes os

In this book, as in most of Oxford World's Classics translations that are included in each chapter, preference is given to the familiar Latin forms, though a few Greek spellings appear in the text and in translations of Greek literature. The index helpfully provides Greek forms should readers encounter any variants.

A NOTE ON DATES

Dates for historical events and figures, works of art, and periods of time are often a matter of well-reasoned conjecture based on available sources, whether written texts or material evidence. The dates for the periods, people, and events in Greek history provided in the Timeline follow *Ancient Greece: A Political, Social, and Cultural History* (Oxford University Press: 3rd Edition, 2011) by Sarah B. Pomeroy,

Stanley M. Burstein, Walter Donlan, Jennifer Tolbert Roberts, and David Tandy. The dates in the Roman and Ancient Near East sections of the timeline and elsewhere in the text reflect general scholarly consensus.

ACKNOWLEDGMENTS

Writing about Dionysus in his book *Coping with the Gods: Wayward Readings in Greek Theology*, Henk S. Versnel notes that the Greeks did not try to coordinate and organize their many different ways of thinking about their gods. He warns that "inconsistency, confusion, and conflict looms large" whenever we attempt such a feat. His suggestion, then, "is to follow the Greeks in *not* doing that, or if you must, for instance when you suffer from the regrettable ambition to write a textbook, consistently to avoid generalizing statements (which would, as I well realize, make it a particularly unreadable textbook . . .)." Now that this textbook about Greek gods and goddesses has been written, I can say that my regrets were few, and all of them were balanced by the pleasures that accrued from trying to effectively communicate what is beautiful, compelling, and mysterious about Greek gods and Greek myths to all readers, especially to students.

A textbook is about instructing and learning, about one's life as a student and a teacher. And for me life in the classroom has been wonderful—beginning with Mrs. Klein of Public School 160 in Brooklyn, New York, who with her wisdom and kindness made learning a possibility and offered a harbor in the storm. In college and graduate school, I had the good fortune to learn all things Greek from Deborah Boedeker, Mary Lefkowitz, and Miranda Marvin at Wellesley College. At Princeton University, I first studied myth with Richard P. Martin. I would have never earned my degree or been able to write this textbook if I had not worked with him. I am more grateful than I can express, and I know that this textbook represents but a small nugget of what I learned from him. With W. Robert Connor I studied Greek religion and learned above all else how to love the Greeks with abandon. What a whirlwind it has been since learning that lesson. Although there are many more teachers, and indeed many students, I could thank, and with good reason, I turn to colleagues and friends who were present during the time of writing of this textbook.

Bates College has provided a congenial environment in which to work. I am grateful for its sabbatical policy as well as many supportive colleagues and wonderful students whose curiosity and industriousness have contributed to this book in many ways. In particular, my colleague and friend Harry Walker has been generous with his time. He entertained fancies and sometimes, it seemed, spun gold from straw as he helped transform inklings into ideas. Other colleagues and friends have offered conversation, meals, laughter, and good ideas and good desserts, thereby helping this project along.

They include, in no particular order, Misty Beck, Loring Danforth, Elizabeth Eames, Sue Houchins, Kirk Read, Rebecca Herzig, Camille Parrish, Myron Beasley, Aslaug Asgeirsdottir, and Karen Melvin.

Among those who have contributed to the writing of this book in various ways from a distance, I thank Deborah Lyons, Moshe Sluhovsky, David Frankfurter, Anath Golomb, Matthew P. Dillon, Esther Eidinow, and most of all Flora Kimmich, who offered sage advice serendipitously but seemingly just when needed. Most serendipitously of all, Ian Morris first suggested this project and so to him I offer big thanks. Special thanks are due to Eric Cline who kindly and thoroughly reviewed early chapters that included material on the Ancient Near East.

At Oxford University Press in New York City, I have had the good fortune of working with two editors who have made this textbook both conceivable and possible. Charles Cavaliere consistently offered assistance, support, and energy. He has been the guiding genie behind this work, and his efforts and enthusiasm have made all the difference, perhaps more than he realizes. Meg Botteon has infused this textbook with her intelligence, wit, and insight. I wish I could thank her enough. So often we had (and I don't believe I imagined this) fun collaborating on a project that took shape before our eyes and grew in promise: the promise of offering the student and intelligent reader approaches to the vibrant and tangled world of Greek myths that in some small way matched the exuberance of the myths themselves. Barbara Mathieu, with imperturbable calm and organizational acumen, oversaw the production of the book; Francelle Carapetyan, polyglot and wise purveyor of images, managed the artwork; David Kear made the index especially robust and useful, by dexterously weaving a glossary and pronunciation guide into its entries; Laura Wilmot performed the Herculean and unsung task of copy-editing, while Lynn Luecken seemed to manage all manner of work that no one else did or could, with patience and competence. Michele Laseau's design is readily visible and readily beautiful for all to see and appreciate as they navigate this book.

In no small measure, I thank my very own heroine, Margaret, who encouraged, cajoled, inspired, supported, and spent many nights alone while I wrote this textbook. She is my lifeline and my love who brightens dark places.

Finally, to the many anonymous reviewers who now are named and who read many chapters and commented at length, I offer my gratitude. I have very much appreciated the conversation that their willingness to review this textbook has generated, albeit a conversation that took place through paper and e-mail and at a distance. Their comments often included their own experiences in the classroom. Reading them renewed my confidence in the deep and abiding pleasures and learning that can happen when teachers and students study Greek gods, goddesses, heroes, and heroines together.

Reviewers

Henry Bayerle, Oxford College of Emory University
Marie-Claire Beaulieu, Tufts University
Eve A. Browning, University of Minnesota Duluth
Joel Christensen, University of Texas at San Antonio
Keith Dickson, Purdue University
Matthew Dillon, Loyola Marymount University
Marcia D.-S. Dobson, Colorado College
Kimberly Felos, St. Petersburg College
Robert Forman, St. John's University
David Frankfurter, Boston University
Krin Gabbard, Stony Brook University
John Gibert, University of Colorado Boulder
John Given, East Carolina University
Fritz Graf, Ohio State University
Daniel E. Harris-McCoy, Wellesley College
Shane Hawkins, Carleton University
Yurie Hong, Gustavus Adolphus College
William Hutton, College of William & Mary
Micaela Janan, Duke University
Rachel Ahern Knudsen, University of Oklahoma
Thomas Kohn, Wayne State University
John R. Lenz, Drew University
Victor A. Leuci, Westminster College
Penny Livermore, Loyola University Chicago
Deborah Lyons, Miami University
Robin Mitchell-Boyask, Temple University
Joseph O'Connor, Georgetown University, Emeritus
Oliver Ranner, Loyola University
Robert Schon, University of Arizona
Judith Lynn Sebesta, University of South Dakota
Christine A. Smith, Washington University in St. Louis
Martha C. Taylor, Loyola University Maryland
Han Tran, University of Miami

Class Testers

Marie-Claire Beaulieu, Tufts University
Victor A. Leuci, Westminster College
Deborah Lyons, Miami University
Christine A. Smith, Washington University in St. Louis

ABOUT THE AUTHOR

Lisa Maurizio is Associate Professor of Classical and Medieval Studies at Bates College in Lewiston, Maine. She received her PhD from Princeton University. She has taught at Wellesley College, Stanford University, and University of Massachusetts at Amherst. She publishes on Greek religious practices, especially divination at Delphi. In addition, she has written several plays on classical themes, two of which have been produced by Animus Ensemble at the Boston Center for the Arts, "Tereus in Fragments" and "The Memory of Salt."

CLASSICAL
MYTHOLOGY
IN CONTEXT

GENEALOGY OF THE GREEK GODS

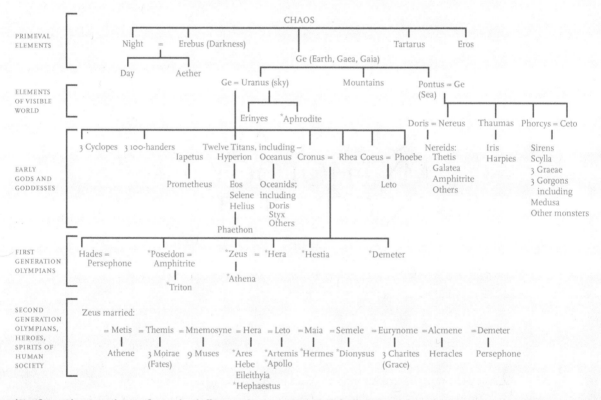

CHAOS

PRIMEVAL ELEMENTS

Night = Erebus (Darkness)   Tartarus   Eros

Day   Aether

Ge (Earth, Gaea, Gaia)

ELEMENTS OF VISIBLE WORLD

Ge = Uranus (sky)   Mountains   Pontus = Ge (Sea)

Erinyes   *Aphrodite   Doris = Nereus   Thaumas   Phorcys = Ceto

EARLY GODS AND GODDESSES

3 Cyclopes   3 100-handers   Twelve Titans, including –

Iapetus   Hyperion   Oceanus   Cronus = Rhea   Coeus = Phoebe

Nereids:
Thetis
Galatea
Amphitrite
Others

Iris
Harpies

Sirens
Scylla
3 Graeae
3 Gorgons
including
Medusa
Other monsters

Prometheus   Eos   Oceanids;   Leto
            Selene   including
            Helius   Doris
                     Styx
                     Others

Phaethon

FIRST GENERATION OLYMPIANS

Hades =   *Poseidon =   *Zeus = *Hera   *Hestia   *Demeter
Persephone   Amphitrite

*Athena

*Triton

SECOND GENERATION OLYMPIANS, HEROES, SPIRITS OF HUMAN SOCIETY

Zeus married:

= Metis   = Themis   = Mnemosyne   = Hera   = Leto   = Maia   = Semele   = Eurynome   = Alcmene   = Demeter

Athene   3 Moirae   9 Muses   *Ares   *Artemis *Hermes *Dionysus 3 Charites   Heracles   Persephone
         (Fates)   Hebe   *Apollo   (Grace)
                            Eileithyia
                            *Hephaestus

*Signifies an Olympian god; = signifies "produced offspring with." From *A Study Guide for Classical Mythology*. John T. Davis. Burgess Publishing Co.

PART I

GODDESSES AND GODS

In the center of ancient Athens, there was the Altar of the Twelve Gods. This monument consisted of a rectangular altar surrounded by a low wall that created a square enclosure of roughly thirty feet on each side. The altar was erected when Athens was ruled by tyrants (522 BCE) and was damaged when the Persians invaded Greece. The Athenians repaired the monument during the apex of their democracy (425 BCE). It was at this time that they came to associate the Altar of the Twelve Gods with the Goddess of Pity, because so many people sought asylum there—and because the Athenians came to believe that offering shelter to suppliants was a measure of the generosity and strength of their democracy and their gods. The Altar of the Twelve Gods had other, more pragmatic, purposes as well: it served as a milestone from which distances in Athens were measured.

The Altar of the Twelve Gods in Athens is important evidence that the Greeks singled out twelve of their many gods to worship as a group (even if the gods included on the altar have not been identified, and even if they differed from groups of twelve gods found in other Greek cities). In depictions of their myths, the Greeks increasingly grouped together twelve gods, known as the Olympians, as their major deities. Not far from the Altar of the Twelve Gods in Athens, for example, a frieze of twelve Olympian gods sitting together in regal repose was carved on the Parthenon, a temple devoted to Athena.

Grouping together the most important Olympians was one way the Greeks organized their gods. The chapters in the first part of this textbook accordingly concentrate on the deities whom the Greeks frequently included in depictions of the twelve Olympians. (In the second part, we turn to the heroes and heroines who achieved mythic stature despite being only partly divine, or even wholly human.) In addition to creating canonical groups of twelve Olympians, the Greeks placed all their gods and goddesses in a large network of family relationships (Genealogy of the Greek Gods, p. 2).

Hesiod's poem the *Theogony* describes this vast network of Greek gods and goddesses. Although not to be considered a sacred text (like the Islamic Qur'an or the Christian Bible), the *Theogony* was important to the Greeks for understanding their theology and cosmology (Chapter 2.1). It provides one way to understand which gods and goddesses came to be important enough to be included among the canonical twelve Olympians. "Olympian" was a general term used to describe the gods who were imagined to dwell on Mount Olympus in the skies. Rhea and Cronus were the immediate ancestors of the Olympians; they themselves belonged to an earlier generation of gods, called Titans, whom the Olympians eventually defeat. Hesiod lists six offspring of Rhea and Cronus who are often counted among the canonical twelve (*Theogony* 374–378). These are as follows:

1. Hestia
2. Demeter
3. Hera
4. Hades
5. Poseidon
6. Zeus

The other Olympians included among the canonical twelve include Zeus's offspring from goddesses and mortal women:

7. Aphrodite, from the goddess Dione (*Iliad* 5.370)
8. Athena, from the goddess Metis (*Theogony* 700–710)
9. Apollo, from the goddess Leto (*Theogony* 726–728)
10. Artemis, from the goddess Leto (*Theogony* 726–728)
11. Ares, from the goddess Hera (*Theogony* 729–730)
12. Hephaestus, from the goddess Hera *without Zeus* (*Theogony* 734)
13. Hermes, from the nymph Maia (*Theogony* 744–745)
14. Dionysus, from the mortal woman Semele (*Theogony* 746–748)

It is worth noting that Aphrodite is always included among the twelve Olympians, although she was born before Rhea and Cronus in Hesiod's *Theogony* (156–170). Only in the *Iliad* is she described as the daughter of Zeus and the goddess Dione. Also of note is that Hephaestus is the son of Hera alone in the *Theogony*, although elsewhere he is the son of Zeus and Hera.

This list, as you will no doubt have noticed, contains *fourteen* Olympians; all of their names can be found in the titles of the chapters in Part I. This expansion suggests the variations that can be found in ancient groupings of the twelve Olympians. For example, Hades and Hestia were often not included in such groups. Hades was frequently excluded because he dwelled almost exclusively in the Underworld, not on Olympus with the other gods. He is granted a prominent role here, in Chapter 4.1, for two reasons. First, he is implicated in a myth that is critical to understanding Demeter and her worship in Eleusis. Second, he plays an important role in Greek concepts about the Underworld and death. Hestia is the firstborn of Cronus and Rhea; however, she is seldom represented in written or visual sources and has few forms of worship. Nonetheless, she is included here in Chapter 7.1 because she offers a compelling contrast to the god Hermes. Interestingly, Hermes and Dionysus are sometimes excluded from the twelve Olympians—in part because their mothers are not goddesses. However, both gods were widely worshipped and were often represented in myths. Organizing the following chapters around fourteen Olympians follows ancient practices by including those deities of greatest importance to the ancient Greeks.

Although it may seem entirely sensible to organize a book about Greek mythology around the major Olympian gods and goddesses, it is worth considering if this is the ideal (or, indeed, the only) way to arrange this material. To use the gods and goddesses as organizing principles for these chapters suggests that Greek deities can, and perhaps should, be understood as characters with consistent and coherent psychological profiles who operate in an extended family. To do so enhances our sense of the myths as "stories," and of the deities as literary characters whose motives and deeds can be understood as (almost) human. The Greek texts and illustrations in each chapter show that the Greeks did, in fact, represent the gods as tangibly and unapologetically human. As depicted in myth, drama, verse, and the visual arts, these gods appear both beautiful and vain, passionate and cruel, and creative and destructive—as both upholders of order and instigators of rebellion.

Yet the Olympians (and all of the other Greek gods) were emphatically *not* human beings. Their attributes and their personalities varied according to time, place, and custom. Above all, Greek gods and goddesses were *religious* conceptions—they came to life, so to speak, when they were worshipped. They were also aesthetic conceptions, which took form when artists painted them on vases, carved them in stone, or evoked them in verse. Different worshippers and different artists had different understandings of the gods. It becomes clear that although Greek gods and goddesses have recognizable traits, they do not have coherent psychological profiles.

To understand Greek deities as religious and aesthetic conceptions, Part I investigates the most important Greek gods as objects of worship that changed over time and place, that influenced and were influenced by local deities and practices as well as in the Ancient Near East and Mediterranean basin (Timeline of Classical Mythology, pp. 6–7), that prompted a range of theoretical inquiries across academic disciplines, and that inspired modern and contemporary artists. Approached from these four different contexts, a rich and varied understanding of Greek gods and goddesses and the mythological web in which they were woven can be perceived. Finally, and most importantly, by presenting a number of contexts in which to observe Greek gods and goddesses, these chapters ask you to investigate the appeal and meaning they had for the ancients and their continued resonance in our culture today.

Timeline of Classical Mythology

	GREECE	ANCIENT NEAR EAST	ITALY
EARLY BRONZE AGE 3000–2100 BCE		**MESOPOTAMIA (SUMER)** Writing systems develop (c. 3000 BCE) **MESOPOTAMIA** Gilgamesh rules the city of Uruk (c. 2800 BCE) **MESOPOTAMIA** Sargon of Akkad defeats the Sumerian states (c. 2300 BCE)	
MIDDLE BRONZE AGE 2100–1600 BCE		**MESOPOTAMIA** *In the Desert of the Early Grass* (1750 BCE) **ANATOLIA** Rise of Hittite Empire (1750 BCE) **EGYPT** *Hymn to Thoth* (1332 BCE)	
LATE BRONZE AGE (MYCENAEAN) 1600–1150 BCE	Linear B used in mainland Greece Mycenae and other cities destroyed (1200–1150 BCE)	**MESOPOTAMIA** *Epic of Gilgamesh, Enuma Elish,* and *The Descent of Ishtar* (early versions) **ANATOLIA** Troy destroyed (1200–1150 BCE)	
IRON AGE 1150–750 BCE	First Olympics (776 BCE)	**MESOPOTAMIA** *Epic of Gilgamesh, Enuma Elish,* and *The Descent of Ishtar* (standard versions) **ANATOLIA** Height of the Phrygian Empire and worship of Cybele (eighth century BCE) **LEVANT** Israelites, Philistines, and Phoenicians flourish in the region **LEVANT** Portions of the Hebrew Bible, including Genesis, composed	Traditional founding date of Rome (753 BCE)

	GREECE	ANCIENT NEAR EAST	ITALY
ARCHAIC PERIOD 750–490 BCE	Homer (750 BCE), *Iliad* and *Odyssey* Hesiod (700 BCE), *Theogony* and *Works and Days* Anonymous (700 BCE), *Homeric Hymns* ATHENS Peisistratid tyranny (546–510 BCE) ATHENS Democratic reforms (508 BCE)	LEVANT Portions of Hebrew Bible, including Genesis, redacted	Roman Republic begins (509 BCE)
CLASSICAL PERIOD 490–323 BCE	Persian Invasion of Greece (490–479 BCE) Aeschylus (525–456 BCE), *Prometheus Bound* and *Oresteia* Sophocles (497–406 BCE) Herodotus (484–425 BCE), *Histories* Peloponnesian War (431–404 BCE) Euripides (480–407 BCE), *Medea, Bacchae, Iphigenia among the Taurians* Plato (429–347 BCE), *Symposium*	EGYPT Alexander the Great conquers Egypt (336–323 BCE) MESOPOTAMIA Alexander the Great captures Babylon (331 BCE) and dies in Babylon (323 BCE)	
HELLENISTIC PERIOD 323–30 BCE	Greece comes under Roman control (146 BCE) Apollonius of Rhodes (c. third century BCE), *Argonautica*	EGYPT *Cosmologies at the Temple of Esna* (second century BCE) LEVANT Region conquered by Rome (66–62 BCE) EGYPT Region conquered by Rome (31 BCE)	
IMPERIAL ROMAN PERIOD 30 BCE–476 CE	Plutarch (46–120 CE) Pausanias (115–180 CE), *Description of Greece* Xenophon (c. 150 CE), *An Ephesian Tale* Anonymous (c. 150 CE), *The Acts of Paul and Thecla*	LEVANT birth of Jesus (1 CE) ANATOLIA Ephesus is named the provincial capital of the region under Rome's control (30 CE)	Senate grants Octavian the title of Augustus (27 BCE) Catullus (84–54 BCE), *Attis* Vergil (70 BCE–19 CE), *Aeneid* Ovid (43–17 CE), *Metamorphoses* Seneca (4 BCE–65 CE), *Medea* Apuleius (c. 123 CE), *Cupid and Psyche*

Greece and Greek-Speaking Cities in Anatolia

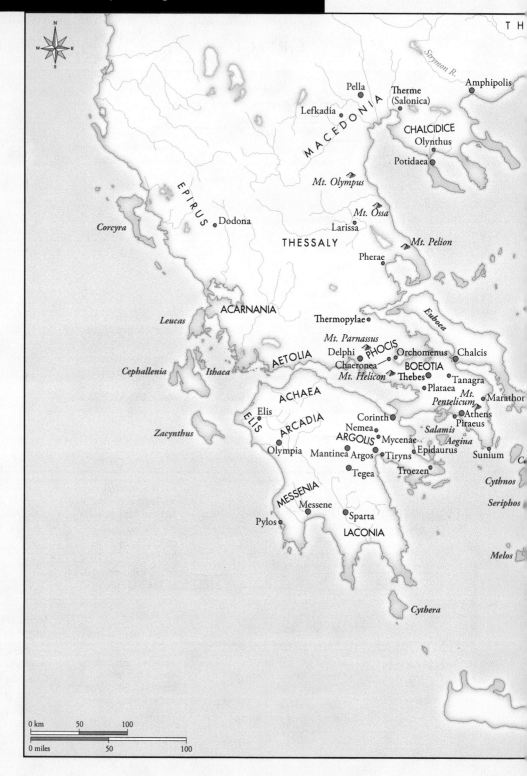

T H

Amphipolis

Pella
Therme
(Salonica)

Lefkadia

MACEDONIA

CHALCIDICE
Olynthus

Potidaea

Mt. Olympus

Strymon R.

EPIRUS

Corcyra

Dodona

Mt. Ossa
Larissa

THESSALY

Mt. Pelion

Pherae

ACARNANIA

Euboea

Leucas

Thermopylae

Mt. Parnassus

AETOLIA

Delphi PHOCIS Orchomenus Chalcis
Chaeronea
Cephallenia *Ithaca* BOEOTIA
Mt. Helicon Thebes Tanagra
Plataea *Mt.*
ACHAEA *Pentelicum* Marathor
Elis Athens
ELIS Corinth Piraeus
Nemea *Salamis*
ARCADIA ARGOLIS Mycenae *Aegina*
Zacynthus Olympia Epidaurus Sunium
Mantinea Argos Tiryns
Tegea Troezen *Cythnos*

Seriphos

MESSENIA
Messene
Pylos Sparta

LACONIA

Melos

Cythera

0 km   50   100

0 miles   50   100

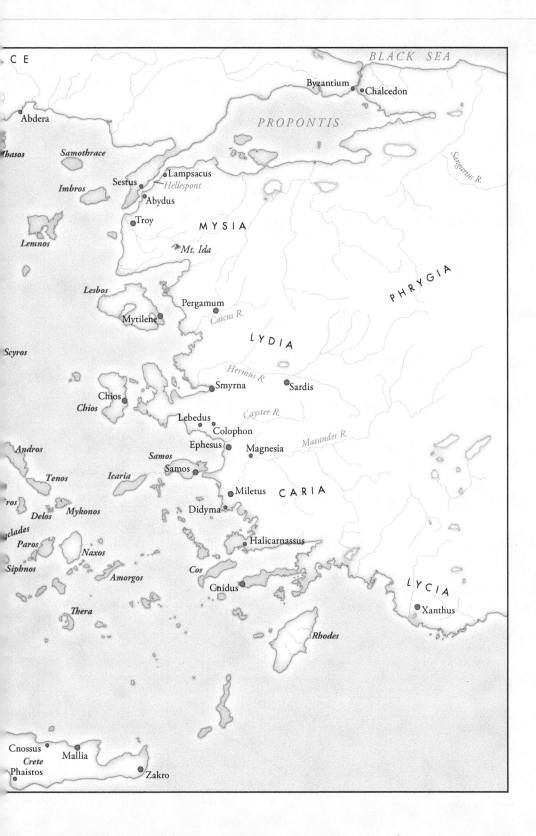

BLACK SEA

Byzantium
●Chalcedon

PROPONTIS

Sangarius R.

CE

Abdera

Thasos   Samothrace

●Lampsacus
Imbros   Sestus ● _Hellespont_
●Abydus
●Troy

MYSIA

Lemnos

Mt. Ida

PHRYGIA

Lesbos

Pergamum●

Caicus R.

Mytilene●

LYDIA

Scyros

Hermus R.

Chios ●Smyrna ●Sardis
Chios

Cayster R.

Lebedus●
Colophon

Andros   Ephesus● ●Magnesia   _Maeander R._

Tenos   Samos

Icaria   Samos●

ros

Delos   Mykonos   ●Miletus   CARIA

clades   Didyma●

Paros   Naxos

Siphnos   ●Halicarnassus

Amorgos   Cos

Thera   Cnidus●   LYCIA

●Xanthus

Rhodes

Cnossus ●
Crete   Mallia●
Phaistos●   ●Zakro

CHAPTER 1

CLASSICAL MYTHS AND CONTEMPORARY QUESTIONS

Myths are not lies. Nor are they detached stories. They are imaginative patterns, networks of powerful symbols that suggest particular ways of interpreting the world. They shape its meaning.

—MARY MIDGLEY, *THE MYTHS WE LIVE BY* (2003)

One of Odysseus's last adventures in his long journey from the battle-field at Troy to his home on the island of Ithaca is his visit to the Under-world. Hordes of souls press against him, trying to drink the blood of the ram he has sacrificed. Although they mean Odysseus no harm, these shades are more terrifying than the Cyclops, who ate Odysseus's men before his eyes, or Scylla, who plucked men off his ship and devoured them. These vast, shadowy throngs threaten to overwhelm Odysseus, even though Odysseus has the means either to animate them—to restore them to life—with a sacrificial ram's blood or to consign them forever to the dark, anonymous silence of the Underworld. These souls, and their stories, are like myths. They exist below the surface of things, embody great knowledge, and yet only have meaning when someone brings them back to life through retelling and listening.

< 1.1 (OPPOSITE): **Odysseus sacrifices a ram at the entrance of the Underworld.** Bas-relief from an Etruscan sarcophagus. Pepper tree wood. Probable copy of a fifth-century BCE painting. Museo dell'Opera del Duomo, Orvieto, Italy. *Erich Lessing / Art Resource, NY ART200190.*

1.1

WHAT IS A MYTH?

What is a myth? Is it a story about the hero Heracles, an ancient Greek poem about the goddess Aphrodite, or the Roman epic *Aeneid*? Is it a sculptural relief of Medusa or Titian's painting of Dionysus swooping up Ariadne from the island of Naxos? Are the German "fairy tales" collected by the brothers Grimm, or the legends of King Arthur and the Round Table, considered myths? Could a Batman comic or a Superman movie or the Harry Potter novels be considered myth? What of Princess Diana of England, whose life and tragic death were frequently compared to a fairy tale? What about the story of George Washington, who never told a lie? Or the tale of Johnny Apple-seed? As any list of the stories and images that might be described as myth inevitably begins to swell, you will find yourself like Odysseus in the Under-world: a vast number of stories and figures will throng your imagination and clamor to tell their tales. Yet are all of these stories myths?

MYTH, LEGEND, AND FOLKLORE

Scholars have repeatedly sought to limit the definition of myth, because there are so many contenders for this title. The work of American folklorist and anthropologist William R. Bascom (1912–1981) offers a useful starting point for any attempt to distinguish myths from other stories. Bascom compared myths with legends and folktales. Although he considered all of them to be prose narratives, he distinguished among them by the characters that appear in them, the time period they describe, and whether their original audiences considered them to be true. Although Bascom notes that different societies may use categories other than myth, legend, and folktale to describe their stories, he nonetheless argues for the usefulness of his template, which he titled "Three Forms of Prose Narratives" (Table 1.1). His template helps lay the groundwork for making very general distinctions among these three sorts of tales that seem to have so much in common.

Bascom argues that myths differ from both legends and folktales because they have "high emotional content" as well as "sacred theology and ritual" and are considered "true accounts of what happened in the remote past." A signif-icant portion of British theologian Don Cupitt's (b. 1934) definition of myth overlaps with Bascom's, filling out some of the details of his template, and including features that are found in many definitions of myth. In his book *The World to Come* (1982), Cupitt writes:

> So we may say that a myth is typically a traditional sacred story of anony-mous authorship and archetypal or universal significance which is re-counted in a certain community and is often linked with ritual; that it tells of the deeds of superhuman beings such as gods, demigods, heroes,

Table 1.1 Three Forms of Prose Narratives

FORM	BELIEF	TIME	PLACE	ATTITUDE	PRINCIPAL CHARACTERS
MYTH	Fact	Remote past	Different world: other or earlier	Sacred	Nonhuman
LEGEND	Fact	Recent past	World of today	Secular or sacred	Human
FOLKTALE	Fiction	Any time	Any place	Secular	Human or nonhuman

spirits or ghosts; that it is set outside historical time in primal or eschato-logical [i.e., last, ultimate] time or in the supernatural world. (29)

Cupitt calls myths "sacred," thereby underscoring Bascom's claim that for a story to be a myth, it must pertain to nonhuman beings, religion, and rituals. Cupitt adds that myths are *traditional*: they represent beliefs shared by a group or society, and they often begin their lives as oral tales passed down anony-mously for generations before they are recorded and enter the written record. For Bascom and Cupitt, then, myth is sacred and traditional and consists of stories that often include nonhuman figures.

common definition

Bascom's and Cupitt's definitions, although satisfyingly clear, are too narrow. First, Bascom limits the *form* of myth to primarily prose narratives or tales and excludes visual arts (such as photography, sculpture, or painting) and literature (such as drama, epics, or poems). For his part, Cupitt, by focus-ing on the oral nature of myths, implies that a work of art with one clearly identified creator might not be traditional and hence might not be mythic. Second, Bascom (and Cupitt to a lesser degree) limits the *content* of myth to supranatural beings who exist in very distant times, whether in the past or the future. Third, both assume that myths *function* to secure or explain religious or sacred beliefs; their definitions exclude myths that may be meaningful to individuals and society but do not concern the sacred realm. Bascom's tem-plate, even when enhanced with Cupitt's ideas, then, limits the category of myth by tying it so closely to religious beliefs.

How do these definitions limit mythology? too narrow

A THREE-POINT DEFINITION OF A MYTHOLOGICAL CORPUS

In his work *Mythography: The Study of Myths and Rituals* (1986), the eminent scholar William G. Doty (b. 1939) develops an inclusive definition of myth.

He offers a seventeen-part definition of "a mythological corpus" that he explains in no fewer than fifty-five pages. His comprehensive definition embraces ancient and modern myths as well as many previous definitions of myth. Like many current scholars working on myths, Doty does not attempt to define a myth but instead takes as his object of study a mythological corpus, a group of myths. Doty's shift in focus immediately alerts us to an important feature of myths: a myth always exists in a context. This context may be a particular society, a religious group within a society, or even a work of art that epitomizes a society's aesthetic values. But one story in isolation from its context cannot be a myth. Therefore Doty defines the mythological corpus as a kind of network. The following definition modifies and organizes Doty's points into the categories of form, content, and function (the same criteria that informed Bascom's and Cupitt's definition of myths).

In Doty's definition, a mythological corpus may contain myths that have many *forms*; they are almost always stories, but they may be conveyed with words or pictures. What is significant is that when these stories are told in words, they are always rich in metaphors and symbols. These stories do not use everyday language, and they are not "straightforward." In other words, myths are not sermons, philosophical tracts, or political speeches. Whatever meaning they hold is hidden in plots, metaphors, and symbols. It is never explicit. When images convey myths, the focus is often on just one key moment or aspect of the larger story. Such images, too, though, are rarely realistic; and even if they are photographs, they often have a timeless quality that points to a broader idea or concept, so that the picture in its totality becomes a metaphor or symbol. To sum up, the form of a myth may be in writing or in a visual medium; it always includes or itself becomes a metaphor or symbol.

These allusive components of myth that Doty highlights often attract and enthrall audiences, frequently compelling the question, "What might that mean?" Thus Doty's observations about the form of myths in a mythological corpus lead to his description of the *content* of myth—which answers, "What might that symbol, story, or metaphor mean?" Doty argues that the content of myth is not to be found on its surface, such as whether gods or the creation of the universe make an appearance (i.e., the very sorts of details that Bascom considered relevant). Instead, the content of a mythological corpus is its religious, political, and cultural values and meanings that connect the individual to society and the cosmos. These values and meanings are often not explicit; instead they are built into—indeed they hide inside—the symbols, metaphors, images, and plots found in myths. Consequently, the content of a mythological corpus is not clearly stated and often eludes discovery by its audiences.

The content of myth (defined as its values and meanings) leads to the *function* of myth. "Function" refers to the purpose that a myth serves for individuals, groups, or society as whole. For example, many scholars argue that myth explains the workings of the natural world, the divine realm, ritual activities, or society; in this case, the function of myth is to explain the cosmos and all its constituents: it is a type of science, theology, or politics, but one that relies on stories, images, symbols, and metaphors, rather than logic or explicitly and clearly stated reasoning. Another functional definition is that myth ameliorates or makes endurable troubling differences and contradictions. For example, myth may ameliorate the difference between life and death by offering stories of an afterlife. Doty captures succinctly all the possible ways that myths may function: "Myths provide systems of interpreting individual experience within a universal perspective" or within a particular society's perspective. The function of myths, therefore, is to offer ways of understanding and integrating one's experience in a broader framework than one's own life, and of understanding these broader frameworks. Here is a summary of this three-point definition distilled from Doty's comprehensive version:

[margin note: myths help people interpret their different perspectives]

1. Whether the form of a myth is an oral story, a written document, or a painted image, it always includes metaphors and symbols that engage viewers' emotions or that compel viewers to search out what its metaphors, symbols, and stories mean.
2. The content of a myth is composed of the religious, political, and cultural values and meanings about self, society, and cosmos that it offers, which are often hidden in a myth's metaphors, symbols, images, and stories.
3. The function of myths is to offer ways of locating one's experience in a broader framework than one's own life and of understanding this broader framework. For this reason, myths must be studied in a particular context and must be part of a mythological corpus.

We now come to one consideration about the form, content, and function of Greek myths: whether contemporary audiences of myths can make sense of a myth in the same way that its original audiences did. Is what myths offered to and required of their original tellers and listeners comparable to what myths offer to and require of their contemporary investigators, like you, or me, or Doty? For many people, the answer to this question seems obvious. Contemporary readers of myths do not believe in Poseidon, Athena, or any of the other gods and goddesses—and even if they did, they live nearly three thousand years after these stories were first told. Thus contemporary audiences are at a great remove from ancient Greece and at a great remove from its mythological corpus. Yet there is one important way in which ancient and modern audiences are alike. The strange metaphors, stories, symbols, and characters that populate a network of myths provoke its audiences, whether ancient or modern, to actively seek out the meanings behind a particular myth. Indeed, we will see that almost as soon as the Greeks started telling myths, they began questioning them much as we do. In the next section, then, we look at myths from ancient Greece, and we consider what the Greeks said about their own

[margin note: Ancient + modern both provoke audience to search for meanings]

myths, to understand better not only who the Greeks were but also how the Greeks themselves developed the field of mythology (the study of myths).

1.2 WHAT IS CLASSICAL MYTHOLOGY?

[handwritten note: Classical mythology are myths from ancient Greece and Rome]

Many university course catalogues, textbooks, and scholarly journals have "classical mythology" in their title, yet what qualifies as a "classical" myth—and what distinguishes "myth" from "mythology"—requires some clarification and explanation. The word "classic" derives from Latin—not Greek—and describes something that belongs to a certain category, group, or class. Over time, however, the word evolved to mean something that exemplifies the best qualities of a particular group or class, and thus is in a class (or league) of its own. To call a car, musician, or novel a classic is to imply that the object or person is somehow exemplary and better than all other members of its group, because she, he, or it embodies the ideal characteristics of the whole group. The adjective "classical" was first used by Renaissance scholars to describe Greek and Roman antiquity, because, in their eyes, Greece and Rome represented the pinnacle of success in the arts, political structures, and philosophy, to name but a few of the areas that Renaissance scholars found worthy of such high praise. Thus "classical" myths are myths from ancient Greece and Rome. Like most of what the West has inherited from Greece and Rome, these myths have been considered classics and are described as classical. Classical myths, especially those from Greece, are considered beautiful, extravagant, expressive, and meaningful, as well as part of a robust mythological corpus. Consequently, Greek myths have played an important role in shaping how scholars think about both the category of myth and mythological systems more generally.

We turn now to a brief survey of the myths of ancient Greece, after which we introduce their relationship to myths from the Ancient Near East, many of which predate and intersect with Greek myths. In so doing, we are deliberately broadening the definition of classical myths by including non-Greek influences on Greek myths. We then look at myths from Rome, which postdate Greek myths and owe much, although not all, of their form and substance to their Greek predecessors. Our goal in this chapter—and throughout this book—is to develop a comprehensive, if schematic, introduction to myths from ancient Greece in relation to myths from the Ancient Near East and Rome.

MYTHS FROM ANCIENT GREECE

"Ancient Greece" refers less to a well-defined geographical area than to the places where Greeks lived. These places include modern Greece and the coast of modern-day Turkey, as well as the eastern edges of present-day Italy and the coast of the Black Sea. The chronological period associated with general studies of ancient Greece begins with the introduction of bronze (c. 3000 BCE) and ends with the Roman conquest of Greece (146 BCE), which then becomes an important province in the Roman Empire.

Throughout this long stretch of time, the Greeks did not organize themselves politically into one nation but instead mainly dwelled in small communities called city-states, each of which had its own independent government. The Greek term for city-state is *polis*; often translated as "city," it is the origin of the English word "political." City-states waged wars with one another and even enslaved one another, although they could, and sometimes did, work together to defend Greece against outside invasions, such as the Persian invasions in the fifth century BCE. Regardless of the hostility or shared purposes that characterized relations among the Greek city-states, the Greeks as a whole had a shared identity, if not a shared government. This shared identity, in the words of the Greek historian Herodotus (484–425 BCE), rested on the fact that the Greeks are defined by a shared language, a shared religion and way of life or culture (*Histories* 8.144). Thus ancient Greece is wherever Greeks dwelled. To this list we might add their shared mythological corpus.

Myths in the Archaic Period The Greek mythological corpus was created and circulated during all periods of Greek history but evolved and changed as Greek city-states and their relations with one another changed. We begin our survey of Greek myths with the Archaic Period (750–490 BCE) and the *Iliad* and the *Odyssey*. These two epics were originally oral compositions developed over many generations before being written down (Figure 1.2). Consequently, they contain descriptions of objects and customs that are found in the Late Bronze Age (1600–1150 BCE), as well as in the Iron Age (1150–750 BCE) and the Archaic Period (750–490 BCE). During the Iron Age and Archaic Period, anonymous poets composed and recited poems in hexameter verse on the subjects found in these epics. Each line of a poem composed in hexameter verse has twelve beats that may vary in rhythmic structure for dramatic

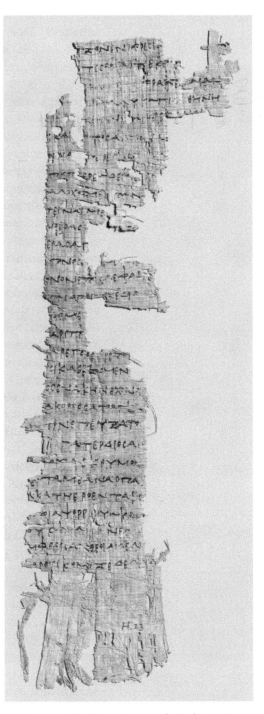

1.2 Fragment of the *Odyssey*. Papyrus with Greek script. Egypt. 285–250 BCE. *Image copyright © The Metropolitan Museum of Art. Image source: Art Resource, NY, ART378594.*

emphasis. This versatile meter enabled poets to remember and combine phrases called "formulae" while adhering to a general story. This method of composition meant that no one oral performance was identical to any other.

These epics are commonly attributed to Homer, yet "Homer" is a short-hand expression for generations of anonymous bards who composed and performed poems in the style of Homer. The *Iliad* and *Odyssey* that we possess are not transcripts of a performance—it would take nearly twenty-four hours to recite either of these epics! Presumably, recitals were much briefer and featured one episode from these longer tales. The epics we possess most likely owe their length and current arrangement of stories to whoever committed them to writing. When and how these epics were first written down is debated; sometimes Peisistratus, the Athenian tyrant, is credited with having them written down in 565 BCE, although some scholars posit that the epics were committed to writing closer to the time that the Greeks adapted the Phoenician alphabet to the Greek language in the eighth century BCE.

In addition to Homer's two epics, the *Homeric Hymns*, poems of varying length in hexameter verse composed in the same manner as Homer's epics, are dedicated to a god or goddess and preceded the performance of epics. Finally, *Theogony* and *Works and Days*, said to be by Hesiod (eighth to seventh century BCE), are also hexameter poems, orally composed by poets and eventually recorded in writing, in a similar manner to Homer's poems.

Although the Homeric epics and hymns and Hesiod's poems were not sacred texts, they were nonetheless important for making sense of Greek gods and goddesses. Again Herodotus is our guide for understanding how Greeks viewed these poems. He writes that Hesiod and Homer described the genealogical relations among the gods and goddesses and detailed their appearance and traits (*Histories* 2.53). Because Greeks lived in small communities that were not unified into a nation, their gods were initially worshipped in local temples and altars. Any one god or goddess therefore might have different characteristics, depending on where he or she was worshipped, and the relationships among a group of local gods were often simply geographical. Herodotus's comments, then, show how important these early Greek poets were in creating a framework (mostly through constructing the gods in one large extended family) in which local deities could be located and organized.

Thus recitations of Homer and Hesiod contributed to the transformation of local deities, worshipped in small communities and city-states, into gods recognizable to all Greeks—that is, into Panhellenic deities. (*Pan* means "all," and *Hellenes* is the word the Greeks use for themselves.) Indeed, these poems were recited at Panhellenic sanctuaries, such as Olympia, during festivals that Greeks from all over the Greek world could attend. Our understanding of Greek myths also relies on the framework and conceptions of the gods found in Homer's and Hesiod's poems. Yet no sooner did these poets name, identify, and describe the gods in a mostly genealogical framework that was committed to writing than the Greeks began to question this framework and all that it implied or taught about the cosmos and the gods.

Myths in the Classical Period Whereas some Greeks already expressed skepticism about the conceptions of the gods found in Homer and Hesiod during the Archaic Period, in the city of Athens during the Classical Period (490–323 BCE) Greeks began to examine their myths in earnest. Their inquiries laid the foundation for all subsequent studies of mythology. Why and how the Greeks became critics of their own mythological systems is linked to the dramatic, even revolutionary, explosion in creative and intellectual activities that prompted later scholars to label the fifth and fourth centuries BCE in Greece the Classical Period. Just as Renaissance scholars first called all of Greek and Roman antiquity "classical" because of the regard in which they held the achievements of those civilizations, this period of time in Greece has come to be known as the Classical Period, because above all others it was thought to embody the pinnacle of the Greek commitment to reason and beauty. In addition, this era in ancient Greece witnessed the development of many scholarly disciplines such as mathematics, philosophy, psychology, and biology (to name but a few) that still shape how we study the world and organize knowledge.

During the Classical Period, Homeric and Hesiodic poems continued to be recited at festivals in Athens; tragedians such as Aeschylus (525–c. 456 BCE), Sophocles (497–406 BCE), and Euripides (480–406 BCE) composed plays about and including gods and goddesses; the historian Herodotus composed and recited his *Histories*, which, although devoted primarily to the Persian Wars, nonetheless contained stories about the gods; and temples such as the Parthenon on the Athenian Acropolis were constructed with sculptures depicting the gods. In other words, the Greek mythological corpus continued to grow in words as well as in the visual arts.

At the same time, *muthos* (the Greek word for myth) became defined and interrogated. The philosopher Protagoras (490–420 BCE), one of the most renowned teachers in Athens at the time, wrote, "Man is the measure of all things," swatting the gods aside and setting human beings at the center of the universe. Plato (428–348 BCE), recognizing that myths persuade their listeners to adopt ideas about the gods that he often judged erroneous, wanted to ban myths from his ideal republic. Not surprisingly, however, Plato himself employed traditional myths and created some of his own, such as the myth of Er or of Atlantis, to teach his philosophical doctrines.

Palaephatus, an obscure figure who wrote at the end of the fourth century BCE, both collected and debunked mythological stories in his book *On Incredible Tales*. For example, he offered this explanation of the tale about a nymph named Callisto whom the goddess Artemis turned into a bear: Callisto walked into the forest and was torn apart by bears; when one of the bears emerged from the forest, witnesses believed it to be the transformed girl. Palaephatus set out to rationalize stories about which audiences were increasingly skeptical—if they ever were believed to be literally true in the first place. But Greek gods and goddesses and the stories about them were not entirely dismissed or considered irrelevant. The trial of the philosopher Socrates (c. 469–399 BCE), in which he was prosecuted for mocking traditional gods, conveys the anxieties generated by the interrogation of tradition and traditional views about gods.

As members of Athenian society continued to question their beliefs and stories about the gods, they also advanced rational arguments, called *logoi* (the singular is *logos*), about the universe, including the gods, society, and humankind. They began to define myths (*muthoi*, the plural of *muthos*) as the opposite of *logoi*. If *logoi* were rational arguments that relied on logic and statements made in straightforward prose, then *mythoi* were not rational and included stories, metaphors, symbols, and images. If *logoi* explained all the cosmos as accurately as human reason allowed, then *mythoi* were inaccurate fictions that did not aim to describe things as they are.

The similarities between the Greek definition of *muthoi* and the modern definitions of myth surveyed earlier in this chapter are not accidental. The Greeks had a rich, vibrant mythological corpus; by the end of the Classical Period, they also had a rich, vibrant critique of *muthoi*. They embraced and continued to develop a wide range of responses to their mythological corpus in ways that proved influential in the Western world.

Myths in the Hellenistic Period and Beyond During the Hellenistic Period (323–30 BCE), one of the key responses to Greece's mythological corpus was less interrogative than retrospective. Educated Greek scholars and teachers who lived in Alexandria, the cultural and political capital of Hellenistic Egypt, began to collect and imitate earlier Greek myths and stories. Callimachus (310/305–240 BCE), for example, composed hymns dedicated to gods and goddesses, but his hymns were witty, urbane, and full of obscure references. Apollonius of Rhodes (third century BCE) composed a relatively short epic in hexameters called the *Argonautica*, about Jason's quest with his Argonauts for the Golden Fleece. In Apollonius of Rhodes's version, the weak-willed protagonist Jason bears little resemblance to Homer's heroes.

When the Romans gained control over wide swathes of the Mediterranean (they decisively took control of Greece in 146 BCE and Egypt in 30 BCE), they began uniting peoples of many different languages and cultures under their rule. Greeks in the elite vanguard of the Roman Empire continued to expand and, increasingly, to explain the Greek mythological corpus. Among these, Plutarch (46–120 CE) wrote treatises on Delphi (where he was a priest), biographies of famous Greek and Roman statesmen, and treatises on Greek,

Roman, and Egyptian philosophy, theology, and customs. Pausanias (second century CE) traveled throughout Greece and described its temples, buildings, and customs, thus preserving many features of Greek culture. By the fifth century CE, the Roman Empire became Christianized, and the Greek mythological system became quiescent.

Classical mythology can now be more accurately defined. Like biology (the study of *bios*, "life") or anthropology (the study of *anthropoi*, "human beings"), classical mythology is the study of myths: that is, the sort of tales that the Greeks themselves labeled *muthoi*. Although classical myths may come from any period in Greek or Roman antiquity, Greek myths from the Archaic and Classical Periods compose the core of most studies of classical mythology. This is because of the vibrant mythological corpus the Greeks created during these periods *and* their contributions to analyzing this corpus. Even so, Greek myths and Greek mythology were never isolated from the myths and peoples that lived among and around Greek-speaking peoples. These include people and myths from the Ancient Near East and the people and myths of Rome. Greece's interactions with the great empires to its east and with Rome to its west were very different. Each contributes to the study of classical mythology in different ways.

MYTHS FROM THE ANCIENT NEAR EAST

The "Ancient Near East" (Map 1.1, pp. 22–23) refers to a large geographical region that has four regions; the peoples who dwelled in each area developed their own mythological corpus. In the north is the large landmass called Anatolia or Asia Minor (modern Turkey), and in the south is Egypt. On the west and bordering the Mediterranean Sea is the Levant (modern Syria, Lebanon, Israel, Jordan, and Palestine). To the east is ancient Mesopotamia, the region between the Tigris and Euphrates Rivers (modern Iraq). The empires and kingdoms in these four regions developed at different paces from one another, as well as from Greece, which was a relative newcomer to the region. For example, the Egyptians and the Sumerians had writing systems and complex hierarchical social structures long before the Greek alphabet was adapted from the Phoenicians. In addition, almost all of these regions and the smaller communities within them were ruled for thousands of years by kings who were believed to be sacred. The lion, as the king of beasts, was often adopted for their insignia and guardians, as is evidenced by the famous gate of Ishtar, which was decorated with lions (Figure 1.3). Greece, by contrast, eventually developed democratic systems of governance.

Beginning in the Bronze Age, when it too was ruled by kings, Greece interacted with the empires and kingdoms in the east through trade, war, travel, and migration. Additionally, it shared a language group with some of its eastern neighbors. One of the two language groups in the Ancient Near East is

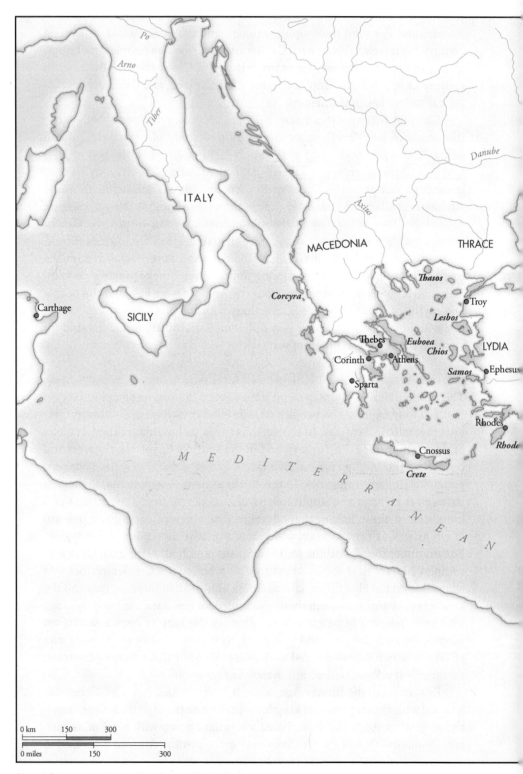

Map 1.1 Greece, the Ancient Near East, and the Mediterranean

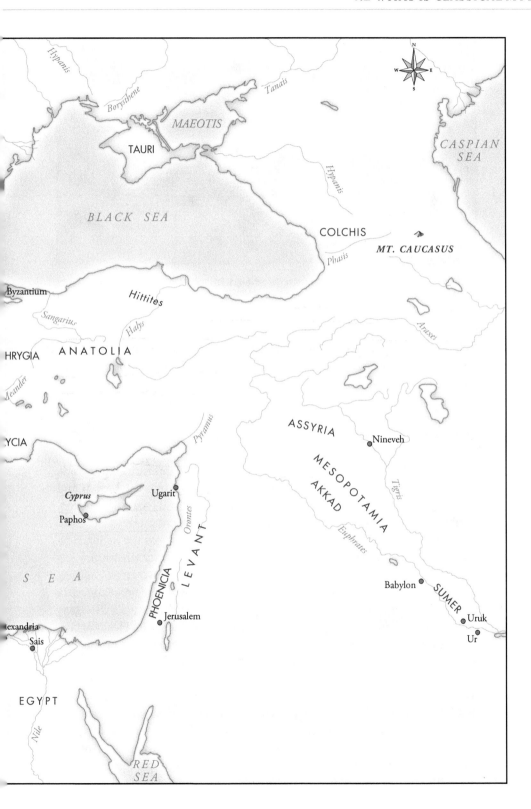

1.3 Lion from the Processional Wall of the Ishtar Gate, Babylon. *Enameled tile and brick. Detail. 575* BCE. *bpk, Berlin/Vorderasiatisches Museum, Staatliche Museen Berlin/Olaf M. Tessner/Art Resource, NY, ART478723.*

Indo-European, which includes Greek as well as Hittite and Vedic Sanskrit, one of the earliest Indo-European languages. The Afro-Asiatic group includes ancient Egyptian and the Semitic languages: biblical Hebrew, Phoenician, Ugaritic, and Akkadian, of which Assyrian and Babylonian were direct descendants. The Sumerian language, spoken in Mesopotamia, belongs to neither of these two language groups.

Anatolia In Anatolia, the Hittite Empire arose in the eighteenth century BCE. By the fourteenth century BCE it had expanded south into the Levant and Mesopotamia before collapsing around 1200 BCE, when wide-scale destruction, attributed to invasions by the Sea Peoples, civil unrest, drought, a series of earthquakes, or a combination of these, swept through across the region. Several important Hittite myths dating to the fourteenth or thirteenth century BCE include the *Song of Kumarbi* (also called *The Kingship in Heaven*) and *The Song of Ullikummi.* Both of these myths, which tell the tale of the god Kumarbi's rise and fall from power, share some similarities with Hesiod's *Theogony* and as a result have raised questions about Eastern influence on Hesiod's tale. The location of the city of Troy in the *Iliad* on the western shores of Anatolia also raises possibilities about the interplay between Greek and Hittite myths. Scholars have suggested that the Greek god Apollo's origin is the Hittite god Appaliunas, whose name appears in a treaty between the Hittite king Muwattalis and Prince Alaksandus of Wilusa. Alaksandus has been suggested by some scholars as the King Alexander (Paris) of Ilios (an alternative name for Troy) mentioned in the *Iliad.* This hypothesis not only offers a reason for Apollo's protection of Troy in Homer's *Iliad* but also raises intriguing questions about the historical reality behind Homer's epic and possible Hittite influences on this foundational text.

In addition to the Hittites, the Phrygian kingdom in the central and western part of Anatolia had many cultural exchanges with the Greeks. In Homer's *Iliad*, the Phrygians fought alongside the Trojans against the Greeks. The kingdom of Phrygia thrived during the eighth century BCE but eventually was conquered and came under the control of the Lydians, a neighboring kingdom in Anatolia, followed by the Persians, and thereafter was conquered and Hellenized by Alexander the Great before being incorporated into the Roman Empire. The Great Mother (also called Cybele) in Phrygia was a considerable religious phenomenon in the whole Mediterranean region. Forms of her worship were adopted in both Greece and the Roman Empire.

The Levant In the Levant (variously called Syria-Canaan or Syro-Palestine), the religions of the Syro-Canaanites, the Phoenicians, and the Israelites developed. The Syro-Canaanite religion is well documented in Ugaritic sources, found in Ugarit (in modern Syria), from the later half of the second millennium BCE. From the Syro-Canaanite religion came the religious traditions of the Phoenicians, who lived on the coast of modern-day Lebanon. Inveterate sailors and traders, the Phoenicians traveled throughout the Mediterranean world and spread religious and cultural ideas from one part of the region to another. The Phoenicians founded the city of Carthage on the northern coast of Africa in 814 BCE, and the Punic people of Carthage trace their descent to the Phoenicians and North African Berbers. Closer to the Levant is the island of Cyprus, where the Phoenicians and the Greeks shared religious shrines and settlements as well as conceptions and representations of goddesses. Cyprus is host to some of the many Phoenician colonies where they exchanged goods and ideas with Greeks.

The Israelites in the Levant provide a detailed account of their history and their worship of Yahweh in the Hebrew Bible but rarely mention their neighbors in the Levant, who in turn seldom mention them. The Israelites formed a nation under King David (1000 BCE) after defeating their neighbors in several small battles. They are most noted for their monotheism (worship of one god only) and increasingly came to believe that the worship of gods other than Yahweh violated Moses's covenant with him. Monotheism distinguished Judaism and then Christianity from neighboring religious systems and led Tertullian (160–225 CE), an early Christian writer from Carthage, to famously ask: "What does Jerusalem have to do with Athens?"

For Tertullian, the monotheism of the Israelites (Jerusalem) has no relationship to the polytheism of Greece (Athens), and consequently, in his reasoning, Greek polytheism should have precluded Christian interest in the myths and gods of the Greeks. Tertullian's successors in the West, however, came to a very different conclusion, finding instead that Athens and Jerusalem have much to do with each other indeed. They have asked what, if anything, both the Greeks and the Hebrews contributed to the development of Christianity. And they have puzzled over both the similarities in Greek and Hebrew narratives of the flood, for example, and the differences between the moral universes created by Yahweh and Zeus.

Mesopotamia The small kingdoms and their religious systems that arose, interacted, and declined in the Levant contrast with the great empires of Mesopotamia, whose size, wealth, and complexity far exceeded them. These empires generated a complex mythological corpus that is succinctly referred to as Mesopotamian, but there are various strands within this large corpus.

The Sumerians were the earliest settlers in the south of Mesopotamia. They developed cuneiform (a mostly syllabic system of writing) just before the start of the third millennium BCE and had a vibrant kingdom until the Akkadian king, Sargon the Great (2334–2279 BCE), defeated and incorporated them into a larger Mesopotamian empire he established and ruled. The Sumerians had a brief resurgence (2112–2004 BCE), and many of their myths are dated to this period, including *In the Desert by the Early Grass* (Chapter 4.3). Sumerian continued as the language of literature and government, while Akkadian (a Semitic language) increasingly became the language used for all other purposes.

Babylonia, with the city of Babylon as its capital, became the next center of power in the region (1900–1550 BCE). The composition and recording of many Mesopotamian myths—including *Gilgamesh*, an epic often compared to Homer's *Iliad* because of its content and its oral composition over generations prior to its recording in writing, and the *Atrahasis*, a creation hymn compared to Hesiod's *Theogony*—date to this period. The similarities in the narrative patterns of Mesopotamian and Greek myths are quite striking, despite the radical differences in the political systems of Mesopotamia, organized around the concept of sacred kingship, and ancient Greece, whose various city-states valued citizen status and resisted seeing their leaders as divine. Not surprisingly, scholars have struggled with the question of whether historical diffusion or common human experiences that transcend cultural differences can explain the similarities between the mythic imaginations of the Mesopotamians and the Greeks.

Egypt On the southern border of the Ancient Near East, the upper and lower regions of Egypt were conjoined shortly before the time Sumer grew in prominence in the third millennium. The Egyptians, like the Sumerians, developed a writing system (hieroglyphics) and built many of the great pyramids that are now the icons of ancient Egypt.

Much of what we know about Egyptian mythology and religion is related to the pyramids. The *Pyramid Texts*, the *Coffin Texts*, and the *Book of the Dead* are collections of texts called mortuary literature. Found in pyramids, temples, and coffins, these texts primarily treat the afterlife and are associated with graves and entombment sites. After the Age of the Pyramids, Egypt witnessed a particularly robust period during the New Kingdom (1550–1292 BCE) and, in particular, rebounded as a powerful empire in the Archaic Period. At that time the ruler Psammetichus I, employing Greek mercenaries, established the independence of Egypt from invading Assyrians and Nubians, presided over an Egypt that was unified once more, and made the city of Sais his capital.

Alexander the Great (356–323 BCE), son of Philip II of Macedon, succeeded his father as king of Macedonia and sought to extend his rule over the Ancient Near East (including Greece). When he established his power in Egypt, he founded the city of Alexandria, not too far from Sais, as his capital (331 BCE). On Alexander's death (323 BCE), Ptolemy I Soter I, one of his Macedonian generals, established his ruling dynasty over Egypt until the Romans took control and made Egypt part of their empire (30 BCE). Alexandria remained a vital and cosmopolitan capital for centuries in the region amid these political upheavals; first Greek and Egyptian and then Greek, Egyptian, and Roman cultural exchanges flourished there.

Although the exchanges between Greece and Egypt from this period are well documented and not disputed, contemporary scholarship often engages, sometimes quite vigorously, the question of Egyptian influence on the development of Greek religion and language in the Bronze Age. Such early Egyptian influence has raised the question of whether Africa, through Egypt, has influenced Greek and hence all of Western culture. Because of its implications for the cultural politics of the present day, this question has garnered a great deal of interest in both ancient Egypt and Greece beyond the traditional community of students and scholars of ancient mythology. Thus one of the projects of this book—to set ancient Greek mythology in the wider context of the Ancient Near East—has both ancient origins and contemporary implications. Comparing Greek myths to those of its neighbors in the region leads to many insights about the nature of Greek myths and myths more generally, as well as cultural and religious exchanges.

MYTHS FROM ANCIENT ROME

During the first century CE, one could reasonably say that all roads led to Rome, as the four regions of the Ancient Near East (Anatolia, the Levant, Mesopotamia, and Egypt) and Greece increasingly came under Roman control. Yet Rome's relationship to Greece was qualitatively different than Rome's relationship to its other conquered peoples, and consequently Rome's mythological system was transformed by contact with Greece in a unique way.

It may come as a bit of a surprise to those who have read Vergil's *Aeneid* or Ovid's *Metamorphoses* to learn that scholars debate whether the Romans

1.4 Romulus and Remus suckling the she-wolf. Rome, Italy. *Timothy McCarthy / Art Resource, NY, ART165537.*

had a mythological corpus to call their own. The Romans, who spoke and wrote the Indo-European language Latin (from which modern Italian, Spanish, and French are derived), not only superimposed the beauty and form of Greek gods on their indigenous deities but also produced no native cosmologies and theogonies of their own. They did have some stories (such as that of Romulus and Remus, the two founders of Rome, shown in Figure 1.4) that are thought to be native to the residents of the Italian peninsula and that predate contact with the Greeks. Yet most of what counts for Roman myths can be found in Vergil, Ovid, and Horace, as well as in Pompeian wall paintings and Roman sculpture, and dates to the late republic (147–30 BCE) and early empire (after Rome's conquest of Greece). These works are judged to be literary confections of considerable sophistication that very consciously and very liberally borrow from Greek predecessors. Moreover, these works (unlike some Greek myths) played no part in rituals, and their references to rituals appear to be deliberately created.

For these reasons, scholars—repeating the sentiment of the Roman poet Horace: *Graecia capta ferum victorem cepit* ("captured Greece captured its fierce victor")—have argued that there was no indigenous Roman mythological system. That is, they, like Horace, endorse the view that although Rome conquered Greece with its army, Rome was conquered by Greece insofar as it owed much of its literary, artistic, philosophical, and religious achievements, including its myths, to the Greeks.

Contemporary scholars, however, are beginning to revise the view that the Romans had a paltry and derivative mythological corpus. Because the Greeks sent out colonies to Italy during the Archaic Period, and because Greece and Rome had contacts long before Rome conquered Greece in 146 BCE, scholars now consider that Greek myths and conceptions of the gods were diffused in Italy before their deliberate adoption by later Roman authors and poets. Thus it may not be possible to isolate Greek elements in Roman myths. Additionally, as the narrow definition of myth as sacred narrative has expanded, so too have scholars expanded the sorts of Roman writings they are willing to categorize as Roman myth.

In the three-point definition described at the beginning of this chapter, the content of a myth includes religious, political, and cultural values and meanings. Because scholars now look at where the Romans made sense of the political and cultural, although not necessarily religious, aspects of their empire, they suggest that Rome's mythological corpus ought to include Roman declamation (wildly fictional law cases that were used to educate young Roman boys and men to become statesmen and lawyers) and historical writing such as Livy's *Histories* (c. 27–25 BCE). In this view, Rome did have its own mythological corpus; nonetheless, because the Romans adapted Greek myths to such a great degree, it seems natural to use the term "classical mythology" to refer to both Greek and Roman myths. Yet, the Greek mythological corpus, like Greece itself, is balanced between the empires and kingdoms in the Ancient Near East and Rome in the West. So too is this study, which takes Greek myths as its vibrant core while acknowledging contributions from Greece's east and west, as well as looking to both Greece's past and its future.

1.3 HOW DO WE MAKE SENSE OF CLASSICAL MYTHS?

The three-point definition of a mythological corpus serves as the foundation for the organization of this book. Because the form of myths may be an oral story, a written document, or an image, this book treats written documents as well as visual and archaeological material as important components of the Greek mythological corpus. Because myth's metaphors, symbols, images, and stories hold important meanings, we explore these facets of myths but do not attempt to rationalize them in the manner of Palaephatus's *On Incredible Tales*. We defined the content of a myth as its religious, political, and cultural values and meanings about self, society, and cosmos. Therefore, we examine Greek myths in their historical context. Because we proposed that myths function to offer ways of locating one's experience in a broader framework than one's own life, as well as understanding this broader framework, we ask how Greek myths functioned in Greek society and what they accomplished for their listeners and tellers. Because every mythological system is complex yet can be understood as having these three different components (form, content, and function), each of the sections in the following chapters provides a different perspective on the Greek mythological system.

- We do not rationaliz
- Examine history
- What functions and accomplishments they made?

The first section of every chapter is labeled "History"; it addresses the form and content of myths by providing an overview of the chapter's god, goddess, heroes, or heroines in their historical setting in ancient Greece. This section concludes with an ancient Greek source that is particularly relevant for constructing an understanding of the chapter's topic. The second section, called "Theory," surveys the different ways scholars have explained the *function* of myth and concludes with a reading that offers a way of interpreting the chapter's content. The third section, called "Comparison," looks at myths from Greece's neighbors in order to offer a regional perspective on the chapter's topic and includes a myth for comparison with the chapter's Greek material. The last section of each chapter, called "Reception," is devoted to modern and contemporary art that alludes to and interprets Greek myths. In this final section, modern and contemporary art (whether poem, painting, sculpture, or photograph) is interspersed throughout, rather than appearing at its conclusion.

Each of these four sections contains an essay coupled with source material: a Greek myth, a scholarly text, a myth from the ancient Mediterranean, and modern or contemporary art. No single essay lays out all the meanings and possible interpretations of the included source; instead each essay seeks to create ways to interpret it. Indeed, the entirety of this book is designed around such sources because the goal of this book is to introduce readers to methods for understanding classical mythology using an approach that is not limited to simply or only supplying facts about such myths.

HISTORY

Very often, indeed too often, a Greek god or goddess is explained by means of a list of attributes. Zeus is the god of thunder and kings; Aphrodite is the goddess of love and sex. Heroes or heroines are defined by means of a single, significant adventure or exploit. Achilles fought at Troy; Medea murdered her two children. These attributes and stories are not incorrect but provide a rather static and limited picture of the mythological system of which they are a part. To the Greeks, the immortals were alive, and they were everywhere; heroes and heroines once walked the earth and now were worshipped at their tombs. What animated these figures and made them live in the imaginations of the Greeks? How do we move beyond lists of attributes and deeds to gain an understanding of how the divine and semidivine figures participated in and defined the world of ancient Greece?

The History section of each chapter examines where and how Greeks encountered and worshipped the deities and heroic figures that are the chapter's topic. We examine various forms of representing these figures, whether through written sources, visual sources (such as a vase or a statue), or material evidence (such as the configuration of a temple). In the case of the immortals, particular emphasis is given to religious practices; in the case of the heroes and heroines, emphasis is given to the stories in which they appear. Each essay uses ancient sources to address one broad question whose answer leads to understanding how these immortals and heroic mortals were imagined and understood by the Greeks. Each of these essays also demonstrates how the content of Greek myths is intimately bound up in the religious, cultural, and political life of ancient Greece, even if these myths have moved beyond that world and have entered our imaginations. One ancient Greek myth is included in its entirety (except for epics, which are excerpted) at the section's end. These myths allow the Greeks to describe their immortals and mortals in a Greek voice. Although the essay portion of the section provides a context in which this myth may be placed as well as offering some insights into its content, you will find the myth more beautiful and complicated than any essay could convey; thus you will want to interpret and make sense of the included myth, perhaps even reading the next section, on theory, to do so.

THEORY

The word "theory" comes from the Greek verb *theaomai*, "to gaze at" or "to contemplate." A theory is a lens held over a myth that enables the viewer to gaze at parts or aspects of the myth that might not be readily visible to the casual observer. If a myth is viewed through the lenses of different theories, it will appear quite different in each instance. Thus theories provide ways of looking at myths, but no one theory explains a myth completely. Most theories provide ways to answer a question implied in our three-point definition of a mythological corpus, namely: how does this myth function? That is, what purpose does this myth serve in its society for its tellers and listeners?

Scholars have developed a range of theories (ways of looking at and asking questions) about how myths worked or functioned in the communities where they were told. Some scholars explore the social purposes of myth, whereas others offer theories that outline the psychological, intellectual, or religious purposes myths serve. Because these theories are complex and because a single reading on any one theory is often not sufficient for understanding it, the sections on theory are paired. In other words, although the book has twelve chapters (excluding this introductory chapter), it offers the reader six theoretical perspectives. The sections on theory in Chapters 4 and 5, for example, address theories of gender in myth, whereas the sections in Chapters 8 and 9 address theories about initiation rituals in myth. The Theory sections conclude with selections from scholars who work on particular theories. The brief essays that introduce these selections often explain what prompted a particular scholar to develop a particular theory, describe what insights the theory does and does not offer, or highlight what is significant or difficult in the theoretical reading. Yet the introductory essays are not summaries; they cannot substitute for the included readings that have been chosen as examples of the sometimes dense and sometimes lively scholarly literature that Greek myths have inspired.

COMPARISON

The third section of each chapter, Comparison, takes as its premise that one of the more fundamental ways to understand something—a butterfly, a novel, a marriage ritual, or a law—is to compare it to other similar items. In the field of mythology, scholars often compare myths from within one society, myths from very different societies, or myths from regions that border one another, through a variety of approaches. Some scholars study one myth that appears in societies that have no known contact with one another in order to draw broad conclusions about the nature of myth. Comparing a myth that appears in different societies is often believed to demonstrate that myths express universal fears, hopes, and desires that all human beings share. Comparativists who are not interested in the universal aspects of myth often study the diffusion of a myth across societies that have had contact with one another, for example, through trade, religious movements, colonization, travel, and wars. They look for the origin of a particular myth, or they examine how myths change over time in different societies. Diffusionists draw historical conclusions about myths in a particular country or regional context.

The Comparison sections take up the various approaches of comparative mythologists in order to develop yet another way of knowing Greek myths: namely, through their similarities to and differences from myths in the Ancient Near East and Rome. Unlike the Romans, who explicitly acknowledged their debt to the Greeks, the Greeks rarely mentioned their neighbors to the east or acknowledged their exchanges and borrowings with and from them. For this reason, the essay portion of the Comparative sections often introduces the historical relationship between Greece and the kingdom or empire under consideration and suggests possible motives and explanations for the similarities and differences between the chapter's Greek myth and its myth from a neighboring society included at the section's close. Each Comparison section draws on myths from the Ancient Near East and Rome. Like the sections on theory, these sections work in pairs so readers have two opportunities to familiarize themselves with different mythological traditions. The first two Comparison sections, for example, in Chapters 2 and 3, focus on Genesis in the Hebrew Bible and its resonances in Greek myths about the creation and the god Zeus.

RECEPTION

Tour any gallery or museum of Western art and a Greek goddess will meet you, or a mysterious name will appear in a painting's title that, on inquiry, will reveal itself to be a mythical Greek monster or place. Western art from every period draws from a deep reserve of artistic interpretations of and allusions to Greek myths. Yet this section of each chapter is necessarily limited in its scope and purpose. It explores Greek myths in modern art (1860–1970) and contemporary art (1970–present) and only occasionally refers to earlier periods, as our study is especially devoted to examining how Greek myth remains a vital force today. And—unlike earlier Western art, which can be difficult to grasp without significant commentary because it is embedded in a particular time and place and uses an idiom or style that is unfamiliar—modern and contemporary art, whether verbal or visual, addresses the world today.

Each Reception section chooses one aspect or feature of the chapter's main topic, often one that did not receive ample attention in the previous sections, and explores the works of visual and literary artists who offer insight into its meaning. Their work is treated not as illustrations or as simple retellings but as innovative re-creations and interpretations of Greek myths. The aim is not to offer a comprehensive catalogue of the chapter's topic in contemporary and modern art or to suggest that earlier treatments of Greek myth are less important. Indeed, these modern and contemporary expressions of Greek myths hopefully will inspire—or provoke—you to trace them back through the corpus of Western art. Yet the focus of this section is decidedly on how artists have mined and revived Greek myths to make sense of the pressing issues of their day and *ours*. We dance on the bridge that modern and contemporary artists have built between the world of Greek myths and the world of today.

Each of the four sections in every chapter, then, enables an exploration of Greek myths in a particular way, and each borrows from and thus introduces a number of academic disciplines. The History sections borrow techniques and tools that historians, archaeologists, and classicists use to explore and explain worlds that existed in the past. The Theory sections borrow primarily from the fields of anthropology and religious studies and include psychology as well as folklore and oral studies. The Comparison sections borrow from comparative studies in history and religion, Ancient Near Eastern studies, and the growing area in anthropology and history called Mediterranean studies. The Reception sections borrow from the disciplines of art history, media studies, and literary and cultural studies. In sum, the study of classical mythology has become a multidisciplinary field, in part because the definition of myth has expanded and myth is no longer defined as a sacred, traditional narrative. As a multidisciplinary endeavor, the study of classical mythology offers an introduction first and foremost to ancient Greece, but also to the many disciplines it deploys. It also illuminates some of the myriad ways that Greece has contributed to the contours of the Western world. As relevant and practical as these reasons are for studying classical mythology, there are yet others.

WHY STUDY CLASSICAL MYTHS IN THE TWENTY-FIRST CENTURY?

1.4

This chapter begins with a definition of myth from philosopher Mary Midgley's book *The Myths We Live By* (2003). Midgley is interested in modern myths, not ancient ones. She observes: "We are accustomed to think of myths as the opposite of science. But in fact they are a central part of it: the part that decides its significance in our lives. So we very much need to understand them." In other words, Midgley argues that mythic forms of thinking still inform how we view and understand our world. For example, she argues that since the age of enlightenment, Westerners conceive of individuals as having rights. Only living creatures, with a certain kind of intelligence and capacity to act, have rights that can protect them in courts of law. Not surprisingly, we debate whether animals have rights, but more importantly—and this is Midgley's point—in a legal and cultural system that recognizes individual rights, the environment has none, because it is not a living creature with a certain sort of intelligence

1.5 Romare Bearden, "Realm of Shades." In this image from modernist artist Romare Bearden's *Black Odyssey*, Odysseus (left) enters the Underworld. Bearden evokes Christian imagery with the flames and frightening figures that are not a part of the Greek conception of the Underworld. *©Romare Bearden Foundation/Licensed by VAGA, New York, NY. Courtesy of DC Moore Gallery, New York.*

and agency. Consequently, the way the environment is imagined and treated rests on a form of thinking that, in Midgley's view, is mythic. Our myths tell us that the environment, just like an animal in many people's thinking, is an object to be used by individuals with rights. Thus Midgley wants us to become aware of our own myths in order not to be controlled by them. In this view, studying classical mythology is one way to develop a set of multidisciplinary tools with which to understand current myths. This is a good reason to study classical mythology in the twenty-first century. Yet there are more.

A robot named Watson, who defeated every human contestant in many episodes of the game show *Jeopardy!*, is now working at Memorial Sloan Kettering Hospital, a premier cancer research hospital in New York City. He is learning more, and more quickly, than any human being could about how to diagnose and treat cancer; soon, his progeny might replace your human doctor. Video lectures and computer programs have already begun to replace teachers and professors. Cloned animals are already penned in farms. Drones, aerial machines carrying only bombs and bullets and guided only by algorithms, can travel halfway across the globe and eliminate their targets. You can watch a tsunami or an asteroid wreak destruction from your couch in real time. Technology is racing around a planet that is slowly warming and destroying species of living creatures every day. We are drawn ever closer together yet are driven ever further apart. We are, all of us are, besieged by information, most of it unpleasant, and rendered unable to sensibly act—sometimes even to think—amid the din of it all. But you can turn off this technological noise and tune your imagination to where Greeks dwell—not in a fit of nostalgia, but in the spirit of an imaginative adventure. There you may find that when Antigone refuses to yield to King Creon in the belief that she must, no matter the consequences, bury her brother, you too experience her desperation and argue her words. When Bellerophon mounts the glorious winged horse Pegasus, you too may feel the wind and freedom of that ride. In such moments, you imagine your way across 3,000 miles and nearly as many years. One reason to study classical mythology, then, is to learn that we human beings live more and live better when we understand ourselves as connected to all peoples, whether past, present, near, or distant, not by means of technology but by an experience of our shared humanity.

But perhaps more importantly, the study of classical mythology allows you—like Odysseus in the Underworld (Figure 1.5)—an opportunity to listen to the tales of shades and shadows, to experience that although that long-lost world may be quiet, it is not dead. Study classical myth to experience once and for all that the world is alive, if you are able to imagine it to be.

KEY TERMS

Folktale 13
Legend 13

Mythological Corpus 14
Roman myths 28

FOR FURTHER EXPLORATION

Csapo, Eric. *Theories of Mythology.* Malden, MA, and Oxford: Wiley-Blackwell, 2005. Csapo surveys theories frequently applied to Greek myths and offers sensible advice about how to deploy these theories to understand myths.

Gardner, Jane. *Roman Myths.* Austin: University of Texas Press, 1993. Gardner's introduction to Roman myths highlights their form and function for Romans and lays out their differences from Greek myth.

Graf, Fritz. *Greek Mythology: An Introduction.* Translated by Thomas Marier. Baltimore, MD: The Johns Hopkins University Press, 1996. This is a clear and concise overview of a select number of theories frequently used to understand Greek myths, along with a review of how the Greeks created and continually reinvented their own myths.

Holland, Glen. *Gods of the Desert: Religions of the Ancient Near East.* Lanham, MD: Rowman & Littlefield, 2010. This is an excellent overview of the religions and gods of Egypt, the Levant, and Mesopotamia.

CHAPTER 2

CREATION

Coming into this particular body, and being born of these particular parents, and in such and such a place, and in general what we call external circumstances. That all happenings form a unity and are spun together is signified by the Fates (Moirai).

—**PLOTINUS**, **ENNEAD** (II.3)

W e think that if we know where we came from, we will know both who we are and who we are meant to be. We believe that our family histories will help us trace the origins of our own personalities and habits. We are told that an understanding of our country's history and the opportunities offered by its political and social organization will help us determine our roles as citizens. Finally, we may feel that an inquiry into the origins of the universe and of the human race will enable us to grasp our purpose in living. When Plotinus (c. 204/205–270 CE), a Greek philosopher living in the Roman Empire, observes that our physical body, parents, and external circumstances are our Fates, he succinctly captures a belief widely held in the ancient world as well as in our own times: that each person's origins and futures are linked.

Just as family stories convey information about your individual past and thus explain the present, stories about the creation of the universe serve a greater purpose than an attempt to explain the beginning of everything. For the ancient Greeks, as in many other cultures, beliefs about the creation of the universe reflect an understanding about the way their world works. Stories about the first humans and their actions are believed to be the foundation of—and to set the pattern for—all subsequent human history. By describing

< **2.1 (OPPOSITE):** Prometheus (seated) molds human beings out of clay and water. Marble sarcophagus. Third century CE. Museum Capitoline, Rome, Italy. *Erich Lessing / Art Resource, NY, ART74681.*

how the world came into being and how the first humans behaved, creation stories are believed to contain ethical, social, and religious patterns for human society. Creation tales thus seek to provide both explanation and justification, whether directly or indirectly, of the present order and to indicate how people ought to behave.

A GREEK CREATION STORY

The Greek text *Theogony*, believed to have been composed around the seventh century BCE by a poet known as Hesiod (dated to c. 750 and 650 BCE), was arguably the most important creation tale among the Greeks. The Greeks saw deeper meaning in and drew life lessons from Hesiod's depiction of the ascent of Zeus to kingship of the universe. In this chapter, we examine Hesiod's complex and often baffling creation story for reflections of the ethical, social, and religious codes of ancient Greece. We briefly survey the historical contexts in which Hesiod as well as Homer worked and seek to explain how both poets became of primary importance to Greek culture. A brief look at alternative creation stories that did not have the widespread currency of Hesiod's *Theogony* is followed by an examination of the major themes in Hesiod's *Theogony*. The emphasis of this further examination is on the religious and cultural relevance of Hesiod's creation story.

HISTORICAL SETTINGS OF HESIOD'S *THEOGONY*

The works attributed to Hesiod and Homer were recited orally by Greek poets for generations before they were ever written down (Figure 2.2). In fact, scholars have long debated whether the poets we know as "Hesiod" or "Homer" actually existed as historical figures. The poets of ancient Greece were able to perform very long works like *Theogony* and *Iliad* in a fairly consistent manner because these poems were composed orally using a type of verse called hexameter ("six feet"; every line of hexameter verse has six stressed syllables). This poetry relied on phrases called formulae (i.e., "so he spoke") and descriptions of people and objects called epithets ("ox-eyed Hera" or "warlike Menelaus") that all fit easily into the hexameter rhythm. Formulae and epithets were both memorable and easily combined, allowing poets to compose lengthy stories. Even after they were recorded in writing (sometime in the Archaic Period), these poems continued to be recited in public performances. Oral poems, then,

2.2 **A lyre player performs in a musical competition.** Detail from an Attic red-figure amphora. Andocides Painter, c. 525–520 BCE. Louvre Museum, Paris, France. @RMN-Grand Palais/Art Resource, NY, ART154717.

were the culmination of many performances of anonymous skilled poets who performed at games and festivals in places like Olympia.

Today, scholars continue to use "Homer" and "Hesiod"—rather than a more cumbersome and perhaps more accurate phrase such as "poets who performed songs in the style of Homer"—to refer to the composers of the *Iliad*, *Odyssey*, *Works and Days*, and *Theogony*. Thus although the first-person speaker who calls himself Hesiod in the opening of the *Theogony* and throughout the *Works and Days* emerges as a full-fledged individual, most scholars argue that this biographical information is more fiction than fact. However, as we have seen, archaeological discoveries suggest that the overall picture of Ascra in Hesiod's *Works and Days* nonetheless preserves some historical truth.

Despite the fundamental importance of its creation stories to many generations of Greeks, Hesiod's *Theogony* was not what could be considered sacred scripture, in the sense of the Hebrew Torah or the Christian Bible. In ancient Greece, there was no single, sacred book about the gods and all their deeds (what we might call "myths"). Hesiod's two great poems, *Works and Days* and *Theogony*, along with Homer's *Iliad* and *Odyssey* and a collection of Homeric hymns thought to be by Homer, were, however, considered to be especially important documents among the abundance of other texts and images that the Greeks considered filled with religious significance, if not quite "sacred." From such written material (as well as temple reliefs, statues, vase paintings, and religious practices) the Greeks learned about their gods and goddesses. How and when the Greeks encountered Hesiod's *Theogony* is taken up later in the sections on the Iron Age and Archaic Period. However, we begin our study with the Late Bronze Age because of its possible influence on the poetry of both Hesiod and Homer and its general relevance for understanding the historical context of myths.

The Late Bronze Age (1600–1150 BCE): Mycenae The Bronze Age—so named because of the use of bronze for tools and weapons—began before the third millennium in Greece. Three distinct regions in Greece had thriving civilizations during the Bronze Age: the island of Crete, where the Minoans dwelled; the Cycladic islands in the Aegean Sea; and mainland Greece (Map 2.1). On mainland Greece, the Late Bronze Age (1600–1150 BCE) is called the "Mycenaean Age" because it is typified by one fortified settlement called Mycenae. In Homer's great epic *Iliad* (Chapter 10.1), the Greek hero Agamemnon is said to have ruled Mycenae before joining his brother Menelaus and sailing off to battle at Troy. Besides Mycenae, important settlements in the Late Bronze Age include Pylos, Thebes, and Sparta, the very places that appear in myths from early Greece, particularly in Homer's epics. Although scholars debate the degree to which Homer's epics describe the conditions of the Late

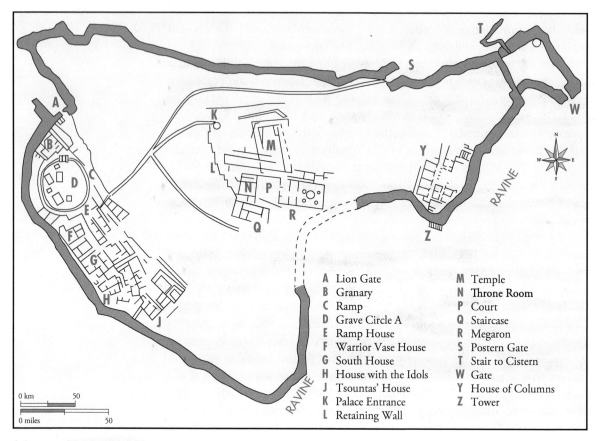

2.3a Plan of Mycenae's Citadel.

A Lion Gate
B Granary
C Ramp
D Grave Circle A
E Ramp House
F Warrior Vase House
G South House
H House with the Idols
J Tsountas' House
K Palace Entrance
L Retaining Wall
M Temple
N Throne Room
P Court
Q Staircase
R Megaron
S Postern Gate
T Stair to Cistern
W Gate
Y House of Columns
Z Tower

2.3b Ruins of Mycenae today. © Florin Stana/Shutterstock 194965928.

Bronze Age, the destruction of Mycenae and other large settlements in Greece ended an era known for its prosperous settlements and powerful kings.

The historical conditions of Late Bronze Age settlements are largely known from archaeological evidence and from documents found on clay tablets in a script called Linear B. The Mycenaeans developed Linear B from a writing system (called Linear A) used among the Minoans, who dwelled in Crete and came under Mycenaean domination by the fourteenth century BCE. Whereas scholars have not been able to decipher Linear A, they have succeeded in deciphering Linear B which the British linguist and architect Michael G.F. Ventris

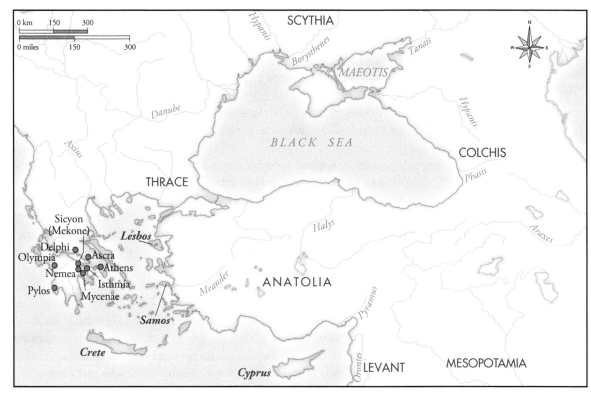

Map 2.1 Greece in the Mycenaean Age and the Archaic Period

(1922–1956) correctly identified as a form of early Greek. The five thousand or so clay tablets in Linear B that have been translated are largely administrative records about the production and distribution of goods. Even more compellingly, these documents also contain the names of some Greek gods and goddesses, including Artemis, Dionysus, Zeus, and Hera, indicating their early worship in Greece.

Located in the Peloponnese in a region called the Argolid, Mycenae was a typical Late Bronze Age settlement. Its center was on a hill, protected by thick walls, where a large building was surrounded by many smaller ones (Figures 2.3a and 2.3b). The central location of this large building suggests that the wealthiest and most powerful among the Mycenaean elite lived there. The Linear B tablets mention a king (*wanax*), ranked above the other elites, who seems a likely candidate for this building's resident. A grand staircase leading to its great court and its central room (*megaron*), which functioned as a place of worship and a reception area, suggest the *wanax*'s activities. The

Linear B tablets also list other elites (such as the "leader of the people," perhaps an army commander) and religious or political administrators who would have lived on the citadel as well. Bronze weapons, pottery, and gold jewelry found in royal graves and beehive tombs (*tholoi*, so named because their shape resembles a beehive) indicate the wealth of these elites. The houses of craftsmen, merchants, and the farmers and herders who provided food for those within the citadel were located on the plains outside Mycenae's massive stone walls.

Mycenae, like other Late Bronze Age communities such as Pylos and Thebes, had complex social and economic networks. The Linear B tablets as well as archaeological evidence indicate that the *wanax* employed perfume makers, bakers, potters, metalworkers, carpenters, spinners, and weavers, among other artisans. Specialization of labor typically indicates that a society was wealthy enough to support workers who do not have to engage in subsistence-level farming to survive. Some farmers and herders in Mycenae tended crops or livestock owned by elites, whereas others maintained smaller plots that they owned themselves (Figure 2.4). These farmers and herders paid taxes in the form of the goods they produced, enabling other residents to engage in activities other than food production. Along with craftsmen, they also served in the armies, whose officers were elite classes who lived on the *wanax*'s citadel. Mycenae was also home to slaves, who had been either captured in war or purchased from overseas.

Why and how Mycenae and similar well-organized and well-defended settlements in Greece and throughout the Ancient Near East disappeared soon after 1200 BCE remains a historical puzzle. The archaeological record neither precludes nor supports any single hypothesis to the exclusion of the others. Natural disasters (such as earthquakes and drought), external factors (such as invasions by the Sea Peoples and constant warfare), and internal factors (such as civil unrest) may have all contributed to the widespread and dramatic decline of Late Bronze Age settlements throughout the region. Whatever the causes, the highly organized social structure of the Late Bronze Age settlements did not reemerge in the subsequent Iron Age. Unlike Mycenae, Hesiod's town of Ascra was small, poor, and less centrally organized. Instead of one *wanax*, it had several rulers (*basileus*; the plural form is *basileis*). Because the powers of these rulers are debated, they are variously called kings, princes, chiefs, lords, or masters. Here we shall refer to them as kings.

2.4 A man with a plow pulling oxen. Terracotta statue from Boeotia, Greece. Seventh to sixth century BCE. Louvre Museum, Paris, France. *Gianni Dagli Orti/The Art Archive at Art Resource, NY, AA379724.*

The Iron Age (1150–750 BCE): Ascra The Iron Age, so named because iron became widely used for tools and weapons, is poorly understood because almost no written records survive to supplement archaeological material. Hesiod's *Works and Days*, composed at the end of the Iron Age, is one exception. Its events take place in Ascra, a small town located on the slopes of Mount Helicon in Boeotia. Along with archaeological evidence, Hesiod's *Works and Days* offers a glimpse of Ascra, as well as of the life of the poet whose *Theogony* influenced and shaped subsequent notions of Greek gods and goddesses.

In the *Works and Days*, Hesiod reports that his father immigrated to Ascra from Cyme on the coast of Asia Minor (Turkey), and that Hesiod and his brother, Perses, fought over their inheritance. Hesiod calls the kings who seemed to have decided this dispute in favor of Perses as "gift-eating." These kings, who were most likely wealthy landowners, had some collective judicial (although not military) power that they exercised over a loosely affiliated farming population. A recent archaeological survey of the slopes of Mount Helicon has revealed roughly sixty acres covered with a large number of artifacts, the remains of a circuit wall, and house walls that archaeologists have identified as Ascra. This area appears to be a farming village lacking both the fortified, grand palace typical of a Late Bronze Age settlement and the well-defined center typical of later Greek cities. This archaeological evidence seems to support Hesiod's description, according to which the Ascran kings did not dwell in centrally located palatial houses on citadels nor have as much wealth, military power, or economic authority as a Late Bronze Age *wanax* and the elites who surrounded him.

Hesiod describes every farmer as dwelling in his own residence (*oikos*) with a wife, children, and perhaps slaves or hired workers who help with the harvest. Every farmer must work the land, help or rely on his neighbor, and store his goods in his own barn. The self-reliance of Ascran farmers is evident in Hesiod's advice to his brother, Perses. He constantly advises Perses to work in order to secure his family's livelihood and warns him of the dangers of poverty. In this small, hardscrabble community with minimal civic structure and oversight, Hesiod also warns, even a man swearing an oath with a brother ought to get a witness. No doubt Hesiod's dispute with his brother Perses has inspired this bitter advice. But more than speaking to Hesiod's own situation, his advice indicates that the residents of Ascra had to rely on one another both to ensure that oaths and agreements were honored and to manage disasters such as drought. Self-reliant farmers such as these were most likely the first audiences of Hesiod's *Theogony*. During the subsequent Archaic Period, Hesiod's poems—his practical (if somewhat pessimistic) sensibilities in the *Works and Days* and his views of the gods and the cosmos in his *Theogony*—gained most of Greece as an audience and shaped Greek views of their gods.

The Archaic Period (750–490 BCE): Olympia An increase in population transformed Iron Age towns into robust cultural and political communities with ties to other communities, ushering in the Archaic Period. (This period was named by later historians for the style of its artistic production, which some historians considered "archaic" [i.e., old fashioned] when compared to art from the Classical Period.) Towns could not sustain their larger populations, prompting one of the major developments of the Archaic Period: colonization. Greeks began to travel, west to Italy and east to Asia Minor and the Black Sea region, establishing cities in lands with harbors and fertile plains. In addition, as towns in Greece became more populated, more extensive systems of government were needed.

The kings described by Hesiod became landed elites who gained more economic resources and who shared power with one another. If, however, one such elite could wrest power away from other elites by aligning himself with merchants, farmers, or tradesmen, he became a tyrant: initially a neutral term that described a sole ruler, "tyrant" eventually acquired negative connotations once such rulers were replaced with other forms of government. In this process, very often those who helped the tyrant gain power developed an identity as a collectivity, or a people (*demos*). This in turn led to cities in the Archaic Period becoming centrally organized—as suggested by laws recorded on stone and the invention of coinage—and developing civic identities. Members of such cities also interacted with one another in ways that began to shape their identity as Greeks, even though they did not develop a shared federal form of government. Shared beliefs and conceptions of the gods contributed to this process as well.

The Greeks, perceiving a common identity in their shared language and religious customs, began to describe themselves collectively as "Hellenes," rather than as members of a particular city (i.e., Athenians, Spartans, or Thebans). During the Archaic Period, Panhellenic (all-Greek) sanctuaries—the four most important were Delphi, Isthmia, Nemea, and Olympia (Figures 2.5a and 2.5b)—contributed to this developing shared identity among Greeks. Governed by neighboring towns or residents, these Panhellenic sanctuaries were understood to serve all Greeks. Their temples and grand quadrennial festivals provided an opportunity for Greek cities to worship their shared gods and to compete with one another in athletic and musical competitions, where they might hear poems such as Hesiod's *Theogony*.

The oral performances of works by Homer and Hesiod in the Archaic Period had a great impact on how the Greeks understood and imagined their gods and goddesses. They contributed to a gradual homogenization of beliefs and worship that was further encouraged by greater social exchanges among Greek-speaking communities. When traveling poets performed the

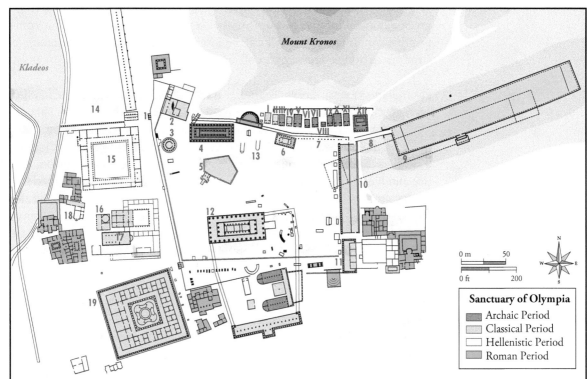

2.5a Plan of Olympia, Greece.

1: Northeast Propylon or Gate 2: Prytaneion 3: Philippeion 4: Temple of Hera 5: Pelopion 6: Metroon 7: Treasuries
8: Crypt (arched way to the stadium)   9: Stadium 10: Echo stoa 11: Hestia stoa 12: Temple of Zeus 13: Altar of Zeus
14: Gymnasion 15: Palaestra 16: Heroon 17: Phidias' workshop and paleochristian basilica 18: Greek baths 19: Leonidaion
I – XII: Treasuries of various Greek city-states.

songs of Homer and Hesiod throughout Greece and at Panhellenic sites, songs and ideas about the twelve Olympians (and the Olympians themselves) became increasingly popular. Wherever these gods were worshipped, they came to take on the characteristics attributed to them by Homer and Hesiod. Herodotus, the fifth-century BCE Greek historian who lived long after Hesiod, said that Greeks turned to Homer and Hesiod to learn about the appearances, ranks, titles, and powers of their gods (*Histories* 2.53). Herodotus confirms what modern historians surmise from studying Panhellenic sanctuaries and

2.5b Ruins of Olympia today: the Palaestra. © *f8grapher/ Shutterstock 138597086.*

greater cultural interactions during the Archaic Period. Even so, some communities maintained their local beliefs about specific characteristics of Greek gods and goddesses, as well as local worship traditions.

Panhellenism and Greek Divinities Most contemporary studies of Greek mythology present gods and goddesses with coherent personalities. This coherence derives from the moment in Greek history when Panhellenism culturally unified the Greeks. Such studies focus on four main types of stories about divinities: their spheres of influence (for example, Zeus oversees justice and Hera oversees marriage); their activities, which often correspond to mortal ones (for example, Athena weaves, as do mortal women); their associates on Olympus and on earth (Artemis, the virgin, is accompanied by young girls on earth and avoids Aphrodite, a goddess of love and sexuality, on Olympus); and their important sanctuaries or rituals (Apollo is often shown at Delphi, where he issues oracles, whereas Demeter is connected to her ritual and sanctuary in Eleusis). When small details about a particular god or goddess contradict one another (Aphrodite is the daughter of Uranus in Hesiod's *Theogony* but is the daughter of Zeus and Dione in Homer's *Iliad*), modern accounts often present the story that recurs most frequently in ancient written and visual sources while ignoring the variations.

Such coherent portraits of gods and goddesses are reasonable and defensible—indeed, they follow ancient representations of the gods, especially in visual media. The Greeks conceived of gods and goddess as having the forms of human beings, and the paintings and statues they made of these divinities can be astonishingly realistic. Greek artists crafted statues in bronze with gleaming marble eyes that seem to blink in the flickering lights of an oil lamp and life-sized marble statues of gods (which many contemporary scholars believe were brightly painted) whose musculature makes them seem about to step off their platforms and stride away. In the Greek theatre, masked actors played the part of divinities, just as masked actors played the part of human characters. With such vivid depictions and sensational stories, it is difficult to resist the allure of imagining the gods and goddesses as having coherent identities, even modern psychological profiles.

Yet ancient or modern depictions that represent a god or goddess with a unified personality, however compelling, are inevitably inaccurate. Greek gods and goddesses were worshipped all over the Greek-speaking world over long stretches of time. Not surprisingly, the ways they were worshipped and the traits attributed to their personalities varied from place to place and at different times. Some communities worshipped gods and goddesses that were indigenous— that is, they came into existence and were worshipped in only one community. Often these local divinities left traces of their existence in local laws or at local sites, but they have no known myths attached to them. Alternatively, local divinities were assimilated to any one of the gods described in Homer and Hesiod. Some communities worshipped gods and goddesses found in many myths but gave them a cult title (a descriptor that is tied to worship and thus has religious connotations) that hints at an aspect of the god that grew out of a particular event or need. (Cults are defined in Chapter 3.1.) For example, Apollo is infrequently labeled "Smintheus" (mouse-killer), an epithet that suggests he had once been called on to rid a community of a plague of mice.

In Part I of this book, we consider gods and goddesses in their Panhellenic aspect (i.e., their traits that are widely shared throughout Greece) as well as some of their local or temporal variations. As an example of this variation, we next turn our attention to alternative creation stories dating to the Archaic Period that did not achieve the popularity nor exert the cultural influence of Hesiod's *Theogony*.

Alternative Creation Stories The technological and cultural developments of the Archaic Period include systems for organizing information and promoting exchanges and communication. In particular, writing and coins rely on equivalences between different things. For example, to measure the worth of a cow in coins requires a symbolic connection between embossed metals and a living animal. Making this connection requires a type of abstract thinking that characterizes the Archaic Period of Greece. Philosophers of that time, such as Thales of Miletus (624–546 BCE) and Heraclitus of Ephesus (535–475 BCE), speculated on the origins of the universe and composed creation tales that reflect this symbolic thinking. These philosophers argued that there was one primary substance that was substituted for or underwent a process that converted it to all other substances. Thales argued that the primary substance was water, whereas others favored fire. Still other philosophers posited that an original principle instigated creation. Heraclitus used the word *logos* to describe this rational principle. In these ways, philosophers imagined that a substance or process created the universe, although they did not deny the existence of gods and goddesses.

In contrast to the philosophers' accounts of the origins of the universe, other stories (like Hesiod's *Theogony*) included generations of divine beings rather than a substance or principle. Among these are the creation stories of the Orphics, a loosely affiliated group of believers who claimed to follow the teachings of Orpheus (fifth century BCE to second century CE). Fragments of Orphic creation stories survive in a number of sources that span centuries. Although they do not agree with one another, they collectively include repeated motifs and gods not found in Hesiod. Most notably, they describe the early gods as Phanes (Light), Protogonus (Firstborn), and Chronus (Time; not to be confused with Cronus in Hesiod's *Theogony*), as well as Zeus and Earth.

In one Orphic hymn, recorded by the Greek philosopher Damascius (458–538 CE), a speaker explains Orpheus's account of creation: Chronus generated an egg that contained male and female natures within it. This egg, along with an unnamed winged god that is part bull and serpent, then generated other gods. Zeus is considered an important early god and acquires names and identities that are particular to Orphism and are not found elsewhere. He is called Pan (All) and Phanes (Figure 2.6).

Although Orphic accounts of creation with details such as these and the speculations of philosophers proliferated, none dislodged or replaced Hesiod's *Theogony* in the imaginations of Greek speakers, whether artists, philosophers, or ordinary citizens.

HESIOD'S CREATION STORY: THE *THEOGONY*

Instrumental in shaping Panhellenic notions of the Greek gods and goddesses, Hesiod's *Theogony* offered a grand vision of the origins of the universe. The *Theogony* is not a single integrated poem but rather a collection of different types of oral poems: hymns (praise poems to gods), catalogues (lists of places or events such as divine marriages and births), and dramatic tales (epic narratives with divine protagonists who take actions) (Table 2.1). Although most analyses of the *Theogony* focus on its dramatic tales, which chart Zeus's rise to power, its hymns and catalogues also contribute to an understanding of the creation of the universe and the birth of the gods. In particular, the two hymns in the poem (one to the Muses and one to Hecate) provide clues about how Hesiod and the audience for the *Theogony* viewed the gods.

2.6 A youthful divinity, perhaps Phanes. Detail from a marble relief. Second century CE. Galleria e Museo Estense, Modena, Italy. *Alinari / Art Resource, NY, ART129980.*

Hymns to Divinities The hymns in Hesiod's *Theogony* and those attributed to Homer were composed in hexameter and were meant to be recited by performing poets. Homeric hymns, especially those dedicated to Demeter, Aphrodite, Hermes, and Apollo, include stories of the god or goddess's birth, his or her relationships with other gods, and his or her acquisition of powers and places of worship. Although hymns convey this information in lively stories, their primary purpose is prayer to and praise of the gods. Although human beings play minor roles in hymns,

Table 2.1: Hesiod, The *Theogony*

HYMNS	
1–94	To the Muses
333–372	To the goddess Hecate

CATALOGUES	
95–125	Chaos gives birth
175–191	Night gives birth
192–332	Gods and goddesses of the sea give birth
591–649	Places in the universe
696–735	Zeus's marriages
736–810	Unions between goddesses and mortal men

DRAMATIC TALES	
126–174	Cronus defeats his father, Uranus
373–416	Zeus escapes from his father, Cronus
417–499	Zeus defeats Prometheus
500–590	Zeus defeats his father, Cronus
650–695	Zeus defeats Typhoeus

the relationship between humanity and divinity as well as religious sentiment can be gleaned from the hymns, making them rich sources for understanding the Greek mythological and religious imagination. We revisit Homeric hymns to specific gods and goddesses in later chapters; here, our focus is on *Theogony*.

2.7 A Muse plays a lyre atop Mount Helicon. Attic red figure (white ground), Lekythos. Achilles Painter, c. 445 BCE. *Staatliche Antikensammlungen und Glypothek München, Photograph by Renate Kühling, S80 Beazley Archive Number: 213977.*

Hesiod begins his *Theogony* with a hymn in praise of the Muses who dwell on Mount Helicon, where Hesiod is pasturing his flocks (1–94) (Figure 2.7). Hesiod makes himself a main protagonist in this hymn. The Muses give him a laurel branch, the emblem of the god Apollo (patron of prophecy, oracles, and song), and they teach him to sing about the gods. At first glance, this apparently autobiographical vignette conveys the source of Hesiod's ability and authority to sing about the creation of the universe: the Muses have inspired him. Yet, as soon as they grant Hesiod the authority to sing about the gods, they take it away, explaining: "Shepherds that camp in the wild, disgraces, merest bellies: we know to tell many lies that sound like truth, but we know to sing reality, when we will" (22–24). Thus, although the Muses may inspire Hesiod to sing the tale of creation, they mockingly imply that they may give him false and misleading information. Their words not only cast doubt on the tale Hesiod will tell but also suggest a world in which the divine is unreliable. Additionally, their words reveal the ignorance and vulnerability of human beings at the mercy of a universe of potentially deceitful divine beings.

In contrast to the hymn to the Muses is the devout, even comforting, hymn to Hecate, who here is presented as a benign and protective goddess (333–372), although she is more frequently associated with the Underworld and witchcraft. This hymn has many puzzling features. First, it describes a world in which Zeus rules the universe and an advanced human society of kings, cavalry, wars, animal husbandry, athletic contests, and courts. Yet in the larger narrative of the *Theogony*, Zeus has not gained control of the universe and human beings have not yet been created. Hesiod's insertion of this traditional hymn to Hecate therefore violates the overall order of his creation story. Such stitching together of traditional tales in inconsistent, even idiosyncratic, fashion is typical of oral composition; a performer mentions a name that reminds him of a long tale or hymn he knows, and he performs it without regard to what has come before.

Hesiod's portrayal of Hecate as a goddess counterbalances his depiction of the Muses. Whereas the Muses are disdainful of shepherds who must eat to survive, Hecate helps men obtain food, victory, and success, if they pray to her and offer her sacrifices. Considered together, these two hymns describe two very different kinds of female deities and perhaps convey the range of views that Hesiod and his audience held about the divine. The Greeks, it seemed, simultaneously imagined both scornful distrust and rapturous harmony between gods and men.

Catalogues Unlike the hymns, Hesiod's catalogues concern only gods and goddesses. The catalogues are a kind of list, and like all lists they contain useful information. The catalogues in the *Theogony* include long genealogies of divine beings that explain how the world became populated. Although they seem dull and impossible to remember to a modern reader, this feature made them particularly enjoyable to the audiences and poets of ancient Greece. They challenged a poet's memory, allowing him to show off his knowledge and skill. It may seem to modern readers that the catalogues, like the hymn to Hecate, are only tangentially important to Hesiod's overall tale. Did the poet simply stitch together traditional tales that were popular with audiences? Or do the catalogues have a larger significance to the creation story of the *Theogony*? A brief survey of three catalogues suggests the latter.

The story of creation that follows Hesiod's hymn to the Muses begins with a catalogue that describes how certain features of the cosmos came into existence. Chasm (Chaos) appears. She is followed by Earth (Gaia), Tartarus (a region in or below Earth), and Eros, a beautiful young male god who "overcomes the reason and purpose in the breasts of all gods and all men" (*Theogony* 98–99). Eros represents passion, and his presence early in the *Theogony* may explain what motivates procreative acts among subsequent generations. After these four elements come into being, Chasm, without a partner, gives birth to Darkness (Erebus) and Night (who are brother and sister). They then mate and give birth to Brighter Air (Aether) and Day. Then Earth, of her own initiative, gives birth to her son Heaven (Uranus), with whom she goes on to bear many offspring, in addition to the "fearsome" offspring she bears on her own.

The next genealogical catalogue furthers this impression of a seemingly random, self-generating universe that relies on a primarily feminine creative power (175–191). Without a male partner, Night produces Doom, Fate, Death, Sleep, Dreams, Cavil (Blame), Misery, the Hesperides (female goddesses), the Fates, the Furies, Resentment, Deceit, Intimacy, Old Age, and Strife (Figure 2.8). Some of these offspring are metaphors for Night, whereas others (such as Sleep and Dreams) represent Night's different

2.8 Strife (Eris). Interior of a black figure cup. Nikosthenes, c. 540–530 BCE. *The J. Paul Getty Museum, Villa Collection, Malibu, California, 86.AE.169.*

features. Both principles of association are typical of catalogues and may explain how oral poets composed and remembered them. Strife, also a female deity, then begets without a male partner a series of offspring more troublesome than those of Night. These include Neglect, Starvation, Bloodshed, Slaughter, Quarrels, and Lies. Significantly, Night and Strife's offspring have no male progenitors. They issue solely from their mothers in a random and uncontrolled fashion. All bring suffering into the world.

A later catalogue presents a contrast to these first two, which were dominated by the female principle. In this catalogue, after defeating Typhoeus, Zeus gains control of the universe and consolidates his rule by distributing honors among the immortals subject to his rule. Zeus then marries female goddesses, who bear him many children, most of whom are female and who represent the qualities of both Zeus and their mother. (For example, Themis, whose name means "established custom," gives birth to the Seasons, Lawfulness, Justice, and Peace.) An important exception to this pattern is Zeus's marriage to Metis, a goddess whose name means "cunning intelligence." Advised by Earth and Starry Heaven that she will give birth to a son who will challenge him, Zeus swallows Metis whole and then gives birth to the child she was carrying, Athena, from his head (Chapter 6.1).

With the exception of the story of Metis, the catalogue of Zeus's marriages offers a sharp contrast to the earlier catalogues of Night's and Strife's offspring. Female deities who are firmly under Zeus's control through marriage give birth to offspring whose attributes benefit mankind, but the offspring of females who produce spontaneously, without a male, have only negative attributes. Hesiod's catalogues suggest two different visions of how the universe might be populated: by females who procreate on their own or by Zeus, who operates through the institution of marriage. The *Theogony* celebrates the second option, presenting the marriages of Zeus as a positive alternative to earlier forms of female reproduction.

Dramatic Tales The dramatic tales in the *Theogony* describe how Zeus came to occupy his supreme position. The first dramatic tale describes the first generation of gods (126–174). Once Earth produces Heaven (Uranus), mother and son mate with each other and produce children called Titans. When the Titans are born, Uranus places them back inside Earth, their mother, prompting her to ask the children trapped inside her to revolt against their father. Only Cronus is willing. With Earth's assistance, he castrates Uranus with a sickle. As a consequence of his violent action, his brothers and sisters (the Titans) are able to leave their mother Earth. From Uranus's bloody genitals Aphrodite is born (Chapter 5.1), along with the Erinyes (female spirits of revenge), giants, and Meliai (nymphs). The catalogues of Night's offspring and the sea creatures immediately follow the castration of Uranus. This violent tale, together with these two catalogues, evokes a tumultuous world with no guiding principle, a seemingly ceaseless stream of monstrous births.

The creation and organization of the second generation of gods is described through three dramatic tales. In the first (373–416), the Titans Rhea and Cronus, who are brother and sister, give birth to the Olympians. These include Hestia, Demeter, Hera, Hades, Poseidon, and Zeus. Like his father, Uranus, Cronus wants to control the new generation of gods and so swallows them whole, confining them in his body, where they cannot resist his rule. Rhea, like her mother, Earth, wants to revolt against her husband but cannot reach her children to ask for their assistance. Yet she is not without advice and help. Her parents, Earth and Uranus, tell her to give Cronus a rock to swallow rather than her next child, Zeus, to whom she secretly gives birth on the island of Crete. On swallowing the rock, Cronus coughs up all his children. For his part, Zeus frees the powerful Cyclopes from Tartarus, where Uranus had imprisoned them.

2.9 **Zeus defeats Typhoeus.** Chalcidian black-figure hydria, c. 540 BCE. *Staatliche Antikensammlungen und Glypothek München. Photograph by Renate Kühling, 596.*

This second dramatic tales closes, like the first, on a note of confusion and impending conflict.

A further dramatic tale is devoted to Zeus's victory in battles and his eventual control of the universe. The monster Typhoeus, who is the offspring of Earth and Tartarus, has many snake-like heads and speaks all sorts of languages: human, divine, and bestial. Zeus battles and defeats the monster, finally consolidating his control of the universe (650–695) (Figure 2.9). Typhoeus embodies a confusion of categories between divinity and humanity, man and beast, and can be seen to represent social anarchy. Curiously, just as Earth prodded Cronus to revolt against Uranus and then helped Zeus revolt against Cronus, Earth's creation of Typhoeus hints that she will challenge all who seek to supplant her. Typhoeus would have ruled the universe had Zeus not defeated him, and his leadership would have been as chaotic and disorganized as his many-headed body—or as the unchecked and spontaneous fertility of Earth, with her seemingly limitless ability to bring forth monsters.

Zeus's defeat of Typhoeus demonstrates that he is able to conquer any martial enemy; the catalogue of his marriages that follows this tale suggests that he has found a way to contain and control female reproduction. The conclusion of the *Theogony* diverts readers from the fact that Zeus did not create the universe. Instead, Hesiod seems to find relief in Zeus's institution of order and justice; Zeus has transformed the universe from a chaotic place to a *cosmos*, a Greek

2.10 The creation of Pandora with Epimetheus, Hermes, and Zeus. Red-figure krater. Fifth century BCE. *Ashmolean Museum / The Art Archive at Art Resource, NY, AA566705.*

word that means "government," "ruler," or "universe," but also means simply "good order." But this good order of Zeus pertains mainly to the gods. The human world, as we shall see, is less well organized.

The story of Prometheus and Pandora, the last of the dramatic tales in the *Theogony* to be considered, addresses both the institution of marriage and the question of order in human society. The first half of the story, set in the divine realm, concentrates on the battle of wits between Prometheus and Zeus; the second half concerns the creation of Pandora and the human world.

Hesiod does not offer an explanation for why Prometheus challenges Zeus to a battle of wits. Prometheus, a Titan, may be innately hostile to Zeus and all the Olympians or may be seeking to wrest control of the universe from Zeus. Hesiod also does not explain when men were created. As the story begins, men and the gods are dining together at Mekone (a mythical place that is sometimes associated with Sicyon in the northeast Peloponnese), and Prometheus tries to trick Zeus into choosing a portion of food that consists of inedible bones hidden in delicious fat. Zeus retaliates against Prometheus for this deception by taking fire away from human beings, even though they played no role in Prometheus's trick. This vengeful action makes sense in the context of other myths that make Prometheus the ancestor or creator of the human race. In some such myths, Prometheus makes human beings out of clay and water (Figure 2.1); in others, his son, Deucalion, and his wife, Pyrrha, the only survivors of a flood, repopulate the earth by tossing rocks onto the ground that are transformed into human beings (Chapter 3.3). Thus, when Zeus takes fire away from human beings, he indirectly punishes Prometheus, who then steals fire and returns it to humankind to keep them from perishing (Chapter 3.1).

After Prometheus's theft of fire, the focus of this tale turns to the human race. Zeus cleverly retaliates, not by taking anything from human beings, but by giving them a gift that transforms their world. He asks the gods to fashion a beautiful maiden who, like the portion of food Prometheus gave him, looks lovely on the outside but whose character is deceitful (Figure 2.10). In many accounts, Pandora marries Epimetheus (Prometheus's brother) and gives birth to several children, including Pyrrha who with her husband repopulates the earth after a great flood (Chapter 3.3). The figure of Pandora, the ancestor of the race of human women, is meant to describe and explain all women, or at least how Hesiod and his audience saw them: "pretty" and necessary, yet "conspirators in causing difficulty" and a "great affliction."

The creation of Pandora and the presence of women among men compel two vital human practices: sacrifice and marriage. Men will no longer dine at Mekone *with* the gods; instead, they will sacrifice *to* the gods. Hesiod writes that, "ever since that [i.e., Prometheus's trick], the peoples on earth have burned white bones for the immortals on aromatic altars" (454–456). In addition, men must marry and produce children with their wives, who stay in the house and take the toil of others into their own "bellies," a word that recalls the Muses' address to Hesiod and shepherds. "Bellies," like the tale of Prometheus, suggests a uniquely masculine perspective on the human condition. Between birth and death, men in ancient Greece toiled to serve the needs of many "bellies": their own, as well as those of their wives and children, through constant agricultural and pastoral labor. Yet their hardships and sufferings had meaning because they were linked to a cosmic order controlled by Zeus that embodied beauty and stability. The alternative to the present order on earth and in heaven, the *Theogony* suggests, is the chaos of Typhoeus or the disorder of Earth.

HESIOD, *THEOGONY*

BEFORE YOU READ

Hesiod's *Theogony* is a treasure trove of information about the origins of the gods and goddesses as well as how the Greeks understood and worshipped them. One useful approach to this text is to identify its hymns, catalogues, and dramatic tales (see Table 2.1, on p. 49) and to make sense of these discrete sections before trying to put them together. (Translated by M. L. West.)

- How do the dramatic tales describe male leaders such as Uranus, Cronus, and Zeus? How is Zeus similar and different from his father and grandfather? What sorts of qualities does Zeus have that they do not?

- Prometheus's deception of Zeus introduces the practice of sacrifice into the world. Can you describe the practice of sacrifice from Hesiod's tale? How does sacrifice define the relationships between mortals and gods?

- Creation stories describe not only how the universe was created but also how human beings ought to behave. What lessons does this poem impart to its male audience? Does it have anything specific to say to a female audience?

- The next section of this chapter introduces the notion of "charter" myths. If you treat Hesiod's *Theogony* as a charter myth, can you list the social practices and values this poem justifies?

HESIOD, *THEOGONY* (EIGHTH CENTURY BCE)

FROM the Muses of Helicon let us begin our singing, that haunt Helicon's great and holy mountain, and dance on their soft feet round the violet-dark spring and the altar of the mighty son of Kronos. And when they have bathed their gentle skin in Permessos, or the Horse's Fountain, or holy Olmeios, then on the highest slope of Helicon they make their dances, fair and lovely, stepping lively in time. From there they go forth, veiled in thick mist, and walk by night, uttering beautiful voice, singing of Zeus who bears the aegis,

and the lady Hera of Argos, who walks in sandals of gold,
and the daughter of Zeus the aegis-bearer, pale-eyed Athene,   10
and Phoebus Apollo, and Artemis the archer,
and Poseidon earth-charioted, shaker of the earth,
and holy Themis, and Aphrodite of curling lashes,
and Hebe of gold diadem, and fair Dione,
Leto, Iapetos, and crooked-schemer Kronos,
Dawn, mighty Sun, and shining Moon,
Earth, great Oceanus, and dark Night,

and the rest of the holy family of immortals who are for ever.
    And once they taught Hesiod fine singing, as he tended his lambs below holy Helicon. This is what the goddesses said to me first, the   20
Olympian Muses, daughters of Zeus the aegis-bearer:

"Shepherds that camp in the wild, disgraces, merest bellies:
we know to tell many lies that sound like truth,
but we know to sing reality, when we will."

So said mighty Zeus' daughters, the sure of utterance, and they gave me a branch of springing bay to pluck for a staff, a handsome one, and they breathed into me wondrous voice, so that I should celebrate things of the future and things that were aforetime. And they told me to sing of the family of blessed ones who are for ever, and first and last always to sing of themselves.   30
    But what is my business round tree or rock? Come now, from the Muses let us begin, who with their singing delight the great mind of Zeus the father in Olympus, as they tell of what is and what shall be and what was aforetime, voices in unison. The words flow untiring from their mouths, and sweet, and the halls of their father, loud-thundering Zeus, rejoice at the goddesses' clear voice spread abroad, and the peak of snowy Olympus

rings, and the mansions of the gods. Making divine utterance, they celebrate first in their song the august family of gods, from the beginning, those
whom Earth and broad Heaven begot, and the gods that were born from
them, givers of blessings. Second they sing of Zeus, father of gods and   40
men, how far the highest of the gods he is, and the greatest in power. And
again they sing of the family of men and of powerful Giants to delight the
mind of Zeus in Olympus, those Olympian Muses, daughters of Zeus the
aegis-bearer.

They were born in Pieria to Memory, queen of the foothills of Eleutherae, in union with the father, the son of Kronos; oblivion of ills and respite
from cares. Nine nights Zeus the resourceful lay with her, going up to her
holy bed far away from the immortals. And when the time came, as the
months passed away and the seasons turned about, and the long tale of
days was completed, she bore nine daughters—all of one mind, their care-   50
free hearts set on song—not far from the topmost peak of snowy Olympus.
There they have their gleaming dancing-places and their fair mansions; and
the Graces and Desire dwell beside them, in feasting. Lovely is the sound
they produce from their mouths as they sing and celebrate the ordinances
and the good ways of all the immortals, making delightful utterance.

So then they went to Olympus, glorying in their beautiful voices, singing divinely. The dark earth rang round them as they sang, and from their
dancing feet came a lovely *estampie* as they went to their father. He is king
in heaven: his is the thunder and the smoking bolt, since he defeated his
father Kronos by strength. He has appointed their ordinances to the immor-   60
tals, well in each detail, and assigned them their privileges.

This is what the Muses sang, who dwell in Olympus, the nine daughters born of great Zeus,

Clio and Euterpe and Thaleia and Melpomene,
Terpsichore and Erato and Polyhymnia and Urania,
and Calliope, who is chief among them all;

for she even attends august kings. Whomsoever great Zeus' daughters
favour among the kings that Zeus fosters, and turn their eyes upon him at
his birth, upon his tongue they shed sweet dew, and out of his mouth the
words flow honeyed; and the peoples all look to him as he decides what   70
is to prevail with his straight judgments. His word is sure, and expertly he
makes a quick end of even a great dispute. This is why there are prudent
kings: when the peoples are wronged in their dealings, they make amends
for them with ease, persuading them with gentle words. When he goes
among a gathering, they seek his favour with conciliatory reverence, as if
he were a god, and he stands out among the crowd.

Such is the Muses' holy gift to men. For while it is from the Muses and far-shooting Apollo that men are singers and citharists on earth, and from Zeus that they are kings, every man is fortunate whom the Muses love; the voice flows sweet from his lips. Though a man's heart be withered with the 80 grief of a recent bereavement, if then a singer, the servant of the Muses, sings of the famous deeds of men of old, and of the blessed gods who dwell in Olympus, he soon forgets his sorrows and thinks no more of his family troubles, quickly diverted by the goddesses' gifts.

Farewell now, children of Zeus, and grant me delightful singing. Celebrate the holy family of immortals who are for ever, those who were born of Earth and Heaven and of black Night, and those whom the briny Sea fostered; and tell how the gods and the earth were born in the first place, and the rivers, and the boundless sea with its furious swell, and the shining stars and broad firmament above; and how they shared out 90 their estate, and how they divided their privileges, and how they gained all the glens of Olympus in the first place. Tell me this from the beginning, Muses who dwell in Olympus, and say, what thing among them came first.

First came the Chasm; and then broad-breasted Earth, secure seat for ever of all the immortals who occupy the peak of snowy Olympus; the misty Tartara in a remote recess of the broad-pathed earth; and Eros, the most handsome among the immortal gods, dissolver of flesh, who overcomes the reason and purpose in the breasts of all gods and all men.

Out of the Chasm came Erebos and dark Night, and from Night in 100 turn came Bright Air and Day, whom she bore in shared intimacy with Erebos. Earth bore first of all one equal to herself, starry Heaven, so that he should cover her all about, to be a secure seat for ever for the blessed gods; and she bore the long Mountains, pleasant haunts of the goddesses, the Nymphs who dwell in mountain glens; and she bore also the undraining Sea and its furious swell, not in union of love. But then, bedded with Heaven, she bore deep-swirling Oceanus,

Koios and Kreios and Hyperion and Iapetos,
Thea and Rhea and Themis and Memory,
Phoebe of gold diadem, and lovely Tethys.   110

After them the youngest was born, crooked-schemer Kronos, most fearsome of children, who loathed his lusty father.

And again she bore the proud-hearted Cyclopes,
Thunderer, Lightner, and Whitebolt stern of spirit,

who gave Zeus his thunder and forged his thunderbolt. In other respects they were like the gods, but a single eye lay in the middle of their forehead; they had the surname of Circle-eyes because of this one circular eye that lay on their forehead. And strength and force and resource were upon their works.

And again there were born of Earth and Heaven three more sons, mighty and stern, not to be spoken of, Kottos, Briareos, and Gyges, overbearing children. A hundred arms sprang from their shoulders—unshapen hulks—and fifty heads grew from the shoulders of each of them upon their stalwart bodies. And strength boundless and powerful was upon their mighty form. 120

For all those that were born of Earth and Heaven were the most fearsome of children, and their own father loathed them from the beginning. As soon as each of them was born, he hid them all away in a cavern of Earth, and would not let them into the light; and he took pleasure in the wicked work, did Heaven, while the huge Earth was tight-pressed inside, and groaned. She thought up a nasty trick. Without delay she created the element of grey adamant, and made a great reaping-hook, and showed it to her dear children, and spoke to give them courage, sore at heart as she was: 130

"Children of mine and of an evil father, I wonder whether you would like to do as I say? We could get redress for your father's cruelty. After all, he began it by his ugly behaviour."

So she spoke; but they were all seized by fear, and none of them uttered a word. But the great crooked-schemer Kronos took courage, and soon replied to his good mother: 140

"Mother, I would undertake this task and accomplish it—I am not afraid of our unspeakable father. After all, he began it by his ugly behaviour."

So he spoke, and mighty Earth was delighted. She set him hidden in ambush, put the sharp-toothed sickle into his hand, and explained the whole stratagem to him.

Great Heaven came, bringing on the night, and, desirous of love, he spread himself over Earth, stretched out in every direction. His son reached out from the ambush with his left hand; with his right he took the huge sickle with its long row of sharp teeth and quickly cut off his father's genitals, and flung them behind him to fly where they might. They were not released from his hand to no effect, for all the drops of blood that flew off were received by Earth, and as the years went round she bore the powerful Erinyes and the great Giants in gleaming armour with long spears in their hands, and the nymphs whom they call Meliai on the boundless earth. 150

As for the genitals, just as he first cut them off with his instrument of adamant and threw them from the land into the surging sea, even so they were carried on the waves for a long time. About them a white foam grew from the immortal flesh, and in it a girl formed. First she approached holy Cythera; then from there she came to sea-girt Cyprus. And out stepped a   160 modest and beautiful goddess, and the grass began to grow all round beneath her slender feet. Gods and men call her Aphrodite, because she was formed in foam, and Cytherea, because she approached Cythera, and Cyprus-born, because she was born in wave-washed Cyprus, and "genial," because she appeared out of genitals. Eros and fair Desire attended her birth and accompanied her as she went to join the family of gods. And this has been her allotted province from the beginning among men and immortal gods:

> the whisperings of girls; smiles; deceptions;
> sweet pleasure, intimacy, and tenderness.   170

As for those children of great Heaven, their father who begot them railed at them and gave them the surname of Titans, saying that straining *tight* in wickedness they had done a serious thing, and that he had a *title* to revenge for it later.

Night bore hateful Doom and dark Fate and Death, she bore Sleep, she bore the tribe of Dreams. And secondly gloomy Night bore Cavil and painful Misery, bedded with none of the gods; and the Hesperides, who mind fair golden apples beyond the famed Oceanus, and the trees that bear that fruit; and the Fates she bore, and the mercilessly punishing Furies who prosecute the transgressions of men and gods—never do the god-   180 desses cease from their terrible wrath until they have paid the sinner his due. And baleful Night gave birth to Resentment also, an affliction for mortal men; and after her she bore Deceit and Intimacy, and accursed Old Age, and she bore hard-hearted Strife.

> Hateful Strife bore painful Toil,
> Neglect, Starvation, and tearful Pain,
> Battles, Combats, Bloodshed and Slaughter,
> Quarrels, Lies, Pretences, and Arguments,
> Disorder, Disaster—neighbours to each other—
> and Oath, who most harms men on earth,   190
> when someone knowingly swears false.

Sea fathered Nereus, reliable and true, the eldest of his children. And they call the old man so because he is *ne'er*-failing and kindly, and does not neglect what is right, but has a just and kindly mind. Then again he fathered great Thaumas and noble Phorcys in union with Earth, and Ceto of the lovely cheeks, and Eurybia, who had a spirit of adamant in her breast.

From Nereus were born numerous goddess-children in the undraining sea, and from Doris, lovely-haired daughter of Oceanus the unending river:

Protho, Eucrante, Sao, and Amphitrite,	200
Eudora, Thetis, Galene, and Glauce,	
Cymothoe, swift Speo, and lovely Thalia,	
Pasithea, Erato, and rosy Eunice,	
delightful Melite, Eulimene and Agaue,	
Doto and Proto, Pherosa, Dynamene,	
Nesaea and Actaea and Protomedea,	
Doris, Panope, and beautiful Galatea,	
lovely Hippothoe and rosy-armed Hipponoe,	
Cymodoce, who stills with ease the waves	
in the misty sea and the gusts of strong-blowing winds	210
with Cymatolege and fair-ankled Amphitrite;	
Cymo and Eïone and fair-diadem Halimede,	
smiling Glauconome and Pontoporea,	
Leagora and Euagora and Laomedea,	
Polynoe, Autonoe, and Lysianassa,	
Euarne lovely of build and perfect to behold,	
and Psamathe of charming body, and gracious Menippe,	
Neso, Eupompe, Themisto, and Pronoe,	
and Nemertes, who has her immortal father's manner.	

These were born of the excellent Nereus, fifty daughters of excellent 220 attainments.

Thaumas married a daughter of deep-flowing Oceanus, Electra, and she bore swift Iris and the lovely-haired Harpies, Aello and Ocypeta, who race with the gusts of the winds and with the birds on swift wings, for they hurl on high.

To Phorcys Ceto bore old women fair of cheek, white-haired from birth: the immortal gods and men who walk on earth call them the Old Women, fair-robed Pemphredo and saffron-robed Enyo. And she bore the Gorgons, who live beyond famed Oceanus at the world's edge hard by Night, where the clear-voiced Hesperides are: Sthenno, Euryale, and 230 Medusa who suffered a grim fate. She was mortal, but the other two immortal and ageless; and with her the god of the Sable Locks lay in a soft meadow among the spring flowers. And when Perseus cut off her head from her neck, out sprang great Chrysaor and the horse Pegasus. He was so named because he was born beside the waters of Oceanus, while the other was born with a golden sword in his hands. Pegasus flew away and left the earth, the mother of flocks, and came to the immortals; and he lives in Zeus' palace, bringing thunder and lightning for Zeus the resourceful. Chrysaor fathered three-headed Geryoneus in union with Callirhoe, daughter of famed Oceanus. The mighty Heracles despoiled him beside   240 the shambling oxen in sea-girt Erythea on the day when he drove off the broad-browed bulls to holy Tiryns, after he had crossed Oceanus and killed Orthos and the herdsman Eurytion in the misty ranch beyond famed Oceanus.

But Ceto bore another impossible monster—not like mortal men nor the immortal gods—in a hollow cave, the wondrous Echidna stern of heart, who is half a nymph with fair cheeks and curling lashes, and half a monstrous serpent, terrible and huge, glinting and ravening, down in the hidden depths of the numinous earth. There she has her cave, down below in a hollow cliff, far away from immortal gods and mortal men, where the   250 gods allotted her a home to dwell.

Grim Echidna is confined underground in the land of the Arimi, immortal nymph and ageless for all time. And they say Typhaon was united with her in intimacy, terrible lawless brute with curly-lashed nymph; and she conceived, and bore stern-hearted children. First she gave birth to Orthos, a dog for Geryoneus. Secondly she bore an impossible creature, unspeakable, the ravening Cerberus, Hades' dog with a voice of bronze, fifty-headed, shy of no one, and powerful. Thirdly she gave birth to the baleful Hydra of Lerna, whom the white-armed goddess Hera fostered in her insatiable wrath towards the mighty Heracles. But the son of Zeus, called son of   260 Amphitryon, Heracles, slew it with merciless bronze, with the help of the warlike Iolaus, and the advice of Athene driver of armies.

But she bore Chimaera, who breathed invincible fire, a terrible great creature, swift-footed and strong. She had three heads: one of a fierce lion, one of a she-goat, and one of a powerful serpent. She was killed by noble Bellerophon with Pegasus. But she, surrendering to Orthos, bore the baneful Sphinx, death to the people of Cadmus, and the Nemean Lion, which Hera, Zeus' honoured wife, fostered and settled in the foothills of Nemea, an affliction for men. There it lived, harassing the local peoples, monarch of Tretos in Nemea and of Apesas; but mighty Heracles' force   270 overcame it.

The youngest that Ceto bore in shared intimacy with Phorcys was the fearful serpent that guards the golden apples in a hidden region of the dark earth, at its vasty limits. That is the descendance of Ceto and Phorcys.

Tethys bore to Oceanus the swirling Rivers,

> the Nile, Alpheus, and deep-swirling Eridanus,
> Strymon, Maeander, and fair-flowing Danube,
> Phasis, Rhesus, and silver-swirling Achelous,
> Nessus, Rhodius, Haliacmon, Heptaporus,   280
> Granicus and Aesepus and wondrous Simois,
> Peneus, Hermus, and flowing Caïcus,
> great Sangarius, Ladon, Parthenius,
> Euenus and Ardescus and wondrous Scamander.

And she bore the holy family of Nymphs, who nurture men on earth with the lord Apollo and the Rivers, having this function allotted by Zeus:

> Peitho and Admete, Vianthe and Electra,
> Doris, Prymno, and godlike Urania,
> Hippo, Clymene, Rhodea, and Callirhoe,
> Zeuxo, Clytia, Idyia, and Pasithoe,   290
> Plexaura and Galaxaura, lovely Dione,
> Melobosis, Thoe, and fair Polydora,
> Cerceïs of lovely form, Pluto of big dark eyes,
> Perseïs, Ianeira, Acaste, and Xanthe,
> lovely Petraea, Menestho, Europa,
> Metis, Eurynome, and saffron-robed Telesto,
> Chryseïs, Asia, and desirable Calypso,
> Eudora, Tyche, Amphirho, Ocyrhoe,
> and Styx, who is chief among them all.

These were the eldest daughters born of Oceanus and Tethys; but there are   300
many others too. For there are three thousand graceful-ankled Oceanids;
widely scattered they haunt the earth and the depths of the waters everywhere alike, shining goddess-children. And there are as many again of the
Rivers that flow with splashing sound, sons of Oceanus that lady Tethys
bore. It is hard for a mortal man to tell the names of them all, but each of
those peoples knows them that live near them.

Thea, surrendering in intimacy to Hyperion, gave birth to the mighty
Sun and shining Moon, and to Dawn, who makes light for all who dwell
on earth and for the immortal gods who live in the wide heaven.

With Kreios Eurybia shared intimacy, noble among goddesses, and   310
bore great Astraeus and Pallas, and Perses, who shone out amongst them
all for his wisdom. To Astraeus Dawn bore the stern-hearted Winds, the
clearing Westerly and the rushing Northerly and the Southerly, goddess

with god bedded in love; and after them the Mist-born one gave birth to the Morning Star, and the shining stars that are heaven's garland.

Styx, daughter of Oceanus, in union with Pallas, bore Aspiration and trim-ankled Victory in her halls, and Power and Strength, outstanding children, who will not live apart from Zeus, nor take their seats, nor go except where the god goes before them, but they sit for ever beside heavy-booming Zeus. For so did Styx, perennial Oceanid, determine, on   320
that day when the Olympian Lightner called all the immortal gods to long Olympus, and said that whoever of the gods would fight the Titans with him, he would not smite any of them down from his privileges, but each one would keep the honour he had had before among the immortal gods. And he said that whoever was unhonoured by Kronos and unprivileged, he would set him in the path of honour and privileges, as is right and proper. And the first to come to Olympus was perennial Styx with her children, on the advice of her dear father; and Zeus honoured her, and granted her exceptional favours. He made her to be the great oath of the gods, and her children to dwell with him for all time. In the same way he   330
fulfilled his promises to all throughout, while he himself has the power and the kingdom.

Phoebe came to Koios' bed of delight; and conceiving then, goddess with god united in intimacy, she bore sable-robed Leto, ever gentle, mild towards men and immortal gods, gentle from the beginning, most kindly in Olympus. She bore also Asteria, whom it is good to speak of; whom Perses later brought home to his great house to be known as his dear wife. There she conceived and bore Hecate, whom Zeus son of Kronos honoured above all others, granting her magnificent privileges: a share both of the earth and of the undraining sea. From the starry heaven too   340
she has a portion of honour, and she is the most honoured by the immortal gods. Even now, when an earthly man sacrificing fine offerings makes ritual propitiation, he invokes Hecate, and great favour readily attends him, if the goddess is well disposed to his prayers, and she grants him prosperity, for she has the power to do so. From all those that were born of Earth and Heaven and were allotted honour, she has a share. The son of Kronos did not oppress her or take away from her anything of what she had been allotted among the Titans, the former gods: she keeps it even as the distribution was first made, from the beginning. Nor does her being an only child mean that the goddess has received less honour and   350
privilege in earth and sky and sea, but much more, because Zeus honours her. By whomsoever she chooses, she comes and stands in full presence and helps him. In time of judgment she sits beside august kings; in the public gathering the man of her choice shines out among the crowd. When men arm themselves for battle and slaughter, there the goddess

comes and stands by whichever side she chooses to grant victory with her favour and hand them glory. She is good for standing by cavalry, when she chooses to; and good again when men compete in athletic contest— there the goddess comes and stands by them too and helps them; and victorious by his strength and power, a man wins the fine prize with ease   360 and joy, conferring glory on his parents. To those too who till the surly grey, and who pray to Hecate and the strong-thundering Shaker of Earth, easily the proud goddess grants a large catch; but easily she takes it away when it is sighted, if she so chooses. She is good for increasing the livestock in the folds together with Hermes. Herds of cattle and broad herds of goats and flocks of fleecy sheep, if so she chooses, she makes great out of small, and less out of many. So, even though she is an only child on her mother's side, she is honoured among the immortals with every privilege. And the son of Kronos made her a fosterer of the young, for those whose eyes since her birth have seen the light of far-sighted   370 day. So she has been a nurse of the young from the beginning, and these are her privileges.

Rhea, surrendering to Kronos, bore resplendent children:

> Hestia, Demeter, and gold-sandalled Hera,
> mighty Hades who lives under the earth,
> merciless of heart, and the booming Shaker of Earth,
> and Zeus the resourceful, father of gods and men,
> under whose thunder the broad earth is shaken.

The others great Kronos swallowed, as each of them reached their mother's knees from her holy womb. His purpose was that none but he of the   380 lordly Celestials should have the royal station among the immortals. For he learned from Earth and starry Heaven that it was fated for him to be defeated by his own child, powerful though he was, through the designs of great Zeus. So he kept no blind man's watch, but observed and swallowed his children. Rhea suffered terrible grief. But when she was about to give birth to Zeus, father of gods and men, then she begged her dear parents, Earth and starry Heaven, to devise a plan so that she could bear her child in secrecy and make Kronos pay her father's furies and those of the children he had been swallowing, great Kronos the crooked-scheming. And they took heed and did as their dear daughter asked, and told her   390 all that was fated to come to pass concerning Kronos the king and his stern-hearted son. And they told her to go to Lyktos, to the rich Cretan land, when she was due to bear the youngest of her children, great Zeus. Mighty Earth accepted him from her to rear and nurture in broad Crete. There she came carrying him through the swift, dark night, not stopping until she came to Lyktos, and taking him in her arms she hid him in a cave hard of access, down in the secret places of the numinous earth, in the Aegean mountain with its dense woods. Then she wrapped a large stone in babycloth and delivered it to the son of Heaven, the great lord, king of the Former Gods. Seizing it in his hands, he put it away in his belly, the   400 brute, not realizing that thereafter not a stone but his son remained, secure and invincible, who before long was to defeat him by physical strength and drive him from his high station, himself to be king among the immortals.

Rapidly then the lord's courage and resplendent limbs grew; and when the due time came round, the great crooked-schemer Kronos, tricked by the cunning counsel of Earth, defeated by his son's strength and stratagem, brought his brood back up. The first he spewed out was the stone, the last he swallowed. Zeus fixed it in the wide-pathed earth at holy Pytho, in the glens of Parnassus, to be a monument thereafter and a thing of wonder   410 for mortal men.

He set his father's brothers free from their baneful bondage, the sons of Heaven whom their father in his folly had imprisoned; and they returned thanks for his goodness by giving him thunder and lightning and the smoking bolt, which mighty Earth had kept hidden up to then. With these to rely on he is lord of mortals and immortals.

Iapetos married a trim-ankled Oceanid nymph, Clymene, and went up to share one bed with her. She bore him Atlas, a stern-hearted child, and proud Menoitios, and Prometheus, subtle, shifting-scheming, and misguided Epimetheus, who from the start turned out a disaster to men who   420 live by bread, since he was the original one who received the moulded maiden from Zeus for a wife. The lawless Menoitios was sent down to the darkness by wide-seeing Zeus with a smoking bolt, because of his wickedness and overbearing strength. Atlas, under strong constraint, holds up the broad sky with his head and tireless hands, standing at the ends of the earth, away by the clear-voiced Hesperides, for Zeus the resourceful assigned him this lot. And he bound crafty Prometheus in inescapable fetters, grievous bonds, driving them through the middle of a pillar. And he set a great winged eagle upon him, and it fed on his immortal liver, which grew the same amount each way at night as the great bird ate in the course of   430 the day. It was killed by trim-ankled Alcmene's valiant son, Heracles, who saved the son of Iapetos from that affliction and set him free from his distress. Olympian Zeus who rules on high was not unwilling, intending that the fame of Heracles, born at Thebes, should be still greater than before upon the wide-pastured earth: this is why he did reverence and honour to his eminent son, and, irate though he was, ended the anger he had before, which was because Prometheus pitted his wits against the mighty son of

Kronos. For when gods and mortal men were coming to a settlement at Mekone, he had carved up a big ox and served it in such a way as to mislead Zeus. For him he laid out meat and entrails rich with fat in the hide, 440 covering it in the ox's stomach, while for men he laid out the ox's white bones, which he arranged carefully for a cunning trick by covering them in glistening fat. Then the father of gods and men said to him,

> "Son of Iapetos, outstanding among all the lords,
> my good sir, how unfairly you have divided the portions."

So chided Zeus, whose designs do not fail. But crooked-schemer Prometheus, smiling quietly and intent on deceit, said to him,

> "Zeus greatest and most glorious of the eternal fathers,
> choose then whichever of them the spirit in your
>   breast bids you."

He spoke meaning trickery, but Zeus, whose designs do not fail, recog- 450 nized the trick and did not mistake it, and he boded evil in his heart for mortal men, which was to come to pass. With both hands he took up the white fat; and he grew angry about the lungs, and wrath reached him to the spirit, when he saw the white oxbones set for a cunning trick. Ever since that, the peoples on earth have burned white bones for the immortals on aromatic altars. In great ire Zeus the cloud-gatherer said to him,

> "Son of Iapetos, clever above all others,
> my good sir: then you are still intent on deceit."

So spoke Zeus in his wrath, whose designs do not fail. And after that, with his anger ever in mind, he would not give to the ash-trees the power of 460 untiring fire for mortal men who live on earth. But the noble son of Iapetos outwitted him by stealing the far-beaconing flare of untiring fire in the tube of a fennel. And it stung high-thundering Zeus deep to the spirit, and angered him in his heart, when he saw the far-beaconing flare of fire among mankind.

At once he made an affliction for mankind to set against the fire. The renowned Ambidexter moulded from earth the likeness of a modest maiden, by Kronos' son's design. The pale-eyed goddess Athene dressed and adorned her in a gleaming white garment; down over her head she drew an embroidered veil, a wonder to behold; and about her head she 470 placed a golden diadem, which the renowned Ambidexter made with his own hands to please Zeus the father. On it were many designs fashioned, a wonder to behold, all the formidable creatures that the land and sea foster: many of them he put in, charm breathing over them all, wonderful designs, like living creatures with a voice of their own.

When he had made the pretty bane to set against a blessing, he led her out where the other gods and men were, resplendent in the finery of the pale-eyed one whose father is stern. Both immortal gods and mortal men were seized with wonder then they saw that precipitous trap, more than mankind can manage. For from her is descended the female sex, a   480
great affliction to mortals as they dwell with their husbands—no fit partners for accursed Poverty, but only for Plenty. As the bees in their sheltered nests feed the drones, those conspirators in badness, and while they busy themselves all day and every day till sundown making the white honey-comb, the drones stay inside in the sheltered cells and pile the toil of others into their own bellies, even so as a bane for mortal men has high-thundering Zeus created women, conspirators in causing difficulty.

And he gave a second bane to set against a blessing for the man who, to avoid marriage and the trouble women cause, chooses not to wed, and arrives at grim old age lacking anyone to look after him. He is   490
not short of livelihood while he lives, but when he dies, distant relatives share out his living. Then again, the man who does partake of marriage, and gets a good wife who is sound and sensible, spends his life with bad competing constantly against good; while the man who gets the awful kind lives with unrelenting pain in heart and spirit, and it is an ill without a cure.

Thus there is no way of deceiving or evading the mind of Zeus, since not even Iapetos' son, sly Prometheus, escaped the weight of his wrath, and for all his cleverness a strong fetter holds him in check.

When their father first became hostile towards Obriareos, Kottos, and   500
Gyges, he bound them in powerful fetters, indignant at their overbearing strength and aspect and stature, and settled them below the wide-pathed earth. There they sat at the world's end, living in misery below the earth, at the great world's limits, and for a long time they were suffering there with great pain at heart. But the son of Kronos, and the other immortal gods whom lovely-haired Rhea bore in intimacy with Kronos, brought them up again into the light, on Earth's advice. For she told them everything at length—that with their help they would win victory and their proud claim. For long they had fought against each other in fierce combat, and the struggle gave them pain at heart, the Titan gods and those that were born   510
of Kronos: the proud Titans from high Othrys, and from Olympus the gods, givers of blessings, whom lovely-haired Rhea bore bedded with Kronos. They had been fighting each other continually now for ten full years, and the fight gave them pain at heart; and to neither side came solution or end

of the bitter strife, and the outcome of the war was equally balanced. But when Zeus provided those allies with full sustenance, nectar and ambrosia, such as the gods themselves eat, and the proud spirit waxed in all their breasts, then the father of gods and men spoke to them:

"Hearken to me, proud children of Earth and Heaven, and let me say what the spirit in my breast bids me. For long now we have been fighting   520 each other for victory and power, day after day, the Titan gods and we who were born of Kronos. But now you must display your great strength and your terrible hands against the Titans in the fearful slaughter, remembering our faithful friendship, and how much you suffered before our decision brought you back into the light from your dismal bondage down in the misty darkness."

So he spoke, and the excellent Kottos straightway replied:

"Friend, what you say is not unfamiliar to us. We know that you have exceeding intelligence and exceeding insight, and that you have been the immortals' saviour from chilling peril, and that it is by your providence that   530 we have come back up from the misty darkness and our harsh bondage, lord, son of Kronos, after sufferings we never anticipated. So now in turn, with fixed purpose and willing spirit, we will secure your supremacy in the terrible slaughter by fighting the Titans in fierce combat."

So he spoke, and the gods, givers of blessings, applauded when they heard his words. Their spirits began to yearn for battle even more than before, and they raised such conflict as none would find fault with, all of them, both females and males, on that day, the Titan gods and those born of Kronos, and those whom Zeus brought to the light from the gloom beneath the earth, fearful and powerful ones with overbearing strength. A   540 hundred arms sprang from the shoulders of each of them, and fifty heads grew from their shoulders above their stalwart limbs. These then engaged the Titans in grim slaughter, with sheer cliffs in their stalwart hands, while the Titans on the other side strengthened their battle lines with a will. Both sides displayed a feat of main force; and the boundless sea roared terribly round about, the earth crashed loudly, and the broad sky quaked and groaned. Long Olympus was shaken to its foundations by the onrush of the immortals; the heavy tremors from their feet reached misty Tartarus, and the shrill din of the indescribable onset and the powerful bombardment. So it was when they discharged their woe-laden missiles at each other. The   550 voices of the two sides reached the starry heaven as they called out, clashing with loud battle-cries.

Now Zeus held in his strength no longer. Straightway his lungs were filled with fury, and he began to display his full might. From heaven and from Olympus together he came, with continuous lightning flashes, and the bolts flew thick and fast from his stalwart hand amid thunder and lightning, trailing supernatural flames. All around, the life-bearing earth rumbled as it burned, and the vast woodlands crackled loudly on every side. The whole land was seething, and the streams of Oceanus, and the undraining sea. The hot blast enveloped the chthonic Titans; the indescribable flames reached the divine sky, and the sparkling flare of the thunderbolt and the lightning dazzled the strongest eyes. An amazing conflagration prevailed over the Chasm: to see it directly with the eyes and to hear the sound with the ears, it seemed just as if Earth and broad Heaven above were coming together, for even such a mighty din would be arising with her being crashed down upon and him crashing down from above. So great a din there was as the gods clashed in strife; and in addition the winds magnified the quaking and the dust and the thunder and lightning and smoking bolt, great Zeus' wizardries, and carried the noise and shouting of both sides together. The din that rose from the terrible conflict was immense, and it was a powerful action that was displayed.

560

570

The scales of battle turned. But until then, they attacked each other, fighting furiously in fierce combat. In the forefront Kottos, Briareos, and Gyges, who was never sated with battle, raised bitter conflict. Three hundred rocks from their stalwart hands they discharged in a volley, darkening the Titans' sky with missiles. And they dispatched them below the wide-pathed earth, and bound them in painful bondage, having defeated them by force for all their pride: as far below the earth as heaven is from the earth, for so far it is from earth to misty Tartarus. For nine nights and days a bronze anvil might fall from heaven, and on the tenth reach the earth; and for nine nights and days a bronze anvil might fall from earth, and on the tenth reach Tartarus. Round it a brazen barrier is driven, and darkness is spread about its neck in three layers, while above it grow the roots of the earth and of the undraining sea.

580

There the Titan gods are hidden away down in the misty gloom, by decision of Zeus the cloud-gatherer, in a place of decay, at the end of the vast earth. They have no way out: Poseidon fastened brazen doors thereon, and a wall is driven up to the doors from both sides.

There Kottos, Gyges, and brave Obriareos live, trusty guardians of Zeus who bears the aegis.

590

And there are the sources and extremities of dark earth and misty Tartarus, of the undraining sea and the starry heaven, all in order, dismal and dank, that even the gods shudder at; a vast chasm, whose floor a man would not reach in a whole year if once he got inside the gates, but storm-wind upon terrible stormwind would carry him hither and thither. It is a cause of fear even for the immortal gods, this marvel. And there stands the fearful house of gloomy Night, shrouded in clouds of blackness.

Next to that the son of Iapetos stands holding the broad heaven firmly upon his head and untiring hands, where Night and Day approach and greet each other as they cross the great threshold of bronze. One goes in, one comes out, and the house never holds them both inside, but always there is one of them outside the house ranging the earth, while the other waits inside the house until the time comes for her to go. One carries far-seeing light for those on earth, but the other, baleful Night, shrouded in clouds of mist, cradles Sleep, the brother of Death.   600

There the sons of gloomy Night have their dwelling, Sleep and Death, fearsome gods. Never does the shining Sun look upon them with his rays when he goes up into heaven, nor when he climbs down from heaven. The one of them ranges the earth and the broad back of the sea gentle and mild towards men, but the other has a heart of iron and a pitiless spirit of bronze in his breast. That man is his whom he once catches, and he is hateful even to the immortal gods.   610

There, further on, stands the echoing house of the chthonic god, and in front of it a fearsome hound stands guard. He is pitiless, and he has a nasty trick: those who enter, he fawns upon with his tail and both his ears, but he does not let them come out again, but watches, and devours whoever he catches going out of the gates.

And there dwells a goddess who makes the immortals shudder, awful Styx, eldest daughter of Oceanus that flows back into itself. Apart from the gods she has her famed home, roofed with long rocks, and on every side it is fastened to the sky with silver columns. Rarely does Thaumas' daughter, swift-footed Iris, go errands there over the broad back of the sea. When quarrel and strife arise among the immortals, if one of them that dwells on Olympus speaks false, Zeus sends Iris to bring the gods' great oath from far off in a golden jug, the celebrated cold water that drops from a high, sheer cliff and, far below the wide-pathed earth, flows from the holy river through dark night, a branch of Oceanus. A tenth part is her share: nine parts Oceanus winds round the earth and the broad back of the sea with his silver eddies, and falls into the brine, while that one part issues forth from the cliff, a great bane to the gods. Whosoever of the immortals that possess the peak of snowy Olympus swears false upon making a libation of that water, he lies without breathing for a full year, and never lays hands on ambrosia and nectar by way of food, but lies breathless and voiceless on his bed, wrapped in a malignant coma. When he completes his long year of malady, another more trying ordeal succeeds the first. For nine years he is cut off from the gods who are for ever, and does not join them once in council or feast for nine whole years; but in the tenth he rejoins the company of the immortals who dwell in Olympus. Such is the oath   620   630

the gods have made of Styx's perennial water—elemental water, that flows
through a rugged region.   640

There are the sources and extremities of dark earth and misty Tartarus,
of the undraining sea and the starry heaven, all in order, dismal and dank,
that even the gods shudder at; and there are the shining gates and the
bronze threshold, firmly fixed with long roots, made by no craftsman's
hand. And beyond, excluded from the company of gods, the Titans live, on
the far side of the gloomy Chasm. But the renowned allies of loud-crashing
Zeus have their home at Oceanus' foundations—Kottos and Gyges; but
Briareos was so worthy that the heavy-booming Shaker of Earth made him
his son-in-law, giving him his daughter Cymopolea in marriage.

Now when Zeus had driven the Titans out of heaven, the huge Earth   650
bore as her youngest child Typhoeus, being united in intimacy with Tartarus by golden Aphrodite. His arms are employed in feats of strength, and
the legs of the powerful god are tireless. Out of his shoulders came a
hundred fearsome snake-heads with black tongues flickering, and the eyes
in his strange heads flashed fire under the brows; and there were voices in
all his fearsome heads, giving out every kind of indescribable sound.
Sometimes they uttered as if for the gods' understanding, sometimes again
the sound of a bellowing bull whose might is uncontainable and whose
voice is proud, sometimes again of a lion who knows no restraint, sometimes again of a pack of hounds, astonishing to hear; sometimes again he   660
hissed; and the long mountains echoed beneath. A thing past help would
have come to pass that day, and he would have become king of mortals
and immortals, had the father of gods and men not taken sharp notice. He
thundered hard and stern, and the earth rang fearsomely round about,
and the broad heaven above, the sea and Oceanus' stream and the realms
of chaos. Great Olympus quaked under the immortal feet of the lord as he
went forth, and the earth groaned beneath him. A conflagration held the
violet-dark sea in its grip, both from the thunder and lightning and from
the fire of the monster, from the tornado winds and the flaming bolt. All the
land was seething, and sky, and sea; long waves raged to and fro about   670
the headlands from the onrush of the immortals, and an uncontrollable
quaking arose. Hades was trembling, lord of the dead below, and so were
the Titans down in Tartarus with Kronos in their midst, at the incessant
clamour and the fearful fighting.

When Zeus had accumulated his strength, then, and taken his weapons, the thunder, lightning, and smoking bolt, he leapt from Olympus and
struck, and he scorched all the strange heads of the dreadful monster on
every side. When he had overcome him by belabouring him with his blows,
Typhoeus collapsed crippled, and the huge earth groaned. Flames shot
from the thunderstruck lord where he was smitten down, in the mountain   680

glens of rugged Aïdna. The huge earth burned far and wide with unbeliev-able heat, melting like tin that is heated by the skill of craftsmen in crucibles with bellow-holes, or as iron, which is the strongest substance, when it is overpowered by burning fire in mountain glens, melts in the divine ground by Hephaestus' craft: even so was the earth melting in the glare of the con-flagration. And vexed at heart Zeus flung Typhoeus into broad Tartarus.

From Typhoeus are the strong winds that blow wet, except for the Southerly and the Northerly and the clearing Westerly: these are from the gods by birth, a great blessing to mortals, but the other winds blow hap-hazard on the sea. Falling upon the misty waves, a great bane to mortals, 690 they rage with evil gusts; they blow different at different times, scattering ships and drowning sailors. There is no help against disaster for men who meet with them at sea. And some of them even on land, the boundless realm of flowers, destroy the fair husbandry of earthborn men, filling it with dust and troublesome refuse.

When the blessed gods had completed their work and settled the matter of privileges with the Titans by force, then on Earth's advice they urged that Olympian Zeus the wide-seeing should be king and lord of the immortals. And he allotted them privileges satisfactorily.

Zeus as king of the gods made Metis his first wife, the wisest among 700 gods and mortal men. But when she was about to give birth to the pale-eyed goddess Athene, he tricked her deceitfully with cunning words and put her away in his belly on the advice of Earth and starry Heaven. They advised him in this way so that no other of the gods, the eternal fathers, should have the royal station instead of Zeus. For from Metis it was des-tined that clever children should be born: first a pale-eyed daughter, Trito-geneia, with courage and sound counsel equal to her father's, and then a son she was to bear, king of gods and men, one proud of heart. But Zeus put her away in his belly first, so that the goddess could advise him of what was good or bad.   710

Second he married sleek Themis, who bore the Watchers, Lawful-ness, Justice, and flourishing Peace, who watch over the works of mortal men; and the Fates, to whom Zeus the resourceful gave the most privi-lege, Clotho, Lachesis, and Atropos, who give mortal men both good and ill.

Eurynome, a daughter of Oceanus with lovely looks, bore him the three Graces, Aglaïa, Euphrosyne, and fair Thalia. From their eyes love that dissolves the flesh seeped down as they looked; beautiful is their glance from under their brows.

And he came to the bed of Demeter abundant in nourishment, and she 720 bore the white-armed Persephone, whom Aïdoneus stole from her mother, Zeus the resourceful granting her to him.

Again, he took love of Memory with her beautiful hair, from whom the Muses with their gold diadems were born to him, nine of them, whose pleasure is in feasts and the delights of song.

Leto gave birth to Apollo and Artemis the archer—lovely children above all the Celestials—in shared intimacy with Zeus who bears the aegis.

Last of all he made Hera his fertile wife, and she bore Hebe and Ares and Eileithyia, sharing intimacy with the king of gods and men.   730

And by himself, out of his head, he fathered the pale-eyed Tritogeneia, the fearsome rouser of the fray, leader of armies, the lady Atrytone, whose pleasure is in war and the clamour of battle; while Hera, furying and quarrelling with her husband, gave birth to the renowned Hephaestus, who is endowed with skills beyond all the Celestials.

From Amphitrite and the loud-booming Shaker of Earth great Triton was born, whose strength extends widely, who occupies the bottom of the sea, dwelling in a golden house with his dear mother and the lord his father; a formidable god.

To Ares the piercer of shield-hides Cytherea bore Terror and Fear,   740 formidable gods who rout tight battlelines in the chilling conflict together with Ares sacker of cities; and Harmonia, whom proud Cadmus made his wife.

To Zeus Atlas' daughter Maia bore glorious Hermes, the herald of the immortals, after going up to his holy bed.

Cadmus' daughter Semele bore him a resplendent son in shared intimacy, merry Dionysus, immortal son of mortal mother, but now they are both gods.

Alcmene bore the mighty Heracles, in shared intimacy with Zeus the cloud-gatherer.   750

Hephaestus, the renowned Ambidexter, made Aglaïa his fertile wife, the youngest of the Graces.

Golden-haired Dionysus made auburn Ariadne, Minos' daughter, his fertile wife, and the son of Kronos made her immortal and ageless for him.

Fair-ankled Alcmene's valiant son, the mighty Heracles, after completing his oppressive ordeals, made Hebe his modest wife in snowy Olympus, child of great Zeus and gold-sandalled Hera; fortunate Heracles, who performed a great feat among the immortals, and now lives free from trouble, free from old age, for all time.

To the tireless Sun the renowned Oceanid Perseïs bore Circe and king   760 Aeetes. Aeetes, son of the Sun who makes light for mortals, married by the gods' design another daughter of Oceanus the unending river, fair-cheeked Idyia; and she bore him the trim-ankled Medea, surrendering in intimacy through golden Aphrodite.

Farewell now, you dwellers in Olympus, and you islands, continents, and the salt sea between. But now, Olympian Muses, sweet of utterance, daughters of aegis-bearing Zeus, sing of the company of goddesses, all those who were bedded with mortal men, immortal themselves, and bore children resembling the gods.

Demeter, noble among goddesses, gave birth to Wealth, in union of 770 intimate desire with the hero Iasius in a thrice-turned fallow field, in the rich Cretan land: Wealth, a goodly god, who goes over all the earth and the broad back of the sea, and whoever encounters him, into whosever hands he comes, he makes him rich and bestows much fortune upon him.

To Cadmus Harmonia, daughter of golden Aphrodite, bore Ino, Semele, and fair-cheeked Agaue, and Autonoe whom Aristaeus of the luxuriant hair married, and Polydorus, in well-walled Thebes.

Oceanus' daughter Callirhoe, sharing golden Aphrodite's intimacy with stout-hearted Chrysaor, bore a son, the strongest of all mortals, Geryoneus, whom mighty Heracles killed for his shambling oxen in sea-girt 780 Erythea.

To Tithonus Dawn bore Memnon, bronze-armoured king of the Ethiopians, and the lord Emathion. And to Cephalus she produced a resplendent son, doughty Phaëthon, a man resembling the gods. While he was young and still had the delicate bloom of his glorious prime, a boy with childish thoughts, Aphrodite the lover of smiles snatched him away and made him her closet servant in her holy temple, a noble Hero.

The son of Aeson took from Aeetes the daughter of that Zeus-fostered king by the design of the gods, the eternal fathers, after completing the many oppressive ordeals enjoined upon him by the great overbearing 790 king, the brute Pelias, who was wicked and stern in action. Having completed them, Aeson's son reached Iolcus after long sufferings, bringing the curly-lashed girl on his swift ship, and made her his fertile wife. And surrendering to Jason shepherd of peoples, she bore a son, Medeios, whom Chiron the son of Philyra brought up in the mountains in fulfilment of great Zeus' purpose.

As for the daughters of Nereus, the Old Man of the Sea, Psamathe, noble among goddesses, bore Phocus in shared intimacy with Aeacus through golden Aphrodite, while the silverfoot goddess Thetis, surrendering to Peleus, gave birth to Achilles lionheart, breaker of men. 800

Cytherea with the fair diadem bore Aeneas in union of intimate desire with the hero Anchises among the peaks and glens of windy Ida.

Circe, daughter of the Sun, the son of Hyperion, in shared intimacy with Odysseus the enduring of heart, bore Agrius and Latinus, the excellent and strong, who were lords of all the famous Tyrrhenians far away in a remote part of the Holy Isles. And Calypso, noble among

goddesses, bore Nausithous and Nausinous to Odysseus in union of
intimate desire.

These were bedded with mortal men, immortal themselves, and bore
children resembling the gods.   810

THE SOCIAL WORLD SHAPES MYTH

The work of anthropologist Bronislaw Malinowski (1884–1942) has profoundly influenced the study of myth. Early in his career, Malinowski read a
book that changed the course of his life: *The Golden Bough* by James Frazer
(1854–1941), a magisterial work on comparative myth and ritual. Although
Malinowski's later fieldwork on islands near New Guinea led him to challenge
Frazer's understanding of myth, magic, and science, his contribution to the
field of mythology begins with Frazer.

In *The Golden Bough* (1890) Frazer examined myths collected from the
reports of European missionaries, traders, and explorers during and after the
age of exploration (1400–1700), the period when Europeans traveled to and
colonized Africa, Asia, the Americas and Oceania. These reports inaugurated
the study of myths, as Europeans became increasingly aware of the diversity
of human societies and the sorts of tales they tell. Frazer collected and compared not just myths but also rituals and magical practices, which he treated
as related phenomena. Relying on Charles Darwin's newly influential ideas
about evolution, Frazer argued that all human societies pass through three
stages of development: magical practices, formalized religions, and finally
scientific reasoning. He argued that societies that engage in magical practices
and lack certain technologies (such as writing) are at one end of this evolutionary spectrum, even if they are contemporaneous with Europe, whereas
societies that rely primarily on scientific reasoning are at the other.

For modern scholars, there are fundamental weaknesses in Frazer's understanding. To construct his evolutionary scheme, Frazer treated the myths,
rituals, and magical practices he collected in isolation from the societies they
came from; he did not try to connect them to education, marriage patterns,
economics, or other social institutions and structures. Rather, for Frazer,
myths and rituals only had meaning in terms of Frazer's ability to plot them
on his spectrum of man's intellectual progress. In part, Frazer's decontextual-
ized approach to this material results from his status as an "armchair mythologist." He did not travel to the societies from which these myths originated.
Rather, he relied on myths from vanished societies and distant continents,
transcribed into English from languages he did not read and collected by
others whose accounts may have been biased or inaccurate. Malinowski's

great and lasting contribution was to understand myths in their social context, an approach enabled by his fieldwork.

Malinowski began his fieldwork in the Trobriand Islands, north of New Guinea in the Pacific Ocean. These islands were his laboratory, where his training as a scientist influenced his methods in the field. Malinowski chose a theme (such as kinship, marriage, magic, or myth) from the controversial topics discussed in anthropological literature. Based on data he collected in the field, he developed general principles that, he argued, would be applicable to all societies. In this sense, his book *Myth in Primitive Culture* (1926) is as much about the myths of the Trobriand islanders as the myths of the Greeks.

Malinowski argued that a society and its culture form a coherent and integrated system in which people develop ways to cope with problems and to satisfy their needs. Culture includes not only education, economics, beliefs, marriage, and kinship but also agriculture, tools, houses, artistic expression, and symbols or signs (Figure 2.11). All the components of a culture serve a purpose or function. What function or need does myth satisfy? In the introduction to his essay "Myth in Primitive Psychology," Malinowski proposes:

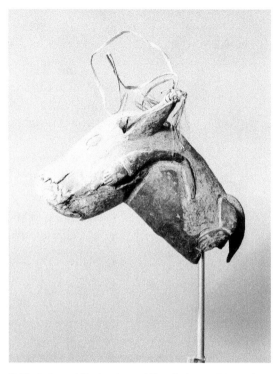

2.11 **Pig figure.** Wood, paint, and fiber. Early to mid-twentieth century. Papua New Guinea, Prince Alexander Mountains, Middle Sepik River. *Image copyright © The Metropolitan Museum of Art. Image source: Art Resource, NY, ART500336.*

> Myth . . . is not of the nature of fiction, such as we read today in a novel, but it is a living reality, believed to have once happened in primeval times, and continuing ever since to influence the world and human destinies. . . . Myth fulfills in primitive culture an indispensable function: it expresses, enhances, and codifies belief; it safeguards and enforces morality; it vouches for the efficiency of ritual and contains practical rules for the guidance of man. Myth is thus a vital ingredient of human civilization; it is not an idle tale, but a hard-worked active force; it is not an intellectual explanation or an artistic imagery, but a pragmatic charter of primitive faith and moral wisdom. (81 – 82)

Unlike Frazer, Malinowski insists that myth can only be understood within a social context because only its social context can indicate its function. In particular, he showed how a myth could be a "charter" or "practical guide" about how to act and behave.

IVAN STRENSKI, *FROM* "INTRODUCTION" *TO MALINOWSKI AND THE WORK OF MYTH*

In this introduction to a collection of Malinowski's writing, Ivan Strenski, a religious studies scholar, summarizes Malinowski's thinking about how to define myth as well as how creation myths serve as charters—an especially important insight of Malinowski's work.

- What does Malinowski mean by a "charter" myth? How is the story of Adam and Eve in Genesis in the Hebrew Bible a charter myth? (The relevant portion of Genesis is included in the next section.)

- According to Malinowski, does a myth need to be "literally true" to serve as a charter myth? Why or why not?

- Malinowski says that myths must be measured by what they "achieve." What sorts of things do myths achieve or accomplish for those who tell them?

IVAN STRENSKI, *FROM* "INTRODUCTION" *TO MALINOWSKI AND THE WORK OF MYTH* (1992)

WHAT SHOULD SURVIVE OF MALINOWSKI'S THEORY OF MYTH?

THEIR "LILI'U" IS REALLY OUR "MYTH"

Malinowski did what every myth theorist ought to do but which few, if any, have done. He understood that using the word "myth" is to mark a category of story.[1] "Myth" is not just the name of any story. The term "myth" singles out a class of story, just as the terms "art" or "literature" do the same for their referents. Thus, using the word "myth" is a way of evaluating stories, or of describing them as special or important stories.

In addition to myth theorists' general obliviousness to the marking process, the main problem in the development of a theory of myth has been that myth theorists broadly disagree about at least two things: First, what should make up the content, function, or structure of the marked category "myth"? For example, do myths have to contain some reference to gods, heroes, creation, origins, spirits, and so on? Or must they *function* religiously, to evoke mystery and to create existential realizations, or socially, to charter institutions? Second, to which particular stories should we apply this term "myth"? Is the story of Adam and Eve myth or is it revelation? Are the gospel stories of the life of Jesus myth or are they history, legend, or an heroic tale?

What makes something a work of art or literature? Is art distinctive because of what it *depicts* (e.g., satyrs and nymphs, rather than humble peasants), or the way it *functions* (e.g., to create the feeling of the sublime)? But having agreed, for the sake of demonstration, that art must create the feeling of the sublime, we might disagree that a certain *depiction* in a portrait or landscape does so. The Naturalist painters created precisely this kind of dilemma by trying to create a sense of the sublime while depicting objects not previously thought capable of creating intense emotional reactions. For this reason, a good myth theorist, like a theorist of art or literature in a comparable situation, will have to defend why they think a certain story should be called myth. Myth theorists have to take responsibility for their concept of myth by recognizing that in calling something a myth, they are marking that something off as a distinct category.

Malinowski operates with some awareness that he is involved in a marking process when he deals with "myths." In "Myth in Primitive Psychology" Malinowski writes that "the most important point of the thesis which I am urging" is that "I maintain that there exists a class of stories"[2] that he calls myths.

How did Malinowski determine what a myth was? How did he decide what fit the category? What did "myth" mean for him, even before he arrived in the Trobriand Islands?

We might begin by recognizing that the term "myth" had a rich and controversial history in Malinowski's Europe. In this context, myth primarily meant a radiant and important story. The Romantic culture which Malinowski inherited in late nineteenth- and early twentieth-century Polish society had to some degree overcome the Enlightenment's disparagement of myths as simpleminded false stories.

As a recent Polish study of Malinowski's romantic background concludes: "Even Malinowski's biography turned out to be a model biography of Polish romanticism."[3] Even more, Malinowski's sensibilities were shaped specifically by a local Polish version of the European "modernist" or neoromantic movement.[4] The original British and German romantics of the late eighteenth and early nineteenth centuries did much to collect and popularize the stories of ancient Greece and Rome, as well as those of the northern peoples, the Scandinavian Eddas or the German stories collected by the brothers Grimm or those put into epic operatic form in the Ring Cycle of Richard Wagner. In like manner, the Polish neoromantics expressed their sensibilities in scientific, ethnographic, and folklorist work. During the last quarter of the nineteenth century, Malinowski's own linguist father and his academic friends formed a loosely connected intellectual circle in Krakow devoted to such interests as local ethnology and Polish folk culture.[5] High on the list of things that interested these neoromantic intellectuals of Malinowski's milieu were stories; these stories were routinely called "myths."

Malinowski was drawn to stories in part because, like all anthropologists who harbored empirical and "scientific" aspirations, he needed data. Now, stories are relatively easy to convert into data. In large part, they are publicly available for recording in the notebook of the anthropologist. This distinguishes them from many of our cultural beliefs, which often are presumed, but not explicitly available to consciousness. Further, stories are "portable" and their removal does not really make much of an impact upon the cultural environment of the society in question, compared with the legion of problems—even in the heyday of imperialism when Malinowski flourished—in collecting so-called "primitive art," and the problems of making it "data." In many cases, statues or masks are not portable simply because of their size, but equally they often cannot be taken away (secretly or openly) for display and discussion because of cultural restrictions. They are holy objects, the removal of which would be inconvenient or conspicuous, and moreover a grave wrong to the people being studied. While it is true that many stories are sacred in this sense, many are not subject to restrictions (nor even the possibility of enforcing them) against retelling them or writing them down.

Malinowski was drawn to the stories his hosts in the southwestern Pacific told among themselves and, sometimes, to him. But why call these stories "myth" rather than "literature" or "art"? These stories were different from each other and had many indigenous names (but none of these names was of course "myth"). The Trobrianders had what Malinowski just called "stories."[6] But they also had their *"lili'u," "libogwo," "kukwanebu," "wosi," "vinavina," "megwa,"* and *"yopa."*[7] How should Malinowski talk about these classes of stories? Should he just use these raw terms unfamiliar to his readers, or should he try to invent equivalents in Western culture, and then translate the names of the different kinds of native stories into terms his readers might better understand? And which native story, if any, was equivalent to our notion of "myth" which Malinowski and others took for granted as a result of their European romantic nurture?

In trying to answer this question, Malinowski assumes what most of our theorists of myth assume as well, yet in ways that show a somewhat higher degree of self-awareness about what he was doing.

What makes Malinowski somewhat admirable, and thus what should contribute to the survival of his approach to myth, is that he chose deliberately to try to convey the sense of the unfamiliar by the familiar, the new by the old, by having recourse to the *marking process.* He knew that in labeling a story a "myth," he was marking it in a particular way—just as surely as when we call a painting "art," or a novel "literature." This is one reason it is instructive to read Malinowski on myth, and to look at his effort to render native stories intelligible to Western readers.

As a Romantic, Malinowski assumed that the stories he should study and feature as "myths" were those stories especially marked as "sacred" among the Trobrianders. In doing this, rightly or wrongly, he imported fundamental assumptions from Western culture which almost all theorists of myth do as well. We have given importance to certain stories, such as the Greek myths, the Bible stories, the folktales of northern Europe; we have tended to call them all "myths," and have linked them with religion. They are the "sacred" narratives, even when "myth" is taken pejoratively to mean "false story."[8] In this case, typically its falsity is itself important. Attempts to debunk biblical narrative as merely mythical are so fervent partly because critics believe that these stories have done real damage in leading people astray. Malinowski assumed that the Trobrianders mark off some stories for special religious reasons, and that they would name them as well.

This then leads Malinowski to seek out a class of stories for special treatment among the Trobrianders. He chose the Trobriand *"lili'u,"* and equated them straightaway with our (originally Greek) term, "myth." Why? Malinowski says that the *lili'u* are the "most important class" of stories—adding that this is "reproducing *prima facie* the natives' own classification and nomenclature."[9] Identifying it with "myth," Malinowski notes that the *lili'u* is "true, venerable and sacred," and plays a "highly important cultural part."[10] Thus it is because both are the important or sacred stories of a given society, that we can speak of their *"lili'u"* as equivalent to our "myth."

I am not uncritically celebrating this equating of terms from different cultures in the way Malinowski does. In many ways, his approach could be indicted for engaging in a massive imperialist projection of Western romantic notions upon the Trobrianders. Our word, "myth," henceforth swallows up their word, *"lili'u,"* without any sense that *"lili'u"* might contain different non-Western features. More than that, from here on, Malinowski assumes both that stories have an equally special value in all societies, and that "myth" swallows up all non-Western "important narratives."

Nevertheless, Malinowski is to be commended for being as explicit as he was about the marking process. His example, rightly read, enables us to see that all talk about "myth" across cultures involves the kinds of conceptual marking of choice features of the cultures of others. Since there is no accepted definition of "myth" and since "myth" is our word—not theirs—whenever we want to talk about another culture, we will inevitably need to work out acceptable ways of using terms familiar to our readers. Malinowski was very far from perfect in this regard, but he at least opens the door a crack, allowing us to see further.

FUNCTIONALISM: MYTH IS AS MYTH DOES

If any word is always associated with Malinowski, it is "functionalism." Despite many critical attacks on Malinowski's functional theory, it continues to hold many adherents. But what is functionalism in respect to myth? How can we understand why it has managed to retain the interest and devotion of students of myth and religion? An inquiry into Malinowski's functionalism is doubly important, because he held different functionalist positions at different times in his life. Let us start simply by asking what central claims are embedded in Malinowski's functionalism.

First, there is generic or "broad" functionalism. To be this kind of functionalist means little more than to view society as an interdependent organic whole.[11] This generic functionalism calls attention to the ways culture or society coheres, hangs together, works—how it *functions*. Here Malinowski does not differ significantly from Durkheim or even Aristotle. On this view, such functionalists view myth as a part of the social or cultural whole, a piece of the mechanism of society performing its tasks in maintaining the whole. In particular, Malinowski says that the job of myth is "a warrant, a charter, and even a practical guide to the activities with which it is connected." Myths are not actually meant to be read as explanations, but are active parts of culture like commands, deeds, or guarantees, certifying that some sort of social arrangement is legitimate; they are the "backbone of primitive culture."[12] They maintain the legitimacy of our social arrangements. The story of Adam and Eve, for example, may or may not be literally true, but its literal truth is irrelevant to its *function*. The story has functioned in the past, among other things, to charter the institutions of wearing clothes, bearing children in pain, or working by the "sweat of our brows."

But a second, riskier, and more interesting, sense of functionalism can also be found in Malinowski.[13] It has two parts as well. Malinowski asserts, first, that myth functions *unconsciously* as far as the actors in question are concerned. Second, myth functions as "an indispensable ingredient of all culture";[14] it fulfills objective, even biological, needs essential to the survival of the culture in question.

What distinguishes Malinowski's second pragmatic sense of functionalism from the first broad or generic variety is the idea that *all* the elements of a cultural whole serve a *necessary* practical function for the survival of the institution. *Everything* in society functions to fulfill basic needs. And when Malinowski speaks of the "basic needs," he has biology in mind—so much so that he speaks of the "biological utility" of culturally functioning institutions.[15] This extreme biological functionalist interpretation of human culture developed gradually for Malinowski. Early in his career, Malinowski argued that only so-called "primitive" culture was exclusively pragmatic. Thus at one point Malinowski believed that even language was used in exclusively pragmatic ways: "primitive" cultures simply had no other choice, since they lived precarious existences and needed to make everything in their culture count. As Malinowski says, "language in its primitive function and original form has an essentially pragmatic character . . . [It is] a mode of behavior, an indispensable element of concerted human action."[16]

Myth thus follows the lead of language. The so-called "primitive" is "an eager actor, playing his part for his own benefit, trying to use all the means in his power towards the attainment of his various needs and desires. . . . He is interested in all things which subserve these ends and are thus immediately useful. Round these he develops not only his magic . . . but also his myths."[17]

This assertion occurred in the context of Malinowski's point that "primitive" folk were not idle and ignorant.[18] Their cultures showed admirably that they worked with a hardheaded practicality. But to some extent Malinowski also disparaged practicality—native or otherwise— as sign of a certain lack of refinement or aristocratic cultivation. At the same time as he was saying that primitive language was essentially pragmatic, he believed that Western scientific language rose above practicality and moved in realms of pure thought.

But later in *Coral Gardens* (1935) Malinowski changed his mind. He extended his pragmatic reading of "primitive" culture to "us" "moderns" as well. "Even literary and scientific language" is subject to the same pragmatic interpretation as primitive language:

> in one of my previous writings [above], I opposed civilized and
> scientific to primitive speech, and argued as if the theoretical uses of
> words in modern philosophic and scientific writings were completely

detached from their pragmatic sources. This was an error, and a serious one at that. Between the savage use of words and the most abstract and theoretical one, there is only a difference of degree. Ultimately all the meaning of all the words is derived from bodily experience.[19]

Pragmatism is everywhere.

As for myth, it is here in this fundamental, biological, and universal human pragmatism, that we find the origins of myth. Myth for Malinowski is "indispensable" and "vital"[20]—something a society needs—and without which it cannot materially persist. Tradition here takes a special role in this indispensable job which myth performs for culture: "Myth expresses, enhances and codifies belief; it safeguards and enforces morality; it vouches for the efficiency of ritual and contains practical rules for the guidance of men . . . a pragmatic charter of primitive faith and moral wisdom.[21] Myth is thus a "hard-worked active force," covering the "whole pragmatic reaction of man towards disease and death" and expressing "his emotions, his foreboding."[22] For Malinowski, myth is practically linked with our basic biological needs.

As if this pragmatic biological sense of functionalism were not radical enough, Malinowski also claimed that the actors in question were *unconsciously* serving these functions.[23] Myths work on us subrationally, below our threshold of awareness. We may be moved by stories of the return of a dead loved one such as in the play *Blithe Spirit*. Malinowski would say that this is not because we consciously recognize the truth of these accounts, and rationally conclude that they are so. Rather, the promise of neverending life and the desire to avoid death, which are embodied in such a play, speak directly to us, straight to our organism as Malinowski might say. Our will to believe myths of life beyond the grave testify to the natural built-in drives and instincts of our animal nature. These visceral reactions translate into emotions which overwhelm our rational critical calculating mind, and thus make believers out of every one of us—all without our being necessarily aware of it. "There are no atheists in foxholes," the saying goes. Thus Malinowski can earnestly assert that myth is "born from the innermost and emotional reaction to the most formidable and haunting idea"[24]—death.

Whatever doubts we may have about Malinowski's viewpoint, there is power in this position—the power of the "bottom line." Malinowski forces us to measure myths by what they can really seem able to achieve—by their observable effects. Thus at one level, myths may provide access to the stated beliefs of people. They are "founts of ethnographic information,"[25] as Malinowski calls them. But if we take them literally, we will soon become baffled. For example, what are we to make of tales of miracles, ghosts, or persons surviving death to live in another world? If we take the storytellers at their literal word, we would have to conclude either that they knew about the mysterious technology of living forever or, since people die and do not seem to live forever, that they were not telling the truth. Either way, we arrive at a dead end. The technology of life eternal would probably transcend our understanding, leaving us dumbfounded and unable to make intelligent comments or, if untrue, such a narrative simply shuts us out.

Malinowski's answer to this difficulty is to say that what people really mean in relating such narratives was not what they literally (or symbolically) said. Rather, what they meant could be discovered in what the stories did for them. Telling myths about life everlasting does not really give a report about life in another state; rather, these stories are about how they affect an audience—how they demonstrably make people feel better about their inevitable fates. The bottom line about such a myth is what it *does*—it boosts our morale. Malinowski's perspective turns attention to the behavioral consequences of certain stories, rather than their literal meaning: if we really want to understand myths, look at what myths *do*, not what they *say*.

NOTES

1. See especially Bronislaw Malinowski, *Argonauts of the Western Pacific* (1922), pp. 299 (pp. 10–11 this volume), 301–3, and "Myth in Primitive Psychology," *Magic, Science and Religion*, Robert Redfield, ed., p. 107f (p. 86ff this volume), and "The Foundations of Faith and Morals," *Sex, Culture and Myth*, p. 304f (pp. 140–41 this volume).
2. Malinowski, "Myth in Primitive Psychology," p. 108 (p. 87 this volume).
3. Jan Jerschina, "Polish Culture of Modernism and Malinowski's Personality," *Malinowski between Two Worlds*, p. 136.
4. Ibid., pp. 128–48, esp. 128, 130, 136. Ivan Strenski, "Malinowski: Second Positivism, Second Romanticism," *Man* 17 (1982): 766–71.
5. Paluch, "Malinowski and Cracow Anthropology," p. 5, and Grazyna Kubica, "Malinowski's Years in Poland," pp. 88–89, 94 in *Malinowski between Two Worlds*.
6. Malinowski, *Argonauts*, pp. 291–95 (pp. 3–6 this volume).
7. Ibid., p. 299 (pp. 10–11 this volume).
8. Malinowski, "The Foundations of Faith and Morals," p. 312 (p. 148 this volume).
9. Malinowski, "Myth in Primitive Psychology," p. 107 (p. 86 this volume).

10. Ibid., p. 107 (p. 86 this volume).

11. Malinowski, "The Foundations of Faith and Morals," p. 324 (p. 160 this volume).

12. Malinowski, "Myth in Primitive Psychology," p. 108 (p. 87 this volume).

13. A. Pierce, "Durkheim and Functionalism," in K. Wolff, ed., *Essays on Sociology and Philosophy* (New York: Harper and Row, 1964), p. 154.

14. Malinowski, "Myth in Primitive Psychology," p. 146 (p. 115 this volume).

15. Bronislaw Malinowski, "The Problem of Meaning in Primitive Languages," Special Appendix to C. K. Ogden and I. A. Richards, *The Meaning of Meaning* (London: Kegan, Paul, Trench and Trubner, 1923), p. 332.

16. Ibid., p. 316.

17. Bronislaw Malinowski, "On Sir James Frazer," *Sex, Culture and Myth* (New York: Harcourt, Brace and World, 1962), p. 272.

18. Malinowski, *Argonauts*, p. 166.

19. Bronislaw Malinowski, *Coral Gardens* (London: Allen & Unwin, 1935), vol. 2, p. 58, quoted by D. T. Langendoen, *London School of Linguistics* (Cambridge: MIT, 1968), p. 34.

20. Malinowski, "Myth in Primitive Psychology," p. 101 (p. 82 this volume).

21. Ibid., p. 101 (p. 82 this volume).

22. Ibid., p. 132 (p. 105 this volume).

23. Pierce, "Durkheim and Functionalism," p. 157.

24. Malinowski, "Myth in Primitive Psychology," p. 110 (p. 89 this volume).

25. Bronislaw Malinowski, "Baloma," *Magic, Science and Religion*, p. 239, and *Argonauts*, p. 317 (p. 25 this volume).

2.3 COMPARISON

LEVANT: CREATION STORIES

The most straightforward way to understand something is to compare it to other similar items. In the field of mythology, scholars often compare myths from one society, myths from very different societies, or myths from neighboring regions. In *Mythology* (1924), Jane Harrison, an influential British scholar of mythology of the late nineteenth and early twentieth century, compared Greek religions and myths with those from Greece's neighbors. She wrote,

"We are all Greeks," says Shelley, in words thrice memorable, "our laws, our religion, our art, have their roots in Greece." True, but with one large deduction. Our religion is not rooted in Greece; it comes to us from the East, though upon it, too, the spirit of the West and of Greece itself has breathed. What Greece touches she transforms. Our religion, Oriental as it is in origin, owes to Greece a deep and lasting debt. To formulate this debt—this is the pleasant task that lies before us. (p. xi)

In Harrison's day, European and American scholars typically referred to the Ancient Near East as "the Orient" and, unfortunately, often categorized the cultures of the Orient as inherently inferior to those of the West. Although readers today may reject Harrison's valorization of Western and Greek myths, the insights she and other comparative mythologists gain by understanding Greek myths in the context of a broader geographical region remain both provocative and fruitful to the study of myth.

"The Mediterranean" refers to areas that border the Mediterranean Sea and does not designate any particular time period. One can speak about the Mediterranean in the twenty-first century as well as in the eighth century BCE. "The Ancient Near East," on the other hand, is a term that specifies both time (roughly 4000–400 BCE) *and* place. It refers to the large landmass that stretches from Anatolia (also referred to as Asia Minor) in the north (modern Turkey) to Egypt in the south. It includes the Levant (modern Syria, Lebanon, Israel, Jordan, and Palestine) as well as Mesopotamia, the region between the Tigris and Euphrates Rivers (modern Iraq) in the east (Chapter 1, under "What Is Classical Mythology?"). Although Greece is considered part of the Mediterranean region only, archaeological as well as textual and other evidence proves that it was greatly influenced by the societies of the Ancient Near East (see Map 1.1, Greece, the Ancient Near East, and the Mediterranean, on pp. 22–23). Thus comparative mythologists study Greek myths in the context of both regional associations. Whereas they tend not to follow Harrison in elevating Greece above its neighbors, their studies shed light on the myths, rituals, and peoples in the Mediterranean region and in the Ancient Near East.

There are two main approaches to comparative mythology, both of which we shall apply in the comparative sections of this book. Some scholars study a single myth that appears in societies that have no known contact with one another; this approach allows scholars to draw broad conclusions about the nature of myth. Comparing a myth that appears in different societies, such scholars argue, demonstrates the fears, hopes, and desires that all human beings share. A different approach, taken by scholars who are not interested in the universal aspects of myth, is to study the diffusion of a myth across societies that have had contact with one another. Diffusionists study the ways

Map 2.2 Creation Stories in the Ancient Near East

in which ideas move among societies (such as trade, colonization, travel, or war) to determine the origin of a particular myth or how myths change over time in different societies. Diffusionists draw historical conclusions about myths in a particular country or regional context.

Scholars have noted the similarities between several creation myths from the Ancient Near East and Hesiod's *Theogony*. These include a Hittite creation myth called *Kingship in Heaven,* as well as Egyptian myths about Osiris, Horus, and Set. This section and Chapter 3.3 focus on two creation myths from the Levant, namely the Babylonian *Enuma Elish* and Genesis in the Hebrew Bible (Map 2.2). Both myths offer parallels to Hesiod's *Theogony*. Both of these myths were recorded in languages from the Semitic group of languages, which includes biblical Hebrew, Phoenician, Ugaritic, and Akkadian (from which Assyrian and Babylonian are directly descended). Greek, by contrast, belongs to the Indo-European language group, which includes Hittite and Vedic Sanskrit (Figure 3.12, p. 126).

The *Enuma Elish,* sometimes called *The Epic of Creation* or *When on High* in English, shares more features with Hesiod's *Theogony* than it does with Genesis. Although it was written on clay tablets during the first millennium BCE, its stories circulated orally during the second millennium BCE and thus might have influenced oral poetry in Greece. In the Babylonian tale as in Hesiod's, male gods succeed one another as the universe becomes increasingly well defined. Apsu, Anu (with his son Ea), and Marduk can be compared to Uranus, Cronus, and Zeus. The goddess Tiamat produces monstrous offspring, just as Earth (Gaia) creates Typhoeus. Marduk successfully leads the other gods against Tiamat and her offspring and then establishes and rules an orderly universe; his victory over chaos is like Zeus's victory over Typhoeus. Just as Zeus establishes his home on Olympus, Marduk makes Babylon his home, and the text lists fifty names, some of which originally described other gods in the Mesopotamian pantheon, that are applied to him.

Although Genesis in the Hebrew Bible is more different from than similar to either the *Enuma Elish* or the *Theogony*, it still has much to offer to a careful comparative study. In the Ancient Near East, the Hebrews were distinguished by their monotheism—their belief in one god. Although there is evidence of polytheistic religions and myths in the Hebrew Bible (dragons, angels, giants, and other gods are mentioned), creation proceeds from the intention and thought of a single god who is unchallenged by other gods. The centerpiece of his creation is the human race, and this is one of the most important differences between Hesiod's *Theogony* and Genesis. Yet Genesis describes the creation of the world and the human race twice, and this repetition requires some explanation (Figure 2.12).

Not unlike the *Theogony*, Genesis also contains hymns, catalogues, and dramatic tales that may have been woven together from different sources to create the account we now have (sometime during ninth and sixth centuries BCE). Such a process would explain why Genesis has two creation stories, rather than one, as many people think. The first story of creation (Genesis 1:1–2:4a) belongs to a source scholars label the Priestly document. The Priestly document contains both genealogical catalogues and dramatic stories. In the Priestly document, God is called "Elohim," often translated simply as "God." His creation of the world is described in a way that emphasizes order and balance. The cosmos at first is formless, dark and watery, until God wills its parts into being: "Then God said, 'Let there be light'; and there was light." On each of the following days he creates plants, animals, and finally men and women: "So God created humankind in his image, in the image of God he created them; male and female he created them" (1:27). After instructing human beings to multiply and to be stewards of the earth, God rests on the seventh day. Here the Priestly document concludes (2:4a), and the second account begins.

In what scholars call the Yahwist narrative, God is called "Yahweh" (often translated as "Lord" or "the

2.12 Illuminated medieval manuscript of Genesis 1 from the Hebrew Bible. The Xanten Bible. Germany, thirteenth to fourteenth century CE. Spencer Collection. *The New York Public Library / Art Resource, NY, ART497620.*

Lord God"). The Yahwist narrative differs from the Priestly document in both content and style. It contains stories in which Israelites, both men and women, are lively protagonists to whom the Lord God offers protection and blessings. The Yahwist narrative begins by describing the Lord God's creation of the earth and heavens with one lengthy sentence spread over four verses. The creation concludes after the Lord God creates a man, Adam (not human beings), from clay and relieves Adam's loneliness by creating a woman, Eve, from Adam's rib (2:4b–8). It is in the Yahwist source that we find the stories of the tree of knowledge, the serpent, Eve's disobedience, and Adam's complicity. If all is order and calm in the Priestly document, where God (Elohim) is distant, serene, and transcendent, in the Yahwist narrative, the Lord God, human beings, the serpent, and the natural world are all intertwined and interact with one another. But however many differences there are between the two creation tales in Genesis, none are as great as their differences from the *Theogony*. Nonetheless, a comparison between the Priestly document (1–2:4a), the Yahwist document (2:4b–3:24), and the *Theogony* reveals the uniqueness of each tale.

GENESIS 1:1–3:24

Creation stories do not simply tell how the world began; they offer a vision of divinity, of men and women, of the natural world including plants and animals, and of the relationship between divinity and humankind. The following questions direct attention to key differences in the plot of each creation story so that the values, morals, and worldview of each tale can be found.

- What is the first act of creation in each creation story? What does this first act tell you about Elohim, Yahweh, and Zeus, respectively?

- How does each creation story function as a charter myth that tells human beings how they should treat animals and the natural world?

- Compare the details of the creation of the first woman in the Priestly document, the Yahwist document, and Hesiod's *Theogony*. What message does each story convey about the nature of women and their relationship to men?

- What is the attitude of Elohim, Yahweh, and Zeus toward human beings, specifically toward men?

GENESIS 1:1–3:24

1 In the beginning when God created the heavens and the earth, ²the earth was a formless void and darkness covered the face of the deep, while a wind from God swept over the face of the waters. ³Then God said, "Let there be light"; and there was light. ⁴And God saw that the light was good; and God separated the light from the darkness. ⁵God called the light Day, and the darkness he called Night. And there was evening and there was morning, the first day.

⁶And God said, "Let there be a dome in the midst of the waters, and let it separate the waters from the waters." ⁷So God made the dome and separated the waters that were under the dome from the waters that were above the dome. And it was so. ⁸God called the dome Sky. And there was evening and there was morning, the second day.

⁹And God said, "Let the waters under the sky be gathered together into one place, and let the dry land appear." And it was so. ¹⁰God called the dry land Earth, and the waters that were gathered together he called Seas. And God saw that it was good. ¹¹Then God said, "Let the earth put forth vegetation: plants yielding seed, and fruit trees of every kind on earth

that bear fruit with the seed in it." And it was so. ¹²The earth brought forth vegetation: plants yielding seed of every kind, and trees of every kind bearing fruit with the seed in it. And God saw that it was good. ¹³And there was evening and there was morning, the third day.

¹⁴And God said, "Let there be lights in the dome of the sky to separate the day from the night; and let them be for signs and for seasons and for days and years, ¹⁵and let them be lights in the dome of the sky to give light upon the earth." And it was so. ¹⁶God made the two great lights—the greater light to rule the day and the lesser light to rule the night—and the stars. ¹⁷God set them in the dome of the sky to give light upon the earth, ¹⁸to rule over the day and over the night, and to separate the light from the darkness. And God saw that it was good. ¹⁹And there was evening and there was morning, the fourth day.

²⁰And God said, "Let the waters bring forth swarms of living creatures, and let birds fly above the earth across the dome of the sky." ²¹So God created the great sea monsters and every living creature that moves, of every kind, with which the waters swarm, and every winged bird of every kind. And God saw that it was good. ²²God blessed them, saying, "Be fruitful and multiply and fill the waters in the seas, and let birds multiply on the earth." ²³And there was evening and there was morning, the fifth day.

²⁴And God said, "Let the earth bring forth living creatures of every kind: cattle and creeping things and wild animals of the earth of every kind." And it was so. ²⁵God made the wild animals of the earth of every kind, and the cattle of every kind, and everything that creeps upon the ground of every kind. And God saw that it was good.

²⁶Then God said, "Let us make humankind in our image, according to our likeness; and let them have dominion over the fish of the sea, and over the birds of the air, and over the cattle, and over all the wild animals of the earth, and over every creeping thing that creeps upon the earth."

²⁷So God created humankind in his image,
  in the image of God he created them;
  male and female he created them.

²⁸God blessed them, and God said to them, "Be fruitful and multiply, and fill the earth and subdue it; and have dominion over the fish of the sea and over the birds of the air and over every living thing that moves upon the earth." ²⁹God said, "See, I have given you every plant yielding seed that is upon the face of all the earth, and every tree with seed in its fruit; you shall have them for food. ³⁰And to every beast of the earth, and to every bird of the air, and to everything that creeps on the earth, everything that has the breath of life, I have given every green plant for food." And it was so. ³¹God saw everything that he had made, and indeed, it was very good. And there was evening and there was morning, the sixth day.

2 Thus the heavens and the earth were finished, and all their multitude. [2]And on the seventh day God finished the work that he had done, and he rested on the seventh day from all the work that he had done. [3]So God blessed the seventh day and hallowed it, because on it God rested from all the work that he had done in creation.

[4]These are the generations of the heavens and the earth when they were created.

In the day that the Lord God made the earth and the heavens, [5]when no plant of the field was yet in the earth and no herb of the field had yet sprung up—for the Lord God had not caused it to rain upon the earth, and there was no one to till the ground; [6]but a stream would rise from the earth, and water the whole face of the ground—[7]then the Lord God formed man from the dust of the ground, and breathed into his nostrils the breath of life; and the man became a living being. [8]And the Lord God planted a garden in Eden, in the east; and there he put the man whom he had formed. [9]Out of the ground the Lord God made to grow every tree that is pleasant to the sight and good for food, the tree of life also in the midst of the garden, and the tree of the knowledge of good and evil.

[10]A river flows out of Eden to water the garden, and from there it divides and becomes four branches. [11]The name of the first is Pishon; it is the one that flows around the whole land of Havilah, where there is gold; [12]and the gold of that land is good; bdellium and onyx stone are there. [13]The name of the second river is Gihon; it is the one that flows around the whole land of Cush. [14]The name of the third river is Tigris, which flows east of Assyria. And the fourth river is the Euphrates.

[15]The Lord God took the man and put him in the garden of Eden to till it and keep it. [16]And the Lord God commanded the man, "You may freely eat of every tree of the garden; [17]but of the tree of the knowledge of good and evil you shall not eat, for in the day that you eat of it you shall die."

[18]Then the Lord God said, "It is not good that the man should be alone; I will make him a helper as his partner." [19]So out of the ground the Lord God formed every animal of the field and every bird of the air, and brought them to the man to see what he would call them; and whatever the man called every living creature, that was its name. [20]The man gave names to all cattle, and to the birds of the air, and to every animal of the field; but for the man there was not found a helper as his partner. [21]So the Lord God caused a deep sleep to fall upon the man, and he slept; then he took one of his ribs and closed up its place with flesh. [22]And the rib that the Lord God had taken from the man he made into a woman and brought her to the man. [23]Then the man said,

"This at last is bone of my bones
    and flesh of my flesh;

this one shall be called Woman,

    for out of Man this one was taken."

24Therefore a man leaves his father and his mother and clings to his wife, and they become one flesh. 25And the man and his wife were both naked, and were not ashamed.

3 Now the serpent was more crafty than any other wild animal that the LORD God had made. He said to the woman, "Did God say, 'You shall not eat from any tree in the garden'?" 2The woman said to the serpent, "We may eat of the fruit of the trees in the garden; 3but God said, 'You shall not eat of the fruit of the tree that is in the middle of the garden, nor shall you touch it, or you shall die.'" 4But the serpent said to the woman, "You will not die; 5for God knows that when you eat of it your eyes will be opened, and you will be like God, knowing good and evil." 6So when the woman saw that the tree was good for food, and that it was a delight to the eyes, and that the tree was to be desired to make one wise, she took of its fruit and ate; and she also gave some to her husband, who was with her, and he ate. 7Then the eyes of both were opened, and they knew that they were naked; and they sewed fig leaves together and made loincloths for themselves.

8They heard the sound of the LORD God walking in the garden at the time of the evening breeze, and the man and his wife hid themselves from the presence of the LORD God among the trees of the garden. 9But the LORD God called to the man, and said to him, "Where are you?" 10He said, "I heard the sound of you in the garden, and I was afraid, because I was naked; and I hid myself." 11He said, "Who told you that you were naked? Have you eaten from the tree of which I commanded you not to eat?" 12The man said, "The woman whom you gave to be with me, she gave me fruit from the tree, and I ate." 13Then the LORD God said to the woman, "What is this that you have done?" The woman said, "The serpent tricked me, and I ate." 14The LORD God said to the serpent,

    "Because you have done this,

        cursed are you among all animals

        and among all wild creatures;

    upon your belly you shall go,

        and dust you shall eat

        all the days of your life.

15I will put enmity between you and the woman,

        and between your offspring and hers;

    he will strike your head,

        and you will strike his heel."

16To the woman he said,

    "I will greatly increase your pangs in childbearing;

in pain you shall bring forth children,
yet your desire shall be for your husband,
and he shall rule over you."
[17]And to the man he said,
"Because you have listened to the voice of your wife,
and have eaten of the tree
about which I commanded you,
'You shall not eat of it,'
cursed is the ground because of you;
in toil you shall eat of it all the days of your life;
[18]thorns and thistles it shall bring forth for you;
and you shall eat the plants of the field.
[19]By the sweat of your face
you shall eat bread
until you return to the ground,
for out of it you were taken;
you are dust,
and to dust you shall return."
[20]The man named his wife Eve, because she was the mother of all living. [21]And the LORD God made garments of skins for the man and for his wife, and clothed them.

[22]Then the LORD God said, "See, the man has become like one of us, knowing good and evil; and now, he might reach out his hand and take also from the tree of life, and eat, and live forever"—[23]therefore the LORD God sent him forth from the garden of Eden, to till the ground from which he was taken. [24]He drove out the man; and at the east of the garden of Eden he placed the cherubim, and a sword flaming and turning to guard the way to the tree of life.

2.4 RECEPTION

TITANS IN MODERN ART

Ever since Zeus defeated the Titans, fallen gods have haunted the collective imagination of the West. Trapped in darkness and immobilized, these old gods are emblems of resistance against Zeus's rule. Their monstrous size and their vague shapes suggest the potentially disruptive force of the emotions they represent. For these reasons, modern artists have used the enemies of Zeus to symbolize what lies buried in the human mind as well as the ever-present danger and temptation of rebellion against order.

And yet, there are other ways of representing the Titans, namely, as emblems of strength. Thus some artists have represented the Titans as providers of systemic order to the social world. If their approaches differ, however, modern artists who contemplated the Titans did so in an effort to recover origins—narratives that could explain the human condition in a world tottering on the brink of change and destruction. Here we examine how two iconic sculptures in Rockefeller Center created during the Great Depression (1929–1939) offer two different views of Titans.

The construction of Rockefeller Center, located in midtown Manhattan, was very much a project of the Great Depression. John D. Rockefeller, after whom Rockefeller Center is named, leased the land from Columbia University only shortly before the stock market crash in October 1929. As a consequence, financial backers and institutions such as the Metropolitan Opera who were interested in the project withdrew their support, and Rockefeller became its sole financial backer. Undeterred, Rockefeller continued to pursue his building plans and in so doing counteracted the devastation of the Depression. The project employed some 40,000 people during its construction, from 1930 to 1939, including the artists who decorated its facades and designed its sculpture in the art deco style that was current. The statues of the two Titans, Prometheus and his brother Atlas, were created and built during this time and reflect the determination and grit of Rockefeller as well as the anxieties generated by the Depression.

The American artist Paul Manship (1885–1966), born in St. Paul, Minnesota, was a prominent sculptor of public art in the United States between the First and Second World Wars. Manship studied at the American Academy in Rome from 1909 through 1912. During this period, he began to investigate the archaic art of Greece, India, and the Ancient Near East. This research profoundly influenced his later work, including the sculpture he was commissioned to design for Rockefeller Center. In Manship's most iconic work, his gilded bronze *Prometheus* (located in the center's lower plaza), the Titan is shown carrying a ball of fire to humanity (Figure 2.13). Prometheus emerges from a ring featuring the signs of the zodiac into a horizontal plane, a striking contrast to the vertical skyscrapers surrounding the fountain in which the bronze sculpture is placed. The zodiac ring marks the border between the world of the gods under Zeus's management and the world of men, recently condemned by Zeus. The stolen fire that Prometheus bears will allow men to escape the destruction Zeus had planned for them.

A quote adapted from Aeschylus's tragedy, *Prometheus Bound*, is inscribed on a wall behind the statue. In Aeschylus's play, Prometheus describes the

2.13 *Prometheus, the Light Bringer.* Paul Manship, c. 1934. Rockefeller Center, New York, USA. *Melvyn Longhurst/Alamy, E6RE48.*

2.14 *Atlas.* Lee Oscar Lawrie, c. 1937. Rockefeller Center, New York, USA. *imageBROKER/Alamy, CY0A65.*

stolen fire as the teacher who will equip mortals to survive (Chapter 3.1). In contrast, the inscription to Manship's *Prometheus* ascribes the role of teacher to the Titan himself: "Prometheus, Teacher in Every Art, Brought the Fire That Hath Proved to Mortals a Means to Mighty Ends." This inscription suggests great faith in technology and industry, and in their ability to transform human landscapes, cultures, and lives for the better. Manship's *Prometheus* is not the rebel of Hesiod's *Theogony* but a teacher. In the context of the difficult economic and political times in which Prometheus was designed, his golden color, fluid posture, and fire seem to promise a way to achieve "mighty ends." In these respects, Manship's *Prometheus* can be contrasted with the other Titan in Rockefeller Center, Prometheus's brother Atlas.

Designed by Lee Oscar Lawrie (1877–1963) with Rene Chambellan (1893–1955), *Atlas* also suggests a promise that technology will solve social ills. Nestled among the skyscrapers of Rockefeller Center, Lawrie's *Atlas* reaches four stories high (Figure 2.14). His machine-like muscles seem invincible as he climbs onto the massive square plinth with an astrolabe straddling his shoulders. Looking up at the statue from the ground, the building behind *Atlas* appears to be inside his astrolabe, so that his cosmic burden and the achievements of men appear to rest on his mighty shoulders.

Atlas, like Prometheus, captures the spirit of his times in all its anticipatory excitement about the bright future that technology and industrialization might bring. He imparts a sense of stabilizing strength and fortitude. Yet, although it is impossible not to see the hopeful strength that Lawrie's Atlas represents, it is equally difficult not to see the enormity of his task: carrying the world and its inhabitants on his shoulders throughout eternity. Atlas's decisively human form and his burden compel the viewer to wonder whether the Titan can succeed. Lawrie's Atlas poses this anxious question: can one individual save a failing society or planet? It is an anxiety that was likely shared by the workers and artists who built Rockefeller Center during the Great Depression, and even by Rockefeller himself. Prometheus, on the other hand, seemingly lofted by the hurly-burly of the crowds that so often surround him, remains wholly an emblem of promise and progress: gilded, fiery, and (dangerously) proud.

KEY TERMS

Ascra 43	Metis 52	Rhea 53
Cronus 52	Mycenae 39	Themis 52
Cult title 47	Night (goddess) 51	*Theogony* 38
Earth (Gaia) 51	Olympia 44	Typhoeus 53
Hesiod 38	Pandora 54	Uranus 51
Homer 38	Panhellenism 46	

FOR FURTHER EXPLORATION

Alter, Robert. *The Art of Biblical Narrative.* New York: Basic Books, 1981. Alter offers a distinctly literary and lively interpretation of the Hebrew Bible.

Cline, Eric H. *1177 BC: The Year Civilization Collapsed.* Princeton New Jersey: Princeton University Press, 2015. Relying on a wide range of literary sources and archaeological evidence, Cline provides a dramatic and engaging account of the collapse of the Bronze Age—which he dates to 1177.

Lamberton, Robert. *Hesiod.* New Haven, CT: Yale University Press, 1988. This well-reviewed handbook provides readers with a comprehensive introduction to Hesiod's world and poetry.

Pomeroy, Sarah B., Stanely M. Burstein, Walter Donlan, Jennifer Tolbert Roberts, and David Tandy. *Ancient Greece: A Political, Social, and Cultural History, 3rd Edition.* Oxford, UK: Oxford University Press, 2011. This is a well-organized introduction to ancient Greece; its dates for the chronological periods in ancient Greece have been followed here.

Roussel, Christine. *The Art of Rockefeller Center.* New York: W. W. Norton, 2005. A well-illustrated and comprehensive review of the artworks in Rockefeller Center and the artists who created them.

Strenski, Ivan (ed.). *Malinowski and the Work of Myth.* Princeton, NJ: Princeton University Press, 1992. Strenski's introduction (excerpted previously) and his inclusion of Malinowski's essays offer a thorough introduction to Malinowski's contribution to anthropology and the study of myth.

CHAPTER 3

ZEUS AND HERA

Watch it now. The Boss checks everything out.

—**AESCHYLUS, *PROMETHEUS BOUND* (119)**

I n the opening scene of Aeschylus's play *Prometheus Bound*, the god Prometheus is shackled to a mountain and tortured by Hephaestus, the god of metallurgy. Although in most Greek tragedies such violence takes place offstage, this explicit scene reveals the absolute rule of Zeus over gods. Power, Zeus's servant, makes clear that Zeus is ever present and ever ready to punish those who (like Prometheus) disobey him: "Watch it now," he cautions. When, over the course of the play, audience members learn that Zeus once tried to destroy the human race, they come to realize that Zeus's harsh treatment of Prometheus is typical, rather than exceptional, and this vividly dramatizes his attitude toward the human race.

< 3.1 (OPPOSITE): Heracles (left) kills the eagle eating Prometheus's liver. Detail from a black-figure krater with lid. Nettos Painter, c. 610 BCE. National Archaeological Museum, Athens, Greece. *Gianni Dagli Orti / The Art Archive at Art Resource, NY, AA389426.*

THE ESSENTIALS ⊰ ZEUS AND HERA

ZEUS (Jupiter, Jove), Ζεύς

PARENTAGE Cronus and Rhea

OFFSPRING Artemis and Apollo (with Leto), Athena (from Metis), Dionysus (with Semele), Hermes (with Maia), and Persephone (with Demeter), as well as many others

ATTRIBUTES Thunderbolt, lightning, eagle

SIGNIFICANT CULT TITLES
- Horkius (Guardian of Oaths)
- Meilichius (Mild One)
- Ombrius (Stormy)
- Philius (Guardian of Friendship)
- Xenius (Guardian of Hospitality)

SIGNIFICANT RITUALS AND SANCTUARIES
- **The Diasia** A carnival-like ritual in which adults and children played games, exchanged gifts, and offered animal-shaped cookies to Zeus.
- **Olympia** Zeus was honored in a quadrennial festival at Olympia with sacrifices and athletic and musical competitions.
- **The Pompaia** A parade around Athens during which a ram's skin was carried to ensure the city's protection.

HERA (Juno), Ἥρα

PARENTAGE Cronus and Rhea

OFFSPRING Hebe (the goddess of youth); Eileithuia (a goddess of childbirth); Hephaestus (the god of metallurgy); and Typhaon (a snaky dragon sometimes identified with Typhoeus, the offspring of Gaia)

ATTRIBUTES Scepter, crown, peacock

SIGNIFICANT CULT TITLES
- Argeia (Argive)
- Nympheuomene (Bride-to-Be)
- Telea (Fulfiller of Marriage)

SIGNIFICANT RITUALS AND SANCTUARIES
- **The Hecatombaia** A procession and a sacrifice of one hundred oxen at Argos.
- **The Tonaia** During this ritual at Samos, a statue of Hera was bound to a tree.

3.1 HISTORY

ORDER AND REBELLION

This chapter surveys myths and religious practices devoted to Zeus in order to understand how the Greeks viewed the god who, as the "boss" of their universe, was at the center of their mythology. Particular attention is given to how Zeus maintains order in the cosmos, especially when challenged by the gods and mortals he governs. This chapter also considers Hera, Zeus's wife and sister, and seeks to understand the ways in which she (like Prometheus) resists and challenges Zeus. Along the way, this chapter highlights two key concepts that pertain to Greeks gods and goddesses. First, the "personalities" of gods and goddesses are variable: they change over time and place and in different written and visual representations. Second, however beautiful and compelling Greek gods and goddesses may be, they are not role models for human beings. They are to be worshipped and revered, but not imitated. Divine powers and passions far exceed those of humankind; they cannot and should not be sustained by mere mortals or their communities.

ZEUS

At the end of the *Theogony*, Hesiod describes Zeus's many marriages to goddesses and the offspring they produce. As the husband of Themis (Established Custom), Zeus sires several daughters whose names suggest the cosmic spheres he oversees and the values he introduces into the universe. These daughters are the Seasons (sometimes called "Watchers"), Lawfulness, Peace, and Justice (Chapter 2.1). The fact that the Seasons are Zeus's daughters suggests that although Zeus did not create the cosmos—as Hesiod writes, the universe originated with Chaos spawning other deities—Zeus nonetheless ensures its orderly continuance through natural processes, such as the seasons. Additionally, despite being called "the father of gods and mortals," Zeus created neither all the divine beings in the universe nor the human race. Nonetheless, he oversees peace and justice among both groups, enabling them to carry on successfully despite their frequent warfare and strife. Zeus secures his rule by maintaining order in three key spheres: the cosmic sphere, which concerns celestial phenomena; the human sphere, which concerns the actions of human beings on earth; and the divine sphere, which concerns gods and goddesses.

3.2 Zeus with a thunderbolt. Corinthian, bronze statuette. Circa 530–520 BCE. Glyptothek, Munich, Germany. © Vanni Archive / Art Resource, NY, ART382686.

Cosmic Order: Thunder and Lightning The name "Zeus" is associated with the Indo-European root *dyeu-*, which refers to the bright sky of the day rather than the night. This suggests that the Zeus whom the Greeks worshipped derived from a widely worshipped Indo-European sky god. Even though he is a sky god, however, Zeus is associated only with particular meteorological phenomena. He is not associated with the sun, for example, which the Greeks identified with the god Helios, or with the dawn, which the Greeks called the goddess Eos. Zeus is specifically connected with the thunderbolt and lightning (Figure 3.2). These are simultaneously his weapons by which he asserts his power over other gods as well as the sources of the celestial phenomena he does control, namely, rain and storms.

In the *Iliad*, Homer includes a snippet from a creation story not found in Hesiod's *Theogony* that emphasizes Zeus's association with the sky. He writes that, when Poseidon was quarreling with Zeus, the two brothers (along with Hades) drew lots to determine who would get which part of the universe. Poseidon received the salty seas, whereas Hades drew the dark Underworld, and Zeus drew the upper sky and clouds. This divine lottery provides a mythical explanation of Zeus's location in the sky, where thunder and lightning secure his dominance over his brothers (*Iliad* 15.187–193).

Religious imagination translated the myth of Zeus's inheritance of the sky into the belief that Zeus dwelled on the mountains. Sanctuaries devoted to Zeus located on lofty peaks suggest that the Greeks understood Zeus to control rain and storms. Mount Lycaeus in Arcadia, a mountainous region in central Peloponnese, was one such mountaintop where Zeus had a "cult." ("Cult" refers to *repeated actions* directed toward specific divinities in a particular place, such as on Mount Lycaeus. "Ritual" describes these actions; they include sacrifice, dedications of objects, prayer, dance, songs, and processions.) On Mount Lycaeus, archaeologists have found an ash altar to Zeus, a large mound composed of ashes mostly from burnt animal bones, dedications such as pottery, drinking cups, coins, a statue of Zeus, and fulgurite, a glassy substance made from sandy soil that has been petrified by lightning. Priests on Mount Lycaeus, which at 4,500 feet above sea level allows for cloud and weather patterns to be easily observed, performed rain magic. For example, if there was a drought, a priest would pray, offer sacrifices, and dip an oak branch in a spring that was believed to generate a rain-producing mist. Because oak trees were sacred to Zeus, the priest's gesture may have been a form of sympathetic magic, that is, a gesture intended to encourage Zeus to send rain-filled clouds.

Similarly, Zeus was worshipped on Mount Hymettus, southeast of the Acropolis in central Athens. On the summit of this mountain, which permitted a clear view of cultivated fields as well as cloud formations, dedications have been found in a pit near a curved wall. Those with inscriptions that refer to Zeus, which began to be offered around 700 BCE, identify the site as his. The word "Stormy" (Ombrius), a cult title that associates Zeus with rain and weather, appears on one pot recovered from the site. Because the dedications on Mount Hymettus cease around 600 BCE, some archaeologists argue that as Athenians increasingly imported rather than cultivated grain, easing their dependence on favorable weather for their crops, their worship of Zeus on Mount Hymettus diminished. The rain rituals on Mount Lycaeus as well as the dedications on Mount Hymettus suggest that worshippers had a practical understanding of Zeus as a god who dwelled in the sky and sent rain for their fields. Curiously, Zeus's control of rain and stormy weather is closely intertwined with his role as the ensurer of justice among humankind.

Human Order: Justice In the *Theogony* (Chapter 2.1) as well as in *Works and Days*, Hesiod weaves together Zeus's function as weather god with his

Map 3.1 Zeus and Hera in Greece

oversight of human deeds and justice. In the *Works and Days*, Zeus exhibits a particular interest in the dealings of princes. Whereas the *Theogony* shows him in relation to other gods, the *Works and Days* depicts Zeus as deeply engaged with the human and natural world. Hesiod and the farmers of Ascra who toil in the fields worship Zeus as a giver of rain and judge of men's deeds. Hesiod suggests how these two activities—meting out justice and sending rain—are intimately connected to each other (translated by M. L. West):

HESIOD, FROM *WORKS AND DAYS*

As for those who give straight judgments to visitors and to their own people and do not deviate from what is just, their community flourishes, and the people blooms in it: Peace is about the land, fostering the young, and wide-seeing Zeus never marks out grievous war as their portion. Neither does Famine attend straight-judging men, nor Blight, and they feast on the crops they tend. For them Earth bears plentiful food, and on the mountains the oak carries acorns at its surface and bees at its center. Their fleecy sheep are laden down with wool; the womenfolk bear children that resemble their parents; they enjoy a continual sufficiency of good things. Nor do they ply on ships, but the grain-giving ploughland bears them fruit.

But for those who occupy themselves with violence and wickedness and brutal deeds, Cronus' son wide-seeing Zeus, marks out retribution. Often a whole community together suffers in consequence of a bad man who does wrong and contrives evil. From heaven, Cronus' son brings disaster on them, famine and with it plague, and the people waste away. The womenfolk do not give birth, and households decline, by Olympian Zeus' design. At other times he either destroys those men's broad army or city wall, or punishes their ships at sea.

Hesiod's remarks connect Zeus's distribution of justice to the conditions in the natural environment. A ruler who gives "straight" (i.e., fair) judgments governs a peaceful community that "flourishes" and "blooms" with abundant crops, wooly sheep, and thriving children. However, violent and wicked men bring suffering to their "whole community" in the form of famine, plague, and sterility of the earth and humankind. When these catastrophic events occur, they are understood not as random events but, rather, as punishments inflicted by Zeus on whole communities in which rulers or lesser individuals have not acted justly. The justice of Zeus, then, dictates that the actions of a single ruler or individual may lead to the devastation of an entire community.

The worship of Zeus Meilichius (Mild One) in Athens provides a religious counterpart to Hesiod's description of Zeus's oversight of weather and justice in *Works and Days*. Zeus Meilichius is represented as a bearded man or as a snake (Figure 3.3). As snakes were linked by the ancient Greeks to the earth and the Underworld, the depiction of Zeus Meilichius as a snake suggests his connection to the Underworld, from where he sent the earth's fruits upward. At the carnival-like Diasia festival in Athens, adults and children from both the city and rural areas gathered to play games, exchange presents, and offer cakes in the shape of animals to Zeus. In this way, they thanked him for beneficial weather as well as propitiated him to ensure a successful harvest. Thus Zeus Meilichius was linked to the fertility of the crops through his connection to the earth as a snake and to rain in his aspect as a sky god.

Zeus Meilichius was also connected to justice. He had to be supplicated if any murder had been committed in Athens, and

3.3 Votive relief for Zeus Meilichius. Circa fourth century BCE. *bpk, Berlin/Antikensammlung, Staatliche Museen, Berlin, Germany / Ingrid Geske / Art Resource, NY, ART358210.*

in the Pompaia (Parade), another ritual dedicated to him, a ram's skin was carried around the city to protect it from pollution caused by any ritual violations, including bloodshed. The shrine of Zeus Meilichius, then, illustrates Greek religious habits and attitudes as well as the many dimensions of Zeus. He oversees community welfare by attending to its agricultural and human fertility as well as to the moral and ethical behavior of its members: he will ensure successful harvests if a community does not harbor murderers or any other polluted persons. In these ways, the worship of Zeus Meilichius in Athens translates the religious thinking about Zeus in Hesiod's *Works and Days* into ritual action.

Zeus had many other cult titles (in addition to Meilichius) that demonstrate his concern with justice in human communities. As a king of gods, he was especially important to Greek kings, who claimed him as their protector and patron. But Zeus also protected those on the margins of society. Zeus's cult title Xenius (Guardian of Hospitality) refers to his oversight of ethical and religious obligations between guests and hosts, obligations that had great importance for intercity commercial, social, and political exchanges. Other cult titles, such as Horkius (Guardian of Oaths), Philius (Guardian of Friendship), and Polius (Guardian of the City), further indicate that Zeus's oversight of human communities and customs was just as important as his control of the weather.

Divine Order: Kingship If Hesiod's Zeus in *Works and Days* is a judge of men, in Homer's *Iliad*, Zeus is a king who works to keep balance in a world at war, both on Olympus and on earth. Zeus is firmly in control of the gods by virtue of his physical strength—a fact Hephaestus reinforces when he tells the other gods about the time Zeus threw him from Olympus because of his disobedience. Hephaestus asks them, "Why, what if the Olympian, master of lightning, wished to blast / us from our seats? For his strength is much the greater" (*Iliad* 1.570–571). Despite his superior strength, however, Zeus must work to maintain his position of authority among the gods, who often try to evade his dictates in order to help human beings they love or to harm those they dislike.

Homer shows repeatedly that, despite his supreme power over the Olympians as their ruler, Zeus is nonetheless constrained by his obligations to other gods and goddesses, whose allegiance Zeus values in his quest to maintain his sovereignty without strife. When, for example, Zeus wants to rescue his beloved son Sarpedon from death on the battlefield, he asks Hera if he should whisk him away while he is still alive (Figure 3.4). Hera reminds him that the mortal Sarpedon's destiny is to die and then warns him, "Go, do it; but all we other gods will not approve it" (*Iliad* 16.443). Hera explains that all the gods have children with human beings and other mortal favorites they would like to save. If Zeus were to rescue Sarpedon, it would disrupt tacit

3.4 Sarpedon, Zeus's son, is lifted by Hypnos and Thanatos in the presence of Hermes. Red-figure calyx-krater. Euphronius Painter, c. 515 BCE. National Museum of the Villa Giulia, Rome, Italy. *Scala/Minestero per I Beni e le Attivita culturali/Art Resource, NY, ART407274.*

agreements among the gods about how they ought to behave toward mortals and one another alike. By reminding him of the obligations he owes other gods, Hera makes clear that although Zeus is the king of Olympus and has the authority to rescue his son, he exercises that authority among other deities whose powers must be respected, if cosmic warfare is to be avoided.

Hera's comments also shed light on why Zeus does not always respond to human requests and even why human beings suffer. When Zeus is bound to meet his obligations to other immortals, he often cannot respond to human prayers and sacrifices. Because these divine obligations may be unknown to human beings, his actions appear fickle, unclear, even cruel. When, for example, Achilles sends his companion Patroclus into battle on his behalf, he prays to Zeus for two things: that Patroclus beat back the Trojans from the Greek ships and that he return from battle alive. Homer says that Zeus heard both prayers but granted only one: Patroclus would beat back the Trojans but would not survive. We know that Zeus is obliged to the goddess Thetis, Achilles's mother, to ensure that Achilles and not Patroclus gains honor in battle. We surmise that Zeus uses the death of Patroclus to incite Achilles to fight the Trojans and thus win honor. But Achilles himself does not know about Zeus's promise to Thetis or how he will meet it—he only knows that Zeus did not fulfil his prayer to keep Patroclus alive.

There are other examples of human actors in the *Iliad* either not understanding or misinterpreting the actions of Zeus. The most dramatic of these involves the destruction of Troy. Agamemnon rallies his troops by convincing them they have Zeus on their side because the Trojans have violated the religious and social customs of hospitality (*xenia*) by taking Helen from Sparta. Agamemnon confidently asserts, "Zeus will not help liars" (4.235). Yet Zeus's motive for wanting Troy destroyed has no relationship to Agamemnon's claims. In a conversation with Hera, Zeus says that his altar in Troy "has never lacked in the equal feast, or in the offerings of wine, / or in the scent of burned flesh" (4.47–48). In Zeus's view, contrary to Agamemnon's beliefs, the Trojans are properly respectful of all the gods, and the city of Troy is "the most honored in [his] heart." Yet, in order to maintain equilibrium on Olympus among the gods as well as to honor his pledge to Thetis, Zeus reluctantly agrees to let Hera destroy Troy, a city she despises. In return, Zeus demands that Hera pledge to allow Zeus to destroy any city he chooses in the future, even if it is dear to her. Hera readily promises that Zeus may ruin even her beloved cities of Sparta, Argos, or Mycenae, if she can raze Troy (4.50–54).

The wide gap between Agamemnon's claims about Zeus and Zeus's bargain with Hera is a measure of how little human beings understand the workings of the divine. Human actors in the *Iliad* lack the capacity to understand the constraints on Zeus's prerogatives, making Zeus appear incomprehensible, indifferent, and even unconcerned with justice. In emphasizing those aspects of Zeus that best fit his tale of war and suffering, Homer portrays Zeus as seen through the eyes of the warriors at Troy, and perhaps by extension Homer's audience, many of whom would have been soldiers. In the *Iliad*, survival on the battlefield seems arbitrary; the fate of soldiers seems to have little to do with their moral fiber. Thus Zeus is understood to be an inscrutable god of warriors and kings; he embodies the cruelty they both inflict and suffer. The Hesiodic Zeus, in contrast, judges people's actions. He does not cut deals with other gods to destroy cities.

Neither Hesiod nor Homer is more "correct" about Zeus. Neither *Works and Days* nor the *Iliad* was considered sacred scripture. Neither poem was meant to express a coherent religious theology, nor should a reader combine the poems in an effort to create one. It is more consistent with Greek thinking to treat each poem as an expression of how different people in different circumstances made sense of Zeus. Behind the Iliadic Zeus of the battlefield, the Hesiodic Zeus of thunder and justice, and Meilichius's snaky visage, we sense how the Greeks attempted to understand Zeus's oversight of the human race and the causes of human suffering. A prayer to Zeus as unknowable and all-encompassing and a collection of myths about Zeus in the form of an animal also address the nature of Zeus and the question of human suffering. The following section examines these two very different representations of Zeus.

Violence and Grace In Aeschylus's play *Agamemnon*, after the chorus describes Agamemnon's sacrifice of his daughter, its members are filled with fear and foreboding. They pray to Zeus and in so doing express how they (and perhaps the audience of the play) understand his mysterious governance of the cosmic, divine, and human realms (translated by Alan Shapiro and Peter Burian).

 ### AESCHYLUS, FROM *AGAMEMNON* (179–210)

Whoever Zeus may be,
if it pleases him by this
name to be called, by this
name then I call to him.
I have weighed this with that,
and, pondering everything,
discover nothing now
but Zeus to cast for good
the anxious weight of this
unknowing from my mind.

He who was once great, boundless
in strength, unappeasable, is now
unnamed, unsung, as if
he never was, and he
who threw him, only to be
thrown in turn, losing
the third fall, he
is gone, too, past and gone.
But he who sings glad praise
of Zeus' victory
strikes to the heart of knowledge:

For it was Zeus who set
men on the path to wisdom
when he decreed the fixed
law that suffering
alone shall be their teacher.
Even in sleep pain drips
down through the heart as fear,
all night as memory.
We learn unwillingly.
From the high bench of the gods
by violence, it seems, grace comes.

In the first stanza, the chorus expresses both its members' reverential piety and their limited understanding of Zeus and the world in which they live. They seem to suggest that the name "Zeus" does not quite capture the nature of the god to whom they pray, yet it is the only one they have to describe him. In the second stanza, the chorus recalls Hesiod's account of how Zeus came to power: "He who was once great" refers to Uranus, and "he who threw him" refers to Cronus. Here we see how seamlessly mythic tales and religious piety intersect with each other.

The chorus concludes with a picture of Zeus that seems distinctly Greek. It sees benefit in the inevitable suffering of human beings: "suffering alone shall be their teacher." This expression became well known, in part because of its brevity and rhythmic structure in Greek (*pathei mathos*). The chorus also links the judgments of Zeus and the other divinities to "grace," something equally beautiful and divine. We might say that although Zeus's violence causes suffering, that suffering allows (perhaps even compels) human beings to develop a perspective on their condition. Grace and beauty complement that perspective and lead to a state of awe or appreciation. Divine violence coupled with divine grace: these are Zeus's gifts to humanity. Thus the chorus's view of Zeus expands his oversight of the human world beyond the spheres of a single cult (like that of Zeus Meilichius) or any single myth, and perhaps ventures beyond the question of Zeus's justice to a contemplation of his very being.

One collection of myths offers further insight into the violence and grace associated with Zeus. These are the stories in which Zeus disguises himself, often as an animal, in order to rape or seduce (if that is the right word) a human being, usually (but not always) a woman. These stories too are meditations on Zeus's relationship to the human race. In one such myth, Zeus appears to the Phoenician princess Europa disguised as a sweet-smelling bull. Persuaded to sit on his back, she is then carried off by the god. In another myth, Zeus assumes the form of an eagle and seizes the handsome young Trojan prince Ganymede, taking him to Olympus, where he achieves immortality as Zeus's servant. In the form of golden rain, Zeus pours into the tower where Danaë's father, King Acrisius, has hidden her; the son that results is the hero Perseus (Chapter 12.1). Sometimes Zeus took on the identity of a mortal man in order to seduce or rape a woman he desired. For example, disguised as Amphitryon, the husband of Alcmena, he impregnates Alcmena, who later gives birth to Heracles, the greatest of Greek heroes (Chapter 10.1).

These tales of Zeus in disguise frequently appear in collections of children's myths, where their sexual and violent content is minimized. Yet these sexual and violent aspects contribute to their religious meaning. The story of Leda and Zeus, in particular, offers a case study through which to explore what these stories convey about the relationship of Zeus to mortals.

3.5 Leda and the Swan. Marble relief. Fifth to fourth century BCE. Greek National Archaeological Museum, Athens, Greece. *Gianni Dagli Orti/The Art Archive at Art Resource, NY, AA389421.*

Zeus approaches Leda, wife of the Spartan king Tyndareus, in the form of a swan. He impregnates her, and she gives birth to Helen and Pollux. At the same time, she gives birth to Clytemnestra and Castor, who were fathered by Tyndareus. (The last section of this chapter explores how modernist poets respond to this particular myth about Zeus.) Two representations of Zeus and Leda indicate that the ancients depicted this encounter sometimes as a violent, nonconsensual act and at other times as a playful seduction. In the marble relief, the strangeness and violence of Zeus's attack is emphasized as Leda tries to release her thighs from his talons (Figure 3.5), whereas the standing sculpture shows Leda embracing the swan (Figure 3.6). Among the many depictions of Zeus and Leda found on vases, oil lamps, mirrors, and sculptural reliefs, relatively few depict the swan overpowering her with physical force as in Figure 3.5. Zeus, like all the gods, has other means at his disposal when he wishes to seduce—beauty, grace, divinity, even a sweet fragrance. Why, then, would he resort to violence?

The struggle portrayed on the marble relief suggests that human beings cannot escape the will of Zeus or the limits of their mortality. It also conveys a palpable fear that the gods may be indifferent or cruel in their passion toward humankind. On the other hand, the beauty and hope of semidivine offspring (many of whom grow up to be legendary heroes and heroines) may be a consolation for the human condition. Moreover, it is precisely the fluctuations between female consent and resistance and between divine violence and grace in these tales that convey a range of human sentiments, even ambivalence, toward Zeus. Greek myth evokes what one eminent scholar calls the "hard realism" of early Greek religion. The gods lent beauty and grace to the human world, but they did not offer relief for (and indeed in some instances they directly caused) human suffering. Neither negated or compensated for the other. In Greek myths and religious practices, the world was imagined to be eminently beautiful as well as difficult; so, too, were the gods, with Zeus at their helm.

HERA

Zeus and Hera are brother and sister, the children of Rhea and Cronus. They are also husband and wife, which makes them unique among the Greek gods (who do not, as a rule, marry their siblings). Their marriage is characterized by Hera's fidelity and Zeus's philandering. Hera remains monogamous and marries no other god. She bears only the offspring of Zeus: Ares, the god of war; Hebe, a goddess who represents youth and becomes Heracles's bride; and Eileithuia, a goddess of childbirth, an area of women's lives also overseen by Hera. On her own, without Zeus or any other male, Hera also bears Hephaestus, a god who is known for his lameness and his association with metallurgy, and Typhaon, a snaky, dragon-like monster who seems to be a shadowy double of Typhoeus in the *Theogony*.

Zeus, on the other hand, produces many offspring outside of his marriage with Hera, provoking Hera's infamous wrath. Hera's anger leads her, for example, to pursue and torment Heracles, the son of Zeus and the mortal woman Alcmene, throughout his life (Chapter 10.1). In *Prometheus Bound*, we learn that Hera has turned one of Zeus's mortal lovers, Io, into a cow. Hera instructs Argus, a many-eyed guardian, to follow Io in order to keep her from Zeus.

Hera's inability to curtail her husband's infidelities provides one explanation of Hera's anger. Zeus compounds her anger by refusing to share the governance of the cosmos with Hera. Like all the other gods and goddesses, Hera is subject to Zeus's rule. Hera's subservience to her husband is reflected in architecture, art, and ritual. At Olympia, for example, Zeus's temple, ash altar, and athletic games were all on a grander scale than Hera's. (The statue of Zeus in his temple there was so colossal that it was considered one of the Seven Wonders of the Ancient World.) Yet neither Zeus's dominance nor his philandering fully explain or justify her common portrayal as a chronically angry and jealous wife.

3.6 Leda and the Swan. Marble Statue. Roman copy (second century CE) after a Greek original attributed to Timotheos, c. 370 BCE. *Yale University Art Gallery / Art Resource, NY, ART325369.*

To understand Hera's wrath, we must turn not to myth but to historical developments in Greek religious practice. There are religious and historical dimensions of Hera's worship that are independent of Zeus and provide a different lens through which to understand their contentious relationship. At Argos, Corinth, and Perachora in Greece; at Samos in Ionia; and in the Argive colonies in Italy, Hera was a powerful goddess who was worshipped in magnificent temples (Figure 3.7). This Hera oversaw a range of human endeavors unconnected to her mythic profile as the wife and sister of Zeus.

Goddess of Heroes at Argos Hera's temple at Argos and the festivals celebrated there in her honor demonstrate her intimate association with the region

3.7 Colossal limestone head from the cult statue of Hera in the Heraion of Olympia. 580 BCE. Archaeological Museum, Olympia, Greece. *Erich Lessing / Art Resource, NY, ART105413.*

3.8 Model of a temple dedicated to Hera, from Argos. Temple date is c. 700 BCE. National Archaeological Museum, Athens, Greece. *Nimatallah / Art Resource, NY, ART85617.*

of Argos and its heroes. Hera's festival was one of the grandest in the region. Taking place at the beginning of the new year, the festival included a procession in which a priestess rode on a cart pulled by oxen (the ox was associated with Hera), athletic competitions, the dedication of a new garment for Hera, the lighting of new fire (a ritual typical in new year's festivities), and the sacrifice of one hundred oxen. This sacrifice gives the festival its name, Hecatombaia (sacrifice of one hundred cattle). Coupled with numerous terracotta figurines of mother and child and model houses (Figure 3.8), these festivities suggest the many facets of Hera's identity among the Argives.

Although scholars debate the origins of her name, the word "Hera" may be connected to the Greek words for hero (*hērōs*) as well as their word for seasons (*horae*). If these linguistic connections are correct, they suggest the two main ways in which Hera's sanctuary and rituals define her. These two ways are also reflected in her statue in the temple, in which she is shown holding a scepter (a sign of political power) and a pomegranate (a sign of fertility). Hera protected the political integrity of the region of Argos and the military might of its male citizens, who fought in ways that recalled the Iliadic heroes at Troy. She also oversaw the protection of young women and their children, regulating birth and nurturance of the human community as well as the seasons. Her temple in Samos provides a similar picture of Hera, connecting her with Greek heroes, political sovereignty, and the prosperity and continuity of communities reflected by a growing population.

Goddess of Fertility and Protection at Samos
Located off the coast of modern-day Turkey, the island of Samos was a wealthy and vibrant Greek community, where Hera had an equally wealthy and vibrant sanctuary. Herodotus reports that her temple there was one of the largest he had ever seen (*Histories* 3.60). Hera's sanctuary was said to have been founded by Jason and the Argonauts when they sailed east to get the Golden Fleece (Chapter 12.1). From the

tenth century BCE, Hera's sanctuary was of regional importance, as shown by the Egyptian and Babylonian dedications of considerable value that have been found there. Visitors from outside the island attended her festivals, which featured athletic and choral competitions and sacrifices at her altars (one was an ash altar, and the other was made of stone).

One particularly interesting ritual in Hera's honor was the Tonaia (Binding), during which Hera's statue was washed in the sea and then bound to a *lugos* tree (sometimes identified as a willow tree, a symbol of sexual abstention) and offered barley cakes. A founding story is offered for this ritual: when pirates tried to steal Hera's statue, she made their ship unable to move. Frightened, the pirates returned the statue to shore with offerings. Although the ritual mimics this event and may be an attempt to keep the goddess on the island and thus secure her protection, it is also possible that the ritual suggests Hera's connection to fertility. The annual purification and imagined disappearance of the statue suggests the cycle of agricultural fertility, in which seeds disappear in the earth and then eventually sprout and reappear. (Compare this story and ritual to rites associated with Demeter in Chapter 4.1). Offerings of pomegranates and pinecones, symbols of fertility, found in Hera's sanctuary reinforce this possibility, as does animal iconography (Figure 3.9) that associates Hera with the natural world. In addition, statues of female figures with bands crossing their wombs also suggest that the Samian Hera was associated with fertility.

3.9 Three women in long dresses with two crouching lions. Base of a marble basin from Hera's temple on Samos, Greece. Seventh century BCE. Staatliche Museen, Berlin, Germany. *Erich Lessing / Art Resource, NY, ART204850.*

It is noteworthy that Zeus had no presence in Samos until the seventh century BCE, when a wooden statue of male and female figures, identified as Zeus and Hera, was dedicated. Although the statue does not definitively indicate that Zeus was worshipped at this time, there was nonetheless a gradual disappearance of dedications of pinecones and pomegranates. Joan O'Brien, a classical scholar, has suggested a connection between these two events. She argues that Hera was a goddess worshipped independently of Zeus for her protection and fertility. Once she became more widely known as Zeus's wife and sister, Hera's position as a goddess who oversees fertility in all realms diminished, and instead she became more associated with the production of offspring in marriage. In Greece, several of Hera's cult titles link her with marriage and thus to Zeus (Figure 3.10). She is called Telea (Of Fulfillment), in reference to marriage (an

3.10 The marriage of Zeus and Hera. Metope from temple E at Selinunte. Fifth century BCE. National Archaeological Museum in Palermo, Italy. *Erich Lessing / Art Resource, NY, ART200891.*

act believed to fulfill a woman's life), as well as Nympheuomene (Bride-to-Be). O'Brien writes, "This later stage of the cult, in which fertility became muted and marriage to Zeus became the cornerstone, probably developed imperceptibly, as the *Iliad*'s portrait had entered the popular imagination." In other words, conceptions of Hera the goddess in both myth and ritual evolved over time, suggesting that Greek gods and goddesses may have different attributes depending on the time and place of their worship.

Divine Consort of Zeus One myth about Hera may explain the connection between worship of Hera as a goddess independent of Zeus and her role in myths as the angry wife of Zeus. Hera is often associated with the peacock, on whose feathers she placed the eyes of Argus, the many-eyed guardian of Io (on the orders of Zeus, Hermes killed Io; Hera retrieved his eyes) (Figure 3.11). She is also associated with the cuckoo (*kokkux*), a bird known to place its young in the nest of other species in order to trick them into raising its (the cuckoo's) young. An ancient Greek scholar, commenting on a poem by Theocritus, recounts how Zeus disguises himself as a cuckoo to trick Hera into mating with him:

 SCHOLIAST, *TO THEOCRITUS*

Mythologists say that Zeus was plotting to mate with Hera, when he saw her sitting apart from the other gods. Wanting to become invisible and not be seen by her, he changed his appearance into a cuckoo bird and sat on a mountain that had been called Mt. Thronax but is now called Mt. Cuckoo. Zeus caused a terrible storm on the day when Hera traveling arrived at the mountain alone, and sat where there is now the temple of Hera Telea. The cuckoo looking about flew and alighted near Hera's knees, shivering and rigid because of the storm. Hera seeing the bird pitied it and took it upon her lap. Zeus immediately changed his appearance and grabbed hold of Hera. When Hera asked her mother for permission to mate with Zeus, Zeus undertook to make Hera his wife.

Many scholars think this story reflects the historical process that O'Brien describes. Hera was at first worshipped independently of Zeus, with whom she was not closely connected. Once the Greeks, perhaps prompted by changing social circumstances, began to worship Zeus's sovereignty, they began to conceive of a family of gods unified under his rule (as Hesiod describes in his *Theogony*, and Homer in his *Iliad*). As these myths circulated, they began to shape the worship and understanding of the gods among Greek-speaking peoples. In this view, myths about the hostility between Zeus and Hera may reflect some historical fact about the collapse of their independent worship. Such a developing system of religious practices provides one way to explain how Hera (and perhaps other gods for whom there is less evidence) became both subordinate and hostile to Zeus in myth. In sum, myth and ritual influenced each other; similarly, myth and politics also influenced each other.

ZEUS AND *PROMETHEUS BOUND*

Evolving religious and social practices may explain not only Hera's hostility to Zeus in myth but also Zeus's cruelty in Aeschylus's *Prometheus Bound*. Composed and staged in fifth-century BCE Athens, *Prometheus Bound* reflects its era of great political

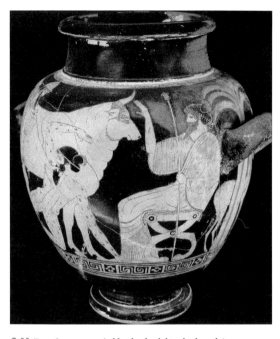

3.11 Zeus is accompanied by the dead, hundred-eyed Argos, who guarded Io and was killed by Hermes. Red-figured Attic stamnos, terracotta. Kunsthistorisches Museum, Vienna, Austria. *Erich Lessing / Art Resource, NY, ART21449.*

and cultural upheavals. The social and political context of *Prometheus Bound* informs its startling presentation of Zeus, discussed in the opening of this chapter.

Like many cities in Greece during the Archaic Period, Athens was ruled by a tyrant, Peisistratus ("tyrant" was initially a neutral term for a sole ruler, without the negative connotations of modern usage), and his sons. Whereas Peisistratus benefited the city in many ways—he granted powers and prerogatives to those who were not aristocrats, instituted festivals, and sponsored the construction of public buildings—his sons became increasingly autocratic and cruel and were eventually overthrown (510 BCE). Shortly thereafter, Athens began to develop democratic forms of governance. Power to govern was vested in all adult male citizens, not only landed aristocrats. Mechanisms of voting, courts, and military units were reorganized and institutionalized to enable the adult male populace to govern effectively, although women were still excluded from public life and slavery was still maintained as a viable economic and social institution.

Concurrent with the development of democracy in Athens, all Greeks had to defend themselves against the Persian kings Darius (c. 550–486 BCE) and his son Xerxes (519–465 BCE), who had invaded their lands. The Greeks were successful despite their smaller numbers and attributed their victory to their freedom from tyranny and kingship. (Herodotus describes the Persian wars in his *Histories*.) No Greek man was conscripted to fight the Persians. Instead, each man fought for himself, for his land, and for laws shared by all, not on behalf of a single king.

After the defeat of the Persians, and throughout the Classical Period, Athens began to assume leadership of the Delian League, a federated group of Greek cities committed to protecting Greece from further invasions. Athenians garnered funds from the league and used its increasing wealth to make their city a cultural, educational, and commercial center in the Greek world. Two central sites in Athens were enlarged and embellished during this prosperous age. The Acropolis (high city), a massive, rocky bluff that was the religious center of Athens, was adorned with even more temples, gates, altars, and statues. In the theater of Dionysus on its south slope, tragedies and comedies were performed. The Agora, the city's commercial and social center to the west of the Acropolis, saw the construction of temples and statues alongside governmental and educational buildings. Here Socrates, Plato, Aristotle, and other philosophers lectured on mathematics, philosophy, and physics to their young male students, and Athenians debated the existence of the gods. Myths were recounted and disputed. The philosopher Protagoras (c. 490–c. 420 BCE) captured the spirit of the age when he claimed that "man is the measure of all things," placing human beings above the gods. Yet in the Agora, Athenians still marched in religious parades (such as the Panathenaia [Chapter 6.1]) and worshipped gods at altars.

In this intellectually, politically, and religiously vibrant city, *Prometheus Bound* was first staged. A close reading of its depiction of the conflict between Prometheus and Zeus suggests that the play reflects theological, religious, and political concerns alike, at a time when the nature of divinity was being publicly debated on city streets. Zeus's rule as a king, and as the sole ruler of Olympus, may have offered a vision of the divine world that no longer mirrored Athenian democracy. In *Prometheus Bound*, the kingship of Zeus is criticized. This skepticism, however, should not be considered unusual; earlier representations of Zeus, as we have seen, were not considered sacred. Indeed, myths about Zeus (along with all Greek divinities) compose a historically conditioned, imaginative, and emotionally resonant network that the Greeks used to understand themselves and their world.

The Greek understanding of Zeus evolved over time to accommodate the ideals and needs of a changing society. Any individual myth or ritual offers us only a partial view of him. We can attempt to combine these fragments, stitching together a homogenized picture of Zeus with a list of his attributes, activities, and rituals. But a more productive approach would be to try to understand what people who recounted myths as well as worshippers were trying to express about the moment Zeus's thunderbolt touched earth and inspired a story. This is the approach offered in the following introduction to *Prometheus Bound*.

AESCHYLUS, FROM *PROMETHEUS BOUND*

BEFORE YOU READ

Prometheus Bound was part of a trilogy, along with *Prometheus Unbound* and *Prometheus the Fire-Bringer*. The order of these plays, as well as their dating and authorship (they are most often attributed to Aeschylus), has been debated. Most scholars agree only that this trilogy comes from the fifth century BCE after the Persian Wars, and that the trilogy's resolution involved some sort of reconciliation between Zeus and Prometheus.

In *Prometheus Bound*, generally considered to be the first play of the trilogy, Zeus is a cruelly methodical ruler, whereas Prometheus is a sympathetic (if self-congratulatory) protector of human beings who has disobeyed Zeus and is punished on a lonely mountain in Scythia. Those who visit him assess the fairness of his punishment; in so doing, they contemplate Zeus's nature and rule. Io, the only mortal in the play, arrives on Prometheus's mountain in the form of a cow. Driven from her home by Zeus, transformed by Hera into a cow, and pursued by a stinging gadfly, Io's great suffering testifies to the cruelty of Zeus and his indifference to human beings. Unlike Prometheus, who knowingly and willingly challenged Zeus, Io bears no responsibility for her condition.

The chorus of Oceanids, daughters of the god Ocean, provides the emotional ballast of the play and offers a relief from suffering. Prometheus and the Oceanids repeatedly use the words "pity" and "love" to describe Prometheus's relationship to human beings and to describe the Oceanids' relationship to Prometheus. These emotional commitments become moral ones over the course of the play and enable Prometheus and the Oceanids to stand together at the play's end. The Oceanids' refusal to desert Prometheus cannot stop Zeus from exercising his will against Prometheus. Yet their choice offers a form of resistance to Zeus's power: love, pity, and friendship.

Prometheus's actions on behalf of humanity and the Oceanids' decision to stay with him suggest how even a king may fall: the alliances among and knowledge possessed by those ruled (especially if they are ruled unjustly) may prove too powerful to ignore or suppress. The tense relationships between power (Zeus), knowledge (Prometheus), and empathy or solidarity (Oceanids) offer a distinctly human-centered response to suffering in the face of indifferent gods. Although *Prometheus Bound* does not assert that "man is the measure of all things," it does imply that human connection may be one powerful response to a hostile divinity. (Translated by James Scully and C. John Herington.)

- Compare Zeus in the opening scene of *Prometheus Bound* to Zeus in Hesiod's *Theogony*, in Hesiod's *Works and Days*, in the choral ode of Aeschylus's *Agamemnon*, and in the sculptural depictions of Leda and the swan. Are there any commonalities in Zeus's character in these different representations?

- In the opening scene, Hephaestus does not want to punish Prometheus, yet he does. How do his protests contribute to an evaluation of Zeus and Prometheus? How does Prometheus explain his role in the Titanomachy to the chorus? How is his account different from Hesiod's description of the Olympian conquest of the Titans during the Titanomachy?

- What gifts does Prometheus give to humankind in *Prometheus Bound*? How does his account compare with that of Hesiod?

AESCHYLUS, FROM *PROMETHEUS BOUND* (FIFTH CENTURY BCE)

POWER And so we've come to the end of the world.

    To Scythia: this howling waste

                            no one passes through.

    Hephaistos, now it's up to you.
    What the Father wants done
        you've got to do.
    On these overhanging cliffs
        with your own shatter-proof irons
    you're commanded:
    Clamp this troublemaking bastard to the rock.   10

    After all, Hephaistos, it was *your* glowing flower
            FIRE
        —the power behind all
                works of hands—
    he stole it, he gave it away
    to *human beings*.
    That's his crime, and the Gods demand
        he pay for it.
    He must submit
        to the tyranny of Zeus   20
    and like it, too.
    He'll learn.

    He's got to give up
    feeling for humanity.

HEPHAISTOS Power and Violence . . . you've already carried out
            your orders from Zeus.
        you're free to go now.

But me, I haven't the heart to chain this god
    this brother!
to this stormbeaten ravine.   30
       And yet I must.
    It's heavy business
to shrug off the Father's word . . .

Prometheus, I know you for what you are:
the headlong, steep thinking son
      of Themis: your levelheaded mother.
Yet against my will, as against yours
I'll spike you to this
    inhuman cliff.
Nobody's here, no human voice   40
will come through to you.
When the bloom on your cheek is burnt
    black by the sun
you'll be glad when night with her veils of starcloud
covers up the glare,
And again glad when at dawn, the sun
      scatters the hoarfrost off.
But always you'll be crushed by the load
    of each, every moment.
The one who will set you free   50
hasn't even been born.

This is what you get
for loving humankind.

You, a god, outraged the Gods.
Weren't you afraid?
You gave mere people
what people should not have
    Prometheus!
Now you must stand watch
over this brute rock   60
and never bend your knee,
you won't sleep, won't move,
no you'll
      sigh and howl
and won't be heard. No

Zeus is not
    about to mellow.
Every ruler who's new
is hard.

POWER MOVE damn it! What good's your pity?   70
    Why don't you hate the god
        the Gods hate?
    Didn't he betray you? He gave humans a power
    meant for you!

HEPHAISTOS We're family, we're friends: there's power in that, too.

POWER Sure. But how can you refuse the Father's
        orders!
    Don't *they* scare you even more?

HEPHAISTOS (*groaning*)
    You *are* pitiless . . . shameless too. You always were.

POWER No use whining about it. He's had it.   80
    Don't work yourself up
        over a lost cause.

HEPHAISTOS It's this work, these masterful hands of mine—
    that's what I hate!

POWER What for? Fact is, the craft you work at
    wasn't to blame for this.

HEPHAISTOS Still, I wish it had fallen to someone else.

POWER Every job's a pain, except
        for the God at the top.
    Only Zeus is free.   90

HEPHAISTOS (*gesturing toward* PROMETHEUS)
    Obviously. What can I say.
POWER THEN GET A MOVE ON! Throw the chains on him—
    before Zeus sees you loafing on the job.

HEPHAISTOS Look here, the iron's at hand. You aren't blind.

POWER Clamp his wrists, real hard. Now the sledge: with all
   your might, quick, spike him to the rock!

HEPHAISTOS OK, OK, I'm doing my job. I'm doing it right.

POWER Strike! Strike! Harder. Squeeze. He's too shrewd:
   where there's no way out, still, he'll find one.

HEPHAISTOS Well, here's one arm he'll never work free.   100

POWER Then spike the other, hard. He's got to learn:
   "intellectual" that he is, next to Zeus he's stupid.

HEPHAISTOS No one can say I didn't do
              justice to this job!
   Except Prometheus.

POWER Now the arrogant jawbone, of *wedge*: batter
   it hard, you, crunch through his chest!

HEPHAISTOS (*cries out: striking, recoiling*)
   PROMETHEUS! it's *your* agony I cry for!

POWER You shying off again? Moaning over enemies of Zeus?
   Watch out, or you'll be moaning for yourself.   110

HEPHAISTOS You see something no one should see.

POWER I see this bastard getting what he deserves.
   Now! Slap those iron bands around his ribs.

HEPHAISTOS I do what I have to do. Don't push it.

POWER I'll push you alright! the way a hunter sics his dogs.
   Now get under. Shackle those legs.

HEPHAISTOS (*having gotten under, getting hastily back up*)
   There, the job's done. I've made short painless work of it.

POWER Now, hard as you can, hammer the shackles INto him!
   Watch it now. The Boss checks everything out.

HEPHAISTOS I can't tell which is worse: your looks or your loud mouth.   120

POWER So *be* a bleeding heart! Me, I'm thick-skinned,
    but don't blame me for that. I am what I am.

HEPHAISTOS Let's get out of here. He's ironbound, hand and foot.
                                      (HEPHAISTOS *hobbles off.*)

POWER (*finally addressing* PROMETHEUS)
    You cocky bastard: *now* steal
        powers from the Gods.
    And for what?
             Things that live and die!
    Tell me sir, can humanity drain off
        a single drop of your agony?   130
    The Gods called you "Resourceful,"
        that's a rich one.
    You'll need resources, to squirm out of this
    first-rate ironwork.

[Omitted: The chorus of Oceanids (young daughters of the god Ocean) followed
by their father Ocean arrive on the mountaintop where Prometheus is shackled.
While Ocean soon departs, the Oceanids remain with Prometheus.]

PROMETHEUS I say nothing, but don't think that means I'm   620
    arrogant or stubborn.
    I see myself abused, bullied, and . . .
        Brooding
    eats my heart away.
    After all, who apportioned the privileges
        among these latter-day Gods?
        Who but I?
    But I won't go into that,
    you've heard it all before.
        Instead, hear   630
    what wretched lives people used to lead,
    how babyish they were—until
    I gave them intelligence,
        I made them
    masters of their own thought.

I tell this
    not against humankind, but only to show
how loving my gifts were . . .

Men and women looking
    saw nothing,   640
they listened
    and did not hear,
but like shapes in a dream dragging out their long lives
        bewildered
they made hodgepodge of everything, they knew nothing
                  of making

    brick-knitted
     houses the sun warms,
nor how to work in wood.
They swarmed like bitty ants
    in dugouts   650
in sunless caves.
They hadn't any sure signs of winter, nor spring
      flowering,
nor late summer when the crops come in.
All their work was work without thought,
until I taught them to see
what had been hard to see:
             where and when the stars
             rise and set.

What's more, for them I invented   660
    NUMBER: wisdom
above all other.
        And the painstaking, putting together of
LETTERS: to be their memory
of everything, to be their Muses'
      mother, their
        handmaid!
And I was the first to put brute beasts
under the yoke, fit them out
    with pack saddles, so they could take   670
the heaviest burdens off the backs of human beings.
Horses I broke and harnessed
    to the chariot shaft
so that they loved their reins, they showed off

the pride and wealth of their owners.
I, I alone invented
   the seawandering
     linen wingd
chariots for sailors.

All these devices, I invented for human beings.   680
Yet now in my own misery, I can't devise
   one single trick
to free myself from this agony.

CHORUS You've been tortured, humiliated, so that your mind
          wanders
driven to distraction.
Like a bad doctor fallen sick
   you grope, desperate
for what you can't find:
the drugs that will make you well.   690

PROMETHEUS But hear the rest, you'll be more amazed:
   what arts, what
     resources I worked out!
And the greatest was this . . .
If someone fell sick
   there was nothing for it: nothing to eat, drink
nor rub into the skin.
Without drugs
people wasted away,
until I showed them how to mix   700
   soothing herbs
to ward off every sort of disease.

I marked out the many ways men might
     see into the future.
I was the first to realize what dreams are bound
to wake up: real.
And snatches of speech
   caught in passing, and chance meetings along the road,
these too have secret meanings.
I showed them this.   710
      And clearly analyzed the flight
   of birds with crookt claws—
     what ones

          bring luck, and which
       are sinister—
and the way each species lives,
what hates it has, what loves,
what others it settles with.
I looked into
      the silky entrails, I showed them   720
what color gall bladder meant the Gods were pleased,
and the liver's
      lovely marbled lobe.
And thigh bones wrapped in fat, and long backbones
        I burned,
I showed humans the pathway into an art
hard to figure.
I gave the fire
      eyes, so that its signs
        shone through   730
where before they were filmed over.

So much for these. As for the benefits to humankind
hid under the earth (the copper the iron
              the silver the gold)
who but I could claim he discovered them?
No one, except a babbling idiot.

In a word: listen!
All human culture comes from Prometheus.

UNIVERSAL QUESTIONS SHAPE MYTH

Bronislaw Malinowski argued that a myth is a "pragmatic charter" that justifies a society's beliefs, practices, and institutions and must therefore be examined in its social context. Almost a century later, many mythologists still treat myth and society as interlocking parts that must be studied together. Yet they also find that myths are more than the "dogmatic backbone" of society that Malinowski believed them to be (Chapter 2.2). Because myths often engage perplexing questions about such profound matters as good and evil and life and death, they are suggestive of much more than merely their social context. When myths from different societies are compared—a style of inquiry that

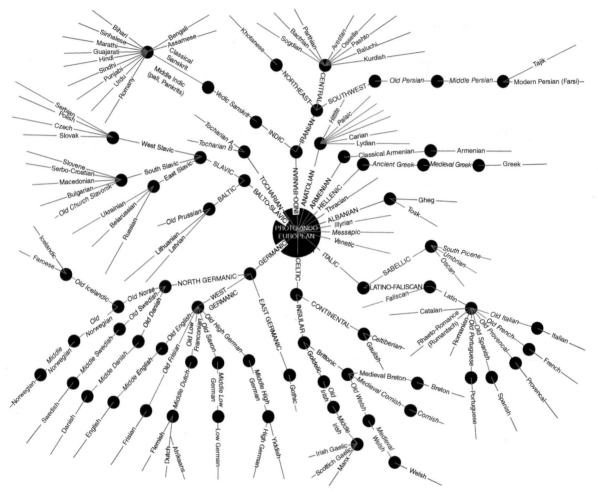

3.12 Chart of Indo-European Languages.

Malinowski rejected—these questions and their universal aspects become apparent.

One scholar interested in the profound and universal questions addressed by myths is Wendy Doniger (b. 1940). Doniger, a scholar of Hinduism and Sanskrit, is a prolific author—writing about mythology, Hinduism, religion, and gender—as well as an eminent translator of Hindu texts. Doniger does not argue with or against Malinowski's way of understanding myths. But her approach allows us to see the various ways scholars have understood myths since the time of Malinowski.

Doniger approaches myth as a rich cultural product that potentially has many meanings and thus demands to be studied from many different perspectives. Doniger's eclectic approach to myth is distinguished by her commitment to identifying universal questions about human existence posed by myths from many cultures, and to comparing the answers such myths provide. In this way Doniger may seem to be an acolyte of James Frazer, the great comparativist of myth and ritual whose approach to myth was rejected by Malinowski (Chapter 2.2). But this would be a simplification of Doniger's approach.

Instead, Doniger attempts to bridge the distance between the two main approaches modern scholars take to myths—that is, between the study of myths within their unique historical contexts and the study of shared features among myths from several societies. Her argument is that scholars must use a variety of approaches in order to determine a myth's unique features as well as the features it may share with other myths. These shared features, she argues, originate in "certain shared human experiences." To explain the shared experiences behind different myths, Doniger uses historical linguistics. All Indo-European languages, including ancient Greek and modern romance languages, have different words for the same object. Yet, by studying their similarities, linguists are able to detect one original language (*proto-Indo-European) from which all these different languages have evolved (Figure 3.12). Similarly, myths that exhibit similarities despite their differences have evolved from experiences shared by all human beings. In Doniger's view, these experiences are as worthy of study as the particular social, religious, and historical circumstances of myths.

WENDY DONIGER, FROM *THE IMPLIED SPIDER: POLITICS AND THEOLOGY IN MYTH*

BEFORE YOU READ

Doniger looks at how shared and repeated experiences among human beings may explain similarities in myths from different societies. She uses the images of a spider and spider's web to illustrate her understanding of myth. Myths from around the world compose a spider's web (of interrelated stories with shared themes or threads). The existence of this web of stories *implies* that there must be a spider, and this spider is the shared human experiences that come before human beings weave the web or compose myths.

- What does Doniger claim is behind the repeating patterns of myths from different societies?

- How does Doniger use the concepts of language and pain to explain the similarities between myths from different societies?

- Do you think that myths are culturally specific tales and must be treated as such, as Malinowski suggests (Chapter 2.2), or do you think that myths have universal features that are best studied through comparison, as Doniger claims?

WENDY DONIGER, FROM *THE IMPLIED SPIDER: POLITICS AND THEOLOGY IN MYTH* (1998)

What do we mean by saying that a story is "the same as" or even "similar to" another story while acknowledging that the context is different? We often feel that the various tellings of a much-retold myth are the same, at least in the sense that they do not disappoint us by omitting what we regard as essential parts of the myth, without which it would lose at the very least some of its charm, and at the most its meaning. When we say that two myths from two different cultures are "the same" we mean that there are certain plots that come up again and again, revealing a set of human concerns that transcend any cultural barriers, experiences that we might call cross-cultural or transcultural. As Marina Warner puts it,

> Of course there are fairy tales unique to a single place, which have not been passed on. But there are few really compelling ones that do not turn out to be wearing seven-league boots. The possibility of holding a storehouse of narrative in common could act to enhance our reciprocal relations, to communicate across spaces and barricades of national self-interest and pride. We share more than we perhaps admit or know, and have done so for a very long time.[1]

We share, for instance, the realization that we are separate from our parents, the knowledge that they will die ("Thou know'st 'tis common"), that we will die. And we share the experiences of joy: sex, food, singing, dancing, sunrise, sunset, moonlight, puppies, going to the seashore. People all over the world fall in love and have babies; stories about these experiences must have *something* in common. As C. S. Lewis put it, "Myth is the isthmus which connects the peninsular world of thought with the vast continent we really belong to."[2] We share certain dispositions and predilections, and that's why coffee and tea catch on everywhere once they are brought from the Orient[3]—and why certain myths catch on when they are brought from the Orient.

And certain questions recur in myths, which I would call religious questions: Why are we here? What happens to us when we die? Is there a God? How did men come to be different from women? Questions such as these, which are the driving force behind myths, have no empirical answers, and there is much disagreement about the nonempirical answers that have been advanced. Different cultures predispose their members to perceive shared experiences differently and to ask shared questions differently. Cross-cultural comparisons therefore have much to contribute to the insoluble chicken-and-egg paradox of nature vs. nurture: if we suspect that certain things are culturally constructed but several different cultures construct them in the same way, that sameness strikes a blow on the side of nature.

The themes held in common with other texts may not constitute the most important aspect of a myth, but they do make a useful base from which to ask questions about differences. Some of the questions posed by myths and some of the images and the naked outlines of a narrative are cross-cultural, but the shared images and ideas are structured in a narrative in different ways, so as to give very different answers and sometimes to ask different questions. Onto the shared base, each telling adds something unique, sometimes transformingly unique. And a shared meaning need not be an identical meaning. Jonathan Z. Smith has rightly faulted comparatists for assuming that they must "assert either identity or uniqueness."[4] Indeed, perhaps the claim of the comparatist should be not that two stories are identical but merely that they share some meanings.

Accounting for mythological themes that appear in different cultures by assuming that they derive from certain shared human experiences frees us from the obligation of specifying a mechanism (such as C. G. Jung's collective unconscious, or, more respectably—but no more convincingly—historical diffusion) by which a universal theme might be perpetrated. All we need point out is that the same forms do appear in many different places, in response to human experiences that appear to be similar on at least one level, and that they take on different meanings to the extent that those experiences turn out to be dissimilar on other levels.

As Shylock said in defense of one minority group, "Hath not a Jew eyes? Hath not a Jew hands, organs, dimensions, senses, affections, passions? If you prick us, do we not bleed? If you tickle us, do we not laugh? If you poison us, do we not die? And if you wrong us, shall we not revenge?"[5] Note the different sorts of things that he implicitly holds up for comparison: physical organs and physiological processes, which most of us would agree are universal; but also affections and passions, laughter and revenge, which some of us would regard as far more culturally constructed. President John F. Kennedy, in his epoch-making speech at the American University in 1963, trying to end the cold war, named what he regarded as "our most common link": "We all inhabit this small planet, we all breathe the same air, we all cherish our children's futures, and we are all mortal." The arguments of Shylock and Kennedy arose out of political rather than academic debates, but their point is also useful in a more general humanistic argument. Indeed, we might even aspire to generalize beyond human commonality and include animals among those who share our experiences—they too, after all, breathe air, care for their young, and are mortal—though it is unlikely that they share with Shylock and Kennedy the awareness of their own mortality.[6]

Plato discussed the relationship between such shared experiences and the myths that refract them in a discussion of myths about the change in the direction of the sun and moon:

> Every one of these stories comes from the very same experience (*pathos*), and in addition to these thousands of others even more amazing (*thaumastotera*), but in the course of time some of them have been lost and others have been scattered in diaspora (*diesparmena*) and are told each one separated from the others. But the thing that is the cause (*aition*) of all of these, the experience, no one has told.[7]

Plato's single, seminal experience is a cosmic one that occurred only once: the withdrawal of the creator from the universe after he had created it. My single, seminal experience (for each myth) is a human one that occurs again and again, such as the withdrawal of a mother at the moment of inevitable separation. The parallelism between these two events is obvious: both are about the loss of a creator, though Plato's loss occurs on what I would call the level of the telescope, mine on the level of the microscope. I would take from Plato not the specific content of his theory but the outlines of the process that he specifies: the fragmentation of myths from a single experience.

Behind a narrative is an experience, real or imagined: something has happened—not once, like a historical event, but many times, like a personal habit. Narrative does not receive raw experience and then impose a form upon it. Human experience is inherently narrative; this is our primary way of organizing and giving coherence to our lives. But we can never give an exact account of an experience, any more than we can retrieve a dream without any secondary revisions or elaborations. However close we get, we can never reach it, as in Zeno's paradox of Achilles and the tortoise—we get halfway there, and half the remaining distance, and so on, but never all the way.[8] There must be an experience for all the retellings to refract it as they do, but all we have are the refractions (some closer to the experience, some farther), the tellings, which are culturally specific, indeed, specific to each individual within the culture. And we can get close (as close as Achilles got) to this ideal raw experience by extrapolating from what all the myths have in common, modified in the light of what we can simply observe about the human situation in different cultures.

A parallel to the Platonic experience behind the myth may be seen in linguistics (an area from which other mythologists, notably F. Max Müller[9] and Claude Lévi-Strauss, have drawn their inspirations). Certain words are strikingly similar in a number of Indo-European languages: *foot* (English), *pied* (French), *fuss* (German), *ped* (Latin), *pada* (Sanskrit), etc. Following linguistic rules such as Grimm's Law, which tell us how sounds change through time, it is possible to construct the one *proto-Indo-European word that could have given rise to all the words in the group. That word does not exist; the asterisk that precedes it marks it as a purely theoretical construct. Yet the hypothesis of its existence solves the riddle of the relationship among all the other words. One cannot follow this method too slavishly; the fact that there is no common Indo-European word for *hand* might lead to the conclusion that the *proto-Indo-Europeans had feet but no hands. Nor can one trace Indo-European myths back to a theoretical origin as easily as one can trace Indo-European words; Max Müller and Georges Dumézil tried, with varying degrees of success, but it remains highly problematic.[10]

The linguistic analogy is nevertheless appropriate, because one thing that these myths have in common to one degree or another is language. That is, although language is often thought (by people like the Pumpkin-head of Oz, whom we met in the introduction) to be an uncrossable barrier beween people, some people think, as I do, that it is one of the great things that humans share, and that it offers a way across all barriers. Michael D. Coe describes both ends of the continuum between universal and culturally specific linguistic characteristics. First he speaks of cultural specificity: "It seems that the unborn fetus must already react to language, for experiments with four-day-old French infants show that they suck much harder while hearing French than while hearing Russian." (I wonder if the babies listening to French also called for wine instead of milk, and corrected the experimenter's accent.) Other experimenters have reported that Chinese babies babble single syllables with different tones.[11] Mr. Coe's experiments are somewhat reminiscent of one that Herodotus reported over two thousand years ago, in which the Egyptians isolated infants at birth to see what language they would "naturally" speak (it turned out to be *bekos*, the Phrygian word for "bread").[12] But then Mr. Coe speaks of universality: "Even though there are 4,000 to 6,000 languages today, they are all sufficiently alike to be considered one language by an extraterrestrial observer. In other words, most of the diversity of the world's cultures, so beloved to anthropologists, is superficial and minor compared to the similarities. Racial differences are literally only 'skin deep.' The fundamental unity of humanity is the theme of Mr. Chomsky's universal grammar."[13] Noam Chomsky's grammar is hardwired for all of human nature (and even applies to some primates, as is evident from the study of a talented chimp named, appropriately, Nim Chimpsky).[14] Coe's basic point—or rather, his basic two points, for difference and for sameness—are well taken.

Elaine Scarry has argued similarly for the universality of the relationship between language and pain:

> Even if one were to enumerate many additional examples, such cultural differences, taken collectively, would themselves constitute only a very narrow margin of variation and would thus in the end work to expose and confirm the universal sameness of the central problem, a problem that originates much less in the inflexibility of any one language or in the shyness of any one culture than in the utter rigidity of pain itself: its resistance to language is not simply one of its incidental or accidental attributes but is essential to what it is.[15]

There is therefore a level of human experience—pain is a vivid example—that precedes and even resists any language, including the language in which myths are told; yet that very experience that resists language is something that binds us to one another. The universality of pain, even in its wordlessness, is an example of the experience behind the narrative, before language, that both deconstructionists (like Mark Taylor) and post-Freudian feminists (like Julia Kristeva, following and modifying Lacan) have tried to reach in very different ways. So too, the many languages in which myths are told, despite their enormous variations, have in common their very inability ever to express those experiences, and their continuing, quixotic attempts to do so.

NOTES

1. Marina Warner, *From the Beast to the Blonde: On Fairy Tales and Their Tellers*, 414.
2. C. S. Lewis, cited by Michael Nelson in "One Mythology Among Many: The Spiritual Odyssey of C. S. Lewis," 628.
3. Sir Ernest Gombrich, *The Sense of Order*, 191–92 (see also the critical discussion of Jung on 246–47); and *Topics of Our Time*, 43–44.
4. J. Z. Smith, *Drudgery Divine*, 47.

5. Shakespeare, *Merchant of Venice*, 3.1.

6. See O'Flaherty, *Other Peoples' Myths*, chapter 4, "If I Were A Horse"; and Doniger, "The Mythology of Masquerading Animals."

7. Plato, *The Statesman*, 269B.

8. O'Flaherty, *Dreams, Illusion*, 203.

9. F. Max Müller, *Lectures on the Science of Language*; see esp. "Metaphor."

10. I tried it too, with only middling success, in *Women, Androgynes, and Other Mythical Beasts*.

11. Joan Aitchison, *The Language Web*, 44.

12. Herodotus, *History*, 2.2.

13. Michael D. Coe, review of Steven Pinker's *The Language Instinct*, 7–8.

14. H. S. Terrace, *Nim*.

15. Elaine Scarry, *The Body in Pain*, 5.

LEVANT: FLOOD STORIES

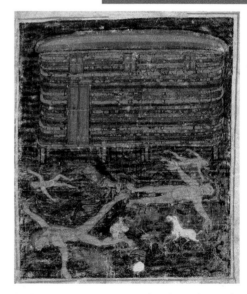

In the Ancient Near East, floods were considered sacred because they were believed to be caused by divine powers. One of the earliest documented floods occurred at the beginning of the third millennium in the Sumerian city of Shuruppak (Tell Fara in present-day Iraq) on the banks of the Euphrates. Its buildings and people were devastated, and the dynastic rule of its king ended. The city of Kish, located upstream (Tell al-Uhaymir in present-day Iraq), became the new center of power, in part because its king could control the irrigation of Shuruppak and other cities downstream and thus assert his power over other kings and cities in the region. The *Sumerian King List*, a catalog of Sumerian and neighboring dynasties, explains this shift in power a bit differently, stating simply, "After the flood the kingship was handed down from Heaven a second time." This suggests that kings were considered to be gods, the sons of a god, or the deputies of gods whose rule came from the heavens. A king's power to ensure the fertility of the lands through complex irrigation systems reflected a god's power to send (or withhold) rains. Thus, in the Ancient Near East, a flood, whether from natural or man-made sources, was never simply ascribed to the weather but instead was a sign of divine favor or displeasure.

3.13 **The Flood and Noah's Ark.** The ark is at the top of the image; drowned people, giants, and animals float in the waters below. From the Ashburnham Pentateuch (Pentateuch of Tours). Northern Africa, Spain, or Italy. Circa fifth to sixth century CE. NAL 2334 Folio9. Bibliothèque Nationale de France (BnF), Paris, France. © BnF, Dist. RMN-Grand Palais / Art Resource, NY, ART488780.

Map 3.2 Floods and Flood Stories in the Ancient Near East

The many flood stories from the Ancient Near East may contain the memory of historical floods, such as the one in Shuruppak. In such stories, floods are the actions of gods who want to destroy the human race. In the eleventh tablet of the *Epic of Gilgamesh*, Utnapishtim, a wise man or priest from Shuruppak, explains to Gilgamesh that the great gods swore an oath to destroy the city by means of a flood (Chapters 10.3 and 12.3). All the gods agreed to this plan except Ea, known for his cleverness. Ea revealed the news of the impending flood to Utnapishtim and told him to build a large boat and to save his family and other living creatures.

The Babylonian *Epic of Atrahasis* (c. seventeenth century BCE) tells a similar tale. When the gods want to destroy the human race because it has become so populous, they send a flood. Enki (another name for the god Ea), who created the race of human beings, advises a wise man named Atrahasis to build a large boat in order to save his family and other living creatures. Many other flood stories from this geographical area have a similar plot: a god or gods decide to send a flood to destroy the human race, which is saved by one god who advises one man to build a boat with which to save his family and the creatures of the earth.

One Greek flood story, which involves Zeus and Prometheus, follows the plot typical of this group of tales: A god wants to destroy humankind; another god saves them. The Greek flood story appears in *The Library*, an ancient forerunner of modern collections of Greek myths, whose author is unknown (translated by Robin Hard).

UNKNOWN, FROM *THE LIBRARY* (c. FIRST TO SECOND CENTURY CE)

Prometheus had a son Deucalion, who ruled the area around Phthia, and married Pyrrha, the daughter of Epimetheus and Pandora, whom the gods had fashioned as the first woman. When Zeus wanted to eliminate the race of bronze, Deucalion, on the advice of Prometheus, built a chest, and after storing it with provisions, climbed into it with Pyrrha. Zeus poured an abundance of rain from heaven to flood the greater part of Greece, causing all human beings to be destroyed, apart from those few who took refuge in the lofty mountains nearby. It was then that the mountains of Thessaly drew apart and all the lands outside the Isthmus and Peloponnese were submerged. But Deucalion was carried across the sea in his chest for nine days and as many nights until he was washed ashore at Parnassos; and there, when the rain stopped, he disembarked, and offered a sacrifice to Zeus, God of Escape. Zeus sent Hermes to him and allowed him the choice of whatever he wished; and Deucalion chose to have people. On the orders of Zeus, he picked up stones and threw them over his head; and the stones that Deucalion threw became men, and those that Pyrrha threw became women. That was how people came to be called *laoi*, by metaphor from the word *laas*, a stone.

The story in *The Library* is brief. In order to make sense of it, details from other myths must be supplied. The author mentions the "race of bronze," referring to Hesiod's tale of five races of men in *Works and Days*. Hesiod's tale describes the increasing degradation of each race, which may suggest why Zeus wants to destroy human beings. Even so, *The Library*'s author does not explain why Prometheus wants to save them. We must infer that there was a conflict between the two gods, as described in *Prometheus Bound*. There, Prometheus says that he decided to save human beings when Zeus wanted to destroy them. Although he does not mention that Zeus planned to send a flood to rid the earth of human beings, many commentators have seen this detail as a reference to the flood story recounted in *The Library*.

The flood story in the Hebrew Bible offers a very different resolution to the problem of a hostile deity who wants to destroy the human race (Figure 3.13). In this case, there is no other god to save them. The flood story in Genesis appears after the two creation stories we examined in Chapter 2.3 (one from P, the Priestly document, in which the divine is called Elohim or "God," and one from J, the Yahwist narrative, in which the divine is called Yahweh or "Lord"). Whereas these two sources are separated and follow each other sequentially in the opening of Genesis, they are interwoven with each other in the flood story (6:1–9:22). Elohim (God) and Yahweh (Lord) alternate in the text. Each distinct character has different reasons for sending the flood and different approaches to human beings after the flood. Thus the following discussion treats each source separately.

Yahweh/Lord sets out to destroy human beings because he "saw that the wickedness of humankind was great in the earth, and that every inclination of their thoughts was only evil continually" (6:5–6). When Noah disembarks from the ark, he burns offerings on an altar. Pleased, Yahweh/Lord says, "I will never again curse the ground because of humankind, for the inclination of the human heart is evil from youth; nor will I ever again destroy every living creature as I have done" (8:21). Yahweh/Lord refers to and now appears to accept the inborn evil in human nature that the flood has not altered in any way.

Alternatively, in the Priestly document, Elohim/God sends the flood to cleanse the "corruption" of the earth created by human beings. "Now the earth was corrupt in God's sight, and the earth was filled with violence. And God saw the earth was corrupt; for all flesh had corrupted its ways upon the earth" (6:11–12). After the flood, Elohim/God ignores a consideration of human nature and instead gives commands about how to keep the earth free from corruption. Elohim/God tells Noah that he should "be fruitful and multiply," that he may eat animal flesh but must not eat live animals or animal blood, and that anyone who kills a human being forfeits his own life. Elohim/God then says that the rainbow in the sky will remind him of his promise never to destroy the living creatures of the earth (9:1–28).

Some scholars argue that the differences between Elohim and Yahweh and the repetitions in and contradictions between their different motives and behaviors can be explained by considering the influence on Genesis of the flood stories in the *Epic of Atrahasis* or the *Epic of Gilgamesh*. These polytheistic stories, they argue, were continually revised and eventually converted into a monotheistic tale that celebrates one God. Thus Genesis may reflect two different gods who have been incompletely fused into one seemingly capricious god. In this view, Elohim and Yahweh act differently because they were originally two different gods.

Other scholars minimize the influence on Genesis of polytheistic flood stories and seek to unify the contradictory actions of God in Genesis. God causes the flood to purify and cleanse the earth because it has become corrupted and polluted by human beings, who were and always will be prone to evil. He lays down laws to help human beings refrain from corrupting the earth again, which they will no doubt do because of their inborn inclinations. In this view, God's laws are a coherent and consistent solution to the dilemma he faced before the flood (the evil in human nature and the corruption of the earth). Whether or not we acknowledge that two or more sources have been compiled to create this story, we still are left wondering how to understand the relationship between this god and human beings. In this light, viewing the flood story in Genesis alongside other flood stories from the Ancient Near East suggests that they all address profound questions, perhaps even anxieties, about the relationship between the human race and the divine.

GENESIS 6–9

BEFORE YOU READ

The story (or stories) of the flood in Genesis shares a key element with other flood stories from the region: a god wants to destroy the human race because it has become displeasing to him. Although the *Epic of Gilgamesh*, *Prometheus Bound*, and *The Library*'s stories include several gods, they share with Genesis an attempt to capture the feeling a stormy sky provokes: a sense of human fragility coupled with incomprehension of the divine and the desire for divine protection. Each of these myths poses profound questions: is individual existence significant to a great and transcendent god? Is the whole human race visible and meaningful to this god or merely a nuisance to be ignored or even destroyed?

- What does the flood story in Genesis suggest about the relationship between God and human beings?

- How would you compare Zeus's relationship to human beings in *Prometheus Bound* to Elohim's and/or Yahweh's relationships to human beings in Genesis?

- Wendy Doniger argues that myths express universal experiences, questions, and dilemmas. What universal experiences and dilemmas do you think the flood story in Genesis expresses? Are these questions the same as those posed in *Prometheus Bound*?

GENESIS 6–9

6 When people began to multiply on the face of the ground, and daughters were born to them, ²the sons of God saw that they were fair; and they took wives for themselves of all that they chose. ³Then the LORD said, "My spirit shall not abide in mortals forever, for they are flesh; their days shall be one hundred twenty years." ⁴The Nephilim were on the earth in those days—and also afterward—when the sons of God went in to the daughters of humans, who bore children to them. These were the heroes that were of old, warriors of renown.

⁵The LORD saw that the wickedness of humankind was great in the earth, and that every inclination of the thoughts of their hearts was only evil continually. ⁶And the LORD was sorry that he had made humankind on the earth, and it grieved him to his heart. ⁷So the LORD said, "I will blot out from the earth the human beings I have created—people together with animals and creeping things and birds of the air, for I am sorry that I have made them." ⁸But Noah found favor in the sight of the LORD.

⁹These are the descendants of Noah. Noah was a righteous man, blameless in his generation; Noah walked with God. ¹⁰And Noah had three sons, Shem, Ham, and Japheth.

¹¹Now the earth was corrupt in God's sight, and the earth was filled with violence. ¹²And God saw that the earth was corrupt; for all flesh had corrupted its ways upon the earth. ¹³And God said to Noah, "I have determined to make an end of all flesh, for the earth is filled with violence because of them; now I am going to destroy them along with the earth. ¹⁴Make yourself an ark of cypress wood; make rooms in the ark, and cover it inside and out with pitch. ¹⁵This is how you are to make it: the length of

the ark three hundred cubits, its width fifty cubits, and its height thirty cubits. [16]Make a roof for the ark, and finish it to a cubit above; and put the door of the ark in its side; make it with lower, second, and third decks. [17]For my part, I am going to bring a flood of waters on the earth, to destroy from under heaven all flesh in which is the breath of life; everything that is on the earth shall die. [18]But I will establish my covenant with you; and you shall come into the ark, you, your sons, your wife, and your sons' wives with you. [19]And of every living thing, of all flesh, you shall bring two of every kind into the ark, to keep them alive with you; they shall be male and female. [20]Of the birds according to their kinds, and of the animals according to their kinds, of every creeping thing of the ground according to its kind, two of every kind shall come in to you, to keep them alive. [21]Also take with you every kind of food that is eaten, and store it up; and it shall serve as food for you and for them." [22]Noah did this; he did all that God commanded him.

7 Then the LORD said to Noah, "Go into the ark, you and all your household, for I have seen that you alone are righteous before me in this generation. [2]Take with you seven pairs of all clean animals, the male and its mate; and a pair of the animals that are not clean, the male and its mate; [3]and seven pairs of the birds of the air also, male and female, to keep their kind alive on the face of all the earth. [4]For in seven days I will send rain on the earth for forty days and forty nights; and every living thing that I have made I will blot out from the face of the ground." [5]And Noah did all that the LORD had commanded him.

[6]Noah was six hundred years old when the flood of waters came on the earth. [7]And Noah with his sons and his wife and his sons' wives went into the ark to escape the waters of the flood. [8]Of clean animals, and of animals that are not clean, and of birds, and of everything that creeps on the ground, [9]two and two, male and female, went into the ark with Noah, as God had commanded Noah. [10]And after seven days the waters of the flood came on the earth.

[11]In the six hundredth year of Noah's life, in the second month, on the seventeenth day of the month, on that day all the fountains of the great deep burst forth, and the windows of the heavens were opened. [12]The rain fell on the earth forty days and forty nights. [13]On the very same day Noah with his sons, Shem and Ham and Japheth, and Noah's wife and the three wives of his sons entered the ark, [14]they and every wild animal of every kind, and all domestic animals of every kind, and every creeping thing that creeps on the earth, and every bird of every kind—every bird, every winged creature. [15]They went into the ark with Noah, two and two of all flesh in which there was the breath of life. [16]And those that entered, male

and female of all flesh, went in as God had commanded him; and the LORD shut him in.

[17]The flood continued forty days on the earth; and the waters increased, and bore up the ark, and it rose high above the earth. [18]The waters swelled and increased greatly on the earth; and the ark floated on the face of the waters. [19]The waters swelled so mightily on the earth that all the high mountains under the whole heaven were covered; [20]the waters swelled above the mountains, covering them fifteen cubits deep. [21]And all flesh died that moved on the earth, birds, domestic animals, wild animals, all swarming creatures that swarm on the earth, and all human beings; [22]everything on dry land in whose nostrils was the breath of life died. [23]He blotted out every living thing that was on the face of the ground, human beings and animals and creeping things and birds of the air; they were blotted out from the earth. Only Noah was left, and those that were with him in the ark. [24]And the waters swelled on the earth for one hundred fifty days.

8 But God remembered Noah and all the wild animals and all the domestic animals that were with him in the ark. And God made a wind blow over the earth, and the waters subsided; [2]the fountains of the deep and the windows of the heavens were closed, the rain from the heavens was restrained, [3]and the waters gradually receded from the earth. At the end of one hundred fifty days the waters had abated; [4]and in the seventh month, on the seventeenth day of the month, the ark came to rest on the mountains of Ararat. [5]The waters continued to abate until the tenth month; in the tenth month, on the first day of the month, the tops of the mountains appeared.

[6]At the end of forty days Noah opened the window of the ark that he had made [7]and sent out the raven; and it went to and fro until the waters were dried up from the earth. [8]Then he sent out the dove from him, to see if the waters had subsided from the face of the ground; [9]but the dove found no place to set its foot, and it returned to him to the ark, for the waters were still on the face of the whole earth. So he put out his hand and took it and brought it into the ark with him. [10]He waited another seven days, and again he sent out the dove from the ark; [11]and the dove came back to him in the evening, and there in its beak was a freshly plucked olive leaf; so Noah knew that the waters had subsided from the earth. [12]Then he waited another seven days, and sent out the dove; and it did not return to him any more.

[13]In the six hundred first year, in the first month, on the first day of the month, the waters were dried up from the earth; and Noah removed the covering of the ark, and looked, and saw that the face of the ground was

drying. ¹⁴In the second month, on the twenty-seventh day of the month, the earth was dry. ¹⁵Then God said to Noah, ¹⁶"Go out of the ark, you and your wife, and your sons and your sons' wives with you. ¹⁷Bring out with you every living thing that is with you of all flesh—birds and animals and every creeping thing that creeps on the earth—so that they may abound on the earth, and be fruitful and multiply on the earth." ¹⁸So Noah went out with his sons and his wife and his sons' wives. ¹⁹And every animal, every creeping thing, and every bird, everything that moves on the earth, went out of the ark by families.

²⁰Then Noah built an altar to the LORD, and took of every clean animal and of every clean bird, and offered burnt offerings on the altar. ²¹And when the LORD smelled the pleasing odor, the LORD said in his heart, "I will never again curse the ground because of humankind, for the inclination of the human heart is evil from youth; nor will I ever again destroy every living creature as I have done.

²²As long as the earth endures,
> seedtime and harvest, cold and heat,
summer and winter, day and night,
> shall not cease."

9 God blessed Noah and his sons, and said to them, "Be fruitful and multiply, and fill the earth. ²The fear and dread of you shall rest on every animal of the earth, and on every bird of the air, on everything that creeps on the ground, and on all the fish of the sea; into your hand they are delivered. ³Every moving thing that lives shall be food for you; and just as I gave you the green plants, I give you everything. ⁴Only, you shall not eat flesh with its life, that is, its blood. ⁵For your own lifeblood I will surely require a reckoning: from every animal I will require it and from human beings, each one for the blood of another, I will require a reckoning for human life.

⁶Whoever sheds the blood of a human,
> by a human shall that person's blood be shed;
for in his own image
> God made humankind.

⁷And you, be fruitful and multiply, abound on the earth and multiply in it."

⁸Then God said to Noah and to his sons with him, ⁹"As for me, I am establishing my covenant with you and your descendants after you, ¹⁰and with every living creature that is with you, the birds, the domestic animals, and every animal of the earth with you, as many as came out of the ark. ¹¹I establish my covenant with you, that never again shall all flesh be cut off by the waters of a flood, and never again shall there be a flood to destroy the earth." ¹²God said, "This is the sign of the covenant that I make

between me and you and every living creature that is with you, for all future generations: ¹³I have set my bow in the clouds, and it shall be a sign of the covenant between me and the earth. ¹⁴When I bring clouds over the earth and the bow is seen in the clouds, ¹⁵I will remember my covenant that is between me and you and every living creature of all flesh; and the waters shall never again become a flood to destroy all flesh. ¹⁶When the bow is in the clouds, I will see it and remember the everlasting covenant between God and every living creature of all flesh that is on the earth." ¹⁷God said to Noah, "This is the sign of the covenant that I have established between me and all flesh that is on the earth."

¹⁸The sons of Noah who went out of the ark were Shem, Ham, and Japheth. Ham was the father of Canaan. ¹⁹These three were the sons of Noah; and from these the whole earth was peopled.

²⁰Noah, a man of the soil, was the first to plant a vineyard. ²¹He drank some of the wine and became drunk, and he lay uncovered in his tent. ²²And Ham, the father of Canaan, saw the nakedness of his father, and told his two brothers outside. ²³Then Shem and Japheth took a garment, laid it on both their shoulders, and walked backward and covered the nakedness of their father; their faces were turned away, and they did not see their father's nakedness. ²⁴When Noah awoke from his wine and knew what his youngest son had done to him, ²⁵he said,

"Cursed be Canaan;
    lowest of slaves shall he be to his brothers."
²⁶He also said,
"Blessed by the LORD my God be Shem;
    and let Canaan be his slave.
²⁷May God make space for Japheth,
    and let him live in the tents of Shem;
    and let Canaan be his slave."

²⁸After the flood Noah lived three hundred fifty years. ²⁹All the days of Noah were nine hundred fifty years; and he died.

LEDA AND THE SWAN IN MODERNIST POETRY

Of all the tales of Zeus assuming the guise of an animal to seduce a mortal, the myth of Leda and the swan is one that has attracted the attention of artists for centuries. And as we observed earlier, the sculptural representations from ancient Greece present this interaction between the mortal and

3.14 *Leda and the Swan*, **1923**. Marie Laurencin (1883–1956).
Oil on canvas, 26½ × 32 inches (67.3 × 81.3 cm). *The
Philadelphia Museum of Art / Art Resource, NY, ART318651.*
© *Fondation Foujita / Artists Rights Society (ARS), New York /
ADAGP, Paris 2015.*

the divine differently; in some instances, it is represented as a gentle union, and in others, as a violent rape. The French Cubist painter Marie Laurencin (1883–1956) conceived of the encounter in the first category (Figure 3.14). Here, Leda wears a diaphanous gown that suggests but almost conceals her nakedness. The presence of a chair between her and the swan suggests an interior space, yet there is green foliage behind and between them. A blue feather in Leda's hair further suggests her link to nature, specifically birds. Moreover, Leda's white arm and black, almond-shaped eyes are identical to the swan's. Laurencin's painting suggests intimacy, but not violence. In this regard, Laurencin's painting has much in common with a poem by the modernist H.D. (Hilda Doolittle, 1886–1961). H.D. too offers a dreamy, gentle, and colorful union between Leda and the swan. Her poem "Leda" offers a stark contrast to the far more well-known poem, "Leda and the Swan" (1924), by William Butler Yeats (1865–1939).

Yeats graphically describes the swan's attack on Leda and its violent repercussions. One result of Zeus's "great wings beating" and Leda's "loosening thighs" is Helen, who will cause the Trojan War; Troy's destruction is evoked as "the broken wall" and "burning roof and tower." This rape, Yeats reminds us, will also result in the birth of Clytemnestra, who will murder Agamemnon when he returns from Troy. Thus Yeats also alludes to the great works of art, such as the *Iliad*, that provide an antidote to Zeus's violence. Zeus is "the brute blood of the air," and his beak is "indifferent," yet he is also the source of knowledge, power, and even beauty.

 ## WILLIAM BUTLER YEATS, "LEDA AND THE SWAN" (c. 1928)

A sudden blow: the great wings beating still
Above the staggering girl, her thighs caressed
By the dark webs, her nape caught in his bill,
He holds her helpless breast upon his breast.

How can those terrified vague fingers push
The feathered glory from her loosening thighs?
And how can body, laid in that white rush,
But feel the strange heart beating where it lies?

A shudder in the loins engenders there
The broken wall, the burning roof and tower
And Agamemnon dead.
                    Being so caught up,
So mastered by the brute blood of the air,
Did she put on his knowledge with his power
Before the indifferent beak could let her drop?

In the last four lines of the poem, Yeats's question echoes a distinctly Greek concern: Even if we acknowledge that contact with Zeus serves as a prelude to knowledge and power, is such contact worth the suffering that follows? Do the gods love us, or are they indifferent even when they are compelled by us mortals?

Hilda Doolittle (H.D.), a contemporary of Yeats, examines Leda and the swan in a manner that critics have argued is distinctly feminine. In her poem "Leda" (1919), Zeus as a red swan with a soft purple breast caresses and flecks with gold a lily that represents Leda. H.D. describes Zeus and Leda's encounter as a soft fluttering, or quivering, without violence or force. Rather than knowledge or power, this Leda is freed from regret and moves toward "bliss." Thus H.D. removes sexual violence from the encounter between Leda and the swan and suggests that contact with the divine exceeds human dimensions, comprehension, or regret.

 ## HILDA DOOLITTLE, "LEDA" (c. 1919)

Where the slow river
meets the tide,
a red swan lifts red wings
and darker beak,
and underneath the purple down
of his soft breast
uncurls his coral feet.

Through the deep purple
of the dying heat
of sun and mist,
the level ray of sun-beam
has caressed
the lily with dark breast,
and flecked with richer gold
its golden crest.

Where the slow lifting
of the tide,
floats into the river
and slowly drifts
among the reeds,
and lifts the yellow flags,
he floats
where tide and river meet.

Ah kingly kiss—
no more regret
nor old deep memories
to mar the bliss;
where the low sedge is thick,
the gold day-lily
outspreads and rests
beneath soft fluttering
of red swan wings
and the warm quivering
of the red swan's breast.

The differences between these two poems are as great as the difference among ancient representations of the encounter of Leda and the swan (Figures 3.5 and 3.6). Taken together, these poems offer readers a way to discover the range of ancient perspectives not only on the myth of Leda and the swan but also on the possibilities and perils of an encounter with the divine. At the same time, these modernist poems offer new perspectives and ideas not found in the original myth. In either case, these modernist artists bring one disturbing, yet strangely beautiful, myth into the present for consideration and provocation.

KEY TERMS

Argos 111

Io 111

Leda 109

Meilichius 104

Prometheus 99

Samos 112

Sarpedon 105

FOR FURTHER EXPLORATION

Cohn, Norman. *Noah's Flood: The Genesis Story in Western Thought*. New Haven, CT, and London: Yale University Press, 1999. This book surveys flood myths in mythical and religious traditions from the ancient world to the present.

Doniger, Wendy. *The Implied Spider: Politics and Theology in Myth*. New York: Columbia University Press, 1998. This is a brief and lively (at times quite dense) overview of Doniger's current thinking on myths.

Dowden, K. *Zeus*. New York and London: Routledge, 2006. This succinct introduction to Zeus examines his myths and rituals with great clarity and insight.

O'Brien, Joan V. *The Transformation of Hera: A Study of Ritual, Hero, and the Goddess in the Iliad*. Lanham, MD: Rowman & Littlefield, 1993. Although intended for scholars, O'Brien's book is comprehensible and one of the few thorough treatments of Hera.

ΕΝΙΑΥΤΟΣ   ΕΛΕΥΣΙΣ

DEMETER AND HADES

When Demeter came to our land, in her wandering after the rape of Korê (Persephone), and, being moved to kindness towards our ancestors by services which may not be told save to her initiates, gave these two gifts, the greatest in the world—the fruits of the earth, which have enabled us to rise above the life of the beasts, and the holy rite which inspires in those who partake of it sweeter hopes regarding both the end of life and all eternity.

—ISOCRATES, *PANEGYRICUS* (4.28)

The Greek orator Isocrates (436–338 BCE) made an oblique but tantalizing reference to the rituals with which the goddess Demeter was commemorated. Figure 4.1 illustrates the attributes and gifts that Isocrates described, and for which Demeter was revered. In this vase painting, a young boy named Eniautus (Year) holds a cornucopia (or horn of plenty) filled with stalks of grain. He represents the "fruits of the earth" that Demeter provides to humankind through her oversight of agriculture, a role suggested by her very name. "De" is linked to *Ge*, the Greek word for the earth, and "meter" to *mater*, the Greek word for mother; "Demeter" thus means "Earth Mother." The fertility of the earth, and to a lesser degree that of women, is the primary sphere of influence of this goddess.

But it is a small detail on this vase that indicates the "holy rite" Isocrates mentions: visible above Demeter's head is the word "Eleusis" (in Greek, ΕΛΕΥΣΙΣ), the town where her holy rite, called the Mysteries, was celebrated. Initiates at this festival held torches (like the one shown here in Demeter's

< **4.1 (OPPOSITE):** Demeter (right) accompanied by a young boy, Eniautus (Year). Detail from an Apulian red-figure loutrophoros. Painter of Louvre M NB1148, c. 350–340 BCE. *The J. Paul Getty Museum, Villa Collection, Malibu, California. 86.AE.680. The Theoi Project: Greek Mythology. Website © 2000–2011 Aaron Atsma.*

THE ESSENTIALS ⊰ DEMETER AND HADES

DEMETER (Ceres), Δημήτηρ

PARENTAGE Cronus and Rhea

OFFSPRING Persephone

ATTRIBUTES Wheat stalk, torch

SIGNIFICANT CULT TITLES
- Chloe (Green Shoots)
- Horaphorus (Bringer of the Seasons)
- Thesmophorus (Bringer of Law)

SIGNIFICANT RITUALS AND SANCTUARIES
- **The Eleusinian Mysteries** A week-long initiation ceremony that began in Athens and concluded in Demeter's sanctuary in Eleusis, where initiates received secret knowledge.
- **The Haloa (Fields)** A festival for women meant to protect newly planted seeds to ensure an abundant harvest.
- **The Proerosia (Before Plowing)** A ritual plowing that preceded the actual plowing of fields in preparation for planting. Demeter, along with Zeus and Persephone, was offered gifts and was honored.
- **The Thesmophoria** A three-day celebration, for women, to ensure successful marriage and childbirth.

HADES (Hades or Pluto), Ἄιδης

PARENTAGE Cronus and Rhea

OFFSPRING None

ATTRIBUTES Scepter, throne, cornucopia

SIGNIFICANT CULT TITLES
- Chthonian Zeus (Zeus of the Underworld)
- Pluton (Of Wealth)
- Polydegmon (Receiver of Many)

SIGNIFICANT RITUALS AND SANCTUARIES
- No temples or festivals were dedicated to Hades.
- **Caves** Caves dedicated to Hades, such as the one at Eleusis, were believed to be entrances to the Underworld.
- **Funerals** Funerary rituals for the dead consisted of three parts: a laying out of the corpse (*prosthesis*), a procession to the gravesite (*ecphora*), and subsequent feasts at the gravesite for a brief period of time. Although these rites were not performed in honor of Hades, their purpose was to guarantee that the souls of the dead entered his kingdom.

hand) during nocturnal rituals and processions. During their initiation in Demeter's holy rite, they received knowledge and blessings that would give them "sweeter hopes" for a better life after death.

4.1 HISTORY

LIFE AND DEATH

It may seem puzzling from a modern perspective that Demeter, a goddess whose primary association is with fertility, also offers solace for human beings at the end of life. Indeed, most gods and goddesses did not oversee similarly opposing spheres of human experience; for example, Ares, the god of war, plays no part in peace or civic concord. On the one hand, Demeter's connection to death can be explained through myth: Persephone, her daughter, is married to Hades, the god of the Underworld. On the other hand, a complex network of symbols that informs funerary and agricultural rituals—as well as her Mysteries at Eleusis—links Demeter to death. These symbols also provide evidence of how the Greeks understood the processes of life and death.

In this chapter, then, we take two approaches to exploring the connection between Demeter's two gifts, "the fruits of the earth" and her holy rite. First we examine the myth that connects Demeter, Persephone, and Hades. Then we consider the rituals associated with Demeter that concern the processes of life and death. We begin with the god Hades, who rules the Underworld, and with Greek notions of death, before turning to Demeter and fertility.

HADES

Hades, the god of the Underworld, is the son of Cronus and Rhea, and thus the brother of Zeus and the other Olympians. Although he fights the Titans alongside his siblings in Hesiod's *Theogony*, he is different from the other Olympians because he resides not on Olympus but in the Underworld, located under the earth. Additionally, his association with human mortality causes all the gods to have an aversion toward him. In Euripides's *Hippolytus*, for example, when Artemis's beloved servant, Hippolytus, is about to die, Artemis leaves him, refusing to witness his death and thus become polluted by it. Even so,

4.2 **Hades (right) and Persephone in a temple-like building.** Detail from a red-figure krater. Circa 350 BCE. Museo Archeologico Nazionale, Naples, Italy. *Erich Lessing / Art Resource, NY, ART200836.*

Hades is not without honor among gods and human beings. He is considered a king much like Zeus. Hades is often depicted sitting on a throne with a scepter in his hands, accompanied by Persephone, his wife (Figure 4.2). One of his titles, "Zeus of the Underworld" (Chthonian Zeus), suggests that he rules below in the Underworld as Zeus rules above in Olympus.

Regal and aloof, Hades seems to take little interest in the inhabitants of the vast, dark kingdom he governs. He neither judges nor punishes the souls of the dead. Although he is considered "hateful" because death is unwelcome to and despised by all human beings, he is not feared. For Hades does not demand the death of individuals or cause death to the living in a general way. He was not imagined as a grim reaper who stalks humankind. That task sometimes falls to a figure called Thanatus (Death). In Euripides's play *Alcestis*, for example, Thanatus appears on stage and claims he is eager to snatch the princess Alcestis and take her to the Underworld. Thanatus, along with Hypnus (Sleep), has also been shown as a winged man carrying off the fallen warrior Sarpedon, the son of Zeus (Figure 3.4, p. 106). Here, Thanatus seems to be a gentle rather than rapacious figure. Hades, by contrast, does not greedily snatch souls or even gently carry them away, nor does he escort them to his kingdom. He simply receives souls in his realm, as his title "Receiver of Many" (Polydegmon)

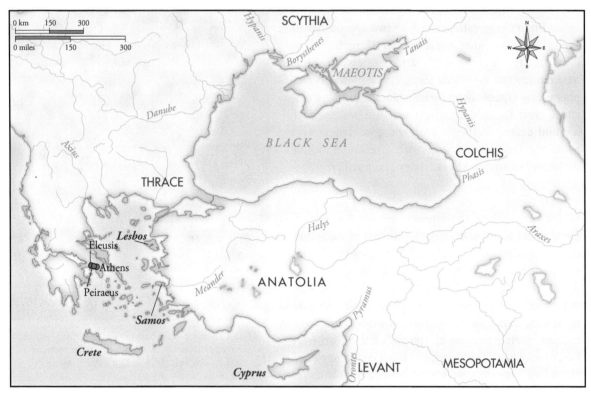

Map 4.1 Demeter and Hades in Greece

implies. Both titles, "Chthonian Zeus" and "Receiver of Many," suggest that Hades bears no ill will toward human beings, whether living or dead.

There are almost no temples or sanctuaries where festivals were held in Hades's honor. Instead, Hades is associated with caves, which were sometimes imagined to be entrances to the Underworld. The most famous of these caves can be found at Eleusis in Demeter's sanctuary (Map 4.1). The absence of worship in Hades's honor suggests that Hades cannot fend off death (because he is not imagined to be the cause of it in the first place) and that Hades cannot alter or improve one's lot in the Underworld. Thus the absence of worship in his honor has less to do with Hades's character and actions than with Greek notions of the Underworld and death. Neither was frightening, but both were unavoidable.

The Geography of the Underworld Although Greek beliefs about death evolved over time, the generally inconsistent outline of the geography of the Underworld found in Homer's *Odyssey* and *Iliad* dominated Greek representations long after Homer. Homer locates the Underworld in three different places. Toward the end of the *Odyssey*, Hermes leads the souls of the suitors whom Odysseus has killed to the Underworld with his wand (*Odyssey* 24.1). They pass over the streams of Ocean, a river that was believed to continuously flow around the earth and through the Gates of the Sun to finally reach fields of asphodel (a spiky white flower common across the Mediterranean), where they will dwell forever. The Underworld appears to be located on the same flat surface as the earth, in the west where the sun sets. Yet Homer then describes the Underworld as the "secret places of the earth," that is, underneath the earth. When Odysseus, following Circe's directions, travels to the Underworld, he beaches his ship on the misty shores of the land of the mythical Cimmerians, who dwell in the north. Thus Homer locates the Underworld in three different places: the west, under the earth, and in the north. Most often, however, the Underworld was believed by the Greeks to be under the earth, not at its edges. One of Hades's titles (which served as an alternative name), Pluton (Of Wealth), confirms this idea. "Pluton" refers to the belief that Hades is responsible for sending the earth's wealth up to human beings in the form of minerals and plants. For this reason, Hades is also imagined as bountiful and is even frequently shown carrying a cornucopia. The Romans also called the god of the Underworld by these two names, Hades and Pluto.

Five rivers were imagined to divide the land of the living from the Underworld, and to provide a protective barrier to keep the souls of the dead from wandering back among the living. These rivers were Styx (Hated), which if sworn upon makes an oath inviolable; Lethe (Forgetfulness), also imagined as a spring of water in the Underworld or a plain near a river, whose waters—however described—were believed to cause forgetfulness to all who drink them; Acheron (Sorrows), a river whose banks were described as covered with lotuses; and Pyriphlegethon (Fiery) and Cocytus (Wailing), which flow into Acheron. After Homer, Greeks began to identify these mythological rivers with real ones and disputed their geographical location.

Myths about these rivers bordering the Underworld were also developed after Homer. A boatman named Charon who demanded a payment of a coin or a cake from those who recently died and wished to reach the Underworld was depicted on vases with increasing frequency. Often Hermes escorted souls to Charon's boat, although Hermes, unlike Charon, is not a permanent resident of the Underworld (Figures 4.3 and 4.4). Charon was imagined to keep guard over the waters dividing the living and the dead and to refuse passage to souls who want to return to the land of the living. Similarly, the mythic watchdog Cerberus, who is frequently depicted with two or three heads (but is described by Hesiod to have fifty heads), was also imagined to guard the entrance of the Underworld, welcoming the souls who enter Hades's realm but refusing to let them leave. One of the twelve labors of Heracles involved retrieving Cerberus from the Underworld (Chapter 10.1). This labor ended happily for all concerned; Heracles subdued Cerberus, brought him

4.3 (left) and 4.4 (right) Charon (left) waits as Hermes (right) leads the soul of a deceased person to his boat. White-ground lekythos (oil jug). Sabouroff Painter, c. fifth century BCE. *bpk, Berlin/ Antikensammlung, Staatliche Museum, Berlin/Johannes Laurentius/Art Resource, NY, ART301136 and ART301171.*

(with the permission of Hades) to show to Eurystheus, and then safely returned the beast back to his position at the gates of the Underworld. A vase depicting this scene shows Cerberus with two heads and a rather gentle demeanor (Figure 10.4, p. 441).

Homer mentions two other geographical components of the Underworld: the Elysian Plain and Tartarus. The Spartan king Menelaus receives a prophecy that when he dies he will go the Elysian Plain, a place of perpetual springtime. Menelaus does not earn this reward because of virtuous behavior (*Odyssey* 4.561). Rather, it is a gift from Zeus, who is the father of Menelaus's wife, Helen. Other heroes are sometimes said to dwell in the Elysian Plain, also called the Islands of the Blessed (Hesiod, *Works and Days* 166). In general, heroes may achieve some sort of afterlife that is better than others (Chapters 10.1 and 12.1), but not necessarily in the Elysian Plain, which is seldom mentioned in early Greek sources and seems to be an oddity even in Homer. Thus, the idea that the dead might dwell in verdant green fields such as the Elysian Plain remains peripheral to Greek ideas about the afterlife.

Tartarus, the fourth element in the universe in Hesiod's *Theogony* (Chapter 2.1) as well as a region under the earth where Zeus imprisons the Titans, seems to be an even deeper and darker region than the Underworld and is the site of many gruesome eternal punishments; yet this region too is not central to Greek conceptions of the afterlife. Both the Elysian Plain and Tartarus, however, do not alter the general Greek view that the souls of all the dead, whether their lives were exemplary or undistinguished, wander eternally in the dark and dank expanses of Hades's realm.

Souls in the Underworld Souls in the Underworld were believed to retain the appearance and personality they had at the moment of death. When the soul of Patroclus visits Achilles in his tent, for example, he has the same stature, the same beautiful eyes, the same voice, and even the same clothing as he had when living. He looks so much like his former self that Achilles reaches out to touch him, but Patroclus's soul dissipates and flits away. Their thwarted embrace suggests that the souls of the dead, however convincingly lifelike, cannot be physically touched by the living (*Iliad* 23.103–104). In most literary and visual depictions, as in this passage, souls have the appearance of the living person. (There are exceptions: the souls of the suitors in Homer's *Odyssey* are depicted as small, winged, and bat-like as they fly with Hermes to the Underworld.)

With their personalities intact, the souls of the dead were depicted as gossiping with one another, playing checkers and other board games, and welcoming newly arriving family members to the Underworld. They even have disagreements with one another. When Odysseus sees King Minos in the Underworld, the ruler is passing out judgments in disputes among the souls of the dead, an activity connected to his role in life as king of Crete. However, Minos does not mete out eternal punishments for behavior during life (only in later literature are he and King Rhadamanthys perceived in this role). Instead, he moderates legal disputes, which, Homer implies, are like those heard in the courts among the living. Similarly, because Hades does not judge the souls of the dead or inflict punishments for their behavior during life, when he is seen dispensing judgments in the Underworld, it is to resolve disputes among the dead.

This view of the Underworld as a place where the souls of the dead have a leisurely, if litigious, existence contradicts other descriptions of the afterlife found in Homer. Homer, who sometimes calls the dead "strengthless heads," seems to suggest that souls retain their consciousness but experience no emotions and have no vitality. They exist in a sort of suspended animation, devoid of pleasure and meaning, as they wander aimlessly over a dank landscape. The eternal futility of existence within Hades's realm was considered a "hateful," although not frightening, prospect. Moreover, in Homer, the ethical or moral behavior of the living person—however excellent—did not and could not provide relief from such a tedious eternity.

And yet other tales suggest that there were both rewards and punishments after death depending on how one lived one's life or attracted the favor of the gods. Menelaus, as we saw earlier, enjoyed an eternity in the blissful Elysian Plain. Among those who were condemned to an eternity of punishment and pain in Tartarus is the giant Tityus, who attempted to rape Leto, the mother of Apollo and Artemis. He spends eternity strapped down while two vultures eat his liver, believed to be the source of passion. Tantalus, who stole ambrosia and nectar from the gods while at their table in Olympus, cannot drink the water he stands in nor eat the fruit on nearby trees. The deceitful king Sisyphus must repeatedly push a boulder up a hill; each time he almost gets it to the top, it rolls back down again. Ixion, like Tantalus, is punished for betraying his host; invited to dine with Zeus at Olympus, Ixion lusted after Hera. In Tartarus, he is strapped to a wheel that never stops spinning. Punishments in Tartarus are not just reserved for treacherous and lecherous kings. Fifty Danaids, daughters of the mythical king Danaus, who murdered their husbands must spend eternity attempting to collect water in leaky vessels.

Although the Greeks did not conceive of a coherent system of rewards and punishments for the dead in the Underworld, they did, however, believe that behavior (good or evil) had consequences on earth. They also increasingly developed rituals, such as the Eleusinian Mysteries (discussed subsequently), to mitigate the eternal darkness that is death.

Crimes and immoral acts had consequences for the living, and not only for the victims of such deeds. One's own behavior was believed to shape the fortunes of one's descendants. Herodotus tells the tale of Croesus, the king of Lydia (560–547 BCE), who sends envoys to Delphi to ask why he, being a pious man who often gave Apollo great offerings, lost his kingdom in war. Apollo answers that Croesus had to pay for his ancestor Gyges's crime of regicide some five generations earlier. This example demonstrates that although some were punished for wrongdoing by being condemned to Tartarus, it was more generally believed that evil deeds in this life would result in suffering and punishment for future generations. On the other hand, in Homer, heroic feats generate a sort of immortality through remembrance in song. Such re-membrance benefited one's descendants, just as an inheritance of wealth and reputation would. But neither fame nor admirable or even heroic behavior allowed one to escape an eternal—and eternally bleak—existence in the Underworld.

In the centuries following Homer, alternative belief systems about the fate of the soul after death gradually arose. Greek philosophers, including Pythagoras, Empedocles, and their followers, developed ideas about reincar-nation. Although such ideas did not erase or replace the Homeric view of Hades and the Underworld, they did offer those who believed in them a very different vision of their soul's trajectory over time. More common than the idea of reincarnation, but also indicating a concern about the soul, were ritu-als and beliefs that offered some hope for a better afterlife. Groups such as the Orphics (who claimed the legendary Orpheus as their founder) elaborated beliefs about happier prospects for the soul in the afterlife. Additionally, ritu-als in honor of Dionysus or Demeter (such as the Eleusinian Mysteries) also were believed to help participants achieve a better life for their souls after death. Thus, after Homer, notions and rituals concerning the afterlife began to evolve. Scholars have ascribed different motives to this shift in attitude: perhaps the bleakness of the Homeric view became insufferable, or anxiety about death increased. Funeral rituals and inscribed grave markers too became more important after Homer. Whereas inscribed gravestones en-sured the remembrance of the deceased among the living, funerary rituals ensured the safe journey of the soul to the kingdom of Hades.

Funerary Rituals Funeral rituals in Greece served to help the soul of the dead reach the Underworld. Such rituals also helped community and family members endure the loss of the deceased through ritualized forms of remembering. Both men and women participated in the funeral rituals, which can be divided into three stages: laying out the corpse for burial, escorting the dead to the gravesite while singing lamentations, and visiting the grave for a set period of time after burial. Although both men and women participated in funerary rituals, women had an especially prominent role in each stage of this process.

Women prepared the dead for the first stage of the funeral, the laying out of the body (*prosthesis*). Immediately after a death, kinswomen washed the body of the deceased, closed its eyes and mouth, and dressed it in a special garment and crown before laying out the body for family and friends to mourn. Funerary plaques, which were small painted clay rectangles displayed in tombs, typically depicted the *prosthesis* (Figure 4.5). Women, who in some cases had scratched their faces and shaved their heads, are shown standing close to the corpse, while small children hover under the bier. Men stand further from the corpse and raise their hands in a mourning gesture.

After the corpse had been mourned in the home, the funeral procession (*ecphora*) took place. Women lamented and sang dirges while the dead were transported to the cemetery (cremation was less common) as well as at the tomb. Their laments were well-wrought songs, not simply spontaneous outbursts of emotion; they had repeating themes and metrical patterns. After the burial, there was a feast in which the deceased was believed to partake. The soul was believed to hover near its body at the gravesite, where it could be called on by the living; the influence of these souls is suggested by the magical curse tablets found in graves that contain requests to the dead to perform acts of vengeance. During an interim period lasting roughly one month after the burial, offerings to the dead were made so that the person's soul might go to the Underworld.

Women were charged with overseeing death processes in funerary rituals because of their cultural and symbolic association with the body. The prevalence

4.5 Plaque of a funerary ritual (*prosthesis*). Black-figure plaque. Attributed to the Burgon Group, c. 560–550 BCE. Louvre Museum, Paris, France. © *RMN-Grand Palais / Art Resource, NY, ART147733.*

of this social pattern, as scholars of anthropology and gender studies have argued, derives from practical considerations concerning pregnancy, childbirth, and nursing. These are seen to bind women to the domestic world of the house, as well as to the needs of their bodies and their children's bodies. Thus women became mentally and symbolically linked to all bodily concerns. Women's intimate association with life and death through childbirth and funerary rituals is reflected in Demeter's oversight of fertility as well as her mythological connection to Hades, the king of the Underworld, by his marriage to her daughter, Persephone. Her two gifts to humanity, the fruits of the earth and her holy rite at Eleusis, can be understood to match the cultural and ritual patterns of women's lives. Not surprisingly, then, many of Demeter's agricultural rituals that celebrate fertility include symbolic representations of death. It is to these rituals that we turn before examining her Mysteries at Eleusis, which were celebrated by participants from all over the Mediterranean world for a period lasting longer than a thousand years.

DEMETER

The goddess Demeter is an Olympian; she is the daughter of Cronus and Rhea, and thus sister to Zeus. She is the mother of one child, Persephone, whose father is Zeus. The Homeric *Hymn 2* (*To Demeter*), which describes her search for her daughter, Persephone, is also connected to a ritual known as the Eleusinian Mysteries that ensured participants a better life after death. As we noted earlier, Demeter's name suggests her connection with agriculture; she was often shown carrying a wheat stalk. She is also frequently shown with Triptolemus, an adolescent boy who rides a winged chariot, to whom she gives the knowledge of agriculture to share with humanity (Figure 4.6). Many of her cult titles, such as Chloe (Green Shoots) and Horaphorus (Bringer of the Seasons), underscore her association with agriculture and growth. Demeter was also associated with rituals that were designed not only to ensure agricultural success but also to link the fertility of the earth to the fertility of women.

Agricultural Rituals The Proerosia and the Haloa are two rituals directly tied to the agricultural cycle of planting and harvesting the crops. Each makes use of symbols that connect Demeter to human fertility as well as mortality. (The Thesmophoria, a ritual concerning human fertility that uses agricultural imagery, is discussed separately later.) Occurring during the planting season (October through

4.6 Triptolemus on a winged chariot with Demeter. Detail of an Attic red-figure krater. The Niobids Painter, c. 460 BCE. Archaeological Museum Ferrara, Italy. *Alfredo Dagli Orti / The Art Archive at Art Resource, NY, AA356430.*

December), not during the harvest (May and June), these all-female rituals were a counterpart to men's agricultural work and were intended to ensure the success of the year's crops.

The Proerosia (Before Plowing) included a ritualized plowing of the fields before the actual plowing and sowing took place. Sacrifices were offered to Demeter, Persephone, Zeus, and a goddess named Daira. Women may have gathered separately from·men, although little more is known about this festival. The Haloa (Fields) festival, which was for women only, took place in late December, when the seeds would have been in the ground for a month or so and at risk from rainfall or cold weather. The Haloa was meant to ensure the safety of the planted seeds and thus the season's harvest. An anonymous ancient Greek scholar provides a lengthy description of this all-female festival: women play with pastries in the shapes of sexual organs, drink wine, tell obscene jokes, and display food on tables that have been supplied by *archons* (male political leaders) who themselves do not participate in the women's activities. As the Greeks frequently compared human sexuality and fertility to agriculture, the bawdy character of the Haloa can be interpreted as a metaphor for the season's agricultural labor and concerns.

The parallel between agriculture and human reproduction rests on a nearly universal metaphor of the earth as female and the cultivator as male, a metaphor that permeated the Greek language. The comic playwright Menander (c. 341/42–c. 290 BCE) records a formula used when brides were betrothed to their husbands in which plowing is compared to the sexual act: "I give her to you for the plowing (*aroto*) of legitimate children." Similarly, the Greek verb *ergein* (to work) can mean the agricultural labor of men to make the earth fertile as well as their "work" to impregnate their wives. In the divine realm, Zeus sends rain to fertilize Demeter's earth. A Greek prayer, "Rain! Give Birth!" (*Hue! Kue!*), also relies on this analogy, for the Greek word *kue* describes women's pregnancy.

In a world where the metaphorical connection between agricultural and human reproduction is so prevalent, the obscene words and sexual gestures of the Haloa took on symbolic and ritual significance for agricultural production. By ritually mimicking the sexual union between men and women with objects and words, women were encouraging and ensuring the growth of the season's crops through sympathetic magic—that is, the belief that the ritual enactment of a desired outcome will conjure and produce that outcome. In other words, women ritually enacted human sexual consummation to "make" seeds planted in the fields take hold in the ground and grow into the next season's harvest.

Thesmophoria: A Fertility Ritual The Thesmophoria, an all-female ritual that occurred before sowing (October to November), relied on the same network of symbols and objects as the Haloa. The cult title Thesmophorus (Bringer of Law), applied to Demeter as well as Persephone, suggests that Demeter conveys something established and customary, such as agricultural practices. This cult title may pertain to myths in which Demeter teaches her Mysteries and agricultural knowledge to Triptolemus, a mythical Eleusinian prince. He, in turn, imparts the knowledge of agriculture to the people he visits by depositing wheat across the earth from his flying chariot.

The Thesmophoria took place over the course of three days. During the first day, Anodos (Ascent), women left their houses and walked to where they would worship Demeter and Persephone. On the second day, the Nestia (Fast), no public business or sacrifices were conducted throughout the cities where the Thesmophoria was celebrated. Women fasted, insulted one another, and made obscene jokes. They may have ritually beaten each other with sticks, an activity believed to enhance fertility. The title of the third day, Calligenia (Beautiful Births), suggests that the day's observances were concerned with human fertility. Women broke their fast, sacrificed, and feasted; men may have joined them.

The most intriguing component of the Thesmophoria took place late on the second day of the festival, when women purified by a ritual entered pits and dug up a mixture of dirt containing items that had been deposited several months earlier. In archaeological sites dedicated to Demeter all over Greece, there are pits containing pigs' bones. In addition to being relatively inexpensive and thus readily available, pigs have a symbolic importance that may explain their use (Figure 4.7). Pigs were a symbol of fertility, and the ancient Greek word for pig was also a slang word for a young girl and/or female genitals.

Along with the decayed pigs, cakes shaped like genitalia, snakes, and pinecones (which may have served to represent male genitalia) that had been buried sometime earlier were also dug up. Although the Greeks may have used a similar mixture of organic waste as a kind of compost to fertilize their fields, the rotting mixture dug up as part of the Thesmophoria did not serve such a practical purpose. Instead, it was offered to Demeter on the third day of the festival. The curious mixture makes symbolic sense if we consider that its components stood for female and male sexual organs. In this way, the Thesmophoria (like the Haloa) included aspects of sympathetic magic,

4.7 Baubo (also called Iambe) on the back of a pig. Terracotta. Circa first century BCE. Antikensammlung, Staatliche Museen, Berlin, Germany. *bpk, Berlin/Antikensammlung, Staatliche Museum, Berlin/Johannes Laurentius/Art Resource, NY, ART450592.*

as symbols and symbolic evocations of human sexuality were used to conjure agricultural success.

Whereas the Thesmophoria celebrates human fertility to ensure agricultural success and honors Demeter, the decayed material dug up during the festival's second day also suggests mortality and death. Even though women's ritual manipulation of the compost and their offering of it to Demeter are connected to generating life, culminating in the celebration of "beautiful births," the symbolic objects and activities of the Thesmophoria collectively introduce death into a celebration of life. In this way, the festival compels an acknowledgment among its female participants that death and life processes are inextricably linked.

The Eleusinian Mysteries Demeter's festival at Eleusis is very closely connected to the Homeric *Hymn 2* (*To Demeter*). The hymn not only explains why Demeter is worshipped in Eleusis but also describes Demeter's activities in such a way that they seem closely coordinated with the initiates' ritual activities.

Demeter wanders to Eleusis when she is searching for her daughter, Persephone, whom Zeus had given to Hades in marriage without Demeter's knowledge. Demeter grieves as she wanders in search of her missing daughter. The king of Eleusis, Celeus, and his wife Queen Metaneira, offer her hospitality; their servant Baubo (Iambe) manages to make her smile (*Hymn 2* [*To Demeter*] 195–204). In return, Demeter tries (and fails) to make their young son, Demophoon, immortal. Filled with rage at her losses, Demeter demands that a temple be built in her honor at Eleusis. She also exiles herself from the gods and destroys the earth's harvests. To avoid the disastrous consequences of Demeter's actions for mortals and immortals alike, Zeus allows Persephone to leave the Underworld for part of each year. The hymn culminates in a reunion between Demeter and Persephone and refers to the benefits that initiates in the Eleusinian Mysteries will gain after death. Many scholars compare the initiates' journey to Eleusis during the festival to Demeter's journey, whereas others compare their journey to Persephone's descent into the Underworld. Both interpretations are valid, and each provides a way of understanding the initiates' activities in the Mysteries.

The week-long festival of the Mysteries took place in September, before the Thesmophoria, the Haloa, and the Proerosia. Eleusis was a small area located northwest of Athens that came under Athens's control during the seventh century BCE. Eleusinian families, nonetheless, retained control of the Mysteries, providing its priests, priestesses, and attendants and overseeing the maintenance of the area sacred to Demeter and Persephone. Any Greek-speaking person—including women, men, and slaves—who was ritually pure (i.e., had not committed murder) could participate in the Mysteries. Participation was not compelled by virtue of membership in a city; it was a voluntary and personal, not a civic, act. Initiates (*mustai*) had to be sponsored by a previous initiate and had to provide a baby pig in order to participate. The sacrificial pig may symbolize Persephone because "pig" was a slang word for a girl or because, in one version of her abduction story, a swineherd named Eubouleus is tending his pigs at the spot where Hades emerges from the earth to kidnap Persephone; the pigs fall into the Underworld with the girl. Through the sacrifice of the pig, the initiates may be encouraged to identify with Persephone, who must find her mother.

The festival began in Athens, where Eleusinian officials gathered initiates and directed them to bathe themselves and their sacrificial pigs in the port of Peiraeus. Officials and initiates then walked the fourteen miles to Eleusis. When they reached the Cephisus River, which they had to cross, a curious ritual activity took place: masked individuals (perhaps initiates from the previous year) teased and mocked the initiates. This introduction of bawdy humor into an otherwise solemn occasion may have recalled Baubo (Iambe), the Eleusinian servant who roused Demeter from her grief with jokes.

Once at Eleusis, the initiates, who had abstained from food since the beginning of the festival in imitation of Demeter, broke their fast. They sacrificed their pig (if they had not already done so in Athens) and offered seed mixtures and barley cakes to Demeter. In Eleusis, they would also walk by a rocky cave associated with Hades and Kore (Young Girl), one of Persephone's cult titles, and the "mirthless rock" where Demeter was said to have sat and mourned Persephone's absence. After feasting at Eleusis and viewing sacred places in Demeter's sanctuary, the initiates were prepared to enter Demeter's temple, the Telesterion, and receive secret knowledge that would complete their initiation (Figure 4.8).

What exactly happened in the Telesterion? Initiates were forbidden from revealing their experiences, and even though the festival persisted for a thousand years, not a single initiate is known to have left a record of what happened during the ceremonies. Some of what we know about the Eleusinian Mysteries is derived from the structure of the Telesterion itself. Its design differs from other temples because it was built to accommodate worshippers. The typical Greek temple was rectangular and housed a statue of the god or goddess. As it was considered the house of the divinity, the temple was not suitable for human worshippers to enter. Instead, sacrifices were performed outside on an outdoor altar in front of the temple. The Telesterion, on the other hand, was a

4.8 The temple called the Telesterion at Eleusis, Greece. The Solonic Telesterion was erected about 600 BCE. *HIP/Art Resource, NY, AR9146068.*

square building with eight tiers along its interior walls that provided seating for the initiates. In this large, enclosed space, the initiates were shown or taught something sacred.

Clement of Alexandria (150–215 CE), an early Christian scholar whose writings attempted to persuade Greeks to convert to Christianity by debunking ancient "pagan" rituals, has left a brief statement about the Eleusinian initiation ceremony. He reports what he believes the initiates said during the ceremony when Demeter's mystery was revealed to them: "I have fasted. I have drunk the barley ale. I have taken out of the sacred box, worked and deposited into the sacred basket and out of the sacred basket and into the sacred box." The first two parts of this saying are clear: initiates fasted and broke their fasts with a drink brewed from barley. But what was in the boxes and baskets, and what kind of "work" did it require of the initiates?

Over the centuries, scholars have suggested many different possibilities. Some argue that a stalk of grain was displayed. Other scholars suggest that an infant was presented, and still others that cakes in the shape of genitalia, like those used in the Thesmophoria, were shuffled in and out of the boxes and baskets. Some argue that relics at the shrine were revealed, although this conjecture has received little widespread acceptance. Each hypothesis is plausible and corresponds to some aspect of the festival and Demeter. A stalk of grain, for example, would emphasize Demeter's oversight of agriculture to her initiates. An infant or cakes in the shape of genitalia would reinforce the symbolic analogy between the fertility of women and that of the earth. In the end, we may never know what exactly was displayed or revealed during the initiation ceremony in the Telesterion. What we can say with more certainty is that participation in the Eleusinian Mysteries, a ceremony that culminated in some sort of celebration of fertility and life, was believed to ensure a better afterlife for initiates.

The power of Demeter's Great Mysteries for her initiates is a consequence of the complex network of symbols that operated in the rituals and myths of the goddesses Demeter and Persephone as well as in funerary rituals. Its underlying logic links Demeter's role as an overseer of both agriculture and death with the everyday lives of Greek women as overseers of childbirth as well as the rituals associated with death. In ancient Greece, it was women who directly experienced the seasons of planting as well as harvest, between birthing and burying and between life and death. The Mysteries, which deployed symbols and ritual actions that evoked these eternal rhythms, were not restricted to women. The rituals thus granted everyone an experience of the inextricable, necessary, and perhaps even comforting cycle between life and death. Demeter's two gifts to humankind—"the fruits of the earth" and "sweeter hopes" regarding dying—were truly a blessing if understood and experienced together as one united gift. This unity of vision was made possible for all initiates through their participation in the Mysteries.

UNKNOWN, *HYMN 2: TO DEMETER*

Hymn 2 (*To Demeter*), like all Homeric hymns, was orally composed and performed by anonymous bards at religious festivals long before it was recorded in writing. Yet this hymn is distinguished from all the other Homeric hymns because it is considered to be very closely connected to the Eleusinian Mysteries. Indeed, it is often treated as a liturgy (script) that corresponds to the Mysteries. Just as Persephone is eventually reunited with Demeter, an initiate's journey to Eleusis culminates in an encounter with Demeter. Every initiate is Persephone, Demeter's beloved child whom she cannot save from death but whom she can tend in life (and even in death) by offering sweet hopes for a better afterlife. In this respect, the hymn is also a compelling poetic treatment of the bond between mother and child that captures the poignancy of their inevitable separation as the child reaches adulthood. *Note:* Ancient texts, whether written on stone or papyrus, often contain illegible words or have been partially worn away or destroyed. Editors indicate these places in various ways: barely legible words that have been restored through careful scholarship are placed in brackets, while empty brackets or empty spaces indicate places where words can't be restored or where the text has been lost. Lines 387–404 of *Hymn 2* (*To Demeter*) are an example of reconstructed text. (Translated by Michael Crudden.)

- Make a list of all the correspondences between the hymn and the ritual. (For example, the initiates walk from Athens to Eleusis, just as Demeter walked to Eleusis while searching for Persephone.) Do these correspondences persuade you that the hymn is closely connected to the Eleusinian Mysteries and perhaps was composed as a liturgy or script for the Mysteries?

- One of the more puzzling moments in the hymn is Demeter's care of Demophoon, the Eleusinian prince. Why does Demeter choose to take care of this child and try to make him immortal? How does her care of Demophoon pertain to her search for Persephone and to the goals of initiates to achieve a better life after death by participating in the Mysteries?

- Demeter challenges Zeus's decision to give their daughter Persephone to Hades as his bride. Their conflict is peacefully resolved and does not result in cosmic warfare. Instead, Demeter gains a temple with worshippers in Eleusis and thus more honor among mortals. How does the resolution between Zeus (husband) and Demeter (wife) offer a "charter" (justification) of decision-making and the prerogatives of mortal fathers to give their daughters in marriage? (On charter myths, see Chapter 2.2)

- Two scholars have extensively studied initiation rituals: Arnold van Gennep (Chapter 8.2) and Victor Turner (Chapter 9.2). Their work may be fruitfully applied to the Eleusinian Mysteries. Specifically, van Gennep divides initiation rites into three stages. What are these stages? What events of the Eleusinian Mysteries fit into each of the stages of van Gennep's description? What sort of insight does van Gennep's work offer toward an understanding of the Eleusinian Mysteries?

UNKNOWN, *HYMN 2: TO DEMETER* (c. 700 BCE)

With fair-tressed Demeter, the sacred goddess, my song begins,
With herself and her slim-ankled daughter, whom Aïdoneus once
Abducted—given to him by deep-crashing, far-seeing Zeus—
While remote from Demeter whose sword is golden, of sparkling fruits,
She was joining together with Ocean's full-bosomed daughters in play,
And amidst a soft meadow-field was plucking flowers: the rose,
The crocus and beautiful violet, iris and hyacinth blooms,
And narcissus—grown by Earth through the will of Zeus to please
The Receiver of Many, a snare for the maiden with budding face—
A wondrous, radiant blossom, awesome for all to view,   10
Both for immortal gods and also for mortal men.
From this plant's root a hundred heads had sprouted up,
And scent most sweetly spread; all Heaven wide above
Beamed, as did all Earth, and the salty swell of the Sea.
And she, being struck with wonder, reached out with both of her hands
To grasp this beautiful plaything; but broad-pathed Earth gaped wide
On the Nysion plain where the lord, the Receiver of Many, rushed forth
With his deathless horses, Kronos' son who has many a name.
He seized her against her will, and aboard his golden car
Carried her off, lamenting; she uttered a piercing scream   20
In appeal to her father, Kronos' son, the highest and best.
But there was not any amongst the immortals or mortal men
Who heard her call, nor did the olives with sparkling fruit;
Only Persaios' daughter whose thoughts are of youthful mirth,
The brightly head-dressed Hekate, heard from within her cave,
As did the lordly Sun, Hyperion's splendid child,
When the maiden shrieked in appeal to her father, Kronos' son.
But Zeus sat apart, far away from the gods, in a prayer-filled shrine,
And received the beautiful offerings made by mortal men.
And against her will her father's brother carried her off,   30
The Commander of Many, Receiver of Many, by Zeus' advice
With his deathless horses, Kronos' son who has many a name.
      While the goddess viewed earth and starry sky, and the strong-flowing sea

Teeming with fish, and the rays of the Sun, she still hoped to behold
Her dear mother again, and the tribes of gods eternal in race;
So long did hope soothe her mighty mind despite her grief

. . . .

The mountains' peaks and the depths of the sea rang out at the sound
Of her deathless voice, and her queenly mother caught the cry:
A sharp pain took hold of her heart, and about her heavenly locks
She rent her head-dress, cast from her shoulders her dark veil down,   42
And over both firm and fluid rushed like a bird in her search;
But there was not any amongst the gods or mortal men
Who would tell her the truth, nor from birds did any true messenger come.
For nine days then queenly Deo wandered across the earth,
A flaming torch in each hand, and neither ambrosia touched
Nor sweet-tasting nektar in grief, nor with bath-water splashed her flesh.
But when for the tenth time upon her the radiant Dawn had shone,
Then she was met by Hekate holding a light in her hands,
Who, to report her tidings, addressed her with words and said:
       "Queen Demeter, Bringer of Seasons, Bestower of Splendid Gifts,   54
Who amongst the heavenly gods or mortal men
Carried Persephone off and grieved you within your heart?
For I heard the sound of her voice, yet caught no glimpse with my eyes
Of the one who carried her off: I tell you at once the whole truth."
       So Hekate spoke; the daughter of Rhea whose tresses are fair
Gave her no answer in speech, but together with her in haste
Rushed onward, holding in each hand a flaming torch.
They came to the Sun, the watcher of gods and men, and stood
In front of his horses. The bright one of goddesses questioned him:
       "Sun, as a god for a goddess show your regard for me,   64
If ever by word or deed your heart and spirit I pleased.
The daughter whom I bore, my sweet offshoot of glorious form,
I heard through the murmuring air giving vent to an anguished cry
As though overpowered by force, yet caught no glimpse with my eyes.
But since from the brilliant sky you look down on all earth and sea
With your rays, now tell me the truth: have you anywhere seen my child?
Who took her without my consent against her will by force
And vanished—one of the gods, or was he of mortal men?"
       In this way she spoke, and Hyperion's son responded in speech:
"Daughter of fair-tressed Rhea, lady Demeter, you'll know.   76
For indeed I have great respect and pity for you in your grief
Concerning your slim-ankled child. No one else of the gods was the cause
Save Zeus who gathers the clouds: to be called his flourishing spouse
He gave her to Hades his brother, who snatched her and carried her off

Down to the murky gloom with his horses, shrieking loud.
But, goddess, cease your deep mourning—nor must you at all in vain
Keep hold of boundless rage. A not unsuitable match
Amongst the immortal gods for your daughter to marry is he,
Aïdoneus, Commander of Many, your very own brother by birth,
Sown from the selfsame seed. And as regards honour, he gained   86
His share by lot at the first, when the three-way division was made:
He dwells amongst those whose sovereign it fell to his lot to be."
    With that he called to his horses, and at his behest they began
Quickly to pull the swift car, like birds with their wings outstretched;
But into the heart of Demeter came grief more dreadful and grim.
She then was filled with anger at Kronos' black-clouded son,
And forsaking the gods' assembly and tall Olympos mount,
For a long time through humans' cities and rich tilled fields she went,
Effacing the signs of her beauty; and no one who saw her of men
Or deep-girdled women knew her, until she came to the house   96
Of shrewd-minded Keleos, sovereign of fragrant Eleusis then.
She sat near the road, her heart full of woe, by the Maiden's Well,
Where the townsfolk drew water in shade—above it an olive-bush grew.
She resembled an aged woman born many years before,
Now deprived of the power of birth and the gifts that the goddess
    bestows,
Aphrodite the lover of garlands; one such as those who nurse
The children of doom-dealing kings and serve in their echoing halls.
    The daughters of Keleos, son of Eleusinos, saw her there,
As they came for the easy-drawn water, to bring it in pitchers of bronze
To their father's beloved halls, like four goddesses, blooming with youth: 108
Amongst them Kallidike came, Kleisidike too was there,
And Demo the lovely came, and Kallithoe eldest of all.
They did not know her—but hard are gods for mortals to see.
And standing close near by, they addressed her with winged words:
    "Who are you, of all the humans born many years ago,
And from where do you come, old woman? And why have you taken yourself
Outside the city's bounds, and don't draw near the homes
Where women of your age and younger dwell in the shadowy halls
Who would receive you kindly in word and also in deed?"
    So they spoke; and she, a queen amongst goddesses, answered
    with words: 118
"Dear children, whoever you are of female womanhood, hail!
I'll tell you; it's only good manners to answer your questions with truth.
My name is *Doso*—my queenly mother called me that.
Yet now from Crete I've come upon the broad back of the sea,

Not willing; with violence, rather, against my will by force
Pirate men carried me off. They beached their swift ship next
At Thorikos; there the women stepped on shore in a throng,
As did the men also themselves. They began to prepare a meal
By the ship's stern-cables; within me, however, I felt no desire
For the honey-sweet savour of supper, but rushing unseen I passed   131
In flight from my arrogant masters over the land's black soil,
Lest they sell me—picked up for free—and enjoy the price that I'd fetch.
So here I've arrived in my wanderings, having no notion at all
What country this is that I've come to and who its natives are.
But may all who have homes on Olympos grant husbands to you and the birth
Of children, as parents wish—but, maidens, take pity on me

· · · · · · · · · ·

With a ready mind, dear children: whose house may I approach,
The home of what husband and wife, to perform with a ready mind
Such tasks for them as belong to a woman past her prime?
I could hold and finely suckle a new-born babe in my arms,   141
And could keep an eye on the house; I could strew the master's bed
In a nook of the well-built rooms, and could teach the women their tasks."
      The goddess spoke; to her the maiden as yet untamed,
Kallidike, fairest of Keleos' daughters, at once replied:
      "Mother, the gifts that the gods bestow we humans endure
Perforce, though filled with grief: for they are more mighty by far.
But what you seek to know I'll pass on exactly and name
The men who here possess the great power that honour brings,
Who amongst their folk stand first, and guard the town's head-dress of walls
By means of their plans and straight judgements: Triptolemos shrewd
      in thought,   153
Dioklos and Polyxeinos, Eumolpos free of fault,
Dolikhos and our brave father—of all these men there are wives
Who manage their household affairs, and amongst these wives there is none
Who would scorn at first sight your appearance and shut you out from her home;
No, they will bid you welcome, for you have the look of a god.
But if you wish, wait here, while we go to our father's halls
And tell Metaneira, our deep-girdled mother, all this right through,
In the hope that she asks you to our house, and not to seek others' homes.
She has a darling son being reared in the well-built hall,
Whose birth, coming late, answered many a prayer, and was greeted
      with joy.   165
If you were to rear this child, and he reach his measure of youth,
It wouldn't be hard for any of female womanhood then
To feel envy on seeing you, such rewards for his rearing she'd give."

So she spoke; and with her head Demeter nodded assent.
Having filled their bright vessels with water, the maidens bore them away,
Exulting. They speedily reached their father's great abode,
And lost no time in telling all they had seen and heard
To their mother; she lost no time in urging them to go
And call Demeter to her, pledging a boundless wage.
And as hinds or heifers in springtime over the meadow leap   175
When their hearts are sated with forage, so did the maidens sweep
Along the hollowed cart-track, restraining their billowing garb,
And about their shoulders went streaming locks like the crocus' bloom.
      They found her, the glorious goddess, beside the road, where before
They had left her; without delay to their father's beloved halls
They led her; behind, her heart full of woe, completely veiled,
She followed them; round the goddess' slim feet her dark robe swirled.
And soon they reached the halls of Keleos cherished by Zeus,
And crossing the portico found their queenly mother there,
Where she sat alongside a pillar that propped the solid-made roof,   186
With her child on her lap, her young offshoot. The maidens ran over to her,
But onto the threshold stepped the goddess: the beam of the roof
She touched with her head, and filled the doorway with heavenly light.
Metaneira was seized with reverence, awe, and pallid fear;
She surrendered her chair to the goddess, and on it she urged her to sit.
But Demeter, Bringer of Seasons, Bestower of Splendid Gifts,
Had no desire to sit upon the gleaming chair,
But continued to wait in silence, her beautiful eyes cast down,
Till Iambe who knew her duties set a compact stool
Beside her, and over it threw a fleece of dazzling white.   196
Then, sitting down, the goddess hid herself under her veil;
For a long time bereft of speech she sat full of woe on the stool.
To no one did she give greeting with either a word or sign;
She had no laughter within her, no hunger for food and drink;
But, with longing pining away for her deep-girdled daughter, she sat,
Till Iambe who knew her duties with jokes and by mocking induced
Queenly and holy Demeter to smile and laugh and be kind;
And Iambe has pleased her temper then too in later times.
Metaneira proffered a goblet that brimmed with honey-sweet wine;
With an upward nod she refused it—it was not permitted, she said,   207
For her to drink red wine—but bade her to give her instead
A draught of barley and water mixed with tender mint.
She prepared and handed the goddess the potion as she required;
And when for the sake of the rite most queenly Deo received

. . . .

Metaneira whose girdle was fair amongst them was first to speak:
    "Hail to you, lady, since you, I believe, were not given birth
By parents of low estate, but by parents of noble blood:
You've the grandeur and grace in your gaze that doom-dealing kings display.
But come, the gifts that the gods bestow we humans endure
Perforce, though filled with grief: for upon our neck lies the yoke.   217
But now, since you've made your way here, all I have will be yours
    to command.
Rear me this boy that I'm holding, whose birth, coming late, beyond hope,
The immortals conferred upon me in answer to my many prayers.
If you were to rear this child, and he reach his measure of youth,
It wouldn't be hard for any of female womanhood then
To feel envy on seeing you, such rewards for his rearing I'd give."
    Demeter whose crown is fair then spoke to her in turn:
"And hail to you also, lady; may heaven grant you what is good!
With a ready mind I'll take this boy in my care as you bid:
Rear him I shall, and it's not my belief that he'll suffer harm   228
Through the folly of mind of his nurse from a spell or the cutter of roots,
For I know a strong counter-cut of more might than the cutter of wood,
And I know a safeguard that's good to ward off a baneful spell."
    When so she had spoken, the goddess took to her fragrant breast
The boy in her deathless hands, and his mother felt gladness at heart.
So in the halls she reared Demophoön, splendid son
Of shrewd-minded Keleos, whom Metaneira whose girdle was fair
Had borne, and he grew like a god. Neither tasting then food nor milk

       . . . .

With ambrosia she would anoint him, as if he were sprung from a god,
Shedding sweet breath upon him, and clasping him to her breast.   238
But by night she would keep him concealed in the mighty fire like a log,
In secret from his dear parents—it was a great wonder to them,
How he grew in advance of his age, and in looks resembled the gods.
And then she would have made him free of age and death,
If in her folly of mind Metaneira whose girdle was fair
Had not kept watch in the night and seen from her fragrant room.
Shrieking, she beat her breasts in fear about her boy,
Being much misled at heart, and in grief spoke winged words:
    "Demophoön, child that I bore! The stranger keeps you concealed
In the blazing fire, and causes me sorrow and wretched woe."   249
    In this way lamenting she spoke, and the bright one of goddesses heard.
Demeter whose crown is lovely, filled with anger at her,
Put away from herself on the ground with her deathless hands the dear boy—
Whom she, Metaneira, had borne beyond her hope in the halls—

Having snatched him up from the fire with dreadful fury at heart,
And at the same instant addressed Metaneira whose girdle was fair:
    "Ignorant humans, who lack the discernment to know in advance
Your portion of good or ill, as one or the other draws near!
Woman, your folly's misled you beyond all chance of a cure.
For let the gods' oath know this, the implacable water of Styx,   259
That I would have made your dear boy ever free of death and age,
And would have conferred upon him honour that does not fade;
But he now has no means of escaping death and the spirits of fate.
But an honour that does not fade will always belong to him,
Because he has climbed on my knees and slept in my arms' embrace.
And in due season for him, as the years come rolling round,
Together with one another the boys of Eleusis town
Will always wage for ever war and dreadful strife.
I am the goddess Demeter, holder of honour, who is
For immortals and mortals alike the greatest boon and joy.   269
But come now, let the whole people build a great shrine for me,
And an altar to stand beneath it, under the town and sheer wall,
Above Kallikhoros spring, upon the projecting hill;
And I myself will lay down for your instruction my rites,
So that then, by performing them piously, you might appease my mind."
    When so she had spoken, the goddess altered her stature and form,
Casting old age away, and round about her then
Beauty began to be breathed: a delightful perfume spread
From the fragrant robes that she wore, a radiance shone out far
From the goddess' immortal flesh, to her shoulders golden hair
    streamed,   279
And the solid-made house was filled with a light like the lightning-flash.
She went from the halls, and at once Metaneira's knees were loosed;
For a long time she lay there mute, not even thinking to lift
Her darling boy from the floor. But his sisters caught the sound
Of the piteous squall that he raised, and leaped down from their well-
    strewn beds.
Then one, having lifted him up, to her bosom clasped the boy;
Another kindled the fire; and a third on tender feet rushed
To help their mother stand and emerge from her fragrant room.
Gathering round, they began to bathe the struggling boy,
Whom they hugged in a loving embrace; but his spirit was not
    soothed,   290
For inferior nurses and nurturers held him now in their grasp.
    Through all the hours of night, though shaking with terror, they sought
To appease the glorious goddess; but at the appearance of Dawn

They informed wide-ruling Keleos truly of what was prescribed
By the fair-crowned goddess Demeter. Calling his numerous folk
To the place of assembly, he gave them the order to make a rich shrine
And an altar for fair-tressed Demeter upon the projecting hill;
And they at once obeyed him, complied with his word, and built
The shrine in the way he prescribed, and it grew by the goddess' decree.
  When they finished and ceased from their labour, they each
   set off for home;   302
But gold-haired Demeter sat there, far from all blessed gods,
And, with longing pining away for her deep-girdled daughter, she stayed.
On the earth that nurtures many she brought to pass a year
Most dreadful for humans and grim, when the soil made sprout no seed,
For Demeter whose crown is lovely was keeping it then concealed.
In the fields the oxen were dragging many curved ploughs in vain,
And upon the soil to no purpose fell much white barley grain.
And now she would have destroyed the whole of the human race
By means of grievous famine, and robbed of their glorious due
Of portions of honour and offerings those with Olympian homes, 312
If Zeus had not perceived and taken note in his mind;
And first he stirred into motion Iris whose wings are of gold
To summon fair-tressed Demeter who has a delightful form.
So to Iris he spoke; and she obeyed Zeus, the black-clouded son
Of Kronos, and ran with her feet at speed through the space between.
Reaching her journey's end at fragrant Eleusis town,
She found within the shrine Demeter the darkly robed;
And Iris, speaking aloud, addressed her with winged words:
  "Demeter, you're summoned by Father Zeus who knows deathless
   schemes
To come amongst the tribes of gods eternal in race.   322
Now don't leave lacking fulfilment the word that I bring from Zeus."
  In this way entreating she spoke, but Demeter paid no heed.
Then every one of the blessed gods who always exist
The Father dispatched to her, and drawing near in turn
They invited her and offered many most beautiful gifts
And such honours as she might choose amongst the immortal gods.
But there was not one who was able to change her mind or intent
As she seethed with anger in spirit: sternly she spurned their pleas,
For never on fragrant Olympos would she, she told them, set foot,
Nor make the crop sprout from the earth, till she saw her fair-faced
  child.   333
  When deep-crashing, far-seeing Zeus heard this, to Erebos then
He sent the Slayer of Argos who bears the rod of gold
To bring Hades round with soft words and holy Persephone lead

From the murky gloom to the light amongst the other gods,
So that her mother, on seeing her, might desist from her wrath.
Hermes did not disobey, but speedily hurtled down
At once from Olympos' seat to the hidden places of earth;
And the lord in his halls he discovered seated upon a couch,
And he had his revered spouse by him, though much against her will,
Since she longed for Demeter, her mother—who had to the blessed
    gods'   345
Unbearable deeds replied by devising her deadly scheme.
The mighty Slayer of Argos stood close near by and said:
    "Hades whose hair is dark, who rule over those who have died,
Zeus the Father has ordered that I from Erebos lead
Splendid Persephone out amongst the other gods,
So that her mother, on seeing her, might pull back from the wrath
And the dreadful rage that she nurtures against the immortal gods.
For she's thought of a monstrous deed, to wear down the feeble tribes
Of humans born on earth, concealing the seed in the soil,
And destroying immortals' honours. She nurtures her dreadful wrath   354
And does not mix with the gods, but far away she sits
In her fragrant shrine and presides over rocky Eleusis town."
    In this way he spoke; Aïdoneus, Lord of Those Below,
With his eyebrows signalling pleasure, did not disobey King Zeus'
Commands, but speedily urged Persephone shrewd in thought:
    "Go, Persephone, now to your dark-robed mother's side,
Keeping within your breast your temper and spirit mild,
And be in no way despondent too much in excess of the rest.
For amongst the immortals you'll find that I'm no unsuitable spouse,
Being Father Zeus' own brother. Going there, you'll rule   365
Over all that lives and moves; amidst the immortals you'll have
Honours of greatest worth; and vengeance for ever will come
Upon those who act unjustly and fail to appease your heart
By performing your offerings piously, paying you fitting gifts."
    In this way he spoke, to the joy of Persephone shrewd in thought.
She quickly leaped up in delight, but secretly, glancing round,
He gave her to eat a pomegranate's honey-sweet seed, so that there
By revered Demeter the dark-robed she would not for ever stay.
Aïdoneus, Commander of Many, in front of a golden car
Then harnessed two deathless horses, and she got on board;
    alongside,   377
The mighty Slayer of Argos with reins and whip in his hands
Made the pair race from the halls, and they not unwillingly flew.
They completed with speed their long journey; the deathless horses' career
By sea or the water of rivers, by grassy glens or peaks

Was not delayed, but above these they clove the thick mist as they went.
He brought to a halt the horses where fair-crowned Demeter remained,
In front of her fragrant shrine; and she, when she saw them, rushed
As a raving Maenad might down a mountain shaded with wood.
[From the] other [side] Persephone [   ]
Of her mother down [   ] 388
She bounded [to] run [   ]
And to her [   ]
[   ]
Ceasing [   ]:
         'Child, now tell me, you surely didn't anything [   ]
Of food? Speak out [   ]
For so, ascending [   ]
Beside myself and the Father, [Kronos' black-clouded son,   ]
You then could have your home, by all [the immortals esteemed];
But if you partook, you'll return [to the hidden places of earth]   398
And dwell for one-third of the seasons [   ]
But the other two-thirds by me and [the rest of the deathless gods.]
When the earth is blooming with every sweet-scented flower of spring,
Then from the murky gloom you will once more ascend,
And will be a mighty wonder for gods and mortal men.

· · · · · · · · · ·

And the mighty [Receiver of Many] duped you by means of what trick?"
         In answer most lovely Persephone spoke to her in turn:
"Mother, for you I shall indeed recount the whole truth.
When the speedy Slayer of Argos as messenger came to me
From the Father, Kronos' son, and the rest of the heavenly gods,   408
And passed on the news that he bore—that from Erebos I was to go,
In order that you, on seeing me, might desist from the wrath
And the dreadful rage that you nurture against the immortal gods—
I at once leaped up in delight, but Hades secretly put
A food as sweet as honey, a pomegranate's seed, in my hand,
And using violence forced me to taste it against my will.
And how he snatched me up and departed, bearing me off
To the hidden places of earth through the cunning plan devised
By my father, Kronos' son, I'll recount and tell all as you ask.
We were all in the lovely meadow—Leukippe and Phaino were there,   418
Elektra, and also Ianthe; Melite, Iakhe too,
Rhodeia, and also Kallirhoe; there was Melobosis too,
With Tykhe, and also Okyrhoe, nymph with budding face;
Khryseïs too, Ianeira, Akaste, Admete too,
Rhodope also, with Plouto; delightful Kalypso was there,
With Styx, and also Ourania; fair Galaxaure was there,

With Pallas the waker of battle, and archeress Artemis too.
We played and plucked fair blossoms, tender crocus mixed
With iris, hyacinth, rose-buds and lilies, a wonder to view,
And narcissus—grown by broad Earth, and resembling the crocus'
    bloom.   428
But as in delight I plucked it, the ground gave way from below,
And there the lord, the mighty Receiver of Many, leaped out.
He bore me away in his golden chariot under the ground,
Though much against my will, and I uttered a piercing cry.
In these words for you I've spoken, despite my grief, the whole truth."
      So then, throughout the whole day, at one with each other in mind,
They cheered their hearts and spirits much, embracing with love,
And their thoughts were turned from sorrow, each taking and giving joy.
The brightly head-dressed Hekate came from near at hand,
And lavished fond embraces on holy Demeter's child: 439
Her usher and helper the Lady from this time forward has been.
And deep-crashing, far-seeing Zeus as messenger sent to them
The fair-tressed Rhea to lead amongst the tribes of the gods
Demeter the darkly robed, and promised that he would give
Such honours as she might choose amongst the immortal gods;
And he signalled assent with a nod, that her daughter would make her home
For one-third of the circling year down in the murky gloom,
By her mother passing two-thirds with the rest of the deathless gods.
So to Rhea he spoke; and the goddess did not refuse to convey
The message entrusted by Zeus, but setting off at speed   449
Shot down from Olympos' peaks. She reached the Rarion plain,
In times past an udder of ploughland bearing the nurture of life,
But it bore no nurture now: it stood idle, devoid of all growth,
And kept the white barley concealed, as Demeter the fair-ankled planned.
Yet in future it soon would be sprouting with slender ears of corn,
As spring came waxing round; on the earth with ears of corn
Would the fertile furrows be burdened, while others lay bound in sheaves.
This was the place where first she arrived from the murmuring air;
Seeing each other with joy, they exulted within their hearts,
And the brightly head-dressed Rhea spoke to Demeter these words: 459
    "Come now, my child, you are called by deep-crashing, far-seeing
        Zeus
Amongst the tribes of the gods: he promised [that he would give]
[Such] honours [as you might choose] amongst the immortal gods;
[And he signalled assent with a nod, that your daughter would make her home]
[For one-third of the] circling [year down in the murky gloom,]
[But would pass two-thirds by you and the rest of] the deathless gods.

[So did he say it would be,] and nodded his head in assent.
[Come then,] my [daughter,] obey, and don't so [implacably rage]
At Kronos' black-clouded son; [instead, without delay,]
Make grow for humans [the harvest] that bears the nurture of life."   469
　　　[In this way she spoke;] and fair-crowned Demeter did [not] disobey,
But sent up from the clod-rich ploughland the harvest without delay,
And all broad earth was burdened with leaves and blossoms' weight.
The goddess Demeter then went and [showed] to the doom-dealing kings—
To Triptolemos, chariot-driving Diokles, Eumolpos the strong,
And Keleos leader of peoples—the way to perform her rites,
And disclosed sacred actions to all that can be in no way [transgressed,]
Learnt, or divulged, for the tongue is curbed by the gods' great awe.
Blessed is he who has seen them of humans who walk on the earth;
But he who has not been enrolled in the rites, who is lacking a share,   481
In death has no matching portion down in the mouldy gloom.
　　　But when by the bright one of goddesses all her rites were laid down,
They set off for Olympos and entered the concourse of other gods.
Having their dwelling there by Zeus whom thunder delights,
They are sacred and held in reverence. Greatly blessed is he
Of humans who walk on the earth whom they in goodwill hold dear:
Without delay they send to the hearth of his great abode
Ploutos, the giver of wealth to humans doomed to death.
　　　But come now, you who preside over fragrant Eleusis' land,
Over Paros that waters flow round, and Antron where rocks abound,   491
You queenly Bringer of Seasons, Bestower of Splendid Gifts,
Lady Deo, yourself and your daughter, Persephoneia most fair:
In goodwill return for my song life's nurture that pleases the heart.
But I will call to my mind both you and another song.   495

4.2 THEORY

MYTHS REINFORCE SOCIAL NORMS

"Goddess feminism" is a curious phrase. Whereas "goddess" evokes the myths of ancient Greece, "feminism" recalls the civil rights and women's movements of the 1960s. It was at that time that new forms of spiritual feminism, "thealogy" (as opposed to the masculine "theology"), and other forms of goddess-centered worship were created. "Goddess feminism" was a term associated with feminist teacher and author Carol P. Christ (b. 1945) and was used to describe a neopagan goddess worship that, according to its practitioners, would generate and support a reshaping of cultural and social norms that have for millennia oppressed women. Goddess feminism, once widely adopted, would usher in a nonviolent, egalitarian, and spiritual renewal of society. "Goddess feminists," "spiritual feminists," and "thealogians" are all closely connected terms used to describe individuals who study the spiritual dimensions of feminism and consider how the gender of the divine in different religious traditions might be reconceptualized so that women are not seen as or treated as inferior to men.

Spiritual feminists who seek to discover goddesses in societies where women held positions of power and worshipped have often turned to the work of Marija Gimbutas (1941–1994), the scholar most closely associated with what has come to be known as "matriarchy studies." An archaeologist with an interest in linguistics and folklore, Gimbutas argued that there were "matristic" societies in Neolithic Europe (7000–1700 BCE) in which the "Great Goddess" was worshipped. She called these societies "matristic" to suggest that although women had power, they used it not to dominate men but instead to establish egalitarian relationships and arrangements. According to Gimbutas, matristic societies valued peace, religion, the arts, and the natural world. What happened to these matristic societies? Gimbutas suggests that, at the start of the Bronze Age, a patriarchal and warlike people living in Eastern Europe (called "Proto-In-

4.9 Demeter, Triptolemus, and Persephone. Marble votive relief from Eleusis. Circa 440–430 BCE. Museum of Archaeology, Athens, Greece. *Nimatallah / Art Resource, NY, ART18.*

do-Europeans" or "Kurgans") invaded Central Europe and eventually overcame the existing peaceful matriarchies. They established hierarchical societies in which men were at the top of the social and political pyramid and women were at the bottom, and they imagined pantheons in which gods had more prestige and power than goddesses.

Gimbutas's far-ranging hypothesis about the matristic societies of Central Europe has been challenged by scholars working in archaeology, linguistics, and myth, to name just a few. Archaeologists argue that there were forts and weapons in Neolithic Europe, a fact that suggests that Neolithic European societies were not the peaceful societies Gimbutas posited. Others argue that the numerous female figurines, sometimes depicted with infants in their arms, that Gimbutas claims indicate the worship of the Great Goddess are not in fact attached to any particular cults or temples and may not represent goddesses at all (indeed, some are clearly not female). Most importantly, there is no archaeological evidence that supports the broad and far-reaching conclusions that Gimbutas draws about the ancient social world from these figurines.

Despite the fact that archaeologists have discredited Gimbutas's claims, her work continues to have an enormous impact outside the academy. The prehistorical world Gimbutas conjures supplies a foundation story (one could call it a myth) for imagining a world that was egalitarian, peaceful, artistic, and respectful of nature, with goddess worship and women at its center. Spiritual feminists have found Gimbutas's depiction of matristic societies especially inspiring and even acknowledge (as Foley points out) that they are engaged not in the historical recovery but in the creative interpretation of the past to serve their own spiritual and political agenda. Thus, the scholarly rejection of Gimbutas's work has not discouraged its social and spiritual application. Spiritual feminists and thealogians continue to look to the ancient worship of goddesses, as Gimbutas describes it, in order to develop their religious system. The study *and* worship of goddesses of ancient Greece are a part of their work of recovery, even though spiritual feminists are aware that ancient Greece was a patriarchal society and that Zeus, the father of gods and men, was the ruler of Olympus.

What, we might wonder, is the relationship between contemporary goddess feminism and the goddesses of ancient Greece? Did the worship of goddesses like Demeter and Persephone empower Greek women, as modern-day goddess worshippers claim to be empowered by their spiritual practices? Did the goddesses of Greece and their associated cults celebrate women and women's lives? It is precisely these questions that classical scholar Helene P. Foley (b. 1942) explores in her article "A Question of Origins: Goddess Cults Greek and Modern." Foley considers how Greek women participated in religious practices and how (if at all) Greece's polytheistic system of gods and goddesses offered women the sorts of empowerment claimed by spiritual feminists and thealogians. She offers an interpretation of Demeter's myths and cults that borrows both from Malinowski's notion (Chapter 2.2) that myths and rituals justify social norms and from contemporary scholarship about the relationship between gender and religion.

Specifically, Foley addresses the interests of spiritual feminists and asks whether the myths and worship of these goddesses in archaic and classical Greece offered Greek women some form of empowerment. To accomplish this goal, Foley considers myths about Demeter and Persephone in relation to the historical and social conditions surrounding their worship at Eleusis. In Greece, fathers chose marriage partners for their daughters as well as for any other young girls (such as nieces) for whom they served as legal guardians. These girls, like Persephone in *Hymn 2* (*To Demeter*), had little or no choice in the selection of their husbands. In the *Hymn*, Demeter and Persephone are initially displeased with Zeus's choice of Hades as Persephone's husband. Yet both mother and daughter gain honor when they accept the marriage Zeus has arranged. Persephone becomes queen of the Underworld, and Demeter is worshipped in Eleusis. Together they are able to help human beings gain a better life after death through the ritual at Eleusis. In Foley's view, then, both the *Hymn* and the ritual at Eleusis teach Greek women to accept patriarchal rules (especially those concerning marriage) in order to reap social rewards. Indeed, many depictions of Demeter show her with her daughter Persephone and Triptolemus (the adolescent boy who brings the knowledge of agriculture to the human race), thereby emphasizing her role as a mother and encouraging other women to adopt this role (Figure 4.9).

Foley, borrowing Malinowski's approach to myth, argues that *Hymn 2 (To Demeter)* is "first and foremost an aetiological justification of mortal marriage" that illustrates on a divine level how goddesses benefit by accepting marriage and male decisions. Consequently, women's worship of Demeter and Persephone was *compensatory*. It compensated women for the fact that they had relatively little power in society, particularly in marriage, and had to accept the decisions that husbands and fathers made on their behalf. Additionally, myths concerning Demeter that describe Athens as the place where agriculture was invented emphasize and thereby celebrate the role of men— not women—in agriculture. In Foley's analysis, then, the myths and cults of Demeter served the patriarchy in Athens and developed over time "to support its evolving cultural agenda," namely, marriage and the prerogatives of Athens and its men.

HELENE P. FOLEY, *FROM* "A QUESTION OF ORIGINS: GODDESS CULTS GREEK AND MODERN"

BEFORE YOU READ

Foley's interpretation of Demeter's myths and cults is programmatic: that is, it may be used to understand all myths and cults, especially those associated with women. Foley takes as her premise that myths and rituals must be understood in their historical context, and that they always reinforce its dominant ideas and practices. In a patriarchal society such as Greece, then, myths and associated rituals will always support patriarchy, instructing women to accept their secondary status and then compensating them for their lack of power (by praising them for obedience, for example). Thus Foley assumes that a myth or a ritual has one dominant message: it supports the ideas and beliefs of its social setting. If that setting is patriarchal, myths and rituals will support men's agenda for themselves as well as for women. Although Foley's argument is quite convincing, John Winkler offers a very different way to explore women, myth, and ritual. He argues that myth did not always enforce cultural norms but sometimes provided a way to criticize them (Chapter 5.2).

- Do you think that a myth has a single meaning that reflects, supports, and reinforces the status quo, as Foley argues?

---------- ☙ ----------

**BEFORE YOU READ
CONTINUED**

⚼

- Do Greek myths reflect and codify men's perspectives because Greece was a patriarchal society? If so, do Greek myths and their accompanying rituals completely exclude women's voices and experiences?

- Do you think different audiences for myths had different interpretations based on their own experiences and perspectives, or did all people share the same interpretations? Are there any sorts of evidence from ancient Greece that might help formulate an answer to this question?

- Could the elaborate and lengthy ritual at Eleusis have held different meanings for the different people—women and men, free and enslaved individuals—who participated in it?

HELENE P. FOLEY, *FROM* "A QUESTION OF ORIGINS: GODDESS CULTS GREEK AND MODERN" (1994)

I turn now to Demeter and Persephone, a myth that has been appropriated and re-interpreted by spiritual feminists. In Greek versions of the myth, the goddess Persephone is raped by the god of the underworld Hades. In angry response, her mother, the goddess of grain Demeter, produces a famine on earth. Zeus, the ruler of the gods, capitulates; Persephone will divide the year between her mother in the world above and her spouse in the world below. The spiritual feminist reading aims to strip the myth of its patriarchal overlay, and to preserve its celebration of what such a reading defines as pre-Olympian female power and female bonds.[1] Charlene Spretnak and Carol Christ, for example, offer a re-working of the myth that censors the rape as a patriarchal addition, and makes Persephone's voluntary visit to the underworld part of a process of acquiring maturity that separates and then reunites her with her mother.[2] Spretnak's version has Persephone choose a temporary separation from her mother because of her concern for the fate of the dead. She cites the classical scholar Gunther Zuntz's study of Persephone (75–77) in support of the view that the rape is a later addition to the myth.[3] My first point will be that more is involved in the shaping of this myth than patriarchy—imperialism, democracy, different ritual contexts, the nature of the audience, to name a few almost certain influences—and that the significance and meaning of the myth is so thoroughly shaped by these forces that it is unlikely that we can legitimately extricate from it an original core reflecting a historical female experience and female deity untainted by patriarchal society. I will then turn to the implications of the spiritual feminist version of the myth in a modern context.

The Demeter/Persephone myth is of particular interest in part because it played a role in several important religious contexts in Athens. It was the central myth in virtually all of the major cults celebrated exclusively by women of Athens,[4] but above all in the three-day festival of the Thesmophoria, as well as the basis for Eleusinian Mysteries, the most important and longlasting mystery cult of Antiquity. Some scholars have argued that the cult at Eleusis began as a rite exclusive to women,[5] but in historical times at least, initiation was open to all who spoke Greek: male and female, slave and foreigner. The cult promised initiates increased wealth and happiness in the world above and a better existence in the world below. Initiates received these benefits through the beneficence of two powerful goddesses, one who controlled fertility on earth as the goddess of grain, the other a queen in the world below. On the one hand, in the Thesmophoria the myth was enacted by women who were performing an important civic ritual to insure the fertility of the year's crops just before the autumn sowing. Since the proceedings of the rite were kept secret, however, only traces of this version of the myth exist. We know that the women fasted and mourned in imitation of Demeter on the second day of the rite, and may well have celebrated the reunion with Persephone on the final day.[6] On the other hand, we have more extensive, although often fragmentary, knowledge of variants on myths that explained the origins of the cult at Eleusis. Again, many aspects of the cult were secret, and we do not know the relative status of different versions of the myth by the classical period.

Examining two major variants of the Eleusinian myth—that in the Homeric *Hymn to Demeter* and that offered in a local Attic variant—will help to show us some of the probable functions that the Demeter/Persephone myth had in Greek culture and the complex forces that may have shaped it.[7] I shall argue that only by looking at the myth in context can we fully understand the implications of attempts by spiritual feminists to appropriate or revise it in a modern context. In the only complete Greek version of the myth, the archaic Homeric *Hymn to Demeter*, the story of the rape takes place in a civilized world: human beings already have agriculture, sacrifice, and marriage. After the rape, Demeter discovers from the sun god Helios that Persephone is trapped in the impenetrable underworld. In disguise as a mourning old woman, she descends to earth, engages herself as a nurse to the young Eleusinian prince Demophon, and attempts to make the child immortal. Interrupted by the child's mother, Demeter abandons her disguise, demands that a temple be built in her honor, and withdraws fertility from the earth. The gods, deprived of their accustomed sacrifices, try and fail to persuade Demeter to abandon her wrath. Zeus then agrees to Persephone's return. But because Hades tricked Persephone into eating a pomegranate seed in the world below, she must spend one third of the year with her husband as the great queen of the underworld. Demeter then teaches the Eleusinians how to become initiates in her cult and its benefits.

The *Hymn* concentrates on the goddesses' encounter with the world of death and mortal experience. Both goddesses suffer the separation from each other that mortals experience in death and face new limits on their powers. Demeter cannot immortalize the child Demophon, and must accept her daughter's marriage to Hades. Zeus' attempt to give his daughter in marriage to Hades without the knowledge of mother and daughter imposes patriarchal marriage—that is, the exchange of women by men and patrilocal residence for the wife—on divinities who have no experience of it.[8] Yet during her stay on earth, Demeter encounters mortal women who accept marriage and affirm the authority it brings to the wife. Hence the concluding resignation of the goddesses to Persephone's lot is prefigured in the mortal context and made to seem inevitable. In addition, Persephone's marriage to Hades becomes the basis for a new mortal experience after death promised in the cult; for prior to this event, the spheres of heaven, earth and underworld were not reliably linked.[9]

The *Hymn* implies that the mysteries are established as a result of the goddesses' encounter with something analogous to mortal limits.[10] As Jenny Clay has recently argued, this hymn, like the other Homeric hymns, belongs to a time imagined to be between the establishment of the reign of Zeus and a period when the rest of the Olympian divinities acquired the spheres of influence and cults for which they were later known ("Politics of Olympus," esp. 3–15). These poems tell us how our world got to be the way it is and why. Ostensibly about divine experience, the *Hymn to Demeter* actually represents first and foremost an aetiological justification of mortal marriage by making the marriage of Persephone the source of her power and divine identity. The myth also explains a significant change in the relation between gods and mortals. As the goddesses adopt and nurture their initiates, their relation to mortals becomes specifically maternal. Their gifts are reliable, unlike those of other gods, and the cult promises for the first time to ordinary humans an alleviation of the gloomy afterlife we find in the Homeric poems—not as in Homer, by acquiring immortal fame, but as a divine gift.

In the Homeric *Hymn's* version of the myth, then, the mother's and daughter's psychological confrontation with death, separation, and marriage results in a transformation of the human relation to both deity and death. Above all, a specifically female experience of limit makes possible the greatest of all gifts to humankind—a better life after death. Like the tragedies, then, this myth serves to compensate the female sex for the loss of autonomy and emotional fulfillment inflicted by patriarchy. The plot patterns of *Iphigeneia in Tauris* and *Helen* discussed earlier actually resemble that of the Demeter/Persephone myth. Both the *Hymn* and *Helen* use their myths to critique patriarchy even while capitulating to it, in the first case by completing the rescue of its protagonists only in the religious sphere, and in the other by direct compromise. In the divine case, Demeter's wrath and power accomplish a resolution for herself and her daughter not available to the mortal wife and mother. Yet in the *Hymn to Demeter* even divine females cannot escape a closer brush with mortality and nature than their male counterparts, and the acceptance of patriarchy is precisely what permits the two deities to become of transcendent value to humanity.[11]

In other versions of the Demeter/Persephone myth, including other Attic versions, the story occurs before humankind has agriculture.[12] Demeter also gives mortals the knowledge of agriculture in gratitude for their benefits to her. Here the Goddess descends to earth in search of her daughter and discovers her whereabouts from mortals rather than from the sun god, Helios. Local versions in many parts of Greece in fact claimed the role of informant for their own inhabitants. In Attic versions, the Eleusinian Triptolemus embarks on a winged chariot to spread agriculture from Attica to the rest of the Greek world. The Homeric hymns were generally designed as a prelude to the recitation of the major archaic epics. Although composed by poets from specific localities like Eleusis, they were in all probability designed for panhellenic audiences.[13] The *Hymn to Demeter*, by assigning the role of informant to Helios, adapts itself to a panhellenic audience by avoiding the need to take sides on the controversial question of which mortals were the first to assist Demeter on earth. Local Attic versions, on the other hand, in claiming for Attica the origin of agriculture and in developing male roles in the story more extensively, served the interests of the Athenian polis and its imperialism. The cult at Eleusis also resonated with democratic ideology at Athens, both by countering archaic epic's emphasis on mitigating death through the glorification of exceptional individual (usually masculine and aristocratic) achievement and by the cult's inclusiveness.[14] Furthermore, the status Demeter acquired at Eleusis and Athens seems to have been part of her transformation from a deity whose cult existed at the margins of civic spaces and who played an unimportant role in mainstream epic poetry to one who became central to civic worship. Important throughout Greece from a very early date, and above all in female cults such as the Thesmophoria, Demeter's myths and cults gained international prominence once Athens understood the propagandistic value of the mysteries.

In other words, it may not be historically the case, as the spiritual feminists claim, that with Demeter and Persephone patriarchy suppressed the worship of powerful pre-historic goddesses, but that patriarchy increased their powers precisely to support its evolving cultural agenda. I do not mean to deny the antiquity of Demeter's cult or its significant association with women. Yet rather than preserving the relics of a pre-Olympian past, it is entirely possible that this myth transforms or interprets a particular set of "original" powers of Demeter that are imagined to be relatively free from patriarchal influence precisely so that they can be replaced by honors and powers that appear considerably more significant even while they simultaneously involve the incorporation of the goddesses into the patriarchal system. In other words, the myth may well operate in a manner analogous to the South American myths of matriarchy studied by Joan Bamberger, that which posit an entirely invented past era in which women were in control in order to explain why women are subordinate to men at the present time ("Myth of Matriarchy").[15] Only in the slightly different case of the Demeter/Persephone myth, the present compensates for the loss of a female autonomy imagined to have existed in the past through the goddesses' acquisition of greater cultural authority.

The attempt by spiritual feminists to rescue the myth from the distortions imposed on it by patriarchal culture—in particular, the diminution and transformation of female power by rape and patriarchal marriage—also raises several important questions. Human relations in the modern world are still shaped by patriarchy. Christ's and Spretnak's version of the myth, which censors the rape and trivializes the power of marriage to shape female existence, eliminates the anger of Demeter toward acts and institutions still central in modern life. In their reading, the "pre-Olympian" story also becomes the daughter's story more than the mother's, thus attenuating one of the very few powerful representations of maternal experience in western literature before the twentieth century. Yet the expression of maternal anger, desire, and bereavement in this text is precisely what has made it of special interest to feminist literary critics like Marianne Hirsch. Hirsch argues that the infantile plentitude of the initial mother/daughter relation requires male intervention to become a story; nevertheless, it is a story that defies traditional modes of literary resolution, since the relation between Demeter and Persephone is cyclical and Persephone eternally divides her loyalties between husband and mother. "The 'Hymn to Demeter' thus both inscribes the story of mother and daughter within patriarchal reality and allows it to mark a feminine difference."[16] By contrast, the spiritual feminist myth, which avoids recognizing Persephone's emerging sexuality and the inscription in patriarchy, can provide only vague and unconvincing motives for the separation between mother and daughter.

In all ancient versions of the Demeter/Persephone myth, female experience remained at the center of the cult, so that the central pagan mystery revolved around the relation of mother to daughter rather than, as in Christianity, of father to son. Spiritual feminists use this element of the myth to assert the priority of the mother/daughter paradigm in religious history. Yet it might be far more valuable to examine critically the forces that gave this female-centered story its cultural prominence and maintained its importance for many centuries to Greek women in their Thesmophoria (a rite of course also shaped by patriarchy and politics), to the city of classical Athens, and to the larger Greco-Roman world.[17]

NOTES

1. Christ, "Laughter," 286, also admires the mother's struggle against patriarchy and marriage in order to rescue her daughter.
2. Christ, "Laughter," 201, and Charlene Spretnak, "The Myth of Demeter and Persephone," in Plaskow and Christ, *Weaving the Visions*, 72–76. See also the discussion of the significance of the Demeter myth to modern women by Christine Downing, *The Goddess: Mythological Images of the Feminine* (New York: Crossroad, 1988). For a spiritual feminist reading of the myth not discussed here, see Carol Orlock, *The Goddess Letters: The Myth of Demeter and Persephone Retold* (New York: St. Martin's, 1987). For a discussion of other feminist reactions to the Demeter/Persephone myth, see Helene P. Foley, *The Homeric Hymn to Demeter: Translation, Commentary and Essays* (Princeton: Princeton University Press, 1993).
3. Gunther Zuntz, *Persephone* (Oxford: Oxford University Press, 1971) is here attempting to reconcile through the story of the rape two possibly separate myths, a putatively Indo-European myth about mother and daughter corn goddesses and a putatively pre-Greek myth about Persephone goddess of the underworld. This intriguing reconstruction is entirely speculative, but in any case there is no evidence that pre-Greek culture in southern Greece was pre-patriarchal or matrifocal.
4. The less important Adonia may have included male participants.
5. See George Thomson, *Aeschylus and Athens* (New York: Haskell House, 1972), 119–23, T. W. Allen and E. E. Sikes, *The Homeric Hymns* (London: MacMillan and Co., 1904), 292, and Jane Harrison, *Prolegomena to the Study of Greek Religion* (Cambridge: Cambridge University Press, 1903), 120–62. This supposition derives from the role of women in other Demeter cults, not from any certain evidence. If the Thesmophoria pre-dated the Mysteries, women probably did play a

role in creating the Eleusinian myth and the cult at its earliest phases. The earliest physical remains at Eleusis are Mycenaean, although they may not be indicative of a cult at this early date. Only if the cult began at an earlier stage that was in some sense pre-patriarchal (a strictly hypothetical speculation), can the myth as we now have it represent a patriarchal re-shaping of pre-patriarchal material.

6. The activities on the opening day of the festival seem to have evoked a primitive context in which humans did not yet have all the benefits of culture (Diodorus Siculus, *Bibliotheca* 5.4.7); hence it seems likely that the myth used at the Thesmophoria, unlike that in the *Hymn to Demeter,* situated the Demeter/Persephone story at a time before humankind had received the benefits of agriculture from the goddesses (see Foley, *Hymn to Demeter,* 100, n. 64).

7. For a fuller discussion of these mythical variants, see Foley, *Hymn to Demeter,* esp. 97–103 and Jenny Clay, *The Politics of Olympus* (Princeton: Princeton University Press, 1989), 224–65 passim.

8. Like other divine marriages, the marriage of Zeus and Hera—an endogamous and incestuous marriage between brother and sister—does not involve the exchange of women by men or the imposition of patrilocal residence on the wife. For a detailed discussion, see Foley, *Hymn to Demeter,* 104–112.

9. See Jean Rudhardt, "A propos de l'hymne homérique à Déméter," *Museum Helveticum* 35 (1978): 1–17, translated in an abridged form in Foley, *Hymn to Demeter,* 198–211.

10. See further, Foley, *Hymn to Demeter,* 83–97.

11. For further discussion of the dynamics of the mother/daughter relation in the poem and the female confrontation with patriarchy, see Marylin Arthur, "Politics and Pomegranates: An Interpretation of the Homeric *Hymn to Demeter,*" *Arethusa* 10 (1977): 7–47 reprinted in Foley, *Hymn to Demeter,* 21–42 and Foley, *Hymn to Demeter,* esp. 112–37 with further bibliography.

12. See especially Orphic frag. 49 Kern, *Orphicorum Fragmenta* (Berlin: Weidmann, 1922) and Apollodorus, *The Library* 1.5.1–3.

13. See Clay, "Politics of Olympus," esp. 3–16 and Foley, *Hymn to Demeter* 175–78.

14. See further, Foley, *Hymn to Demeter,* 142–46.

15. In contrast to Bamberger, Peggy Reeves Sanday, *Female Power and Male Dominance: On the Origins of Sexual Inequality.* (Cambridge: Cambridge University Press, 1981), 179–81, 197 interprets these myths as, in some cases, a response to the disorder following Europeanization; in other cases the myths are produced by cultures in which women have considerable informal power. Bamberger's interpretation seems to fit

the Greek context better (see the use of Bamberger by Zeitlin in "Dynamics of Misogyny").

16. Marianne Hirsch, *The Mother/Daughter Plot; Narrative, Psychoanalysis, Feminism* (Bloomington and Indianapolis: Indiana University Press, 1989), 5–6; see also 102–03. The plot pattern of wrath, withdrawal, return was in fact common to both male and female stories in epic (e.g., Achilles in the *Iliad*), but the resolution of the Demeter/Persephone story marks its difference from the mortal and masculine version.

17. For short summaries of both the Eleusinian mysteries and their role in Antiquity and the Thesmophoria, see Foley, "Hymn to Demeter," 65–75.

MESOPOTAMIA: A SUMERIAN MOTHER GODDESS

A woman approaches a ferryboat as it is about to cross a river. She asks to board, but the ferryman hesitates. She sings a mournful poem; impressed by its beauty, he allows her to board, and she reveals that she has been searching for her son, whom slave traders took from her home a year earlier. As the boat arrives at the other side of the river, a ceremony is being performed in front of a gravesite. The ferryman reports that a young boy was buried there a year ago. The mother begins to call out the name of her son, and his ghost appears. She tries to grasp him, but the ghost flits away, as she continues to call him and lament.

This story sounds like an ancient Greek myth. Indeed, its general outline is not that different from the Homeric *Hymn 2* (*To Demeter*). Yet this is *Sumida River*, a Noh drama from medieval Japan. The story of a mother who overcomes all obstacles to find her missing child is so familiar and appears in so many different societies that it is tempting to ask if a universal impulse generates this recurrent tale. And, indeed, many interpreters of *Hymn 2* (*To Demeter*) take this approach. In this section, we compare the *Hymn* to Mesopotamian myths of goddesses who seek a lost son, lover, or brother; the comparisons suggest what is distinctly Greek about the story of Demeter and Persephone.

The word "Mesopotamia," Greek for "between rivers," refers to the land between the Tigris and Euphrates Rivers. The Sumerians first occupied Mesopotamia in roughly 5000 BCE. Their origins are unknown, and their language does not belong to the two large language groups in the ancient Near East, the Semitic and Indo-European groups. Sumerian city-states were independent until an Akkadian

4.10 Dumuzi the Shepherd. A clay impression or "printout" from a marble cylinder seal. 3200–3000 BCE. *bpk, Berlin/ Vorderasiatisches Museum, Staatliche Museen, Berlin, Germany/Olaf M.Teßmern/Art Resource, NY, ART497597.*

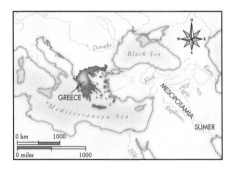

Map 4.2 A Sumerian Mother Goddess

king, Sargon the Great (2334–2279 BCE), united them. Although the Sumerians briefly reestablished their political hegemony, the Akkadians became dominant again, and eventually their language was used throughout the region, whereas the Sumerian language ceased to be spoken around 1800 BCE. Written Sumerian, however, continued to be used for many more centuries. Additionally, the Akkadians adapted the Sumerian writing system for their language. The political intermingling of these two peoples in Mesopotamia and their shared writing systems explain why Sumerian and Akkadian beliefs eventually combined to form a unified Mesopotamian system of beliefs and myths.

Two popular Mesopotamian myths, the Sumerian *Descent of Inanna* and the Akkadian *Descent of Ishtar*, describe a goddess who goes to the Underworld to rescue her lover (Chapter 5.3). The Sumerian goddess Inanna—like her Akkadian counterpart, Ishtar—was associated with war, fertility, beauty, sexuality, and cities where she was sometimes referred to as the king's consort. Her lover, Dumuzi, was a divine being (if not quite a god) associated with the changing seasons (Figure 4.10). The plot of this Mesopotamian myth in both of its versions is very similar to that of *Hymn 2 (To Demeter)*: a goddess attempts to rescue a young adult who has been taken rather suddenly to the Underworld; she is not wholly successful because, although she wins the young adult's release from the Underworld, it is only for part of the year.

Like Dumuzi and Persephone, other gods in the Mediterranean region were believed to annually descend into the Underworld and return. These gods are often described as "dying and rising gods," although scholars increasingly find this terminology imprecise, because these gods do not "die" in the Underworld in the manner of mortals; in some instances, they do not return, and when they do, their return is not the resurrection that the word "rising" suggests. Nonetheless, these gods have some similarities to one another. They were worshipped annually, and their rites consisted in lamentations over their departure that coincided with the wilting and dying of vegetation. These gods include Tammuz (the Babylonian name for Dumuzi), Greek Adonis (whose name may be from the Hebrew word for "Lord"), and the Phrygian god Attis. Significantly, Persephone is the only female among these divinities. And this distinction casts Demeter's hymn in a different light than the Mesopotamian myths of Inanna and Ishtar. The love between mother and daughter, Demeter and Persephone, conflicts with an agreement between Zeus (Persephone's father) and Hades (her uncle and husband). A stark contrast is drawn between gods and goddesses, and it is the goddesses who assume center stage in both the *Hymn* and Demeter's rituals. Persephone, unique among such figures in the ancient Mediterranean, is a dying and rising *goddess*. Thus we see through this comparison a feature that distinguishes Greek myths from those of Mesopotamia.

The following excerpt from the Sumerian poem *In the Desert by the Early Grass* tells the story of Dumuzi's death and the attempts of his lover, sister, and mother to protect and rescue him. Like the tales of Inanna and Ishtar's descent, it too has many parallels with *Hymn 2 (To Demeter)*. Most notably, the greatest portion of the poem is devoted to the quest of Duttur (mother) for her son Dumuzi, a shepherd. (Dumuzi is also identified with a parallel god, Damu, a youth associated with the rising sap of trees in springtime.) These figures, associated with the burgeoning of the natural world, both disappear at the beginning of the summer heat and drought. Duttur, searching for her son in the mountains and desert, tries to bribe the demons of the Underworld to let him live and works to revive him with beer she has brewed.

For his part, although Dumuzi seeks to contact and return to his mother, he also tries to persuade Duttur to not follow him to the land of the dead. Indeed, more than its narrative action, the poem is memorable for the poignancy of the exchanges between mother and son and the depths of Duttur's sorrow in refusing to accept the loss of her child. Duttur's plight recalls that of Demeter. Each of these myths, one Greek and one Sumerian, separated by a sea and a millennium, derives its emotional intensity from a mother's recognition of the inevitability of her child's death. Although the Greek insistence on a dying *goddess* is distinctive, the myth's central concentration on maternal loss is a powerfully resonant and enduring theme.

UNKNOWN, FROM *IN THE DESERT BY THE EARLY GRASS*

BEFORE YOU READ

Many portions of this poem are laments that may be linked to ritual. Other portions narrate events in Duttur's search for her son, who is called both Dumuzi and Damu. Translator Thorkild Jacobsen has noted the poem's "eerie and dreamlike quality," suggesting one way to read the poem. In this dreamscape, which seems to merge with the natural world of the desert, the emotional connection of son and mother stands out, making the poem strangely familiar and understandable even at a distance of some three thousand years. *Note:* Ancient texts, whether written on stone or papyrus, often contain illegible words or have been partially worn away or destroyed. Editors indicate these places in various ways: barely legible words that have been restored through careful scholarship are placed in brackets, while empty brackets or empty spaces indicate the spaces where words can't be restored or where the text has been lost. (Translated by Thorkild Jacobsen.)

**BEFORE YOU READ
CONTINUED**

- In contrast to *Hymn 2* (*To Demeter*), where Demeter and Persephone have few exchanges with one another, Duttur sings several dirges to which her son responds. What information can you glean about what has happened to Damu, the son? What is the emotional impact of the lost child's response to the mother, and how does this compare to Persephone's absence and silence?

- Compare the reactions of Duttur and Demeter to the loss of their children. In what ways are they similar? In what ways are they different?

- In the last excerpt ("Songs of the Reviving Beer"), Duttur prepares beer to revive her son. How does Duttur's action here compare to Demeter's treatment of Demophoon or Persephone?

FROM *IN THE DESERT BY THE EARLY GRASS* (c. 1750 BCE)

DAMU'S MOTHER CURSES THE DAY HE WAS CONSCRIPTED. MOURNERS TAKE UP THE CRY

"I am the mother who gave birth!
    Woe to that day, that day!
    Woe to that night!"
O Mother of the lad,
    Woe to that day, that day!
    Woe to that night!
"The day that dawned for my provider,
    that [dawned] for the lad,
    my Damu!
A day to be wiped out,   10
    that I would I could forget!
Yon night, [. . . .] that should [never]
    have let it go forth,
when my rangers, shamelessly,
    made their way
    into my [presence.]
The lad—Woe! The day destroyed him,
    lost me a son!
The lad, my Damu [. . . .]
With the nails [most] burningly   20
    [I clawed my face . . . . . ."]

                        (lacuna of unknown length)

THE DEAD GOD TRIES TO DETER HIS MOTHER FROM FOLLOWING HIM

"Mother who gave birth,
    how [could you eat the food,]

[how could you drink that water?)
Mother of the lad,
 how could you eat the food,
 how [could you drink] that water?
That food,
 the surface of it has gone bad,
 how [could you eat] that food?   30
That water,
 the surface of it has gone bad,
 how [could you drink] that water?
The food I have eaten since yesterday
 my mother [should not eat,]
the water I have poured for myself
 my mother should no[t drink!"]

"I am the mother who gave birth,   **THE MOTHER**
 but neither of heaven are you,   **RECOGNIZES NOT**
 nor are you of earth!   **THE VOICE**
I am the mother who gave birth,   40
 but neither my husband [are you,]
 [nor are you my son!]
I am the mother who gave birth,
 [in my] burning with grief
 [may you not(?) . . . .]
I am the mother who gave birth,
 but neither of heaven are you,
 nor are you of earth,
I am the mother who gave birth,   50
 but neither my husband are you,
 nor are you my son!"

"Mother who gave birth,   **THE SON CONTINUES**
 cow, low not for the calf,   **TRYING TO DETER HER,**
 turn your face toward me!   **THE AUTHORITIES**
Cow who will not make the calf answer,   **WILL NOT GIVE THE**
 turn your face toward me!   **SON BACK**
The constable will not
 give you your son,
the lord (in charge) of the plowland   60
 will not give him to you,
the lord, chief herdsman (?)
 will not give him to you!"

THE MOTHER TELLS HOW THE PITILESS RECRUITERS NOW TOOK BOTH HER SON AND HER HUSBAND

"The man, cause of dirges,
　　the lord constable,
　　　what sought he from me?
The constable, lord of the manor,
　　what sought he from me?

In Girsu on the bank of the Euphrates
He forced apart my thighs,   70
　　robbed me of my husband,
forced apart my knees,
　　robbed me of my son!

SHE WILL CLAIM HIM

"In the constable's gate
　　let me tread—
In the constable's gate
　　let me tread my mournful measure,
the 'Woe the lad!' that goes with it
　　let me dolorously say,
'He was my good fortune!'   80
　　dolorously let me say,
and my 'I, a mother who gave birth,
　　driven like an ox!' burningly let me say!

SHE ASSURES HERSELF THAT HE IS IN FOR A TERM ONLY

"After the term they have set
　　for the lad, my Damu,
　　he will come back,
　　out of the spring grass!
After [the lad] passes the day set,
　　he will come back,
　　out of the spring grass!"   90
After [the days] are full [for my Damu,]
　　he will come back,
　　out of the spring grass!"

[Omitted: A parallel myth about a mother (Mother Ninnibu) who is searching for her son interrupts the story of Dumuzi and her son.]

NARRATOR TELLS HOW THE MOTHER IN HER SEARCH IS GETTING CLOSE TO THE MOUNTAINS, THE REALM OF DEATH

From the cow its calf is gone
from the mother who gave birth
　　that which was her pleasure
　　is gone,
the waters have carried off
　　the precious one
　　from her.   100

To the mother who gave birth,
    enquiring, searching,
    the foothills
    were getting close,
like a ewe separated from the lamb
    she could not hold back.
like a goat separated from the kid
    she could not hold back.
The foothills were getting close.
    The mountain rises   110
    were getting close.
Before her rushes were rising high,
    halfa grass was rising high,
over the lad's mother
    the canebrake was rising high,
and on reed hummock after reed hummock
    the mother of the lord
    was letting tears fall.

"He who will show me my provider
who will show me   120   **THE MOTHER OFFERS**
    where my provider is   **REWARD**
to that man let me give
    things (numerous as)
    the stars of heaven!
"O lad, the things (numerous as)
    the stars of heaven,
    pertaining to you,
    things as of sounds of a hue and cry,
    come nearer and nearer,
the things (numerous as)   130
    the stars of heaven,
    pertaining to you,
    that come to me,
keep frightening me,
    and I,
with hand stretched out,
    bless toward yonder.
"Where my calf is I know not,
I am wending my way,
search according to my own judgment,   140
noon has turned into evening for me,
    the things as of sounds of a hue and cry

come nearer and nearer,
while it will come to me
    as were it illusion,
    it is true! It is true!
I am the mother who gave birth!
    I shall make Earth tremble
    like a cedar forest!"

THE DEAD SON AGAIN TRIES TO DISSUADE HER FROM SEEKING HIM

"Mother who gave birth,   150
    cow, low not for the calf!
    Turn your face toward me!
O you, cow who cannot
    make the calf answer,
the lord (in charge) of the plowlands
    is not giving it to you,
the lord (in charge) of . . . . .
    is not giving it to you!
Cow, from the riverbank
    turn your face toward me!   160
Aurochs, from Arali and the high desert
    turn your face toward me!

                             (lacuna of unknown length)

THE MOTHER DECIDES TO FOLLOW HER SON EVEN INTO THE REALM OF DEATH

"If it be required, you lad,
    let me walk with you
    the road of no return.
Alas, the lad! The lad, my Damu!"

NARRATOR

She goes, she goes
    toward the breast of the mountains,
the day waning, the day waning,
    toward the mountains, still bright,   170
to him who lies in blood and water,
    the sleeping lord,
to him who knows no healing lustrations,
to the road making an end
    of the one who walks it,
to the traces of the kings,
to the grange of the anointed ones.

The wind blew off a pure reed
    from the gipāru,
the wind blew off a pure reed, the lad,   180
    from the gipāru.

"Since I am one lying in the south winds
    lying in all the north winds,
since I am lying in the little ones
    that sink the ships,
since I am lying in the big ones
    that drown the crops,
since I am lying in the lightnings
    and in tornados,
she should not be
    where (I,) the lad, am!
    Why does she follow me?
She should not be
    where (I,) Dumuzi, am!
Again, she who cries 'alas!' for me,
    why does she follow me?"

THE DEAD DUMUZI'S DISEMBODIED SPIRIT IS A WIND BLOWING WITH OTHER WINDS

190

"For the [. . . .] who will come,
    who will take refuge with me,
who in his fleeing before him
    will take refuge with me,
my head (in readiness to leave)
    is covered with a (head)cloth.
He will escape their capture,
    and in his running
    he will take refuge with me!

THE MOTHER IS SURE THE SON WILL DESERT AND IS READY TO FLEE WITH HIM

200

"Lie down! [I shall say,]
    [as I] cover up the lad,
in his loins [I shall restore]
    the (power) to run,
the grip (?) on his pinioned arms
    [I shall loosen.]
He may say: 'My hands!'
    and the hands I shall [. . . . .]
He may say: 'My head!'
    and I shall [bandage] it
    with a piece of cloth.

SHE IMAGINES HOW SHE WILL RECEIVE HIM

210

"Food that is not food
    let me [eat] with him,
milk that is not milk
    let me drink with him.
Alas! Woe! Be off! Be off!

SHE IS READY FOR HADES

220

Go out and away!
Never [. . . . . . .]
[Alas! Woe!] My Damu,
Be off! Be off!
[Go out and away!"]

[Omitted: Dumuzi asks those he meets to take a message to his mother; he appears not to understand that he and they are ghosts.]

(SONGS OF THE REVIVING BEER)

RETURN TO THE THEME OF SEARCH THE MOTHER WILL PREPARE A REVIVING MEAL

[Your mother is approaching]
   [the gr]ange of the [anointed] ones,
for your mother's] approaching
   the grange of the anointed ones   230
your mother has laid out a meal,
   she is calling,
   your mother is calling,
your mother has brewed beer,
   she is calling,
   your mother is calling!
When your mother who bore you
   has served
   her meal which she has laid out,
   may you eat of it!   240
When your mother who bore you
   has poured
   her beer which she has brewed,
   may you drink of it!
And may your mother,
   after she has come near,
   step with you
   (up) from the bank!
(In her stepping) toward
   the bank of the river   250
   may you still be a ghost.
(In her stepping) from
   the bank may you,
   eyes healthy, cheeks healthy,
   be a man!

PERSEPHONE IN CONTEMPORARY WOMEN'S POETRY

The Homeric *Hymn 2* (*To Demeter*) tells the story of Demeter and Persephone's separation and reunion. Although the plot turns on Persephone's disappearance, it is Demeter who has the starring role. We see events unfold from her perspective, even though the hymn is written in the third person. We follow Demeter as she roams the earth, grieving and raging over the loss of her daughter. We watch her try to immortalize Demophoon, destroy the earth's flowers and fruit, demand a temple for her worship in Eleusis, and bargain with Zeus for Persephone's return from the Underworld. About Persephone's actions and emotions, we know little: she is picking flowers in a field; she is abducted by Hades against her will; she weeps; she hopes she will see her mother again. And then she disappears for most of the hymn until she is reunited with her mother.

In the hymn, we do not witness Persephone's life in the Underworld. Nor do we know how she feels about having to move between worlds every year through the deal Demeter brokers with Zeus. Throughout the hymn, Persephone is a passive victim, except for one stray detail: although the Homeric hymn says that Hades tricked Persephone into eating pomegranate seeds (line 374), Persephone tells Demeter he used force (line 414). Has Persephone lied? Has she tried to cover some untoward fact from her mother? If eating Hades's seeds is a symbol for gaining sexual knowledge or for sexual consummation, then Persephone suddenly seems an active agent in what now appears to be another perspective of a universal drama: the daughter's separation from her mother in favor of her husband (Figure 4.11).

The question of Persephone's desire is one that contemporary poets have pursued. Rita Frances Dove's *Mother Love* (1995), Rachel Zucker's *Eating in the Underworld* (2003), Louise Gluck's *Averno* (2006), Lynn Lifshin's *Persephone* (2008), and Alison Townsend's *Persephone in America* (2009) all engage this timeless tension between mother and daughter, and daughter and lover. In this section, we examine three poems that explore Persephone's perspective.

Rita Frances Dove (b. 1952) was the first African American woman to be appointed poet laureate of the United States (1993–1995). In *Mother Love*, she interweaves the myth of Demeter and

4.11 *Persephone.* Gouache on paper. Janet Gorzegno, 2010. Resembling a fresco (a painting on plaster), this painting introduces the idea of Persephone' death: she seems to be decomposing before the viewer's eyes. Persephone, though, is serene and seemingly unaware of her own dissolution. As such, she is an icon for our relationship to our own mortality as much as she is the lost daughter of Demeter. *Janet Gorzegno.*

Persephone with a modern tale of a mother, her college-aged daughter spending her junior year abroad in Paris, and her daughter's suitor, a slick Parisian who persuades her to pose nude for his paintings and then rapes her. In "The Narcissus Flower," a girl, presumably Persephone, describes her experience of rape in a way that differs from the Homeric hymn, in which Persephone tells Demeter that when Hades took her against her will, she grieved and cried (*Hymn 2 (To Demeter)* 417–432). Dove's Persephone, in contrast, conveys an intensity of emotion.

 ### RITA FRANCES DOVE, "THE NARCISSUS FLOWER" (1995)

I remember my foot in its frivolous slipper,
a frightened bird . . . not the earth unzipped

but the way I could see my own fingers and hear
myself scream as the blossom incinerated.

And though nothing could chasten
the plunge, this man
adamant as a knife easing into

the humblest crevice, I found myself at
the center of a calm so pure, it was hate.

The mystery is, you can eat fear
before fear eats you,

you can live beyond dying—
and become a queen
whom nothing surprises.

Dove's Persephone explicitly describes not only the physical impact of the rape but its devastating aftermath: while she maintains a calm in the center of violent chaos, the experience of that "calm" is transformed into pure hatred. Persephone survives this trauma through an internal stilling of her senses, a form of living death. She will be both half-alive to the world around her and half-dead—nothing will surprise her. Thus Persephone will forever be defined and transformed by trauma and circumstance, the conditions and restrictions imposed on all women. Hades's rape has rendered Persephone capable of being a queen of the dead.

In *Eating in the Underworld* (2003), Rachel Zucker (b. 1971) describes a Persephone who is not abducted by Hades but, rather, chooses him. In addition, and rather surprisingly, this Persephone rails against Demeter for refusing to accept her choice to be with Hades. The poems in Zucker's book take the form of letters and diary entries. In "Diary [Underworld]," Persephone offers an account of her relationship with Hades in a way that completely subverts the Homeric hymn.

RACHEL ZUCKER, "DIARY [UNDERWORLD]" (2003)

Only a mother could manufacture such a story:
the earth opened and pulled her down.

She shows my picture all over town
and worries the details of my molestation.

Terrified she screamed for mother . . .
but I did not scream.

She says it is like having an arm ripped
from her body. But think, Mother,

what it is to be an arm ripped from a body.
Bloody shoulder bulb, fingers twitching, useless.

Did she expect me to starve?
To wither away, mourning the tulip, primrose, crocus?

And if I have changed, so be it.
He did not choose me for my slim ankles or silken tresses.

She moans and tears her hair   *Unfair!*
There was so much I longed to teach her.

In this diary entry, Persephone calls Demeter's account of Hades's kidnapping a story her mother has manufactured to garner sympathy and attention for her own suffering. Moreover, Demeter's broadcasting of this misrepresentation serves Demeter's own ends—a glorification of her mourning and loss that comes at the cost of Persephone's identity. Persephone seems to suggest that Demeter, not Hades, has objectified and dehumanized her; it is the mother's possessive love, not the actions of Hades, that she sees as violent.

Zucker, then, gives voice to Persephone imagining events from her perspective and expressing thoughts the Greeks might have found shocking: when Persephone writes in her diary "the fields await instruction," she scornfully refers to Demeter's oversight of agriculture and suggests that she is unimpressed with her mother's expertise. In this way, she attempts to diminish her mother and thereby claim her own identity.

Alison Townsend also changes the plot of the Demeter and Persephone myth. In her collection of poems *Persephone in America*, Persephone loses and mourns her mother. Townsend, whose own mother died at an early age, focuses on Persephone's experience of loss. It is the mother, not the daughter, who dies and disappears from the storyline; in this way, Townsend inhabits the character of Persephone as she weaves myth and autobiography together. In the first poem of her collection, Townsend describes her adaptation of Persephone's story.

 ### ALISON TOWNSEND, "PERSEPHONE IN AMERICA" (2009)

Because the body is a map
and the because the map I know best
is the one of this country, I pluck her
from the pages of the book of myth
and paste her down here,
on a page in my journal,
in the middle of my life,
in the middle of the country,
wind from the end of a century
whistling around our face and ears.

I make her walk beside a wagon to get here.
I pick her up, like Midge or Barbie,
and say, *Listen, I know you're a goddess.*
But those white robes won't cut it.
I dress her the way I dressed myself
in high school so that I can remember
before it is gone—skirts
rolled up too short, white lipstick,
black fishnet stockings that left
our knees printed with diamonds.
I teach her to hitchhike
and take her to Woodstock,
skin bronzed with Bain de Soleil,
her hair streaked California blonde
the way my own once was with Sun-In.

I tell her, *In this country*
girls grow up too young, already
worried about their weight at ten.
But I take her out dancing at midnight
across the tawny fields—the Monkey,

the Frug, the Swim—all the way up
through break and line dancing,
the years humming through us
like a fast-forward film,
while she lies down with the boys
and men I remember, and the delicate,
pink rock roses of our bodies bloom and burn
but refuse to die, their petals a flag sewn
in the shape of a woman printed with stars.

I take her back. I make
her mother die when she is young
and hold her in my arms afterwards
the way I never was. I give her
a tongue, flickering like a small
green flame or a sprout of corn
in her mouth, and whisper *America*,
America in her ear while she sleeps.
I snap down the faded oilskin
Mercator projection and teach her
the names of the states, letting her love
California best for its Mediterranean air,
her feet fast in a pair of red Keds
that carry her all the way
from one coast to the other,
western meadowlark purling
a goldrush in our heads,
the history of what the body
can become here as spacious
as the sky arching above us.

I tell her the pause between breaths
is what she must always return to.
These mountains, this blue
clarity of thought and air,
golden poppies and owl's clover
blooming in clefts left
by earthquake, landslide, the flash-
fire-rape of clinical depression
that abducts us but cannot
keep us down, air breathed
from my mouth to hers, life

animating the pale white form
of a woman I walk back into daylight
with from the world below, making
of us both something greater
than loss, inscribing our names
beside those of Homer, Walt Whitman,
Zeus, and God, because it is already
the twenty-first century, and this
is America, where I say
things like this can happen.

By providing Persephone with the attributes of a twentieth-century American girl, Townsend reveals both mundane and pivotal details of her own life: trips to Woodstock, hitchhiking, and white lipstick as well as encounters with boys and men and the death of her mother. The spaciousness and beauty of the American landscape offer consolation for what Townsend describes as "the flash-fire-rape of clinical depression that abducts us," threatening to pull goddess and American girl alike into the Underworld. The poem concludes with a hope that America will allow both females to return to light and air and see their names endure, like the names of male poets and gods cited in the final lines of the poem. On this cautiously triumphant note, Townsend uses the myth of Persephone to imaginatively recover the lives, experiences, and voices of women from ancient Greece as well as our own times.

KEY TERMS

Cerberus 151

Charon 151

Demeter 156

Demophoon 159

Eleusinian Mysteries 159

Eleusis 150

Elysian Plain 152

Funerary rituals 155

Hades 149

Persephone 149

Tartarus 152

Thanatus 149

Thesmophoria 157

Triptolemus 156

FOR FURTHER EXPLORATION

Foley, Helene P. *The Homeric Hymn to Demeter: Translation, Commentary, and Interpretative Essays.* Princeton, NJ: Princeton University Press, 1993. This book collects essays from a range fields (mostly classics and psychology) on Demeter, the Homeric *Hymn to Demeter*, the Eleusinian Mysteries, and the Thesmophoria. Foley's essay, in particular, collates and addresses approaches to this material in a sophisticated yet accessible way.

Garland, Robert. *The Greek Way of Death.* Ithaca, NY: Cornell University Press, 2001 (1995). Drawing on a range of sources from poetry to gravestones, Garland offers a general picture of Hades, the Underworld, funerary rituals, and the Greek notions about death and dying that inform these expressions.

Jacobsen, Thorkild. *The Treasures of Darkness: A History of Mesopotamian Religion.* New Haven, CT: Yale University Press, 1978. Jacobsen covers both Sumerian religion and mythology in this comprehensive overview. A section on Dumuzi addresses the myths discussed here.

Parca, Maryline, and Angeliki Tzanetou (eds.). *Finding Persephone: Women's Rituals in the Ancient Mediterranean.* Bloomington: Indiana University Press, 2007. The introductory essay by the editors to the essays they have collected offers a comprehensive and balanced overview of scholarship on women's rituals that addresses the question of whether they conformed with or challenged larger social norms.

CHAPTER 5

APHRODITE, HEPHAESTUS, AND ARES

Eros, unconquered in
  Combat! Eros, that
Leaps down upon
  The herds! You
That pass the night-
  Watch on a girl's
Soft cheeks . . .
  You that stir up this
Strife between two
  Men of the same
Blood, while victory
  Goes to the force
Of love in the gaze; the
  Desiring eyes of
The bride shine with
  Wedding joy—this Power on its throne rules
Equally with the great
  Laws, for the goddess
Aphrodite at her play
  Cannot be conquered.
  —SOPHOCLES, *ANTIGONE* (781–805)

< **5.1 (OPPOSITE): Eros playfully blindfolds a woman.** Attic red-figure skyphos. Workshop of the Ilioupersis Painter, c. 375–350 BCE. Museum of Art, Rhode Island School of Design, Providence, Rhode Island. *RISD Museum Appropriation Fund, 25.089.*

THE ESSENTIALS ⚔ APHRODITE, HEPHAESTUS, **AND** ARES

APHRODITE (Venus), Ἀφροδίτη

PARENTAGE Zeus and a goddess named Dione; alternatively described as the "daughter" of Cronus's blood on the sea

OFFSPRING Eros, Erotes, and Peitho (Persuasion) (with no male) and Aeneas (with Anchises)

ATTRIBUTES Birds, the Erotes

SIGNIFICANT CULT TITLES
- Limenia (Of the Harbor)
- Pandemus (Of All the People)
- Philommedes (Laughter-Loving or Genital-Loving)

SIGNIFICANT RITUALS AND SANCTUARIES
- **Aphrodite Pandemus** A sanctuary dedicated to Aphrodite and Peitho on the Acropolis in Athens.
- **The Adonia** A festival for women only that recalled the death of Adonis.
- **Corinth** A sanctuary on Acrocorinth with sacred female servants.

HEPHAESTUS (Vulcan), Ἥφαιστος

PARENTAGE Hera alone or Zeus and Hera

OFFSPRING Twin sons, the Cabeiri (with Cabeiro) and Erichthonius (with the involvement of Athena)

ATTRIBUTES Hammer, tongs

SIGNIFICANT CULT TITLES
- Chalceus (Of Bronze)
- Cyllopodium (Of Dragging Feet)
- Polytechnes (Of Many Crafts)

SIGNIFICANT RITUALS AND SANCTUARIES
- **The Chalceia** A festival for bronze workers in Athens.
- An unnamed fire festival on Lemnos to purify the island.
- **Hephaesteion** A temple in Hephaestus's honor in Athens.

ARES (Mars), Ἄρης

PARENTAGE Hera alone or Zeus and Hera

OFFSPRING Harmonia, Deimus (Terror), and Phobus (Fear) (with Aphrodite); the Amazons (with Harmonia); and many more children with mortals

ATTRIBUTES Helmet, spear, shield, greaves

SIGNIFICANT CULT TITLES
- Andreiphontes (Manslaying)
- Deinus (Fearsome)

SIGNIFICANT RITUALS AND SANCTUARIES
- Altars in various Greek cities.

Aphrodite and Eros, her son or companion, are associated with desire, attraction, and romance. In Figure 5.1, for example, Eros rides on the back of a woman, covering her eyes as he steers her blindly forward in a game whereby players must find rocks on the ground. On the other side of the vase (not shown) a young man stands in front of a seated woman who may be Aphrodite. A bird, a frequent attribute of Aphrodite, is delicately perched on the goddess's finger; at a moment's notice, it might flit away. Both the bird and Eros's playful behavior hints at the fickle and flighty nature of desire, which Aphrodite and Eros oversee. Although the images on this vase suggest the playful and mischievous aspects of Aphrodite and Eros, the pair was also associated with conflict and violence.

In the choral ode from Sophocles's tragedy *Antigone* that introduces this chapter, Eros hovers near brides and weddings. Yet Sophocles also says that Eros leaps on herds of animals, emphasizing that Eros is a random life force that compels both human beings and animals to mate. Sophocles also credits Eros with provoking strife in families. His tragedy *Antigone* illustrates both these sides of Eros. Antigone defies state laws to bury her brother, whom she loves above all else, and is condemned to death. Her fiancé, Haemon, who loves her in defiance of his father, the king, kills himself on finding Antigone dead. Thus Sophocles suggests that Eros and Aphrodite inflame passions that are potentially disruptive and do not support familial or civic communities. The ominous mood of this ode is in stark contrast with the frivolity of the comic scene of this chapter's opening image.

LOVE AND STRIFE

This chapter examines myths and cults of Aphrodite that suggest the great ambivalence the Greeks felt toward the passions she and Eros provoke. Her worship by brides and prostitutes as well as by magistrates and citizens is explored. Myths about the disastrous unions that Aphrodite instigates among human beings, as well her own foibles with lovers both mortal and divine, are considered. Her husband, Hephaestus, the god of metallurgy, and her adulterous lover Ares, the god of war, are introduced and compared. Finally, philosophical and artistic attempts to understand Eros as a force of unfettered and compulsive desire are surveyed. Particular attention is given to how myths and cults present Aphrodite's ability to inspire love and laughter as well as sorrows and conflicts.

APHRODITE

Two different myths describe the birth of Aphrodite (Figure 5.2). In Homer's *Iliad*, she is the daughter of Zeus and Dione, a goddess about whom little else is known (*Iliad* 5.370). In Hesiod's *Theogony*, when Cronus castrates his father Uranus and tosses his genitals on the sea (Chapter 2.1), the foam (*aphros*) that collects around them becomes Aphrodite; the blood of Uranus that falls on the earth produces the Erinyes (female spirits of revenge) and the war-loving giants (*Theogony* 152–155). Hesiod says that when Aphrodite walks out of the sea onto the island of Cyprus, grass grows around her feet; this evokes her association with the earth's fertility and suggests that she is endowed with the generative abilities of her father's organ.

Hesiod calls Aphrodite "Philommedes," a title that conveys her association with sexual desire unmitigated by social consideration. If the word *medes* is interpreted as "genitals," then "Philommedes" is translated as "genital-loving." Yet many scholars think

5.2 Birth of Aphrodite. Detail of the Ludovisi Throne. Greek marble relief. Circa 460–450 BCE. Museo Nazionale Romano (Palazzo Altemps), Rome, Italy. *Erich Lessing / Art Resource, NY, ART58590.*

5.3 Aphrodite surrounded by Erotes and an attendant holding a swan. Detail from a red-figure lekythos (oil flask). Circa late fifth century BCE. *Gianni Dagli Orti / The Art Archive at Art Resource, NY, AA393928.*

"Philommedes" is an alternate form of her more frequently used cult title "Laughter-Loving," which (in Greek) has an almost identical spelling and is an equally appropriate description of Aphrodite. Indeed, Hesiod describes how Aphrodite receives "the whisperings of girls; smiles; deceptions; sweet pleasure, intimacy, and tenderness" (*Theogony* 169–170) as her portion of honors when she enters Olympus after her birth. Aphrodite's birth in the *Theogony*, then, begins in a violent cosmic struggle that hints at her connection to conflict, whereas the growth of grass and her list of honors signal that she oversees not violence but desire and attraction, both in the natural world and among mortals.

Marriage and Love Brides prayed to Aphrodite before their wedding day (Pausanias 2.34.12). From a modern perspective, it might seem perfectly natural that love and desire would be associated with marriage. In ancient Greece, however, the relationship between desire and marriage was decidedly different. Our understanding of how Aphrodite functioned as a goddess of desire must be embedded in a particularly Greek appreciation of the role of emotions in shaping marriage and other institutions. A number of visual and literary depictions of Aphrodite hint at why the Greeks did not consider love and desire necessary to the arrangement of marriages.

Aphrodite is often depicted in the company of divine winged beings and birds, such as doves, swans, swallows, and sparrows. She is also frequently shown with two goddesses: Harmonia (Harmony) and Peitho (Persuasion, or "Agreeable Compulsion"). Harmonia and Peitho are sometimes described as Aphrodite's daughters. The divine winged beings include Eros, Pothos (Longing), and Himeros (Desire), who are collectively called Erotes (plural of Eros) (Figure 5.3). Eros, the most important of these three, is generally considered a god; the other two, though divine, seem to be manifestations or personifications of Aphrodite's powers. Fleeting and flighty, the winged creatures suggest that the emotions that Aphrodite inspires are impossible to restrain or confine, perhaps hinting at why such emotions were not imagined to provide an appropriate foundation for a social institution such as marriage.

Aphrodite's involvement in causing the Trojan War suggests that love (or desire) and marriage were not always aligned in ancient Greece. A key early event in myths about the Trojan War, commonly called the "Judgment of Paris," begins at the wedding of Thetis, a sea goddess. Predicted to give birth to a son who would topple Zeus, Thetis was compelled to marry a mortal man, Peleus, with whom she eventually gives birth to Achilles, the greatest Greek warrior at Troy (Chapter 10.1). All the gods and goddesses were invited to the wedding ceremony except for one: the goddess Eris (Discord). Angered, Eris sent a golden apple inscribed with the word "beautiful" on it to the celebration. The Trojan prince Paris was asked to choose the most beautiful goddess from among Athena, Hera, and Aphrodite to be the recipient of the apple. Aphrodite promised him the most beautiful woman in the world—Helen, the wife of the Spartan king Menelaus—if he gave her the apple. Paris, unable to resist such an offer, bestows the apple on Aphrodite.

Now intent on obtaining Helen, Paris goes to Sparta and abducts (or, in some versions, seduces) her. In doing so he destroys her marriage to Menelaus, provoking the king and his brother, King Agamemnon, to marshal a Greek army to attack Troy and avenge the abduction, leading to the catastrophic Trojan War. This is perhaps the ultimate example of the ways in which the forces of desire represented by Aphrodite disrupt and destroy (rather than inspire and sustain) marriage. In many such stories, this desire is often unreciprocated: one person passionately desires another who is indifferent (or, in some cases, repulsed). Such is the case with Paris and Helen.

The abduction of Helen—the moment when Helen and Paris leave Sparta—is frequently depicted in visual arts and scrutinized in literary accounts. Whether Paris takes Helen against her will or whether she desires to go with him was a matter of debate in antiquity, and Helen's volition was depicted differently in accounts. In Figure 5.4, Aphrodite follows Helen, adjusting her headdress, while Peitho stands behind Aphrodite. Eros flits above the place where Paris and Helen physically unite as Paris holds Helen by the wrist. Interestingly, in many other images (not specifically of Paris and Helen) men are shown using this gesture in both wedding and abduction scenes. Whereas this gesture suggests their control over women, it also evokes the unknown quality and even irrelevance of female intentions. This ambivalence over Helen's participation in her abduction attaches to every bride in Greece. Marriages in ancient Greece were arranged; fathers selected suitable husbands for their daughters, whose consent (not to mention desire) was neither required nor considered. Marriages were not a consequence of love or attraction

5.4 **Paris leads Helen by the wrist, while Aphrodite adjusts her hair.** Red-figured skyphos. Circa fifth century BCE. *Museum of Fine Arts, Boston, Massachusetts, USA / Francis Bartlett Donation / Bridgeman Images, BST487717.*

between bride and groom; rather, they were strategic alliances between families who sought to consolidate power, property, and social ties.

Myths about the abduction of Helen, then, offer some insight into Aphrodite and Peitho's oversight of marriage: they secure unions that depend less on female desire than on the prerogatives of fathers and grooms. Peitho's name, "Agreeable Compulsion," captures well the role that she may have been imagined to play at such marriages. Whereas bride and groom may be compelled to marry, Peitho signals the hope that both will nonetheless find each other agreeable. Similarly, Aphrodite expresses the hope that desire and offspring will subsequently attend their union. In other words, Aphrodite and Peitho represent not the instigators of marriage but its anticipated outcomes. Thus Aphrodite's gift of Helen to Paris shows that desire inspired by Aphrodite, unlike marriages arranged by families, may be quite dangerous. Conversely, Paris's abduction of Helen also suggests that female consent of any sort in the marriage is not necessary: her groom, with her father's consent, will lead her by the wrist to her new home, no matter her wishes.

Humor and Laughter Whereas Aphrodite provokes and often disrupts marriages or causes war among mortals, among the gods Aphrodite is often connected with humor. Two myths—Aphrodite's love triangle with Hephaestus and Ares and her bickering with Persephone over Adonis—generate carefree laughter among the gods while hinting at the serious consequences of sexual infidelity in the human world.

In a comic tale in the *Odyssey*, Aphrodite's husband, Hephaestus, the god of metallurgy, decides to expose Aphrodite's infidelity with Ares, the god associated with war and aggression (8.266–366). He forges metal chains that no man or god may escape and casts them over Aphrodite and Ares while they are making love. He then invites all the gods to view the trapped couple and thus condemn their adulterous behavior. When the gods arrive, however, they marvel at Aphrodite's beauty, envy Ares's good fortune, and find no cause to be outraged on Hephaestus's behalf as he had hoped. Apollo and Hermes even snicker that they would happily be caught with Aphrodite in chains.

Aphrodite's infidelity with Ares may provoke laughter among gods, but in the context of the *Odyssey*, it also points toward the dangers of infidelity among mortals, particularly with respect to Odysseus's return to Ithaca. All the Greek men returning from Troy face a dangerous situation. If their wives have committed adultery or forgotten them, they will have no home in Greece. The most extreme formulation of this dilemma is the myth of Agamemnon's return from Troy: his wife, Clytemnestra (who is also Helen's sister), who is having an adulterous affair, kills Agamemnon on his return home. Odysseus's homecoming also depends on the fidelity of his wife, Penelope. Thus in the

Map 5.1 Aphrodite, Hephaestus, and Ares in Greece

story of Aphrodite, Ares, and Hephaestus, the laughter of human audiences who hear this tale may be like that of the gods: it may express a certain amusement at the foibles of desire and the disruptive ways of erotic attractions. Yet the laughter of human audiences may also express a measure of the anxiety they feel when they consider the consequences of Aphrodite's power to disrupt the social institution of marriage.

A myth about Aphrodite's attraction to a mortal boy named Adonis and a ritual connected to their romance are both filled with laughter, although again this laughter expresses more than simply joy and pleasure (Figure 5.10). In Paphos, the city sacred to Aphrodite on the island of Cyprus, Smyrna (or Myrrha) did not properly worship Aphrodite. To punish her, Aphrodite made her fall in love with her father. Helped by her nurse, she tricked her father into sleeping with her for several nights. Once he discovered how he had been tricked, he set out to kill Smyrna. The gods in pity turned her into the myrrh tree—a small, thorny tree that exudes a medicinal and fragrant resin. After nine months, Smyrna (in the form of the tree) gave birth to Adonis.

In some tales, Aphrodite immediately falls in love with the boy and hides him away from the other gods. Persephone, on seeing him, also falls in love with Adonis. Zeus then intervenes and forces the goddesses to share the handsome youth: he must spend part of the year in the Underworld with Persephone, and part of the year with Aphrodite. In other tales, Aphrodite falls in love with Adonis when she sees him after being accidently pricked by one of Eros's arrows, which were believed to compel attraction. Adonis is later killed by a boar when out hunting (in some versions, a jealous Ares incites the boar to kill Adonis). Aphrodite ministers to Adonis in his death; from the mixture of his blood with divine nectar the anemone flower is created. In both versions of the story of Aphrodite's love for Adonis, humor is invoked by the idea of a mighty goddess being smitten with an unquenchable desire for a mortal boy as well as the undignified squabbling her passion evokes. But that humor—like mortal love affairs—is also shadowed by the very human grief Aphrodite experiences over his loss. Both Aphrodite's laughter and her sorrows are part of a ritual called the Adonia.

The Adonia recalls the Eleusinian Mysteries of Demeter: both rituals concern a deity (Persephone or Adonis) who travels to and from the Underworld (Chapter 4.1). Yet, unlike Demeter's Mysteries in Eleusis, only women celebrated the Adonia. They placed small containers of plants that would sprout quickly and die on rooftops. These plants represented Aphrodite's lover Adonis, who died while still a young man. The women would stage a mock funeral for Adonis, lamenting his brief life and death. Classicist John J. Winkler (1946–1990), whose essay on the Adonia appears in the next section, focuses on the women's laughter, not their mourning. He argues that the quick sprouting and withering of the plants, which imitated male sexual functioning, prompted women's laughter. Laughing at the withering may have been a way to diminish Aphrodite's powers in the sexual realm, or at least keep them at a distance. It may also be an anxious laughter, an attempt to fend off Aphrodite, who inspires bonds of affection that death tears apart. Some scholars argue that women's mourning during the Adonia had important social significance in Athens, particularly during the Peloponnesian War. The festival allowed women to lament the male relatives they lost at war but were prohibited from lamenting publicly.

Aphrodite's laughter has many facets that go beyond romance. Indeed, the bonds of affection she could inspire were vital ingredients in many relationships, especially civic ones, for Aphrodite was worshipped in city centers. She was also honored at the seaports, where commercial, political, and personal interactions took place.

Civic Harmony Aphrodite (along with Peitho) was important in the establishment and governance of cities. In part, the role Peitho and Aphrodite played in courtship and marriage illuminates why this was so. If "agreeable compulsion" is an apt way to describe marriages that depended on familial agreements rather than individual (especially female) choice, it also fittingly describes shared governance among citizens, who have not chosen to be in a community with one another but nonetheless dwell in the same city. They must find ways to govern themselves. The amatory persuasion that Peitho oversees in romance and marriage finds its counterpart in the rhetorical persuasion used in courts and assemblies; the amorous attraction overseen by Aphrodite is parallel to the bonds among citizens that create social and communal cohesion. Aristotle acknowledges these similarities when he compares the relationship husbands have with their wives to shared governance among citizens, further indicating that Greeks drew comparisons between marital and civic bonds (*Politics* 1259a37–b10).

Aphrodite's cult title "Pandemus" (Of All the People) also suggests her role as a unifying force. Pausanias describes Aphrodite Pandemus's cult in Athens, reporting that when Theseus, the legendary king of Athens, joined all the people of Athens into one civic body, he established a cult to Aphrodite Pandemus and Peitho on the south slope of the Acropolis. Whereas ancient scholars attribute the establishment of this cult to Solon (638–538 BCE), an Athenian lawmaker who instituted many economic and political reforms that helped to unify Athens, some modern scholars argue that the cult was established when Cleisthenes (570–507 BCE), a founder of Athenian democracy, reorganized the political units in Athens in order to establish democratic principles of governance. A common thread in all these possible origins explains the cult's significance: the worship of these goddesses is associated with the unification of Athens and communal bonds among its members. A festival called the Aphrodisia in Athens celebrated Aphrodite's assistance in the unification of Athenians.

Aphrodite, in her guise of overseeing communal sentiments and camaraderie, often found a place in ports and harbors, where economic and cultural exchanges were common. In addition to her cults in the Acropolis, Aphrodite had several cults around the Athenian port of Peiraeus. She also had many cults in harbors, on islands, and on the tips of peninsulas throughout Greece. In Corinth, a thriving port city, Aphrodite had a temple on Acrocorinth, a high, rocky outcropping above the city's harbor. There she had many female servants, who may have been prostitutes whose earnings supported the sanctuary. (Scholars dispute the religious and commercial aspects of their activities.) Her cult title Limenia (Of the Harbor) confirms this association. Aphrodite's amatory, political, and nautical aspects all have a common denominator: when more than one person is present and mutual cooperation is vital, Aphrodite is nearby.

HEPHAESTUS

Aphrodite is paired with different male companions, two of whom are Olympian gods. Hephaestus, the god of metallurgy, is her husband, whereas Ares, the god of war, is her lover. These two gods, unlike the other Olympians, are seldom worshipped: they have few sanctuaries or festivals in their honor. Of the two, Hephaestus appears in more myths and has more rituals, but neither was as important as Aphrodite or the other twelve Olympians.

Hephaestus is unusual among the gods because of his very human infirmity: he is lame. One of his titles is Cyllopodium (Of Dragging Feet). There are many versions of the story of his parentage and birth. In some myths, he was conceived by and born to Hera without any male assistance. At his birth, when Hera saw his lameness, she tossed him out of heaven. He landed in the sea, where he was tended to by Thetis, the sea goddess, and her nymphs. Hephaestus, angry with Hera for her mistreatment, crafts a throne that binds whoever sits in it and sends it to Hera as a gift. When she becomes trapped on the throne and cannot be freed by any amount of force or cunning, Zeus promises Aphrodite in marriage to whoever can release her. Dionysus plies Hephaestus with wine, encouraging him to return to Olympus to free Hera and gain Aphrodite. Dionysus then places the drunk Hephaestus on a donkey and leads him to Olympus. The visual representations of "the return of Hephaestus" are rather comic: Hephaestus slumps on a well-endowed donkey as Dionysus and satyrs prance about (Figure 5.5). This undignified procession and its accompanying myth offer one explanation of why Hephaestus and Aphrodite are married.

In other myths, Hephaestus is not born lame but, rather, is injured when Zeus tosses him out of heaven (this time for helping Hera escape from fetters by which Zeus bound her during one of their many feuds). Hephaestus lands on the island of Lemnos in the northern Aegean. There, with an island nymph he sires twin boys called the Cabeiri, who become ancestors of a race of semidivine male figures, linked to religious cults on the island of Lemnos and Samothrace.

As the god of metallurgy, Hephaestus was associated with fire and volcanoes. He was said to have a forge on Lemnos, and he was associated with a perpetual fire from the island's volcanic Mount Mosychlos. He also had a festival on the island in his honor that was connected to Aphrodite. As the story goes, Aphrodite, angry that the women of the island did not worship her, gave the women such a foul odor that their husbands turned to Thracian slave women. In revenge,

5.5 The Return of Hephaestus to Olympus. Red-figured stamnos. Group of Polygnotus, c. 440 BCE. *bpk, Berlin / Antikensammlung, Museumslandschaft Hessen Kassel, Kassel, Germany/ Art Resource, NY, ART497600.*

the Lemnian women killed their husbands (as well as all other men on the island) and were subsequently ruled by Hypsipyle, a queen. When Jason and the Argonauts land on the island, they sire offspring with the Lemnian women, thereby "breaking the spell" that Aphrodite had cast on the island (Chapter 12.1). A fire festival in honor of Hephaestus on Lemnos entails getting new fire (perhaps from Mount Mosychlos) and using it purify the island of the women's "Lemnian crimes," in part by restarting the ovens and forges of potters and blacksmiths. Hephaestus was associated with other volcanoes, particularly in Magna Graecia (the name given to the area encompassing Sicily and southern Italy colonized by the Greeks), including Sicily's Mount Etna.

Many myths and cults about Hephaestus pertain to his skills in manufacturing and technology, especially metalwork. For this reason, he is called Polytechnes (Of Many Crafts). In Athens, he was linked to Prometheus and Athena, who were associated with the crafts of pottery and weaving, respectively. Hephaestus was also associated with a festival for bronze workers called the Chalceia (Bronzes) and had a cult title, Chalceus (Of Bronze). In Athens, also, he had a temple called the Hephaesteion, appropriately located next to the Agora in Athens, a commercial center where his crafts would have been traded, bought, and sold. In myths, he constructs unbreakable chains to trap Aphrodite and Ares in the act of making love and a throne to trap Hera. He is also said to have helped with the creation of the first woman, Pandora (Chapter 2.1), and in some versions of the myth of Athena's birth is said to have assisted by splitting Zeus's forehead with an axe so the goddess can leap out (Figure 6.2, p. 249). He forges armor for Achilles in the *Iliad* (Chapter 10.1) and binds Prometheus to a mountain at Zeus's behest (Chapter 3.1). The constant attention to Hephaestus's work at his forge, his lameness, and the divine laughter (if not ridicule) that accompanies his exploits makes Hephaestus seem more human than divine. His unlikely pairing with Aphrodite, noted for her beauty and grace, suggests the humor and even unglamorous side of attraction and marriage.

ARES

Aphrodite's pairing with Ares illustrates a much less humorous aspect of her inescapable powers as well as the serious consequences of human passion and desire (Figure 5.6). Ares is the son of Zeus and Hera. His sister is the goddess Eris (Quarrels), who instigates war. With Aphrodite, he sires three offspring: Deimus

5.6 Ares and Aphrodite. Marble votive relief. Circa late fifth century BCE. *bpk, Berlin/Museo Archeologico, Venice, Italy/ Alfredo Dagli Orti/Art Resource, NY, ART332617.*

(Terror), Phobus (Fear), and Harmonia (Harmony). Deimus and Phobus accompany him on the battlefield, representing the emotional effects of battle, and Ares represents a bloodlust unmitigated by any other considerations. He represents neither courage in war nor military strategy. Ares is pure aggression, rage, and destruction and was despised by the gods and mortals alike. Even in the *Iliad*, an epic devoted to war, Homer's view of Ares is singularly negative. He describes him as a slaughterer of men: screaming, gory, insatiable in battle, and most hateful among gods. Two titles, Deinus (Fearsome) and Andreiphontes (Manslaying), summarize his character and main activity. The *Iliad* does not praise Ares but instead portrays his lack of intelligence and skills, noting that both Athena and the Greek warrior Diomedes wounded Ares on the battlefield.

The Greeks' low regard for Ares is indicated by the fact that he inspired no religious devotion and was linked to no social institutions. It is true that young military recruits from various Greek cities took oaths of allegiance to their country in his name, treaties between warring nations invoked him, and some Greek cities had altars dedicated to him. Yet the martial arts, whereby men fight in units and follow a code of conduct, fall under the purview of Athena (Chapter 6.1), not Ares. Similarly, few myths concern him. One cluster of myths associates Ares with the Amazons, a warlike race of women who dwell in Scythia, north of Greece. Ares and the nymph Harmonia are said to be the ancestors of the Amazons, thus explaining their warlike nature. The Areopagus (Rock of Ares), a rocky outcropping near the Acropolis in Athens where homicide trials were held, was where Theseus was said to have defeated the invading Amazons. In sum, Ares was a baleful figure who embodied what the Greeks understood to be man's worst instincts on the battlefield. His pairing with Aphrodite reminded the Greeks of the dangers of impossibly powerful emotions, placing the madness of war alongside the madness of the bedroom.

EROS

Like Ares, the god Eros also points to the dangerous madness associated with Aphrodite and desire. Eros is frequently described as Aphrodite's son, although in Hesiod's *Theogony* he is the fourth element in creation, following Chaos, Gaia, and Tartarus (97–99). He is described as beautiful as well as strong enough to conquer the limbs and minds of gods and mortals alike. Eros's placement at the start of Hesiod's tale indicates that he was not an Olympian, as he was born before them, and also offers an explanation of the propulsive quality of the various sorts of creation and procreation that follow. Greater than the human sexual drive, Eros is an animating, creative force that propels all living creatures not simply to reproduce but also to thrive and take

action. At Aphrodite's birth, however, Eros appears to be one of her servants. The broad scope of Eros's activities and powers now seems to be
in her control, and she assumes a more elevated position among the
gods than he. Subsequent philosophical discourses and the visual arts
indicate the varied ways the Greeks attempted to understand Eros. They
imagined him alternately as a powerful force that drives creation in
nature or culture, an adolescent boy, and even a cherubic baby. Eros as
an adolescent is often shown carrying a bow and a quiver of arrows
(Figure 5.7). These arrows, which were believed to cause anyone they
touched to fall immediately in love with the next person who came near,
represent the inexplicable and overwhelming feelings of attraction that
are as likely to lead to comic or even disastrous effect as they are to true
love.

The Philosophy of Passion More than other immortals, Aphrodite and
Eros have attracted the attention of many philosophers, who treat them
not as divinities but rather as metaphors to explain passion, love, and
lust. Empedocles (c. 490–c. 430 BCE), a philosopher from Sicily, describes how love (variously called Aphrodite, Harmony, Joy, and Friendship) acted together with strife on the four elements (earth, air, fire, and
water) to create the world. In the first stage of creation, he speculated,
parts of human and animal bodies wandered around either unattached
or incorrectly attached, until Aphrodite brought creatures and their
parts together, securing their survival. Although at times Empedocles
seems to describe Aphrodite as an evolutionary process of attraction, at
other times she retains her divinity.

In Plato's *Symposium*, perhaps the most famous Greek philosophical writing on attraction and love, Aphrodite and, especially, Eros function as metaphors more than immortals. The *Symposium* describes a
lengthy dinner conversation whose participants discuss the nature of
love. Among the guests is the comic poet Aristophanes, who provides
a myth about three types of creatures. Each is composed of two people:
either two men, two women, or a man and woman. These creatures
propel themselves by rolling instead of walking. When Zeus becomes angry
with them for their arrogance, he cuts them in two and rearranges their
arms, legs, heads and genitals so that they may walk upright as well as physically reunite with one another and thus quell their longing to return to
their original, unitary state. Despite the comic image of these roly-poly creatures, Aristophanes's tale of two souls somehow recreating their original
oneness captures the feeling of wholeness people experience when they fall
in love. No other speech in the dialogue has been as popular among ancient

5.7 Eros in the role of archer. Red-figure
lekythos, c. 500–480 BCE. *Kimbell Art
Museum, Fort Worth, Texas / Art
Resource, NY, ART334291.*

and modern audiences, except for Socrates's speech at the dialogue's conclusion.

Socrates claims he learned about love from a woman named Diotima. To explain the nature of love, Socrates describes the birth of Eros (Love). (Translated by Robin Waterfield.)

PLATO, FROM *SYMPOSIUM* (c. 385–370 BCE)

Once upon a time, the gods were celebrating the birth of Aphrodite, and among them was Plenty, whose mother was Cunning. After the feast, as you'd expect at a festive occasion, Poverty turned up to beg, so there she was by the gate. Now, Plenty had got drunk on nectar (this was before the discovery of wine) and he'd gone into Zeus' garden, collapsed, and fallen asleep. Prompted by her lack of means, Poverty came up with the idea of having a child by Plenty, so she lay with him and became pregnant with Love (Eros). The reason Love became Aphrodite's follower and attendant, then, is that he was conceived during her birthday party; also he is innately attracted towards beauty and Aphrodite is beautiful.

Now because his parents are Plenty and Poverty, Love's situation is as follows. . . . He takes after his mother in having need as a constant companion. From his father, however, he gets his ingenuity in going after things of beauty and value, his courage, impetuosity, and energy, his skill at hunting (he's constantly thinking up stratagems), his desire for knowledge, his resourcefulness, his lifelong pursuit of education, and his skills with magic, herbs, and words.

This tale of Eros's parentage explains how and why individuals pursue a lover and knowledge. Later in the *Symposium*, Socrates says, "If a person isn't aware of a lack, he can't desire the thing which he isn't aware of lacking." That Eros's mother is Poverty explains why Eros (or desire) makes one feel keenly the "lack" of something or someone; that his father is Plenty suggests how desire makes one seek a solution to this lack. According to Socrates, Eros will compel a man to desire a young man who embodies beauty. The man will then begin to desire the quality of beauty itself, leading to a desire to understand the nature and meaning of beauty. Finally, at its most refined, this desire will compel a man to take up philosophical inquiry. Thus, what first appeared to be an erotic lack that can be fulfilled by a lover evolves into a desire for the pursuit of knowledge.

The philosophical ideas embedded in Eros's birth story suggest that Socrates is creating a myth to explore the nature of passion, beauty, and philosophy, rather than exploring the nature of the god Eros. Instead, Socrates distills the mythological and religious essence of Aphrodite and Eros as a driver of cosmic and human unions and uses their essence as a metaphor to explain his own intellectual project, the quest for truth. Through his abstraction of Eros, Socrates separates Eros and the search for truth from bodily contingencies. More importantly, he elevates and nearly deifies the search for truth and beauty. For most Greeks, however, Eros, like Aphrodite, retained his compelling force as a divinity.

From Eros to Cupid(s) The visual representations of Eros from the Classical Period in Athens seem to reflect a particular cultural and social moment. Vases that depict Eros are inscribed with the word "beautiful" (*kalos*), as are many vase paintings that depict young boys being pursued by older men. The winged figure of Eros is shown with long hair and without a beard, two markers of adolescence, the age when boys had not developed the restraint and composure of an adult male citizen and were considered by the Greeks to be most desirable (Figure 5.8). In these images, Eros is an idealized young man, the sort whom elite male citizens would pursue as lovers and sexual partners. By the cultural logic of Athens at that time, such relationships facilitated the development of youth as successful citizens and soldiers of Athens. This social practice, wherein older men had relationships with younger ones, is described in literary evidence, such as Plato's *Symposium*, legal speeches, and erotic poetry. This Eros, then, is a desirable yet potentially fickle adolescent; he has not yet learned the restraints imposed by adulthood. His depiction not only alludes to a social-sexual practice among Athenian men but also suggests that Eros is a desire that requires control and constraint.

5.8 **Eros chases Atalanta.** Detail from a red-figure lekythos. Attributed to Douris, c. 500 BCE. *Cleveland Museum of Art, OH, USA / Leonard C. Hanna, Jr. Fund / Bridgeman Images, CVLI761955.*

Over time, however, Eros was increasingly shown not as an adolescent but as an infant, or even a group of infants. (Rather confusingly, these infants are called Erotes, the same term used to refer to Eros, Himeros [Desire], and Pothos [Longing] when they are depicted as adolescents.) The infant Erotes are often not individually named and appear in even greater numbers than three. The transformation of Eros from a single adolescent, winged boy to several pudgy infants is variously called "pluralization" or "infantilization." Increasingly common in the third century BCE in Greece, this change reached its conclusion in the Roman world, where Eros was called either Amor or Cupid (with no difference in meaning). Cupids (or Amores) are depicted in Roman literature and images as making perfume, playing hide-and-seek, hunting, driving chariots, or holding fishing rods, or are depicted simply entwined with ribbons as decorative elements in Roman wall paintings, mosaics, and reliefs (Figure 5.9). These cavorting infant Cupids seem to have little, if any, association with their identity as divine figures associated with desire.

These changing representations of Eros, then, are not simply aesthetic choices; rather, they capture different responses to Eros over time. Erotes (or Cupids) as several babies are charming and inconsequential; they portray an aspect of passion in human life that is quite different than that depicted by the

5.9 A group of Cupids make perfume. Plaster and pigment. Detail from a mythological scene on a wall. Circa 50–75 CE. *The J. Paul Getty Museum, Malibu CA 72.AG.81. Digital image courtesy of the Getty's Open Content Program.*

muscular, winged adolescent Eros. Infantilization and pluralization make it difficult to find any trace of Hesiod's elusive and primordial Eros on Roman walls. The diminution of Eros may suggest that less value was placed on human sexuality in Rome, or it may be an attempt to lessen the importance placed on the passions in human life. In either view, the Roman Cupids seem a world apart from the Greek Aphrodite and Eros and the gravely serious roles they played in the sexual, social, and political institutions, as indicated by Greek myths and rituals.

BEFORE YOU READ

UNKNOWN, *HYMN 5: TO APHRODITE*

Aphrodite appears as a gloriously powerful and vital goddess in the Homeric hymn in her honor. She seduces the mortal Anchises, conceiving and then giving birth to Aeneas, the legendary founder of Rome. Aphrodite inspires great desire in Anchises, but also fear; the tale, which evokes the limits of human mortality, infuses the hymn with solemnity. Not only will Anchises die, but so too will her son Aeneas. This sobering thought does not detract from the wonder of Aphrodite's visit to Anchises in the hills of Ida. Nor does it detract from the humor generated by Aphrodite's outsized body, her shame at loving a mortal man, and the various ways she tries to hide her own desire. Laughter, beauty, danger, and even sorrow accompany Aphrodite and the desire she inspires wherever she goes. (Translated by Michael Crudden.)

- Why does Zeus cause Aphrodite to fall in love with Anchises? What are the consequences of her actions?

- What particular moments in Anchises and Aphrodite's interactions are amusing? How is the laughter (or amusement) these moments create similar to other instances in which Aphrodite is associated with laugher?

- How does this hymn represent relationships between gods, goddesses, and mortals? Can you draw any conclusions about whether and how the gods love human beings?

UNKNOWN, *HYMN 5: TO APHRODITE* (c. 700 BCE)

Speak to me, Muse, of golden Aphrodite's works,
The Cyprian's—she who sends sweet desire on the gods, and subdues
The tribes of mortal men, the birds that fly through the air,
And all the many wild beasts that are nurtured by land and sea:
The works of Kythera's fair-crowned goddess concern all these.
    There are three whose minds she cannot persuade or beguile—
        and the child
Of Zeus who bears the *aigis*, bright-eyed Athena, is one.
For not pleasing to her are golden Aphrodite's works,
But what is pleasing to her are wars and Ares' work,
Combats and battles, and being busy with splendid works—   11
She was the first who taught the craftsmen on earth to make carts
And chariots gleaming with bronze, and she taught her splendid works
To the soft-skinned maidens in halls, inspiring each one's mind.
    Aphrodite the lover of smiles can also never subdue
Artemis—goddess with distaff of gold, whose cry resounds—
In love: for what is pleasing to her is the bow and to kill
The beasts on the mountains, lyres and dances, piercing cries,
Shaded groves, and the city belonging to righteous men.
    Aphrodite's works fail to please the revered maid Hestia too,
Whom Kronos the cunning of mind begot as his first-born child,   22
But then as his youngest he gave her a second birth, through the will
Of Zeus who bears the *aigis*, his queenly goddess child
Whom Poseidon wooed and Apollo. But she, unwilling to wed,
Firmly rejected her suitors, and swore a mighty oath
(Which has been brought to fulfilment), when by his head she had grasped
Father Zeus who bears the *aigis*, a virgin to be for all time,
Brilliant amongst the goddesses. Father Zeus then gave
A beautiful share of honour to her in marriage's place,
And taking the choicest portion she sat in the midst of the house.

She is a holder of honour in all the shrines of the gods,   31
And by all mortals is counted the eldest amongst the gods.
     The minds of these three she cannot persuade or beguile; none else
Can escape Aphrodite, of blessed gods or mortal men.
She even misled the wits of Zeus whom thunder delights,
Who has the greatest power, of honour the greatest share:
Deceiving even his shrewd mind whenever she wished,
She easily joined him together with mortal women in love,
Having made him forgetful of Hera, his sister and wife, who is
Of all the immortal goddesses much the fairest in form—
The most glorious daughter that Kronos the cunning of mind begot   42
With Mother Rhea, and Zeus who knows unperishing schemes
Caused her then to become his revered and true-hearted wife.
     But Zeus put the sweet desire even in Aphrodite's heart
That she be joined together in love with a mortal man,
To ensure with the utmost speed that she herself might be
To a mortal's bed no stranger, nor ever be making the boast
Amidst the gods' assembly, laughing sweetly, that she,
Aphrodite the lover of smiles, had joined together the gods
With mortal women who bore to immortals mortal sons,
And that she had the goddesses joined in love with mortal men.   52
So Zeus put sweet desire for Ankhises within her heart:
On the lofty peaks of Ida where many fountains flow
He was grazing cattle then, and was like the immortals in build.
     Aphrodite the lover of smiles, when once she set eyes on him,
Was filled with yearning; desire completely conquered her mind.
She went to the island of Cyprus, and entered her fragrant shrine
At Paphos, the place where her precinct and fragrant altar are found;
There, having gone inside, she closed the gleaming doors.
And there the Graces washed her, anointed her there with oil,
With the deathless oil that covers the gods who always exist,   62
Heavenly, sweet-smelling oil which had been perfumed for her.
And when she had clothed herself well with fair robes all about her flesh,
And was decked with golden adornments, on toward Troy then rushed
Aphrodite the lover of smiles, leaving fragrant Cyprus behind,
Completing the journey at speed high up amongst the clouds.
     To Ida, where many fountains flow, the mother of beasts,
She came, and over the mountain straight for the farmstead she aimed.
Grey wolves and bright-eyed lions fawning behind her went,
Bears and swift-moving panthers never sated with deer.
Delighted at heart by the sight, she put in their breasts desire,   73
And all together they mated in pairs through the shadowy vales.

But she herself arrived at the finely constructed huts,
And found left behind at the farmstead, alone, apart from the rest,
Ankhises, the hero possessed of beauty derived from the gods.
While over the grassy pastures the others all followed the herd,
He, left behind at the farmstead, alone, apart from the rest,
Was strolling now this way, now that, and was piercingly playing the lyre.
But then before him stood Aphrodite daughter of Zeus,
And in stature and form she resembled a maiden as yet untamed,
So that when with his eyes he perceived her he would not succumb
      to dread.   83
Ankhises, on seeing, took note, and was struck with awe at her form,
Her stature, her glossy clothes. For she had put on a robe
That blazed more brightly than fire, and was wearing twisted whorls
And gleaming floweret-cups; and chains surpassingly fair
About her tender neck were hanging, beautiful, gold,
Of exquisite craft right through—it seemed as though the moon
About her tender breasts were shining, a marvel to view.
Ankhises was seized with passion, and to her spoke these words:
    "You are welcome, Queen, to this house, whoever you are of the Blest,
Whether Artemis, Leto, golden Aphrodite perhaps,   93
Themis of noble birth, or Athena whose eyes are bright.
Or you that have come here perhaps are one of the Graces, who serve
As companions to all of the gods, and are called immortals themselves;
Or else you're one of the nymphs who inhabit beautiful groves,
Or one of the nymphs who make this beautiful mountain their home,
And the springs whence rivers flow, and the meadows where grasses grow.
On a summit seen from all sides I'll build an altar for you,
And in every season I'll make you beautiful offerings there;
But let you have a kindly heart, and grant that I be a man
Of distinction amongst the Trojans; offspring blooming with health   104
Bestow in future on me, and permit me to lead myself
A long and happy life, to see the light of the Sun
With blessings amongst my people, and reach the threshold of age."
    To him then in answer spoke Aphrodite daughter of Zeus:
"Ankhises, greatest in glory of humans born on earth,
I am no god. Why think that I'm like the immortals? No,
I'm just a mortal, a woman the mother that gave me birth.
My father is Otreus, whose name is renowned—you've heard it, perhaps—
Who over the whole of strongly fortified Phrygia rules.
But I have perfect knowledge of your people's language and ours.   113
For the nurse who reared me at home was a Trojan; right from the first
She received me, a tiny babe, from the hands of my mother, to tend;

And that's how I've also good knowledge of your people's language,
    at least.
But now the Slayer of Argos who bears the rod of gold
From the dance of Artemis, goddess with distaff of gold, whose cry
Resounds, has snatched me away. We were playing, many nymphs
And cattle-yielding maidens, ringed by a measureless throng;
But then the Slayer of Argos who bears the rod of gold
Snatched me and carried me over the many worked fields of men,
And over a vast expanse of land unallotted, untilled,   123
Where wander through shadowy vales wild beasts that eat raw flesh,
And I thought that I wouldn't touch the grain-growing earth with my feet.
But the god said that I would be called Ankhises' wedded wife,
Who would lie in your bed and give birth to splendid children for you.
The mighty Slayer of Argos pointed and showed me the way,
And then departed amongst the tribes of immortals once more;
But here to you I came, and upon me was mighty constraint.
But I beg you, by Zeus and your parents—and they, I think, must be
Worthy folk, for none who are base could beget such a man—
Take me now and show me, untamed and untried in love,   133
To your father and true-hearted mother, your brothers who share your blood:
They'll find me not an unfit, but a suitable daughter-in-law.
But send a messenger quickly to Phrygia's swift-mounted folk,
To tell my father the news, and my mother, who'll now be distressed.
To you they'll send an abundance of gold and of woven garb,
And let you accept as payment their many and splendid gifts.
When you have done all this, prepare then to hold the feast
Of desirable marriage, which men and immortal gods esteem."
    When so she had spoken, the goddess put sweet desire in his heart.
Ankhises was seized with passion; he spoke, and addressed her aloud: 144
    "If a mortal is what you are, and a woman gave you birth,
If Otreus is, as you say, your father whose name is renowned,
If the will of the deathless Conductor, of Hermes, has brought you here,
If you'll always be called my wife, then of gods and mortal men
There's none who'll stop me from joining in love with you right now—
Not even Apollo the Far-shooter launching arrows of woe
From his silver bow. I'd be willing, Lady with goddesses' looks,
Having once climbed into your bed, to enter Hades' abode."
With these words he took her hand; Aphrodite the lover of smiles
Turned herself round and walked, her beautiful eyes cast down,   156
To the bed that was finely strewn in the place where for the lord
It had already with blankets been softly spread—but on top
Were lying the skins of bears and of lions with deep-throated roar,

Beasts that upon the high mountains the hero himself had slain.
And when the pair climbed into the finely constructed bed,
Ankhises first took from her flesh the gleaming adornments she wore,
The brooches and twisted whorls, the floweret-cups and chains;
He loosed her girdle next, slipped off her glossy clothes,
And laid them down on a chair that was studded with silver nails.
By the gods' will then and fate he lay, a mortal man,   167
Beside an immortal goddess, and knew not what he did.

  But as the time approached when herdsmen drive back to the byre
Their cattle and flocks of fat sheep from the pastures where flowers bloom,
Then on Ankhises she poured a pleasant draught of sweet sleep,
And put on her beautiful clothes. In all her fine attire,
Brilliant amongst the goddesses, there in the hut she stood:
Her head reached the well-wrought roof-beam, and deathless beauty shone
From her cheeks, such as to Kythera's fair-crowned goddess belongs.
Waking him up from slumber, she spoke, and addressed him aloud:

  "Stir yourself, son of Dardanos. Why this unwaking sleep?   177
Consider now if the same as when first you saw me I seem."

  In this way she spoke, and he from slumber heard her at once.
As soon as he saw Aphrodite's neck and beautiful eyes,
He felt his heart stricken with dread, and turned his gaze aside.
Back down again he sank, and with a blanket hid
His handsome face. In plea he addressed her with winged words:

  "From that very moment, goddess, when first I set eyes on you,
I knew that you were divine; but you didn't tell me the truth.
Yet by Zeus who bears the *aigis* I beg you, don't let me dwell
Amongst humans in strengthless existence, but show me your mercy—
  the man   189
Who sleeps with deathless goddesses has no flourishing life."

  To him then in answer spoke Aphrodite daughter of Zeus:
"Ankhises, greatest in glory of humans doomed to die,
Fill yourself now with courage, and don't be so frightened at heart.
You've no reason to fear that you'll suffer some evil inflicted by me
Or the other blessed immortals, since you are dear to the gods.
You will have a son of your own, who amongst the Trojans will rule,
And children descended from him will never lack children themselves.
His name will be *Aineias*, since a *dreadful* pain
Has seized me, because I fell into the bed of a mortal man.   199

  But those who in form and appearance most resemble the gods
Amongst humans doomed to die have always sprung from your race.
Sagacious Zeus, indeed, because of his beauty snatched
Blond Ganymedes away, amongst the immortals to live

And within the abode of Zeus to pour out drink for the gods.
It's a wonder to see him there, by all the immortals esteemed,
As he draws the ruddy nektar from his golden bowl.
But unforgettable sorrow was gripping Tros at heart,
And he had no notion at all of where his beloved son
Was brought when the stormwind sent from heaven snatched him away;   208
So then for him he was making constant, unending lament.
Zeus took pity and gave him horses with nimble hooves,
Of the sort that convey the immortals, as payment for his son.
These he gave him to keep as a gift; and at Zeus' command
The Conductor, the Slayer of Argos, told him all he desired,
How his son was now deathless and ageless, exactly as are the gods.
When he heard the message of Zeus, no longer did Tros lament,
But within his heart felt gladness; and in his gladness he drove
A chariot pulled by the horses with hooves moving swift as the storm.
     And so too by golden-throned Dawn was Tithonos snatched away,   218
A man who was sprung from your race, who resembled the deathless gods.
And Dawn went to seek as a favour from Kronos' black-clouded son
That Tithonos be free of death and live throughout all time;
Zeus gave her his nod in promise, and brought her wish to pass.
But the thought never entered the head of queenly Dawn (the fool!)
To ask that Zeus grant him youth and strip off him destructive age.
So long then as he remained possessed of gorgeous youth,
Delighting in Dawn whose throne is golden, the early-born,
He dwelt by Ocean's streams at the outermost limits of Earth.
But when the first grey hairs appeared on his handsome head   229
And grew in his noble beard, away then from his bed
Queenly Dawn was staying, but kept him within her halls
And nursed him with food and ambrosia, giving him beautiful clothes.
But when he was fully bowed under the weight of hateful age,
And was not able to move or raise a single limb,
Then the best course to adopt seemed to Dawn in her heart to be this:
She set him down in a chamber, and closed the gleaming doors.
From him flows ceaseless speech, but he has no vigour left
Of the sort that in former times was found in his pliant limbs.
     I would not have it that you amongst the immortals be   240
In this way free of death and live throughout all time.
If in form and build you could live as you are, and be called my spouse,
Then the shrewd mind within me would not be enfolded by grief.
But merciless, levelling age will soon be enfolding you now,
That never departs from humans when once beside them it stands,
Old age that wastes and wearies, shuddered at even by gods.

But a great disgrace will be mine amongst the immortal gods
For ever, throughout all time, that I'll suffer because of you.
Before today they feared the murmurs and cunning plans
That I used to join together at some stage every god   250
In love with mortal women: my thought subdued them all.
But now I'll have no longer this boast on my lips to tell
Amongst the immortals, since into an act of pure folly, perverse,
That I can't bear to name, I've been tricked, been led astray from my wits,
And under my girdle conceived a child in a mortal's bed.

   As soon as he sees the Sun's light, the nymphs with ample breasts
Who inhabit this tall, divine mountain will bring the child up in their care.
They follow neither mortals nor immortal gods;
Long is the span of their lives, and deathless the food that they eat;
And amongst the immortal gods in beautiful dance they swirl.   261
They join with Seilenoi in love in the nooks of enticing caves,
And the keen-eyed Slayer of Argos is also joined with them there.
Fir-trees and high-topped oaks on the earth that nurtures men
Sprout at the birth of these nymphs; the trees with beautiful growth
Stand tall on the lofty mountains—immortals' precincts they're called,
And no mortals hew them with iron. But when the doom of death
Beside the nymphs is standing, first the beautiful trees
Dry up in the earth, the bark shrivels round them, their boughs fall down,
And it's then that the souls of the nymphs depart the light of the Sun.
These nymphs, keeping with them my child, will bring him up in their
      care.   273

   As soon as upon him comes the time of gorgeous youth,
Here will the goddesses bring and show to you the child.
But I, to inform you further of all the plans in my mind,
After four years have passed shall return, bringing with me our son.
As soon as you set your eyes upon this offshoot of ours,
You'll be filled with joy at the sight, for he'll be very like the gods;
And you at once will bring him to Ilios swept by the wind.
If any of mortal men inquire who the mother may be
That under her girdle conceived a beloved son for you,
To him let you, remembering, answer as I command: 283
   'They say he's the offspring born of a nymph with budding face,
One of those who have as their home this mountain that forest clothes.'

   But if with a senseless heart you speak and make it your boast
That you were joined with Kythera's fair-crowned goddess in love,
Zeus in his anger will blast you with thunder's smouldering bolt.
To you now all has been spoken; let you, taking thought in your mind,
Desist, don't utter my name, but dread the wrath of the gods."

When she had in this way spoken, she shot to the windswept sky.
Farewell to you, goddess who over firm-founded Cyprus reign.
From you I began; I will now move on to another hymn.   293

5.2 THEORY

MYTHS CHALLENGE SOCIAL NORMS

Speculation about how individuals (rather than entire cultures) experience rituals and interpret myths has become increasingly relevant in the fields of anthropology, classical studies, and literary studies. Since the middle of the twentieth century, women have emerged both as important subjects of research in these fields and as, increasingly, researchers themselves. It is evident that if anthropologists like Bronislaw Malinowski (Chapter 2.2) spoke only to male informants, they would not gain access to women's lives and would not be able to understand a female perspective. As female ethnographers began to conduct fieldwork and interview female informants, they found that men and women (as well as different social groups or classes) often participated in and interpreted social practices in very different ways. These differences were especially pronounced in sex-segregated societies like ancient Greece. This raised an intriguing question for classicists who study Greek myths: Was it possible that men and women experienced or understood myths and rituals differently from each other? And how might this question be answered, given the scarce textual evidence left by ancient Greek women?

Classical scholar John J. Winkler (1943–1990) takes up the challenge of determining a specifically female perspective on myth and ritual. Winkler's approach to the Adonia in his essay "The Laughter of the Oppressed: Demeter and the Gardens of Adonis" contrasts with Helen Foley's interpretation of the Great Mysteries of Demeter (Chapter 4.2). Foley concentrates on how myth and cult support and justify social structures for individuals and argues that the Mysteries encourage women to accept men's control over marriage. Winkler, on the hand, tries to determine how individuals might use myths and rituals to express their beliefs and to criticize social norms. His approach assumes that women were "vital protagonists" who

5.10 Aphrodite and Adonis accompanied by Eros and a woman. Red-figured aryballesque-lekythos. Circa 410 BCE. Louvre Museum, Paris, France. © RMN-Grand Palais / Art Resource, NY, ART433916.

actively interpreted and defined their world, rather than passively accepting male definitions of their lives. In Winkler's view, the Adonia, an all-female festival concerning sexuality and fertility, provides evidence of women's perspective on at least one myth. His study suggests the limitations of assuming that myths and rituals reinforce and impose on women the patriarchal norms of Greek society; not all myths, he argues, were men's stories that taught women to be docile and dominated.

Winkler's interpretation of the Adonia and myths about Aphrodite and Adonis serves as a reminder that much of our evidence about women in ancient Greece is based on textual evidence created and interpreted by men and is therefore not completely reliable. Winkler sees ancient Greece as androcentric—that is, focused on and concerned primarily with men. This concept, although related to patriarchy, emphasizes men's cultural practices (such as athletics, sex, or other social activities) rather than their formal roles (such as political, economic, and ritual functions) that grant them power. In an androcentric society, Winkler argues, men's talk was a "calculated bluff" to present themselves as powerful, confident, and crucial to society, while simultaneously downplaying women's activities in both the public and private domains. Although there are very few documents authored by women from ancient Greece, the female poet Sappho is a powerful exception. Winkler's interpretation of the Adonia begins with Sappho's treatment of several myths about goddesses and their male lovers, including Adonis.

JOHN J. WINKLER, *FROM* "THE LAUGHTER OF THE OPPRESSED: DEMETER AND THE GARDENS OF ADONIS"

BEFORE YOU READ

In this essay, Winkler explores what the women in Adonia were laughing about. Why did they find the myth about the death of a beautiful young Adonis and the ritual of watching plants wilt on the rooftops funny? His answer is, simply, men. Women see in this story and ritual an allegory for men's sexual activity. He observes, "Women saw their own work as sustaining and globally encompassing that of men, whose contribution to the production of children and crops is, though indispensable, relatively brief and short-lived." The women's laughter and their perspective on men's limited contributions to childbirth and childrearing reinforce neither the androcentrism of Greek society nor its patriarchal structures. Thus Winkler's approach to the Adonia challenges the notion that myths and rituals always support the premises of a society.

BEFORE YOU READ
CONTINUED

- Foley (Chapter 4.2) argues that myths and rituals reinforce and reflect social norms; Winkler argues that people can interpret and experience myths and rituals in ways that subvert or criticize social norms. Whose approach do you find more persuasive? What sorts of available evidence can you find to support your view?

- To explore the possibilities that Winkler's approach offers, speculate about how men and women might interpret the Homeric *Hymn 2* (*To Demeter*) and participate in Demeter's Eleusinian Mysteries in different ways depending on their gender. Compare your reasoning to Foley's analysis of the Mysteries (Chapter 4.2).

- If Greece was a patriarchal and androcentric society in which women were not able to leave their words in documents or contribute their perspectives to the stories we consider myths, should we think of Greek myths as exclusively Greek *men's* myths?

JOHN J. WINKLER, *FROM* "THE LAUGHTER OF THE OPPRESSED: DEMETER AND THE GARDENS OF ADONIS" (1990)

THE ENCLOSING GODDESS

To launch our own attempt to read women's meanings for the Thesmophoria and Adonia, let us turn to the work of Eva Stehle (forthcoming). In a very elegant and insightful talk to the Berkshire Conference on Women's History, Stehle noted a certain preference in Sappho for the tales of great goddesses carrying off young mortal lovers. These stories are not the exclusive property of Sappho but their occurrence in her work is suggestive.

The best documented is Dawn (Eôs), who was much given to snatching up and carrying off beautiful young men. Homer and Hesiod mention in passing that at one time or another she carried off Orion (*Od.* 5.121), Kleitos (*Od.* 15.250), Kephalos (*Theog.* 986), and Tithonos (*Theog.* 984). The story of Tithonos is told at some length in the Homeric Hymn to Aphrodite (218–38): after seizing Tithonos for his beauty, Dawn asked Zeus to make him immortal, which he did, but she forgot to ask for eternal youth as well. For a while she enjoyed his company but when the first grey hairs appeared she stopped sleeping with him; she kept him fed and clothed in her quarters, but as he got older and older and finally could not move at all she put him away in a room and closed the door. Only his voice lived on. Sappho fragment 58 is very broken but it contains the lines "rosy-armed Dawn . . . carrying off to the ends of the earth" along with references immediately before that to old age visible on one's skin and black hair turned [white] and weak knees. The conclusion seems inevitable that in some fashion or other Sappho dealt with Dawn's seizure of Tithonos and with his eventual fate.*

What Sappho sang about Selene (Moon) and the young hunter Endymion is not as clear. We simply know (from a scholiast on Apollonios of Rhodes 4.57) that she told the story. From other sources we know that Endymion was a young hunter associated with a cave on Mount Latmion in Karia: he is usually said to have been cast into an eternal sleep. Stehle perceives a pattern here. The ever-aging Tithonos and the never-aging Endymion have this in common—after the goddess has enjoyed them, both are put away in an enclosed space and are forever powerless, quiescent either in perfect sleep or in perfect senescence. If it is fair to put these two side by side we have an underlying story-pattern in which the male figure, after the goddess has loved him, is either eternally young and helpless or eternally old and helpless. In either case he has been placed outside the rhythms of ordinary human time as he has been placed outside ordinary social space. That the goddess carries the man away to her own house is a reversal of the patrilocal or virilocal pattern prevalent (though not universal) in Greek towns. The implied permanence of the union makes it a quasi-marriage. This is quite different from what gods do when they desire mortal women. Male deities come down and consummate their desire on the spot, then leave the maiden behind to become the founding mother of an important race or noble family line, usually after much suffering and disgrace.

The third Sapphic story of this type joins youth and age together. An old man named Phaon ran a ferry across one of the straits of Lesbos. Aphrodite took on the appearance of an old woman and after he had ferried her across he asked for no payment, so she rewarded him by transforming him into a young and exceedingly handsome man. According to Pliny (*nat. hist.* 22.20), the folklore of plants entered the story. The *eryngê* or sea-holly has a root which takes the form of either male or female genitals; if a man finds one with the male-shaped root he becomes sexually attractive. Pliny connects this bit of lore with Sappho and Phaon. But if nature has powers to turn a withered old man into an attractive young man, she also has powers to reverse the effect. Aelian (*var. hist.* 12.18) records that Aphrodite hid Phaon among the

---

*Ibykos (frag. 8 Page) mentioned Dawn's rape of Tithonos in tandem with Zeus' of Ganymede.

lettuces. The comparison with Tithonos and Endymion leads us to expect that the goddess will put her mortal lover away in a space removed from ordinary civilization, but why in a lettuce patch? The answer depends on herbal knowledge which few of us have occasion to use, but in Greek culture the antaphrodisiac properties of lettuce were well known and frequently referred to (Detienne 1977:67–8).

Moreover the lover hidden in the lettuce bed is not Phaon but Adonis, who is our fourth example. Sappho records that the dead Adonis was laid out by Aphrodite in a lettuce bed (frag. 211 b iii) and the same association is reported by Kallimakhos and by two Attic comedians, Kratinos and Euboulos, the latter in a play called *The Impotent Men* (*Astutoi*), literally "Those who are not erect." On the level of surface narrative the details vary: Kallimakhos and Kratinos say that Aphrodite *hid* Adonis in a lettuce bed, which might suggest that she was trying to save him from the wild pig which killed him. Sappho and Euboulos say rather that Aphrodite laid out the dead Adonis in a lettuce bed after the boar gored his thigh. The variation of details serves to show us what features of the myth are not important. In contrast to Frazer and all those who saw in Adonis a vegetation spirit, it does not matter whether Adonis is dead or not. Like Tithonos, Endymion, and Phaon, Adonis' essential fate is to be no longer erect, decisively and permanently so. Tithonos' permanent aging, Endymion's permanent sleep, Phaon and Adonis tucked away in the lettuce patch are four versions of the same exemplary tale. He whom a goddess loves ceases to be a phallic man, enters instead a state of permanent detumescence. The goddess still cares for him but puts him away in a cradle or cupboard somewhere in her house or in that part of nature which is her territory—a mountain cave or a garden.

It is not clear how this whole set of stories was taken. The same narrative can always be told with very different emphases and to support quite different points of view. Greek men undoubtedly told such tales as warnings about what dangerous female powers could do to them. Fears of impotence and castration ran high in the phallocentric half of Greek society. Even to peek at a powerful woman in the privacy of her own territory brought blindness to Teiresias and sudden death to Aktaion, both of whom were young hunters like Endymion (Kallimakhos *Hymn* 5.75, 109). For men, such stories may serve as fearful images which justify their keeping away from women's spaces.

. . .

But though we cannot go very far in establishing the sense and tenor which Sappho gave to these four myths, we can ask a slightly different question: How do these myths connect with what we know of women's rites? Adonis gives us the direct connection. Stehle provides the intepretive context. If we cut out the intrusive phallic elements from Detienne's account, we may yet be able to see the Adonia as Greek women saw it. There *is* a real contrast drawn between the eight-month agricultural labor needed to produce Demeter's grain and the eight-day sprout-and-fizzle of Adonis' gardens. The Demeter festival, as our sources say, promotes the generation both of crops and of humans. Men's role in both cases is to plow and to plant the the seed. It is Mother Earth who does the eight months' labor, as it is human mothers who carry the long burden of human generation. It is women who civilize Demeter's wheat, turning it first into flour, then into bread; it is women who nurture and train children. If any contrast is to be drawn between the respective roles of the sexes in cultivating these natural processes, men must be placed squarely on the side of Adonis, Aphrodite's eager but not long enduring lover. What the gardens with their quickly rising and quickly wilting sprouts symbolize is the marginal or subordinate role that men play in both agriculture (vis-à-vis the earth) and human generation (vis-à-vis wives and mothers).*

So I would suggest that in the growing and wilting of the sprouts we can see, among many other meanings, a sexual joke of the sort for which other women's festivals were a primary location. One may detect a small gleam of misandric humor about men's sexuality as a thing which disappears so suddenly: "O woe for Adonis!" Poor little thing, he just had no staying power. There is a vase which illustrates such an interpretation, a red-figure pelike in the British Museum (see frontispiece). A woman with an extraordinarily sweet and knowing smile on her face is tending a crop of phalloi, growing like asparagus in front of her. The lines of white paint from her right hand seem to indicate that she is sprinkling water on them. Deubner associated it with the Haloa, seeing the phalloi as real objects that have been placed in the ground, but this is to overestimate the documentary value of the picture. I suggest rather that the scene is humorous fantasy, not necessarily associated directly with the Adonia (since the plants are not in pots) but illustrating the same cultural equation.

On the surface the myths of Dawn and Aphrodite might look as if they were simply about women's *erôs*, their desire sometimes for handsome young men. But in each case the narrative brings the lover quickly to a dormant state which can be read not only as a genital but also as

---

*"Male symbolism is not absent in the [Thesmophoria], but is merely an adjunct, reduced to instrumental terms, objects which the women handle and use to enhance their own dominant role in procreation" (Zeitlin 1982: 146).

a social allegory, a statement that women and goddesses have primary control of the processes of production and reproduction, that women enjoy relative independence from male performance in the basic life processes. And it is incidentally a joke on men's *erôs*. In the communities of women such knowledge is shared, passed around, and passed on. The many religious-social gatherings of ancient Greek women, so few of which were noted by men, are the obvious location for sharing knowledge about male adequacy—or inadequacy.

The limitations constraining this essay should be obvious enough, but perhaps it is worth spelling them out. The limited question "What were women laughing at?" is just a small facet of the ensemble of meanings that must have been involved in the Demetrian festivals. I have made no attempt to give a general theory of Demeter and Korê and their separation, of the Eleusinian initiations shared by men and women alike, or of the antique agricultural significance of the rites and their incorporation into the political life of Athens. Further, the sources are evidently male authors, whose sense of shock at ritual obscenity may have exaggerated its role beyond what it would have seemed to women participants. And finally I am limited by my own partial perspective and set of interests as a American male Classicist, groping to recover by means of ancient and modern texts a more lively and authentic sense of Mediterranean sex/gender relations. The resulting account may, I fear, still be overly preoccupied with phallic issues of interest to men: instead of claiming that "phallic men are central," as Detienne's account does, mine claims that "phallic men are peripheral and their pretensions amusing." In both cases the focus is on men. And, in a sense, the energy of this essay has been directed as much or more towards Detienne as towards Demeter, and it may appear to some to be an undignified male squabble rather than the feminist exploration we would really like. But each scholar must contribute what he or she can to the corporate enterprise.

The question of how women in male-dominant cultures define and interpret reality, particularly the social and erotic aspects of their own sexuality, is extremely hard to answer for ancient societies, easier but still very difficult for contemporary societies. Safa-Isfahani, for instance, reports on the musical mimes and skits at women's parties in Iran. Though not entirely unknown to men, who occasionally parody womens' skits in bawdy songs, these little plays are almost exclusively performed by and for women.* Sex and the problems of gender feature prominently

---

*Pictures of these parties will appear in Bauer (forthcoming).

in them: a woman giving birth to a child without the support of her husband or family, a woman seducing a vegetable seller (played by a woman in drag) in the marketplace with suggestive and aggressive language, a striptease game ("I have ants" "Where do you have them?" "Here, and here, and here; what am I to do?" "Take it off! Take it off!"), and the selection of a husband. A young female character explains why each of her suitors is unacceptable in terms of his work, punning on the double meaning of "work" as making love: the grocer works with short weights, the butcher minces his meat, the mullah works bent over, the army colonel works with guns and cannons.

In this collection of texts women's consciousness about their sexuality is framed within the terms and problems created for them by normative conventions, but the women are not passive participants in their own domination, rather they are "vital protagonists interacting with the structures of their domination, necessarily exercising some degree of autonomy, not only in defining and interpreting but in redefining and reinterpreting how the dominant structures define and interpret them" (Safa-Isfahani 34). Women in these skits are active sexual and social subjects, often defying or thumbing their noses at the public conventions which supposedly determine the limits of their behavior.*

Women's alternate and subordinate discourses take many forms in different cultures, with various relations of resistance and accommodation to patriarchal standards (Warren and Bourque). On the basis of such fragile evidence as we have, it would be temerarious to insist that we have now recovered the sense of ancient Greek women's laughter, but the picture here drawn is at least more consistent with the reported facts and with comparative studies of women in other male-dominant societies. It also pushes the analysis in a more positive direction, asking us to imagine more fully the subjective world of ancient Greek women apart from the male discourse of bluff and prescription. Instead of assuming that women "accept the [patriarchal] notions of how they are supposed to feel, think, and act, because they are influenced by the weight of moral or mechanical sanctions or because they internalize these structures through socialization and enculturation processes" (Safa-Isfahani 33), ancient scholiasts and modern classicists would have done better to ask "Why are the women laughing?"

---

* When a woman asks about her ailing lover and promises to tend him, some of the therapies she will provide assume that the lover is a woman—applying eye shadow and rouge, rubbing breasts. Safa-Isfahani (43) merely comments that the woman both is the subject of the song and projects herself as the object of it.

5.3
COMPARISON

MESOPOTAMIA: ISHTAR

Many goddesses in the ancient Mediterranean share attributes, such as a connection to the fertility of the earth and human reproduction. There are similarities in their associated myths and stories, too. The Greek *Hymn 2* (*To Demeter*) and the Mesopotamian (Sumerian) *In the Desert by the Early Grass*, for example, both describe a mother goddess's search for her lost child (Chapter 4.3). The similarities in these two tales, however, do not indicate direct influence of the older Mesopotamian goddess on the Greek Demeter. To suggest such influence, historical information about direct contact between the worshippers of these goddesses is needed. Such evidence is available for Aphrodite on the island of Cyprus, where she and the Phoenician goddess Ashtart (who inherited many traits from the still-earlier Mesopotamian goddess Ishtar) were worshipped. Cyprus lies seventy miles west of the Levant (the Phoenician homeland) and six hundred miles east of mainland Greece. At this crossroads of the Mediterranean, Aphrodite came to resemble Ishtar through Ashtart. This section explores first the fusion of Aphrodite and Ashtart on Cyprus and the shared qualities of Aphrodite and Ishtar.

Aphrodite had several temples, altars, and sacred areas on the island of Cyprus, where she first stepped out after her birth (Hesiod, *Theogony* 160–164). So too did several Ancient Near Eastern goddesses. Because Cyprus was inhabited by different ethnic populations who (despite the island's small size) lived peaceably with one another, over time the worship of Aphrodite and these other goddesses came to resemble one another, in a process called syncretism: a blending among the roles, functions, and worship of different gods or goddesses. Herodotus, the Greek historian, offers invaluable insight on how and why the syncretism between Aphrodite and goddesses in the Ancient Near East occurred. He reports that the oldest temple of Aphrodite was in Ascalon (in Syria), and that the Cypriots claim their temple to Aphrodite in Cyprus was modeled on the one in Ascalon (1.105). He then adds by way of explaining why Aphrodite had a temple in Syria that "the Assyrians call Aphrodite Mylitta; the Arabs call her Alilat, and the Persians Mitran" (1.131). In this way, Herodotus indicates his belief that goddesses with different names in different languages and similar attributes are manifestations of the same goddess. Consequently, when people from different cultures recognize that they worship the same divine beings under different names, they integrate their worship practices and their gods, smoothing out any differences among them. (To be sure, this syncretism may occur without such conscious action on the part of worshippers.) Whatever the motive, on the island of Cyprus, where the worshippers of Aphrodite and

Map 5.2 Aphrodite, Astarte, and Ishtar in the Ancient Near East

Ashtart lived in close proximity with one another, the god-
desses were fused with one another. Statues of Aphrodite from
Cyprus (Figure 5.11), which (unlike statues from mainland
Greece) depict the goddess with a rounded stomach and wear-
ing ear caps, closely resemble statues of Astarte from Cyprus
(Figure 5.12).

Mycenaean Greeks settled near Paphos, a port city in
Cyprus, around 1190 BCE. There, they encountered the local
Cypriot population and adopted their worship of a goddess called
variously "Paphian" or "Queen." When the Phoenicians arrived
on Cyprus in 850 BCE, they introduced the worship of the goddess Ashtart, one of the three major Semitic goddesses worshipped in the Levant. The Phoenician Ashtart on Cyprus is a
version of Astarte, a Semitic counterpart of the Mesopotamian
Ishtar (who is herself a composite of the Sumerian Inanna and
the Akkadian Ishtar). It is through Ashtart on Cyprus that
Aphrodite and Mesopotamian Ishtar are linked, for when the
Phoenicians brought Ashtart to Cyprus, they brought Ishtar as
well. Archaeological remains dating from the eighth century
BCE at the settlement at Amathus provide evidence that the worship of these different goddesses fused over time, and the goddesses came to take on each other's characteristics. In this
relatively small geographical area, Cypriots worshipped a goddess they called "Paphian," whom the Phoenicians worshipped
as Ashtart and the Greeks worshipped as Aphrodite.

As a consequence, Aphrodite shares with the Mesopotamian Ishtar certain attributes and associations such as fertility,
sexuality, war, a male consort who dies, the planet Venus, the
sea, and attire. Clothing may seem the least important of these
details, yet it is powerfully symbolic. In *Hymn 5* (*To Aphrodite*),
Aphrodite's clothing is described in detail when she seduces
Anchises (81–90). Anchises must remove each item of her
clothing before they make love (162–166). The undressing of
Aphrodite is not simply a matter of the inclusion of realistic details. Rather, the removal of her clothing signals her loss of
power and status. Similarly, the power of Aphrodite's clothing
is made evident when she lends a remarkable girdle or sash to
Hera (*Iliad* 14.173–187) and when she dresses Pandora (*Works
and Days*). If we look at myths of Ishtar, it becomes clear that
Aphrodite's clothing—what she herself wears and what she
gives Hera and Pandora—in part derives both meaning and
power from Aphrodite's syncretism with Ishtar.

5.11 Cypriot Aphrodite-Astarte. Terracotta figurine.
Anonymous. Circa late seventh century BCE. *Museum
of Fine Arts, Boston, Massachusetts, USA /
Bridgeman Images, BST1762524.*

5.12 Cypro-Archaic Astarte II. Terracotta figurines. Circa 600–480 BCE. *Image copyright © The Metropolitan Museum of Art. Image source: Art Resource, NY, ART500335.*

The saying that "clothes make the man" might apply more accurately to Ishtar, for whom "clothes and jewelry make the goddess." Ishtar is closely connected to the Sumerian Inanna, whose clothes and jewelry are closely associated with her powers. In the Sumerian *The Descent of Inanna*, the goddess descends to the Underworld to retrieve Dumuzi, who is her lover or son; while there she is stripped of her clothing, relinquishing one item at each of the seven gates of the Underworld. The story implies that each item of clothing or jewelry represents one of her specific powers. Similarly, Aphrodite's clothing in the Homeric hymn both represents and contains her powers. The girdle Aphrodite lends to Hera, the clothing she gives Pandora, and the items with which she adorns herself take on additional meanings when seen through the lens of her Ancient Near East parallels. Far from mere signs of (female) vanity, these items are a form of numinous power.

BEFORE YOU READ

UNKNOWN, *THE DESCENT OF ISHTAR TO THE UNDERWORLD*

In *The Descent of Ishtar*, Ishtar, like Inanna, travels to the Underworld. Like her, Ishtar relinquishes one item of jewelry or clothing at each of the seven gates of the Underworld, regaining them when she leaves. Ishtar's belongings, like Inanna's, are imbued with divine power. The overall narrative structure of the story is similar to *Hymn 2 (To Demeter)*. Yet the stripping of Ishtar evokes the stripping of Aphrodite before she makes love to Anchises. *Note:* Ancient texts have often been worn away or destroyed. Editors indicate these places in various ways: barely legible words restored through careful scholarship are placed in brackets, while empty brackets or spaces indicate places where the text has been lost. (Translated by Stephanie Dalley.)

- As you read, make note of the similarities and differences between *Hymn 5 (To Aphrodite)* and *The Descent of Ishtar*. How many similarities can you find in addition to the importance of their clothing?

- Why does Ishtar travel to the Underworld? Is there any clear indication of her purpose either before she departs or after she returns?

- How does this tale describe Ishtar's spheres of influence? To what extent are her spheres of influence like those of Aphrodite?

UNKNOWN, *THE DESCENT OF ISHTAR TO THE UNDERWORLD* (c. SEVENTH CENTURY BCE)

To Kurnugi, land of [no return],
Ishtar daughter of Sin was [determined] to go;
The daughter of Sin was determined to go
To the dark house, dwelling of Erkalla's god,
To the house which those who enter cannot leave,
On the road where travelling is one-way only,
To the house where those who enter are deprived of
    light,
Where dust is their food, clay their bread.
They see no light, they dwell in darkness,
They are clothed like birds, with feathers.   10
Over the door and the bolt, dust has settled.
Ishtar, when she arrived at the gate of Kurnugi,
Addressed her words to the keeper of the gate,
    "Here gatekeeper, open your gate for me,
    Open your gate for me to come in!
    If you do not open the gate for me to come in,
    I shall smash the door and shatter the bolt,
    I shall smash the doorpost and overturn the
        doors,
    I shall raise up the dead and they shall eat the
        living:
    The dead shall outnumber the living!"   20
The gatekeeper made his voice heard and spoke,
He said to great Ishtar,
    "Stop, lady, do not break it down!
    Let me go and report your words to queen
        Ereshkigal."
The gatekeeper went in and spoke to [Ereshkigal],
    "Here she is, your sister Ishtar [. . .]
    Who holds the great *keppū*-toy,
    Stirs up the Apsu in Ea's presence [. . .]?"
When Ereshkigal heard this,
Her face grew livid as cut tamarisk,   30
Her lips grew dark as the rim of a *kunīnu*-vessel.
    "What brings her to me? What has incited her
        against me?
    Surely not because I drink water with the
        Anunnaki,

I eat clay for bread, I drink muddy water for
    beer?
I have to weep for young men forced to abandon
    sweethearts.
I have to weep for girls wrenched from their
    lovers' laps.
For the infant child I have to weep, expelled
    before its time.
Go, gatekeeper, open your gate to her.
Treat her according to the ancient rites."
The gatekeeper went. He opened the gate to her.   40
    "Enter, my lady: may Kutha give you joy,
    May the palace of Kurnugi be glad to see you."
He let her in through the first door, but stripped off
    (and) took away the great crown on her head.
    "Gatekeeper, why have you taken away the great
    crown on my head?"
    "Go in, my lady. Such are the rites of the
    Mistress of Earth."
He let her in through the second door, but stripped
    off (and) took away the rings in her ears.
    "Gatekeeper, why have you taken away the rings   50
    in my ears?"
    "Go in, my lady. Such are the rites of the
    Mistress of Earth."
He let her in through the third door, but stripped
    off (and) took away the beads around her neck.
    "Gatekeeper, why have you taken away the beads
    around my neck?"
    "Go in, my lady. Such are the rites of the
    Mistress of Earth."
He let her in through the fourth door, but stripped
    off (and) took away the toggle-pins at her
    breast.
    "Gatekeeper, why have you taken away the
    toggle-pins at my breast?"
    "Go in, my lady. Such are the rites of the
    Mistress of Earth."
He let her in through the fifth door, but stripped off   60
    (and) took away the girdle of birth-stones
    around her waist.
    "Gatekeeper, why have you taken away the girdle

> of birthstones around my waist?"
> "Go in, my lady. Such are the rites of the
> > Mistress of Earth."

He let her in through the sixth door, but stripped
> > off (and) took away the bangles on her wrists
> > and ankles.
> > "Gatekeeper, why have you taken away the
> > bangles from my wrists and ankles?"
> > "Go in, my lady. Such are the rites of the
> > > Mistress of Earth."

He let her in through the seventh door, but stripped
> > off (and) took away the proud garment of her body.
> > "Gatekeeper, why have you taken away the proud   70
> > garment of my body?"
> > "Go in, my lady. Such are the rites of the
> > > Mistress of Earth."

As soon as Ishtar went down to Kurnugi,
Ereshkigal looked at her and trembled before her.
Ishtar did not deliberate (?), but leant over (?) her.
Ereshkigal made her voice heard and spoke,
Addressed her words to Namtar her vizier,
> "Go, Namtar [   ] of my [   ]
> Send out against her sixty diseases
> > [   ] Ishtar: 80
> Disease of the eyes to her [eyes],
> Disease of the arms to her [arms],
> Disease of the feet to her [feet],
> Disease of the heart to her [heart],
> Disease of the head [to her head],
> To every part of her and to [   ]."

After Ishtar the mistress of (?) [had gone
> down to Kurnugi],
No bull mounted a cow, [no donkey impregnated a
> jenny],
No young man impregnated a girl in [the street (?)],
The young man slept in his private room,   90
The girl slept in the company of her friends.
Then Papsukkal, vizier of the great gods, hung his
> head, his face [became gloomy];
He wore mourning clothes, his hair was unkempt.
Dejected (?), he went and wept before Sin his
> father,

His tears flowed freely before king Ea.
>"Ishtar has gone down to the Earth and has not
>>come up again.
>As soon as Ishtar went down to Kurnugi
>No bull mounted a cow, no donkey impregnated a
>>jenny,
>No young man impregnated a girl in the street,
>The young man slept in his private room,   100
>The girl slept in the company of her friends."
Ea, in the wisdom of his heart, created a person.
He created Good-looks the playboy.
>"Come, Good-looks, set your face towards the
>>gate of Kurnugi.
>The seven gates of Kurnugi shall be opened
>>before you.
>Ereshkigal shall look at you and be glad to see
>>you.
>When she is relaxed, her mood will lighten.
>Get her to swear the oath by the great gods.
>Raise your head, pay attention to the waterskin,
>Saying, 'Hey, my lady, let them give me the   100
>>waterskin, that I may drink water from it.'"

>(*And so it happened. But*)
When Ereshkigal heard this,
She struck her thigh and bit her finger.
>"You have made a request of me that should not have been made!
>Come, Good-looks, I shall curse you with a great
>>curse.
>I shall decree for you a fate that shall never be
>>forgotten.
>Bread (gleaned (?)) from the city's ploughs shall   120
>>be your food,
>The city drains shall be your only drinking place,
>The shade of a city wall your only standing place,
>Threshold steps your only sitting place,
>The drunkard and the thirsty shall slap your
>>cheek."
Ereshkigal made her voice heard and spoke;
She addressed her words to Namtar her vizier,
>"Go, Namtar, knock (?) at Egalgina,
>Decorate the threshold steps with coral,

> Bring the Anunnaki out and seat (them) on
> > golden thrones,
> > Sprinkle Ishtar with the waters of life and conduct   130
> > > her into my presence."
> Namtar went, knocked at Egalgina,
> Decorated the threshold steps with coral,
> Brought out the Anunnaki, seated (them) on golden
> > > thrones,
> Sprinkled Ishtar with the waters of life and brought
> > > her to her (sister).
> He let her out through the first door, and gave back
> > > to her the proud garment of her body.
> He let her out through the second door, and gave
> > > back to her the bangles for her wrists and
> > > ankles.
> He let her out through the third door, and gave   140
> > > back to her the girdle of birth stones around
> > > her waist.
> He let her out through the fourth door, and gave
> > > back to her the toggle pins at her breast.
> He let her out through the fifth door, and gave back
> > > to her the beads around her neck.
> He let her out through the sixth door, and gave
> > > back to her the rings for her ears.
> He let her out through the seventh door, and gave
> > > back to her the great crown for her head
> "Swear that (?) she has paid you her ransom, and   150
> > > give her back (in exchange) for him,
> > For Dumuzi, the lover of her youth.
> > Wash (him) with pure water, anoint him with
> > > sweet oil,
> > Clothe him in a red robe, let the lapis lazuli pipe
> > > play (?).
> > Let party-girls raise a loud lament (?)"
> Then Belili tore off (?) her jewellery,
> Her lap was filled with eyestones.
> Belili heard the lament for her brother, she struck
> > > the jewellery [from her body],
> The eyestones with which the front of the wild cow
> > > was filled.
> > "You shall not rob me (forever) of my only
> > > brother!

> On the day when Dumuzi comes back up, (and)   160
>   the lapis lazuli pipe and the carnelian ring come
>   up with him,
> (When) male and female mourners come up with
>   him,
> The dead shall come up and smell the smoke
>   offering."
>
> (3 lines missing)

5.4 RECEPTION

PYGMALION IN HOLLYWOOD

Ovid tells us an odd story of love from the town of Amathus in Cyprus (Book X, 243–297). Pygmalion, a sculptor, has turned away from women because of his disgust at the practice of temple prostitution in the town's worship of Aphrodite. Additionally, a group of women called Propoetides had angered Aphrodite, either by denying her divinity or by keeping the wages from their prostitution rather than giving them to Aphrodite's temple. Aphrodite turned these women into stone sculptures. Pygmalion, for his part, creates an astoundingly beautiful and lifelike statue of a young woman and promptly falls in love with it. At the next festival to Aphrodite, he prays to the goddess that he be granted a wife as lovely as his statue. When he returns home, he kisses the statue and discovers, to his joy, that it has turned into a human being. She is called Galatea. They marry and have a child.

Ovid's tale of Pygmalion has attracted much attention in contemporary cinema because it permits both a consideration of significant social questions and the exploration of the effects of desire on individual identities. *Trading Places* (1983), for example, examines race, class, and moral corruption. The film is about two corrupt white investment bankers who take up a black street hustler and transform him into a young executive. To resolve their ongoing debate over whether one's fate is determined by nature or nurture, they place their protégé in competition with a rising star at the bank.

Other writers and directors have turned to Ovid's story to explore men's expectations, hopes, and fears about women—rarely is a woman cast in the role of Pygmalion. Some examples are *Ruby Sparks* (2012), *Maid in Manhattan* (2002), *Mighty Aphrodite* (1995), and *Boxing Helena* (1993). This section explores three popular cinematic versions that follow Ovid's plot rather closely: *My Fair Lady* (1964), *Pretty Woman* (1990), and *Lars and the Real Girl* (2007). These films look at the anxiety about a lover's autonomy that desire can arouse. Pygmalion turns away from love, fearful of the ability demonstrated by the Cyprian temple prostitutes to control their own sexuality. He turns instead to a statue that has no sexuality of her/its own and that cannot lure him into a relationship in which he might relinquish his own autonomy. In this reading, Pygmalion ensures his autonomy by loving an object, not a woman. Galatea can never objectify Pygmalion with her desire. By making the object of his affection a literal object, Pygmalion manages the anxiety of love.

George Bernard Shaw (1856–1950), the renowned Irish playwright and social critic, wrote *Pygmalion* in 1912 (Figure 5.13). In his play, a confirmed bachelor named Henry Higgins, a scholar who studies the range of accents in Edwardian London, makes a bet with a friend that he can transform the Cockney flower seller Eliza Doolittle into an upper-class lady simply by teaching her to speak with an upper-class

5.13 Playbill from George Bernard Shaw's *Pygmalion*, 1940. *Everett Collection. MSDPYGM EC001.*

accent. Shaw attempted to resist the romantic theme embedded in the Pygmalion story and to tell instead a tale lampooning restrictions on the political and social autonomy of women as well as what he thought were the perversities of the British class system. Shaw's transformation of the Pygmalion myth in his play, moreover, is unremittingly rational. If Pygmalion's Galatea is stone transformed through divine intervention into flesh, Shaw's Eliza achieves her transformation through the scientific study of language.

Despite his modern, unromantic, and rationalizing approach to the story, Shaw's producers and his audiences demanded at least the possibility of an affectionate relationship between Higgins and Doolittle. For generations, directors have softened the ending of Shaw's play to allow the audience to think that the characters might be in or might fall in love. For Shaw, the play was about the social and economic emancipation of Eliza, and that emancipation required her to resist the subjugation he thought would be inevitable if she married Higgins.

Although he permitted a film to be made of *Pygmalion*, Shaw refused to approve a musical version of his play. It was not until after his death that the Broadway team of Alan Jay Lerner and Frederick Loewe (lyricist and composer, respectively) offered a production of *My Fair Lady* on the New York stage (1956). The play was an instant and wildly popular hit that has enjoyed many revivals. The musical adopts a softer ending with a hint of the romantic possibilities that Shaw despised. So too did George Cukor's movie version of the musical (1964), starring Rex Harrison and Audrey Hepburn.

In all these versions of *Pygmalion* and *My Fair Lady*, the vast gulf between the social status of the male hero, Higgins, and that of his female protégée both explains and instigates the process of transforming her into a social equal, or at least someone who would be socially acceptable in Higgins's class.

Eliza, unlike the statue Galatea, has a voice, identity, and backstory. Yet she and Higgins agree that her voice must radically change in order for her to have any chance to improve her lot in life. Her education begins not with an elocution lesson but with a bath and the burning of her old clothes. Moreover, during Eliza's attempts to try out her newly acquired accent at events involving high society, Higgins advises her to say as a little as possible. Her elaborate outfits and her beauty coupled with her near silence in these scenes make Eliza less lifelike than the scenes in which she is learning from Higgins in the studio. The unsettling aspects of the film revolve around this conundrum: the more Eliza learns to speak with an upper-class accent, the less she has to say. She transforms from a vivid (if slightly vulgar) young woman to a kind of dress-up doll. This tension is only somewhat resolved when, at the movie's conclusion, Eliza decides to marry a man named Freddie who has fallen hopelessly in love with her. Only then, and with the advice of his mother, does Higgins begin to recognize something essential in Eliza's identity, something separate from her value as a successful student of language who proves his skills as teacher. The film ends when Higgins and Eliza acknowledge their attraction to each other. This romantic conclusion bypasses Shaw's social criticism and harkens back to the original Ovid.

Pretty Woman (1990) follows *My Fair Lady* in several ways. Here too the social gulf between the hero, a successful businessman named Edward Lewis, and the female protégé Vivian Ward, a prostitute, instigates their relationship. Edward and Vivian meet when Edward, visiting Los Angeles on business, gets lost and seeks directions. After hiring Vivian for the night, Edward realizes that she would be a useful companion for his week of business engagements, if he can train her to behave in a manner appropriate for the class of clients and associates he must entertain. As in *My Fair Lady*, much attention is paid to cleaning up and dressing Vivian appropriately, and it is through her beauty rather than her speech that she initially succeeds in Edward's world. When Vivian threatens to leave Edward, he realizes that his devotion to business, including his attempt to buy Vivian, has led him to place a monetary value on everything and everyone. Thus Edward has objectified everything in his world and has made himself emotionally dead. Edward realizes then that he cares for Vivian and that she has given him life (her name, Vivian, hints at her capacity to "revivify" Edward). The film ends with the two reunited.

Lars and the Real Girl (2007), in contrast, does not rely on the social gulf between hero and heroine. Instead, the heroine is an inanimate doll and thus closely resembles Galatea. *Lars and the Real Girl* explores the psychological reasons behind Lars's pursuit of a relationship with an inanimate doll. The film locates Lars's anxiety in his troubled childhood and is less about romantic affection than about his ability to support a family that will inevitably arise from his affection. As the film begins, Lars is socially awkward and alienated by his own neuroses from most members of his community. He buys a life-sized female doll, names her Bianca, and treats her in public as though the doll were his girlfriend. To encourage Lars as he comes out of his shell, co-workers, friends, and neighbors begin to treat Bianca as though she were real. In the process, Lars is drawn slowly into the life of the community and is increasingly able to assume socially defined roles like friend, neighbor, and brother.

Eventually, Lars becomes capable of assuming his most challenging social role to date: boyfriend in a committed relationship. Bianca falls ill and dies. She is mourned by the entire community, which has come to cherish the kinds of real connections that the pretense of Bianca's affection fostered. We come to realize that the piece of stone in the film is Lars, and that he is sculpted into humanity both by the reality of human affection and by the processes of ordinary social engagement in a community. In this way, *Lars and the Real Girl*, more explicitly than *My Fair Lady* and *Pretty Woman*, shows that the male hero who seeks to avoid a real girl is emotionally inanimate or dead, and it thus explicitly inverts Ovid's tale to create a modern parable about the dangers of emotional isolation.

KEY TERMS

Adonia 210	Cyprus 205	Peitho 206
Adonis 209	Eros 214	Philommedes 205
Aeneas 218	Erotes 206	Pothos 206
Anchises 218	Himeros 206	Pygmalion 242
Ares 213	Pandemus 211	

FOR FURTHER EXPLORATION

Budin, **Stephanie Lynn**. *The Origin of Aphrodite*. Bethesda, MD: CDL, 2003. This is a detailed scholarly treatment of Aphrodite on Cyprus.

James, **Paula**. *Ovid's Myth of Pygmalion on Screen: In Pursuit of the Perfect Woman*. London and New York: Bloomsbury Academic, 2011. This text offers a thorough study of film versions of the Pygmalion myth with a rich bibliography.

Kondoleon, Christine, Jacqueline Karageorghis, and Phoebe C. Segal. *Aphrodite and the Gods of Love*. Boston and New York: MFA, 2011. Richly illustrated with essays from leading scholars on Aphrodite, this volume accompanied an exhibit on Aphrodite at several museums and offers an up-to-date introduction to the goddess.

Ortner, Sherry. *Making Gender: The Politics and Erotics of Culture*. Boston, MA: Beacon Press, 1996. This collection of essays by Ortner, an anthropologist, does not address Greek material. It nonetheless offers a comprehensible introduction to how to locate women's participation in cults and gender in myths.

CHAPTER 6

ATHENA AND POSEIDON

I will cast my vote for Orestes.

No mother gave me birth, and in all things

But marriage I wholeheartedly approve

The male—I am entirely my father's child.

And this is why the killing of a woman

Who killed her husband, guardian of the house,

Can have no overriding claim on me.

—AESCHYLUS, *EUMENIDES* (853–861)

At the end of Aeschylus's *Eumenides*, Athena explains why she will acquit Orestes, who has murdered his mother, Clytemnestra: Orestes is a man. Curiously, Athena does not apply her characteristic intelligence to the circumstances of Clytemnestra's murder. Athena could have argued for Orestes's exoneration on the grounds that the god Apollo demanded he kill his mother in order to avenge the murder of his father, Agamemnon. Instead, Athena's preference for men over women leads her to declare Orestes's innocence. As she states, "I wholeheartedly approve the male."

< 6.1 (OPPOSITE): Head of Athena. Athena from Piraeus, detail of a bronze statue. Classical Greek. Circa. 350 BCE. Archaeological Museum, Piraeus, Greece. *Marie Mauzy / Art Resource, NY, ART392305.*

THE ESSENTIALS ⊰ ATHENA AND POSEIDON

ATHENA (Minerva), Ἀθήνη

PARENTAGE Zeus and Metis

OFFSPRING Erectheus or Erichthonius (with Poseidon or Hephaestus)

ATTRIBUTES Helmet, shield, spear, owl

SIGNIFICANT CULT TITLES
- Chalcioecus (Goddess of the Bronze House)
- Ergane (Worker)
- Glaucopis (Shining-Eyed)
- Parthenus (Maiden)
- Polias (City Protector)
- Promachus (Front-Fighter)

SIGNIFICANT RITUALS AND SANCTUARIES
- **The Chalceia** A festival for Athenian women during which they wove a garment for Athena.
- **The Panathenaea** A festival in Athens with athletic, military, and beauty contests as well as a procession.
- **Parthenon** The temple of the Acropolis of Athens.
- **The Plynteria** A ritual in Athens during which the statue of Athena Polias and her sacred garment were washed in the sea.

POSEIDON (Neptune), Ποσειδῶν

PARENTAGE Cronus and Rhea

OFFSPRING King Pelias of Iolcus (with Tyro); Theseus (with Princess Aethra of Troezen); Bellerophon (with Eurynome, queen of Corinth); Pegasus, a winged horse, and Chrysaor, a giant (with Medusa); Polyphemus (a one-eyed giant); Laestrygon (a man-eating giant); and many others

ATTRIBUTES Trident, dolphin

SIGNIFICANT CULT TITLES
- Ennosigaeus (Earth-Shaker)
- Hippius (Of Horses)

SIGNIFICANT RITUALS AND SANCTUARIES
- **Erectheum** A saltwater spring in the Erectheum, a temple on Acropolis in Athens.
- **Sounion** A temple on Cape Sounion, near Athens.

6.1 HISTORY

WISDOM AND WAR

This chapter investigates the extent to which Athena's declaration of her loyalty and favoritism of men in this play defines her as a goddess. We compare her oversight of men's activities (plowing, farming, sailing, shipbuilding, taming horses, governing, and warfare) with her oversight of the activities of women (weaving). We consider myths about her founding efforts on behalf of the city of Athens and consider why she, not Poseidon, the god of the seas, was the patron deity of Athens, despite its success as a naval power. Finally, we return to and evaluate Athena's sentiment, "I wholeheartedly approve the male."

ATHENA'S BIRTH

Athena's birth, as she claims, explains not only her affinity with her father Zeus (and with all men) but also her intelligence and martial skills. Of all the gods and goddesses on Olympus, no two have as many affinities or are as linked through their affection for each other as Zeus and Athena. Her birth accounts for their similarities, especially the trait of intelligence.

In Hesiod's *Theogony*, Zeus swallows the goddess Metis, who, Hesiod says, is "the wisest among the gods and mortal men" (700). Fearing a prophecy that Metis would give birth to a son who would topple him, Zeus consumes Metis when she is pregnant with Athena. He gives birth to Athena through his skull with the help of Hephaestus, who serves as a kind of midwife by releasing Athena from Zeus's skull with a whack of his axe (Figure 6.2). Metis thus becomes an attribute of Zeus and Athena. Scholars translate *metis* variously as "cunning intelligence" or "practical intelligence." Athena exhibits both aspects of intelligence in all her endeavors. She is called Glaucopis, "Shining-Eyed" or "Gray-Eyed." This description may allude to her wisdom by suggesting that she sees (that is, she perceives and understands) clearly or well. Her association with the owl may also have arisen in connection with her intelligence as indicated by her eyes.

6.2 Birth of Athena. Black-figure vase (detail). Phrynos Painter, 560 BCE. © The Trustees of the British Museum / Art Resource, NY, ART486123.

As Athena leaps out of Zeus's head, she is armed with a helmet, shield, and spear, the military equipment of a hoplite (or soldier). These attributes further indicate her connection with warfare. Aeschylus says Athena alone has access to Zeus's thunderbolts, thus reinforcing her unique relationship to her father as well as their shared martial skills. Athena's intelligence and martial prowess make her especially suited to be an urban goddess who oversees civic and military affairs. Indeed, Athena rarely appears in natural settings; she is one of the few Greek deities who has no connection to nature or natural phenomena. Born from Zeus's head in a way that is divorced from the female body and human reproduction, Athena's traits and associations pertain to culture and the cities of men.

ATHENA'S PRACTICAL INTELLIGENCE AND MEN'S ACTIVITIES

In her oversight of men's activities, Athena's intelligence appears eminently practical. She is not associated with philosophy or mathematics; she has no use for abstract thought. Her intelligence spurs technological innovations and solves problems that men encounter in their daily lives and work. Athena provides tools and skills that enable men to make use of the materials they find in the natural world, such as clay, metal, horses, trees, wool, or grains, and she is the patron of those crafts she innovates and oversees.

Craftsmen Athena's birth in full armor associates her with warfare and with Hephaestus and the craft of metallurgy, which he oversees. In Sparta, Athena is called Chalcioecus (Goddess of the Bronze House), and in Athens she is worshipped alongside Hephaestus. Whereas Hephaestus represents the power

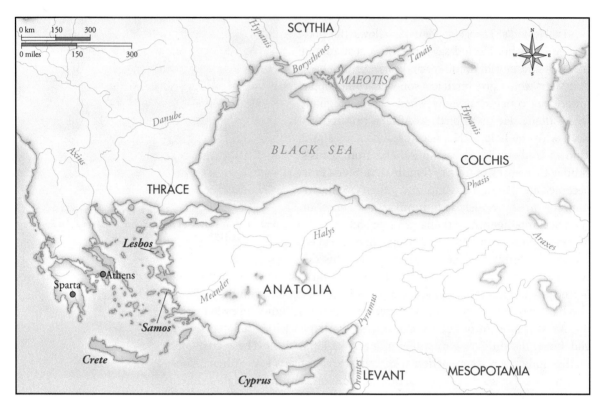

Map 6.1 Athena in Greece

of the forge, Athena imagines the uses to which forged metal may be put: for example, she invents a bridle from bronze for the hero Bellerophon so that he can harness the winged horse Pegasus (Chapter 12.1). Athena is also associated with the skill charioteers use to drive their horses. In Homer's *Iliad*, she often assists charioteers, helping them steer their horses in or out of battle.

Just as Athena devises the uses to which forged metal can be put, so too does Athena devise the varied uses for which carpenters and woodworkers might apply their skills to wood. She is credited with inventing the plough and the art of shipbuilding. Athena supervises a carpenter called Argus, who builds a ship called the Argo, for which they appear to share credit (Chapter 12.1). She also helps Tecton, a Trojan woodworker, to build ships. And just as she helps charioteers use the bridle she invented, Athena also helps sailors navigate their ships.

Similarly, Athena oversees the tools and craft of weaving. Athena's weaving associates her with both women and men. In his *Metamorphoses*, Ovid tells a story that captures Athena's fierce protection of her own role as weaver: Athena turns a girl named Arachne into a spider because she dared to challenge Athena in a weaving contest. Whereas women cleaned, carded, spun, and dyed wool and wove cloth and made clothing in their homes, men also performed a similar range of tasks in small workshops, sometimes employing slaves. Thus Athena's oversight of the various stages of weaving and wool working associates her not only with one of women's primary activities but also with a male profession. Here, as elsewhere, Athena's practical intelligence manipulates items in the natural world in the service of cultural endeavors. With bridles, men tame animals for transportation, work, and battle. With Athena's help, men build and pilot ships in order to travel the seas, and they build plows so that they may harvest grains. And with Athena, men and women shear, card, and comb wool; weave cloth; and make clothes from the animals that pasture in fields.

Soldiers Athena's involvement in war, presaged by her wearing armor even at her birth, depends on the same practical intelligence that she brings to men's professions. Athena oversees martial arts: the skills that men use both to fight their enemies and to control their own aggression. All of her martial inventions are designed to assist in the art of military engagement, by which men act with ferocity but not with blinding savagery. She provides ways of conquering enemies, including ambushes, sallies, and battle-line strategies. But she is not associated with risky confrontations, carried out with little thought and great emotion. Thus Athena's involvement with war does not create any commonality between her and Ares, the god of war, whose presence among the Olympians perhaps recognizes a human propensity toward unfettered aggression and violence in which Athena has no part (Chapter 5.1).

Whether on the battlefield or in political assemblies, Athena assists men as they balance action with thought, and courage with caution. For example, when Achilles must help the Greeks fend off the Trojans but is temporarily without armor, Athena casts her fringed aegis (a breastplate bearing the face of Gorgon) on his shoulders. She stands behind him, and together they let out a shout so terrifying that the Trojans and their horses are routed and then retreat. How could one man alone terrify an army in order to fend off their advance? By means of a well-crafted ruse; that is, by appearing larger than life, like an animal that raises its fur to appear twice its size. So Athena increases the ferocity of Achilles's form and magnifies his presence with the crafts of shouting and shining. In other words, Athena inspires Achilles to appear enraged and ready to go berserk on the battlefield, but to act with restraint and simply strike fear in the Trojans without actually fighting them.

Many of Athena's inventions pertain to warfare and enable military success through restraint, intelligence, and craft. Athena is credited with inventing the Pyrrhic dance, either at the moment of her birth or during the Gigantomachy, the great battle between the Olympians and the Giants. This dance for soldiers in full armor may have been used to develop their strength and coordination. Athena is sometimes said to have invented the technique whereby Greeks fought in ranks (*phalanxes*) and to have taught this technique to Athenians and Egyptians. She is also credited with inventing the military trumpet, called the *salpinx*. In sum, Athena's *metis* is a practical as well as cunning intelligence that solves problems through technological means and helps men subdue the world around them as well as themselves. Her activities by, for, and among men in war and work capture her advocacy of success and victory through reason acting on nature.

Heroes Athena keeps company with heroes whose adventures require varied skills and tactics, military and otherwise. Although she helps many heroes, Heracles and Odysseus are Athena's favorite mortals. When she stands beside Heracles, she is an emblem of the ingenuity he must supply when his indomitable strength is not sufficient to accomplish the labor at hand. For example, Athena assists Heracles in a characteristically practical and clever way when he must clean the stables of the Augean horses: she helps him redirect a river so that it flows through the stables, carrying away all the manure. When Heracles must kill the Stymphalian birds, Athena invents bronze rattles forged by Hephaestus so that Heracles can rouse the birds from the Stymphalian lake. Once the rattles scatter the birds from their nests, Heracles is able to shoot them with his arrows. Athena's appearance always signals that a decisive, clever, and successful choice will be made, as she motivates a man, even a powerful hero like Heracles, to adopt practical intelligence in action.

Similarly, when Perseus must behead Medusa, a Gorgon whose stare has the power to turn men to stone, Athena offers him directions and a polished shield or mirror so that he can fend off Medusa's gaze while approaching close enough to kill her. After Perseus succeeds, he gives Medusa's head to Athena (Figure 6.3). She wears it on her shield (aegis), where it serves as an apotropaic device (that is, a device that wards off the enemy by frightening him or turning him to stone). Not only does Athena deploy Medusa's head as a particularly clever and potent military device, she also invents a flute to mimic Medusa's cries when she is killed. Curiously, Chrysaor, a young man, and the winged horse Pegasus, for which Athena invented the bridle, are born from Medusa's neck when she is beheaded. Medusa's death thus leads to the generation of two living offspring, whereas Athena produces three cultural artifacts from the death: an apotropaic military device; a flute, which she soon gives away; and the bridle.

6.3 **Athena studies the head of Medusa with Perseus.** Detail from an Apulian red-figure krater. Attributed to the Tarporley Painter, c. 400–385 BCE. *Museum of Fine Arts, Boston, Massachusetts, USA / Gift of Robert E. Hecht, Jr. / Bridgeman Images, BST 1121461.*

Of all the heroes that Athena assists, none are more like her than Odysseus; Athena is described as *polumetis* (with much intelligence), as is Odysseus (Chapter 12.1). Athena and Odysseus have a deep and abiding camaraderie. With Athena's aid, Odysseus (unlike most of the Greeks who battled at Troy) successfully returns from war and recovers his house and wife. Athena's assistance always comes in the form of practical and cunning intelligence that converts physical strength into physical prowess. Thus it is no surprise that Odysseus wins the Trojan War with Athena at his side. Odysseus devises the Trojan Horse, a large wooden sculpture hiding Greek warriors in its belly, and Athena helps the carpenter Epeius build it (Figure 6.4). Odysseus and Athena's cunning intelligence wins the Trojan War, which defined and en-

6.4 Athena constructing the Trojan Horse. Red-figured Greek kylix (drinking cup). Sabouroff Painter, c. fifth century BCE. *Museo Archeologico, Florence, Italy. Scala / Art Resource, NY, ART16611.*

compassed Achilles's life, but which he could not win by his strength alone. In myths, Athena's intelligence also allows her to win the city of Athens from the god Poseidon, who wants to preside over it. We turn now to an examination of Poseidon's character and the reasons for Athena's triumph over him.

POSEIDON

Poseidon gained the realm of the sea in a contest with his brothers, Zeus and Hades. When the brothers drew lots, Zeus received the heavens, Hades the Underworld, and Poseidon the sea (Homer, *Iliad* 15.187). Although Poseidon sometimes appears on Olympus among his fellow Olympians, he is more often found in the seas. Residing between the heavens and the Underworld, he has a distinctly different character than other Olympians. Like Zeus, he sires many offspring with nymphs. Among these are Pelias, the king of Iolcus and the uncle of the hero Jason (Chapter 12.1) and the Athenian hero Theseus (Chapter 10.1). Yet Poseidon also sires many giants, the most well-known of which are the man-eating Cyclops, Polyphemus, and Laestrygon (Chapter 12.1). These giants seem to hint at Poseidon's untamed aspect that fits into neither the world of gods on Olympus nor the cities of men on earth. Even so, there were reasons that argued for choosing Poseidon, rather than Athena, as a patron deity for Athens.

Poseidon's dominion over the sea, along with his connection to equestrian pursuits, might seem to indicate a fit between him and Athens because Athens highly valued its cavalry (although it was not militarily significant) and eventually became a naval power. Ships captured from defeated enemies were dedicated to Poseidon, although unlike Athena he was not associated with naval strategies or shipbuilding. Poseidon has the cult title Hippius (Of Horses), and horses (unusually in Greece) were sacrificed to him. He is the

6.5 Poseidon. Detail from an Attic red-figure amphora from Etruria. Kleophrades Painter, 500–490 BCE. *bpk, Berlin / Antikensammlung, Staatliche Museen, Berlin, Germany/Ingrid Geske- Heiden/ Art Resource, NY, ART179889.*

father of Pegasus, the winged horse, with the maiden Medusa (Chapter 12.1). Moreover, Poseidon, like Athena, is sometimes credited with inventing the bridle and teaching mortals equestrian pursuits.

Yet Poseidon is most closely connected to the elemental power of the sea, whose stormy and powerful waves are sometimes imagined as horses (or bulls) who rush from its depths, where Poseidon was imagined to live. He is often called Ennosigaeus (Earth-Shaker), a title that associates him with earthquakes, yet another dangerous elemental force. Earthquakes along with tidal waves and springs of water were believed to be the results of Poseidon striking the ground or ocean with his trident, a three-pronged pole, with which he is often depicted (Figure 6.5). For the most part, Poseidon was worshipped on promontories such as Sounion, near Athens—where the remains of his majestic temple stand along with traces of the markings of a boat slip—and not in city centers, where Athena can be found. Poseidon was associated with the natural world—which was precisely the realm that Athena's practical and cunning intelligence allowed men to overcome.

The Contest for Athens The competition between Athena and Poseidon for the city of Athens explains how Athena came to rule that city and highlights both the commonalities and the differences between Poseidon and Athena. When the god and goddess are vying to become the champions of Athens, Poseidon strikes the ground of the Acropolis with his trident, creating a saltwater spring (which was later believed to be in the Erectheum, a building on the Acropolis dedicated to Erectheus). Athena, in her turn, plants a sacred olive tree. In some versions of this myth, the twelve gods vote to give the land to Athena; in one version, all the men vote to make Poseidon the presiding deity of their land, whereas the women vote for Athena. Because there are more women than men, Athena wins the contest. As a consequence, men deny women the rights of citizenship in Athens to appease Poseidon.

This myth makes women responsible for Athena's patronage of the city (and perhaps explains why a goddess and not a god is their patron deity) while simultaneously offering a reason for their removal from the ranks of citizens. Indeed, the city of Athens, in history not myth, was a city of men, for although it had female residents, it had no female citizens. Women in Athens, as in many Greek cities, did not have the legal standing of citizens. They could neither vote nor testify in court, and they were required to have legal male guardians throughout their lives. Or, to put it another way, this myth establishes Athens as a city of men, whose cunning and practical intelligence stands at the heart of their self-definition and achievement. Poseidon, whose horses rush from the sea and whose power was majestic yet inscrutable and untamed, could not have served to represent and explain the Athenians to themselves and to the Greek world.

ATHENA AND THE CITY OF ATHENS

Although Athena was worshipped in a number of Greek cities, nowhere was her worship and her identity as an urban goddess as developed as in Athens. No fewer than three different representations of Athena stood on the Acropolis, a rocky outcropping at the city's center largely devoted to Athena. The most ancient and holy cult statue of Athena was Athena Polias (City Protector), an olive log believed to have fallen from the sky. The most lavish statue was Athena Parthenus (Maiden), an ivory and gold statue that stood forty feet tall in Athena's temple, the Parthenon, located on the south side of the Acropolis (Map 6.2). Athena Promachus (Front-Fighter), a bronze statue of Athena brandishing her spear, stood guard at the Acropolis's entrance on the west side.

Athena Polias (the olive log) and Athena Parthenus played important roles in the Panathenaea, a festival that celebrated the arts and governance that Athens achieved under Athena's guidance. The Panathenaea was said to be a celebration of Athena's birthday or of her role in the victory of the gods over the giants. It was celebrated in two ways: the Lesser Panathenaea was celebrated every year; the Greater Panathenaea was celebrated every fourth year and had far more events and participants than the annual celebration, including musical, poetic, and athletic competitions, open to all Greek men, and military contests (equestrian and chariot events, boat races, and army maneuvers) restricted to Athenian citizens. Winners received a Panathenaic amphora (a two-handled jug that displayed Athena in full martial splendor on one side and a picture of the competition that the victor had won on the other side) filled with sacred olive oil. Additionally, members of the Athenian empire were compelled to offer a sacrificial cow and a panoply (set of arms) and to thereby acknowledge that Athenian military and political power in Greece was recognized by all of Greece.

Toward the end of the Greater Panathenaea, competitions gave way to a torch race and an all-night festival during which choruses of boys and girls sung hymns in honor of Athena. This was followed by a grand procession in Athena's honor that included women, men, and *metics* (resident aliens) in the city of Athens; the procession traveled toward the Acropolis, where hundreds of animals were sacrificed in Athena's honor. An idealized representation of this procession was carved on stone slabs that were placed on the upper walls

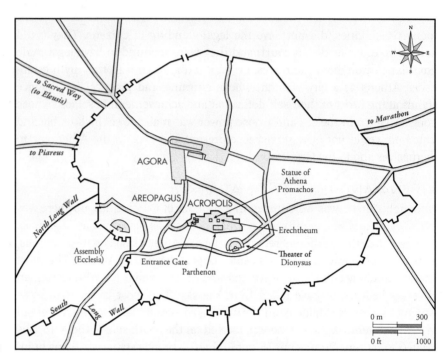

Map 6.2 Athena in Athens

of the Parthenon. In particular, on the frieze at the eastern end of the temple, seated gods calmly observe approaching worshippers. In the center of the gods, above the door of the chamber where Athena Parthenus is housed, five human figures (a man, a woman, and three young girls) are engaged in a sacred activity. One figure, whose gender has been debated, holds what most scholars think represents the gift of a garment (*peplos*) that was dedicated to Athena at every Panathenaea. Because girls and women participated in the weaving of this ritual garment, the *peplos* associates Athena with women's weaving and suggests that women also had a share in Athena's practical and cunning intelligence.

Weaving and the Women of Athens In the earliest literature as well as material evidence, Greek women are shown performing all stages of wool working. They card and spin wool, and they weave on looms that typically produced a rectangular cloth (roughly five feet by six feet) called a *peplos*. This garment was typically folded, belted and pinned to create a woman's dress (Figure 6.6). The *peplos* dedicated to Athena Polias at the Lesser Panathenaea was roughly this size. Women and girls began weaving the *peplos* for Athena Polias nine months prior to the Panathenaea at a festival called the Chalceia. The women who wove Athena's annual *peplos* were called *ergastinai* (workers); in Athens, Athena had the cult title Ergane (Worker). Young girls from elite families who were selected to worship Athena during a yearlong service called the Arrephoria participated in this weaving ritual. In yet another festival, called the Plynteria, the *peplos* was washed, and the wooden Athena Polias was escorted to the sea, where she too was ritually cleansed. During the Arrephoria, the Chalceia, the Plynteria, and the Lesser Panathenaea, women and girls cared for and dedicated woven garments to Athena, who emblematized the craft of weaving, one of the primary activities of women.

The *peplos* dedicated to Athena at the Greater Panathenaea, on the other hand, was so large that it was displayed on the mast of a ship that was wheeled to the Acropolis. Most likely, this *peplos*, remarkable for its saffron and hyacinth colors, was for Athena Parthenus and was hung on a wall in her chamber. Scholars have recently discovered from inscriptions that it may not have been women but, rather, men who wove this enormous *peplos*; these men most likely were professionals, because they were paid for their work. Thus, although weaving was widely represented and recognized as women's work, in some instances, such as Athena's sail-sized *peplos*, it was not exclusively women's province. In the Greater Panathenaic festival, women were recognized and were accorded a place of pride in the parade. Yet the largest portion of Athena's festival program celebrated the practical and cunning intelligence Athena offers her city of men, ensuring their military and political success.

6.6 **The preparation of wool and the weaving of cloth.** Black-figured lekythos (oil flask). Attributed to the Amasis Painter, c. 550–530 BCE. *Image copyright © The Metropolitan Museum of Art. Image source: Art Resource, NY, ART322634.*

The Origins of Athens In myths about early Athens, just as in the Panathenaic festival, women play a smaller role than men. Whereas Hesiod's *Theogony* offers one account of the origins of humankind, many cities had their own foundational myths. In such myths, a city's residents are frequently described as having descended from a god or goddess and/or arisen from the earth on which the city stood, thus giving them an unassailable claim to the place.

Athenian origin myths reveal how and why men created a goddess who served political exigencies and who loved them deeply, for Athena remains a virgin yet gives birth to a son who becomes one of Athens's first kings. She accomplishes this feat with a piece of wool. Resisting Poseidon (or, in some

6.7 Gaia (Ge) hands the baby Erichthonius/Erechtheus to Athena (standing). Red-figure kylix (drinking cup). Kodros Painter, c. 440–430 BCE. *bpk, Berlin / Antikensammlung, Staatliche Museen, Berlin, Germany/Johannes Laurentius/ Art Resource, NY, ART300746.*

versions, Hephaestus) as he ejaculates on her leg, she wipes away his semen with a piece of wool and tosses it on the ground. There, it fertilizes the earth and produces a boy named Erichthonius. In one depiction of this myth (Figure 6.7), the goddess Ge hands Erichthonius to Athena while Hephaestus and a legendary king named Cecrops, whose snaky lower half suggests his connection to and birth from the earth, watch. Erichthonius is also considered an early king of Athens, as is Erechtheus, who is sometimes considered his son and sometimes conflated with him. These early kings were believed to have overseen the transformation of Athens from a plot of land into a political space under Athena's guidance by establishing customs that define Athens as civilized. For example, Cecrops introduced the institution of marriage, and Erichthonius inaugurated the Panathenaic festival.

All of these early figures were considered autochthonous (born from the earth). Because the Athenians claimed they descended from these figures, the Athenians also claimed to be autochthonous. These earth-born figures justified and provided the Athenians with a vital connection to their land and their city as a political unit, and to its protection. Because Athena gave birth to a child from whom all Athenians claimed descent, the Athenians claimed her as a virgin and as their divine ancestor. Although these myths portray Athena as a mother, they emphasize the political dimensions of Athens and Athena, not her generative capacity as a female. Indeed, the mythic assertion that the Athenians were born from the earth occludes the role of women in procreation more generally.

Greek men and women knew that human beings were born from women and not soil, but these early myths allowed Athenian men to imagine an intimate connection with the goddess Athena. Additionally, by ignoring the importance of women in the production of citizens in Athens, these myths convey that, with Athena's help, men are political beings who are sufficient without women. Athenian men did not so much live in houses with wives as in a city with brothers, guided by a goddess born from her father's head. In tragedies, in statues, and in temples, Athenian men created an Athena who unwaveringly supported them as they sought to understand the various strands of their identity as craftsmen, soldiers, and citizens. Athenian men imagined and devoted themselves to a goddess who exemplified an ideal vision of themselves, and who, they believed, had little to do with women. In this way, they freed themselves from their debt to women for bearing their offspring and for ensuring the city's success through subsequent generations. Athena comes to us in the myths of men, particularly Athenian men, who esteemed Athena as "wholeheartedly" as they believed she approved the male. And so, in their writings and myths, she devoted herself to them.

AESCHYLUS, FROM *EUMENIDES*

BEFORE YOU READ

Aeschylus's *Eumenides*, the last play of his trilogy called the *Oresteia*, uses the language of myth to describe the nature and governance of Athena's city, as well as the roles and perceptions of men and women in relation to Athena. The plot of the first two plays of the trilogy consists of a series of revenge murders. In the opening play, *Agamemnon*, Agamemnon sacrifices his daughter Iphigenia in order to appease the goddess Artemis so that she will allow the Greek fleet to sail to Troy. On Agamemnon's return to his city of Argos after the war, his wife, Clytemnestra, kills him and usurps his throne. In the second play, *Libation Bearers*, Electra and Orestes, the children of Agamemnon and Clytemnestra, plot to kill Clytemnestra to avenge their father. Orestes murders his mother and is hounded by the Furies, female spirits of revenge who attack those who have spilled kindred blood (Chapter 11.1).

The *Eumenides* replaces the murders in the two previous plays with a trial in Athens on the Areopagus, a rocky outcropping near the Acropolis where Athena establishes a court for trying homicide. Orestes's murder trial is the court's first case. (This mythic foundation of the Areopagus marks a historical reform of this court in the 460s BCE, shortly before Aeschylus wrote his trilogy.) At Orestes's trial, Apollo defends Orestes, while the chorus of Furies prosecutes his murder. When the human jurors are tied, Athena gives the speech cited at the opening of this chapter and casts the deciding vote to acquit Orestes. Afterward, she persuades the Furies not to harm Athens or the Areopagus in anger but instead to reside in the city and serve the newly established court. The trilogy ends with torchlights and a procession that is reminiscent of the Panathenaea. (Line numbers correspond to the full text.) (Translated by Alan Shapiro and Peter Burian.)

- Why did the chorus of Furies ignore Clytemnestra's murder of Agamemnon (her husband) yet pursue Orestes for the murder of Clytemnestra (his mother)?

- What is Apollo's explanation for why Orestes's matricide is not as important as the murder of a father or husband (lines 768–787)?

- How do Athena's speech and actions in this trial characterize her *metis*? How do this trial and its outcome characterize the city of Athens?

AESCHYLUS, FROM *EUMENIDES* (c. 458 BCE)

ATHENA The case is now before us. Plaintiffs speak first.
It's only right you should, for the pursuer,   680
telling the story from beginning to end,
can best explain the nature of the case.

CHORUS LEADER Though we are many, we'll keep our speeches short.

(*addressing* ORESTES)

Answer our charges, each one, as we present it:
First, did you kill your mother? Yes or no.

ORESTES Yes, I killed her. I never said I didn't.
CHORUS LEADER The first fall goes to us. Two more to go.
ORESTES Or so you boast, but no one's thrown me yet.
CHORUS LEADER Then tell us how you killed her, since you must.
ORESTES Yes. I drew my sword and slit her throat.   690
CHORUS LEADER By whose persuasion? By whose sage advice?
ORESTES By this god's oracle. He is my witness.
CHORUS LEADER The god taught you it's right to kill your mother?
ORESTES Yes, and till now I have nothing to complain of.
CHORUS LEADER But when the verdict snares you, you'll change your
         tune.
ORESTES I trust him; and my father will help me from the
         grave.
CHORUS LEADER Good, kill your mother, and then trust in corpses!
ORESTES Yes, I killed her since she was doubly defiled.
CHORUS LEADER How exactly? Explain it to the judges.
ORESTES She killed my father when she killed her husband.   700
CHORUS LEADER Death freed her from her guilt, but you're still living.
ORESTES Why didn't you hunt her down while she still lived?
CHORUS LEADER The man she killed was not her flesh and blood.
ORESTES You think I have the same blood as my mother's?

CHORUS LEADER How else could she have fed you in her womb,
         you killer? You spurn the mother blood you live by?

ORESTES Now testify, Apollo, on my behalf
         and teach the law to show whether I did
         or didn't act with justice when I killed her—

for I did kill her, that I don't deny.   710
But you determine whether or not this blood
was justly shed, so I can make my case.

APOLLO I say to all of you, to this high court
established by Athena, he acted justly.
I am a prophet; I can never lie.
Not once from my far seeing throne have I
said anything concerning a man, a woman,
or even a city that Zeus himself, father
of the Olympians, did not command.
Be mindful of how powerful this plea   720
for justice is. Follow my father's will.
No oath is stronger than almighty Zeus.

CHORUS LEADER So you want us to believe that Zeus gave you
this oracle to pass on to Orestes,
told him to avenge his father's murder
and, in the process, cast aside, trample
to nothing, the respect he owed his mother?

APOLLO Yes, I do. For it's a different thing
entirely when a noble man who holds
the scepter Zeus bestows is murdered, struck down   730
not even by the far-shot arrow of
some Amazon, but by a woman's hand,
and in a manner I'll describe to you,
Athena, and to all you seated here
to judge the case by vote. Once he returned
from war where he did well enough, on balance,
the woman made a show of being kind,
seemed anxious to please him, fuss over him like a
     wife,
until, as he was stepping from the bath,
there at the very end, she swaddled him   740
in a winding cloth, tangling him up from head
to toe within the endless fold on fold
of the embroidered robe, then struck, him down.
This is how wretchedly he died, a man
all men revered, commander of the fleet.
I've spoken as I have to whip up anger
in you who are called to set this matter right.

CHORUS LEADER So it's your view that Zeus's main concern
is for a father's death. Yet didn't he
himself chain up his aged father, Cronus?   750
How do you square this with your argument?
Heed what you just heard, judges. Remember it.

APOLLO You stinking, hideous filth, shunned by the gods,
we can break bonds, we can slip out of shackles!
There's
a cure for ills like those, yes, countless ways
of getting free. But once a man is dead,
and the ground has sucked dry all his blood,
nothing can ever raise him up again.
My father made no healing spell for that,
though he can turn all other things, at will,   760
inside and out, and not pant from the effort.

CHORUS LEADER See where your way of pleading for this man
has led you: he has spilled his mother's dear
blood on the ground—so how can he live in Argos,
take possession of his father's house?
What public altars could he use? How can he touch
the cleansing water at his kinsmen's shrine?

APOLLO I'll tell you something else, to show how right
I am: the so-called mother of the child
isn't the child's begetter, but only a sort   770
of nursing soil for the new-sown seed.
The man, the one on top, is the true parent,
while she, a stranger, fosters a stranger's sprout,
if no god blights it. And I can prove it to you:
a father can give birth without a mother.
And here before us is our witness, child
of Olympian Zeus, daughter who never fed
and grew within the darkness of a womb,
a seedling that no goddess could bring forth.
In all things, Pallas, and with all my power,   780
I'll glorify your people and your city;
for that's the very reason I sent this man
here to your house and hearth so he could be
a constant friend to you for all time to come,

a friend and ally, goddess, he and his heirs,
each one of their descendents who will keep
this sacred bond, this covenant forever.

ATHENA Have we now heard enough? Should I tell these
              judges
        to cast their votes where they think justice lies?

APOLLO Our quiver's empty, all our arrows shot.   790
        I'll wait to see which way the trial goes.

ATHENA

                              (*turning to the* CHORUS)

        And what must I do now to avoid your reproach?

CHORUS LEADER You've heard what you've heard, and as you vote, my
              friends,
        with all your heart respect the oath you've sworn.

ATHENA Now hear my ordinance, you men of Athens,
        you who have been chosen to decide
        this first trial ever for the shedding of blood.
        Now and in future time, this court of judges
        will continue to exist for the people of Aegeus,
        here on this hill of Ares where the Amazons   800
        pitched their tents when they invaded, armed,
        and angry at King Theseus, raised up
        against the city the towering walls of their
        own battlements, and slit the throats of beasts
        in sacrifice to Ares. This is why
        we call this place the rock and hill of Ares.
        Here the people's awe and innate fear
        will hold injustice back by day, by night,
        so long as the people leave the laws intact,
        just as they are, and never alter them   810
        with foul infusions: muddy the cleanest spring,
        and all you'll have to drink is muddy water.
        I urge my people to follow and revere
        neither tyranny nor anarchy,
        and to hold fear close, never to cast it out

entirely from the city. For what man
who feels no fear is able to be just?
And if you fear and justly revere this court,
then you will have a bulwark for your land,
the city's guardian, the like of which   820
nobody else on earth possesses, not even
the law-abiding Scythians, or Spartans.
This council I establish will be immune
from greed, majestic, poised for wrath, the country's
wakeful watchman over those who sleep.

I've given this long advice to all my people—
it's for the future. But now you must stand up,
take up your ballots and decide the case,
respecting your sacred oath. My speech is done.

> *During the following exchange, the jurors arise,*
> *proceed to the voting urns, deposit their ballots,*
> *and return to their seats.*

CHORUS LEADER I warn you all—if you dishonor us,   830
    we'll be a crushing burden on your land.

APOLLO And I tell you to fear the oracles,
    Zeus's and mine. Don't keep them from bearing fruit.

CHORUS LEADER You honor bloody crimes that aren't your business.
    Your oracles will never now be pure.

APOLLO So Zeus made a mistake when Ixion,
    the first to kill, appealed to him for help?

CHORUS LEADER You said it, I didn't. But if I don't get justice,
    I will come back to crush this land forever.

APOLLO How so? You have no honor among gods,   840
    young or old. I will win this case.

CHORUS LEADER You did the same thing, too, in Pheres' house:
    you persuaded the Fates to let men hide from death.

APOLLO Is it unjust to treat someone so kindly,
        someone that pious, in his time of need?

CHORUS LEADER You overturned the age-old covenant
        by duping those ancient goddesses with wine.

APOLLO And when you lose this trial, you'll vomit all
        your venom at the ones you hate—quite harmlessly.

CHORUS LEADER Young one, since you would trample down your
           elders,   850
        I'll have to wait to hear if the court will give me
        justice, or the city feel my wrath.

ATHENA My office makes me last to judge this case.
        And I will cast my ballot for Orestes.
        No mother gave me birth, and in all things
        but marriage I wholeheartedly approve
        the male—I am entirely my father's child.
        And this is why the killing of a woman
        who killed her husband, guardian of the house,
        can have no overriding claim on me.   860
        Orestes wins, even if the votes be equal.
                            (*turning to the jurors*)

        You jurors who have this duty to fulfill,
        quickly spill out the ballots from the urns.

                Two jurors return to the urns and begin the count.
                      ATHENA *takes a place behind the urns.*

ORESTES Phoebus Apollo, how will it be decided?
CHORUS LEADER Black Night, our mother, are you watching this?
ORESTES It's time now—to feel the noose, or see the light!
CHORUS LEADER To be disgraced, or forever keep our honors!

APOLLO Count up the spilled out votes precisely, friends,
        make no mistake, be sure the sum is just.
        Out of bad judgment comes catastrophe,   870
        But when the judgment's sound, a single vote
        can reestablish order in a house.

ATHENA *(examining the ballots)* This man's acquitted on the
charge of murder—
the number of votes for both sides is the same.

ORESTES O Pallas Athena, you have saved my house!

6.2
THEORY

THE MIND STRUCTURES MYTH IN OPPOSITIONS

Greek myths may seem to share elements with dreams, if not nightmares. The actions, monsters, and scenarios of dreams, such as the ability to fly, often appear in myths. For example, the hero Bellerophon flies on a winged horse named Pegasus and defeats a sea monster. Daedalus makes wings of feathers and wax so that he and his son Icarus can escape from the island of Crete, where they are being held against their will. But, flying over the Aegean Sea, Icarus climbs too close to the sun; the wax in his wings melts, and he plunges into the sea. The myth, like a dream, ends abruptly. The dreamer wakes; the reader wonders what flying might mean.

Not surprisingly, psychologists have noticed the similarities between myths and dreams, daydreams, and even the creative processes of artists. Some have looked to myth to learn how the human mind (or parts of it that they label the unconscious or subconscious) works. They have asked how myths might provide insight into the ways human beings encounter, understand, and then process their experiences.

Sigmund Freud (1856–1939), the Austrian neurologist who founded the discipline of psychoanalysis, explored the connection between myths and dreams. Just as the dreams of individuals express their past and present fears and wishes in fantastical and symbolic ways, he argued, so too do myths express the past and present fears and wishes of a society or most of its people. In this view, myths are an elaborate (if frequently obscure) record of the history and culture of how a particular society is shaped by human desire and anxieties. Freud conjectured that myths offered potentially useful material for his explorations of why and how the unconscious perceives reality and then produces elaborate and obscure accounts of its fears and wishes, especially in dreams and psychosis.

Carl Gustav Jung (1875–1961), Freud's most famous student (who eventually came to disagree with him on many issues), argued that myths—like dreams—convey messages from the unconscious, although in Jung's view these are not limited to hopes and fears. Both Freud and Jung have influenced the subsequent study of Greek myths. (In Chapter 7.2, we make use of Jung's concept of the "archetype" in our study of Hermes as a trickster figure.) In recent years, however, the ideas of Freud and Jung have fallen out favor, as they are perceived to offer interpretations of myths imbedded in complex theories that many scholars no longer find persuasive and that do not sufficiently take into account social and historical issues.

The anthropologist Claude Lévi-Strauss (1908–2009), although not a psychologist, was also interested in how the human mind perceived and organized (the term he used was "structured") experiences and then created similarly structured stories and codes of behavior. Lévi-Strauss's theories fall into a larger category of analysis called structuralism. Indeed, Lévi-Strauss borrowed a structural analysis of language developed by Ferdinand de Sausurre (1857–1913), applying it to kinship and marriage customs as well as to myths. Because Lévi-Strauss's analyses were concerned with structures (and less so with figures or images, as in Freud and Jung's work), his writings have a scientific aspect. This has made his work seem paradoxically reductive as well as unnecessarily complex to many scholars. Even so, his analysis of how the mind structures myth has been profoundly influential, especially as it is more attuned to social realities than the theories of Freud and Jung.

Lévi-Strauss began to develop his ideas after conducting fieldwork in Brazil, where he tried to discover the underlying patterns of thinking that governed the marriage and kinship practices he observed. Although the rules governing marriage he observed at first seemed "absurd" and "meaningless," Lévi-Strauss discovered on further research that such rules are found in many different societies. Because these rules reappear, Lévi-Strauss reasoned that they could not be as absurd and meaningless as he initially imagined.

In his lecture "The Meeting of Myth and Science," Lévi-Strauss explains that he turned to myths rather by accident and discovered the same situation. "Mythical stories, are, or seem, arbitrary, meaningless, absurd, yet nevertheless they reappear all over the world. My problem was trying to find out if there was some kind of order behind this apparent disorder," he wrote (11–12). The order that Lévi-Strauss traced behind marriage rules and myths alike resided, he argued, in the human mind. The mind, he went on to claim, organizes information or reality in terms of oppositions. A simple example might be that night is the opposite of day. Such oppositions can

6.8 Pensive Athena. Marble votive relief from the Acropolis. Circa 470–450 BCE. Acropolis Museum, Athens, Greece. *Nimatallah / Art Resource, NY, ART36206.*

multiply endlessly: north/south, male/female, good/evil, life/death, and so on. Of course, not all oppositions are so stark; dawn and dusk are in-between stages that allow day and night to gradually blend into each other. "Middle age" might cover a long stretch in a human life. In other words, there are many subtle shades of difference between the oppositional categories that the mind uses to organize its perceptions of complex experiences. In Lévi-Strauss's view, then, if one wants to understand myths, one must look for the underlying opposition or oppositions (not the underlying wishes and fears, as Freud argued) that structure their images and events.

The challenge of applying Lévi-Strauss's ideas to myths is in identifying the underlying binary oppositions. To find them, one must break down a myth into smaller units, which Lévi-Strauss called "mythemes." (One strategy for breaking down myths into smaller units can be found in Propp's and Raglan's analyses [Chapters 10.2 and 11.2].) Mythemes may be an event, place, or character that is very different from or opposes another event, place, or character. For example, in Hesiod's *Theogony*, Zeus and the Olympians fight the Titans and send them to Tartarus, while he and the other Olympians remain in the heavens (Chapter 2.1). Zeus also fights Typhoeus, the many-headed monster that is sent by Gaia. After Zeus defeats Typhoeus and casts him too into Tartarus, the universe becomes peaceful. Zeus then marries and produces offspring such as Law, Justice, and the Seasons. He also produces Athena, who, along with her mother Metis, embodies intellectual skill and cunning of the sort necessary for diplomacy to succeed and for war to be avoided. Athena, the consummate warrior, is also the consummate thinker and planner (Figure 6.8).

In this view, we might associate Zeus with order and youth and the Titans, Typhoeus, and even Gaia with chaos and confusion and an old world order. So too we might reason that when Zeus is in control and manages the reproductive capacities of females, he oversees the production of good things, whereas Gaia and other older female divinities (such as the goddess Night) produce dangerous monsters, like Typhoeus. If we make a list of these paired events, personages, and concepts in the *Theogony*, we get something that looks like this:

Order	⟷	Chaos
New	⟷	Old
Olympian	⟷	Titan
Sky	⟷	Tartaros or under the ground
Zeus	⟷	Typhoeus (Gaia)
Marriage	⟷	Female reproduction without males
Diplomacy	⟷	War

If we read this list vertically as well as horizontally, we can draw a series of conclusions about Greek society. For example, Olympus, where the gods rule, is associated with order, whereas under the earth, where the Titans and

Typhoeus dwell, is a place of chaos. Marriage in which the male exercises authority over the female, too, is associated with order, whereas female goddesses who reproduce outside of marriage are associated with chaos. In other words, if we break up myth into smaller units and place them in oppositions, we begin to see the underlying social values of Greek society.

SIMON GOLDHILL, FROM *AESCHYLUS: THE ORESTEIA*

BEFORE YOU READ

Athena, a goddess imbued with many qualities and traits that the Greeks associated with men, has often been the object of structural analyses, because she exhibits both male and female traits and thus mediates this fundamental binary opposition. In an important essay on Aeschylus's *Oresteia*, classical scholar Froma Zeitlin (b. 1933) used structuralist ideas to analyze how this trilogy and the goddess Athena's role in it illuminate Greek views of gender. In the following excerpt from his study of the *Oresteia*, classicist Simon Goldhill (b. 1957) builds on Zeitlin's analysis, offering an analysis of Athena that draws on structuralist approaches to myth. He looks at the conflict between male and female in the *Oresteia* and concludes by commenting on Athena's androgyny, thus suggesting that she mediates the opposition between male and female.

- Beginning with the opposition between male and female, make a chart of oppositions in the last scene of Aeschylus's *Eumenides*. To accomplish this task, you may rely on Goldhill's analysis as well as the excerpt from the *Eumenides* in the previous section.
- Use the chart you have constructed to describe the values that Greeks associate with each gender. According to this chart (and the *Eumenides*, which it summarizes), what sorts of family relationships do females favor?
- What compromise does Athena reach with the Furies? Does this compromise mediate or resolve the conflict between male and female? How or how not?

SIMON GOLDHILL, FROM *AESCHYLUS: THE ORESTEIA* (2004)

At each point of the narrative where tragic conflict takes place, this conflict is depicted as a conflict between the genders. Agamemnon, sent by Zeus, a god, hindered by Artemis, a goddess, is forced to choose between becoming the slayer of his daughter or deserting the men of the military expedition to avenge his brother. Clytemnestra is faced by Agamemnon, to be a husband killer to avenge her daughter. Orestes is faced by Clytemnestra, to be a mother killer to avenge his father. Apollo, a god, faces the Furies, female divinities, in a trial which turns on who is the true parent, the male or the female.

What is more, at each point in these conflicts the female tends towards the support of a position and arguments that are based on the values of ties of blood to the point of the rejection of the ties of society, whereas the male tends to support a wider outlook of social relations to the exclusion of the claims of family and blood. Thus Agamemnon sacrifices his own daughter, "glory of the household," to enable the panhellenic fleet to sail. He rejects his duties as a father to maintain his position in society as king and leader of an international military force. Clytemnestra rejects the social tie of marriage, both by killing her husband and by her adultery, in part at least to avenge her daughter. Orestes rejects that apparently most "natural" of blood ties, between mother and son, to regain his patrimony and reassert the social order of patriarchy. Apollo is a god of state religion, the great civilizer from the international oracle at Delphi. The Furies are depicted as female who seem ready to ignore any claim of society in their pursuit of those who have killed their own kin, their own blood.

The seemingly endless pattern of revenge and reversal, then, is also a pattern of male–female opposition, that itself tends towards an opposition of social and political obligations to familial and blood ties.

Let us now return to the final scenes of the trilogy. Apollo's argument, in support of Orestes' action, seeks to remove the female from any significant role in the production of children (and we may here remember the story of "birth from the soil" which I mentioned in the opening chapter as part of the Athenians' charter myths). The Furies seek to ignore any mitigating circumstances or reasoning for an act of intrafamilial violence. It is clear that the opposition of Apollo and the Furies stresses in an extreme form the radical opposition of male and female, social ties and blood ties. What then, of Athene? She is, of course, a goddess: but she is a goddess who has many of the attributes associated with masculinity in the fifth century. She is a warrior who wears armour and fights; she is associated with the head, as a goddess of wisdom and of guile, and because she sprang fully armed from the head of her father Zeus. She is also a virgin goddess without a male partner. This strange status of Athene must be remembered when she gives her reasons for voting for Orestes—reasons which are instrumental in his preservation and thus the trilogy's conclusion (*Eum.* 735–41):

I will cast this vote for Orestes.
For no mother exists who bore me.
I favour the male in all things, except in attaining marriage,
With all my spirit. I am wholly of the father.
Thus I will not privilege the fate of a woman
Who has killed her husband, the overseer of the house.

Athene's reasons start from the fact that she has no mother. The importance of parental relations has, of course, been emphasized throughout the trilogy, and here Athene is separated from any associations with a mother, with a female line, with female blood. She favours "the male"—note the general category—in all things with all her spirit, except for marriage, that is, except for the one basic role assigned to females within a rigidly patriarchal order. Athene who favours the male does not conform to the female's role within the male dispensation. Thus, she concludes, she is "wholly of the father." I have used this rather strange phrase in English to try to capture some of the range of the Greek, which implies "I am wholly my father's child" (as Athene can claim to be); "I am wholly on the side of the father," that is, in any conflict between a mother's and a father's rights; "I am a faithful follower of my father" (Apollo has claimed that Zeus ordered and supports Orestes' actions). The combination is significant, linking as it does the specifics of Athene's status and Orestes' case to the general social position of "the father" in patriarchy. This collection of reasons leads directly ("thus") to her conclusion, that she cannot grant respect to a woman who has killed her husband, who is "overseer of the house," that is, who holds the authority and status of master within the *oikos*.

Athene's vote, then, has two crucial aspects. On the one hand, it is given for reasons fundamentally linked to the social expectations of gender. Athene supports Orestes because of the unchallengeable role of the man as head of the household, with all the implications of such authority for the position of "the father" and for the status of "the male." On the other hand, the vote is delivered by someone who fits uneasily into such categorizations: a virgin warrior goddess, a female without links to the mother, a female who does not enter marriage. As the narrative has been structured around the polarized oppositions of the genders, so the narrative's ending depends on a figure who does not fit easily into such an opposition.

This may help us to see how her conflict with the Furies ends in resolution. For the first time in the trilogy we do not have the polarized opposition of male and female, each seeking for dominance. Rather, it is an opposition of this strange figure, Athene, and the female Furies, where Athene is aiming at reconciliation rather than at victory through destruction. The diffusion of the rigid and sharply focused opposition of male and female helps achieve the trilogy's conclusion, as it has motivated its action throughout.

Athene persuades the Furies to be assimilated into her city Athens, but the status they are to hold is expressly that of "metics," resident aliens. They are to remain apart from the city in which they are to play a part. Since the Furies have come to stand not merely for the claims of punishment for transgression but also for the claims of blood ties and the female, this positioning has often been seen as particularly significant. For Kitto and those who follow his line of interpretation, this resolution represents the transcendence of Apollo's rejection of the role of the female, and a recognition for the city of the necessary place for what the Furies represent. For an extensive tradition of feminist scholarship, this conclusion represents rather the justification of a subordinate position for the claims of the Furies—with an obvious social analogue for the position of women in Athens. The *Oresteia* becomes viewed as a complex example of what anthropologists have called the "myth of matriarchy overturned," that is, a story that tells of the overthrow of female authority or female search for power as a way of justifying the continuing status quo of male authority in society (Bamberger). Certainly, the final scenes of the trilogy praise the *polis* and its logic of control of women, established laws of marriage, production of legitimate children and restricted rights of women within the state. Yet before the play is taken just as a reaffirmation of the city's order, it must be remembered first that this resolution is effected by Athene, a figure whose representation—even as the goddess of Athens—offers such a complex example for the norms of gender roles; and secondly, that this representation of Athene—as male-like, warrior, persuasive female—comes perilously close to the figure of Clytemnestra (Winnington-Ingram). Whatever the sense of triumph and reconciliation at the end of the *Oresteia*, there remains a powerful sense of potential transgression within the system of gender relations.

6.3 COMPARISON

EGYPT: NEITH

Athena appears in the provocative title of historian Martin Bernal's three-volume *Black Athena: The Afro-Asiatic Roots of Classical Civilization* (1987–2006), and she plays a key role in the contentious debates on the relationship between Greece and Egypt generated by Bernal's work.

In his controversial book, Bernal (1937–2013) argues that Egypt influenced Greece far more than scholars have recognized and that Greek gods have their origins in Egyptian models. In particular, he argues that Athena's name, as well as her attributes, are a result of Egyptian influence on Greece during the second millennium BCE. Although Bernal's arguments from linguistics and myths have not gained widespread support among most classical scholars, his work has invigorated the comparative study of Greek myths and raises one question in particular: what did the Greeks themselves say about the similarities between Athena and the Egyptian goddess Neith, whose worship Bernal claims influenced the Greek conception of Athena? This section looks at the relationship between Greece and Egypt in the Archaic Period, a later period than the one that concerns Bernal, and explores what the relationship between Athena and Neith might tell us about how the Greeks viewed their gods.

Promising evidence for studying the interactions between Egyptians and Greeks, and the correspondences between Athena and Neith, begins in the Archaic Period when the Egyptian king Psammetichus I (664–610 BCE) employed "bronze men," Greek hoplites who wore bronze armor, as mercenaries. With the help of these soldiers, he joined Upper and Lower Egypt and established his dynasty in the city of Sais, where Neith was worshipped. After his reign was secured, Psammetichus I settled the Greek mercenaries on the Nile, near the city of Bubastis, in return for their military service. Subsequent Egyptian rulers also relied on Greek mercenaries; Greek inscriptions recording battles have been found some seven hundred miles south of Lower Egypt, near Nubia.

Most of the interactions between Greeks and Egyptians revolved around trade, not war, and were centered in Naucratis, a settlement of Greeks located ten miles east of Sais in Lower Egypt. The archaeological evidence of altars and temples from different Greek cities in Naucratis indicates that it was different from typical Greek colonies, which were founded by one Greek city and existed on foreign territory without control of locals. Yet Naucratis was not a typical trading post either, as trading posts usually lacked temples and other forms of civic life. In addition, Greek merchants, poets, and statesmen from various cities resided there along with Egyptians, who most likely worked at factories that produced goods for import and export.

The unique organization of Naucratis likely reflects Egyptian control from its founding at the end of the seventh century BCE. All goods from outside of Egypt had to enter through Naucratis, where they were taxed by Egyptian administrators. Additionally, a nearby garrison kept Greek and other traders from the Mediterranean region out of other parts of Egypt. Thus the interactions between the Greeks in Naucratis and the Egyptians appear to have been economically beneficial to both

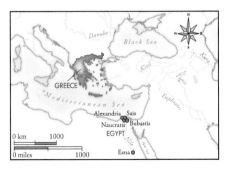

Map 6.3 Egypt (Neith)

parties, yet highly regulated and restricted. By the time that Herodotus wrote about Egypt, Naucratis was thriving.

In the second book of his *Histories* (fifth century BCE), devoted to Egypt, Herodotus not only describes Egyptian geography, animals, vegetation, history, cities, customs, temples, and religious practices but also offers a view of Greek and Egyptian relations that contributes to understanding the possible relation between Athena and Neith. Herodotus compares Egyptians and Greeks and claims that the names of many Greek gods come from Egypt. He writes, "The names of almost all the gods came to Greece from Egypt. My inquiries led me to discover that they are non-Greek in origin, but it is my belief that they came largely from Egypt" (*Histories* 2.50). Herodotus goes on to observe that early inhabitants in Greece (called Pelasgians) worshipped undifferentiated and unnamed gods. The Egyptians introduced the gods' names and personalities and then Homer and Hesiod placed the gods and goddesses in a system for the Greeks (2.52). Yet, when Herodotus describes the worship of Neith in Sais and equates her to Athena, he expresses a Greek tendency to consider the gods as everywhere the same, but with different names and varied attributes in different places. Such are the comments Herodotus makes about Aphrodite and Anath/Astarte, and they suggest his understanding of Neith and Athena is the same (*Histories* 1.131 is discussed in Chapter 5.3).

Herodotus does not state that his identification of Neith with Athena depends on the influence of Egyptians on Greeks. He describes a "lamplight festival" in Neith's honor that took place in Sais. During this festival, oil lamps were kept lit all night. Even those Egyptians who do not actually attend the festival wait for the night of the rite and burn lamps, so there are lamps alight throughout Egypt, not just in Sais. Herodotus then states that there is a sacred story that explains why this night receives light and honor (2.62). This story was very likely depicted on the walls of the Temple of Khnum in the city of Esna (an excerpt from which is included subsequently).

Yet the Temple of Khnum was built several centuries after Herodotus lived, when Egypt was under Roman rule. No earlier attestations of this creation story have been found. And this is not surprising, as very few complete written narratives of Egyptian myths describing the actions of gods (and their interactions with humans) have survived. Information about Neith (and most Egyptian gods and goddesses) comes from mortuary literature (such as the *Pyramid Texts*) in the tombs of pharaohs; the *Coffin Texts*, found on the coffins of dignitaries; and the *Book of the Dead*. From these sources, some of Neith's traits can be gleaned.

Neith is often shown wearing the Red Crown of Lower Egypt and is described as a protector of this region and its king (Figure 6.9). In the *Pyramid Texts*, she and three other goddesses surround and protect the king as he proceeds to the realm of the dead. In general, her fierceness and strength, conveyed by the arrows and shield she often carries, serve to protect cities and men, rather than to attack enemies. In the *Coffin Texts*, Neith is described as protecting the god Osiris. Because every dead person was associated with Osiris, she protects both the god and the dead person in the coffin wherever this invocation is found.

In one instance in the *Coffin Texts*, a mummy's linen wrappings are credited to Neith's weavers, indicating that she, like Athena, is associated with weaving. In the *Book of the Dead*, a spell promises that Neith will come and wrap the petitioner's body in linen strips. Here Neith's association with weaving and her role as a guardian who provides the linens that will protect the body after death are combined. Scattered references such as these give an indication of Neith's spheres of influence. In particular, Neith's role as a guardian, her protection of Sais, and her lamplight festival are reminiscent of Athena's protection of Athens and the Panathenaea, which is preceded by an all-night celebration featuring songs and torches. Thus it becomes understandable why, when Herodotus observed Neith's festival and learned about the traits she shares with Athena (weaving, protection, city patronage, and androgyny), he hypothesized that the two goddesses represent one deity. The historical question that Bernal raised about the manner and extent of the influence of Neith on Athena remains a line of inquiry that will continue to spur research into the relationship between the ancient Greeks and the Egyptians—a relationship that intrigued the Greeks themselves.

6.9 **Neith (left), wearing the Red Crown.** Wall painting, Temple of Khnum, Esna, Egypt. *Jane Taylor / The Art Archive at Art Resource, NY, AR9151364.*

UNKNOWN, *FROM* "COSMOGONIES AT THE TEMPLE OF ESNA"

BEFORE YOU READ

In the creation story from the Temple of Khnum, Neith and the ram-headed god Khnum create the world. In her role as creatrix, Neith is described as two-thirds masculine and one-third feminine. As the creator of the universe, Neith, existing in the midst of primeval waters, says, "let there be land." Proceeding in this way, she then creates many gods and goddesses including her son Re, whom she,

BEFORE YOU READ
CONTINUED

while in the form of a cow, carries between her horns. Defeating enemies, Neith travels with Re from Esna to the city of Sais, where she rules. The festival Herodotus describes in Sais, with its burning of torches, both reenacts Neith's creation of the world from darkness as well as her triumphant entry into the city of Sais carrying Re and concludes with her return to Esna. (Translated by Marshall Clagett.)

- Make a list of the similarities between Neith in the following reading and Athena in *Eumenides*. Are these sufficient to assume that either goddess contributed to the character of the other?

- What conclusions might be drawn about the differences between Athena and Neith from their modes of giving birth to Erectheus and Re, respectively?

UNKNOWN, *FROM* "COSMOGONIES AT THE TEMPLE OF ESNA" (SECOND CENTURY BCE)
TEXT 206: NEITH

(1) Father of the fathers, mother of the mothers, the divinity who began to come into being in the beginning was in the midst of the Abyss. She appeared out of herself while the land was [still] in the shadows and no land had [yet] appeared and no plant had sprouted. . . . She turned herself into a cow so that no divinity wherever he would be could recognize her. Then she changed herself into (*lit.* renewed her appearance as) a lates-fish (2) and started off. She made luminescent the glances of her eyes, and light came into being. Then she said: "Let this place (where I am) become for me a platform of land in the midst of the Abyss in order that I might stand on it." And this place became a platform of land in the midst   10 of the Abyss, just as she said. And [thus] came into being "the land of the waters" (=Esna), which is also Sais. . . .

Everything which her heart conceived came into being immediately. (3) Thus she felt happy about this emergence [of the land] and so Egypt came into being in this happiness.

She created thirty gods by pronouncing their names, one by one, and she became happy when she saw them. They said: "Hail to you, Mistress of divinities, our mother, who has brought us into being. You have made our names before we knew them (i.e. yet had cognizance of them) . . . you have made [for us] the land upon which we can stand, you have separated   20 [for us] the night from the day. . . . How very beneficial is everything which comes from your heart, O Sole One, created in the beginning. Eternity and everlastingness pass before your face. . . . [[4) Then Neith establishes the gods on the emergent land, and they ask (5) what is going to be created.]

Neith then said: "I shall cause you to know what is coming into being. Let us count the four spirits. Let us give form to what is in our bodies (i.e. in our hearts?) and then let us pronounce our forms. So, we shall recognize everything the same day." Everything she said took place, and the eighth hour (i.e. the culminating time) occurred in the space of a moment.   30

The Ahet-cow (*or* Ihet-cow; *here* Neith) began to think about what she was going to create. She said: "An august god will come into being today. When he opens his eyes, light will come into being; when he closes them, (6) darkness will come into being. People will come into being from the tears of his eye, gods from the spittle of his lips. I will strengthen him by my strength, I will make him effective by my efficacy, I will make him vigorous by my vigor. His children will rebel against him, but they will be beaten on his behalf and struck down on his behalf, for he is my son issued from my body, and he will be king of this land forever. I will protect him with my arms. . . . (7) I am going to tell you his name: it will be Khepri in the morn-   40
ing and Atum in the evening; and he will be the radiating god in his rising forever, in his name of Re, every day."

Then these gods said: "We are ignorant of the things we have heard." So the "Eight" became the name of these gods (i.e. the Ogdoad) and also the name of this city (i.e. "Eighttown," i.e. Hermopolis or Ashmunein).

So this god was born from the excretions that came forth from the body of Neith and which she placed in the body of this [primordial] egg. . . . (8) . . . . When it broke the shell, it was Re who was hidden in the midst of the Abyss in his name of Amun the Elder and who fashioned the gods   50
and the goddesses with his rays in his name of Khnum.

His mother, the cow goddess, called out loudly: "Come, come, you whom I have created. Come, come, you whom I have conceived. Come, come, (9) you whom I have caused to come into being. . . . I am your mother, the cow goddess." This god then came forth, his mouth open, his arms opened toward this goddess. . . . And this day [of the sun's birth] then became the beautiful day of the beginning of the year.

Then he cried in the Abyss when he did not see his mother, the cow goddess, and mankind came into being from the tears of his eye; and he salivated when he saw her again, and the gods came into being from the   60
saliva of his lips.

(10) These primordial gods [now] rest in their shrines; they have been pronounced [by creative word] just as this goddess conceived them in her heart. . . .

They (the ancestor gods) thrust aside (11) a wad of spittle from her mouth which she had produced in the Abyss, and it was transformed into a serpent of 120 cubits, which was named Apep (Apophis). Its heart conceived the revolt against Re, its cohorts coming from its eyes.

Thoth emerged from his (i.e. Re's) heart in a moment of bitterness, which accounts for his name of Thoth. He speaks with his father, who sent   70
him against the revolt, in his name of Lord of the Word of God. And this is how Thoth, Lord of Khmun, came into being, in this place, as well as that of the Eight-gods of the first company of gods.

. . . . [Then Neith goes to her city of Esna (i.e. Sais) with her son to establish his name there. She will suckle him until he is strong enough to massacre those plotting against him. Then we are told that the seven propositions that she declared in the course of creation became seven divinities].

. . . (13) And so came into being the Seven Proposition-Goddesses of Methyer. . . .

6.4
RECEPTION

ATHENA AS A POLITICAL ALLEGORY

In ancient Greece, Athena was both a virgin and warrior and was renowned for her intelligence. Although female, Athena did not represent women's lives nor embody the traits they were believed to possess. She was neither a role model for women nor a feminine ideal. Curiously, this disjuncture between Athena and the reality of women's lives allowed her to preside over Athens and represent the ideals to which Athenian men aspired. Freed from the constraints that limited the scope of women's lives in Greece, Athena was able to become a political, military, and unifying goddess and symbol for the Athenian state. Subsequently, female figures modeled on Athena have served a similar role for nations, particularly modern (post-Enlightenment) ones. The figure of Marianne in France and the Statue of Liberty in America can be traced back to Athena. Both are allegories for certain abstract political values. This section addresses why and how these two figures have become such enduring allegories for their nations and what they have in common with Athena.

The word "allegory" comes from two Greek words: *allos*, which means "other," and *agoreuein*, which describes speaking in the *agora* (marketplace)—that is, speaking in public. An allegory may be a character, event, or story that represents or symbolizes an idea, concept, or value that is very different from (or other than) its surface meaning. For example, tales about animals are often allegories for the actions of human beings (George Orwell's grim novel *Animal Farm* may be the best-known such modern allegory).

Of all the Greek gods and goddesses, Athena is particularly suited to represent an idea other than herself. First, in Greek as well as in most Indo-European languages (such as French or Spanish), nouns are classified as male, female, or neuter. Abstract concepts, such as liberty, justice, reason, or temperance, almost always have a female gender. Hence their personification almost "naturally" requires a female form. Second, Athena's virginity means that she, of all the Greek goddesses, exhibits few, if any, desires or emotions of her own, and she has no agenda except for the exercise of her characteristic practical intelligence and her martial skills. Athena somehow remains untainted by the pettiness and jealousies that so many of the other Olympians display. Even when acting in battle, she does not become wild or uncontrolled; instead, she remains impenetrable in her armor, restrained, and com-

6.10 Eugene Delacroix, *Liberty Leading the People* (1830). Oil on canvas. Louvre Museum, Paris, France. *Erich Lessing / Art Resource, NY, ART76327.*

pletely focused on the causes of those she supports. And, when Athena creates or gives birth to Erichthonius, the ancestor of all Athenians, she does not demonstrate any desire of her own. For these reasons, Athena has more similarity to goddesses like Nike (Victory) or Dike (Justice), who embody and exemplify abstract ideas. Like them, she serves a purpose outside of herself.

During the several revolutions over the course of the eighteenth and nineteenth centuries that transformed France from a monarchy to a republic, Athena inspired two political allegories: Liberté and Marianne, figures who represented the values of liberty, equality, and fraternity—ideals borrowed by revolutionary leaders from ancient Greece and Rome. Marianne, who appears on a seal of the republic established during the French Revolution (1789–1799), was designed to represent the French Republic and to provide it with a symbol that would be as potent and unifying as the hereditary French kings that the Revolution overthrew. On the seal, Marianne appears as a young woman dressed in classical garb, holding a spear with a red cap on it and Roman *fasces*. Marianne's red cap (*bonnet rouge*) is similar to a cap worn by Roman slaves who had been granted their freedom and thus it stood for liberty. Her name itself was one of the most popular women's names among the French people and suggests equality, whereas her *fasces* (a bundle of sticks tied together that Roman magistrates carried) symbolized the unity or fraternity of French people. Finally, Marianne's classical dress gave her a noble and enduring quality that lent to the Revolution a history that skipped over France's monarchs. She stood, much as Athena did, as the mother of the common people (as she was sometimes called). Marianne was depicted to embody and thus ensure the stability and unity of the fledgling republic. However, during turbulent events, she often was represented as stepping forward, raising her arm and rallying fighters.

Liberté in *Liberty Leading the People* (1830) by Eugene Delacroix (1798–1863) is one such example of a more active and martial Marianne (Figure 6.10). Delacroix's painting commemorates the July Revolution of 1830, when the Bourbon monarchy, which ruled France by hereditary right, was overthrown and was replaced by a monarch who ruled by popular consent. Although the figure of Liberté carries some of the same emblems as Marianne, she differs from her in several important ways. Whereas she wears a Phrygian cap like the one Marianne carries, Liberté also wears the dress of a commoner, not a classical garment. She carries the tricolor flag of the Revolution, symbolizing liberty, equality, and fraternity.

This depiction of Liberté also differs from the cool and classical images of Marianne in the actions she is shown taking. In Delacroix's painting, Liberté steps forward on top of fallen bodies that serve as a pedestal. Among these is one of the more shocking details of the painting: a fallen fighter is stripped naked from the waist down and is sprawled in a way that reveals his pubic hair. Liberté is also stripped, but from the waist up. Her nudity, unlike that of the fallen fighter's, bespeaks strength. Far from appearing erotic or vulnerable (like the fallen fighter), the nudity of Liberté is heroic and makes her seem fearless. Liberté was Marianne without her armor or classical dress and without her restraint. For these reasons, Delacroix's painting of Liberté was considered too inflammatory to be displayed, even for the post-Revolutionary government of 1830. The French government bought the painting, but, rather than display it, they returned it to Delacroix.

Over the next few decades, depictions of Marianne varied between the more reserved figure that appeared on the seal of the republic and a more bellicose Marianne, who, like the Liberté of Delacroix, was bare breasted. In 1879, a competition was held to select a statue of Marianne that would be located in the Place de la République in Paris. A more staid and reserved Marianne, designed by François-Charles Morice (1848–1908) and Léopold Morice (1846–1919), won first prize (Figure 6.11). But the more assertive Marianne was not easily left behind. A depiction of a bare-breasted and martial Marianne by the artist Aimé-Jules Dalou (1838–1902), which won second prize, was built on the Place de la Nation, also in Paris. Over time, however, as the French Republic left behind its wars of the previous decades, the Marianne who presides over the Place de la République has become the enduring representation of the republic, appearing on French currency and stamps and in numerous statues standing in town squares throughout France. This Marianne stands on a marble pedestal with three female figures personifying liberty, equality, and fraternity. She wears a Phrygian cap and a classical garment with a belt holding a sword across her shoulder. Her raised left hand holds an olive branch, not a spear, and she rests her other hand on a large tablet inscribed "The Rights of Man and the Citizen." Her stance recalls Athena Parthenus, who holds Nike in her outstretched hand and rests the other on her shield.

The Statue of Liberty, who holds a torch aloft in one hand and carries a tablet with the date July 4, 1776, inscribed on it in her other hand, recalls both Marianne and Athena (Figure 6.12). Given to America by France on the centennial celebration of the American Declaration of Independence, the Statue of Liberty celebrated the friendship between the two nations. It also stood for their shared commitment to liberty and reason and, by virtue of the statue's size and grandeur, established France's stature in the eyes of the world.

The Statue of Liberty was designed by Frédéric Bartholdi (1834–1904), who wanted to build a colossus (large statue) in the 1860s, when Europe became interested in the Seven Wonders of the Ancient World, especially the Lighthouse of Alexandria and the Colossus of Rhodes. Bartholdi's grand ambitions were realized when he was commissioned to build France's monumental gift to the United States of America. Yet, soon after its arrival in America, Bartholdi's statue ceased to be celebrated for its similarity to the Colossus of Rhodes, and its meaning shifted from a celebration of liberty and kinship with France to a symbol of a distinctly American experience. A poem by the American writer Emma Lazarus

6.11 François-Charles Morice and Léopold Morice, *Statue of the Republic* (1879). Place de la République, Paris, France. *Agencja Fotograficzna Caro/Alamy, CRFH69.*

(1849–1887), written to commemorate the statue, was later engraved on a bronze plaque and mounted to the statue's pedestal. This poem has shaped how most Americans understand the Statue of Liberty.

EMMA LAZARUS, "THE NEW COLOSSUS" (1883)

Not like the brazen giant of Greek fame,
With conquering limbs astride from land to land;
Here at our sea-washed, sunset gates shall stand
A mighty woman with a torch, whose flame
Is the imprisoned lightning, and her name
Mother of Exiles. From her beacon-hand
Glows world-wide welcome; her mild eyes command
The air-bridged harbor that twin cities frame.
"Keep ancient lands, your storied pomp!" cries she

6.12 Frédéric Bartholdi, *Statue of Liberty* (*Liberty Enlightening the World*) (1876–1886). Liberty Island. New York, NY. © DeA Picture Library / Art Resource, NY, ART341305.

With silent lips. "Give me your tired, your poor,
Your huddled masses yearning to breathe free,
The wretched refuse of your teeming shore.
Send these, the homeless, tempest-tost to me,
I lift my lamp beside the golden door!"

Lazarus's poem transforms the Statue of Liberty from a guardian of liberty into a "mother of exiles" who welcomes immigrants and exiles to American shores. Although its title acknowledges the ancient precedents that inspired Bartholdi, the poem begins with an emphatic negation—"Not"—and then proceeds to mark the statue's difference from the Colossus of Rhodes. The statue's limbs do not stride and conquer. She is not a "brazen giant." Instead, she commands with "her mild eyes," not with force. Her torch signifies "world-wide welcome," rather than the more abstract concept of "liberty," as implied by the statue's original title, *Liberty Enlightening the World*. Indeed, "Give me your tired, your poor . . ." are the most remembered and readily quoted words of her poem. These lines made the statue an allegory of America's identity as a nation of immigrants "yearning to breathe free." Thus Lazarus's poem shifts the overall meaning of the statue. But Lazarus's transformation is only partially complete.

The Statue of Liberty retains many similarities with Athena. Like her, the statue is both mother and virgin. She does not give birth to America's future citizens but instead welcomes immigrants and exiles as they pass her on the way to Ellis Island. Similarly, Athena did not give birth to the Erichthonius but handed him from Gaia, the earth where he was born, to the daughters of Cecrops for rearing. This kind of virginity characterized by both Athena and the Statue of Liberty is politically useful. As neither can be claimed by any one group of citizens, both can serve as unifying icons, or mother figures, for all citizens. These citizens are then free to define themselves as brothers, despite having no cultural or ethnic affinities with one another. Thus the statue, like virginal Athena, lacking any desires of her own, is available to serve the political agenda and desire of her makers.

KEY TERMS

Acropolis 255

Areopagus 256

Athena Polias 255

Autochthonous 258

Erichthonius 258

Furies 259

Metis 249

Oresteia 259

Orestes 247

Panathenaea 255

Parthenon 255

Peplos 256

Poseidon 253

FOR FURTHER EXPLORATION

Deacy, Susan. *Athena*. New York and London: Routledge, 2008. This compact and comprehensive introduction to Athena is readable and reliable.

Leach, Edmund R. *Claude Lévi-Strauss*. Chicago: University of Chicago Press, 1970. Leach's book remains one of the more comprehensible and reliable introductions to many aspects of Lévi-Strauss's thought.

Traunecker, Claude. *The Gods of Egypt*. Translated by David Lorton. Ithaca, NY: Cornell University Press, 2001. Traunecker provides a succinct, yet thorough, introduction to Egyptian gods and goddesses, while also addressing more complex and nuanced aspects of the Egyptian religious imagination.

Warner, Marina. *Monuments and Maidens: The Allegory of the Female Form*. Berkeley and Los Angeles: University of California Press, 1985. This engaging and lively book considers many allegorical female figures that appear with frequency in European art, with a particular emphasis on Athena, including an overview of her worship and representation in antiquity. Chapter 6.4 relies on Warner's argument.

CHAPTER 7

HERMES AND HESTIA

What distinguishes gods from men? . . . Man is a contradictory being who participates in many conditions of existence. Day and night, heat and cold, serenity and storms, all have claims on him. . . . Only for moments can man be wholly swept into the enchantment of singular being, and then he touches upon the perfect and the divine. . . . But earthly nature cannot abide in this majestic singularity and wholeness; that only the god can do.

—WALTER F. OTTO, *THE HOMERIC GODS* (1954)

Walter F. Otto (1874–1958), a scholar of ancient Greek religion, asks a general question about Greek gods that is particularly relevant to Hermes: what distinguishes gods from humans? Otto points out that although Greek gods are anthropomorphic (they have human traits and a human form), they are nonetheless very different from human beings because they are not affected by circumstances. Instead, each god is distinguished by one essential and unchanging trait. In Otto's words, each deity has a "majestic singularity" that can be discerned behind his or her different features and activities.

Hermes's singular majesty, in Otto's estimation, is joy. He writes that Hermes is "the friendliest of gods" and represents the "favorable moment and its profitable exploitation." Hermes escorts human beings as they travel. He is associated with the acquisition of goods, especially those that are found and not acquired with labor. Indeed, on the island of Samos, the ancients called Hermes "Giver of Joy" because he oversaw a festival in which participants were granted the privilege of stealing without punishment. Although many of Hermes's spheres of influence and playfulness (described in the Homeric

< **7.1 (OPPOSITE):** Three herms. Red-figure pelike. Pan Painter, c. 470 BCE. Louvre Museum, Paris, France. © RMN-Grand Palais / Art Resource, NY, ART194441.

THE ESSENTIALS ⚔ HERMES AND HESTIA

HERMES (Mercury), Ἑρμῆς

PARENTAGE Zeus and the nymph Maia

OFFSPRING Pan (with the nymph Penelopeia), Hermaphroditus (with Aphrodite), the ancestor of the Tanagran people (with the nymph Tanagra), Ceryx (with Agraulos), and Eudorus (with Polymele)

ATTRIBUTES Cap, winged sandals, wand

SIGNIFICANT CULT TITLES
- Agonius (Of Contests)
- Charidotes (Luck-Bringer)
- Criophorus (Ram-Carrier)
- Cynagches (Dog-Strangler)
- Enodius (Of the Road)
- Epimelius (Guardian of Flocks)
- Psychopomp (Escort of Souls)

SIGNIFICANT RITUALS AND SANCTUARIES
- **The Anthesteria** An Athenian festival in honor of Dionysus in which Hermes escorted the souls of the dead back to the Underworld.
- **Kato Syme (Crete)** A place where games for young men under Hermes's tutelage were held.
- **Mount Cyllene in Arcadia** One of Hermes's birthplaces, with many shrines in his honor, including a large phallus that was venerated.
- **Tanagra** A purificatory festival in commemoration of Hermes's assistance.

HESTIA (Vesta), Ἑστία

PARENTAGE Cronus and Rhea

OFFSPRING None

ATTRIBUTES Veil, branch

SIGNIFICANT CULT TITLES None

SIGNIFICANT RITUALS AND SANCTUARIES
- **The Amphidromia** A ritual in which a father runs around the hearth (Hestia) in his house with his two-week-old infant.
- **Prytany Building** A public building found in many cities that kept a pure fire constantly burning on a hearth (Hestia).

hymn included in this chapter) support Otto's description of Hermes's majestic singularity, there are other aspects of Hermes that do not quite fit within this rubric.

7.1 HISTORY

FROM HERMS TO HERMES

This chapter first surveys Hermes's different representations and different activities and then turns to Hestia, goddess of the hearth, with whom the Greeks paired Hermes. The differences between Hermes and Hestia bring to light a quality of Hermes that describes all his activities and is quite different from what Otto describes as his majestic singularity. Comparing Hermes with Hestia and studying the contrasts offers a model for studying Greek deities (their identities become clearer through comparisons) and leads to identifying a unique quality that defines Hermes.

HERMES'S HILLS

Hermes was represented in two distinctly different ways: as a fully human man (sometimes a beardless youth or a bearded adult) or as a statue. These statues consist of a square stone pillar, called a herm (Figure 7.1), which features a head and a phallus. Herms are thought to derive from piles of rocks, called "Hermes's hills," typically found at the sides of roads. Eumaeus, Odysseus's swineherd, says that as he was walking above the city, he passed the "hill of Hermes" (*Odyssey* 16.471). One of the many ancient scholiasts (scholars) who comments on this passage gives the following explanation of a Hermes's hill: in the distant past, Hermes made roads safe for travelers, who consequently honored him as the purifier and guardian of roads by throwing stones into a pile called Hermes's hill. The scholiast adds that, even in the Roman Empire, such piles of rocks could be seen on roads; they eventually were used to mark distances. From the ancient scholiast's comments, subsequent scholars have concluded that Hermes was a patron of travelers, both when they travel through the countryside and after death, when their souls travel to the Underworld. He was also a patron of messengers, who often traveled long distances. Indeed, Hermes was himself a messenger: he brought messages from gods (most often from Zeus) to mortals and other gods. He also conveyed messages from human beings on earth to the souls of the dead in the Underworld.

To and from Olympus and on Earth Hermes is frequently depicted as a messenger who brings messages from Zeus on Olympus to earth. In the *Odyssey*, Zeus calls on Hermes to tell Calypso that she must release Odysseus from her island. Homer describes how Hermes flies just above the spray of the ocean to reach Calypso's distant island, where he gracefully delivers Zeus's unwelcome message. First, however, Hermes puts on his characteristic travel gear: his traveler's cap, which in some instances can render him invisible; his winged sandals, which suggest he moves quickly; and his wand, which marks him as inviolable as a messenger (Figure 7.2). Hermes's wand, called a "caduceus" (a Latin alteration of the Greek *kerykeion*), is a staff with two snakes wrapped around it. Auctioneers in markets and announcers who kept order in political assemblies or at festivals carried this wand; in our own times, it is used as a symbol of the medical profession. Hermes is said to be the father of Ceryx, who founded a family (called Ceryces) in the town of Eleusis, near

7.2 Hermes with winged sandals, cap, and wand. Red-figured lekythos (oil flask). Attributed to the Tithonus Painter, c. 480–470 BCE. *Image copyright © The Metropolitan Museum of Art. Image source: Art Resource, NY, ART414543.*

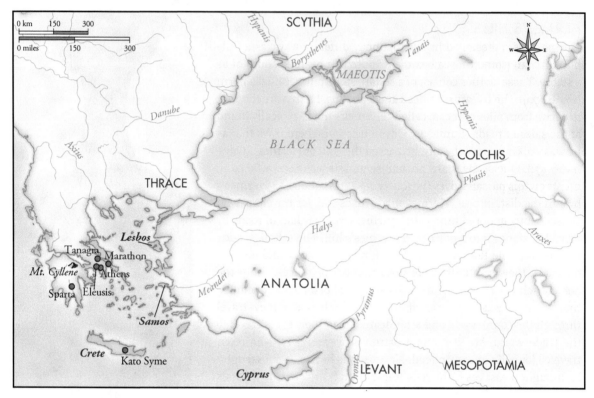

Map 7.1 Hermes and Hestia in Greece

Athens, whose members served as magistrates for the Great Mysteries of Demeter (Chapter 4.1). Hermes was the patron god of the Ceryces and messengers more generally.

Hermes was venerated by travelers as well as messengers, because he helped all who travel dangerous roads. One of his cult titles, Enodius (Of the Road), suggests his constant journeying on behalf of gods and men. In the *Iliad*, for example, Hermes is called on to help the Trojan king, Priam, travel through the enemy territory of the Greek camps in order to ransom his son Hector's body from Achilles, the Greek warrior who killed him. On Priam's nighttime journey through the countryside, Hermes appears as a charming young prince who offers to help Priam. He reassures Priam that his son's body has not been harmed and takes the reins of Priam's chariot to lead him to Achilles's tent. He puts to sleep all the Greek soldiers with his wand, silently opens the heavy bolts of Achilles's enclosure, and delivers Priam safely to his destination. Hermes exhibits his characteristic skills here. As he guides and protects Priam's travels, Hermes is evasive, like a cat burglar; he open bolts with no noise and disrupts no soldier's sleep. He is also a benevolent and beautiful young man, and he thus conjoins male beauty and excellence with nighttime tricks, rather than excellence on the battlefield in daylight.

To and from the Underworld Hermes's hills were not only found on roadsides but also thought to have been used as grave markers. This usage connects Hermes's hills to his function as a messenger and escort from Olympus and earth alike to the Underworld. For example, at her father Agamemnon's gravesite, Electra tries to enlist help from the Underworld as she takes revenge for his murder. She prays: "Greatest Herald of the world above, / and the world below, O Hermes of the dark / earth, help me now. Call on the nether spirits . . ." (Aeschylus, *Libation Bearers* 120). Similarly, Hermes was often called on in curse tablets that were placed in the graves of the recently deceased (or in other places associated with pathways to the Underworld, such as caves) to solicit the assistance of their souls. Curse tablets were thin, rectangular lead sheets that were inscribed with curses before being rolled up and pierced with nails. They often contained herbs or the hair of animals—or even the hair of the intended human victim of the curse. Curses were directed at neighbors, love rivals, or business competition. In curse tablets, Hermes is often grouped with other deities associated with the Underworld (such as Persephone or Gaia) and is called to facilitate communication between those living on earth and those below.

The association of Hermes with the Underworld was also evident during an Athenian festival called the Anthesteria (Flower Festival), which although primarily dedicated to Dionysus also served to worship Hermes. The festival took place at springtime when the year's wine casks were opened, an event that also signaled the opening of the Underworld (Chapter 9.1). The festival included drinking contests, a sacred wedding, and parades of masked participants wandering the streets, who were believed to represent the dead. The festival concluded with the closing of the Underworld and banishment of the souls of the dead from the city. Participants dedicated mixtures of beans and honey in special pots to Hermes and to the dead, and they raised a cry demanding that the dead depart and return to the Underworld. Presumably, Hermes would escort the dead as they departed from the land of the living at the festival's end. Hermes's cult title Psychopomp (Escort of Souls) indicates his role in accompanying the dead as they go to the underworld—a function he performed not only during the festival but also for all who died throughout the year (Chapter 4.1). As Psychopomp, Hermes's presence as escort seems to be a gift or aide to the souls of the newly dead.

Whether Hermes's hills served as road or grave markers, their connection to Hermes explains his role as messenger and escort among the gods on

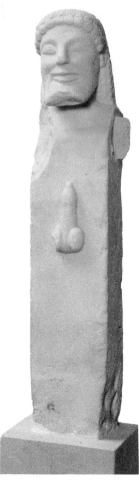

7.3 **Ithyphallic herm**. Marble relief from Siphnos. 510 BCE. National Archaeological Museum, Athens, Greece. *Bridgeman-Giraudon / Art Resource, NY, ART99250.*

Olympus, human beings on earth, and the souls of the dead as they travel to the Underworld. As herald, messenger, and escort, Hermes offers welcome assistance to those he serves or accompanies.

ITHYPHALLIC HERMS

Many scholars reason that Hermes's hills were replaced by herms (Figure 7.3). Although such a development cannot be proven, it is the case that herms most often are found outdoors—at the gates and doors of cities, houses, and temples. Yet the two salient features of herms—their head and erect phallus—suggest spheres of Hermes's influence other than travel and roads. The importance of the phallus to Hermes is evident in Cyllene, a mountainous region of Arcadia, which was believed to be Hermes's birthplace. A statue of an erect phallus there was venerated as Hermes (Pausanias 6.26.5). Specifically, the erect phallus of the herm suggests his connection to fertility, especially that of flocks of certain animals, and his role as a protector.

Fertility Hermes's oversight of fertility is limited to goats, sheep, and swine. No titles, stories, or rituals connect him with the fertility of plough animals (such as oxen and mules), the fertility of crops (which is the domain of the grain goddess, Demeter), or human procreation. The specific nature of Hermes's oversight of fertility is hinted at in a story from the *Iliad.* Hermes falls in love with and impregnates a girl named Polymele. She gives birth to a son, Eudorus (*Iliad* 16.179). Because Polymele means "rich in flocks" and is often used to describe lands that have good pasturage for herds, and because Eudorus means "generous," both mother and son seem to represent this aspect of Hermes's identity.

Hermes is also connected to good luck and to lucky finds; this aspect of the god may be an extension of his origins as a fertility god. Hermes increases one's possessions, whether flocks or other material goods. He is called Charidotes (Luck-Bringer) and is associated with sudden windfalls. When a fisherman in ancient Greece pulled up his nets and found them filled with fish, he described his haul as a *hermaion*, a lucky catch. In this instance, the abundance of fish seems to be a magical or unexpected form of increase, because no labor was required for their sudden arrival. Hermes's beneficence in increasing flocks, bestowing wealth, and supplying lucky finds is consistent with his overall beneficent character.

Protection The phallus on herms is thought to indicate Hermes's role as a protector as well as his role as a fertility god, for several reasons. Most convincing among these is the Greek use of the phallus as an apotropaic (that is, capable of warding off evil) symbol. Apotropaic devices were placed at entryways of shops, houses, and temples, as well as on streets and plazas. In the ancient Mediterranean, images of eyes were also commonly used as apotropaic devices. Another well-known apotropaic device was Medusa's head, which as part of Athena's aegis (shield) was believed to ward off enemy advances in battle. Apotropaic amulets made from clay and metals and featuring eyes, phalluses, and Medusas have been found throughout ancient Greece, suggesting their widespread use. The erect phallus on herms, then, may indicate Hermes's role as a protecting deity associated with flocks and the countryside, which also extends to his protection of human communities and individuals. Herms located at the doors and gates of temples, houses, and cities suggest that Hermes stands ready to defend residents. Herms were also placed at the entry of bedrooms, implying that sleepers sought his protection, and perhaps even his encouragement of procreation.

Hermes's association with the protection of herd animals is captured by his epithet Epimelius (Guardian of the Flocks). The prayers and offerings of Odysseus's swineherd Eumaeus, for example, indicate that Hermes was a god on whom shepherds relied for protection and success. Before every meal Eumaeus prays to Hermes; the nymphs who lived in mountains, waters, and trees; and Pan. Eumaeus's prayers complete and ensure his careful protection of Odysseus's swine: Eumaeus places pens for swine next to where he sleeps and keeps four dogs near precious boars to protect them. Hermes's strange epithet Cynagches (Dog-Strangler) suggests a certain antagonism between him and such protective dogs. Hermes can evade and silence dogs (perhaps by strangling them) when he prowls at night helping travelers, such as Priam. Yet Hermes also has a kind of kinship with dogs because they, like him, guard flocks.

Hermes protects communities of people as well as flocks, as a ritual dedicated to Hermes in Tanagra, in Boeotia, makes clear. The Tanagrans claimed that Hermes was born on Mount Cerycaeus (Mountain of Heralds) in Boeotia and that he married a nymph named Tanagra, who is the ancestor of Tanagra's residents. Pausanias reports that Hermes once protected the city of Tanagra from a plague by carrying a ram around the city walls. The Tanagrans dedicated an annual festival to him, during which a handsome young man imitates Hermes's actions and carries a ram around the city (9.22.1–2). Hermes also acquired the epithet Creophorus (Ram-Carrier), and statues of Hermes carrying a ram recall his protective function in Tanagra (Figure 7.4).

In Athens, the dedication and destruction of herms—and, curiously, a myth about Hermes's son Pan—offer further evidence of the protective function of herms. Pan, the son of Hermes (with the nymph Penelopeia), is also frequently represented as ithyphallic. Part man and part goat, Pan has certain affinities with satyrs, who are also part goat and part man, ithyphallic,

7.4 Hermes Criophorus (Hermes carrying a ram). Parian marble statue. Imperial Roman copy of an early fifth-century BCE classical Greek original by Kalamis. Museo Barracco, Rome, Italy. © Vanni Archive / Art Resource, NY, ART405260.

and roamers of the countryside (often in the company of Dionysus) (Chapter 9.1). Although Pan can cause panic (the word "panic" comes from his name) to shepherds who tend their flocks far from their homes, he also protects the lands he roams. Pan makes a rare appearance in a military setting in tales of the battle of Marathon, when the Greeks repulsed the Persian invasion (490 BCE). It was said that Pan spread panic among the Persian troops, which allowed the Athenians to defeat them. In later conflicts with the Persians, the Athenians led a campaign against the Persians and succeeded at a siege in Eion (476 BCE). In an area of the Athenian Agora that was called simply "the herms" because so many of these statues were set up there, the Athenians dedicated three herms (each inscribed with a poem) to celebrate their victory at Eion. Significantly, the citizens of Athens decided not to inscribe the names of those who died in the victory poems. These three undifferentiated herms were thus representative of all democratic citizens, who, through fighting in phalanxes, were to be equal with one another before the law as well as in death. Moreover, these unnamed citizens who died in battle were to be understood as defending Athens, like Herms or like Pan.

The monument of Eion helps to explain the notorious mutilation of the herms that took place in Athens in 415 BCE. On the morning when the Athenian fleet was set to depart for a controversial military campaign in Sicily at the height of the Peloponnesian War, all the herms in the city of Athens were destroyed in a very particular way. Their phalluses were hacked off, and, in some instances, their faces were also attacked. The perpetrators were put on trial for sacrilege, so seriously did the Athenians regard this act. What exactly did the perpetrators mean to convey through their mutilation of the herms? One of the more convincing interpretations is that when the herms were mutilated, the god Hermes was not the target of the attack. Neither was the fertility of the land or of people implicated, nor was Hermes's role as a messenger or escort challenged. Rather, the Athenian people themselves were the target of the attack. Because these herms represented the democratic citizens of Athens, all of whom were charged with protecting Athens, the perpetrators meant to suggest that by participating in the (ultimately disastrous) Sicilian expedition the citizens were not fulfilling their protective duty.

BEARDLESS HERMES

Whereas Hermes appears as a bearded adult man on herms, he is also occasionally represented as a young and beardless man. The association of Hermes with both young and adult males, and more specifically with the transition between adolescence and adulthood, has also been linked to both Hermes's hills and herms. Whereas the Hermes's hills alongside roads marked distances and offered protection to travelers, they are also found in fields, where they mark property boundaries. Herms, too, were placed at the boundaries of temples, cities, houses, and even rooms within houses. Beardless Hermes is a young man on the cusp or boundary of adulthood. He stands on a social or psychological boundary.

Contests in Hermes's honor were held throughout Greece and indicate Hermes's ongoing association with the passage of males into adulthood, as does Hermes's cult title Agonios (Of Contests). These contests usually involved athletics and music and gave young males on the brink of adulthood an opportunity to prove their mettle. One instance of Hermes's association with a man's transition from adolescence to adulthood is a sanctuary dedicated to Hermes and Aphrodite in Kato Syme on the island of Crete. Here, votives from the seventh and sixth centuries BCE in the form of bronze plaques depict both beardless youths and bearded men, carrying animals in the manner of Hermes Creophorus, wrestling, hunting, playing music, and courting one another. The votive plaques demonstrate Hermes's oversight of contests in which young men strove to demonstrate their worthiness to pass over the boundary dividing youth from adulthood.

One activity that young men pursued as part of their maturation in ancient Greece and in many places across the Mediterranean was cattle raiding. In many stories of Greek heroes (including the Homeric *Hymn* 4 [*To Hermes*], in which Hermes steals the cattle of his older brother Apollo), young heroes steal cattle. The result of raiding cattle is usually the development and recognition of a young man's skills, such as stealth, and the development or renewal of ties between the cattle thief and the owner. Thus, Hermes's raid on Apollo's cattle suggests his connection to yet another practice that young men pursued on the way to adulthood.

Hermes's hills, ithyphallic herms, and depictions of a beardless Hermes, then, express a range of activities associated with Hermes. Many of these suggest the joyful and friendly aspects of Hermes that Otto defined as Hermes's majestic singularity. But the friendliness of Hermes might be best understood as his style, not a trait that informs all his actions. Jean-Pierre Vernant (1914–2007), a French scholar of Greek religion, has offered an alternative definition of the majestic singularity of Hermes. Using an approach called structuralism, Vernant studied how the gods functioned in relation to one another, rather than how they developed through time. (Structuralists study

7.5 Hestia, Greek goddess of the hearth. Detail from a red-figure kylix. Circa sixth century BCE. Archaeological Museum, Tarquinia, Italy. *Gianni Dagli Orti / The Art Archive at Art Resource, NY, AA389250.*

how a society constructs oppositions, such as man versus woman, night versus day, or nature versus culture, to organize its political, social, and religious values [Chapter 6.2].) Vernant explores how Hermes and Hestia oppose and thereby explain each other in Greek religious thought. Hermes and Hestia are depicted next to each other on the pedestal of the statue of Zeus in his temple in Olympia, where the gods are paired for reasons that often are readily apparent (Pausanias 5.11.8). Zeus is paired with his wife Hera; Aphrodite is paired with her son Eros; Artemis and Apollo are paired because they are brother and sister. Although Hermes is rarely coupled with Hestia in art, ritual, or myth, Vernant explores the ways in which these two deities are opposites of each other. He thereby offers another method for interpreting gods and a different interpretation of Hermes's singular majesty. To follow Vernant's reasoning, we look at Hestia before returning to Hermes.

HESTIA

Hestia, the firstborn child of Cronus and Rhea, is an Olympian. Yet, unlike many Olympians, she has almost no temples, rituals, or cult shrines in her honor. An eternal virgin, often shown veiled and/or carrying a flowering branch (Figure 7.5), Hestia means "hearth" in Greek. She is closely connected to this fire at a household's center. Although seldom represented, Hestia was frequently worshipped in the life of every Greek because of her presence in every house. In the center of cities, a public building often contained a city hearth, whose fire had to be pure; that is, it had be kept burning, for if it was extinguished, it had to be renewed in ways that preserved its purity. Whether in a house or in a city, the hearth was also considered a place of asylum for those seeking protection. Additionally, as the hearth, Hestia was considered to partake of all sacrifices that required fire or cooking.

Hestia (or the hearth) is the center around which each family defined itself as a vital generative unit. Similarly, in every city, she symbolized and ensured the vitality of the civic community over time. Her role as the stable and unmoving center of each family through time is evident in a ritual called the Amphidromia, performed roughly two weeks after a child was born.

During the festival the child's membership in the family is ritually assured. The father of the child runs around Hestia (that is, the household's hearth) three times before placing the child on the ground near the hearth. Hestia's steadfastness ensured the child's legitimacy, and its placement near the hearth established the child's membership in the family. Thus Hestia defined a fixed center around which a family built itself.

Hestia's fixity in every house contrasts with Hermes's journeys on roads across the countryside and through city centers. Hestia is a goddess attached to the interior of houses, a place where residents retreat from contact with outsiders. Hermes, in contrast, enables exchanges, movement, and contacts. Hestia links females with the house, and Hermes links males with public places. The two deities, Vernant argues, thus represent a "polarity" or "complementarity": each exists in relation to the other. Vernant defines Hestia as the "starting point of orientation and arrangement of human space," whereas "nothing about [Hermes] is settled, stable, permanent, restricted, or definite." He is "the outside world, opportunity, movement, interchange with others."

As we have seen, all of Hermes's endeavors involve movement. Escorts and messengers obviously rely on movement. His increase and protection of flocks allows both their movement through space (the countryside) and their continuance in time. His attendance of young men's maturation enables them to move to adulthood. He is associated with the movement of both manufactured and naturally occurring goods and ideas, whether by way of thievery, trade, travel, conversation, commerce, or political assemblies. In this way Hermes was a most suitable god for Athenian citizens to embrace, because democracy is predicated on the movements of goods and ideas among all (not just elite) citizens. In Vernant's formulation, "the medium of movement" may be the simplest yet best summation of Hermes's majestic singularity, because it makes sense of all his traits and roles.

UNKNOWN, *HYMN 4: TO HERMES*

BEFORE YOU READ

The Homeric hymn to Hermes is one of the longest literary treatments of the god Hermes. In the hymn, Hermes is born, invents the lyre, steals Apollo's cattle, lies, and achieves a place on Olympus, although he was born in a cave on earth. (Translated by Michael Crudden.)

- Make a list of the activities that Hermes pursues and the traits he displays. Organize these according to the survey of Hermes's activities offered

**BEFORE YOU READ
CONTINUED**

previously (travel, messages, protection, fertility, and maturation). Does the hymn offer any evidence about Hermes that does not fit into these categories?

- Does the hymn represent Hermes as joy or motion?

- In the following section (Chapter 7.2), Hermes is described as a trickster figure. In what ways does Hermes exemplify the five-point description of a trickster offered there?

- Hermes lies and steals in this hymn; yet Zeus rewards him. If we assume that this hymn was written to encourage such behavior, how do you explain Hermes's rewards?

UNKNOWN, *HYMN 4: TO HERMES* (c. 700 BCE)

Sing of Hermes, Muse, of Zeus and Maia's son,
Who over Kyllene reigns and Arkadia rich in flocks,
The immortals' speedy messenger. Maia gave him birth,
That nymph whose tresses are fair, having joined in love with Zeus,
Being worthy of reverence. Shunning the throng of blessed gods,
She dwelt in a deep-shaded cave, where Kronos' son used to join
With the nymph whose tresses are fair at the milking-time of night,
While Hera whose arms are pale in the sweetness of sleep was clasped,
And neither immortal gods nor mortal humans knew.
But when to its end was approaching the plan of mighty Zeus—   10
And now for Maia in heaven her time's tenth moon had come—
The issue was brought into daylight, and what had been done was made clear:
It was then that she bore a child who was shifty and cunning in mind,
A seeker of plunder, a rustler of cattle, a leader of dreams,
A spy who keeps watch in the night, who lies in ambush at gates,
And would soon show glorious works amongst the immortal gods.
At dawn he was born, at midday was playing the lyre, and stole
At evening cattle owned by Apollo who shoots from afar,
On the day that queenly Maia bore him, the fourth of the month.
      When he leaped from his mother's deathless limbs, he did
         not for long   21
Remain in the sacred winnowing-fan, but jumped up to search
For Apollo's cattle, and over the vaulted cave's threshold he went.
He found a tortoise there, and vast good fortune gained:
Hermes it was who made the tortoise a singer first.
At the courtyard gates she met him, grazing in front of the house

On the thickly flourishing grass, and moving with waddling steps.
The speedy son of Zeus with a laugh at the sight at once said:
     "Already I have a sign of great profit: I make no complaint.
Hello there, shapely charmer who beat out time for the dance,
You feast's companion who come most welcome to view! But where   32
Did you get this beautiful toy, a glittering shell, to put on,
You tortoise who live in the mountains? No matter, into the house
I will bring you; no slights will you get from me in return for your help,
But you will profit me first. It is better to be at home,
Since harm lies out of doors. You will ward off baneful spells
While you live; if you die, most beautiful then your singing would be."
     In this way he spoke, and raising her up with both of his hands
He returned back into the house, the lovely toy in his grasp.
There tossing her up, with a knife of grey iron he scooped out the flesh
Of the tortoise that dwelt in the mountains, and like the quick passing
     of thought   43
Through the mind of a care-haunted man, or the whirling of gleams from eyes,
No sooner said than done was what glorious Hermes devised.
Cutting reed shafts to measure, he fitted them, piercing the back,
Through the shell of the tortoise; about it he stretched with his cunning the hide
Of a cow, affixed the arms and fastened the yoke to them both,
Then stretched seven cords of sheep's gut to serve as harmonious strings.
But when he had finished, he tried with the plectrum string by string
The lovely toy that he bore, and beneath his hand it made
An astonishing sound. The god began singing a beautiful song
To the tune, exerting himself impromptu, like youths who at feasts   56
Give voice to impudent taunts. Declaring his famous descent,
He sang how Kronos' son Zeus and Maia whose sandals are fair
Had been wont to hold converse once in the friendly union of love;
He extolled the nymph's servants and splendid abode, the tripods throughout
Her home, her numerous cauldrons, but had in the midst of his song
Still other desires in mind. He set down the hollow lyre
In the sacred winnowing-fan, and lusting for meat he leaped
Down the peak from the fragrant hall: he was plotting an outright trick
In his mind, of the sort that thieves carry out in the time of black night.
     As the Sun sank under the ground toward Ocean with horses
          and car,   69
At Pieria's shadowy mountains Hermes in haste arrived,
Where deathless cattle were stabled, owned by the blessed gods,
On meadows unspoiled and lovely taking of pasture their fill.
The keen-eyed Slayer of Argos, the son whom Maia bore,
Cut off then fifty cattle, whose lowing was loud, from the herd;

Turning aside their steps, he drove them by wandering paths
Through sandy ground, and did not forget his fraudulent craft,
Reversing their hooves, the fore-hooves behind, the hind-hooves in front,
While walking backwards himself. But at once at the sands of the sea
With withies he plaited sandals beyond the description of speech,　　　80
Beyond the grasp of mind, miraculous works that he made
By mixing tamarisk stalks together with myrtle-like shoots.
Of this freshly sprouting wood together an armful he tied,
And bound to his feet without pain the light sandals with leaves still attached.
The glorious Slayer of Argos plucked these, avoiding the walk
From Pieria, as making speed a long journey . . .
　　　By an old man who toiled at a vineyard where flowers bloomed
　　　　　　he was seen,
As he sped to the plain through Onkhestos bedded with grassy meads.
Glorious Maia's son was the first of the pair to speak:
　　　"Old man who dig at your plants with shoulders curved
　　　　　　in a stoop,　　　90
Wine will be yours in plenty, whenever all these bear fruit.
Although you have seen, be blind; be deaf, although you have heard;
And be silent, when you on your part suffer no harm at all."
　　　He said no more, but hurried the herd of strong cattle on.
Glorious Hermes drove them through many shadowy peaks,
Valleys resounding with echoes, and plains where flowers bloomed.
Of the helpful gloom of godly Night the greater part
Was passing, quickly the Morning when folk begin work drew near,
And the daughter of lordly Pallas, Megamedes' son,
Brilliant Selene, the Moon, had newly reached her post,　　　99
When the mighty son of Zeus beside Alpheios' stream
Drove the broad-browed cattle that Phoibos Apollo owned.
Although unbroken, they came to a high-roofed byre and troughs
Before a magnificent meadow. There having on fodder well fed
The cattle whose lowing was loud, and then driven them into the byre
In a throng, as they chewed on lotos and galingale moist with dew,
He brought many sticks together, and strove for the craft of fire.
He seized and stripped with iron a bay-tree's splendid bough

　　　　　　. . . . .

That was firmly fixed in his grasp, and upwards heat was breathed:
Hermes it was who first discovered fire-sticks and fire.　　　111
Taking many dry logs entire, in abundance he piled them up
In a pit that was sunk in the ground, and a flame began shining there
That sent far out a blast of fiercely blazing fire.
While the might of renowned Hephaistos kindled the flames, close by

A pair of lowing black heifers Hermes dragged outside;
Possessed of great power, he hurled them both gasping onto their backs
To earth, inclined and rolled them, piercing their spines straight through,
And followed one task with another, cutting their fat-rich meat.
Transfixed on wooden spits he roasted together the flesh,
The chines of honour's share, the black blood crammed in the guts.   123
While these on the ground were lying there, on a rugged rock
He stretched out the hides, as still they are now after all this time,
A long time since these events, and will unceasingly be.
But then Hermes the joyful at heart drew onto a smooth, flat stone
The rich fruits of his labour, divided twelve portions for lots to assign,
And added to each in perfection honour's share of chine.
Then glorious Hermes craved the meat of the rite, for the scent
Distressed him, immortal though he was, with its sweetness; but not
Even so did his bold spirit yield, for all that he yearned to thrust
The meat down his sacred throat. He set down in the high-roofed byre   134
The fat and the plentiful meat, but at once he raised them aloft,
The sign of his youthful theft. Collecting dry sticks, he destroyed
The whole feet, the whole heads with the breath of fire. But when the god
Had fittingly finished it all, in Alpheios where eddies swirl deep
He cast his sandals, quenched the embers, and spent all the night
Spreading black ash with sand in Selene's beautiful light.
　　　To Kyllene's brilliant peaks he quickly came once more
By morning; none of the blessed gods or mortal men
In his long journey's course had met him, and not a dog had barked.
The speedy son of Zeus, having turned himself sideways, passed   146
Through the chink of the hall-door's lock like a harvest-time breeze or a mist.
He went straight on and reached the rich inner shrine of the cave,
Moving with soft steps forward—his walk was so silent, it seemed
His feet were not touching the ground. In the winnowing-fan in haste
Glorious Hermes climbed; around his shoulders he wrapped
The swaddling-bands, and lay like an infant child, having fun
With the sheet that he held at his hams, while keeping enclosed on his left
The lovely tortoise-lyre. But the god did not escape
His goddess mother's sight, and she then spoke these words:
　　　"What are you up to, subtle rogue, arriving here   155
In the night from who knows where, parading your barefaced cheek?
It is now my firm belief that with bonds about your ribs
Against which struggle is futile, bonds that nothing can loose,
You will pass out through the porch in the grasp of Leto's son,
Rather than that you will plunder and rob when you please in the glens.
Be off back where you came from! In you your father begot

A vast vexation for mortal men and immortal gods."
　　To her in answer Hermes spoke these cunning words:
"Mother, why aim this abuse at me, as if I were
An infant child who knows but a few naughty tricks in his mind,　　164
A timid babe, whose mother's rebukes make him cower in fright?
I shall enter whatever craft is best, so keeping us both
In clover for ever: the two of us will not endure
Staying here in this place, the only immortals deprived of gifts
And prayers, as you are bidding. Better that all one's days
Be spent conversing amongst the immortals with riches, wealth,
And plenty of booty, than sitting at home in a murky cave.
As for honour, I too shall enter that rite which Apollo enjoys.
If my father will not allow me, then I shall try—it is in
My power—to be the leader of thieves; and if the son　　176
Of glorious Leto comes in search of me, I think
Something else even worse will happen to him, for I shall go
To Pytho, to break my way inside his great abode.
From there I shall plunder in plenty tripods surpassingly fair,
Cauldrons and gold, and gleaming iron in plenty as well,
And a lot of clothes—and you will see it, if you wish."
　　So they addressed one another, the son of Zeus who bears
The *aigis* and queenly Maia, as Dawn the early-born
Was rising from deep-flowing Ocean, bringing to mortals her light.
But Apollo had reached Onkhestos, the lovely, hallowed grove　　186
Of the loud-roaring Holder of Earth. He found the old man there
Grazing a beast, his vineyard's bulwark, beside the road.
Glorious Leto's son was the first of the pair to speak:
　　"Old man, you bramble-plucker of grassy Onkhestos there,
I've reached this place from Pieria, searching for cattle that came—
All of them heifers, all with twisted horns—from my herd.
The black bull was grazing alone away from the rest, and behind
Him followed the bright-eyed dogs, like four men with one purpose in mind.
These dogs and the bull were left there, and that is a marvel indeed;
But the heifers, just as the Sun was setting, went from the soft　　198
Meadow-field, away from sweet pasture. Tell me, aged one born
Long ago, have you seen any man who with them travelled the path?"
　　The old man, making his answer, addressed him with these words:
"My friend, it's a difficult task to tell all you might see with your eyes.
Many wayfarers travel the road: intent on much evil are some,
While others have worthy ends, and it's hard to know each one.
But I spent the whole day till sunset digging around the ridge
Of the vineyard whose soil yields wine; now I cannot swear to it, sir,

But I thought that I saw a child, and this child, whoever he was,
Was following fine-horned heifers, although a mere infant babe.   210
He was grasping a stick and walking from side to side, from the rear
Of the herd was pressing them back, and was keeping turned towards him
    their heads."
      The old man spoke; the god, when he heard, advanced along
The road with greater speed. He was watching a long-winged bird,
And suddenly knew that the thief was the son of Kronos' son Zeus.
In haste toward holy Pylos Apollo the lord son of Zeus
Rushed on in his search for the shambling cattle, his broad shoulders wrapped
In purple cloud. The Far-shooter noticed the tracks and said:
      "Well now, a mighty marvel is this that I see with my eyes!
Those at least are tracks of cattle with upright horns,   220
Yet back to the asphodel meadow they're turned. But these are steps
That belong to no man or woman, to no grey wolves or bears
Or lions, nor do I think to some Centaur with shaggy-maned neck,
Whoever with swift feet takes such astounding strides as these.
Strange as they are over there, these here are stranger still."
      Apollo the lord son of Zeus with these words rushed onward and came
To Kyllene's wood-clad peak and the deep-shaded lair in the rock
Where the heavenly nymph had borne the child of Kronos' son Zeus.
A lovely scent was spreading throughout the holy peak,
And upon the grass went grazing many slender-legged sheep.   232
Across the threshold of stone and into the murky cave
Quickly then entered the Far-shooter, mighty Apollo himself.
      When Zeus and Maia's son saw Apollo who shoots from afar
Raging about his cattle, he snuggled down amidst
The fragrant swaddling-bands: like ash enfolding a pile
Of tree-stump embers, Hermes curled himself up when he glimpsed
The god who works from afar. In a small space together he pressed
His head, his hands, his feet, like a babe who is fresh from the bath
And is summoning pleasant sleep, though wide awake he was,
And kept the tortoise-lyre beneath the pit of his arm.   242
But Zeus and Leto's son knew well without mistake
The beautiful mountain nymph and her son, a child who, though small,
Was cloaked in deceitful guile; and peering throughout each nook,
With a gleaming key he opened three secret chambers filled
With nektar and lovely ambrosia. Lying inside was gold
And silver in plenty, and plenty of clothes that belonged to the nymph
Of crimson and silvery hue, such treasures as sacred abodes
Of blessed gods contain. When Leto's son had explored
The nooks of the spacious abode, to glorious Hermes he said:

"You child who lie in the winnowing-fan, inform me at once   255
Of my cattle, or soon we'll differ, and not in a seemly way.
For into murky Tartaros, into the dreadful doom
Of darkness that none can escape, I'll toss you. You'll not be released
By mother or father to see the light again, but beneath
The earth you'll be gone, and will rule amongst the little men."
     To him in answer Hermes spoke these cunning words:
"What's this unfriendly speech, son of Leto? You've come here in search
Of cattle whose haunts are the fields? Not a sight did I see, not a fact
Did I learn, not a word did I hear from another's lips, I could
Not reveal the least information, I could not at all collect   264
An informer's fee. I don't even look like a mighty man
Who rustles cattle, and that is no business of mine—till now
Other matters have been on my mind. What's been on my mind is sleep
And the milk of my mother, keeping the swaddling-bands wrapped round
My shoulders, and warm bath-water. No one had better find out
The cause of this quarrel—it would quite astound the immortals to learn
That a new-born babe had passed through his porch with cattle whose haunts
Are the fields! But that's an implausible claim you make: I was born
Just yesterday, soft are my feet, and rough underfoot is the ground.
Yet by my father's head I'll swear, if you wish, a great oath: 274
I neither declare myself to be guilty, nor have I seen
Anyone else who stole your cattle, whatever it is
These 'cattle' may be—about them this rumour is all that I hear."
     In this way he spoke, and had in his eyes a knowing gleam,
As he tossed about with his brows while gazing now here, now there,
Giving long whistles, paying the other's words no heed.
To him with gentle laughter Apollo the Far-worker said:
     "My fine, deceitful schemer, it is my firm belief
That during the hours of night you'll often break your way
Inside the well-built home of more than one man alone,   284
And stripping his house without noise you'll force him to make the ground
His seat, to judge by your talk! And in glens of the mountain you'll vex
Many herdsmen whose haunts are the fields, whenever lusting for meat
You encounter herds of cattle and sheep with woolly fleece.
But unless you desire to take your last and final nap,
Get down from the winnowing-fan, companion of gloomy night.
For this then indeed will be your share of honour amongst
The immortals: you will for ever be called the Leader of Thieves."
     With these words Phoibos Apollo, to carry him, seized the child.
But the mighty Slayer of Argos, while being raised up in his hands,   295
Took thought and sent out an omen, the brazen labouring man

Of his belly, a wicked messenger, after which quickly he sneezed.
Apollo heard it and threw illustrious Hermes to earth,
Seated himself before him, though eager to speed on the way,
Aiming his taunts at Hermes, and to him spoke these words:
    "Take courage, swaddled infant, Zeus and Maia's son.
I shall then indeed discover where my strong cattle are,
By means of these omens—and you, moreover, will lead the way."
    In this way he spoke, but Kyllenian Hermes swiftly jumped up,
Moving with haste. With his hands he pushed about both of his ears   305
The swaddling-bands entwined around his shoulders, and said:
    "Where are you bearing me, Far-worker, fiercest of all the gods?
Is it anger over your cattle that makes you annoy me like this?
May the race of cattle perish! For I stole no cattle of yours,
Nor have I seen any other who stole them, whatever it is
That 'cattle' may be—about them this rumour is all that I hear.
But pay and receive satisfaction with Kronos' son Zeus as the judge."
    But when the shepherd Hermes and Leto's splendid son
Had explored all these points in detail, their minds on different ends—
Apollo, speaking unerringly, not without justice desired   316
To lay hands on glorious Hermes because of his cattle, while he,
The Kyllenian, wanted to dupe with tricks and with cunning words
The God of the Silver Bow—but when Hermes, for all his wiles,
Found him well able to cope, then quickly he walked through the sand
In front, and behind him followed Zeus and Leto's son.
On the summit of fragrant Olympos the beautiful children of Zeus
Came at once to their father, Kronos' son, since there for them both
The scales of justice lay waiting . . . held snowy Olympos,
And the deathless immortals were gathering after golden-throned Dawn.
With Hermes stood Apollo, God of the Silver Bow,   327
In front of the knees of Zeus; and Zeus who thunders on high
Questioned his brilliant son, and to him spoke these words:
    "Phoibos, from where have you rustled this pleasing plunder, a babe
Who's just been born, who has about him a herald's look?
A serious matter is this that's come to the council of gods!"
    The lord Apollo who works from afar addressed him in turn:
"Father, no trifling tale will you be hearing soon,
Although it is your taunt that I am the only one
Who has a liking for plunder. I found a certain child—
This outright brigand here—amongst Kyllene's peaks,   337
When I'd crossed a vast tract of land. An impudent rogue he is,
And never have I, at least, seen any who'd be his match,
Of gods or those men who swindle mortals over the earth.

He stole from their meadow my cattle, at evening he drove them away
By the shore where waves were crashing, and straight for Pylos he aimed.
And the tracks were twofold, prodigious, fit to marvel at,
And a marvellous deity's work. For while the black dust displayed,
Turned back to the asphodel meadow, prints that those cattle made,
This impossible beggar himself was crossing the sandy ground
Neither on feet nor hands, but by means of some other scheme   348
He left an astounding trail, as though walking on saplings of oak.
So long as he sped over sand, all the tracks were distinct in the dust;
But when he had passed beyond the great path that led through the sand,
The cattle's trail and his own soon vanished upon the hard ground—
Though a mortal man perceived him driving toward Pylos the herd
Of cattle whose brows are broad. But when he had shut them away
To rest in quiet repose, and hurtled then hotfoot along
From this side to that of the road, he lay down in the winnowing-fan,
Looking like gloomy night, in a murky cave's deep shade,
Where he could not be reached by even an eagle's piercing gaze.   360
And he gave his eyes a good rub with his hands, as he busied himself
With deceit, then without more ado he uttered in forthright terms
This speech: 'Not a sight did I see, not a fact did I learn, not a word
Did I hear from another's lips, I could not reveal the least
Information, I could not at all collect an informer's fee.'"

    When he had in this way spoken, Phoibos Apollo sat down;
But Hermes in turn replying spoke from the other side,
And pointed at Kronos' son, the master of all the gods:

    "Father Zeus, to you of course I'll tell the truth,
For I am honest, and don't know how to tell a lie.   369
In search of shambling cattle he came to our house today,
Just as the Sun was rising, and brought no blessed gods
As witnesses or observers. Many a threat he made
That he would in broad Tartaros hurl me, since his is the tender bloom
Of youth that loves renown, while I was but yesterday born—
He himself is aware of these facts—and have not at all the look
Of a mighty man who rustles cattle. Believe me, since you
Proclaim yourself my father. May I be blessed so sure
As I drove no cattle home, nor over the threshold went—
And I'm telling the perfect truth. I have great respect for the Sun   381
And other deities; you I love and him I dread.
That I am not guilty you are yourself aware, but I'll give
A mighty oath besides: I am not, by this well-adorned
Front door of immortals! Some day I'll pay him back for his harsh
Inquisition, strong though he be; let you give the younger your help."

The Kyllenian Slayer of Argos winked as he uttered these words,
And he kept without casting aside the swaddling-bands on his arm.
Loud was the laughter of Zeus when he saw the roguish child
Denying about the cattle in fine and skilful speech.
But he ordered them both to make search, at one with each other in mind,   391
And instructed Conductor Hermes to lead the way and reveal—
Without any mischievous plots—where he had the strong cattle concealed.
The son of Kronos nodded, and splendid Hermes obeyed,
Persuaded with ease by the mind of *aigis*-bearing Zeus.
   Rushing toward sandy Pylos, these beautiful children of Zeus
Both came to Alpheios' ford, to the fields and high-roofed byre
Where during the hours of night the livestock were given their feed.
There, while Hermes then passed inside the cave of stone,
And began to drive out the strong cattle into the light of day,
The son of Leto, glancing aside, observed the hides   403
Upon the steep rock, and of glorious Hermes was quick to inquire:
   "How were you able, you trickster, to flay two heifers' hides,
Although you're just a new-born infant child? I'm amazed
Myself at what in future that strength of yours will be—
Kyllenian, son of Maia, you must not grow up tall."
   He spoke these words and started to wind with his hands strong bonds
Of withy about him; but these beneath his feet in the earth
Upon that selfsame spot took root at once, like grafts
Entwining one with another, and spreading with ease over all
The cattle whose haunts were the fields through deceitful Hermes' will,   413
While Apollo looked on with wonder. Then sidelong his gaze at the ground
The mighty Slayer of Argos aimed, being eager therein
To hide the gleaming fire; but he soothed with perfect ease—
Strong though he was—the Far-shooter, glorious Leto's son,
In accord with his own desire. He tried with the plectrum string
By string the lyre, which he took on his left; beneath his hand
It made an astonishing sound, and Phoibos Apollo laughed
For joy. The lovely burst of heavenly music passed
Through his mind, and while he listened sweet longing seized him at heart.
But Maia's son, while playing to lovely effect on the lyre,   423
Took courage and stood on the left of Phoibos Apollo; at once,
As he played the clear notes, he started in prelude to sing—and the sound
Of his voice was lovely—bringing to pass the immortal gods
And shadowy Earth in his song, recounting how first they were born,
And how each obtained his share. Of the gods he first honoured in song
Mnemosyne mother of Muses, for she was assigned Maia's son;
To the other immortal gods the splendid son of Zeus

Gave honour according to age and as they each were born,
Telling all in a seemly way, while playing the lyre on his arm.
Love that he could not resist took hold of Apollo at heart,   434
And he in speech to Hermes gave voice to winged words:
    "Slayer of Cattle, Contriver, Performer of Toil, you Feast's
Companion, fifty heifers is your invention's worth!
I think then indeed in our quarrel we'll part from each other in peace.
But now come, tell me this, you shifty son of Maia, from birth
Did you have these miraculous skills, or was there one amongst
The immortals or mortal men who gave you the marvellous gift
And revealed to you heavenly song? For with wonder my ears are filled
At this sound for the first time uttered that never has yet, I declare,
Been learnt by men or immortals who dwell in Olympian homes,   445
Except by you, you robber, Zeus and Maia's son!
What is the craft, the music of sorrows that none can resist,
The beaten track? For truly can merriment, love, sweet sleep
Be gained all three together. I serve the Muses who dwell
On Olympos, whose joy is in dancing, the splendid path of song,
Melody's sprightly strains, the delightful wailing of flutes;
But not yet have I felt in my mind such joy as this at aught else,
Of all those dextrous skills that the young display at feasts—
I'm amazed, son of Zeus, how lovely these tunes that you're playing sound.
But now since, despite being small, you have knowledge of glorious
        schemes,   456
Sit, my fine fellow, and praise your elders at heart. For now
Renown will be yours and your mother's amongst the immortal gods—
And this is the truth that I'll tell you, yes, by this cornelwood spear!—
I'll seat you in glory and wealth amongst the immortals as Guide,
I'll give you splendid gifts, and I'll not play you false in the end."
    To him in answer Hermes spoke these cunning words:
"You take great care in asking me, god who works from afar;
Yet I don't grudge at all that you enter this craft of mine—
You'll know it this very day. I want to be kindly to you
In counsel and speech—but you know everything well in your mind.   467
For you, son of Zeus, are the first amongst the immortals to sit,
Being so noble and strong; sagacious Zeus with all
Due reverence loves you, to you he has granted splendid gifts
And honours. They say you've learnt prophecies, Far-worker, spoken by Zeus—
From Zeus come all things decreed. Now in these I've learnt myself
That you, my boy, are rich—but you can freely choose
To learn whatever you wish. Well, since your heart is set
On playing the lyre, make melody, play, and busy yourself

With splendid celebration, receiving the lyre from me—
But furnish me, friend, with renown. Produce melodious tunes,   478
As you hold in your hands your clear-voiced companion, expert in speech
That is fair and fine and seemly. Bring it then at your ease
To the bounteous feast, the delightful dance, the revel that loves
Renown, a source of merriment by both night and day.
When one who has learned the knowledge puts to it questions with craft
And wisdom, it cries out and teaches joys of all sorts that charm
The mind, being easily played with a gently familiar touch,
Escaping painful exertion; but when at the outset one
Who lacks knowledge puts to it questions with violence, then it will yield
A pointless, high-pitched jangle—but you can freely choose   489
To learn whatever you wish. Now I shall grant you this,
You splendid young fellow of Zeus, but let us then, Far-worker, graze
The cattle whose haunts are the fields on the pastures of mountain and plain
That gives nurture to horses. The heifers will then be mated with bulls,
And will bear in abundance together calves both female and male—
But you must not grow fiercely angry, despite your greed for gain!"
    With these words he proffered the lyre. Apollo, accepting the gift,
Put in Hermes' palm the gleaming whip that he held, and bestowed
Upon him the tending of herds of cattle; Maia's son
Accepted these gifts with joy. Then Leto's splendid son,   500
Lord Apollo the Far-worker, tried with the plectrum string by string
The lyre, which he took on his left; beneath his hand it made
An astonishing sound, and the god sang a beautiful song to the tune.
    When the two of them then had turned toward the divine meadow-field
The cattle, they themselves, the beautiful children of Zeus,
Rushed back to snowy Olympos, taking delight in the lyre;
Sagacious Zeus rejoiced, and brought them together as friends.
Hermes without reserve felt love for Leto's son—
As still he does even now—when for a token he put
The lovely lyre in the palm of the god who shoots from afar,   509
And he, having learnt, began to play it upon his arm.
But Hermes sought out for himself the craft of another skill:
He made the syrinx' piping that can far away be heard.
And then the son of Leto to Hermes spoke these words:
    "I'm afraid, son of Zeus, Conductor, subtle in guile, that you'll steal
The lyre back and my curving bow. For you hold the honour from Zeus
Of founding acts of barter for humans all over the earth
That gives to many their nurture. But if you could bring yourself
To swear the gods' great oath, by either nodding your head
Or making your vow upon the potent water of Styx,   519

You would accomplish everything pleasing and dear to my heart."
        And then the son of Maia promised with downward nod
Never to steal away whatever the Far-shooter owned,
Or approach his solid abode. In turn with downward nod,
To mark their alliance and love, Apollo, Leto's son,
Declared that amongst the immortals no other would be more dear,
Neither god nor man begotten by Zeus. And out a perfect

.   .   .   .

Amongst immortals and humans I'll make a sign which I trust
And honour at heart. But I'll give you besides a beautiful rod
Of fortune and riches, golden and branching in three; unscathed   530
It will keep you while bringing to pass all decrees of words and of deeds
That are good, all those that I claim to have learnt from the voice of Zeus.
But prophecy, splendid fellow, about which you ask without end,
It's decreed that neither yourself nor another immortal may learn.
For this is a matter known to the mind of Zeus, while I
In pledge have nodded down and sworn a mighty oath
That I alone of the gods who live for ever shall know
The shrewd-minded counsel of Zeus; and let you not command,
Brother with rod of gold, that I disclose the decrees
That far-seeing Zeus devises. Of humans one I'll harm   541
And profit another, while many times around I herd
The tribes of unenvied humans. My voice will profit him
Whose coming is guided by speech and flights of birds that bring
Fulfilment—my voice will profit him, and I shall not
Deceive him. But he who trusts in birds of idle talk,
Who wants to inquire of our prophecy more than reason permits
And have more knowledge than gods who always exist, I say
His journey will be in vain—though I would accept his gifts.
But there's something else that I'll tell you, glorious Maia's son
By *aigis*-bearing Zeus, the immortals' speedy god.   551
For certain holy virgins, sisters by birth, there are,
Who all three exult in quick wings. They have white barley bestrewn
On their heads, and inhabit dwellings down in Parnassos' fold,
Teachers far-off of a prophecy practised by me when still
A boy with the cattle I was, and my father paid no heed.
Flying in one way now, and now in another, from there,
They feed on combs of honey and bring all things to pass.
And when they are inspired from eating pale honey, they wish
To speak truth of their own free will; but if deprived of the gods'
Sweet food, they quiver then amongst one another and lie.   563
These then I grant you: by making exact inquiry delight

Your own mind; should you teach a mortal man, he'll often hear
Your voice, if he's lucky. Possess, son of Maia, these gifts, and take care
Of black cattle whose haunts are the fields, of horses and hard-working mules

.   .   .   .

And that over bright-eyed lions and boars whose tusks are white,
And that over dogs and flocks, as many as broad Earth rears,
And that over all cattle glorious Hermes hold sway, and alone
The appointed messenger be to Hades, who, though he gives
No gifts, will yet of honour give not the smallest share.
    In this way the lord Apollo showed love for Maia's son   574
With friendship of every sort, and the son of Kronos bestowed
Favour upon him besides. With all mortals and immortals both
He has dealings; seldom though does he help, but unceasingly cheats
Throughout the gloomy night the tribes of mortal men.
    And so farewell I bid you, Zeus and Maia's son;
But I will call to my mind both you and another song.   580

THE MIND STRUCTURES MYTHS IN ARCHETYPES

**7.2
THEORY**

The concept of the trickster offers yet another way to understand Hermes's majestic singularity. This additional perspective is loosely connected to the definition of Hermes as a principal of motion offered earlier in this chapter. "Trickster" is a designation for a certain kind of character, found in myths and folktales, that was at first linked to the psychologist Carl Gustav Jung's concept of archetypes. After reviewing Jung's ideas about the trickster, we consider a more widely held definition of this figure that evaluates his social and cultural dimensions before turning to a lively essay by Lewis Hyde that considers both Hermes and abolitionist Frederick Douglass (1818–1895) as trickster figures.

    Jung defined characters or events that recur in myths from around the world as archetypes. Archetypes, Jung argued, are generated by a psychic facility called the "collective unconscious"—an area of the mind that uses patterns or images, rather than linear logic and words, to process and organize experiences. In part, Jung used the term "collective" to indicate that all people organize their experiences in such patterns, or archetypes. Jung considered archetypes to be shared mental models that people in a given society use to describe and make meaning out of their experiences. Although experiences are limitless, the patterns or archetypes by which they are understood are fewer in number. Archetypal characters that appear repeatedly in

7.6 **Hermes Trismegistus.** Detail of a marble pavement. Giovanni di Stefano da Siena, 1488. Duomo, Sienna, Italy. *Scala / Art Resource, NY, ART22288.*

myths from around the world include the Great Mother, the child, the father, the sage (Figure 7.6), the hero, the god, the animal, the shadow, and the trickster. Tricksters, for Jung, are intimately related to the shadow archetype. Both of these figures appear in an essay Jung wrote for an early and influential study, *The Trickster: A Study in American Indian Mythology,* by folklorist Paul Radin (1883–1959). Radin had collected tales from the Winnebago Indian tribe that featured a character called Wakdjunkaga, a word Radin translated as "Trickster."

In Jung's explanation of the trickster figure, he argued that, in the scheme of the psyche, every person must develop a persona, which is the amiable, well-intentioned, and conformist identity every person presents to the world. The shadow is the opposite of the persona. The shadow, which embodies a person's socially unacceptable response to social demands and often has characteristics that society does not value, expresses the emotions and thoughts that the persona cannot acknowledge if it is to maintain its acceptance in society. Like all archetypes, the shadow has different names and features in different societies. For example, Jung argues that Satan is the shadow of Christ in the Christian church. Although a shadow figure can be truly frightening, in some cases it may also be a rather benign figure who expresses antisocial tendencies with humor. The archetype of the trickster, then, is closely related to the shadow archetype. Characters in stories labeled as tricksters are often more benign than those that can be traced back to the shadow archetype, but they share with them an attempt to criticize or subvert, whether for good or ill, the social order.

Many subsequent studies of trickster figures attempt to locate and define tricksters as well as explain their frequent occurrence in stories from around the world. Because most scholars no longer accept Jung's conception of the collective unconscious and archetypes, these more recent studies catalogue the traits that tricksters exhibit and consider their social, rather than psychological, dimensions. Most working definitions of tricksters include the following criteria:

- Tricksters are known for their—often crude—mockery of social, religious, political, or moral laws, institutions, or authorities.

- Tricksters overturn and disrupt any situation they enter into to their bene-fit and sometimes to their detriment by means of their tricks, antics, and deceptions.

- Tricksters have the ability to change their bodily form, which often is animal or animal-like, phallic, and male. (Most tricksters are male, al-though as scholars pay more attention to the female in different cultures, they are finding more female tricksters.)

- Tricksters' creativity and boundless energy allow them to invent objects or stories to serve their ends.

- Tricksters often are classified as "culture heroes" because they frequently give their inventions to humans who previously did not have them. These inventions are often stolen from the gods, and indeed tricksters are often the messengers of gods. Prometheus's list of his gifts to humankind, including the stolen fire, in *Prometheus Bound* offers a succinct example of why and how one figure can be both a trickster and culture hero (Chapter 3.1).

This list of five traits borrows from *Mythical Trickster Figures: Contours, Contexts, and Criticisms*, by William J. Hynes and William G. Doty (1997); Hynes and Doty summarize tricksters as "fundamentally ambiguous, anomalous, and polyvalent," which may account for why tricksters can at once mock society and yet be culture heroes.

This working definition of tricksters has allowed for a focus on the social, rather than psychological, needs fulfilled by trickster figures. Poking fun at a society's customs or public figures is one way to make evident a society's explicit and implicit values and beliefs. Such comic play, whether verbal, dramatic, visual, or ritual, is often a form of social commentary and critique. Humor can also reaffirm the social order by inspiring laughter rather than action, although humor can certainly be considered dangerous and even revolutionary. Yet a trickster's humorous and energetic qualities mask his intentions and thus enable him to escape social censure.

As tricksters mock, challenge, and outwit their social superiors, they create an opportunity for the socially marginalized to serve their own best interests, rather than acting in obedience to social customs and laws. They are often the heroes of marginalized and powerless groups within society. From this perspective, it is not surprising that the trickster figure is a staple in the folktales that Africans brought with them to America. He is also an emblem more broadly of the complexity of African American literature and speech. In *The Signifying Monkey* (1988), scholar and critic Henry Louis Gates (b. 1950) canonizes the African American trickster figure, Monkey, for his prodigious talents of doublespeak and verbal acrobatics. Gates locates the roots of Monkey among West African trickster figures and treats his critical, artful speech as exemplifying the tactics that diasporic Africans have adopted in their lives and arts throughout their history in America. To the degree that tricksters are viewed as coarse and vulgar, or as liars and cheats, the social space they create and the opportunities that space promises are rendered suspect, and their social critique is diminished. To view tricksters as coarse and vulgar, then, is a tactic that allows those with power to discredit tricksters whom they find dangerous and even criminal.

BEFORE YOU READ

LEWIS HYDE, FROM *TRICKSTER MAKES THIS WORLD: MISCHIEF, MYTH AND ART*

In the following essay, scholar and critic Lewis Hyde (b. 1945) studies Hermes as a trickster figure who represents the socially marginalized. Hyde begins his interpretation of Hermes by pointing out the social dimensions of Hermes as a god of the merchant classes, who were viewed with suspicion by the landed elites. Hyde argues that the god Hermes was associated with a less socially powerful group of people in Greece and that his tricks and stratagems to get to Olympus are his way of succeeding in world where he, and those he represents, do not have social power. Then Hyde examines the affinity between the great abolitionist Frederick Douglass and Hermes. Hyde, like a trickster, asks the reader to travel with him between ancient Greece and America as he explores the unexpected parallels between a Greek god and one of America's most eloquent and powerful reformers. Hyde's essay relies on the reader to be familiar with *Hymn 4* (*To Hermes*), included in the previous section.

- Does Doty and Hynes's definition of the trickster adequately define the Hermes of the Homeric *Hymn*? Does Hermes fulfill the criteria for a culture hero?

- Develop a list of traits and actions that might allow you to classify Athena (Chapter 6.1) or Prometheus (Chapter 3.1) as a trickster. Do either of these immortals qualify? Why or why not?

- Compare Hermes's and Douglass's acts of thievery. Are they at all similar?

- Do you think Hermes and Douglass serve the same social function in their respective societies?

LEWIS HYDE, FROM *TRICKSTER MAKES THIS WORLD: MISCHIEF, MYTH AND ART* (1998)

HERMES OF THE LIGHT, HERMES OF THE DARK

When Hermes comes home after stealing Apollo's cattle, he and his mother Maia have the archaic mom-boy argument over his behavior. In reply to her scolding, Hermes explains to her that he doesn't believe they should go on living obscurely in a cave. They deserve better:

> "I'm ready to do whatever I must so that you and I will never go hungry. . . . Why should we be the only gods who never eat the fruits of sacrifice and prayer? Better always to live in the company of other deathless ones—rich, glamorous, enjoying heaps of grain—than forever to sit by ourselves in a gloomy cavern. And as for honor, my plan is to have a share of Apollo's power. If my father won't give it to me I intend to be—and I mean it—the Prince of Thieves."

When he speaks of "Apollo's power" Hermes may be referring to the art of prophecy or to the guardianship of the herds, but however we read the line, the general point is not obscure: if his father won't give him honor and wealth, Hermes will steal them.

This opposition between gift and theft was one of the things that initially drew me to trickster figures, and to this story about Hermes especially. There have always been communities in which some wealth circulates through the exchange of gifts, rather than through purchase and sale. Tribal groups are the typical case; in many tribes it is thought improper to buy and sell food, for example; instead of a market, an elaborate system of gift exchanges assures that every mouth has food to eat. Such a circulation of gifts is an agent of social cohesion; it can even be argued that a group doesn't become a group until its members have an ongoing sense of mutual indebtedness, gratitude, obligation—all the social feelings that bind human beings together and that follow automatically in the wake of a system of gift exchanges. Nor are these phenomena limited to tribal or "primitive" situations. Individual scientists are drawn together into a "scientific community," for example, only to the degree that they treat their data and ideas as contributions to the group (while, conversely, the community fragments when ideas become proprietary, guarded by secrecy and fees).

All of which is very fine if you are one of the in-group. But what if you're an outsider, or what if you're inside but the customary commerce always leaves you beneath your "betters"? All the wonderful gift exchange in tribe A is little help if you've had a crop failure and belong to tribe B. The small-business club down the street may have a fine program for start-up capital, but what if it's for white folks only? What if all the male scientists swap data and you happen to be a woman? What if students at your high school always get scholarships to trade schools, never to elite universities? In cases such as these, you may have to resort to some form of subterfuge to get ahead; if the others won't give, you may have to steal.

By his own description, some such tension lies behind Hermes' thefts. For this and other reasons I read the *Homeric Hymn* as the story of how an outsider penetrates a group, or how marginalized insiders might alter a hierarchy that confines them. Hermes has a method by which a stranger or underling can enter the game, change its rules, and win a piece of the action. He knows how to slip the trap of culture.

His thieving is only one part of his method, of course, just as exclusion from gift exchange is only one way a group might keep someone in his or her place. There are many more. I opened this book with a discussion of actual traps attributed to trickster's intelligence, but it soon became clear that tricksters work with more ethereal snares than those that hunters use. The webs of signification by which cultures themselves are woven are the more complex and enduring sites of trickster's labor. To look at Hermes debating gift and theft is to watch a trickster disturbing but one knot in the almost unlimited number of knots that hold such a web together. Cultures take their shape from distinctions such as "gift and theft" or, to recall others we have seen, "the clean and the dirty," "the modest and the shameful," "essence and accident." These exactly are the joints of the cultural web and therefore the potential sites of trickster's play.

There are as many tricks as there are traps, of course, and I mean to use Hermes' stealing only as my point of departure, adding as we go along the other cunning wiles by which he unravels a particular cultural artifice and weaves a new one in its stead. In this way, by describing it carefully, I would like to abstract from Hermes' method a pattern or template with which to look at other cases of the marginalized undoing the snares that bind them.

As for other cases, I will turn my attention in the next chapter to the story of an African-American slave freeing himself from the plantation culture into which he was born. As I address myself to the *Homeric Hymn* I am therefore going to juxtapose language from the classic

Narrative of the Life of Frederick Douglass, an American Slave. I shall quote Douglass without much comment, as the connections are not obscure, though it will help at the outset to know the simple facts of his life. Douglass was born in 1818 in Talbot County, Maryland, on the eastern shore of Chesapeake Bay. His master (and probably his father) was a small landowner, Aaron Anthony, who worked as overseer on the plantation of one Colonel Edward Lloyd. Douglass was sometimes a field slave in Talbot County and more often a house slave in the Baltimore home of Aaron Anthony's in-laws, Hugh and Sophia Auld. He escaped from slavery in 1838 and settled in New Bedford, Massachusetts, where he became active in abolitionist circles, giving a famous first speech about his experiences to an anti-slavery convention in Nantucket in 1841.

With this in mind, let us return to Hermes and the *Hymn.*

. . .

As is apt for an interpretation guided by Hermes, I want to read the *Hymn* on several levels, to take it as a story about creativity, about the psyche, about social change, about an actual history. To begin with this last, the question is: If tricksters disrupt cultures that exclude or confine them, is there a particular historical context to which the *Hymn* itself belongs, and if so, what historical changes does it record? Norman O. Brown proposed one answer to these questions in his 1947 book, *Hermes the Thief.* Brown set out to chart the ways in which the mythology of Hermes altered from one era to the next, from the Helladic to the classical periods, a thousand years—1500 to 500 B.C.—during which Greek society moved from tribalism through a long period of agrarian kingship to end, for Brown's interest in Hermes, with fifth-century Athenian democracy. Brown places the *Hymn* during the last of these shifts, arguing that it was written down in Athens around 520 B.C., toward the end of a long tension between agrarian kingship and mercantile democracy.

He therefore proposes this parallel: just as Hermes acquires a place alongside Apollo in the course of the *Hymn*, so in the course of the sixth century the "Athenian industrial and commercial classes achieved equality with the aristocracy." That equality was not easily won; it required the resolution of a whole series of differences. In the aristocratic era, wealth came from herding and farming the soil; in Athenian democracy those sources of wealth still existed but were increasingly challenged by a craft economy and commercial exchange with strangers. Agrarian aristocracy was organized around hierarchical kinship ties; Athenian democracy retained such ties but added a new ethic of equality symbolized by the fact that many political positions in Athens were filled by a lottery in which all citizens could participate, regardless of family or status. Most important, the emerging cosmopolitan democracy brought with it a "new ethics of acquisitive individualism [that] conflicted with the traditional morality which the Greeks called Themis—the body of customs and laws inherited from the age of familial collectivism." The older morality took *any* deviation from "the archaic form of commerce by mutual exchange of gifts" to be an immoral thieving (even what we would now call fair trade was taken to be robbery). In short, during the sixth century, a world organized through kin relationships and a collective ethic of gift exchange gave way to a world in which hierarchy could be periodically revised and social relations were increasingly articulated through the individualist (which is to say, thieving) ethic of the marketplace.

As for those who were excluded or marginalized, we should remember that, in a society where the dominant values are kin ties and agrarian wealth, those whose identity is bound up with trade are typically consigned to a subordinate place in the order of things. They are, so to speak, "low caste" (as they have been historically in India, where merchants and artisans fall into the lower two of the four *varnas*). If, in the Greek case, such people hope to place themselves on an equal footing with the warriors and family farmers of ancient days, they will have to subvert that order and reshape it on their own terms. Such, Brown argues, is exactly what happened: the "regime of the landed aristocracy was overthrown, its agrarian economy yielding to a new economy based on trade and handicraft industry, its political oligarchy yielding to the politics of ancient democracy." The *Hymn* reflects that change: "The theme of strife between Hermes and Apollo translates into mythical language the insurgence of the Greek lower classes and their demands for equality with the aristocracy."

Brown's claims cover a lot of ground and his talk of class conflict gives off an air of retrospective Marxism, but the *Hymn* itself, however we fit it into actual Greek history, sets up a tension in accord with the one that Brown suggests. There is little doubt that in the classical period Hermes is associated with artisans, merchants, and thieves, and the poem itself makes it clear that some kind of "outsiderness" is at issue, and that Hermes hopes to change it.

To effect that change he has, as I said earlier, a method by which the excluded can enter a group, change its structure, and give themselves a place at the table. A whole range of cunning tricks makes up this method, but its underlying structure is quite simple: no matter what he does, Hermes is either an enchanter or a disenchanter. The simplest way to imagine him in this double field of action is to picture him at that moment, early in the story, when he emerges from his mother's cave:

> He didn't lie around in his sacred cradle, no, the minute he slipped from his mother's immortal arms he leapt up and set out to find Apollo's herds. As he crossed the threshold of that roomy cave he happened on a turtle and got himself an endless source of wealth.

"He crossed the threshold": here is the boundary-crosser on the boundary itself. He is leaving his mother, his cradle, the earth, the underworld, the private, the dark; he is entering the sunlight, the public, the uncovered, the outer and upper worlds of the sky gods (Zeus, Apollo, Helios). Poised on the threshold, he is in *his* world, the crepuscular, shady, mottled, ambiguous, androgynous, neither/nor space of Hermetic operation, that thin layer of topsoil where all these things are not yet differentiated. From this position Hermes can move in either direction or, more to the point, act as the agent by which others are led in either direction.

It is this double motion that makes Hermes at once an enchanter and a disenchanter. In his enchanting phase, he often begins by going after the border guards, for if they have their wits about them he cannot operate. Earlier we saw how he cast a lazy forgetfulness over the watchdogs guarding Apollo's cattle. In speaking of shame, we saw how he mesmerized Argus with song and story, then sealed the giant's sleeping eyes with a magic wand. Hermes drops the sentinels who watch the peripheries into a stupor, and impermeable boundaries become porous.

This is only the beginning of his enchanting/disenchanting power, too, for once the border is breached, Hermes will deliver a soul into whatever world or mental state lies across the line. He carries his charges into the underworld or out of it, into dreams or into wakefulness, into mythologies or out of them, into foreign countries or back home. When Odysseus has slain the suitors, it is Hermes who carries their souls down into Hades; in another story, it is Hermes who guides Persephone out of Hades and into the daylight. In one story, it is Hermes who puts to sleep the watchmen encircling Achilles's camp; in another, it is Hermes who awakens Odysseus as he walks toward Circe's house, so as to be sure that her magic cannot touch him.

Depending on which way he is moving across the threshold, I call him Hermes of the Dark or Hermes of the Light. Hermes of the Dark is the enchanter or hypnagoge who moves us into the underworld of sleep, dream, story, myth. This darkening motion is a precondition of belief; with it Hermes delivers you to one of the gods and puts you under his or her spell. He dissolves time in the river of forgetfulness, and once time has disappeared the eternals come forward. Hermes of the Dark is the weaver of dreams, the charmer who spins a compelling tale, the orator who speaks your mother tongue with fluid conviction.

Hermes of the Light is the disenchanter or awakening angel who leads you out of the cave. There the bright light prepares the ground for doubt. There he kills and roasts the sacred cattle. He dissolves eternals in the river of time, and when they have disappeared, the world becomes contingent and accidental. Hermes of the Light translates dreams into analytic language; he rubs the charm from old stories until they seem hopelessly made up and mechanical. He walks you inland until you stop dreaming in your mother tongue.

Hermes himself is neither one of these alone but both at once. He is neither the god of the door leading out nor the god of the door leading in—he is the god of the hinge. He is the mottled figure in the half-light, the amnigoge who simultaneously amazes *and* unmazes, whose wand *both* "bewitches the eyes of men to sleep and wakes the sleeping," as Homer says in the *Iliad*. I sometimes wonder if all great creative minds do not participate in this double motion, humming a new and catchy theogony even as they demystify the gods their elders sang about. Pablo Picasso had that double motion, disturbing classical perspective while presenting a strange new way of seeing, one so hypnotic it shows up decades after his death on billboards and children's printed pajamas. Sigmund Freud had that double motion, dragging slips of the tongue into the daylight, or "explaining" Moses, while simultaneously retelling the old story of Oedipus in a manner so compelling that, decades after his death, Ivy League literary critics can't get it out of their heads. Or there is Vladimir Nabokov: if you think his deft language magic is serious, you're wrong, and if you think it's just a game, you're wrong.

To see how this double motion serves Hermes' purposes in the *Hymn* itself, let's begin by watching him disenchant the world into which he has been born. He has several ways to drag it into the light. Theft necessarily comes first. Somehow he must make an entry; few groups go out of their way to embrace the marginal or foreign. All cultures set watchful dogs around their eternal cattle. All cultures guard their essences. If Hermes hopes to create a new home for himself against the grain of the old, he can only begin by stupefying those dogs and making a raid on the middle. And so he steals the cattle, moves them to Pieria, slaughters two of them, and so on. This theft alone is a disenchantment, for with it Hermes, like Loki and Monkey, brings time and death to what was formerly timeless and immortal. (In the situation of archaic Greece by which Brown reads the *Hymn*, the "sacred cows" are kingship, gift exchange, and the like; in the classical period, Hermes types "steal" these eternals and drag them into time where they become history.) Hermes' theft proves the boundary between his world and Apollo's is porous; it implies that the rules by which Apollo operates are contingent and arbitrary. Deftly done, a trickster's thieving calls into question the local property rights. Who gave Apollo those cattle in the first place? Who decided he could set guard dogs around that field?

> [From Frederick Douglass's *Narrative*:] Colonel Lloyd kept a large and finely cultivated garden. . . . It abounded in fruits of almost every description from the hardy apple of the north to the delicate orange of the south. This garden was not the least source of trouble on the plantation. Its excellent fruit was quite a temptation to the hungry swarms of boys, as well as the older slaves, belonging to the colonel, few of whom had the virtue or the vice to resist it. Scarcely a day passed, during the summer, but that some slave had to take the lash for stealing fruit.

> All the education I possess, I may say, I have stolen while a slave. I did manage to steal a little knowledge of literature, but I am now in the eyes of American law considered a thief and robber, since I have not only stolen a little knowledge of literature, but have stolen my body also.

To call the local property rights into question, one must forgo the pleasures of conforming to the local moral code. Hermes willingly submits to being seen as a thief in local terms, even if in his own amoral space or by some different morality the term does not apply. When the local code is insufficient to describe the situation (is stealing from Colonel Lloyd "virtue or . . . vice"?), the creative person is the one who will readily endure that insufficiency and, from an "immoral" position, frame a new set of rules.

7.3 COMPARISON

EGYPT: THOTH

7.7 Thoth with ibis head. Gilded wood and bronze. Circa 600 BCE. Werner Forman Archive / Schultz Collection, New York, New York. Location: 47. *HIP / Art Resource, NY, AR9150290.*

When Herodotus described the festival of the Egyptian goddess Neith in the Egyptian city of Sais, he identified her with Athena. The Greeks, as we saw in our studies of Aphrodite and Athena (Chapters 5.3 and 6.3), often drew connections among their gods and goddesses and those of their neighbors. Such is also the case with Hermes and Thoth, both of whom share a number of attributes and can be viewed as tricksters in their respective systems. However, unlike Athena and Neith (whom the Greeks viewed as two different names for the same goddess), the Greeks not only identified Hermes and Thoth with each other but also, over time, fused these two gods and developed a new deity or semidivine figure named Hermes Trismegistus (Thrice-Blessed).

Hermes Trismegistus emerges from interactions among Greek, Egyptian, and Roman cultures. Although the Egyptians initially resisted the blending of their god Thoth with Hermes, by the time Egypt was under Roman rule (after 30 BCE), Hermes Trismegistus had been created from the integration of Hermes and Thoth. Hermes Trismegistus then became a vehicle through which pagans in late antiquity throughout the Roman Empire articulated abstract, philosophical arguments about the nature of divinity.

The Egyptian god Thoth reminded the Greeks of their own deity, Hermes, despite the fact that the Egyptians represented Thoth either as a baboon or as a man with a head in the form of an ibis (a kind of bird) (Figure 7.7). Originally, Thoth was a creator god credited with the creation of eight Egyptian gods who each represented a different force of nature. The various traditions about the birth of Thoth are contradictory: in one tradition, he is self-generated, hatching from an egg, whereas in others he is the son of Nut (Night). Finally, in some accounts Thoth is born from the head of the god Set, after Set was raped by Horus. In that version, Thoth's birth is similar to Athena's birth from Zeus's head; not surprisingly, both Set and Athena are associated with wisdom.

By the second millennium BCE, Egyptians began to associate Thoth with law, language, medicine, mathematics, and magic. Egyptians also believed Thoth to be an advocate for the dead during the judgment of their souls. Thoth plays an important role in the Egyptian legend of Osiris and Isis, whose currency dates to the earliest Egyptian religious texts, in which many of Thoth's attributes are revealed. Because of Thoth's associations with cultural activities (such as law) as well as with death, the Greeks came to believe he was the Egyptian equivalent of Hermes. Indeed, both Thoth and Hermes can be described as cultural heroes as well as tricksters.

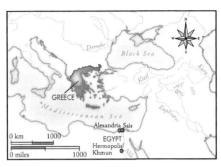

Map 7.2 Egypt: Thoth and Hermes Trismegistus

Plutarch (46–120 CE), a Greek writer and public servant who became a Roman citizen, has provided a systematic account of the Egyptian legend of Osiris that highlights Thoth's connection to law and death. When Osiris, the mythical king of Egypt, is killed and dismembered by his brother Set, Isis, the wife of Osiris, reunites all the parts of his corpse and brings him back to life for a brief period during which she conceives their son Horus. Thoth defends Horus when Set challenges his legitimacy as king. Plutarch's account recalls the much earlier version of Thoth's presentation in the Egyptian pyramid texts (c. 2400–2300 BCE), which also refer to Thoth's defense of Osiris when Osiris's soul is weighed in the Underworld. The trial of Osiris became a template for describing the journey after life of all Egyptians and also illuminates Osiris's role as lord of the dead. This tale also explains Thoth's patronage of legal officials like scribes, arbitrators, and lawyers as well as his role as advocate for the dead. The mythical trials in which Thoth's counsel is invaluable were said to take place before the gods of the city Khmun, which was the center of cultic worship in honor of Thoth in Egypt.

The invention of language and of writing was also attributed to Thoth. Plato, who lived centuries before Plutarch and before the arrival of Alexander in Egypt, knew this aspect of Thoth well. In his *Phaedrus* (excerpted subsequently), he describes Socrates contemplating the role of the Egyptian god Thoth (whom he calls Teuth) in all the arts that require reason and abstraction. In his criticism of the relatively new (to the Greeks) technology of writing, Socrates discusses Thoth because Thoth's association with languages and systems of abstract and symbolic analysis was so well known that Plato could be confident that his readers would understand the reference. Greeks, in fact, had been in contact with Egypt since the seventh century BCE, when traders and mercenary soldiers lived in Naucratis (Chapter 6.3). Thus Plato and his Greek readers would have easily recognized the similarities between Hermes and Thoth.

It is not surprising then, that when Alexander and the Greeks conquered Egypt in the late fourth century BCE, the Greeks continued to assume that Thoth was the Egyptian version of their own god, Hermes. Like Hermes, Thoth was associated with the journey of the soul to the afterworld and served as a messenger and scribe for the gods. Even so, the Egyptians resisted seeing Hermes in Thoth. Although the Greeks were able to conquer Egypt on the battlefield, the Egyptians resisted the cultural process of Hellenization that often accompanied Alexander's triumphant armies. When Alexander's Greek general, Ptolemy I Soter, established himself as the ruler of Egypt after the chaotic period that followed Alexander's death in 323 BCE, he adopted distinctly Egyptian forms of rule and ritual to articulate his authority to the people of Egypt. Ptolemy, for example, took the title "pharaoh." He, and his successors, also spent vast sums building new temples in honor of the Egyptian gods and sharply limited the number of settlements in Egypt that were organized like Greek city-states. This was one of the many ways that the ruling Greeks recognized and blended Greek and Egyptian cultural forms and ideas.

The Ptolemys also settled thousands of Greek mercenaries on land grants throughout Lower Egypt. These Greeks emerged as a leadership class in Egypt, largely displacing native Egyptians who had served the pharaohs and the Persians as administrators and bureaucrats. The Greeks in Ptolemaic Egypt enjoyed a Greek education and the privilege of being subject to Greek, rather than Egyptian, law. They married Egyptians, and in time a Greco-Egyptian elite culture and class, bilingual in both Greek and Demotic (the form of the Egyptian language spoken and written during this period), emerged. Because Egyptians refused to allow non-Egyptians to enter their priesthoods, the influence of Egyptian modes of religious thought was far greater than that of Greek modes in this hybrid community. For this reason, the gods whom the Greeks worshiped in Egypt quickly became imbued with an Egyptian sensibility. Over this time period, despite Egyptian resistance, Hermes and Thoth became increasingly aligned with each other.

In Hermopolis, the name the Greeks gave to Thoth's city, Khmun, Greeks celebrated their festival in honor of Hermes at the same time as Egyptians celebrated their festival in honor of Thoth. Similarly, in the texts of the Greek *Magical Papyri* (second century BCE to fifth century CE), ordinary Greeks living in Egypt invoked the aid of a Hermes who had assumed many of Thoth's traits. Beginning in the third century BCE, Hermes is referred to by the title "a twice great god" (*megistus kai megistus theos*). This is a Greek adaptation, if not literal translation, of a traditional formula used for Thoth. In Egyptian texts Thoth is often referred to as many times great: for example, "eight times great," "twice great," and "thrice greatest." In this way, a new god emerged from the interpolation of Egyptian religious patterns of thought and Greek formal descriptions of their gods. Beginning in Roman times, this god would be called Hermes Trismegistus.

Hermes Trismegistus emerged as a figure inhabiting a region somewhere between the heroic and divine. Eventually, however, largely through his association with Thoth, he became one of the great gods of the late antique world. He is believed to be the author of the *Hermetica*—a collection of astrological, medical, alchemical, and philosophical texts written in Greek, Latin, and Coptic (a later stage of the Egyptian language that evolved from Demotic). Those who worshipped Hermes Trismegistus believed that he wrote these books originally in Egyptian hieroglyphics (i.e., as Thoth) and translated them into Greek, in his incarnation as Hermes. Hermes the translator, however, is conceived of as a second Hermes, a grandson of the original.

The notion that a god might have multiple and varying incarnations would not have struck Romans or Greeks as odd at the time that Rome took control of Egypt. Cicero, for example, in his 45 BCE book *De Natura Deorum* (*On the Nature of the Gods*), describes a number of gods from Asclepius to Vulcan (Hephaestus) who possess multiple manifestations. According to Cicero, Mercury (Hermes) enjoyed five different identities, including the Mercury who taught the inhabitants of Egypt laws and letters. Cicero writes, "The Egyptians call him Theuth, and the first month of the year is known amongst them by the same name."

Hermes Trismegistus, moreover, is not simply an example of a god with multiple manifestations. He is also an example of a god who is born human and becomes divine. The followers of Hermes Trismegistus believed that he first was a wise man (*sophos aner*) or sage who conversed with the gods and eventually became a god himself. Like the Greek god Hermes and the Egyptian god Thoth, Hermes Trismegistus is well suited to mediate between the divine and mortal spheres of existence, and among Greek, Egyptian, and Roman civilizations.

UNKNOWN, "THE HYMN TO THOTH" & PLATO, FROM *PHAEDRUS*

BEFORE YOU READ

"The Hymn to Thoth" is found inscribed on a life-sized statue of Haremhab, a military official during the reign of Tutankhamun. The statue, which is now in the collection of the Metropolitan Museum of Art in New York City, may once have stood near a temple in Memphis, Egypt, where Haremhab and his troops were stationed. The hymn, which is carved on a scroll on Haremhab's lap, describes the spheres and duties of Thoth. These include driving the "night-bark" and the "day-bark," also called the "Ship-of-millions." Ra (or Re), a solar god, is usually depicted driving these two ships. As he crosses over the earth during the day, bringing light, he drives his day-bark, and he drives his night-bark in the Underworld. Thoth destroys a "fiend" (the serpent Apopis) who threatens Ra on his night-bark and thereby becomes the champion of Harakhti, another name for Ra. The term "Ennead" refers to nine Egyptian deities, whereas "Hesret" refers to a sacred place in Khmun (also called Hermopolis), the city sacred to Thoth.

——— ☖ ———
BEFORE YOU READ
CONTINUED
——— ☖ ———

In Plato's dialogue *Phaedrus*, Socrates tells a story about Thoth (Theuth) to his companion Phaedrus. Although Socrates—or, rather, his student Plato, who wrote this dialogue—has contrived this particular story of Thoth, he nonetheless offers a snapshot of Greek notions about Thoth that have contributed to his conflation with Hermes in the figure Hermes Trismegistus. ("The Hymn to Thoth" translated by Miriam Lichtheim. *Phaedrus* translated by Robin Waterfield.)

- Which of Thoth's traits do "The Hymn to Thoth," composed in Thoth's honor, and Plato's *Phaedrus* highlight?

- Which of these traits did the Egyptians and Greeks adopt to create Hermes Trismegistus?

- To what extent might Thoth be considered a trickster or a culture hero in these readings?

UNKNOWN, "THE HYMN TO THOTH" (THIRTEENTH CENTURY BCE)

(1) Adoration of Thoth, Son of Re, Moon,
Of beautiful rising, lord of appearings, light of the gods,
By the Prince, Count, Fan-bearer on the King's right,
Great Troop-commander, Royal Scribe, Haremhab, justified, he says:
Hail to you, Moon, Thoth,
Bull in Khmun, dweller in Hesret,
Who makes way for the gods!
Who knows the secrets.
Who records their expression,
Who distinguishes one speech from another,   10
Who is judge of everyone.
Keen-faced in the Ship-of-millions,
Courier of mankind,
Who knows a man by (5) his utterance,
Who makes the deed rise against the doer.
Who contents Re,
Advises the Sole Lord,
Lets him know whatever happens;
At dawn he summons in heaven,
And forgets not yesterday's report.   20

Who makes safe the night-bark,
Makes tranquil the day-bark,
With arms outstretched in the bow of the ship,
Pure-faced when he takes the stern-rope,
As the day-bark rejoices in the night-bark's joy,
At the feast of crossing the sky.
Who fells the fiend,
Sunders western lightland,
The Ennead in the night-bark worships Thoth,
They say (10) to him: "Hail, [Son of] Re,   30
Praised of Re, whom the gods applaud!"
They repeat what your *ka* wishes,
As you make way for the place of the bark,
As you act against that fiend:
You cut off his head, you break his *ba*,
You cast (15) his corpse in the fire,
You are the god who slaughters him,
Nothing is done without your knowing,
Great one, son of a Great one, who came from her limbs,
Champion of Harakhti,   40
Wise friend in On,
Who makes the place of the gods,
Who knows the secrets,
Expounds their words.

Let us give praise to Thoth,
Straight plummet in the scales,
Who repulses evil,
Who accepts him who leans not on crime.
The vizier who settles cases,
Who changes turmoil to peace;   50
The scribe of the mat who keeps the book,
Who punishes crime,
Who accepts the submissive.
Who is sound of (20) arm,
Wise among the Ennead,
Who relates what was forgotten.
Counselor to him who errs,
Who remembers the fleeting moment
Who reports the hour of night,
Whose words endure forever,   60
Who enters *dat*, knows those in it,
And records them in the list.

PLATO, FROM *PHAEDRUS* (c. 370 BCE)

SOCRATES: All right. The story I heard is set in Naucratis in Egypt, where there was one of the ancient gods of Egypt—the one to whom the bird they call the "ibis" is sacred, whose name is Theuth. This deity was the inventor of number, arithmetic, geometry, and astronomy, of games involving draughts and dice—and especially of writing. At the time, the king of the whole of Egypt around the capital city of the inland region (the city the Greeks call "Egyptian Thebes"), was Thamous, or Amon, as the Greeks call him. Theuth came to Thamous and showed him the branches of expertise he had invented, and suggested that they should be spread throughout Egypt. Thamous asked him what good each one would do, and subjected   10
Theuth's explanations to criticism if he thought he was going wrong and praise if thought he was right. The story goes that Thamous expressed himself at length to Theuth about each of the branches of expertise, both for and against them. It would take a long time to go through all Thamous' views, but when it was the turn of writing, Theuth said, "Your highness, this science will increase the intelligence of the people of Egypt and improve their memories. For this invention is a potion for memory and intelligence." But Thamous replied, "You are most ingenious, Theuth. But one person has the ability to bring branches of expertise into existence, another to assess the extent to which they will harm or benefit those who use them. The loyalty you   20
feel to writing, as its originator, has just led you to tell me the opposite of its true effect. It will atrophy people's memories. Trust in writing will make them remember things by relying on marks made by others, from outside themselves, not on their own inner resources, and so writing will make the things they have learnt disappear from their minds. Your invention is a potion for jogging the memory, not for remembering. You provide your students with the appearance of intelligence, not real intelligence. Because your students will be widely read, though without any contact with a teacher, they will seem to be men of wide knowledge, when they will usually be ignorant. And this spurious appearance of intelligence will make them difficult company."   30

7.4 RECEPTION

HERMAPHRODITUS IN PRE-RAPHAELITE ART

Just as Hermes is a trickster figure who challenges and subverts authority, so too is Hermaphroditus, the son of Hermes and Aphrodite, who can seemingly change his form at will. In Greek and Roman myths, the name "Hermaphroditus" is masculine, and masculine pronouns like "he" and "his" are used to refer to him. And yet Hermaphroditus is both male and female. Greek statues dating from the fifth and fourth centuries BCE portray "Hermaphroditus Exposed" (Hermaphroditus Anasuromenos) as a predominantly female figure lifting her skirts to reveal an erect penis. In Greece, Hermaphroditus was primarily a deity associated with fertility and sexual abundance. And although a god, Hermaphroditus sometimes appeared on earth in the form of human hermaphrodites, who likewise had a bisexed body with male and female parts. In the *Metamorphoses*, Ovid describes Hermaphroditus as *neutrumque et utrumque*—neither and both.

In this section, we trace how Hermes's subversive and creative energies resonate in the art, poetry, and culture that the figure of the hermaphrodite inspired in the Pre-Raphaelite artistic movement of Victorian England. But before we examine these relatively modern cultural expressions, we turn to the ancient literary tradition of hermaphrodites that inspired those later interpretations.

In the *Metamorphoses*, Ovid tells the tale of the unusual Greek god Hermaphroditus, the child of Hermes and Aphrodite. When the adolescent Hermaphroditus wanders through the countryside, he encounters Salmacis, a nymph who dwells in a meadow pond of the same name. Salmacis immediately falls passionately in love with Hermaphroditus, but the youth rejects her advances. Believing he is alone, he swims in her pool; Salmacis embraces him, and despite his resistance, their bodies merge into one. Thus, Hermaphroditus's body combines the attributes of both male and female, with the breasts of a woman and the genitals of a man.

Ovid's recounting of this myth reveals that hermaphrodites, at least in the eyes of Ovid and presumably his readers, are effeminized men. For despite the *addition* of Salmacis's female body parts and attributes, Hermaphroditus is *less than* the man he was prior to his union with Salmacis. He is enervated and

7.8 Sleeping Hermaphroditus. Marble. Roman copy of a Greek original, second half of the second century BCE. Louvre Museum, Paris, France. © *RMN-Grand Palais / Art Resource, NY, ART434602.*

weakened, and he asks that the waters of Salmacis henceforth weaken and enervate those who swim in them. Thus Ovid's tale explains the effects Salmacis's pool was said to have on bathers, as well as the nature of hermaphrodites. Further, Ovid's tale of Hermaphroditus and Salmacis, and not the generative powers and worship of the Greek Hermaphroditus, has shaped subsequent treatments of hermaphrodites in literature, art, law, and medicine.

The Pre-Raphaelites were a group of artists in Victorian England who founded an association they called the "Brotherhood" in 1848. Seeking to overturn prevailing conventions in painting and in poetry, they first expressed their intention to offer a new kind of art through their manner of representing the female form. Eventually, they turned their attention to hermaphrodites and androgynes (biologically male or female figures who nonetheless display the traits and manners of both men and women).

The Pre-Raphaelites' interest in both these figures harkens back to earlier idealizations of the hermaphrodite. To the Pre-Raphaelites, the hermaphrodite and the androgyne suggest an escape from, even a refusal of, a normalizing social and artistic discourse about sexual difference and identity. These figures provided the artists with an opportunity to explore different ways of presenting the human body and to celebrate its beauty above any moral or social dictates. Charles Algernon Swinburne (1837–1909) thought that beauty, whatever its form, not social or religious dictates, must be worshipped without any reservations. One of the Pre-Raphaelites' harshest critics, the Scottish poet and critic Robert Buchanan (1841–1901), countered that attention to beauty over morals and conscience was "morbid" and dangerous to society.

In 1863, Swinburne visited the Louvre, where he saw the second-century BCE sculpture known as the Sleeping Hermaphrodite (Figure 7.8). His poem in response to this image, in which he imagines himself to be addressing the hermaphrodite directly, describes the emotions and desires it aroused. In his 1868 book on the visionary poetry of William Blake, Swinburne wrote that "the two sexes should not combine and contend; they must finally amalgamate and be annihilated" (278). Yet Swinburne's poem conveys not an annihilation by the hermaphrodite of the two sexes but rather an arousal of excessive desires for both males and females that can find no release or resolution. The poem begins with Swinburne standing behind the statue and addressing it.

CHARLES ALGERNON SWINBURNE, "HERMAPHRODITUS" (1863)

I

Lift up thy lips, turn round, look back for love,
   Blind love that comes by night and casts out rest;
   Of all things tired thy lips look weariest,
Save the long smile that they are wearied of.

Ah sweet, albeit no love be sweet enough,
    Choose of two loves and cleave unto the best;
    Two loves at either blossom of thy breast
Strive until one be under and one above.
Their breath is fire upon the amorous air,
    Fire in thine eyes and where thy lips suspire: 10
And whosoever hath seen thee, being so fair,
    Two things turn all his life and blood to fire;
A strong desire begot on great despair,
    A great despair cast out by strong desire.

II
Where between sleep and life some brief space is,
    With love like gold bound round about the head,
    Sex to sweet sex with lips and limbs is wed,
Turning the fruitful feud of hers and his
To the waste wedlock of a sterile kiss;
    Yet from them something like as fire is shed   20
    That shall not be assuaged till death be dead,
Though neither life nor sleep can find out this.
Love made himself of flesh that perisheth
    A pleasure-house for all the loves his kin;
But on the one side sat a man like death,
    And on the other a woman sat like sin.
So with veiled eyes and sobs between his breath
    Love turned himself and would not enter in.

III
Love, is it love or sleep or shadow or light
    That lies between thine eyelids and thine eyes?   30
    Like a flower laid upon a flower it lies,
Or like the night's dew laid upon the night.
Love stands upon thy left hand and thy right,
    Yet by no sunset and by no moonrise
    Shall make thee man and ease a woman's sighs,
Or make thee woman for a man's delight.
To what strange end hath some strange god made fair
    The double blossom of two fruitless flowers?
Hid love in all the folds of all thy hair,
    Fed thee on summers, watered thee with showers,   40
Given all the gold that all the seasons wear
    To thee that art a thing of barren hours?

IV

Yea, love, I see; it is not love but fear.
    Nay, sweet, it is not fear but love, I know;
    Or wherefore should thy body's blossom blow
So sweetly, or thine eyelids leave so clear
Thy gracious eyes that never made a tear—
    Though for their love our tears like blood should flow,
    Though love and life and death should come and go,
So dreadful, so desirable, so dear?   50
Yea, sweet, I know; I saw in what swift wise
    Beneath the woman's and the water's kiss
    Thy moist limbs melted into Salmacis,
And the large light turned tender in thine eyes,
And all thy boy's breath softened into sighs;
    But Love being blind, how should he know of this?

Au Musée du Louvre, Mars 1863.

In the first stanza, Swinburne announces the desire and the despair that the Sleeping Hermaphrodite arouses in him. The hermaphrodite has "two loves at either blossom of thy [its] breast," arousing contradictory emotions in the viewer: What does the viewer desire? Whose love, the hermaphrodite's or the viewer's, is "sweet, albeit no love be sweet enough"? In the second stanza, a divine figure (perhaps Eros), here called Love, "made himself of flesh" in the figure of the hermaphrodite. In so doing, Love has become a human hermaphrodite, who is not an ideal embodiment of plenitude. The hermaphrodite's combination of both male and female results only in a "sterile kiss." In the third stanza, the poet laments that because the hermaphrodite is neither fully male nor fully female, the hermaphrodite cannot satisfy the desires of either a man or a woman, even if the hermaphrodite is able to arouse desire in each. Finally, the poet addresses the sleeping hermaphrodite as if he were Hermaphroditus in Ovid's tale. The Hermaphrodite is a "boy's breath softened into sighs"; he is blind, like Love. If Swinburne's ambivalent language is a deliberate choice, he strives to capture the contradictory and painful emotions that the Sleeping Hermaphrodite arouses in viewers about their own identity and desires.

Just as Victorian critics abhorred the sexual ambiguity in Swinburne's poetry, they also criticized the androgynous qualities of men and women in the paintings of the Pre-Raphaelite artist Edward Burne-Jones (1833–1898). Because androgynes (like hermaphrodites) defy or collapse the distinctions between male and female, Burne-Jones's figures were seen as challenging Victorian social and sexual norms, particularly with respect to masculinity.

The male figures he painted were often passive, languorous, and feminine. They were perceived to have lost their masculinity rather than having gained any positive attributes associated with femininity. To a Victorian audience, this blurring of conventional differences between male and female, along with a certain strange beauty, made Burne-Jones's androgynous figures particularly disturbing.

Two of Burne-Jones's more controversial paintings, *Phyllis and Demophoon* (1870) and a later version renamed *The Tree of Forgiveness*, capture a moment of male and female entanglement that recalls the moment that Salmacis and Hermaphroditus merge. In the myth to which both paintings refer, Phyllis (the daughter of a king of Thrace) believes herself to be abandoned by her husband, the Athenian king Demophoon, son of Theseus and Phaedrus (not to be confused with the Eleusinian prince of the same name in Chapter 4.1). She commits suicide and is transformed by the gods into an almond tree. When Demophoon learns of her fate, he embraces the almond tree in his grief. Burne-Jones modeled *both* Demophoon and Phyllis on his lover, Maria Zambaco, and portrayed Demophoon naked in his early painting *Phyllis and Demophoon*. When this painting was displayed in the Old Watercolour Society for the summer exhibition of 1870, Demophoon's nudity and the similarities between him and Phyllis were so scandalous that Burne-Jones removed the painting and withdrew from the society.

In *The Tree of Forgiveness* (Figure 7.9), Phyllis curls out of the tree trunk to her left, while De-

7.9 Edward Burne-Jones, *The Tree of Forgiveness* (1881–1882). Oil on canvas. © Lady Lever Art Gallery, National Museums Liverpool / Bridgeman Images, WGL110282.

mophoon twists at the torso in a way that mimics her embrace. In this painting, too, the figures are nearly mirror images of each other: they are identical in size, color, and pose. Not only are Phyllis and Demophoon entwined with each other, they are also enmeshed in a lush environment. Burne-Jones's swirl of delicate white almond flowers and rich golden brown and yellow tree limbs and torsos, crossed by Phyllis's red hair, compels the viewer to locate and separate the figures from each other and the elaborate foliage that surrounds them. The viewer must discern the nature of their entanglement and separateness, their similarities and their differences. Curiously, Burne-Jones emphasizes Phyllis's embrace of Demophoon and his confusion about,

7.10 Aubrey Beardsley, *Hermaphrodite amongst the Roses* (1894). Black ink lithograph. *Private collection. Private Collection/ Prismatic Pictures/Bridgeman Images, DGC747049.*

perhaps even resistance to, her attention. Here, as in Ovid's story of Salmacis and Hermaphroditus, the female is active and the male passive, and the distinctions between male and female become blurred. Burne-Jones's painting implicitly poses two interrelated questions: Who is desiring whom? And whom do you, the viewer, desire, and why? In other words, these androgynous figures, like the hermaphrodite in Swinburne's poem, provoke viewers to speculate on the nature of desire, including their own.

Finally, we turn to the illustrator Aubrey Beardsley (1872–1898). Beardsley is associated with the art nouveau movement, which shared affinities with the earlier Pre-Raphaelite movement while foreshadowing modern sensibilities. A member of the artistic circle that included the critic and playwright Oscar Wilde (1854–1900), Beardsley's sexuality (like that of Wilde) was the subject of speculation and scandal. Beardsley used the term "grotesque" to describe his frankly erotic art. Like Burne-Jones, who had been a mentor, Beardsley used the figure of the hermaphrodite to explore inherent tensions in the Victorian sexual code, which demanded sexual purity of women and compelled men to transgress that purity.

Beardsley's hermaphrodites are frequently depicted in natural settings, evoking Pan and satyrs. In his *Hermaphrodite amongst the Roses* (Figure 7.10), one of his illustrations for an edition of Thomas Malory's *Morte d'Arthur* (a fifteenth-century collection of stories about the legendary King Arthur), Beardsley creates a hermaphrodite with breasts and a penis climbing on and surrounded by vines of roses. Less explicitly feminine than the ancient Greek statues of Hermaphroditus Exposed, Beardsley's figure could be interpreted as either a boyish girl with a penis or a girlish boy with breasts. This ambiguity offers a critique, if not an outright parody, of the explicit Christian moralism of the *Morte d'Arthur* as well as the Victorian reimagination of medieval tales.

In all of these ways, the adoption of Hermaphroditus by the Pre-Raphaelite artists to criticize social restrictions and artistic conventions recalls, however distantly, the subversive energies of Hermaphroditus's father, Hermes, the trickster.

KEY TERMS

Anthesteria 289

Caduceus 287

Cyllene 290

Herm 290

Hermaion 290

Hermes's hill 287

Hestia 294

Mutilation of the herms 292

Pan 291

FOR FURTHER EXPLORATION

Bullen, J. B. *The Pre-Raphaelite Body: Fear and Desire in Painting, Poetry, and Criticism.* Oxford: Oxford University Press, 1998. A brief scholarly look at how the Pre-Raphaelites, especially Edward Burne-Jones, represented the body as androgynous.

Fowden, Garth. *The Egyptian Hermes: A Historical Approach to the Late Pagan Mind.* Princeton, NJ: Princeton University Press, 1993. Fowden provides a brief and insightful review of the social, intellectual, and political conditions that led to the creation of Hermes Trismegistus.

Hynes, William J., and William G. Doty (eds.). *Mythical Trickster Figures: Contours, Contexts and Criticisms.* Tuscaloosa and London: University of Alabama Press, 1993. This collection of essays surveys and summarizes previous writings about tricksters in an accessible and lively way.

Otto, Walter F. *The Homeric Gods: The Spiritual Significance of Greek Religion.* Translated by Moses Hadas. London: Thames and Hudson, 1954. Otto offers a compelling analysis of Hermes and his unique character among Greek gods that remains pertinent.

CHAPTER 8

ARTEMIS AND APOLLO

[In 1304] A certain boy in the region of Hesse was seized. This boy, as was known afterwards, and just as the boy told it himself, was taken by wolves when he was three years old and raised up wondrously. For, whatever prey the wolves snatched for food, they would take the better part and allot it to him to eat as they lay around a tree. In the time of winter and cold, they made a pit, and they put the leaves of trees and other plants in it, and placed them on the boy, surrounding him to protect him from the cold; they also compelled him to creep on hands and feet and to run with them for a long time. . . . When he was seized, he was bound with wood to compel him to go erect in a human likeness.

—**From The Chronicle of the Benedictine Monastery of Saint Peter of Erfurt**

The haunting tale of the boy from Hesse, found in an anonymous chronicle (c. fourteenth century CE) from a German monastery, is an early European example of the almost universal lore about "feral" children—nearly wild children who were said to have lived among animals in woods, forests, and jungles. The story of the Hessian boy recalls a well-known ancient myth about wild children: that of the brothers Romulus and Remus, the founders of Rome, who, like the boy from Hesse, were raised by a she-wolf. Such stories have been shared, collected, and studied since ancient times because of the

THE ESSENTIALS ⁑ ARTEMIS AND APOLLO

ARTEMIS (Diana), Ἄρτεμις

PARENTAGE Zeus and the goddess Leto

OFFSPRING None

ATTRIBUTES Bow, quiver, wild animals (especially deer)

SIGNIFICANT CULT TITLES
• Lochia (Protector of Women in Labor)
• Potnia Theron (Mistress of Animals)
• Agrotera (Of the Wilds)

SIGNIFICANT RITUALS AND SANCTUARIES
• **The Brauronia** An initiation ritual for young girls before marriage that took place in Brauron, a region east of Athens.
• **Ephesus** The provincial capital of the Roman Empire on the coast of Anatolia, where the Ephesian Artemis was patron goddess.
• **Sanctuary of Artemis Orthia** The location of initiations for adolescent boys, near Sparta.

APOLLO (Apollo), Ἀπόλλων

PARENTAGE Zeus and the goddess Leto

OFFSPRING Asclepius (with Coronis); Linus and Orpheus (with Calliope, a Muse); and many others

ATTRIBUTES Beardless, long-haired, bow, quiver, lyre, laurel branch

SIGNIFICANT CULT TITLES
• Catharsius (Purifier)
• Musagetes (Leader of the Muses)
• Paean (Healer)
• Pythian (Pythian)

SIGNIFICANT RITUALS AND SANCTUARIES
• **Delos** The island where Leto gave birth to Apollo and Artemis; there Apollo had a sanctuary and an annual festival in his honor.
• **Delphi** An oracular shrine in central Greece where Apollo, through his priestesses the Pythias, dispensed oracles.
• **The Hyacinthia** An initiation ritual for young boys near Sparta and a neighboring town, Amyclae.

questions they raise about human nature. Are human children so pliable that their bodies and minds may be molded by whomever—or whatever—rears them? Does nature or nurture shape human development? Are affinities between human beings and animals deeper and more abiding than "civilized" culture acknowledges? Ancient myths and modern tales of feral children alike address, albeit in different ways, the shifting boundaries between nature and culture, between animals and humans, in the process of defining human identity. Anxieties about these boundaries can be detected in the adolescent initiation ceremonies of ancient Greece, in particular those ceremonies connected with Artemis and Apollo.

8.1 HISTORY

FROM ADOLESCENCE TO ADULTHOOD

The gods, of course, were imagined as ageless. But Apollo and Artemis, as the children of Zeus and the goddess Leto, were seen as especially youthful. They do not mature but rather maintain their youthful identity as siblings;

as such, they are charged with helping young Greeks make the fraught transition from childhood to maturity.

In this chapter, we first examine the spheres of influence of each sibling, apart from his or her role in initiation rituals. We focus on Artemis's association with wild animals, young girls, and childbirth; turning to Apollo, we examine his association with music, poetry, medicine, and prophecy. Regarding their roles as initiatory deities, we consider how initiations associated with Artemis were designed to tame (or eradicate) what were believed to be the wild or even animal-like tendencies of girls, whereas initiations of boys under Apollo's auspices more often were designed to cultivate the skills necessary for Greek adult males. Initiation rituals and observances convey Greek ideas about the differences between boys and girls in their relation to human culture and nature. Artemis and Apollo, in all their aspects, epitomize these differences.

8.2 **Sacrifice of Iphigenia.** Calchas, the priest, stands behind the altar next to Iphigenia, while Apollo (upper left, seated and holding a laurel branch) and Artemis (upper right, holding her bow), watch the proceedings. Detail from an Apuleian red-figure volute krater. Kinship with the Iliupersis Painter, c. fourth century BCE. © The Trustees of the British Museum / Art Resource, NY, ART497993.

ARTEMIS

Among the Olympian goddesses, three were eternal virgins: Athena, Hestia, and Artemis. The character of Artemis's virginity, however, is different from that of Athena and Hestia. Hestia, the goddess of the hearth, is associated with domestic space or city centers. She stands for the integrity of the household in which she resides, and more specifically of the wife of the household. Athena's virginity marks her distance from the domestic sphere of women, allowing her the freedom to associate with men and involve herself with masculine concerns. An urban goddess, Athena has no connection with nature or the outdoors.

Artemis's virginity, on the other hand, forges a connection between her and the nymphs with whom she is frequently depicted. These nymphs are the mythical counterparts to the mortal young girls who worshipped Artemis in rituals devoted to her. Artemis's virginity associates her closely with the life cycle of young women. Finally, Artemis, unlike Athena and Hestia, haunts the forests and open spaces outside cities, houses, and cultivated fields. She keeps company with wild and undomesticated animals.

Wild Animals, Young Girls, and Childbirth In his epics, Homer refers to Artemis as Potnia Theron (Mistress of Animals) and Agrotera (Of the Wilds).

Both titles describe Artemis's connection to wild animals (not domesticated animals or livestock) who dwell in the forests and the mountains where she roams. Among wild animals, bears often appear in myths and rituals associated with Artemis, whereas deer are most precious to her. Yet, paradoxically, Artemis is also often depicted with a bow in her hand or a quiver of arrows on her back (Figure 8.2). Her bow is not a weapon of war but a tool of the hunt. Thus Artemis is represented as both protecting and hunting animals in the wild.

Artemis is often portrayed as leading groups of nymphs in song or dance, and protecting their virginity as well as her own. In one of the more famous stories of Artemis's fierce protection of herself and her nymphs, the hunter Actaeon, in pursuit of game, accidentally sees Artemis and her female followers bathing together in the woods. Angered that she has been violated by Actaeon's gaze, Artemis turns him into a stag, and he is then attacked and killed by his own pack of hunting dogs. Whereas written accounts emphasize that Artemis makes Actaeon's own dogs unwittingly kill their beloved master, many depictions equate Actaeon's dogs with Artemis's arrows: both animals and arrows are at her disposal, and both are equally lethal (Figure 8.12). When a hunter, Orion, attempts to rape Artemis (or, in some accounts, her companion Opis), Artemis kills him directly with her arrows. In other versions, however, Orion is a beloved hunting companion of Artemis who carelessly provokes Hera or Gaia with his boasts about his abilities to hunt and bring down all the earth's animals. As punishment for his pride, Hera (or Gaia, depending on the telling) sends a scorpion to kill him. In these stories, a grieving Artemis (or Zeus at her behest) transforms Orion into a constellation of stars set in the heavens near the constellation Scorpio.

In a variation on this group of myths, an attempted act of sexual violence against a nymph provokes Artemis to punish the female victim, not her attacker. For example, when Zeus impregnates Callisto, a female follower of Artemis, Artemis observes that Callisto is pregnant and turns Callisto into a bear. In some versions, Hera transforms Callisto into a bear out of jealous anger; in other versions, Zeus transforms Callisto to protect her from Hera's wrath. When Callisto's son Arcas goes hunting in the woods and is about to kill Callisto (who, as a bear, is unrecognizable to him), Zeus transforms her into the constellation Ursa Major (Latin for "big bear"). In some versions, Artemis kills Callisto deliberately with her arrows, whereas in others Callisto's death at Artemis's hands is accidental. Artemis, grieving, then transforms Callisto into the constellation Ursa Major, just as she had transformed (or caused the transformation of) Orion.

Taken together, these conflicting versions suggest the difficulties of determining whether Artemis's actions are offered as protection or punishment. Artemis appears both benevolent and cruel to the young girls in her retinue, just as she seems to the wild animals that surround her. The meaning of Artemis's actions in myth becomes more apparent from the perspective of Artemis's oversight of transitional moments in women's lives: the initiation of girls, rituals before marriage, and childbirth.

Artemis is called Lochia (Protector of Women in Labor), and her own birth illustrates this feature of her character. Angry with Zeus for philandering, Hera would not let any land receive Leto when she was pregnant with Apollo and Artemis. Eventually the small island of Delos in the Aegean allowed Leto to deliver her children on its land. Born first, Artemis then helped Leto give birth to Apollo. All three had temples on the island. Archaeologists have found a cache of especially precious offerings in Artemis's Delian sanctuary; Apollo was worshipped there in an annual festival that involved athletic competitions and choral performances for young boys and girls.

As helpful as Artemis was imagined to be in her role as Lochia, she was also said to shoot women in labor with her "gentle arrows," wounding or even killing them. In the *Iliad*, Hera says that Zeus made Artemis a "lion among women" and allows her to kill whomever of them she pleases (21.483). These gentle arrows of Artemis may have been used to explain the high mortality rate in childbirth (of mother and baby alike) in antiquity. This gentle yet lethal role is reflected in her attentions to nymphs, who represent the young women whom Artemis stands beside during other transitional moments. Even if these moments were not as dangerous as childbirth, Artemis, striking her charges with her gentle arrows, nonetheless appears to have two aspects, benevolent and cruel. Such is the case in the myth of Hippolytus and his associated ritual for brides before their marriage.

8.3 Hippolytus attacked by Poseidon. As Hippolytus (accompanied by an elderly servant) drives his chariot, Poseidon's bull and a Fury attack, causing the horses to rear up and kill Hippolytus. Detail from a red-figured volute-krater. Darius Painter, c. 340 BCE. © *The Trustees of the British Museum / Art Resource, NY, ART375622.*

Hippolytus in Myth and Ritual A myth concerning Hippolytus—one of Artemis's adolescent male worshippers—and a ritual for brides that Artemis establishes in his honor offers a way to understand how Artemis attends to her devotees. In his play *Hippolytus* (c. 428 BCE), Euripides depicts Hippolytus as a young man, a virgin and a hunter who prefers the woods and the company of other young men to the city and the demands of adulthood. Hippolytus hoped to remain forever under the auspices of Artemis and never mature into a married man and warrior.

But Aphrodite, angered by his refusal to acknowledge her spheres of love and marriage, causes Hippolytus's stepmother Phaedra to fall in love with him. When Phaedra tells Hippolytus that she loves him, her confession forces him to acknowledge the power of love and thereby abandon his youthful devotion to Artemis. After being rejected by Hippolytus, Phaedra falsely accuses him of rape, provoking her husband, Theseus (Hippolytus's father), to curse his son and cause his violent death: he is torn apart and trampled by his own horses when they are spooked by a bull sent by Poseidon (Figure 8.3). At the close of the play, Artemis promises Hippolytus that young women in his hometown of

Map 8.1 Artemis and Apollo

Troezen will cut their hair and sing laments for him before they marry. (In other versions of this myth, Artemis rescues Hippolytus and installs him as a king or as a temple servant in Aricia, in Italy.)

At first glance, this wedding ritual seems paradoxical because it requires young brides to commemorate Hippolytus's virginal devotion to Artemis (and, perhaps, his rejection of Aphrodite) and to mourn his death. Yet, if Hippolytus represents the youthful virginity and devotion to Artemis that young girls must relinquish on marriage, then lamenting his death could be seen as a way for girls to recognize and ritually mourn the end of their own youth and virginity. Moreover, the violence and sorrow attached to Hippolytus's death allows a young bride to address her conflicting emotions on her marriage: once she is transferred from her father's household to her husband's, she forever leaves behind her natal family. Hippolytus's myth and the Troezen ritual, then, connect mythic transformation and death with the losses that adolescents experience when they must enter into a new stage of their lives. Artemis oversees this moment that is both joyful and sorrowful; thereby she herself appears both cruel and benevolent, and her roles as protector and punisher seem to overlap. Such is the case in all initiation rites under Artemis's tutelage.

8.4 **Young girl running at Brauron.** Fragment of an Attic krater. Greece, fifth century BCE. Archaeological Museum of Brauron, Brauron, Greece. *Gianni DagliOrti/The Art Archive at Art Resource, NY, AA389360.*

Girls' Initiations: The Brauronia The most important initiation that Artemis oversaw was at Brauron, a region due east of Athens on the Aegean coast. When girls were initiated at Brauron, they were described as "playing the bear" for Artemis in a ritual variously called the Brauronia, a title emphasizing the ritual's location, or the Arcteia, a title that emphasizes the importance of bears in the worship of Artemis (*arctos* is Greek for "bear"). A foundation myth associated with Brauron describes how a tamed she-bear scratches a young girl with whom she is playing and then is killed by the girl's brothers. Afterward, the Athenians become ill until an oracle advises them that in order to be cured they must make young girls "play the bear" for Artemis, who was angered over the death of the she-bear. This story not only explains why playing the bear was part of a ritual required of girls in Brauron but also equates the young girl with the she-bear: they play together until the she-bear draws blood from the girl (possibly representing menarche), at which point the bear is killed and also made to bleed.

Archaeological evidence from the site at Brauron offers information about how girls played the bear for Artemis. A building structure with small rooms for sleeping suggests that girls stayed in Brauron, away from their families, during the festival. Small votive statues and vase paintings of young girls found at Brauron indicate that the age range of girls who played the bear was quite wide—perhaps from five to sixteen years, most certainly before they married (estimated to take place after the age of twelve and ideally between fourteen and sixteen years). Vases from Brauron also suggest what sorts of activities constituted playing the bear: girls ran, danced, and even offered their toys to the goddess (Figure 8.4). These actions prepared them in some essential way to become brides once they had departed from Brauron. Finally, a wall not open to public viewing in the dormitory had depressions in it where clothing might have been dedicated. This wall was most likely used for clothing worn during childbirth. These private dedications indicate Artemis's oversight of childbirth and show that Brauron served females at other pivotal moments throughout their lives.

In addition to the dormitory at Brauron, a small temple dedicated to Iphigenia was located at the site. Her story is most likely related to the Brauronia (Chapter 13.1). When Iphigenia's father, Agamemnon, the great king of Mycenae who led the Greeks in the Trojan War, kills a deer sacred to Artemis on the shores of Aulis en route to Troy, Artemis refuses to let the winds blow, thus stranding Agamemnon's fleet. The goddess demands that Agamemnon sacrifice his daughter to her before she will release the winds and the ships. There are many versions of what happens to Iphigenia at the altar: in some, she is slaughtered; in most versions, Artemis substitutes a deer and whisks Iphigenia to the land of the Taurians to become her priestess or even makes the girl immortal. In Iphigenia's tale, then, she and the deer that substitutes for her are made symbolically equivalent (Figure 8.2). When girls played the bear at Brauron, they ritually enacted a similar equivalence.

The suggestion, then, of these myths and their associated rituals is that girls (even if raised by their human parents) were still believed by the Greeks to be somehow animal-like: wild, undomesticated, and separate from the adult world, with its social responsibilities. They are in Artemis's realm. The goddess accompanies them to their initiations, which are necessary to "tame" them and make them suitable members of human society. She protects them as they ritually enact the loss of their youth: the girls playing the bear symbolically die. In other words, the goal of Artemis's initiation at Brauron is to help initiates give up (or kill off) that which is "wild" (free from adult restrictions) in their youthful selves. The mythical deaths or transformations (into a star or an animal) of young girls, then, capture the experience of an initiate who must abandon her child self to become a socially responsible adult woman.

Boys' Initiations: Artemis Orthia In Sparta, an initiation ritual for boys under Artemis's auspices also requires them to "kill off" a part of themselves that is socially unacceptable, although not "wild." This ritual stands out because male gods, especially Apollo, typically oversaw male initiatory rituals. The sanctuary to Artemis Orthia (Upright) was located along the Eurotas River outside of Sparta. The significance of this title remains unclear. The origin of the ritual to Artemis Orthia is attributed to the murder of inhabitants from four surrounding towns who fought at Artemis's altar. Those who survived fell ill, and an oracle advised that Artemis's altar had to be washed in human blood for them to be released from their illness (Pausanias 3.16.9).

Rather than sacrificing human beings, an action that Greeks did not practice despite myths of human sacrifice, the community established a ritual that came to serve as an initiation for adolescent boys. In order to cover the altar with blood, young men were whipped at Artemis's altar, while a priestess held a statue of Artemis. If the statue weighed down the priestess's hand, the youth were to be whipped more vigorously. In some accounts, the young men had to

8.5 Votive mask from the sanctuary of Artemis Orthia in Sparta. Terracotta. Archaeological Museum, Sparta, Greece. *Vanni Archive / Art Resource, NY, ART331763.*

steal offerings of cheese from Artemis's altar, and, if caught, they were whipped for their failure to steal successfully (not for the act of stealing itself). In other accounts, they were enjoined to laugh riotously at the fact of being whipped; the one who best endured the ordeal without showing signs of pain won a prize. During the Archaic and Classical Periods in Sparta, this ritual was part of an elaborate tiered system of initiating boys so that they could become well-trained hoplites in the Spartan army.

Like the Brauronia, the whipping ritual in front of Artemis's altar was designed to compel initiates to give up certain behaviors that did not comport with the adults they were to become. The whipping ritual took place when the boys were sixteen to nineteen years of age, a period during which they were forced to wear the garments and cropped hairstyles typical of helots. (Helots were residents of towns near Sparta who had been enslaved by the Spartans.) And whereas helots could be (and frequently were) whipped by their owners, Spartan citizens themselves were never subjected to a fellow citizen's physical abuse. Thus the ritual of Artemis Orthia forced the initiates to endure being treated like a helot while acting like a Spartan (i.e., laughing), thereby demonstrating their difference from (and superiority to) helots. In this way, initiates

8.6 Apollo with lyre. Bronze statue found in Pompeii, Italy. *HarperCollins Publishers / The Art Archive at Art Resource, NY, AA337378.*

were taught to desire to be a Spartan and leave behind the socially underprivileged state of helots.

Numerous terracotta masks found at the sanctuary of Artemis Orthia are thought to be connected to the whipping ritual. These masks fall into two categories: most are grotesque masks of satyrs, Gorgons, and wrinkled old men and women (Figure 8.5); the rest depict heroic men of different ages. The masks have been interpreted as representing two possible male identities—the grotesque helots and the heroic Spartans. They represent a divide between what the initiates should strive to become (heroic men) and what they should avoid degenerating into (servile helots). The Spartan initiates, then, were forced to act like helots in a symbolic repudiation of a lesser social status, just as female initiates played the she-bear at Brauron. In both rituals, initiates must prove themselves ready to become the adults society requires.

At Brauron and at Sparta, then, Artemis stands on the threshold dividing childhood from adulthood that initiates must cross, while she herself remains more rooted in the wild and untamed world of childhood and animals. Apollo, her brother, also oversees initiations of boys. He too carries the bow and in myth often kills young men. Yet he is associated with cultural achievements—represented by the lyre he carries—and adulthood in a way that Artemis is not.

APOLLO

In his first appearance in the *Iliad*, Apollo wields his bow and lyre in quick succession. He first sends a plague to the Greek camps on Troy's shores; Homer imagines Apollo descending from Olympus with his bow at the ready and his quiver full of deadly arrows, which he aims at both men and animals. The arrows of Apollo and the plague he sends are one and the same. After killing many Greeks, Apollo returns to Olympus to entertain the feasting gods by singing along with the Muses and accompanying them with his lyre (1.592–593) (Figure 8.6). In a short span of verses, Homer conveys that Apollo's violence is tempered by his embodiment of the cultural arts: poetry and music. Apollo also oversees the cultural accomplishments and practices of medicine and prophecy.

Healing Arts Apollo not only had the capacity to unleash the plague but was also associated with curing or ridding a city of plague, and with the healing arts more generally. (His title "Paean" may have referred to a healing god with whom Apollo was conflated or to a ritual song that worshippers used either to call on Apollo for aid or to thank him for his assistance; for example, when the plague Apollo sends at Troy finally abates, the Greeks sing a paean to him.) Apollo is also connected to healing through his son, Asclepius, the legendary figure or god known for healing the sick (Figure 8.7). When Coronis, Apollo's mortal lover, is pregnant with Asclepius, she has an affair with a mortal man. Learning of her behavior from a crow, Apollo has Artemis slay Coronis and asks Hermes to remove the infant Asclepius from her body when she is on the funeral pyre.

Asclepius is reared and educated by the centaur Chiron (who also taught Achilles and Patroclus), who teaches him the art of medicine. Asclepius presided over Epidaurus, the most renowned healing sanctuary in Greece. Located in the Argolid, this large sanctuary had a theater, baths, a gymnasium, dormitories, meeting rooms, and temples. One form of healing demanded that ill people travel to Epidaurus to sleep in its dormitories, where, it was believed, they would have dreams whose interpretation would lead to a cure.

Oracles and Prophecy Apollo is an oracular god as well as a healing god; like Athena, who has access to Zeus's thunderbolts, Apollo has access to Zeus's thoughts. Apollo often says that his prophetic knowledge comes directly from Zeus. Apollo therefore provides "Zeus's counsel" to men at various sanctuaries, of which Didyma in Asia Minor and Delphi in Greece are the most famous. Men sought oracles on political matters, such as colonization, war, laws, leaders, and treaties; on religious matters, such as whether to plow a field or which god to propitiate; and on personal matters, such as marriage and infertility. Apollo at Delphi was also the source of certain adages, such as "know thyself" and "nothing in excess," suggesting that Apollo is a god of moderation and reason.

Delphi was a cosmopolitan oracular shrine at which many Greek states and individuals, including leaders from the Near East such as King Croesus of

8.7 Asclepius and his daughter Hygeia (Health) with a snake. Funerary marble relief from the Therme of Salonika. Circa last quarter of the fifth century BCE. Archaeological Museum, Istanbul, Turkey. *Erich Lessing / Art Resource, NY, ART21941.*

8.8 Aegeus (right), father of Theseus, consults the Pythia. Attic kylix (drinking cup) from Vulci. Kodrus Painter, c. 440 BCE. *bpk, Berlin/Antikensammlung, Staatliche Museen, Berlin, Germany / Johannes Laurentius / Art Resource, NY, ART479247.*

Lydia, sought Apollo's counsel. It also hosted quadrennial games (as did Zeus's sanctuary in Olympia), and it even offered purification from the crime of murder. Indeed, Apollo has the cult title Catharsius (Purifier) because he purifies murderers of the blood on their hands so that they may return to society and not cause it harm by provoking the wrath of the gods. In the opening scene of Aeschylus's *Eumenides* (Chapter 6.1), Orestes arrives at Delphi to be purified because he has killed his mother.

Delphi also enshrined Apollo's relationship with several female figures: the Pythias (Apollo's priestesses at Delphi), Cassandra (the Pythias' mythical double), and Daphne. The Pythias, the women who served as Apollo's priestesses, were historical figures (Figure 8.8). They participated in oracular consultations at Delphi and were believed to be inspired by Apollo and to bring his divine knowledge to human beings. Cassandra, the Trojan princess, promised herself to Apollo and then retracted her offer. As punishment, Apollo gave Cassandra the gift of prophecy; yet he made her prophecies (unlike those he inspired in the Pythias) appear untrue to all who heard them. Condemned to knowing about future tragedies yet being ignored by those she tried to warn, Cassandra thus was isolated from those who heard her. The nymph Daphne, like Cassandra, also refused Apollo's advances and was transformed into a laurel tree by her father (a river god), who thereby fulfilled her wish to escape Apollo's attentions. (Contemporary explorations of this myth are described in section 8.4.) This tale offers an explanation of why Apollo is often shown carrying a laurel branch, which symbolized prophecy and poetry, and why poets (like Hesiod) also carry laurel branches or wear laurel crowns.

Music and Poetry Apollo's lyre associates him most closely with music. In the Homeric *Hymn 4* (*To Hermes*) (Chapter 7.1), Hermes gives the lyre he has invented to Apollo; in other myths, Apollo himself is credited with inventing the instrument. Apollo's children represent his spheres of influence, especially in the area of music. With one of the Muses, Calliope, Apollo has a son named Linus, a musician who plays the lyre and is killed by Heracles during a music lesson. Poets are said to have mourned Linus at the start and end of their songs, and he is sometimes associated with lamentation. The god Hymenaeus, whose name means "wedding song," was said to be Apollo's son. So too was Orpheus, the great musician and legendary founder of Orphism (Chapter 2.1). Apollo is often seen in the company of the Muses and has the title Musagetes (Leader of the Muses).

8.9 Apollo with long hair. Bronze statue. Circa 330 BCE. Museo Archeologico Nazionale, Naples, Italy. *Scala / Art Resource, NY, ART23319.*

Boys' Initiations: The Hyacinthia In addition to his oversight of the arts of healing, prophecy, and music, Apollo, like his sister Artemis, presides over initiatory rituals for boys and young men. And, like his sister, in myths he often kills or greatly harms young men and women (for example, Coronis, Cassandra, and Daphne). When Cyparissus, a young man Apollo loves, will not cease mourning a beloved pet stag, Apollo turns him into a cypress tree, a symbol of lamentation in ancient Greece. Hyacinthus, as we will see later in this chapter, dies directly (if accidentally) by Apollo's actions. In other words, Apollo's relationships with young adults can be as deadly as those of Artemis. Yet the significance of Apollo to the lives of young Greeks differs from that of his sister in some essential ways: Apollo is linked to cultural achievements of Greek society. This distinction reflects prevailing notions about men and women in ancient Greece. Men (unlike women) were believed to be the agents of culture and political actors whose fulfillment of public duties determined communal life. Apollo leads young men from childhood into public life and helps them achieve status and recognition.

Apollo is almost always depicted as beardless, with long hair. This conveys his connection with young men on the brink of becoming full-fledged citizens. Homer describes the Greeks who fight at Troy as "long-haired Achaeans," a description less about cultural standards of beauty for men (although it does convey these) than about the social position and age of those who are fighting at Troy. Although already at war, these are young men who are in the process of becoming seasoned veterans. When they return to Greece, they will be adult men by virtue of their survival of an overseas war. In one famous scene in the *Iliad*, Achilles cuts his hair and dedicates it to a river when his beloved companion Patroclus is killed in battle. Achilles's gesture recalls a ritual practiced in ancient Greece: the cutting and dedication—often to a river god—of a young man's hair, which signals his entry into adulthood. The length of men's hair in ancient Greece, then, is a way of describing age and social position. Long hair describes young men who are in the process of becoming adults. Thus the depiction of Apollo with unshorn hair indicates his affinity with young men (Figure 8.9).

Among the Dorians (the ethnic group of Greeks who settled primarily in the Peloponnessus), Apollo was worshipped in many festivals that marked the development of young men. In Amyclae, a village southwest of and politically connected to Sparta, Apollo and the beautiful young boy Hyacinthus were celebrated together during the Hyacinthia. Hyacinthus was loved by Apollo, and in some myths also by Zephyrus, the west wind. When Apollo and Hyacinthus were throwing the discus (a sport that is still practiced today), Apollo accidently hit Hyacinthus, causing his death. In some versions, Zephyrus, in a fit of jealousy, sent his winds to blow Apollo's discus off course and thus kill Hyacinthus.

The Hyacinthia, a three-day festival, involved a form of ritualized loss. The first day, on which Hyacinthus was mourned, was generally somber in tone, and sacrifices were offered at his tomb. On the following day, there was a procession from Sparta to Amyclae, a distance of about four miles. Musical and athletic contests for boys were followed by a sacrifice in Apollo's honor and a meal in which slaves and foreigners could partake. Women participated in the procession; they also took part in dancing during the night preceding the procession. The restrictions of the first day, devoted to mourning, were removed, and a generally cheerful mood prevailed on the festival's second day and third day (about which little is known).

The Hyacinthia connected Hyacinthus with the boys who participated in the festival. We have seen that myths about Artemis portray her transforming or killing young women, thereby capturing the psychological costs and real dangers that attended transitional moments in young women's lives. The myth about Apollo's accidental slaying of Hyacinthus similarly evokes the real dangers that will attend young men's lives when they enter adulthood. All boys must trade playful games with the discus at the gymnasium for deadly battles with shields and spears. Apollo's beauty as an unshorn young man is a measure of how much boys must relinquish in order to become men. They must overcome their particular circumstances and identity by cutting their hair to don the hoplite's helmet and by striving to enact the social ideals of masculinity that Apollo embodies.

BEFORE YOU READ

UNKNOWN, *HYMN 3: TO APOLLO*
&
HYMN 27: TO ARTEMIS

Two separate hymns compose the Homeric *Hymn to Apollo*. As is typical of oral poetry (Chapter 2.1), the two hymns have been stitched together but not fully integrated. The first, called the *Hymn to Delian Apollo*, describes Apollo's birth and subsequent worship on the island of Delos. The second, called the *Hymn to Pythian Apollo*, is included here. It describes Apollo's establishment of his shrine at Delphi. (For this reason the line numbering of the hymn starts with 182, not 1.) This mythical account of Delphi's foundation celebrates Apollo's achievements by which he earns, much as Hermes did in the Homeric *Hymn to Hermes* (Chapter 7.1), a place of pride among the Olympian gods.

The *Hymn to Pythian Apollo* can be divided into two parts: Apollo's establishment of his shrine and his acquisition of priests. In the first part, Apollo arrives at Telphousa—the name of a spring in Boeotia as well as the goddess of the spring. Telphousa tells Apollo to establish his temple in Krisa, in the valley of Mount Parnassos, where Delphi is located (lines 243–276). When Apollo arrives at Delphi, he finds a "snake" (also called a "savage monster") guarding the land. This female snake is the caretaker of Typhaon, a monstrous offspring of Hera, until Apollo kills her. The hymn explains Apollo's cult title "Pythian" by connecting it to the Greek word "to rot"—which he tells the snake she will do on the land that will now be his (lines 277–386). (However, the area around Delphi was called Pytho, offering a more plausible explanation of this title.) After building himself an altar, Apollo kidnaps Cretan sailors and makes them his priests (387–end). Just as nymphs were the mythological counterparts of the young girls Artemis initiates, the Cretan sailors may be the mythological equivalents of the young boys Apollo initiates at rituals such as the Hyacinthia.

In contrast to the complex workings of the hymn to Apollo, the brief *Hymn 27: To Artemis* contains little action: Artemis hunts, visits her brother in Delphi, and then sings a hymn. (Translations by Michael Crudden.)

**BEFORE YOU READ
CONTINUED**

- To what degree does the hymn to Apollo encompass and describe Apollo's many spheres of influence as described in this section? Which, if any, are omitted?

- One of Apollo's central acts—killing the snake—allows him to establish his worship in Delphi. Why do you think the story of Typhaon is included here? Can you find any similarities between Telphousa, the snake, and Typhaon? What makes them hostile to Apollo? How does his defeat of Telphousa and the snake define him as a god?

- To what degree do Apollo's activities at Delphi serve as an initiation for him and for the Cretan sailors he kidnaps?

- What sorts of information does the hymn to Artemis convey about how the Greeks imagined Artemis, apart from her role as a hunter and a sister of Apollo?

UNKNOWN, *HYMN 3: TO APOLLO* (c. 700 BCE)

The son of glorious Leto, playing the hollow lyre,	182
Approaches rocky Pytho in deathless, scented robes;	
His lyre delightfully rings beneath the plectrum of gold.	
And then he goes to Olympos, speeding like thought from the earth,	
To the house of Zeus, and enters the concourse of other gods;	
At once the minds of immortals turn to the lyre and song.	
All the Muses with beautiful voices together responsively hymn	190
The gods' undying gifts and those pains that humans endure	
At the hands of immortal gods as they live without wits or resource,	

And can find no cure for death or defence against old age.
But the fair-tressed Graces and cheerful Seasons, with Harmony, Youth,
And the daughter of Zeus, Aphrodite, hold hands by the wrist and dance.
Along with them is singing one neither ugly nor short,
But tall and of wondrous appearance, the archeress Artemis reared
With Apollo; and Ares comes amongst them romping besides
With the keen-eyed Slayer of Argos. But Phoibos Apollo plays,
Stepping fine and high, on the lyre; about him radiance shines,   202
And sparklings flash from his feet and tunic of beautiful weave.
Leto with tresses of gold and wise Zeus in their great hearts
Feel joy, as they watch their son sport amongst the immortal gods.
    How shall I sing a hymn of you, whom hymns have in every way
       praised?
Am I to sing of you surrounded by brides and love,
And tell how you once went wooing Azan's maiden child
Together with godlike Iskhys, Elatos' horse-rich son?
How you went together with Phorbas, son of Triops by birth?
With Erekhtheus? Or with Leukippos, and to Leukippos' spouse

      . . . .

On foot, on a car the other; yet he was Triops' match.   213
Or am I to sing how first you traversed the earth to find
An oracular shrine for humans, Apollo who shoot from afar?
When you descended Olympos, you reached Pieria first;
Passed by sandy Lektos, the Ainienes too,
And amidst the Perrhaiboi folk; to Iolkos quickly came,
And onto Kenaion stepped of Euboia famed for ships.
On the plain of Lelantos you stood, but it did not please your heart
To set up upon this site your shrine and wooded groves.
Crossing from there the Euripos, Apollo who shoot from afar,
You climbed a holy, green mountain; but from it quickly reached   223
Mykalessos, then Teumessos bedded with grassy meads,
And arrived at the seat of Thebes that was covered over with trees—
For no one yet of mortals was dwelling in sacred Thebes,
Nor yet did there then exist any tracks or paths across
The wheat-bearing plain of Thebes, but forest held all in its grasp.
    From there you went on further, Apollo who shoot from afar,
And to Onkhestos came, Poseidon's splendid grove.
There the new-tamed colt draws breath in his distress
At pulling the beautiful chariot; down from his place to the earth
The driver, though skilful, leaps and walks along the road;   233
Then for a time the horses rattle the empty car,
Sending dominion away. But if the chariot breaks

Within the wooded grove, they tend to the horses, but lean
And leave the vehicle be—for so from the first was the rite.
To the lord they pray, and the doom of god then guards the car.
    From there you went on further, Apollo who shoot from afar,
And then arrived at Kephisos, that river whose flowing is fair,
Who from Lilaia pours his water in fair-flowing streams.
Crossing, you reached the town that many a tower protects,
Okalea, Far-worker; came to lush Haliartos next,   243
And went on toward Telphousa. There it pleased your heart
To set up in that tranquil place your shrine and wooded groves.
Close beside her you stood, and to her spoke these words:
    "In this place, Telphousa, I plan to set up a beautiful shrine
As an oracle sought by humans. Whether they're folk who live
On fertile Peloponnesos, or in Europa dwell
And on isles that waters flow round, they'll always bring to me here
Their perfect hundredfold offerings, hoping to hear my response.
I'll give all unerring counsel, responding within my rich shrine."
When he had in this way spoken, Phoibos Apollo laid   254
Wide and long foundations stretching without a break;
But by this sight Telphousa was angered at heart, and said:
    "Lord Phoibos who work from afar, let me put in your mind a thought,
Since in this place it is your plan to set up a beautiful shrine
As an oracle sought by humans, who'll always bring to you here
Their perfect hundredfold offerings; ponder my words in your mind.
Quick horses' clatter, and mules being watered from my sacred springs,
Will always be causing you pain—a human will then more wish
To view the well-made cars and the clatter of quick-footed steeds,
Than he will your great shrine and the treasures lying heaped up inside. 266
But if you would heed me at all—more powerful, lord, and brave
You are, of course, than I, and have the greatest strength—
Make your shrine in Krisa, down in Parnassos' fold.
About your well-built altar there will in that place be
No beautiful chariots' jolting or clatter of quick-footed steeds.
The glorious tribes of humans would rather be bringing their gifts
To you, Ie-Paieon, and joyful at heart you'd take
The beautiful offerings made by humans who dwell round about."
    So she spoke, and persuaded the Far-shooter's mind, so that she
      herself,
Telphousa, might have—and not the Far-shooter—fame upon earth. 276
From there you went on further, Apollo who shoot from afar,
And came to the city peopled by Phlegyai, violent men,
Who, paying no heed to Zeus, used to make their home on earth

In a beautiful valley lying near the Kephisian lake.
Rushing on swiftly from there, you approached a mountain ridge,
And under snowy Parnassos came to Krisa then,
A slope that faces Zephyr. Above it hangs a crag;
A hollow and rugged valley runs below. This spot
Lord Phoibos Apollo marked out as his lovely shrine's site, and said:

    "In this place it is my plan to set up a beautiful shrine   287
As an oracle sought by humans. Whether they're folk who live
On fertile Peloponnesos, or in Europa dwell
And on isles that waters flow round, they'll always bring to me here
Their perfect hundredfold offerings, hoping to hear my response.
I'll give all unerring counsel, responding within my rich shrine."

    When he had in this way spoken, Phoibos Apollo laid
Wide and long foundations stretching without a break;
Upon them a threshold of stone was placed by Erginos' sons,
Trophonios and Agamedes, dear to the deathless gods;
And countless tribes of humans, using finished blocks,   299
Raised about it a shrine to be famed for ever in song.

    But there was near by a fair-flowing spring, and here the Snake
Was slain by the lord son of Zeus with a shot from his mighty bow,
Well-fattened and huge though she was, a savage monster, who caused
Much harm to humans on earth—much harm to humans themselves,
And much to their slender-legged flocks, since she was a blood-spattered
      bane.
From Hera whose throne is golden she once had taken and reared
The dread and fierce Typhaon, a bane to mortal men.
Hera had given him birth in anger at Father Zeus,
When Kronos' son had begotten renowned Athena within   309
His head. At once with anger was queenly Hera filled,
And she amongst the immortals gathered together said:

    "All you gods and goddesses, listen how Zeus who gathers the clouds
Has begun unprovoked to slight me! He made me his true-hearted
      wife,
And now without me has given bright-eyed Athena birth—
Amongst all the blessed immortals she is beyond compare.
But the runt of all the gods is that son whom I bore myself,
Hephaistos with shrivelled feet. I flung him from my grasp
Into the sea's expanse, but he was welcomed there
By Thetis whose feet are silver, the daughter whom Nereus begot,   319
And she brought him amongst her sisters—I wish she had done
      something else
To please the blessed gods. Relentless, subtle in *Craft*,

What else will you now *think up*? How did you dare alone
Give bright-eyed Athena birth? Couldn't I have given her birth?
Even so amongst the immortals who make broad heaven their home
She would have been called your own. Take care now lest I *think up*
Some wicked plan in future—in fact I'll now contrive
How a son of mine may be born who would be beyond compare
Amongst the immortal gods. I'll not bring any disgrace
On your sacred bed or mine, nor shall I be sleeping with you,   329
But remote from you I'll be amongst the immortal gods."
　So she spoke, and far away from the gods she went in her wrath.
At once then did cow-eyed, queenly Hera begin to pray,
And with down-turned palm she smote the ground and spoke these words:
　"Now listen, Earth, to me, and also broad Heaven above,
And you Titan gods who about great Tartaros dwell underground,
From whom come men and gods; let all of you hear me now,
And give me a son without Zeus who'll be no less strong than he—
So much mightier let him be as than Kronos was far-seeing Zeus."
　In this way she spoke, and lashed the ground with a sturdy hand.   340
The Earth that bears life's nurture was stirred into motion; the sight
Gave her joy at heart, for she knew that her wish would be fulfilled.
From this moment onward then, till the year had brought its end,
She neither at any time came to the bed of Craft-filled Zeus,
Nor did she at any time sit on her richly wrought chair as before,
And devise for him shrewd counsels; she stayed in her prayer-filled
　　shrines,
Did cow-eyed, queenly Hera, and took from her offerings joy.
But when the months and days were drawing near their end—
The year in its cycle revolving again—and the seasons advanced,
She bore then one who was like neither gods nor mortal men,   351
The dread and fierce Typhaon, a bane to mortal men.
Then cow-eyed, queenly Hera took and gave him at once
To the Snake, who made him welcome, an evil in evil hands.
To the glorious tribes of humans he used to cause much harm,
While the day of doom used to carry whoever met her away—
Until lord Apollo who works from afar let fly at her
His mighty shaft, and she, being racked with cruel pains,
Was lying, loudly gasping, writhing upon the ground.
An unearthly clamour arose beyond words, as she twisted now here,
Now there through the wood, and expiring departed her bloody life.   361
Then over her in triumph Phoibos Apollo cried:
　"In this place now let you rot on the soil that nurtures men.
You won't be an evil affliction to living mortals who eat

The fruit of the bountiful Earth and will to this place bring
Their perfect hundredfold offerings. Neither Typhoeus will ward
Grim death from you, nor even Khimaira of hateful name,
But black Earth will make you rot, as will beaming Hyperion's rays."
   He spoke these words in triumph, and darkness covered her eyes.
There she was made to rot by the sacred might of the Sun;
And this is the reason why *Pytho* is called by its present name,   372
And they title the lord *Pytheios*, because in that place there
The might of the piercing Sun had *rotted* the monster away.
   And then did Phoibos Apollo see that the fair-flowing spring
Had deceived him; in anger he made for Telphousa, and soon arrived.
Close beside her he stood, and to her spoke these words:
   "Telphousa, you were not destined to keep this lovely spot
By deceiving my mind, and pour forth your fair-flowing water: here
Will my fame also be, and not just yours alone."
   When he had spoken these words, lord Apollo who works
      from afar
Upon her piled a peak with a falling shower of stones.   383
Hiding her streams from view, within the wooded grove
He built for himself an altar close to the fair-flowing spring;
And under the title *Telphousios* all there pray to the lord,
Because he there disfigured sacred Telphousa's streams.
   And then did Phoibos Apollo begin to ponder at heart
What folk he might bring to serve him in rocky Pytho as priests.
While revolving this matter he saw a swift ship on the wine-dark sea;
Aboard her from Minos' Knossos were many fine Cretan men—
It is they who offer the lord his sacrifice, they who report
The decrees of Phoibos Apollo whose sword is of gold, when he
      speaks   395
From the bay-tree proclaiming his oracles down in Parnassos' glens.
On a voyage of business and profit toward sandy Pylos town
And its native Pylian race their black ship's course was bound.
But Phoibos Apollo met them; in shape like a dolphin he leaped
Upon their swift ship and lay, a huge dread monster, on board.
And if amongst the Cretans any was minded to act,
He shook him in every direction and rattled the planks of the ship.
Silent and fearful they sat; throughout the hollow black ship
They were not untying the rigging, nor were they striking the sail
Of the ship with dark-coloured prow, but as they had set it in place   407
At the outset with oxhide ropes, so onward they held their course,
And a southerly gale blew up that roused the swift ship from behind.
They first passed Maleia and came along the Lakonian coast

To a city crowned by the sea and a place that belongs to the Sun
Who brings pleasure to mortals—Tainaros. There are the thick-fleeced
    flocks
Of the lordly Sun ever grazing; he owns this pleasant spot.
And there they wished to drop anchor and when they had disembarked
To examine this great wonder and with their eyes to watch
Whether the monster would stay aboard the hollow ship
Or would leap out into the swell of the salt sea teeming with fish.   417
But the ship which was finely constructed would not answer the helm,
But went on alongside of fertile Peloponnesos; with ease
Lord Apollo who works from afar directed her course with the breeze.
To Arene and lovely Argyphea forging onward she came,
To Thryon the ford of Alpheios, to Aipy that well-built place,
Then to sandy Pylos town and its native Pylian race.
She went past Krounoi and Khalkis, past Dyme and Elis' bright land,
Where power is held by Epeioi; and as for Pherai she aimed
In joy at Zeus' favouring wind, the sheer mountain of Ithake hove
From under the clouds into view, and Doulikhion too was seen   429
With Same and wooded Zakynthos. But when she had passed beyond
The whole of Peloponnesos, and when the vast gulf that sets bounds
To fertile Peloponnesos and stretches toward Krisa appeared,
Then came Zephyr, mighty and clear, in accord with Zeus' decree,
In a headlong swoop from the sky, so that with utmost speed
The ship would hurtle across the salty water of sea.
Back then again to face the Dawn and Sun they began
To sail, and the lord son of Zeus, Apollo, led them on.
At Krisa, clear to view, where vines abound, they came
To harbour; the sea-going vessel scraped the sandy beach.   439
Lord Apollo who works from afar then leaped out over the side
Like a star in the middle of day—there flew from him many sparks,
And radiance shot to heaven. He passed within his shrine
Amidst the precious tripods, kindled there a flame,
Revealing his darting rays, and all Krisa was bathed in light.
The wives and fair-girdled daughters of Krisa's men wailed out
At Phoibos' onrush, for great was the dread that he put in each heart.
But he bounded aloft from there to fly at the speed of thought
Back to the ship again in the shape of a fine strong man
Enjoying the prime of his youth, whose locks about broad shoulders
    hung;   450
And speaking aloud to the Cretans addressed them with winged words:
    "Who are you, strangers? From where do you sail on the liquid
      ways?

Is it on business you travel, or do you recklessly rove
Across the salt sea like pirates, who wander, staking their lives,
Bringing harm to foreign nations? Why sit in such sorrow, and not
Disembark on the shore, or take your black ship's tackle down?
This at least is the custom of men who are eaters of bread,
When sick with fatigue they come in their black ship from sea to land,
And at once their hearts are seized with a longing to taste sweet food."

   In this way Apollo spoke, and put courage within their breasts;   462
And then to him in answer the Cretans' leader said:

   "Stranger—although in truth you haven't about you the build
Or the look of mortal folk, but are like the immortal gods—
May health and great joy be yours, and heaven grant blessings to you!
Now give me an honest answer, to set my mind at rest:
What country is this, what land? What mortals are native here?
With a different route in mind we were sailing across the great gulf,
For Pylos bound from Crete—our birthplace, we proudly boast.
Now here in our ship we've landed, not of our own accord,
By a journey and ways unintended, though yearning to head back
     home.   472
But to this place has some immortal brought us against our will."

   And then to them in answer Apollo the Far-worker said:
"You strangers who dwelt in times past near Knossos where many
     trees grow,
But who now will never again return to your lovely town,
Fair homes, and darling wives, but here will tend my rich shrine
That is honoured by many humans: I am the son of Zeus,
And my boast is that I am Apollo. Across the great gulf of the sea
I've brought you, meaning no harm: no, here you'll tend my rich shrine
That all humans hold high in esteem, and you'll know the plans of
     the gods,
Through whose will you'll always be honoured, for ever, throughout
     all time.   485
But now quickly obey my instructions: take the sail down first,
Untying the oxhide ropes; then dragging ashore the swift ship,
Unload your cargo and gear; and building an altar there
On the strand where the sea's surf breaks, upon it kindle a flame,
Offer white barley and pray while standing about it close by.
As at first in shape like a *dolphin* I leaped on board your swift ship
Amidst the cloud-coloured sea, so to me as *Delphinios* pray;
The altar itself will always be *Delphic* and present to view.
Then prepare for yourselves a meal beside your swift black ship,

And pour for the blessed gods who have Olympos as home.   498
But when you have banished desire for the honey-sweet savour of food,
Come along with me and sing the Ie-Paieon hymn,
Until you have made your way to the place where you'll tend my
    rich shrine."
   When he had in this way spoken, they heeded his words and obeyed.
They took the sail down first, untying the oxhide ropes;
Lowered the mast with the forestays, bringing it home to the crutch;
Next disembarked themselves on the strand where the sea's surf breaks,
And dragged ashore the swift ship high up on the sandy beach,
Drawing long props beside it; and built an altar there
On the strand where the sea's surf breaks, upon it kindled a flame,   509
Offered white barley and prayed while standing as bidden close by.
They made then a meal for themselves beside their swift black ship,
And poured for the blessed gods who have Olympos as home.
But when they had banished desire for drink and for food, they set out;
Apollo the lord son of Zeus was leading them on their way,
Holding the lyre in his hands and playing a lovely tune,
Stepping fine and high; behind him the Cretans, stamping their feet,
Followed toward Pytho and sang the Ie-Paieon hymn—
A hymn such as those that are sung by Cretans within whose breasts
The goddess Muse has placed the honey-sweet sound of song.   519
Unwearied, they reached a ridge on foot, and suddenly came
To Parnassos, that lovely spot where the god intended to dwell,
Honoured by many humans. Leading them further he showed
His holy shrine and rich temple; the spirit was stirred in their breasts.
Putting to him a question, the Cretans' leader said:
   "Since far away from our friends and the land of our fathers, Lord,
As it pleased your heart, you've brought us, how are we now to live?
Consider this point, we ask you. The land here, though lovely indeed,
Neither is fit to yield crops nor offers for pasture sweet grass,
Whereby we might live well and attend to humans' needs."   530
   The son of Zeus, Apollo, smiled and said to them:
"You senseless humans, you wretched creatures wishing at heart
For sorrows, hard toils, and troubles! Your answer I'll give you with ease
And put in your minds to think on. Let every last one of you grasp
A dagger in his right hand and for ever be slaughtering flocks:
They will be there in abundance, all those that are brought for me
By the glorious tribes of humans. Stand guard before my shrine
And welcome the tribes of humans who gather here in search,
Above all, of my guidance; but if there will be a rash word or deed,

And outrageous conduct, which is the custom of mortal men,   541
Then others you'll have as your masters, for ever forced under
    their yoke.
To you now all has been spoken; keep it safe in your thoughts."
    And so farewell I bid you, Zeus and Leto's son;
But I will call to my mind both you and another song.   546

UNKNOWN, *HYMN 27: TO ARTEMIS* (c. 700 BCE)

Of Artemis, goddess with distaff of gold, whose cry resounds,
I sing, the virgin revered, the archeress shooter of deer,
The sister by birth of Apollo, god of the golden sword.
In the chase over shadowy mountains and wind-swept peaks she
    delights,
And takes aim with a bow of pure gold, dispatching arrows of woe.
The heads of high mountains tremble, the thick-shaded forest screams out
A dire echo of bestial clamour, and shudderings shake both the earth
And the sea that is teeming with fish; but she with a heart that is strong
Now this way turns, now that, destroying the race of beasts.
Yet when the archeress tracker of beasts has had pleasure enough   11
From the hunt and has gladdened her mind, she unstrings her
    flexible bow
And goes to her brother's great home, to Phoibos Apollo's abode
In Delphi's rich land, to prepare for the Muses' and Graces' fair dance.
She hangs up there with its arrows her bow that springs back from the pull,
And wearing graceful adornments takes the lead in the dance.
The goddesses, raising their heavenly voices, sing a hymn
Of fair-ankled Leto, and tell how she gave her children birth,
Who are in both counsel and deeds the best of immortals by far.
    Farewell to you, children of Zeus and Leto with lovely hair;
But I will call to my mind both you and another song.

8.2
THEORY

MYTH, RITUAL, AND INITIATIONS

The myth of Niobe portrays the violence of Artemis and Apollo against girls
and boys, thus linking it to their roles as initiatory deities. Niobe, the daughter
of a mythical king, proudly boasts that she has seven daughters and seven
sons, unlike Leto, who has only two children, Artemis and Apollo. To avenge

this insult to their mother, Artemis and Apollo use their arrows to slay all of Niobe's children; Artemis kills her daughters, whereas Apollo kills her sons. As for Niobe, she turns into stone, eternally lamenting the loss of her children (Figure 8.10). Whereas the myth of Niobe, like the other myths in this chapter (and, indeed, like many Greek myths), seems to bear traces of ritual practices, the relationship between myth and ritual is less than clear. This section considers the relationship between myth and ritual by refining the term "initiation" through the work of ethnographer Arnold van Gennep (1873–1957) and others on such rituals.

8.10 **Artemis and Apollo slay the children of Niobe.** Detail from an Attic red-figure krater. Niobid Painter, c.450 BCE. Louvre Museum, Paris, France. © RMN-Grand Palais / Art Resource, NY, ART442238.

JANE HARRISON AND THE CAMBRIDGE RITUALISTS

Early in the twentieth century at Cambridge University, a group of scholars perceived myth and ritual as inseparable. The Cambridge Ritualists, as this group came to be known, were classicists who argued that myths corresponded to rituals in some essential way. One of the most well-known Cambridge Ritualists, Jane Ellen Harrison (1850–1928), stated the relationship between myth and ritual categorically: "Myth is the spoken correlative of the acted rite, the thing done." Harrison conceived of ritual as a series of events that was acted out, much like a drama or performance, often before or on behalf of others who formed an audience. A myth, in her formulation, was the script or libretto for a ritual. Often, when the ritual itself falls out of practice, the myth remains.

Although this hypothetical scenario offers an explanation for the often seemingly illogical moments in Greek myths, it ultimately does not convince. Certainly, Harrison's tidy formulation may work in some instances; for example, the Homeric *Hymn* 2 (*To Demeter*) recounts a myth that is closely connected with initiates' ritual activities at the Great Mysteries at Eleusis (Chapter 4.1). But Harrison's formulation is not clearly applicable to most Greek myths or rituals, even if we acknowledge that we have lost the sorts of data and artifacts, not to mention eyewitness testimony, that might clarify such a connection. Greek myths are too elaborate and too detailed to be reduced to a ritual, no matter how creative their interpreters may be. Thus, although later scholars have rejected Harrison's strong claim that myth correlates to ritual, she and the other Cambridge Ritualists did succeed in shifting the focus of myth studies to their societal contexts rather than their purely literary qualities, and in illuminating the vital connections between myth and ritual in ancient Greece and elsewhere. Van Gennep's work on initiations (or rites of passage) has proved particularly relevant to understanding how myth, although it might be concerned with ritual, is not (as Harrison postulated) a script for ritual.

ARNOLD VAN GENNEP AND RITES OF PASSAGE

At the time that van Gennep was an active scholar, rituals of all societies were divided, classified, and studied by type, such as marriages, funerals, baptisms, exorcisms, and sacrifices. Just as each seemed to serve a distinct purpose (function), each seemed to have a unique structure (form). Amid such diversity, van Gennep discerned a common form and function among one class of rituals that he called rites of passage. All rituals of that class, no matter how different they seem, share a common purpose: they facilitate the transition of participants from one stage to another.

Van Gennep argued that rites of passage "accompany every change of place, state, social position and age." They may accompany the installation of a new king or queen, a community's celebration of a new year, or a change in season. In sum, rites of passage (including initiations) enable individuals as well as entire groups to adapt to change. Initiations that accompany various life stages (birth, puberty, marriage, and death) are called age-grade initiations; they often acknowledge and reconcile the biological determinants (such as menarche and puberty) of an individual's life with his or her social roles (such as marriage and citizenship). They allow an individual to negotiate these transitional moments, while simultaneously ensuring that the individual will conform to the norms that determine his or her social position. In this way, van Gennep argued, rites of passage ensure both a society's internal cohesion, by enforcing individuals' assumption of their expected roles, and a society's continuity over time, by managing reproduction.

Just as van Gennep argued that all initiations share a common purpose (they move individuals from one state or position to another), he also noted that all initiations share a similar structure. Initiations, he observed, consist of three stages: separation, time at the margin (or "limen"), and reaggregation. Borrowing the Latin word *limen*, which means "door" or "threshold," van Gennep also called these stages preliminal, liminal, and postliminal. These three stages are given different labels in subsequent literature but are generally applied to the same three broad categories: every ritual, like every story, has a beginning, middle, and end. The simplicity of this scheme, however, should not obscure its importance to ritual studies. For in addition to directing scholarly attention to the similarities among different rites, van Gennep also demonstrated that rituals were not meaningless acts repeated over and over again in a rote fashion. Rituals help to shape individuals to meet the social demands placed on them.

The first stage, separation, separates an individual (the initiate) from his or her former status or life stage. The initiate may temporarily move to a different place, change clothing or appearance in some way, or cross a boundary, whether real or symbolic.

The second stage, limen, is perhaps the most important. It may last from a single day to a full year and involves activities that are designed to transform initiates so that they can fulfill their new social role. Initiates often must undergo psychologically, emotionally, and/or physically challenging activities that are disorienting and that create a kind of cognitive dissonance. Body modification, such as scarification or circumcision, and activities of inversion (for example, boys may dress as girls, or individuals may do things that are otherwise socially forbidden) are common. Initiates may also be stripped naked, underfed, and thus reduced to a state of helpless infancy. Alternately, they may be kept in darkness, dressed in dark garments, and treated as though they are dead. Such acts are intended to make initiates submissive to those conducting the initiation and receptive to the demanded changes. They may then engage in educational activities such as learning and memorizing important knowledge or acquiring and performing new skills. Such acts also have a symbolic aspect: by treating initiates as infants or corpses, these activities convey that a part of the initiates must die and that they must be reborn into their new state, position, or status.

In the third stage, reaggregation, initiates are reintegrated into society in their newly attained position, status, or state. A procession or ceremony may mark an initiate's completion of his or her rite of passage.

In many cultures, weddings illustrate the elegance and applicability of van Gennep's rites of passage. At the separation stage, the initiates (the groom and the bride) no longer occupy their former position or state in life. Once they are betrothed to each other, they begin to relinquish their identity as a daughter or son and enter their future roles as responsible members of society. A series of rituals may take place at this time to mark their separation from their former identity: for example, an exchange of goods between the families of the bride and groom (or, in many Western cultures, the gift of a ring from the groom to the bride); a sham kidnapping of the bride; educative activities; and tattooing, scarring, and other body modifications. Traces of these more serious rituals can be found in the bachelor and bachelorette parties that precede many American weddings. In the second stage, the bride and groom may wear special clothing and undergo rituals that may last one or more days, at the end of which the couple will have a different legal and social status. These rituals may include dancing, symbolic enactments of the tasks and duties the bride will be required to fulfill, rites that ensure the fertility of the couple, and a further exchange of goods between families. In the third stage, the couple will enter society as husband and wife. They may wear different attire and wedding jewelry and will often change residence.

Van Gennep's rites of passage offer useful insight into the myths and the initiatory rituals for adolescents that Artemis and Apollo oversee. Interestingly, however, there is no one Greek word that corresponds to the English word "initiation" to describe these rituals. Instead, as we have seen, local puberty rites have names such as the Brauronia or the Hyacinthia. These two festivals conform in many, although not all, ways to van Gennep's scheme.

Whereas the Brauronia is closely connected to reproductive biology, and Artemis presides over ritual activities that accompany and facilitate the transitions of the daughters of citizens into wives, initiatory festivals for boys (such as the Hyacinthia) move male youth into the ranks of citizens and soldiers. They too must be trained (or compelled) to assume a range of military and political duties and thus become contributing members of society. Table 8.1 illustrates how both the Brauronia and the Hyacinthia conform to van Gennep's tripartite division of initiatory rites.

Van Gennep offers a clear definition of the form (three stages) and function (to facilitate the transformation from childhood to adulthood) of initiations. But how might initiations seen through his theoretical lens illuminate myths? Myths attached to Artemis and Apollo have a repeating pattern that loosely correlates to their initiations. Walter Burkert (1931–2015), a German scholar of Greek religion, offers a nuanced view of the relationship between myths and rituals in a way that is particularly helpful in the case of initiations: "The mythical tale . . . names that which the ritual intends" (*Homo Necans*, 34). The first step of initiatory rituals, the separation stage, is designed to separate

Table 8.1: The Three Stages of Greek Initiatory Rites

	BRAURONIA	HYACINTHIA
SEPARATION	Girls depart for Brauron (or other sites dedicated to Artemis in Athens's environs).	Boys enter into a state of mourning for Hyacinthus; they observe food restrictions; and they offer sacrifices at the tomb of Hyacinthus.
TRANSITION	Girls "play the bear for Artemis." They wear yellow robes or are naked; they race, dance, and sing; they dedicate votives and toys.	Boys participate in citywide competitions, processions from Sparta to Amyclae, banquets, and the dedication of a robe to Apollo. Slaves and women participate.
INCORPORATION	Girls return home, prepared for the changes that marriage brings.	Little evidence describes the events of this day.

the initiate from his or her former identity in order to enable and promote change and development into the next. An important part of the initiate's identity must symbolically die. In many of the myths attached to Apollo and Artemis, young boys and girls die. Here, then, it seems that the myths of Apollo and Artemis name or clarify the intent of initiatory rituals. The ambiguity about whether such deaths or transformations are meant to punish or protect magnifies the ambiguities of gaining adult status while losing the freedoms of youth.

KEN DOWDEN, "INITIATION: THE KEY TO MYTH?"

Dowden (b. 1950) builds on van Gennep's definition of initiation rituals and then explores myths relevant to girls' and boys' initiations.

BEFORE YOU READ

- After discussing Iphigenia (here spelled "Iphigeneia"; both forms are correct), Dowden turns to the daughters of Protios. How do their myths parallel Iphigenia's? How do they pertain to girls' initiatory rituals?

- How does the myth of Leukippos, who experiences a sex change, compare to myths about Achilles and to boys' initiations? Do these myths offer sufficient proof that boys were considered "feminized" prior to their initiations?

- Do you think that initiatory rites and myths connected with Artemis and Apollo in ancient Greece compelled social conformity? Why or why not?

KEN DOWDEN, "INITIATION: THE KEY TO MYTH?" (2011)

IPHIGENEIA AND GIRLS AS ANIMALS

Greek mythology is concerned, inter alia, with the virtue, or otherwise, of wives. But a remarkable number of girls ("maidens") have trouble reaching that stage at all.[1] They may be turned into animals, plants, or even finally constellations (the Proitids, Daphne, Kallisto); they may need to murder their prospective husbands (the Danaids); they may need to give their lives for the community (the Erechtheids); they may die in the course of a pursuit (Iphinoe); or be slaughtered or sacrificed, preferably by their father (the returning Idomeneus). The most famous example of the last category is Iphigeneia, the daughter of Agamemnon.

Her story, as we know it, is part of the saga of the Trojan War, and its focus falls on her father Agamemnon. Helen, the wife of his brother, Menelaos, has been stolen by Paris, the son of the Trojan king Priam; Agamemnon has assembled the Greek forces that will head to Troy to avenge his brother. Their ships are now at Aulis, on the coast of Boiotia facing the long island of Euboia; but Agamemnon cannot gain favourable winds. This is because he has offended the goddess Artemis by shooting a deer. It is not wholly clear why this action has offended Artemis, but one version goes that he boasted as he shot the deer that "not even Artemis" could have shot like that. The prophet Kalchas now pronounces that Agamemnon must sacrifice his daughter if he is to sail to Troy, and Iphigeneia is sent for, ostensibly in order that she may be married to Achilles. Some authors give the impression she is sacrificed; others report that a deer is substituted by Artemis at the last moment and Iphigeneia herself is whisked off to serve Artemis at her shrine amongst the "Tauroi," a Thracian tribe with a name conveniently similar to Artemis' epithet Tauropolos (she of the "bulls," *tauroi*).

If this were all, we would probably be none the wiser. But there are also related myths told in the next land south of Boiotia, namely Attica (the territory of Athens). On the East coast, at Brauron (near Athens airport), a maiden plays with a wild bear but it scratches her and her brothers shoot it. A plague now descends on the Athenians and an oracle pronounces that their maidens must in future *arkteuein* ("do the bear (rite)") before they can marry. On the West coast, at Mounychia (near the old port of Athens), again a bear is killed by the Athenians and again a plague results. The oracle prescribes the sacrifice of his daughter by someone who is willing. At this point, Embaros (who is a byword for ingenuity ever after) agrees, provided he gains the priesthood for his clan. But he hides his daughter in the inner room of the temple and proceeds to sacrifice a goat which he has dressed in his daughter's clothes.

The common structure of these myths is as follows:

an animal is killed	Artemis is angry	an oracle prescribes a remedy	a girl is to be sacrificed by her father	but she is not and an animal is substituted	the prospect of marriage
			the *Arkteia* is to take place		

The account in which the *Arkteia* becomes a necessity veers from myth to what myth signifies. But in all cases we are at a shrine of Artemis and in two (Aulis, Brauron) the question of marriage arises. The *Arkteia* was indeed a ritual which select Athenian maidens performed prior to marriage. And all versions show an oscillation of identity between girl and animal, emphasizing that one may under special conditions substitute for the other. In two versions (Aulis, Mounychia) the slayer is the father.

An initiatory interpretation works as follows. The sacrifice expresses the dynamics of the key moment of separation in the initiation ceremony. To become marriageable, a girl must leave the control of her father and enter the control of her husband. In the Greek context this happens within the ritual embrace of the relevant goddess, Artemis. This is dramatically, but logically, represented by father and daughter engaging in a ceremony in the Artemis shrine in which the father symbolically kills the daughter. Mock-death and mock-killing are staples of the phase of separation in initiation ceremonies. They are the necessary preliminary to rebirth and are also reflected in the change of names and change of appearance which can occur at this stage. But the girl is not really dead: she has become something outside the human category altogether, namely an animal, if a vulnerable one specially loved by the goddess. The goddess has helped her to survive the transition by adopting the girl into her service for a period, and indeed the example of the *arktoi* shows that girls *did* spend a period in the goddess's service. It is only after this that marriage becomes available, the marriage to which Athenian girls looked forward and the marriage which was offered (albeit deceitfully) to Iphigeneia.

The myth of Iphigeneia would on this view find its formative context in a regional family of rituals. I have argued elsewhere that this includes some traces of a deer-ritual prior to marriage in Thessaly, and maybe also aspects of the Dionysos cult in Boiotia, in particular the ritual garb of the maenads (raving matrons), the deer-dress (*nebris*). It is possible that there is also an outlier in Arkadia, where the nymph Kallisto ("Prettiest") is also turned into a bear and shot, this time maybe by Artemis.[2]

A different region is constituted by the Argolid, Sikyon, and neighbouring areas. There we find a mythology of the daughters of Proitos, King of Tiryns, who offend Hera,[3] perhaps by deriding the appearance of her statue. The result is that they suffer from a whitening disease (leprosy, perhaps), and in their madness become convinced that they are cows, then start roaming over the wilds of the Peloponnese. They must eventually find a place to be cured. According to Bakchylides (*Epinician Ode* 11), it is by their father in the waters of Lousoi (north Arcadia). In the most colourful version of the story, though, it is in a ritual chase by the young men, led by the prophet Melampous ("Blackfoot"), a chase of such vigour that one of them, Iphinoē, dies at Sikyon— and you can see her tomb.[4] This ritual chase of the not-quite married is reflected again in the myth of the Danaids (honoured at Argos), who must escape their would-be husbands, who are the sons of Egypt (and therefore black).

Thus, once again, on an initiatory view, there is a parade of appropriate motifs. The subjects are those on the verge of marriage. The Proitids, in a ritual environment (the temple of Hera), lose their human identity and become confused with animals. Their whitening may reflect the use of white daubs in initiation rituals (part of the scenery of changing identity). They also leave their home and have no bearings. Meanwhile there is a clear hint of a ritual chase of the sexes (one which we also know happened in Boiotia in the Dionysos cult), looking as though the normal paleness of women and tanned skins of men is exaggerated through black and white daubings, maybe washed off at the end. If one of the girls dies, that may indicate that in a sense they all die and that the transition is a difficult one. Are the Proitids attractive enough to marry? No longer. And the Danaids' slaughter of their husbands is as clear a rejection of marriage as you will find in any myth. In this liminal period they are unmarried and unmarriageable.[5]

Somewhere in the background of all this seem to lie organized rites, repeated from year to year (or sometimes maybe at gaps of more than a year). Their function seems to be to take the available girls and convert them psychologically and ritually so that they are ready for marriage. The evidence for the ritual, however, is very thin and this evidence comes from well after the time of formation of these myths; thus, it is possible that the ritual alongside which the myth originally made sense has decayed. We might well ask now whether the *Arkteia* for which we have evidence had not changed significantly over the centuries. Presumably, it had originally not been a ceremony for the Athenian state but for the people of the village of Brauron, where in later years it had come to seem like a colourful local part of the Athenian heritage, with its saffron-dyed robes and running races. In fact, however, it was a survival of rites that had once been held in most places, of which Brauron and (on the other side of Attica) Mounychia were only survivals. The whole of the eligible maidenhood of Attica was scarcely going to assemble at Brauron for the *Arkteia*: thus, by its nature in an amalgamated ("syncretized") Attica, it would be available only to *select* girls. We cannot know whether in origin the ceremony had been restricted to the daughters of leading folk; but it seems unlikely that they would be sufficiently numerous. We do not have evidence for non-mythical girls masquerading as cows at Tiryns, though as Argos destroyed the city and much of its culture in the 470s BC, this is not surprising. But as Spartan boys were dragooned in *agelai* (herds) and led by *bouagoi* (ox-leaders), there is nothing implausible about the young girls of Tiryns and its region practising being cows in the same way that Brauronian girls practised being bears. Given that Hera is standardly "cow-faced" (*boöpis*) in Homer, usually translated "ox-eyed," it would seem appropriate.[6]

THE DESTINY OF THE WARRIOR

Boys' myths do not map so easily onto rites and their patterns. But there exists, all the same, a range of myths addressing the key point at which the boy becomes the warrior. Phaistos is in south-central Crete, a bus ride from Heraklion. Today we visit it for its magnificent Minoan palace. But it was a living community in classical times too, and there we hear of a myth associated with a ritual, which the Hellenistic poet Nicander (third–second century BC) had told in Book 2 of his now lost *Metamorphoses* (we have the story as reported by Antoninus Liberalis (second–third century AD?) in his *Metamorphoses* (17), a prose work which draws extensively on Nicander's poem).[7] A woman called Galateia is pregnant with the child of her husband Lampros ("brilliant") and he prays it will be a boy. But it isn't. So she pretends it is and calls it Leukippos ("white-horse," strangely often the name of the king's son in mythology).[8] Leukippos grows up and her beauty is such that Galateia fears she cannot any longer fool Lampros. So she goes to the temple of Leto and implores her to make Leukippos a boy, which indeed Leto does.

> The people of Phaistos even today commemorate this sex-change and sacrifice to Leto of Growth (*Phytia*), who caused the girl to grow male organs; and they call the festival the *Ekdysia* [the (festival of the) Casting Off (of clothes)], since the girl cast off her *peplos* [robe]. And it is the custom that those who are getting married must first lie beside the statue of Leukippos.

This strange myth concerns the "coming-out" of a male under the auspices of a goddess at maturity, and it is associated with the boundary you must cross to reach marriage and with a specific festival, apparently celebrating male "maturation." The myth is presented as aetiological, that is, as giving the reason why a ceremony is held. But in myth-analysis we regard the chain of causation as being rather in the opposite direction, from ritual to myth: the myth exists because the ritual did, and it serves to explain the dynamics of the ritual. The ritual seems to be in initiatory territory, and the myth exists to explore the dynamics of this moment in human ritual life.

So far this is to interpret a single myth rather heavily. But there are a number of comparable myths. One that is important for us was also mentioned by Nicander and appears in the same chapter of Antoninus' *Metamorphoses* (Galateia's prayer was clearly a fine set-piece in which she cited others who had undergone sex-change in order to support her request). This is the myth of Kaineus, situated in Thessaly in mainland Greece. This character is originally a girl, Kainis, and Poseidon is enamoured of her and agrees to grant her a wish. She wishes to become a man and invincible.[9] The story goes on to tell how Kaineus caused people to swear by his spear, and defeated the Centaurs until they took whole fir trees and pounded him into the ground. The latter part is something of a cautionary story, but the sex-change at adolescence (she is not yet married)—granted by Poseidon, a god sometimes elsewhere associated with youths—seems to be from a similar stable to the story of Leukippos.

We then turn to a more famous story, that of Achilles. This greatest of warriors in the Trojan War was not originally going to join the expedition. Indeed, his mother Thetis, knowing he would die if he went, had "disguised him in women's dress and left him with Lykomedes as a maiden."[10] Achilles comes from Phthia, a region of Thessaly, and Lykomedes is the ruler of the island of Skyros, around 150 kilometres away, on the other side of Euboia. This ruse does not escape the attention of the Greek forces assembling for Troy. An embassy is sent, and Odysseus cunningly lays out a selection of women's goods and weaponry before the royal girls on Skyros, whereupon Achilles' interest in the weaponry gives him away. Achilles has been sent to what is effectively a margin, something that matters for the liminal stage of initiation, as we have seen above in van Gennep's analysis.[11] It is at this point that his gender role is defined and he is no longer counted amongst the females: he can now go to war. So it is that once again, as in the case of Iphigeneia, a story leading up to the Trojan War seems to belong with a family of myths, sometimes local ones not particularly well known, and to concern issues of how you cross the threshold to adulthood—whether to marriage or to war. These are issues that also attract rituals, and the Leukippos case is specifically connected to a ritual, though we know nothing else about it. And just as Artemis holds the ring in the case of several girls' myths and rituals, so we find in these cases too that the crucial act must be performed by a god—Poseidon or Leto, though obviously this may also be a narrative necessity.

Another myth which seems to belong in this area, though it takes rather a different direction, is that of Zeus and Ganymede. The myth is simple: Ganymede is the most beautiful adolescent and Zeus is enamoured of him; so his eagle carries Ganymede to Olympus where he will be Zeus's cup-bearer.[12] This then matches a bizarre ritual in Crete, reported by Ephoros in his lost *History* (*FGrH* 70 F 149). It is the custom for a specially attractive youth, who is called the *kleinos* ("famous") to be ritually abducted by a lover, with the agreement of the friends and family of the *kleinos*, and to be taken into the wilds (with the friends and family) to hunt and feast with the lover for two months. At the end they return to the city (it is not stated which one) and the *kleinos* receives a warrior's outfit, an ox, and a cup. The ox is sacrificed to Zeus; the cup recalls the role of Ganymede, as does the sexuality of this abduction and further details regarding intercourse during the period in the wilds. The warrior's outfit links visibly with the weaponry selected by Achilles to end his own period at a margin as a girl. Thus this ritual is part of a family of myths and rituals which deal with the emerging warrior and more generally the emerging male.

THE THEORY IN A NUTSHELL

At this point I am going to draw out a possible, if rather extreme, version of the thinking behind the initiatory theory of myth. It will be extreme so that it may be as clear as possible and so that we may see where it could be exaggerating and where it needs to be pruned back.

On this theory, the Greeks who generated this mythology used to hold initiation rites both for boys and, separately, for girls. These effected their transition to their adult roles, as warriors and as wives or, rather, mothers. Every year, or maybe every two or four years, the next cohort of boys/girls would go through the rites in honour of a god such as Poseidon, Leto, Hera, or Artemis—whichever was the local guardian of youth or controller of the portal to adulthood. These rites would be characterized by a van Gennep structure: separation, time at a margin or a shrine in a margin, return (or, rather, entry) to the adult community. Girls would tend to be considered as animals or nymphs in the marginal period, boys as wolves or even as feminized. We cannot know whether "training" as we would envisage it was part of these ceremonies, but it is not unlikely that it was—perhaps weaving for girls and the manipulation of weapons, especially in hunting, for boys. Because these rites existed, myths also existed in a sort of dialogue with the rites. The moment of separation above all was dramatized, and we catch some sight of the period in the margins. Return to the "city" is not generally visible. It would be crude to say that myths were invented to explain pre-existing rites, as though the rites had no voice before that, and it would be much preferable to view myth and rite as a counterpoint to each other, each describing in their own language the issues in question. But the fact remains that this view, if accepted, explains why some myths existed and why they existed in the form that they did. It is a historical explanation of Greek mythology. There are many myths that should be explained in this way and if we knew more about rituals it would be easier to identify them. But this is not a universal theory of myth: it explains one class, if an important one, of Greek mythology.

NOTES

1. See Dowden (1989).

2. Dowden (1992: 106–7).

3. Hesiod, *Catalogue of Women* F 130–133 MW (78–83 Most).

4. Apollodoros 2.2; Pausanias 1.43.4 mentions the tomb.

5. On the Proitids, see Dowden (1989: ch. 4, 1992: 108–9), Brulé (1987: 219–21).

6. Interestingly *boöpis* is also used as an epithet for Proitos' wife Stheneboia in Hesiod, *Catalogue of Women* F 129 MW (77 Most).

7. On Leukippos at Phaistos, see Dowden (1989: 65–7, 1992: 118).

8. See Dowden (1989: 62–7).

9. See, for example, Apollodoros, *Epitome* 1.22.

10. See, for example, Apollodoros, *Epitome* 1.8.

11. The theme of margin is explored by Vidal-Naquet in his discussions of the Black Hunter (1986) and of Philoktetes (1992); the margin dominates van Gennep's book (index s.v. 'Transition, Rites of', or in the French original 'Marge (périodes de)'). Achilles' Skyros is the equivalent of Philoktetes' Lemnos.

12. See, for example, *Homeric Hymn 5* to *Aphrodite* 206–17; Apollodoros 3.13 for the role of the eagle.

8.3
COMPARISON

ANATOLIA AND ROME: CYBELE

In *The East Face of Helicon*, M. L. West (1937–2015) writes, "oriental deities seem to have cast some reflection of themselves" on Greek gods and goddesses, especially on Apollo. Despite the fact that many scholars have regarded Apollo as the most Greek of all gods because he embodies the cultural values closely associated with Greek civilization, his name does not appear on Linear B tablets in Greece dating from the Bronze Age (Chapter 2.1). This striking absence suggests that Apollo's origins were outside of Greece.

Many scholars have explored how a linguistic connection between the Anatolian god Appaliunas and the Greek Apollo, as well as Apollo's worship in Lycia (a region in southern Anatolia), might suggest that Anatolian gods and religious practices have influenced the ways in which Apollo was understood. In Lycia, Apollo had oracular temples in Patara and Telmessus and was worshipped alongside his mother Leto at a temple called the Letoon near Xanthus. In northern Anatolia, a treaty between the Hittite kings Muwatallis and Alaksundus of Wilusa (c. 1280 BCE) includes a number of gods' names, one of which is remarkably similar to Apollo: Appaliunas. The city of Wilusa is thought to correspond to Troy, which was also known as Ilion (its Latin form is Ilium). This evidence tantalizingly suggests, rather than proves, Anatolian origins or influence on Apollo. The case for the interaction over centuries between the Greek Artemis and Anatolian Cybele, however, is more convincing.

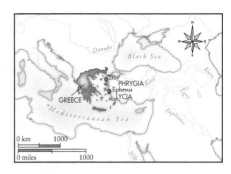

Map 8.2 (Anatolia) Apollo and Artemis

This section traces how Anatolia has cast shadows on Artemis's worship in mainland Greece and, conversely, how Greek conceptions of Artemis, filtered by the Romans, influenced the design of the well-known statue of Artemis of Ephesus, a coastal city in Anatolia. Unlike Apollo, Artemis's name has been found on Linear B tablets in Greece, and thus we can conclude that she was worshipped in Greece during the Bronze Age. Nevertheless, the influence of "oriental deities"—especially the Great Mother (*matar* is the Phrygian word for "mother") from Phrygia, a kingdom in western Anatolia that flourished in the eighth century BCE—can be detected in Greek conceptions of Artemis.

ARTEMIS AND THE PHRYGIAN GREAT MOTHER

The Greeks sometimes referred to the Phrygian Great Mother by the name Cybele, which derives from a Phrygian adjective, *kubeliya*, that means "of the mountains." The Greeks also worshipped a goddess they called "Mother" (*meter*) or the "Great Mother" (*megale meter*) who seems to harken back to the Phrygian Great Mother. Literary and visual evidence from as early as the eighth century BCE in Greece suggests that the Phrygian Great Mother left her imprint not only on goddesses with distinct maternal traits (such as Demeter) but also on Artemis.

In Phrygia, the Great Mother was represented as an older woman, wearing a long, belted gown with a headdress and long veil. On sculptural reliefs, she is often shown standing in a doorway. Accompanied by a predatory bird, such as an eagle or hawk (and, less frequently, by lions or male attendants), she sometimes carries a cup. These reliefs do not appear on temples or palace walls. Rather, they have been found near boundaries, such as city gates and fortification walls, and in rural places apart from human dwellings: on funerary tumuli (mounds), on altars, and especially in the mountains. The iconography and location of these reliefs suggest that the Great Mother was more closely linked to nature than to the political world of the city; yet she facilitated exchanges between natural and civilized spaces. She may have granted to her worshippers power over the natural world, which her attendance by predatory birds suggests she herself had. Curiously, although she is called "mother," she does not appear with infants or children. Thus she seems to be a caretaker of the natural world who ensures its abundance, but not a goddess who oversees human fertility.

8.11 Artemis of Ephesus. Marble statue. Circa first century CE. Museo Archeologico Nazionale, Naples, Italy. *Alinari / Art Resource, NY, ART7892.*

The Phrygian Great Mother's influence can be detected in the attributes of several Greek goddesses, including Artemis, and even in the worship of the Greek god Dionysus (Chapter 9.3). Demeter, for example, inherited the Great Mother's oversight of the abundance of the natural world. Yet Demeter's association with grain and agriculture moves her away from mountains and the wild and toward cultivated fields of grain. Artemis, unlike Demeter, has no maternal traits and nothing to do with agriculture. She wears a short tunic, not the heavy garment of the Great Mother, and she is far removed from maturity or maternity, as she traipses through the woods and keeps company with young adolescent girls. She appears to have inherited the Great Mother's intimate connection to the natural world; scholars have traced Artemis's identity as a "mistress of animals" to the Phrygian Great Mother. Both are accompanied by wild animals and are imagined to dwell outside of civilized spaces. Curiously, when the Greeks migrated east to establish the city of Ephesus in Anatolia and brought Artemis with them, she acquired yet another Anatolian attribute: the many protrusions that have been interpreted as breasts (which suggest the Great Mother's maternity and fecundity), bull's testicles (which were ritually offered to Cybele), or ornaments (such as those that decorate other Anatolian deities).

ARTEMIS IN ROMAN EPHESUS

Once under Roman rule in the first century BCE, Ephesus became an international city that needed a powerful patron goddess. Founded several centuries earlier by the legendary Athenian Androcles, who fought the nearby indigenous Samians, Carians, and Lydians, Ephesus had long been inhabited by both Greeks and Anatolians. Androcles established a sanctuary to Artemis roughly one mile away from the future site of the city (1086–85 BCE), where a temple to Artemis (called the Artemisium) served as a place of asylum as well as a bank that minted coins and took deposits.

The Artemisium was destroyed and rebuilt several times. Its most famous iteration was a marble temple begun in 550 BCE, shortly after the Lydian king Croesus (595–c. 547 BCE) conquered Ephesus and further integrated its Greek and Anatolian populations. This temple was one of the Seven

Wonders of the Ancient World; burned down in 356 BCE, it no longer survives. When Alexander the Great wrested Ephesus from the Persians in 334 BCE, the Ephesians rejected his offer to rebuild the Artemisium. They rebuilt Artemis's temple themselves, a structure that later survived the Romans' conquest of the city (84 BCE) and was Artemis's home when the emperor Augustus declared Ephesus the capital of the Roman province of Asia Minor (30–29 BCE). There the Ephesian Artemis was worshipped by native Anatolians, Greeks, and Romans.

The statue of the Ephesian Artemis (Figure 8.11) is noted for its many egg-shaped protrusions. The various interpretations of these protrusions allowed her to serve Greeks, Anatolians, and Romans alike. Whereas early Christian writers in the third century CE interpreted these as breasts, an interpretation shared by Greeks and Romans in Ephesus, Anatolians would have noted that these protrusions are similar to ornamental jewelry shown on other deities in Asia or to bulls' testicles (which were offered to Cybele in certain rituals). To them, the Ephesian Artemis would have seemed characteristically Anatolian or Eastern. Thus the Ephesian Artemis was neither particularly virginal, like Artemis on mainland Greece, nor maternal, like her distant ancestor the Phrygian Great Mother. Rather, she evolved in response to the fluctuating demographics of Ephesus: her protrusions were depicted with variations so that they could be interpreted as either breasts, testicles, or ornaments. In this way, Artemis offered a vision of wealth, abundance, and protection to all her worshippers.

As the Ephesian Artemis became the patroness of an increasingly cosmopolitan city, she began to resemble the quintessential city goddess, Athena. Indeed, her grand procession, described in *An Ephesian Tale*, bears certain similarities to the Panathenaic procession in Athena's honor conducted in Athens (Chapter 6.1). Thus, from her Greek and Anatolian beginnings, or her "set of prompts" in West's words, the Ephesian Artemis became an international goddess of Asia Minor under Roman rule. She served multiple populations simultaneously until Christianity took hold in the region and made her protection and patronage obsolete.

XENOPHON, FROM *AN EPHESIAN TALE*

BEFORE YOU READ

The procession of the Ephesian Artemis is the backdrop of the opening episode of Xenophon's romance novel, *An Ephesian Tale*. There is little information about the dates of either the author or his work, but most scholars date both to the Roman period of the second century CE. Like most ancient romance novels, *An Ephesian Tale* begins when its two protagonists meet, fall madly in love, and marry, before being separated by pirates, slave traders, a shipwreck, and other harrowing circumstances. Here Xenophon provides

BEFORE YOU READ
CONTINUED

some details of the proceedings and atmosphere of Artemis's procession in Ephesus, where the lovers first meet. (Translated by Stephen M. Trzaskoma.)

- As you read this selection, what details are reminiscent of the Greek myths or Greek rituals that you have already studied?

- Do you find evidence of Artemis's religious identity as a Greek initiatory goddess, a Phrygian Great Mother, or a Greco-Roman goddess who protects her capital city?

XENOPHON, FROM *AN EPHESIAN TALE* (c. SECOND CENTURY CE)

BOOK 1

[1] There was in Ephesos a man named Lycomedes, who was one of the most powerful people there. This Lycomedes and his wife Themisto, who was also an Ephesian, had a son, Habrocomes, a prodigy of exceptional handsomeness. Looks like his had never been seen in Ionia or any other land. This Habrocomes grew more handsome with every passing day, and his intellectual virtues blossomed alongside his physical beauty. He studied every cultural pursuit and practiced various arts, and his regular exercises were hunting, riding, and weapons training.

He was immensely popular with all the Ephesians, but also with those who lived in the rest of Asia, and they had high hopes that he would turn   10
out to be an exceptional citizen. They treated the young man like a god, and there were even those who knelt in reverence and offered prayers when they saw him. The young man was quite egotistical, exulting in his intellectual accomplishments but much more so in his physical beauty. Anything at all that was called beautiful he despised as inferior. Nothing, not a sight, not a sound, seemed to him to measure up to Habrocomes. If he heard that a boy was handsome or a girl beautiful, he scoffed at whoever said it, since obviously they didn't know he was the only one who was beautiful.

In fact, he didn't even think that Eros was a god. He rejected him en-   20
tirely, considering him beneath notice. He said no one would ever fall in love or submit to the god unless they did so willingly. If he happened to see a shrine or statue of Eros, he would laugh at it and announce that he was greater than any Eros, both in physical beauty and in power. And it was

true. Wherever Habrocomes put in an appearance, no one looked at any statues or praised any paintings.

[2] Eros was irate at this. He's a god that loves to fight and grants no quarter to the proud. He began to look for a stratagem to use against the young man—yes, even the god thought he'd have a hard time capturing the young man. Arming himself and cloaking himself with all the power of love magic, he began his campaign against Habrocomes.

There was a local festival of Artemis going on. It was a little less than a mile from the city to the temple, and all the Ephesian maidens, dressed in their finery, had to traverse the distance in a parade, as did all those ephebes who were the same age as Habrocomes. He was about sixteen and a member of the ephebic corps, and he marched at their head in the parade.

A huge crowd made up both of many locals and many visitors had come to watch the parade. It was the custom in that festival, you see, for the maidens to find themselves husbands and the ephebes wives. The participants marched in ranks. First were the holy objects, torches, baskets, and incense offerings. After them were horses and dogs and gear for hunting and warfare, but most of all for peaceful pursuits. < . . .

. . . > Each of them was dressed as if she was meeting a lover. Leading the contingent of maidens was Anthia, daughter of Megamedes and Euippe, both native Ephesians. Anthia's beauty was something to marvel at, far beyond that of the other girls. She was about fourteen years old. Her body was blossoming into beauty, and the stylishness of her look contributed greatly to her loveliness: blond hair—most of it worn loose, a little tied up, all of it moving with the blowing of the breeze; lively eyes— radiant like those of a girl, but unapproachable like those of a chaste woman; clothes—a purple dress, belted to fall at the knee, worn off the shoulder, with a fawn-skin wrap; equipment—a quiver fastened on, a bow, javelins in her hand, dogs at her heel.

Many a time the Ephesians had spotted her in the sanctuary and knelt in reverence in the belief that she was Artemis. On this occasion too when she appeared, a shout went up from the crowd. The spectators made all sorts of comments. Some of them were so stunned they said she was the goddess, others that she wasn't the goddess but had been made by her. All of them offered up prayers and knelt in reverence to her. They remarked how blessed her parents were. "Anthia the beautiful!" was what all the spectators were talking about. And as the group of maidens passed, no one said anything except "Anthia."

But from the moment that Habrocomes showed up with the ephebes, despite how beautiful the sight of the maidens had been, everyone forgot about them as they caught a glimpse of Habrocomes. They turned their eyes to him and, astounded by the sight, shouted, "Habrocomes is so handsome! No one looks more like a handsome god than him!" Some also then added, "How great it would be if Habrocomes and Anthia got married!"

That was Eros warming up for his plan.   70

Soon the two of them began to hear word of each other, and Anthia longed to see Habrocomes, and Habrocomes, though until now unaffected by love, wanted to see Anthia.

[3] When the parade ended, the whole crowd went into the temple for the sacrifice. The order of the procession was broken up as men and women, ephebes and maidens, came together. Then the two saw each other—Anthia was captured by Habrocomes, Habrocomes defeated by Eros. He stared at the girl constantly. He wanted to stop looking but couldn't as the god held him mercilessly in his power.

Anthia had her own problems. She took in Habrocomes' beauty as it   80
flowed into her wide open eyes and soon forgot the proprieties that apply to maidens. Oh yes, she would say things just so Habrocomes would hear them and bare what parts of her body she could so he would see them. He surrendered himself to the sight and became the god's prisoner.

Then the sacrifice was over and they were departing, upset and complaining about how quickly they had to leave. They wanted to keep looking at each other, so they kept turning around and stopping and found many excuses to linger.

They each arrived home, and that's when they realized how bad they had it. Both found their thoughts turning to how the other looked, and love   90
blazed up in them. The rest of the day their desire grew, and when they went to bed they were instantly in turmoil. Their feelings of love were irresistible.

[4] Habrocomes took hold of his hair, tearing at it, and ripped his clothes.

"This is terrible! What bad luck! What's happened to me? Up until now Habrocomes was so manly, he sneered at Eros, he bad-mouthed the god—but now I've been taken prisoner. I'm beaten. I'm being forced to be a slave to a girl. Now I can see that someone is more beautiful than I am, and I'll admit Eros is a god.   100

"What a gutless coward I am! Can't I resist it? Won't I stay strong? Won't I be able to overcome Eros? I have to beat this god. He's nothing! Sure, there's a beautiful girl. So what? Anthia looks good to your *eyes*, Habrocomes, but she doesn't have to look good to *you*. Not if you don't want her to. That's it. My mind's made up. Eros will never get the best of me."

At this the god increased the pressure and dragged him along as he tried to resist, hurting him because he went unwillingly.

When the young man could hold out no longer, he threw himself on the floor. "You've won, Eros! You've raised a great trophy in your victory 110 over the abstinent Habrocomes. Accept him as a suppliant and save him now that he has fled for protection to you, the master of everything. Don't turn a blind eye to me, but also don't punish my impudence for too long. I was still ignorant of your works, Eros. That's why I was arrogant. But give me Anthia now. Don't just be bitter to me because I opposed you—be a patron god to me because I'm surrendering."

But Eros was still angry and planned on exacting a great punishment from Habrocomes for his arrogance.

Anthia too was in trouble, and when she couldn't stand it any more, she pulled herself together in an attempt to hide things from those 120 around her.

"This is not good. What's happened to me? I'm a girl in love, but I'm too young. I'm suffering weird pains that a good girl shouldn't feel. I'm crazy for Habrocomes—he's so handsome . . . but so conceited. How far will my desire go? Where will my trouble end? This man I love only thinks of himself, and I'm a girl who's constantly being watched. Who will I get to help? Who can I share all this with? Where will I see Habrocomes?"

[5] They lamented like this the whole night through and held before their eyes the way the other looked and imagined in their minds each 130 other's appearance. In the morning, Habrocomes went to do his regular exercises, and the girl went to worship the goddess as she normally did. Their bodies were worn out from the night before, their eyes dull, their complexions altered. That was the situation for a long while, and they weren't getting any better.

During this period they spent their days in the goddess' temple, staring at one another. They were too afraid and ashamed to tell each other the truth. It got so bad, Habrocomes would groan and cry, praying pitifully when the girl was within earshot. Anthia's feelings were the same, but she was more deeply affected by her misfortune, because whenever she 140 caught another girl or woman looking at him—and they *all* looked at him—she was clearly pained, afraid that Habrocomes would like one of the others more than her. They both prayed to the goddess in common— even though their prayers were the same, they didn't know it.

As time passed, the young man couldn't stand it any longer. By this point his body was a total wreck and his spirit in despair. It was so bad that Lycomedes and Themisto grew seriously worried. They didn't know what was happening to Habrocomes but were scared by what they saw.

Meanwhile, Megamedes and Euippe were in a similar state over Anthia. They could see her beauty withering away but no apparent reason 150 for her plight. In the end they brought seers and priests to visit Anthia so they could determine how to fix what ailed her. They came and made sacrifices and poured all sorts of libations and recited formulas over her in barbarian languages. They explained that they were placating certain spirits and alleged that her suffering was caused by the gods of the under- world. Lycomedes and his family were also making a lot of sacrifices and praying for Habrocomes. But there was no relief for either one. Their love simply burned more hotly.

They both lay ill, in critical condition, expected to die any minute, unable to confess their misery. At last both fathers sent messengers to con-   160 sult the god about the cause of their illnesses and how to end them.

[6] Not far away is the temple of Apollo in Colophon, a ten-mile trip from Ephesos by boat. This is where the messengers went and asked the god to prophesy truly. They had come for the same reason, and the god gave them in poetic form an oracle that applied to both. This was the poem:

> Wherefore yearn to know the end and start of illness?
>   One illness holds both; the answer lies therein.
> I see terrible sufferings for them and endless troubles.
>   Both will flee across the sea, driven by madness,   170
> will face chains among men with the sea in their veins.
>
> For both a tomb as bridal chamber and destructive fire.
>   And yet, after calamities, a better fate will they have,
>   and by the flows of the sacred river for holy Isis,
>   their savior, furnish rich gifts afterwards.

[7] When this oracle was delivered to Ephesos, the two fathers were immediately baffled and completely lost about what the danger was. They couldn't interpret the god's response. What was the disease? The flight? The chains? The tomb? The river? The help from the goddess? They thought about it a lot and felt it best to go along with the oracle as best they could   180 by joining their children in marriage. They assumed that was the god's will from the prophecy. That was their decision, and they also made up their minds to send the couple away for a while on a trip after their wedding.

Then the city was filled with revelers and everything was covered with garlands. The upcoming wedding was the talk of the town, and the couple was congratulated by everyone, Habrocomes because he was going to marry such a beautiful wife, Anthia because she would get to share her bed with such a handsome young man.

When Habrocomes learned about the oracle's response and the marriage, he was overjoyed that he would have Anthia. He wasn't at all afraid   190
of the prophecy. His feeling was that his current pleasure more than made
up for any suffering. In the same way Anthia was pleased she would get
Habrocomes and could not have cared less about the flight or the misfortunes, since she had in Habrocomes something to comfort her in all the
troubles to come.

[8] When the time for the wedding came, vigils were kept and many
animals were sacrificed to the goddess. Once these preparations had
been completed and the night arrived (Habrocomes and Anthia thought
everything took too long), they brought the girl to the bridal chamber. They
held torches as they sang the marriage hymn and shouted their best   200
wishes. Then they brought her in and put her in the bed.

The bridal chamber had been prepared for them: a golden bed covered with purple sheets, and over the bed a canopy of Babylonian fabric
had been decoratively embroidered—playing cupids, some of them serving Aphrodite (her picture was there too), some riding mounted on sparrows, some weaving garlands, some bringing flowers. That was on one
half of the canopy. On the other side was Ares. He wasn't in armor but
was dressed for his lover Aphrodite, with a garland on his head, wearing
his short cloak. Eros was leading him with a lit torch in his hand. That was
the canopy under which they laid Anthia when they brought her to Habro-   210
comes. Then they closed the doors.

ACTAEON AND DAPHNE IN CONTEMPORARY POETRY

Most Greek myths of transformation, especially transformations of people
into birds, stones, rivers, flowers, or animals, have found their way into the
works of later artists through the Roman epic *Metamorphoses* by Ovid
(43 BCE–18 CE). Contemporary poets have especially revisited Ovid's descriptions of Actaeon's transformation into a stag by Artemis (Figure 8.12) and
Daphne's transformation into a laurel tree, to explore questions of identity
and desire.

Ovid's account of Apollo and Daphne begins with Daphne's petition of
her father, the river god Peneus (1.449–596). She asks him to grant her eternal virginity, and he reluctantly grants her wish. When Apollo, pricked by
Cupid's arrow, sees Daphne in the woods, he immediately desires her and
begins to chase her. As they sprint across the countryside, Apollo regales her

8.12 **Artemis and Actaeon.** Detail from Attic Bell-figure krater. Pan Painter, c. 490 BCE. *Museum of Fine Arts, Boston, Massachusetts, USA / James Fund and by Special Collection / Bridgeman Images, BST196428.*

with boasts of his achievements, as though he were a mortal man trying to convince a woman that he will be a suitable husband. When Daphne can run no more, she prays to her father to change her in a way that destroys her beauty. Ovid describes her arms changing to branches, her hair to leaves, and her head to the green top of a laurel tree. But Apollo's love continues unabated, and he claims the laurel as his, using its leaves to crown his head, lyre, and quiver. Entombed in a tree, Daphne must endure Apollo's claims. Although her father has fulfilled his promise to her, and although she (like Artemis, who in Ovid's telling is called Diana, her Roman name) remains virginal in the woods forever, the reader is left to decide if Daphne has been blessed or cursed.

Contemporary women poets have revisited Ovid's story from Daphne's perspective. Sometimes they conflate the fateful encounter between Apollo and Daphne with a marriage, in which the wood that encases Daphne symbolizes the dullness and routine of married life. At other times, they express the nymph's regret at having refused Apollo. In her poem "Daphne with Her Thighs in Bark," Eavan Boland (b. 1944) writes, "the opposite of passion / is not virtue / but routine" and then goes on to describe herself "cooking" and "making coffee" or "scrubbing wood," when she recalls the wooded forest where she did not yield: "He snouted past. / What a fool I was! / I shall be here forever setting out the tea." Memories of lovemaking, this Daphne imagines, would be better than, or at least a consolation for, being rooted in a marriage whose routines replace passion.

In "Where I Live in This Honorable House of the Laurel Tree," Anne Sexton (1928–1974), like Boland, speaks from the perspective of Daphne and regrets that she has refused Apollo. "Too late / to wish I had not run from you, Apollo, / blood moves still in my bark bound veins," she muses. It is only years after her transformation into laurel (marriage) that Sexton's Daphne recognizes her own desire "for that astonishing rite" (a sexual encounter). Yet, because Sexton's Daphne recognizes her desire too late, it becomes the source of her eternal isolation. Her lament concludes the poem: "how I wait / here in my wooden legs and O / my green green hands."

In both Boland's and Sexton's poems, Daphne, once transformed, is passive and immobile, unable to act on her feelings. In the poem "Daphne" by Alicia E. Stallings (b. 1968), the transformed Daphne is neither passive nor beholden to Apollo. Stallings's Daphne desires, moves, changes, and responds to Apollo as she pleases. Stalling animates the laurel tree so that its biological processes enact Daphne's will; Daphne retains the capacity to choose and act.

ALICIA E. STALLINGS, "DAPHNE" (1999)

> Do what you will.
> What blood you've set to music I
> Can change to chlorophyll,
>
> And root myself, and with my toes
> Wind to subterranean streams.
> Through solid rock my strength now grows.
>
> Such now am I, I cease to eat,
> But feed on flashes from your eyes;
> Light, to my new cells, is meat.
>
> Find then, when you seize my arm
> That xylem thickens in my skin
> And there are splinters in my charm,
>
> I may give in; I do not lose.
> Your hot stare cannot stop my shivering,
> With delight, if I so choose.

Boland, Sexton, and Stallings, like many female poets, take Ovid's poem as an opportunity to meditate not on the violence of Apollo (or on male violence generally), which is unmistakable even in a precursory reading of Ovid's tale, but on female desire for the male. Their transformations of Ovid's tale in which Daphne regrets or rejects a wooded existence as a virgin, like Artemis, highlight the role that desire (or the lack of it) plays in transformations.

Contemporary poets who address the myth of Diana (Artemis) and Actaeon also address the question of desire, yet from a slightly different angle. Following Ovid's lead, they question the connection between desire and guilt. Ovid's tale of Diana and Actaeon begins and closes with a question about Actaeon's guilt (3.131–254). Before describing Actaeon's trespass, Ovid asks the reader to consider if Actaeon should be accountable for losing his way in the woods. Ovid then describes how Actaeon, while hunting in the woods with his pack of hounds, accidentally comes upon Diana bathing naked with her nymphs. Angered by his intrusion, Diana splashes his face with water and tells him he will not be able to tell anyone about what he saw. Diana's threats transform Actaeon: antlers sprout on his head, his hands become hooves, and he is gradually transformed into a stag. His faithful hunting dogs, which no longer recognize any trace of their master in this beast, run him down and tear him to pieces.

Ovid's description of the moment when Actaeon's hounds tear him apart is tinged with pathos and irony. "All changed except his mind," Ovid writes about Actaeon just before his dogs see him in his new form. He imagines the dogs' disappointment in their master's absence and credits them with an almost human consciousness, whereas Actaeon, no longer able to speak, tragically cannot communicate with them. The longing of the dogs for Actaeon, and his own longing to speak to them, confuses the distinction between animal and human, lending poignancy to this horrific moment. Ovid shifts the reader's attention back to the question of responsibility, guilt, and just punishments. He writes, "some believed Diana's violence unjust; some praised it."

The question of Actaeon's culpability occupies a central place in two contemporary poems: "Actaeon," by Seamus Heaney (1939–2013), and "A Call," by Don Paterson (b. 1963). Both poets (among others) were commissioned by the National Gallery in London to respond to three paintings (*Diana and Callisto*, *Diana and Actaeon*, and *The Death of Actaeon*) by Titian (1488–1576) as part of its multimedia production *Metamorphosis: Titian 2012*. (Like Ovid, Titian calls Artemis by her Roman name, Diana.) Neither poet narrates or provides words for Titian's paintings. Heaney responds more to Ovid's myth than Titian's version of it, whereas Paterson superimposes an experience *like* that of Actaeon onto both the myth and the painting.

Heaney's poem begins after Actaeon has been transformed. When Ovid asks whether Actaeon is guilty of simply losing his way at the start of his tale, the reader is invited to consider whether Actaeon may be guilty of something more. The poem invites the reader to speculate about Actaeon's motivations through a series of hypothetical clauses, each beginning with "as if." Through these clauses, Heaney is able to suggest that Actaeon is *like* a stalking beast before he becomes a beast, that his desires are *like* hounds, and that Actaeon is *like* Diana as well as his own hounds in being "impatient for the kill." What Actaeon *like* a stalking beast might do to Diana, Diana does to him. In this way, Heaney makes Actaeon's crime match his punishment yet does not fully offer any resolution as to Actaeon's guilt.

 ### SEAMUS HEANEY, "ACTAEON" (2012)

> High burdened brow, the antlers that astound,
> Arms that end now in two hardened feet,
> His nifty haunches, pointed ears and fleet

Four-legged run . . . In the pool he saw a crowned
Stag's head and heard something that groaned
When he tried to speak. And it was no human sweat
That steamed off him: he was like a beast in heat,
As if he'd prowled and stalked until he found

The grove, the grotto and the bathing place
Of the goddess and her nymphs, as if he'd sought
That virgin nook deliberately, as if
His desires were hounds that had quickened pace
On Diana's scent before his own pack wrought
Her vengeance on him, at bay beneath the leaf-

lit woodland. There his branchy antlers caught
When he faced the hounds
That couldn't know him as they bayed and fought
And tore out mouthfuls of hide and flesh and blood
From what he was, while his companions stood
Impatient for the kill, assessing wounds.

Don Paterson also engages the relationship between desire, violation, and guilt but places the encounter between Actaeon and Diana on a winter train. Diana, in this poem, becomes "Miss Venner." Actaeon is the speaker, and he recalls a time when he was a young boy of six who espied Miss Venner while she was changing her clothes. Despite the fact that the poem is written from Actaeon's/the speaker's perspective, Paterson retains a certain confusion about the speaker's responsibility for his actions.

DON PATERSON, "A CALL" (2012)

vellet abesse quidem, sed adest
Ovid, *Metamorphoses*, III

A winter train. A gale, a poacher's moon.
The black glass. Do I honestly still blame
the wrong turn in the changing rooms I took
when I was six, and stood too long to look?
The scream Miss Venner loosed at me. "The *nerve!*"
I was ablaze. And it was worth the shame,
I thought; of course I did. It was too soon
to tell the dream from what I'd paid for it.
Then soon too late. Two sides of the same door.

So was it the recoil or the release
that lashed the world so out of shape? Tonight
I stare right through the face that I deserve
as all my ghost dogs gather at the shore,
behind them the whole sea like the police.

Here Paterson describes a man who cannot resolve his intentions at the cataclysmic moment of his life: "Do I honestly still blame / the wrong turn . . . ?" Because he was a young child and cannot himself discern his volition in his act of staring at Miss Venner, the act and its consequences seem radically out of kilter. Even as the speaker implies that he might have indeed chosen to take a "wrong turn" in order to spy on Miss Venner, the reader feels less certain. The price—is he standing on the shore contemplating suicide at the poem's close?—seems to be very high indeed for a childhood indiscretion. Both Heaney and Paterson recreate a toxic swirl of desire, violence, and consequences that makes the myth of Actaeon and Artemis/ Diana eternally relevant, and perpetually terrifying.

KEY TERMS

Actaeon 338
Artemis Orthia 343
Asclepius 345
Brauronia 341
Callisto 338

Cassandra 346
Catharsius 346
Daphne 346
Delos 339
Delphi 345

Hippolytus 340
Hyacinthia 346
Iphigenia 342
Orion 338
Pythia 346

FOR FURTHER EXPLORATION

Collins, Billie Jean, Mary R. Bachvarova, and Ian C. Rutherford (eds.). *Anatolian Interfaces: Hittites, Greeks and Their Neighbours.* Oxford: Oxbow, 2010. This exciting collection of essays considers Apollo's origins, among other topics pertaining to interactions between Greece and Anatolia.

Fischer-Hansen, Tobias, and Birte Poulsen. *From Artemis to Diana: The Goddess of Man and Beast.* Copenhagen: Museum Tusculanum Press, 2009. This recent collection of essays addresses different aspects of Artemis from Anatolia to Rome.

Graf, Fritz. *Apollo*. London and New York: Routledge, 2009. Graf provides a comprehensible and thorough overview of Apollo.

Roller, Lynn E. *In Search of the God the Mother: The Cult of Anatolian Cybele*. Berkeley, Los Angeles, and London: University of California Press, 1999. Roller offers a clear and thorough treatment of the evidence for Cybele in Anatolia and her worship in Greece and Rome.

CHAPTER 9

DIONYSUS

O happy the man

Who, blest with knowledge of the mysteries of the gods,

Lives a pure life

And initiates his soul in the Bacchic company

As he celebrates the gods in the mountains

In holy rituals of purity,

Observes the mysteries

Of the great mother Cybele,

And, swinging the thyrsus high,

And garlanded with ivy,

Does service to Dionysus.

—**EURIPIDES, BACCHAE (73–82)**

Dionysus, although the son of Zeus and an Olympian god, is distinguished from other Olympians because of his close connection to human beings. Not only is Dionysus's mother, Semele, a mortal woman, but Dionysus even dies. In a less widely circulated account of his birth and infancy, Dionysus is the son of Zeus and Persephone. For reasons that are not

< **9.1 (OPPOSITE): Birth of Dionysus from Zeus's thigh as Hermes watches.** After Zeus inadvertently immolates Semele while pregnant, Zeus removes Dionysus from her womb, stitches him in his thigh, and gives birth to the infant himself. Detail from a red-figure lekythos. Alkimachos Painter, c. 470–460 BCE. *Museum of Fine Arts, Boston, Massachusetts, USA / Catharine Page Perkins Fund / Bridgeman Images, BST1762525.*

THE ESSENTIALS ⊰ DIONYSUS

Dionysus (Bacchus), Διόνυσος

PARENTAGE Zeus and Semele (a mortal woman)

OFFSPRING Three mortal sons (with Ariadne) and several other mortal and immortal children

ATTRIBUTES Wreath, wine cup, thyrsus (a plant stalk topped with ivy or grape leaves), grapes, vines

SIGNIFICANT CULT TITLES
- Bacchus (a name linked to ritual worship)
- Eleuthereus (from the town of Eleutherae, near Athens)
- Iacchus (a ritual cry)
- Limnaeus (Of the Marshes)
- Lysius (Releaser)

SIGNIFICANT RITUALS AND SANCTUARIES
- **The Anthesteria** A three-day festival in Athens celebrating the opening of the year's wine with drinking contests, parades, and a sacred marriage to Dionysus.
- **The City Dionysia** A week-long festival in Athens that included processions and performances of tragedies, comedies, and satyr plays.
- **The Country Dionysia (or Rural Dionysia)** Local festivals in the Attic countryside with processions, songs, and dramatic performances.
- **Mystery cults** Loosely affiliated, informal groups whose members underwent a secret initiation and then worshipped Dionysus.

made clear, the Titans tear the baby Dionysus apart, until Zeus rescues his heart and limbs. Zeus gives the heart to Athena, so that Dionysus may be reconstituted; his limbs are given to Apollo, who buries them in a tomb near his temple in Delphi. The tale of Dionysus's dismemberment has provoked critical inquiry, not simply because Dionysus, though a god, dies.

The dismemberment of the infant Dionysus resonates in the demise of many mortals in myths who suffer, go mad, and are torn apart after their encounter with Dionysus. The most famous of these is Pentheus, king of Thebes, who is torn apart by Dionysus's worshippers. The depiction of Pentheus's gruesome death in Euripides's tragedy *Bacchae* (discussed and excerpted at the end of this section), coupled with Dionysus's experience at the hands of the Titans, has prompted scholars to investigate the connection between Dionysus and dismemberment in myths and rituals. What symbolic meaning might be assigned to such a brutal act, one that contradicts many descriptions of Dionysus's worshippers as "happy" and "blest"?

9.1 HISTORY

ENCOUNTERING DIONYSUS

Just as we traced the connection between myths of transformation and rituals of initiation when studying Artemis and Apollo (Chapter 8.1), in this chapter too we connect myths of dismemberment with the ritual experiences of Dionysus's worshippers in the three spheres he oversees: (1) viticulture, wine, and fertility; (2) theater and masks; and (3) his mystery cults. In this way, we also try to make sense of an Olympian god who (unlike any others) actually experiences death and even has a tomb in Apollo's sanctuary in Delphi.

VITICULTURE, WINE, AND FERTILITY

Dionysus oversaw both agricultural and human fertility. Augustine, Bishop of Hippo, a Roman province in northern Africa (354–430 CE), wrote knowledgeably about the "pagan" gods he no longer worshipped. He described Dionysus as a god associated with "liquid seeds," including the vital sap and juices from plants and the semen of all living animals, including human beings (*City of God* 7.21). Augustine's phrase "liquid seeds" provides a vivid image that succinctly and plausibly connects Dionysus's oversight of the fertility of the lands (especially grapes) and the fertility of men. In this regard, Dionysus is similar to Demeter, who oversees the fertility of the lands (especially grain) and of women (Chapter 4.1). Unlike Demeter,

9.2 Dionysus (center) accompanied by satyrs and maenads. Black-figure column krater. Painter of Munich, c. 520 BCE. *The John P. Getty Museum, Los Angeles, California. 75.AE.106. Digital image courtesy of the Getty's Open Content Program.*

however, Dionysus's oversight of fertility is very often infused with humor and danger. The Anthesteria, a three-day Athenian festival that conjoined Dionysus's oversight of the land's fertility (in the form of grapes) and the fertility of the human community, had both comic and somber moments.

The Anthesteria The springtime festival of the Anthesteria (from *anthos*, flower) celebrated Dionysus's gift of wine to humankind; it concluded with a sacred marriage that symbolically drew the fructifying powers of the god into the city. Each of the festival's three days, named after a particular vessel associated with the day's activities, composed a complex ritual that symbolically linked Dionysus's wine with human fertility.

The first day of the festival was called Pithoigia (Jar-Opening), after the large storage jars of wine (*pithoi*, the plural of *pithos*) that were brought into the center of Athens from the countryside and opened. Interestingly, *pithoi* were also used for funerary urns in cemeteries; thus, even when used for wine, their opening may have been associated with the release of the dead, who were believed to wander the city during the festival. On this day, too, the city was open not only to the dead but also to the god Dionysus, whose statue was placed on a ship that was mounted on wheels and rolled through the streets.

The second day of the festival was called Choes (Wine Jugs), after the jugs holding roughly two liters of wine that were used in the day's drinking contest. This day was especially eerie, not only because of the presence of the dead but also because of a rather unusual citywide drinking contest, the rules of

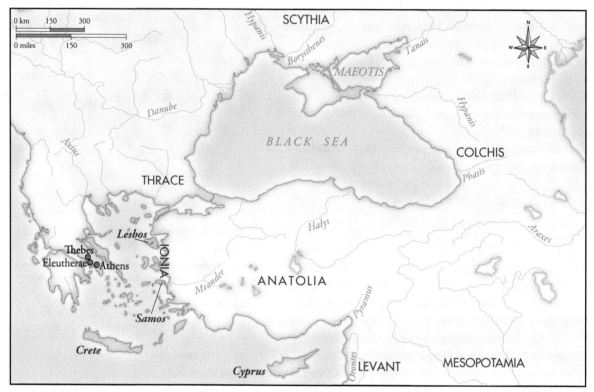

Map 9.1 Dionysus in Greece

which inverted the usual practices at a drinking party (a *symposium* or *symposia* [plural]). The first inversion was the way the wine was distributed. At a *symposium*, all participants drank wine from a large vessel (a *krater*) placed in the center of the room (Figure 9.2). In the Choes contest, however, everyone drank only from his own wine jug and tried to finish his portion before anyone else. Second, whereas Greek *symposia* were defined by conversation, no speaking was allowed during the Choes contest. The Anthesteria's rules did not support conviviality but instead imposed an unusual silence on the city.

After the contest, when the sun had set, participants marched toward Dionysus's temple "in the marshes" (so identified because it was located in a marshy section of the city, which has not yet been conclusively identified). There, they dedicated their *choes* and their garlands to the god. Dionysus's cult title Limnaeus (Of the Marshes) refers to his worship at this temple. Because this day was considered inauspicious, all temples in the city were roped off and closed, while Dionysus's temple in the marshes—which remained closed on all other days of the year—was opened to receive these offerings. During this parade, participants may have worn masks to represent the dead, who were believed to be roaming the city. Thus the opening of Dionysus's new wine, signaling birth, renewal, and agricultural success, also served to remind humans of their mortality.

On the third day of the festival, called Chytroi (Pots), three more events took place (some of these may have taken place on the night of the second day), and the mood of the festival changed from somber to joyful. First, there was a marriage at Dionysus's temple in the marshes. There, fourteen older women conducted secret rites and oversaw a sacred marriage (the details of which remain unknown) between the *basilinna* (queen), who was the wife of the *basileus* (king), an honored official position in Athens, and the god Dionysus. The *basilinna* may be a symbol for the city of Athens, and this ritual marriage can be interpreted as a symbolic marriage between Dionysus and the city itself, one that harnesses Dionysus's exuberant fertility (and perhaps, by extension, that of the city's male residents) to the needs of the city and ensures the reproduction of the next generation. In addition, the ritual suggests that, through marriage, male fertility finds its socially sanctioned place.

This sacred marriage also may have recalled Dionysus's marriage to the Cretan princess Ariadne, whom the god rescues when she is abandoned on the island of Naxos (Chapter 10.1). The marriage of Dionysus and Ariadne, unlike many unions between gods and mortal women, is joyful: it results in three sons, and Dionysus places Ariadne's wedding crown in the sky as the constellation Corona Borealis to commemorate their union.

The second event of Chytroi recalled Dionysus's introduction of wine to Athens. According to that myth, after Dionysus gave wine to Icarius, an Athenian farmer, Icarius shared it with his neighbors. The neighbors, who had never tasted wine before, promptly became intoxicated and passed out. Their families, believing Icarius had poisoned their loved ones, killed the farmer. With the help of Icarius's dog Maera, his daughter Erigone finds his body. Distraught, she hangs herself. To commemorate this myth, during this part of the festival young Athenian girls would play on swings hanging from trees in recollection of Erigone's suicide and the introduction of wine to Athens (Figure 9.3).

The final event of the festival involved offering a mixture of grains and honey boiled in special pots (*chytroi*) to the spirits of the dead to appease them and send them back to the Underworld.

The events of the Anthesteria illustrate many features of the god Dionysus. His association with liquids, especially wine, is evident in the opening of the wine jars and the drinking contest, whereas his association with human fertility is suggested in his marriage to the *basilinna*. These two features of the

9.3 Satyr pushing a young woman on a swing on the last day of the Anthesteria. Attic red-figure skyphos from Chiusi. Penelope Painter, c. fifth century BCE. *bpk, Berlin / Antikensammlung, Staatliche Museen, Berlin, Germany / Eva-Maria Borgwaldt / Art Resource, NY, ART189509.*

festival reflect Augustine's comment about Dionysus's association with liquid seeds in the form of wine and semen. Yet the Anthesteria also highlights other features of Dionysus that Augustine does not mention. As the sacred marriage between Dionysus and the *basilinna* conjoins the human and the divine realms, Dionysus's arrival in the city confuses the categories of the living and the dead. Additionally, the parade to Dionysus's temple and the somber, silent drinking contest illustrate the destabilizing effect of Dionysus on communities. Under his auspices, unorganized groups of citizens wander to a damp and watery region, to a temple open only once each year (in stark contrast to the highly organized daylight processions in honor of Athena during her festivals). The drunk, and perhaps masked, Athenians in this parade under the cover of night would view their city very differently than they would in the daytime. When Dionysus is near, as he is during the Anthesteria, he transforms the ordinary into the extraordinary and the familiar into the strange. To a lesser extent, Dionysus's transformative power through the medium of wine is evident in the tradition of the *symposium*.

The *Symposium* Whereas the Anthesteria celebrates the production of wine from grapes and male fertility in the context of marriage, the *symposium* is a space where Dionysus's wine conjures decidedly male conviviality and sexuality unattached to reproduction. *Symposia* were gatherings of men, particularly those from elite classes, that took place in the male quarters of private houses. *Symposiasts* were waited on by female and male servants, musicians, and female *hetaerae*, a Greek term for women who provided both musical and sexual entertainment. Whereas *symposia* were often congenial and boisterous gatherings fueled by wine, they were also occasions when men could examine their world through dialogue and engage in self-examination. Both kinds of activity were encouraged by Dionysus's presence in the form of wine.

The poet Theognis (sixth century BCE) writes that wine "reveals the mind of a man," whereas the poet Alcaeus (sixth century BCE) writes that "wine is a mirror for man." The drinking cups used at *symposia* often were decorated with large eyes, so that on lifting or draining one's cup, the drinker (or his companions) saw an eye staring back at him. These eyes were often interpreted as apotropaic; that is, they protect the holder of the cup by deflecting an envious stare (the evil eye) of another. Yet these eyes may have served another purpose: they made the drinking of wine mimic the experience of looking into a mirror. They suggest that Dionysus's liquid had the potential to transform men at *symposia* into seekers of wisdom about themselves.

Yet wine did not always have such a positive transformative effect. If it was not sufficiently diluted with water or if it was drunk in excess, wine could transform men into satyr-like creatures whose speech and behavior was ruled by appetite rather than reason. (Satyrs were mythical hybrids with

9.4 Men dance and flirt at a *symposium*. Red-figure wine cup. Briseis Painter, c. 480–470 BCE. *The John P. Getty Museum, Los Angeles, California. 86.AE.293. Digital image courtesy of the Getty's Open Content Program.*

the ears and tails of horses who often accompanied Dionysus and engaged in provocative and burlesque activities, such as drinking to excess, dancing, and singing [Figure 9.2]. Satyrs are frequently depicted in humorous and frankly sexual activities, both with other satyrs and with maenads, mythical females who wear fawn skins and carry snakes and *thyrsi* [a plural form of Greek *thyrsos* (*thyrsus*)], plant stalks topped with ivy or grape leaves.) Male *symposiasts* are often shown dancing, singing, playing musical instruments, engaging in sexual activities with *hetaerae* and men (whether servants or other *symposiasts*), and parading in the streets. Additionally, *symposiasts* often wore wreaths made of ivy or dressed in a manner typical of non-Greeks from Lydia: they carried parasols and wore earrings, boots, ankle-length garments, and turbans (Figure 9.4).

These varied activities and dress imply that Dionysus's wine can temporarily transform men into foreigners or burlesque, oversexed creatures, freed from social conventions, just as easily as it can encourage self-reflection. The theater, where masks and costumes are deployed, is yet another area where the disquieting and liberating effects of encountering Dionysus are felt in the city of Athens.

THEATER AND MASKS

As the patron god of theater, Dionysus is associated with masks, costumes, and dramatic poetry, including tragedy, comedy, and satyr plays (plays that often treat mythic and tragic plots in a humorous way and have a chorus of satyrs). Choral poems (dithyrambs) were also associated with Dionysus and were sung in his honor during his festivals. Three festivals in Athens and its environs included dramatic performances: the Lenaea, a festival in the center of Athens consisting of processions, mystic rituals, and (by the end of the fifth century BCE) tragic performances; the Country Dionysia (also called the Rural Dionysia), small local festivals that took place throughout the Attic countryside; and the City Dionysia (also called the Great Dionysia), which took place in the center of Athens and culminated in the Theater of Dionysus (Figure 9.5). These festivals demonstrate Dionysus's connection with theatrical arts.

The Country Dionysia The Country Dionysia refers to a number of local festivals that took place around the same time every year (approximately December) and consisted of parades in Dionysus's honor followed by performances of tragedies and comedies. Not surprisingly, the Country Dionysia had a rustic flavor. The historian Plutarch (46–120 CE) complains that the festivals of his time, admittedly much after the Classical Period of Greece, had become garish affairs with gold vessels and expensive costumes that were far removed from the City Dionysia of long ago, when the procession was a much more humble affair.

9.5 The Theater of Dionysus at the foot of the Acropolis in Athens, Greece. Fifth century BCE. *Album / Art Resource, NY, alb1462719.*

The playwright Aristophanes, in his comedy *The Acharnians* (c. 425 BCE), confirms Plutarch's vision of such informal and rambunctious celebrations. At the Country Dionysia, Dicaeopolis, the play's protagonist, assigns his daughter to carry a basket and admonishes his two slaves to keep upright a wooden phallus as they parade it through the streets, while he himself drags a he-goat and sings a racy dithyramb in honor of Phales, a god representing the phallus (*The Acharnians* 241–279). Although this procession and the more formal one of the City Dionysia are like those dedicated to other gods and goddesses, the display and parading of a wooden phallus is unique to Dionysus (Figure 9.6). Such "phallic processions" accompanied by bawdy songs are thought by Aristotle to be the origin of comedy. As these phallic processions also represented Dionysus's connection with liquid seeds in festivals celebrating the dramatic arts, one might ask: Is there any underlying or symbolic affinity between Dionysus as the god of liquid seed and drama? Or are these simply two discrete arenas in which Dionysus operates?

9.6 Phallophoria. Attic black-figured kylix. Circa 550 BCE. *Courtesy of the Archeology Authority of Tuscany, Florence.*

The City Dionysia The City Dionysia, a week-long celebration in Athens, began, like the Anthesteria, with the symbolic arrival of Dionysus. At the start of the City Dionysia, a statue of Dionysus Eleuthereus was brought from a temporary lodging to its sacred precinct near the Theater of Dionysus, where Dionysus received sacrifices and offerings. The festival also included processions and several competitions for playwrights and performers.

The various meanings of the title "Eleuthereus" offer insight into the relationship between Dionysus and the theatrical performances in the Theater of Dionysus that were the highlight of this festival. The title "Eleuthereus" refers to the village of Eleutherae, between Athens and Boeotia, and one myth offers a partial explanation of why the Athenians worship Dionysus from this distant town. In this myth, a man from Eleutherae named Pegasus attends a banquet of early Athenian kings. When the Athenians at the banquet refuse to worship Dionysus as Pegasus wishes, the men of Athens develop a venereal disease. The cure entails worshipping Dionysus, and in particular carrying out phallic processions in his honor. This myth explains both the worship of Dionysus Eleuthereus in Athens and the phallic processions in Dionysus's festivals. It also conforms to a significant pattern that appears in many myths about Dionysus, a pattern that will come into sharp relief as we take a closer look at Pentheus later in this chapter: At first, a community rejects Dionysus or his worship. In retaliation, Dionysus drives community members mad and/or causes them to suffer. In the end, the worship of Dionysus is accepted and established by the community.

The title "Eleuthereus," however, has an additional meaning that is not related to the town Eleutherae. The Greek word *eleutherus* means "free." Dionysus has another cult title, Lysius, that means "Releaser." Both titles are often interpreted to describe Dionysus's effects on his worshippers: he "releases" people from their isolated existences and everyday lives as he leads them in groups to his ecstatic worship. This possible meaning of "Eleuthereus" offers an insight into a connection between Dionysus and theater that is easy to overlook, if only because theatergoing is commonplace in the modern world: the experience of theater in ancient Greece had a distinctly Dionysian aspect, because it entailed a release of sorts for the actors and audience.

In ancient Athens, only male citizens were actors. Putting on masks and costumes, they played the parts of male and female characters, as well as slaves and foreigners. Young Athenian military recruits may have composed the choruses, as some scholars argue, because patterned choral dances were useful for practicing military cohesion. Thus the theater provided an opportunity for Athenian men to enact identities that were distinctly different from that of a fully enfranchised male citizen. The audience during the City Dionysia was also composed primarily of male citizens (there is debate about whether female residents attended performances). To the degree that the audience members allowed themselves to identify and empathize with a range of characters that included women, slaves, and foreigners, they were able to adopt identities and perspectives that differed from their everyday life. In this way, actors and audiences were temporarily liberated or freed from their political identities.

This liberating experience is similar to the effects of wine that, as Alcaeus and Theognis write, reveal or unmask the drinker's mind or soul. Thus theater provides opportunities "to stand outside oneself," or, in Greek, *ekstasis* (*ek*, "out," plus *stasis*, "stand"). *Ekstasis*—or "ecstasy"—was the term ancients used to describe the worship of Dionysus in his various mystery cults. Mystery cults, even more than the Anthesteria or theatrical festivals, offered worshippers a direct way of encountering Dionysus that allowed them to leave behind their everyday lives and everyday selves.

MYSTERY CULTS

Dionysus was worshipped in mystery cults throughout the Mediterranean. The term "mystery cult" may also be used to describe Demeter's Mysteries at Eleusis (Chapter 4.1). More often the term refers to religious associations that grew in popularity during the fourth century BCE. Of particular importance are the mystery cults and writings that developed around the figure of Orpheus. Orphic teachings often influenced or blended with the ideas found in other mystery cults, especially those of Dionysus (Chapter 2.1).

Mystery cults are identified by four key criteria that apply equally to the worship of Demeter and Dionysus. First, mystery cults had no civic affiliations and were less restrictive than many civic festivals. They were often open to whomever wanted to join them, whether male or female, citizen or slave. Some, however, were restricted to those who spoke Greek, like Demeter's Mysteries, or to men (as in the case of the god Mithras, whose mystery cults were especially popular in the second and third centuries CE). Second, those who wanted to join had to undergo an initiation. In Aristotle's words, initiates do not learn (*mathein*) about the god or goddess of the cult but endure (*pathein*) an encounter with them; by this he meant that initiates would gain secret knowledge about the god or goddess through a profound experience. Third, mystery cults did not demand an allegiance that precluded belief and participation in other religious practices. Finally, mystery cults offered succor, such as good health, to their members in this life, a better life after death, and a certain intimacy with the god or goddess of the cult. Here the similarities between Demeter's and Dionysus's mystery cults end.

Because Demeter's Mysteries at Eleusis took place only in her temple and were overseen by priests from Eleusis, her worship is distinguished from the mystery cults of Dionysus as well as those of other gods and goddesses (such as Isis) who were worshipped by an informal association (*thiasus*) of individuals that was not linked to a particular temple or priesthood. Scattered evidence suggests that itinerant priests or priestesses could gather worshippers who might pay a small fee to participate. Indeed, unlike in formalized civic religious institutions and practices (or, for that matter, in Demeter's Mysteries at Eleusis), women held particularly prominent roles in Dionysus's cults. Aeschines (389–314 BCE), an Athenian statesman and orator, mentions that his mother led a *thiasus*, in effect serving as its priestess; an inscription from the city of Miletus in Asia Minor stipulates how a priestess is to oversee her mystery cult and how its finances are to be spent. Whereas Demeter's well-established Eleusinian Mysteries remained free of censure, independent Dionysian communities were often viewed

9.7 Villa of the Mysteries. Pompeii, Italy. First century BCE. *Scala / Art Resource, NY, ART70620.*

with suspicion. In part, this suspicion was provoked by the secret rites that these cults were believed to practice.

Initiations There are two types of worship associated with the mystery cults of Dionysus: initiation rites and secret rites called *orgia*. Dionysus's initiations, like those of Demeter, are shrouded in secrecy and must be reconstructed from fragmentary evidence. The Villa of the Mysteries (Figure 9.7), a large Roman house (60–40 BCE) found outside of Pompeii, houses a mural that provides an intriguing visual source of information about initiation into Dionysus's mystery cult. On the central panel of the mural, Dionysus, a satyr, and a winged woman with a whip are portrayed near a woman undergoing an initiatory experience. The initiate unveils a phallus hidden in a basket and is disrobed, possibly prior to being whipped. This scenario, suggesting that initiations into mystery cults include disorienting and terrifying experiences, finds some support in a comment from Plutarch. Plutarch compares the experience of all initiates, not just those of Dionysus, to the experience of the soul in the Underworld after death:

> Then there is every sort of terror, shuddering and trembling and perspiring and being alarmed. But after this a marvelous light appears, and open places and meadows await, with voices and dances and the solemnities of sacred utterances and holy visions. In that place one walks about at will, now perfect and initiated and free, and wearing a crown, one celebrates religious rites, and joins with pure and pious people. (*On the Soul,* fragment 178)

Although Plutarch does not reveal what happened during an initiation in concrete terms, he does convey its emotional tenor as an initiate moves from fear and darkness into relief and light. The mural in the Villa of the Mysteries also suggests that the staging of an initiation was designed to put the initiate in a fearful and confused state before a profound vision of some sort was revealed. On the last panel of the mural, the initiate appears dressed again and finds herself in less threatening circumstances at what seems to be the ritual's conclusion. She sits alone and seemingly at peace. In this way, the mural in the Villa of the Mysteries, as well as Plutarch's observations, suggests that even though initiations were frequently group experiences, their impact was very much individual. They directed initiates to pay attention to the condition of their souls. In this respect, mystery cults were inward looking and differed greatly from the communal religious celebrations and festivals of Greek cities.

Orgia Once initiated into a Dionysian *thiasus*, members then could participate in ongoing Dionysian religious practices (*orgia*). Although these practices were less secret than initiations, the evidence about worshippers' activities is varied and even contradictory. Diodorus Siculus (first century BCE), a historian from Sicily, offers a rather tame picture of Dionysian *orgia* (4.3) that accords with many vase paintings of female worshippers of Dionysus, called Bacchants or Bacchae (Dionysus is also called Bacchus, in both Greek and Latin). Diodorus describes groups of women who, carrying *thyrsi*, dance, pray, and shout in honor of Dionysus. *Orgia* are elsewhere described as taking place outdoors at night and including women only (although the mystery cults of Dionysus did include men). Diodorus's description accords with Euripides's *Bacchae* but leaves out the violent activities depicted in that play—namely, the tearing apart of sacrificial victims (*sparagmos*).

Although not mentioned in Euripides's play or Diodorus Siculus's writings, *sparagmos* is associated with *omophagia* (eating a sacrificial victim raw). Both acts differ from sacrificial customs that demand an animal be properly butchered and cooked. The violent forms of worship in the *Bacchae* offer a portrait of the god and his followers that has puzzled scholars: did women worship Dionysus as Euripides describes, or does Euripides (like Plutarch) attempt to convey the emotional tenor of Dionysus's worship through details that should be viewed as poetic and emotionally rich exaggerations?

EURIPIDES'S *BACCHAE*

Euripides's play *Bacchae*, like many of Dionysus's festivals, begins when the god Dionysus arrives in the city of Thebes. At the play's opening, Dionysus leads a chorus of Bacchants, who have followed him to Thebes from areas in the Ancient Near East (especially the Greek cities of Ionia, Lydia, and Phrygia). He explains to the audience that, although a god, he has disguised himself as a worshipper of Dionysus. The mask he wears serves a double purpose: it is at once a mask just like those worn by any Greek actor, and it marks Dionysus as a god who hides his divinity. Disguised therefore as a human worshipper,

Dionysus proclaims that he wants to introduce the divinity of Dionysus to Thebes, the birthplace of Dionysus. Cadmus, the old Theban king, has sired four daughters with his wife Harmonia: Ino, Autonoe, Agave (the mother of Pentheus), and Semele (the mother of Dionysus). Preferring not to risk offending a god, Cadmus is keen to accept the worship of Dionysus. The women of Thebes at first refuse to worship Dionysus but soon leave their homes and go to the mountains outside the city. But Pentheus, who now rules Thebes, refuses to accept Dionysus. The action of the play is centered on him.

Pentheus views the presence in Thebes of Dionysus, still disguised as a mortal worshipper of Dionysus, as a threat to civic order. He attempts to jail Dionysus but slowly yet inexorably falls under the god's power. Pentheus admits to Dionysus that he desires to spy on the Theban women in the mountains, especially his own mother. With the coaxing of Dionysus, Pentheus dresses as a woman so that he might join the Bacchants unnoticed. Pentheus then has several visions: he sees two suns and two gates at Thebes, and Dionysus appears to him as a bull, an animal frequently associated with Dionysus. (This interchange between Dionysus and Pentheus is included in the following reading.)

Dionysus and Pentheus march to the mountains. Once there, the women first perceive Pentheus as a male intruder and then a lion. In a frenzied ecstasy, they tear him into pieces (Figure 9.8). They return to town, led by Agave, who is holding Pentheus's head (in the theater, the actor's mask would likely have been used for this purpose). She brandishes the head and announces to Cadmus and the Thebans that she has captured a lion. Slowly, though, she realizes that she holds the head not of a lion but of her slaughtered son Pentheus. Her worship of Dionysus has culminated in unbearable suffering. When the play concludes, she and her father, Cadmus, are driven out of Thebes, where henceforth Dionysus will be worshipped.

Euripides's play offers several different perspectives on Dionysus, his initiations, and his *orgia*. The songs of the chorus and the activities of the Theban women suggest that Dionysus's *orgia* are joyful. A shepherd who has spied on the Theban women in the mountains says that they are nursing baby gazelles and wolf cubs, while they themselves drink milk and wine that springs out of the ground. The Theban women have formed a peaceful band that exists in a collective harmony, until they realize shepherds are pursuing them. Unable to catch a shepherd, they seize a cow instead and tear it to shreds (*sparagmos*), as their peaceful revelry becomes violent. Suddenly, their liberation from the strictures of the city and their proximity to Dionysus in the

9.8 **Pentheus with maenads.** Red-figure Attic kylix. Dourisca, c. 480 BCE. *Kimbell Art Museum, Fort Worth, Texas / Art Resource, NY, ART334333.*

natural world become dangerous. Euripides, however, has taken great poetic license, for no historical evidence suggests that female worshippers of Dionysus engaged in such violence.

Yet what Euripides offers is not completely inaccurate. He symbolically expresses the potential dangers of ecstasy, of standing outside of one's social identity (and outside of society in general) while under Dionysus's spell. Euripides presents Dionysus as a disrupter of the status quo and a destroyer of boundaries. The boundaries Dionysus destroys may be between self and other, male and female, city and country, or even self and god. Moreover, the death of Pentheus, which can be considered a *sparagmos*, evokes the story of Dionysus's dismemberment at the hands of the Titans. Dismemberment in myth offers a vivid metaphor for the loss of identity and stability associated with encountering Dionysus in ritual.

Whether Dionysus dresses up or strips down his worshippers, he compels them to see themselves and their world in ways that would not be possible without his influence. Through the influence of wine, he may reveal a man to be a satyr; through the role playing of theater, he may coax a man to experience the completely alien consciousness and experience of a woman or a slave. More radically, Dionysus offered to the members of his mystery cults a psychological dismemberment, that is, a state of being in which human, divine, and animal were undifferentiated and in which social distinctions were destroyed. In his enigmatic and disturbing *Bacchae*, Euripides attempts to convey that encountering Dionysus, whatever one's social station or gender, could be at once a trial and a blessing.

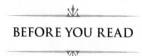

BEFORE YOU READ

EURIPIDES, FROM *BACCHAE*
&
UNKNOWN, *HYMN 7: TO DIONYSOS*

Scholar Richard Seaford (b. 1949) has recently argued that, in *Bacchae*, Euripides warns against the "subjective experience" of worshipping Dionysus. Seaford makes this claim, however, not about the *orgia* of the Theban women but about Pentheus, whom he sees as undergoing a Dionysian initiation of his own. In Seaford's reading, Pentheus's experiences reflect those of an initiate of Dionysus, such as the unnamed woman in the mural in the Villa of the Mysteries (Figure 9.7). His first reaction toward Dionysus's worship conveys an initiate's fear. Pentheus's hallucinatory visions of two suns, two gates, and a bull capture both the confusion and the revelatory vision of an initiate. Pentheus's dressing as a woman refers to an initiate's change in clothing that marks his or her separation from everyday life—a typical feature of age-grade initiations of adolescents

(Chapter 8.2). For these reasons, Seaford draws a parallel between Pentheus and an initiate of Dionysus. (*Bacchae* translated by James Morwood.)

Like most Homeric hymns, *Hymn 7 (To Dionysos)* shows how a god establishes his worship among mortals. Dionysus (spelled "Dionysos" in this translation; both forms are correct) establishes his worship on board a ship and through performance. He transforms himself into a lion and a bull and festoons the ship with grapevines before transforming the sailors who initially refuse to recognize his divinity into dolphins. These visions and transformations evoke the hallucinatory qualities of Pentheus's experiences. (*Hymn 7* translated by Michael Crudden.)

- Dionysus drives Theban *women* into the mountains, and a female chorus of worshippers surrounds him. Speculate on why women may have been especially attracted to Dionysian worship.

- How does the encounter of the Theban women with Dionysus compare with the experience of Pentheus? What might Euripides be trying to convey about Dionysus through these two portrayals?

- Compare Pentheus's dismemberment with those of Actaeon and Hippolytus (Chapter 8.1). What are the similarities among the stories of these three young men? How might van Gennep's definition of initiations explain all of their violent deaths?

- How are the transformations described in *Hymn 7 (To Dionysos)* like (or not like) Pentheus's vision of two suns, two gates, and the appearance of the worshipper of Dionysus (Dionysus himself in disguise) as a bull?

- In what ways is the plot of the Homeric hymn similar to (or different from) the plot of Euripides's *Bacchae*?

EURIPIDES, FROM *BACCHAE* (c. 406 BCE)

Enter PENTHEUS

PENTHEUS. I have suffered terrible things. The stranger who just now was bound fast with rope has escaped me. (*with a start*) But look! Here is the man. What is going on? How can I be seeing you in front of my house? How did you get out?

DIONYSUS. Stand still. Put a stop to your anger and calm down.

PENTHEUS. How have you managed to escape your bonds and come out here?

DIONYSUS. Did I not say—or did you not hear—that someone would free me?

PENTHEUS. Who? You are for ever mentioning new, unexpected things.

DIONYSUS. The one who grows the rich-clustered vine for men. 10

PENTHEUS. . . . .

DIONYSUS. You insult Dionysus over what is his glory.

PENTHEUS. I order that every gate in the circle of walls should be locked.

DIONYSUS. What is the point of that? Cannot gods go over walls?

PENTHEUS. You are clever, clever—except where you should be clever.

DIONYSUS. Where I should be clever, there above all I am so.

A MESSENGER *ENTERS*

But first listen to this man who has come from the mountain to tell you something, and hear what he has to say. We shall remain here, we shall not run away.

MESSENGER. Pentheus, ruler of this Theban land, I have come here from Mount Cithaeron where the dazzling falls of white snow never melt.

PENTHEUS. And what weighty message do you bring?

MESSENGER. I have seen the holy bacchae whose white limbs flashed away spear-swift in their madness. And I have come here wishing to 20 tell you and the city, my lord, that they do strange things, things that go beyond wonder. I want to hear whether I can tell you what has happened there with complete freedom of speech—or should I check my tongue? For I fear your speed of thought, my king, your sharp temper and your all too kingly spirit.

PENTHEUS. Speak—you are in no danger of being punished by me, whatever you say. [After all, it is not right to show anger against just men.] But the more strange the things you say about the bacchae, the more severe the penalty I shall exact from this man who has corrupted the women with his wiles. 30

MESSENGER. The pasturing herds of cattle were just climbing onto the upland country at the time when the sun sends forth its beams to heat the world. I saw three companies of female dancers. Autonoe was in charge of one, your mother Agave of the second, and Ino of the third. And all of them were sleeping, their bodies relaxed, some of them leaning their backs on fir-tree needles, others amid oak leaves, their heads flung down at random on the ground—chastely, and not, as you say, made drunk by the wine-bowl and the music of the pipe, and slinking off on their own to hunt Aphrodite in the wood. But when your mother heard the lowings of the horned cattle, 40 she stood up in the middle of the bacchae and cried her Bacchic cry to make them stir themselves from sleep. The women, casting deep slumber from their eyes, leapt upright, a marvel of good order to look upon, young women and old and maidens still unwed. And first they let their hair down onto their shoulders, and all those whose fawnskins' binding knots had worked loose tied them up and girdled the dappled hides with snakes which licked their cheeks. Some of them held a roe deer or wild wolf-cubs in their arms and all the recent mothers, whose breasts were still swollen for the off-spring they had abandoned, gave to these their white milk. They 50 put on garlands of ivy, of oak, and of flower-clustered bryony. And one of them took her thyrsus and struck it against a rock, from which the dewy wetness of water leapt forth. Another plunged her fennel rod into the earth's surface, and for her the god spurted up a spring of wine. Then all who felt a longing for the while drink scraped at the ground with their fingertips and took jets of milk in their hands. And from their ivy-clad thyrsi dripped sweet streams of honey. So, if you had been there and seen these things, you would have ap-proached this god, whom you now hold cheap, with prayers.

We herdsmen and shepherds came together to outdo each 60 other in our accounts [as we described their strange and wondrous actions]. And someone who had tramped the town and was a glib speaker said to all of us, "You men who live on the sacred upland plateaus, do you want us to hunt Agave, Pentheus' mother, from her Bacchic rites and do our king a favour?" We thought his words made good sense, and we lay in ambush hiding ourselves in the leafy thickets. At the appointed time the women began to rouse their thyrsi for the Bacchic rites, calling in unison on Bromius, the son of Zeus, god of ecstatic cries. And all the mountain and the animals joined them in their Bacchic worship—there was nothing that did not 70 move with the running. Agave happened to be leaping near me and I jumped out, eager to snatch hold of her, emptying the thicket where we were hiding. She shouted out, "O my running hounds, we are the quarry of these men's hunt. But follow me, follow me, with your thyrsi in your hands as weapons." So we ran away and escaped being torn to pieces by the bacchae, while they turned against the young cows which were grazing upon the grass. They held no iron weap-ons in their hands. You would have seen one of them wrenching in two a full-uddered young heifer which bellowed, while others were rending, tearing mature ones apart. You would have seen ribs or a 80 cloven hoof flung up and down. These hung under the fir trees drip-ping, all fouled with blood. Bulls which till then had been arrogant, their anger mounting into their horns, stumbled to the ground dragged down by the countless hands of girls. Their hides were torn apart quicker than you could have closed your royal eyes.

Like birds rising high, they went at a run across the lowland plains which produce fine crops for the Thebans by the streams of Asopus. They swooped down like an enemy on Hysiae and Erythrae which stand in the hill-country of Cithaeron in its lower regions, and ransacked everything from top to bottom. They seized children from 90 the houses and all of these that they placed on their shoulders were held there by no bonds, yet did not fall [to the black ground. Neither did bronze or iron]. They carried fire on the locks of their hair, and it did not burn them. Thus plundered by the bacchae, the villagers resorted to arms in a passion of rage. Thereupon we saw a terrible sight, my lord. The villagers' pointed spears, whether tipped with bronze or iron, drew no blood, while the bacchae shot their thyrsi from their hands and kept wounding them and making them turn and run away. Women did these things to men. A god certainly helped them. 100

Then they went back to where they had started from, to the very springs which the god had sent up for them, they washed off the blood, and the snakes licked the drops from their cheeks making their skin gleam.

And so, my master, receive this god, whoever he is, in this city. For he is great in other respects, and especially in this particular thing that they say of him—that, as I hear, he has given to mortals the vine that puts an end to sorrow. If wine no longer existed, then there would be no Aphrodite or any other sweet delight still left for mortals.

CHORUS. I am frightened to speak out freely what I have to say to the 110 king, but nevertheless it shall be said. Dionysus is inferior to none of the gods.

PENTHEUS. Already this violent blasphemy of the bacchae blazes up close to us like fire. It reflects great discredit on the Greeks. But it is imperative not to hestitate. Off with you, go to the Electran gate. Order all the heavy infantry and those that ride swift-footed horses to assemble—and all who brandish light shields and pluck the bow-string with their hands—since we shall march against the bacchae. For it is certainly beyond endurance if we are to suffer what we now suffer at the hands of women. 120

DIONYSUS. You hear my words, Pentheus, but they make no impression on you. However, even though I suffer this bad treatment at your hands, I still tell you that you should not take up arms against a god. No, you should do nothing. Bromius will not tolerate your dislodging the bacchae from the mountains of joy.

PENTHEUS. Do not tell me what to think. You have escaped from jail. Do you want to stay free? Or shall I renew your punishment?

DIONYSUS. I would pay him sacrifices rather than kick against the goad
in rage—a mere mortal taking on a god.

PENTHEUS. I *shall* pay him sacrifices—in women's blood, as they deserve.   130
I shall shed it in rich measure in Cithaeron's glens.

DIONYSUS. You will all be routed. And this brings disgrace—for bacchae
to turn your shields of beaten bronze with their thyrsi.

PENTHEUS. I am locked together with this stranger and can find no escape
from the hold. He will be silent neither when he suffers nor when he
acts.

DIONYSUS. Sir, it is still possible to set this matter right.

PENTHEUS. By doing what? By being a slave to my slave women?

DIONYSUS. I will bring those women here without the use of weapons.

PENTHEUS. Alas! This is some trick which he is now devising against me.   140

DIONYSUS. How can it be a trick if I am willing to save you by my skills?

PENTHEUS. You have all planned this together so that you can worship
Bacchus in perpetuity.

DIONYSUS. Certainly I planned this—you can be confident of that—
together with the god.

PENTHEUS. Bring me out weapons here, and you, stop talking!

DIONYSUS. Ah!
Do you want to see them sitting together on the mountain?

PENTHEUS. Very much so, and I would give an infinite weight of gold for
that.   150

DIONYSUS. How is it that you have conceived so great a passion for this?

PENTHEUS. I should be sorry to see them drunk.

DIONYSUS. But would you nevertheless be glad to see what is bitter to
you?

PENTHEUS. You can be sure of that—I want to sit in silence beneath the
firs.

DIONYSUS. But they will hunt you out even if you go secretly.

PENTHEUS. No, I shall go openly. This advice of yours is good.

DIONYSUS. Should we lead you then, and will you undertake the
journey?   160

PENTHEUS. Lead me as quickly as you can. I shall hold any delay against
you.

DIONYSUS. Then put fine linen clothes around your body.

PENTHEUS. Why that? Am I to stop being a man and join the female sex?

DIONYSUS. Yes, so that they don't kill you if you are seen there as a man.

PENTHEUS. Another piece of good advice. How clever a fellow you have
been all along!

DIONYSUS. Dionysus gave me full instruction in this.

PENTHEUS. How could your advice to me be successfully realized?

DIONYSUS. I shall come inside your palace and dress you.   170
PENTHEUS. In what clothes? Do you mean a woman's dress?
    But I feel shame at this.
DIONYSUS. Are you no longer eager to be a spectator of the maenads?
PENTHEUS. What do you say you will fling around my body?
DIONYSUS. First I shall make your hair hang long on your head.
PENTHEUS. What is the next feature of my costume?
DIONYSUS. Robes that fall to your feet. And on your head will be a
    headband.
PENTHEUS. And will you put anything else on me in addition to those
    things?   180
DIONYSUS. Yes, a thyrsus for your hand, and a dappled skin of a fawn.
PENTHEUS. I shan't be able to put on a woman's clothes.
DIONYSUS. But you will cause bloodshed if you join battle with the
    bacchae.
PENTHEUS. Rightly said. First I must go to reconnoitre.
DIONYSUS. Yes, it is certainly wiser than to hunt for trouble by inflicting it.
PENTHEUS. And how shall I avoid being seen by Cadmus' people as I go
    through the city?
DIONYSUS. We shall go through empty streets. I shall lead the way.
PENTHEUS. Anything is better than that the bacchae should laugh at me.   190
DIONYSUS. Let us go into the house . . .
PENTHEUS. . . . I shall decide whatever seems best.
DIONYSUS. You may. Whatever you decide, for my part I am ready and
    at hand.
PENTHEUS. I think I shall go in. Either I shall march with arms or I shall
    follow your advice.   *Exit* PENTHEUS.

DIONYSUS. Women, this man is walking into the casting net. He will come to
    the bacchae—and there he will pay the penalty by his death. Dionysus,
    it is your work now. I call upon you, for you are not far away. Let us take
    vengeance on him. First of all, drive him out of his mind, sending dizzy   200
    madness upon him, since if he is sane, he will certainly not be willing to
    put on women's clothes, while if he drives off the track of sanity, he will
    put them on. I want him to raise the Thebans' laughter as he is led
    through the city in a woman's form—after those earlier threats of his
    with which he inspired such terror! But I shall go to dress Pentheus in the
    clothes which he shall take to the Underworld when he goes there
    slaughtered at his mother's hands. He shall recognize Dionysus the son
    of Zeus and see that he is by turns a most terrifying and a most gentle
    god to mortals.   *Exit* DIONYSUS.   210

CHORUS (*sings*). Shall I ever in night-long dance set my white feet

in the Bacchic revel
and fling my head back to the dewy air
like a fawn at play
in the meadow's green joyfulness
when she escapes the fearsome hunt,
leaping clear of the ring of watchers
over the close-woven nets.
And the huntsman shouts
to urge his dogs to speed,
while she, swift as a storm   220
in her effortful racing,
bounds over the water-meadow,
joying in places void of men and the green life
that springs under the shadowy hair of the forest.

What is wisdom? Or what god-given prize
is nobler in men's eyes
than to hold one's hand in mastery
over the head of one's enemies?
What is noble is precious—that ever holds true.

The power of the gods is slow to move   230
but surely none the less.
It corrects those men
who worship senselessness
and in their mad folly
do not magnify the gods
who cover with elaborate devices
the unhastening foot of time
as they hunt down the man without religion.
For in thought and behaviour
one should never go beyond traditional ways.   240
It costs little
to regard these things as having power:
whatever it is that comes from god
and what has always been the tradition established
by nature and long time.

What is wisdom? Or what god-given prize
is nobler in men's eyes
than to hold one's hand in mastery
over the head of one's enemies?

What is noble is precious—that ever holds true.   250

Happy the man who has escaped
from a storm at sea and found harbour.
Happy the man who has overcome hardships.
In various ways one man surpasses another
in wealth and power.
And there remain countless hopes
for countless people. Some of these
find fulfilment for mortals in wealth,
while others vanish.
The man whose life is blessed from day to day—   260
him I count happy.

> *ENTER* DIONYSUS.

DIONYSUS. You who are eager to see what you should not, eager to seek
    what should not be sought, Pentheus I say, come out in front of the
    house. Let me see you dressed in female get-up as a maenad, a
    bacchant, so that you can spy on your mother and her company. You
    look like one of Cadmus' daughters.

> PENTHEUS ENTERS DRESSED AS A MAENAD IN A WIG AND A LONG LINEN DRESS,
> AND HOLDING A THYRSUS.

PENTHEUS. How strange! I think I see two suns and a double Thebes, our
    seven-gated city. And I think that you lead the way before me as a
    bull and that horns have grown on your head. Were you perhaps a   270
    beast all the time? You have certainly been changed into a bull.
DIONYSUS. It is the god who walks together with you. He was hostile
    before but now he is at peace with us. Now you see what you should
    see.
PENTHEUS. How do I look then? Don't I carry myself like Ino or Agave, my
    mother?
DIONYSUS. As I look at you, those are the very women I think I see. But
    this lock of your hair has slipped from its place. It isn't as I tucked it
    beneath your headband.
PENTHEUS. As I shook it backwards and forwards acting my Bacchic role   280
    inside the palace, I must have dislodged it from its place.
DIONYSUS. But I, whose concern it is to be your servant, shall put it back
    where it should be. But hold your head upright.
PENTHEUS. There! You must set me straight. I have put myself in your
    hands.

DIONYSUS. And your girdle is loose and the pleats of your dress do not hang evenly to below your ankle.

PENTHEUS. Yes, I think so too—by my right foot at any rate. But on this side the dress is straight at the tendon.

DIONYSUS. You will certainly regard me as the first of your friends when   290
you see that the bacchae are chaste, contrary to what you expect.

PENTHEUS. Will I be more like a bacchant if I hold the thyrsus in my right hand or in this one?

DIONYSUS. You should lift it up in your right hand, in time with your right foot. I am delighted by your altered mind.

PENTHEUS. Would I have the strength to carry the folds of Cithaeron, bacchae and all, on my shoulders?

DIONYSUS. You could if you wanted to. The way you thought before was unhealthy. Now you think as you should.

PENTHEUS. Should we take along crowbars, or should I put my shoulder or   300
arm beneath the mountain's crests and tear it up with my bare hands?

DIONYSUS. You really mustn't destroy the shrines of the Nymphs and the haunts of Pan where he plays his pipes.

PENTHEUS. Good advice. Women are not to be conquered by brute force. I shall hide myself beneath the firs.

DIONYSUS. You will be hidden as you should be hidden when you come in secret to spy on the maenads.

PENTHEUS. Think of it! I feel that they are in the thickets, caught like mating birds in the delicious nets of love.   310

DIONYSUS. Aren't you on a mission to guard against this very thing? Perhaps you will catch them, if you are not caught first.

PENTHEUS. Escort me through the middle of the land of Thebes. For I am the lone man of them all who dares this deed.

DIONYSUS. You alone bear the burden for this city, you alone. That is why the destined contests lie in store for you. Follow me. I am your guide and shall bring you safely to that place. But another will take you back from there . . . PENTHEUS. Yes, my mother.

DIONYSUS. . . . for all to see. PENTHEUS. That is why I am going.

DIONYSUS. You will not return on foot . . . PENTHEUS. You want to pamper me.   320

DIONYSUS. In your mother's arms . . . PENTHEUS. You are determined to spoil me.

DIONYSUS. Yes, spoil you in my fashion. PENTHEUS. I lay hold on what I deserve.

DIONYSUS. You are an amazing man, truly amazing, and you go to amazing sufferings. Through these you will find a glory that towers to heaven. Stretch out your hands, Agave, and Agave's sisters too, you daughters of Cadmus. I am leading this young man to a great

contest and the winner will be Bromius and myself. Everything else
the event will show.   DIONYSUS LEADS PENTHEUS OUT.   330

UNKNOWN, *HYMN 7: TO DIONYSOS* (c. 700 BCE)

Concerning Dionysos, glorious Semele's son,
I'll remember how once he appeared by the shore of the murmuring sea
Upon a jutting headland, in looks like a young man whose prime
Has just begun; the beautiful hair that round him waved
Was dark, and round his sturdy shoulders he wore a cloak
Of purple. Soon men on a ship benched well for rowers arrived,
Pirates moving swiftly over the wine-dark sea,
Tyrsenians, led by an evil doom. At the sight of him there
They gave each other the nod, and soon leaped out. In haste
They seized and set him on board their ship, exultant at heart.   10
For they said that he was the son of kings who are cherished by Zeus,
And wanted him cruelly bound. But their bonds could not hold him, far
From his hands and feet the withies kept falling, while there he sat,
And with his dark eyes smiled. The helmsman, perceiving the truth,
Called aloud to his comrades without delay, and said:
    "Misguided men, what mighty god is this you seize
And bind? Our ship cannot even bear him, built well though she be.
For Zeus is here, or Apollo, God of the Silver Bow,
Or Poseidon: these are no looks of mortal men, but of gods
Who dwell in Olympian homes. Now come, let's set him ashore   22
On the land's black soil at once. Against him raise no hand,
In case he stirs in wrath cruel winds of hurricane force."
    In this way he spoke; the captain rebuked him with hateful words:
"Misguided man, keep watch for the breeze, and then raise the ship's sail,
With all the ropes in your grasp; this fellow will worry us men.
He is, I expect, for either Egypt or Cyprus bound,
Or else for the Hyperboreans, or further afield. In the end
At some point he'll tell us his kith and kin, and all their wealth,
And who his brothers are, since heaven has sent him to us."
    With these words he started to raise the mast and sail of the ship.   32
A wind bellied out the sail, and on every side they stretched
The ropes taut; but soon before them miraculous works appeared.
Wine at first began along the swift, black ship
To gurgle, sweet to the taste and fragrant—the scent that rose up
Was divine—and all the sailors were seized with awe at the sight.
But at once on either side along the topmost edge
Of the sail a vine was stretched out, and grapes were hanging down

In clusters; dark-green ivy twined about the mast,
Bursting with bloom; upon it delightful berries stirred,
And all the tholes were wearing garlands. The men, when they saw,   42
Then indeed kept bidding the helmsman to steer the ship
Toward shore; but the god within their ship became at the prow
A fearsome lion, roaring loud, and amidships made
A bear with shaggy-maned neck, revealing his portents to view.
It reared up fiercely, the lion upon the upper deck

. . . .

Shooting a fearsome glare; the men fled back to the stern,
And on every side of the helmsman who had a prudent heart
They stood in terror. The god with a sudden rush forward seized
The captain; the men, as they tried to escape from an evil doom,
All together plunged, when they saw, in the brilliant sea,   52
And into dolphins turned. But holding the helmsman back
In pity, he made him in all ways blessed, and spoke these words:
  "Take courage, noble father, you who have pleased my heart.
I am Dionysos who roars out loud, and was given birth
By Semele, Kadmos' child, who was joined in love with Zeus."
  Farewell to you, fair-faced Semele's offspring. It cannot be
That one forgetful of you arrays a song that is sweet.   59

INITIATIONS AND INVERSIONS

The work of anthropologist Victor W. Turner (1920–1983) has greatly influenced the fields of theology, psychology, literature, performance studies, education, and mythology. Turner's influence has been widespread because of what he studied and how he studied it. Whereas Turner's contemporaries in anthropology largely explored areas such as kinship, law, and rituals, seeking to explain how these maintain and support social stability, Turner explored performance genres such as ritual, theater, film, carnivals, and festivals. Importantly, Turner attempted to define how these performance genres challenged social values and structures by offering participants different ways of seeing themselves and their world. He developed the concept of "liminality" to explain these potentially radicalizing and challenging experiences. In the reading at the end of this section, Eric Csapo uses Turner's concept of liminality to explain phallic processions of Dionysian worship.

9.9 Eye cup used at *symposia.* Red-figure drinking cup. Circa 515 BCE. *Werner Forman / Art Resource, NY, AR9156943.*

Here, we define liminality before considering its usefulness for understanding many features of Dionysian worship.

LIMINALITY AND INITIATION RITUALS

Turner began to develop the concept of liminality while studying age-grade initiation rites among the Ndembu of Zambia. To understand these rites, he turned to Arnold van Gennep's definition of rites of passage (Chapter 8.2). Van Gennep separated rites of passage into three stages that facilitate an individual's movement from one social role, status, or state in his or her life to another: (1) the separation or preliminal stage, when individuals leave behind their old identity, often by changing their appearance in some way or moving to another location; (2) the liminal stage, when initiates might endure physical and psychological hardships, learn new skills and secret knowledge, or relinquish possessions or certain behaviors forever; (3) the reintegration or postliminal stage, when initiates re-enter society with a new identity. Whereas van Gennep examined how initiation rites enable initiates to change in a way that reinforces the organization and values of their society, Turner was interested in how the dramatic elements of the second stage might change an initiate in unpredictable ways that do not support social values or structures.

In an influential article, "Betwixt and Between: The Liminal Period in *Rites de Passage*" (1964), Turner examined the liminal stage of initiations more generally, not just those he observed in Zambia. He argued that during this stage initiates are no longer their former selves but have not yet achieved their new status and thus "are at once no longer classified and not yet classified." As van Gennep noted, initiations took place in secluded places outside of cities or towns, or in spaces marked as cut off from everyday life, where initiates' daily routines and social responsibilities were suspended. In places such as these, the initiate was often stripped, left filthy, treated as a newborn infant (or, in Turner's words, a "neophyte"), and/or dressed in black and was placed among masked individuals who represented the dead. Initiates were often symbolically treated as both male and female, whether through clothing changes, body modification, or behaviors allowed only during initiations. Moreover, if initiates were required to act against tradition during an initiation (for example, by acting as the opposite gender or violating other social codes), they did so in obedience to that same tradition. All of the seemingly paradoxical and symbolic activities that fill the liminal stage make initiates socially invisible and push them outside of everyday norms. In this way, initiates are sufficiently removed from their prior social status or role and thus can change.

Turner emphasized how the liminal stage of initiation, or liminality, encouraged initiates to see the provisional nature of all social identities and thereby to develop a critical perspective on their social world. Turner concludes, "During the liminal period, neophytes are alternately forced and encouraged to think about their society, their cosmos, and the powers that generate and sustain them. Liminality may be partly described as a stage of reflection." Thus, unlike van Gennep, Turner does not emphasize the conservative function of initiations—that is, the ways initiations perpetuate social laws and customs in the next generation of adults. Instead, Turner concludes that the varied and complex symbols of the liminal stage provoke reflection. This reflection may lead not to a blind acceptance of social customs but to a complex and rich understanding, and even a critical view, of them.

Turner eventually extended the term "liminality" to include initiations and other religious rituals, as well as theater, carnivals, festivals, and films, or what Turner came to call "performative genres." He argued that liminality in performative genres was "the scene and time for the emergence of society's deepest values in the form of sacred drama and objects. . . . But it may also be the venue and occasion for the more radical skepticism . . . about cherished values and rules" (*The Anthropology of Performance*, 102). Turner's concept of liminality helps us to understand how the performative rituals of Dionysus served to propel participants out of their social world and place them betwixt and between various social categories, whether temporarily or more permanently.

LIMINALITY AND DIONYSUS

Dionysian rituals (the Anthesteria, City Dionysia, Country Dionysia, and mystery cults) as well as *symposia* included theatrical elements (such as costuming, song, and dance) and occurred in spaces and time marked as distinct from daily routines. When accompanied by generous amounts of wine, these celebrations created the opportunity for participants to experience a certain amount of intellectual and emotional freedom, encouraging them to reflect on their social world and their identity (Figure 9.9). The reflection that Dionysus's rituals prompt, however, may be costly to individuals, because such reflection can encourage skepticism about and dissatisfaction with the social world in which participants find themselves. Liminality can create an experience in which an individual's identity is challenged by dressing or acting like (or simply identifying with) someone who is very different from oneself—whether a satyr, a person of the opposite gender, or even (as in the Anthesteria) the dead.

In this light we can understand Pentheus's physical dismemberment in *Bacchae*. Once Pentheus dresses as a female Bacchant and goes to the mountain to worship Dionysus, he finds himself betwixt and between several categories: male and female, king of Thebes and lonely child, commander of the disguised Dionysus and Bacchic servant of the revealed Dionysus. Yet, in this liminal state, Pentheus is not able to sustain reflection on his "cherished values and rules," as the contradictions in his psychological and social identity become increasingly apparent. Euripides expresses this fraying of Pentheus's sense of himself and his world as a physical event, a *sparagmos*: Pentheus is literally torn apart.

ERIC CSAPO, *FROM* "RIDING THE PHALLUS FOR DIONYSUS: ICONOLOGY, RITUAL, AND GENDER-ROLE DE/CONSTRUCTION"

Eric Csapo uses Turner's concept of liminality to explain the "bizarre rite" of phallus riding in Dionysus's phallic processions (Figure 9.6). He argues that although men in these processions parade through the streets carrying a phallus made from a tree trunk, they are nonetheless not hypermasculinized by this ritual activity. Instead, festival antics make it unclear whether the male participants are active wielders of the phallus or its passive recipients. In this sense, phallic processions create ambiguity by placing participants betwixt and between gender roles. Csapo suggests that Turner's concept of liminality explains not only this particular Dionysian ritual but also the pillar used to represent Dionysus in the Anthesteria and elsewhere, Dionysus's association with the phallus, and the prevalence of cross-dressing in Dionysian worship. In exploring these practices associated with Dionysus, Csapo shows the usefulness of Turner's concept of liminality for studying Greek gods, myths, and religious practices, as well as the ways in which van Gennep's three-part schema for understanding initiations illuminates a wider range of rituals than he might have foreseen.

- How does Csapo define *communitas*? How is it related to liminality, and how might it be used to explain Dionysus's *orgia*, *symposia*, or the experience of an actor or audience member in the ancient theater?

- In Csapo's view, what are the connections between humor and liminality?

- What does Csapo find "liminal" about masks and Dionysus's pillar?

- In what ways is Dionysus a "god of two forms"? How does Dionysus embody doubleness and encourage participants in his rituals to do the same?

 ## ERIC CSAPO, *FROM* "RIDING THE PHALLUS FOR DIONYSUS: ICONOLOGY, RITUAL, AND GENDER-ROLE DE/CONSTRUCTION" (1997)

For other Greek gods one can easily distinguish a personality, developed in myth and epic, from the rituals of their worship, which evolved in the separate sphere of cultic practice. Though the rituals are generally suited to the divine personality, they can hardly be said to express it, let alone contain it. It might be argued that Dionysus is unique in this respect: other gods may have developed rituals suited to their personalities, but Dionysus developed a personality to suit his ritual. Moreover, Dionysus, more than any other god, is the expression of a specific type of ritual, which is the most powerful form of ritual, emotionally and psychologically. This is the ritual of inversion, a phenomenon which, though well known and long studied, is variously interpreted. I have chosen (and slightly modified) a model suggested by Victor Turner to help explain the bizarre rite which is the main object of this investigation.

Scholars have already demonstrated the applicability of Turner's concepts of *liminality* and *communitas* to Dionysiac cult; they provide a model which is both simple and powerful and requires no lengthy explanation.[1] Turner picks up from van Gennep's tripartite division of rites of passage: separation from the community, liminality, reintegration. The second phase "liminality" is characterized by disorientation and a breakdown of normal concepts of identity and behavioural norms. Turner calls the social codes which govern behaviour "structure." Opposed to structure are what Turner calls "antistructure" and "interstructure," though he uses the terms indiscriminately in my view. For my own purposes I will call "antistructure" behaviour that is patterned in direct opposition to structural norms.[2] Both structure and antistructure, then, are clear and consistent codes, in fact the positive and the negative of the same code. "Interstructure" exists where there is a confusion of behavioural norms and their opposite, where there is ambiguity and indeterminacy, and a suggestion or illusion, through the disorienting mix of code and anticode, of a virtual codelessness (this meaning, at least, is more in conformity with Turner's usage, esp. 1967: 93–111).

There are two types of liminal rituals: rituals of status elevation and rituals of status reversal. Rituals of status elevation have to do with the permanent transition of individuals from one status category to another. They are organized according to the individual's life-cycle and create irreversible transformations. Rituals of status reversal by contrast involve the entire community, are calendrical, and end in a complete restoration of the status quo. The principal object of liminal ritual is to create "communitas." During these rituals the community is stripped of all social barriers and social distinctions so that members of the community can experience one another "concretely" as equals.

Many are the forms of Dionysiac cult and ritual. Some of them merely articulate or replicate social structure.[3] But the most distinctive Dionysiac rituals are liminal rituals. Dionysus functions in both initiation and carnival rituals as the great leveller and dissolver of social boundaries. The worshippers of Dionysus, free or slave, male or female, young or old, find themselves exalted or humbled to a state of natural equality and cultural indistinguishability. When Dionysiac ritual is viewed in these terms, one can easily see how comedy emerged from the worship of Dionysus. Liminal rituals have a great deal in common with humour: laughter and communitas both spring from incongruity and aggression, the confusion of social categories, and the violation of social taboos. Attic Old Comedy in particular directs its humour towards social hierarchy, debasing the powerful and elevating the low. It is also easy to see why the cult of Dionysus was particularly cultivated by the Athenian democracy, a democracy which was largely content to be ruled by a governing elite, so long as that élite remained under its ultimate control.[4] Liminal rituals dissolve social boundaries by rendering them ambivalent and paradoxical, confusing things with their opposites, until the social status distinctions between them appear artificial and meaningless. Since real community-solidarity can only exist in the most elementary precivilized social formations, where all really are undifferentiated and equal, a divided society will employ such expedients as rituals of status reversal to bolster its sense of community when its social divisions threaten to tear it apart. This function is also a matter of paradox and ambivalence. Though social barriers are temporarily destroyed in rituals of reversal, the destructive act, in the controlled ritual context, largely and normally serves to confirm the importance and sanctity of social divisions once the ritual is over.[5] Like liminal ritual, "Dionysus operates as the principle that destroys differences," as Segal put it (1982: 234). He does so by temporarily merging opposites and rendering them paradoxical. This is at least the principal idea behind Dionysus, and one that is expressed concretely in the god's icon.

Though a god "of many names" and "many forms,"[6] the commonest form of Dionysus in Greek cult is as a post, pillar, or tree-trunk; as a mask; or as a combination of the two, a pillar or tree-trunk to which a mask is attached.[7] These icons express his liminal personality. Masks express liminality in two ways. Modern interpreters tend to focus upon the mask's synchronic ambiguities: that a mask presents and conceals at once, combining an outward fixed personality and a mysterious hidden voluble one. The power of the masked personality resides in the possibility of difference, even polar opposition between the outside and the inside. On this interpretation, the masked icon is a representation of Dionysus' doubleness and duplicity. Indeed the Greeks also called him the "god of two forms,"[8] and this doubleness of the mask might also find expression in the fact that the icon of Dionysus is frequently a double mask—a pillar with two masks affixed to either side and gazing in opposite directions. The uncanny combination of something presented to view and something hidden suggests the portrait of Dionysus we find in myth, with its paradoxical combination of the familiar and the strange. Dionysus is a thoroughly Greek god, yet he is always presented as a foreigner arriving over land or over sea: from

India, Lydia, or Thrace.[9] The story of Dionysus at Thebes best brings out this opposition of familiarity and strangeness: Dionysus comes as a stranger from Lydia to his own birthplace to visit his own family.

But the liminality of the mask may also be interpreted diachronically in terms of transition between states and identities. When you put on a mask you allow your own personality to be submerged in that of another. It is a form of possession and at least a partial expulsion of the familiar self. Frontisi-Ducroux argues that it is this, and not concealment, which the mask signified to the Greek mind: "When put on, the mask served not to hide the face it covered, but to abolish and replace it."[10] If the logic of the mask's doubleness has to do with possession, there is also a certain doubleness in the manner in which the mask seizes its victims. The mask-wearer is invaded by the persona of the mask, but so is the mask-viewer. The mask is a source of fascination, even in the etymological sense of casting a spell (Lat. *fascinare*). In Byzantine art the face of Judas is seen in profile, while all the other apostles are frontal. We are told that this is to encourage communion with the eleven and to avoid possession by Judas.[11]

NOTES

1. For Turner's theories, see esp. 1969: 94–130, 166–203; 1982. The theories are applied to Dionysiac religion by Segal 1982: 13; 1986: 285; Hoffmann 1989.

2. Turner (1982: 44) uses the term "to describe both liminality . . . and 'communitas,' . . . not a structural reversal, a mirror-imagery of 'profane' workaday socioeconomic structure." He is more interested in the experience of liminal rites; I am more interested in the actual mechanics of producing that experience, and so use it in precisely this sense, as a reversal of workaday structure.

3. E.g., the observance of gender, age, and social divisions within cultic roles and hierarchies discussed by Henrichs 1982.

4. For the democratic appropriation of Dionysus, see Dodds 1960: 127–130 *ad* Eur. *Bacch.* 421–423 and 430–433; Connor 1989, 1990 (with Sourvinou-Inwood 1994: 273–277); Versnel 1990: 167; Seaford 1996: 48–49.

5. In Turner's view, liminal ritual is not, as some claim, a kind of social glue binding the community in its terror of disorder, but often more like a solvent, breaking down the rigidity of the social order and saving the community from excessive structuration through "deconstruction and re-construction" (Turner 1982: 83). It is emphatically not, as some deconstructionists claim, a celebration of the chaos beyond structure, as an end in itself, but rather an adaptive mechanism for reconstruction (cf. the criticisms of Friedrich 1996: 266; Seaford 1994: 363–367; 1996:

31, n. 25). Whether or not reconstruction simply refreshes or actually renovates depends entirely upon the social and historical context. Symbols and symbolic acts can acquire new meanings if a culture is ready to receive them. New symbols may be introduced. "Ritual liminality, therefore, contains the potentiality for cultural innovation, as well as the means of effecting structural transformations within a relatively stable sociocultural system" (Turner 1982: 85). For a survey of the literature on the relation of rituals of inversion to the social order, see Goldhill 1991: 176–188; Versnel 1993: 115–121.

6. Soph. *Ant.* 1115; Eur. *Bacch.* 1017–18; *Anth. Pal.* 9.524.13; Plut. *Mor.* 389b.

7. See esp. Casadio 1984.

8. Diod. Sic. 4.5.2. Dionysus' doubleness is a major theme of Otto 1948, *passim.*

9. See esp. Detienne 1986: 21–27; Henrichs 1982: 152–155.

10. Frontisi-Ducroux 1995: 40. The concept of the mask-wearer as displaced by the mask's identity accords well with the archaic concept of mimesis described by Nagy (1996, esp. 55–56 and 81–86) where the performer is conceived not as imitator but as (re)embodiment of the object of mimesis. Diodorus (4.5.3–4) reports two explanations for Dionysus being called the god of two forms, and neither has anything to do with hidden identities. One refers the epithet to an ambivalence in representations of the god's outward appearance, whether old and bearded or young and luxuriant, and the other refers to the two different psychological states induced by wine: mirth and pugnacity.

11. See, e.g., Runciman 1975; 102.

<table>
<tr><td>**9.3**
COMPARISON</td></tr>
</table>

ANATOLIA AND ROME: CYBELE AND ATTIS

At the opening of Euripides's *Bacchae*, Dionysus, disguised as a mortal worshipper of Dionysus, claims he has come to Thebes to establish the worship of the god Dionysus in the city. Despite the fact that Dionysus is a native son of Thebes (his mother, Semele, is a Theban princess) and that his divinity is recognized elsewhere in Greece, Thebes, curiously, has remained indifferent to him. Thebes's indifference and Pentheus's resistance to Dionysus are common themes in myths about him and register the unease that Dionysus's ecstatic worship generated. The Greeks expressed this unease by locating the origins of Dionysian worship in Cybele, the Phrygian Great Mother (Chapter 8.3).

Scholars of the twentieth century accepted the Greek historical construction of Dionysus as an Eastern god. Thus they viewed Euripides's description in the *Bacchae* of Dionysus's departure from Lydia and Phrygia, where he set "Asia dancing and established [his] mysteries," as a historical fact. When Dionysus's name was deciphered in Linear B tablets, indicating that Dionysus was worshipped in Greece during the Bronze Age, scholars realized that Dionysus's ecstatic forms of worship were not necessarily derived from abroad. This section examines how the Greeks, and the Romans who followed them, associated Dionysian ecstasy with Cybele and developed myths about a figure named Attis who was her consort or worshipper.

THE GREAT MOTHER IN GREECE

Euripides's *Bacchae* explicitly associates the ecstatic worship of the Great Mother, called Cybele, with the worship of Dionysus. Before the chorus enjoins its members to accompany Dionysus from Phrygia to Greece, it praises the man who observes the mysteries of Dionysus and Cybele (*Bacchae* 73–82). A Homeric *Hymn* to a Great Mother (c. 700 BCE) describes her as surrounded by torches, drums, rattles, and frenzied dancing, many of which were also to be found in the worship of Dionysus. Yet Cybele's iconography and her ecstatic worship in Greece has only a distant relationship to the serene mature goddess conceived of by the Phrygians (Chapter 8.3).

Similarly, Attis, a mythical figure who came to be worshipped alongside Cybele in Greece, is believed to originate in Phrygia, despite the near absence of Phrygian evidence of him (Figure 9.10). The mythical Greek Attis may refer to Ates, a historical Phrygian royal man, who is honored with the Great Mother on two Phrygian inscriptions and may have been charged with overseeing her worship. Herodotus tells a lengthy tale of how a certain Atys, the son of the Lydian king Croesus, dies in a boar hunt because of the wrath of the goddess Nemesis. Although Cybele is not mentioned, Herodotus's account originates in Lydia, a region near Phrygia, and is distantly echoed in many Greek myths in which Cybele harms Attis (Ovid, *Fasti* 4.222). Thus scholars have argued that Herodotus's tale of the Lydian Atys forges a tenuous connection between the Greek Attis and the Phrygian Ates.

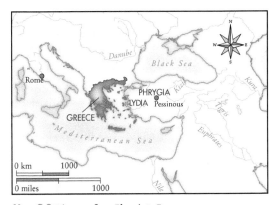

9.10 The goddess Cybele rides a chariot pulled by lions and Attis leans on a pine tree. Relief on a marble altar dedicated to Cybele and Attis. 295 CE. The portions of the inscription visible in this image include the name of the dedicator (L. Cornelius Scipio Oreitus), a priest (augur) who accomplished a bull-killing (*taurobolium*) and dedicated this altar to Cybele and Attis. Archaeological Museum, Ferrara, Italy. *De Agostini Picture Library/A. Dagli Orti/Bridgeman Images, DGA501455.*

Map 9.2 Dionysus from Phrygia to Rome

Although the historical connections between Greek myths about Attis and any Phrygian precedent are few, the Greeks and the Romans nonetheless viewed Attis as Phrygian. They depicted him wearing foreign clothes and a Phrygian cap (Chapter 6.4) in statues and on reliefs. In part, this connection is made because Attis castrates himself in Greek myth; the Greeks and the Romans linked him through this self-mutilation to the Phrygian eunuch priests of the Great Mother, who were also castrated in order to preserve their sexual purity and devotion. Myths of Attis offered an explanation for why Cybele's priests, called Galli (the plural of Gallus), were eunuchs in Greece and in Rome. More importantly, by attributing the Galli's feminine demeanor and ecstatic cult activities to Attis, these myths preserved a Greco-Roman notion of masculinity that excluded such behaviors. In Roman literature especially, the Galli are described with feminine attire, high-pitched voices, and long, perfumed hair. Their frenzied dancing to rhythmic music from the tympanum on the streets of Roman cities attracted censure and disdain. Yet the Romans actively sought the protection of the Great Mother, dedicating a temple in the city center on the Palatine Hill to her and tolerating her priests.

THE GREAT MOTHER IN ROME

The Roman Senate introduced the worship of the Great Mother (Magna Mater in Latin) to Italy after a shower of stones from the skies and recent setbacks in a war had provoked great anxiety (204 BCE). Advised to seek the Great Mother after consulting their prophetic books, they sent an embassy to the city of Pessinous in Anatolia, where the Great Mother was worshipped. The ambassadors secured a large stone representing the Great Mother, brought it back to Rome, and installed it in the Temple of Victory on the Palatine Hill. Subsequently, the stone was moved to a temple built nearby and was dedicated to her (191 BCE); Attis was also honored there.

Terracotta baskets of fruit and figures of sexual organs and human couples have been found at the temple, suggesting that the Romans associated the Great Mother with fertility. A springtime festival in her honor furthered her connection with fertility, whereas her appearance on coins indicates her widespread acceptance. However, the informal and non-state-sanctioned ecstatic worship conducted by her eunuch priests—featuring drums, rattles, music, and frenzied dancing—was viewed less favorably. The Romans attributed such modes of worship, along with the dress and behavior of the Galli, to Phrygia, just as the Greeks before them attributed Dionysian forms of worship to Phrygia. In other words, both the Greeks and the Romans attributed religious customs they found distasteful and certain forms of effeminacy (as represented by Attis) to the peoples of the East.

The Roman poet Catullus (84–54 BCE) offers a psychological portrait of Cybele's ecstatic worship that in many ways reflects Euripides's description of

Pentheus's worship of Dionysus. Swept up in an ecstatic frenzy along with other worshippers, Attis castrates himself, thus becoming one of Cybele's Galli. Once out of his trance, however, Attis is horrified and mourns the loss of the legal rights he enjoyed as a man and his exclusion from activities limited to Roman male citizens. Thus, in complex and unexpected ways, Dionysus's ecstatic worship was linked to the Phrygian Cybele and Attis in the East and to the Great Mother and the Galli in Rome.

CATULLUS, "ATTIS"

BEFORE YOU READ

Catullus gives voice to the experience, both painful and transcendent, of Attis's overpowering encounter with Cybele. The castration of Attis, like the female attire Pentheus puts on before he is dismembered, suggests how great religious passion might emasculate or completely destroy a man. Neither Pentheus nor Attis will ever again live in society as they did before their feverish intimacy with the divine. Seaford argues (see previously) that Euripides's *Bacchae* portrays a "subjective experience" of worshipping Dionysus. "Attis," for its part, offers a first-person narrative of worshipping Cybele. (Translated by Guy Lee.)

- To what degree are Attis's experiences and sensory perceptions similar to those of Pentheus, the chorus of Eastern women, and the Theban women in *Bacchae*?

- Do you think Catullus's poem, Euripides's play, or the Homeric *Hymn* 7 (*To Dionysos*) can be treated as historical documents that reveal the subjective nature of religious experience in Greece or Rome?

CATULLUS, "ATTIS" (FIRST CENTURY BCE)

Over the high seas Attis, carried in a speedy craft,
When he touched the grove in Phrygia eagerly with hurrying feet
And approached the Goddess' gloomy forest-girt domain,
There, by raving madness goaded, his wits astray,
He tore off with a sharp flint the burden of his groin.   5
Then, conscious that the members left him were now unmanned,
Still with fresh blood spotting the surface of the ground,
In snow-white hand she swiftly seized the light tambourine,
Your tambourine, Cybébe, your initiation, Mother,
And tapping hollow bull's-hide with tender fingertips,   10
Proceeded thus, aflutter, to sing to her followers:
"To the heights come quickly, Gallae, together to Cýbele's groves,

Together come, stray cattle of the Mistress of Dindymus,
Who like a band of exiles making for foreign lands
And following my guidance, my comrades, led by me,   15
Have borne the raging salt sea and ocean's savagery,
And through excessive hatred of Venus unmanned yourselves,
With your impetuous wanderings gladden the heart of your Queen.
Rid mind of slow reluctance, together, come, follow me
To Cybébe's home in Phrygia, to the Goddess's Phrygian groves,   20
Where rings the voice of cymbals, where tambourines are banged,
Where Phrygian bass-pipers drone loud on their curved reed,
Where ivy-bearing Maenads violently toss their heads,
Where with shrill ululations they celebrate holy rites,
Where the Goddess's wandering troupers are used to rush around,   25
Thither it is our duty to speed in leaping dance."

Soon as false female Attis had sung her companions this,
Suddenly the procession shrieked with trembling tongues,
The light tambourine was thumping, the hollow cymbals clanged,
The revel rout approached green Ida on hurrying feet.   30
At the same time in wandering frenzy breathless and breathing hard
Attis led on, attended by drums, through gloomy groves,
Just like an untamed heifer avoiding the load of the yoke;
The hurrying Gallae follow her scurry-footed lead.
And so, when those poor tired things arrived at Cybébe's home,   35
After too much effort without Ceres they fall asleep.
Passive slumber covers their eyes with listlessness;
In gentle rest departed their mind's mad paroxysm.
But when the Sun with golden face and flashing eyes
Purified white aether, hard land and wild sea,   40
And drove away Night's shadows with lively clatter-hooves,
Then Sleep from wakened Attis departed, flying fast,
To be welcomed by the Goddess Pasithea with trembling breast.
So, after gentle rest-time, from frenzied madness free,
When Attis' self went over in thought what she had done   45
And in her mind saw clearly where, without what, she was,
She dared with spirit seething return again to the shore.
There, gazing at the lonely sea with tearful eyes,
She thus addressed with sad voice her country piteously:
"O country that gave me being, O country that gave me birth,   50
Whom I wretchedly leaving as runaway servants do
Their masters, to the forests of Ida brought my feet,
That I might be among snow and wild beasts' frosty byres,

And draw near in my madness their every lurking-place,
Where or in what quarter, my country, do I think you lie?   55
My pupils of themselves long to turn their gaze on you,
While my spirit for a short time is free of fierce mania.
Shall *I* rush to these forests far distant from my home?
Be absent from my country, possessions, parents, friends?
Absent from forum, palaestra, stadium and gymnasia?   60
Ah wretched, wretched spirit, you must forever grieve.
What kind of human figure have I not undergone?
A woman I, a young man, an ephebe I, a child.
I've been flower of the gymnasium; I was glory of the oil.
For me the doors were crowded, for me the threshold warm.   65
For me with flowery posies the house was garlanded
When it was time at sunrise for me to leave my bed.
Shall I now be called Gods' handmaid and Cýbele's serving-girl?
Am I to be a Maenad, half me, a male unmanned?
Am I to haunt green Ida's cold, snow-mantled bounds?   70
Shall I spend life beneath the high columns of Phrygia,
With the deer woodland-haunting and forest-ranging boar?
Now what I've done appals me; I'm sorry for it now."

As the sound quickly issued from out her rosy lips
Bearing a new message to the twin ears of the Gods,   75
Then Cybele, unloosing the yoke that joined her lions
And pricking the kine-killer upon the left, spoke thus:
"Be off" she said, "go, Ferox, make frenzy drive him on,
Make him retrace his footsteps to the forest frenzy-struck,
Who desires too freely to escape from my commands.   80
Come suffer your own lashes, flog your back with your tail,
Make every corner thunder again with bellowing roar;
Ferox, go toss the tawny mane on your muscular neck."
So spake Cybébe, threatening, as her hand untied the yoke.
The beast, arousing himself, goaded his spirit to rage,   85
Rushed forward, roared, and trampled the brushwood with roving paw.
But when he approached the moist part of the whitening sea-shore
And saw there tender Attis beside the marbled deep,
He charges. She, demented, runs off to the wild woods;
There she remained at all times, life-long a female slave.   90

Goddess, great Goddess, Cybébe, Goddess Mistress of Dindymus,
Far from my house be all that frenzy of yours, O Queen.
Drive others to elation, drive others raving mad!

DIONYSUS AS A GOD OF THE 1960s

A number of modern and contemporary artists in performance genres have taken up both Dionysus and Euripides's *Bacchae* as vehicles through which to meditate on and challenge entrenched social orders. Some have critiqued the rigidity of gender norms, whereas others have interrogated systems of racial discrimination. Other artists have deployed Dionysian themes to consider issues of class and political corruption within their societies. In the 1960s Dionysus became an especially vital and disruptive figure and was embraced by artists who sought to address the political and social challenges that defined the decade—and that still resonate today.

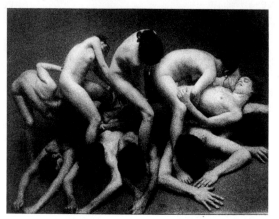

9.11 Birth of Dionysus. From *The Performance Group-Dionysus in '69*, published in Oscar Brockett's *History of the Theatre*. © *Photograph by Max Waldman, Archive USA / All Rights Reserved.*

Classical Scholar Froma Zeitlin (b. 1933) has noted that the late 1960s were a time of radical social transformation in the United States to which the themes of the *Bacchae* were particularly suited. "It seemed in truth like a Dionysiac age in more ways than one," she has observed. Resistance to the war in Vietnam, expanding political rights and social freedom for racial minorities and women, and the emergence of a youth culture that rejected the previous generation's norms relating to sex, the family, and drug use were the hallmarks of the age.

In this section, we explore three influential examples of Dionysian performance: a play (*Dionysus in '69*) that was performed in New York City for a year (1968–1969) before being filmed by Brian De Palma; *The Rocky Horror Picture Show* (1975), a British-American movie directed by Jim Sharman that was based on a British theatrical production (1973); and an adaptation of Euripides's *Bacchae* by the Nigerian playwright and activist Wole Soyinka, commissioned by and performed at Britain's National Theatre (1973).

DIONYSUS IN '69

Directed by Richard Schechner (b. 1934) and conceived by him and the Performance Group, his experimental theater troupe, *Dionysus in '69* was performed for a year in New York City beginning in 1968. The play, an adaptation of Euripides's *Bacchae*, offered its audience a profoundly different experience from conventional theater production. The theater in which it was staged was a square space with wooden scaffolds and ladders against the walls on which the audience could sit, stand, or move about, as the performers themselves did. The play was performed on a mat in the center of the room, yet the performers frequently leapt and crawled on the scaffolding, and the audience members could join the performance; indeed, the play intentionally encouraged and provoked audience participation. This unconventional theatrical experience reinforced the disruptive thematic content of the play, which the young film director Brian De Palma (b. 1940), who would become famous for movies including *Carrie* (1976) and *Scarface* (1983), captured in his documentary film about the play. De Palma created a split screen that simultaneously showed the actors performing and the audience engaging with (or in?) the performance. The split screen also replicated audience participation by forcing the viewer to choose which screen to watch and when.

In addition to its disruption of the typical relationship between theatergoer and performance, the play was also striking for its political commentary, use of nudity, and invocation of homosexuality. Not only did the play open during the American presidential campaign of 1968, but the title, *Dionysus in '69*, is the political slogan for the god Dionysus's political campaign, which he announces at the play's conclusion. The nudity was simultaneously startling to its audience and appropriate for a decade when sexual liberation was celebrated in tandem with the political liberation of the women's rights movement. The play's nudity is not just sexual, however; it was also meant to symbolize a common humanity in opposition to male individuality and prerogatives, as represented by both Pentheus and Dionysus, even if at times they are opposed to each other (Figure 9.11).

In Pentheus and Dionysus's highly sexualized exchanges, Dionysian religion or human beings in a state of nature are not set in opposition to state authority, as in Euripides's *Bacchae*. Pentheus is hostile to and confused by Dionysus's mere presence. To diffuse Pentheus's hostility, Dionysus offers himself or any woman in the room as a sexual partner. When Pentheus refuses, the female chorus members try to calm him. But they fail in their efforts and eventually begin instead to tear Pentheus apart. What motivates their violence is not fully specified. Indeed, a voice-over describes their actions, as their gentle moans become growls and they attack all the male cast members, not just Pentheus. Their act of savagery is not directed against the state (as represented by Pentheus), nor is their savagery an expression of Dionysian energies, or even female forces that require containment by laws and by men. Although all are possible explanations, not one is suggested by the play's conclusion, which instead offers a warning against how individual and communal sentiments can be exploited or manipulated for good or ill.

The play closes with Dionysus, now wearing a suit, announcing his political candidacy. Suddenly both the male and female performers become an enthralled mob—undifferentiated, unthinking, and willingly directing their energies toward Dionysus. As the cast and audience leave the theater and spill out onto the streets, the play's ending raises questions about how individuals who devote themselves to a cause may become blind followers, as the performers at the play's end appear to be. Stefan Brecht, writing in *The Drama Review*, observes that Schechner's play questions whether the anarchic impulses of the hippies and the culture of the sixties can counter a social or political conformism that leads to the blind following of a political leader.

THE ROCKY HORROR PICTURE SHOW

Another movie adaptation of a stage play, *The Rocky Horror Picture Show* (1975; directed by Jim Sharman) achieved greater popularity than De Palma's *Dionysus in '69*. Centered around a Dionysus-inspired leader, Dr. Frank N. Furter, it uses sexual idiom to interrogate conformity and authoritarianism. The film pays tribute to even as it satirizes classic science fiction and horror films.

The movie achieved enduring popularity in the 1970s, when theaters began to show it as a midnight feature. Fans who attended would participate in the performance by shouting abusive or vulgar (but almost always humorous) comments in response to lines in the movie. Eventually, fans who had memorized a character's part began to perform the film at the front of the theater before the movie audience. Over the years, the midnight shows have become increasingly formalized, with "shadow casts" designated to perform the roles, policing of audience members who fail to respond with the appropriate line to the characters on screen, and even initiation rituals for audience members (called "virgins") who are seeing the movie for the first time. Thus, in Dionysian fashion, the experience of *The Rocky Horror Picture Show* breaks the barrier between the audience and the film itself, just as the play *Dionysus in '69* did. *Rocky Horror* also introduces sexuality of all sorts, a birth scene, and even a dismemberment, further highlighting its Dionysian themes.

The wildly convoluted plot begins with a virginal young couple, Brad and Janet, whose car has broken down near a castle. The castle is owned by Dr. Frank N. Furter, a mad scientist and transvestite, who has created Rocky, a Frankenstein-like creature. Brad and Janet arrive just as Frank is hosting a party that is best described as bacchanalian. In the course of the film, he will sleep with both Brad and Janet; kill, dismember, and serve his former lover for dinner; and orchestrate an orgy that will include Brad and Janet. At the end of the film, Frank is revealed to be an alien from the planet Transsexual. He is killed, and Brad and Janet are released but forever transformed.

The Rocky Horror Picture Show, unlike *Dionysus in '69*, emphasizes sexual liberation. Frank N. Furter presents himself as both transsexual and transvestite, and he invites Brad and Janet to join escapades that are outside their ordinary experience. The lyrics are filled with comic sexual allusions that range from coy to explicit. In the song "Don't Dream It, Be It," Frank encourages the couple to surrender "to absolute pleasure" and to "erotic nightmares beyond any measure." Frank's invitation to abandon the self is (like Frank himself) both alluring and alarming and certainly bears some similarity to Dionysus. Yet, by offering only sexual liberation, *The Rocky Horror Picture Show* offers a constrained vision of Dionysian transcendence, suggesting that the Dionysian walk on the wild side, although scary, is all in good fun. Nevertheless, *The Rocky Horror Picture Show* does offer a wickedly subversive critique of, and even release from, the conventional American gender and family roles already under siege in that tumultuous era. Artists of the 1960s, then, found in Dionysus a revolutionary who may bring the blessings of freedom, at a cost. These blessings are largely expressed in terms of sexual freedom and are wholly of this world and appear to have no transcendent quality.

THE BACCHAE OF EURIPIDES: A COMMUNION RITE

The Bacchae of Euripides: A Communion Rite, by Wole Soyinka (b. 1934), was written in Nigeria and performed in England during the time when the theatrical version of *The Rocky Horror Picture Show* was also showing in Britain. Soyinka adapted Euripides's *Bacchae* in very different ways from its contemporary American and British counterparts. The evocative similarities Soyinka finds between ancient Greek and contemporary African religion inform his version of Euripides's play.

Like ancient Greek religion, many African religions (particularly in West Africa) are polytheistic and largely anthropomorphic. Soyinka, for example, suggests correspondences between the African god Ogun and both Dionysus and Zeus. An emphasis on community is articulated in both ancient Greece and contemporary Africa through the importance accorded to the agora (the marketplace that serves political, religious, and economic interests) and to civic festivals. Consequently, Soyinka's *The Bacchae of Euripides: A Communion Rite* omits attention to sexual liberation in favor of addressing political freedom and religious community and in this sense has more affinities with Euripides's original. Soyinka read Euripides in Greek some twenty years before he wrote his version of the play, which was occasioned by his release from prison, where he served two years in solitary confinement for political dissent against Nigeria's military dictators.

Soyinka's play opens not with a birth scene but with Dionysus's entrance onto a stage with two choruses: one of slaves and the other of foreign women from the East. The first half of the play revolves around the chorus of slaves and the beginnings of an annual ritual in which one slave is to be slaughtered on behalf of the community. Although initially frightened of Dionysus, they (along with Cadmus and Tiresias) join forces with the chorus of Theban women and begin to worship Dionysus with exuberant song and dance. They echo Dionysus's opening words—that he will bring freedom from tyranny. At this moment Pentheus enters the stage. He speaks in formal verse, rather than everyday language. His style of speech not only is a nod to Euripides (who, like all ancient Greek tragedians, used verse for all characters and the chorus) but also marks him as a dictator. Constrained by his commitment to order, rules, and tradition, Pentheus tells Dionysus that his powers are weak compared to those of cultured Greece. Soyinka's tragedy closely follows the original plot of Euripides's version, in that Pentheus goes on to hunt the maenads in the woods. When he is discovered, the maenads tear him apart. Yet the conclusion of Soyinka's play is startlingly different from that of Euripides.

In Euripides's original version, Agave returns from the mountains holding the head of Pentheus (which she believes to the head of a lion), and she is gradually brought to her senses and sees her terrible mistake. She leaves Thebes, broken. In Soyinka's play, when Agave returns with Pentheus's head, all the performers drink his blood, which Tiresias tells them is wine. This ritual unites everyone in a mass communion that abolishes boundaries between slaves, Theban rulers, and Eastern chorus members. This communion rite creates liberation from political tyranny. In contrast, in Euripides's *Bacchae*, the Theban women leave their ecstatic state and are left bereft of the god; the boundaries between men and women, human and animal, and human and god that obtained when they worshipped Dionysus in the woods are reestablished in the city. Soyinka's play suggests that the dissolution of differences achieved through ritual can, by implication, be politically revolutionary.

The unsettling, disquieting, liberating, and terrifying promise of Dionysus continues to resonate in popular as well as political culture wherever a society is in a state of tumult. As different from one another as they are from Euripides's original play, *Dionysus in '69*, *The Rocky Horror Picture Show*, and Soyinka's *The Bacchae of Euripides: A Communion Rite* explore the ways in which human beings as individuals and in community alternately bind and dissolve the sexual, political, and religious forces that both constrain and liberate them.

KEY TERMS

Agave 399
Anthesteria 389
Attis 419
Bacchants 398
City Dionysia 395

Cybele 418
Eleuthereus 395
Icarius 391
Maenads 393
Mystery cults 396

Pentheus 399
Satyrs 393
Semele 399
Symposia 392

FOR FURTHER EXPLORATION

Hall, Edith, F. MacIntosh, and A. Wrigley (eds.). *Dionysus since 69: Greek Tragedy at the Dawn of the Third Millennium.* Oxford: Oxford University Press, 2005. A lively collection of essays on recent performances of Greek tragedies, two of which treat Schechner's *Dionysus in '69.*

Roller, Lynn E. *In Search of God the Mother: The Cult of Anatolian Cybele.* Berkeley: University of California Press, 1999. Roller offers a clear and thorough treatment of the evidence for Cybele and Attis in Anatolia and their worship in Greece and Rome.

Seaford, Richard. *Dionysos.* London and New York: Routledge, 2006. A brief overview of the scholarship on Dionysus coupled with Seaford's interpretation of Dionysus and his rituals.

Turner, Victor. "Betwixt and Between: The Liminal Period in Rites of Passage." In: *Forest of Symbols.* Edited by Victor Turner. Ithaca, NY: Cornell University Press, 1967. This much-cited essay, and those that accompany it, introduces readers to key ideas in Turner's thought.

PART II

HEROES AND HEROINES

Asked to define the term "hero," most people might respond that a hero is someone who performs extraordinary acts of courage to serve the common good, often risking his own welfare or even life to do so. When a hero violates society's rules to help another human being, he is still understood to be working for a greater social good that justifies any infractions he might commit. "Ordinary heroes" are also seen to serve the common good, albeit through more humble actions. For such heroes, it is often their daily service over the course of decades that earns our admiration. The terms "hero" and "ordinary hero," then, suggest an almost universal type with universally positive associations: an individual so labeled is committed to protecting and sustaining society, its members, and its values, whether in dramatic episodes of risk or through more quietly consistent deeds. Because the English word "hero" comes from the ancient Greek word for hero, *heros*, it would seem likely that heroes in ancient Greece conform to this common understanding of heroism. And yet this is not the case.

The legendary hero Achilles's supreme feat in the *Iliad* is his action on the plains of Troy: he fights Scamander, the divine god of the Trojan river, and then ruthlessly, even by Homeric standards, slaughters a very large number of Trojans. Moreover, Achilles's entry into battle follows a long absence occasioned by his petulant anger at the Greek leader Agamemnon, during which he watches his fellow Greek soldiers die while he and his troops sit idly. The hero Heracles completes twelve extraordinary feats of cunning and strength (the labors) and earns the highest reward imaginable—he enters Olympus and becomes a god. Yet he also kills his wife and two sons in a fit of madness caused by the goddess Hera. Oedipus frees Thebes from the terror of the

Sphinx and becomes king. And yet he too destroys his family: he kills his father, marries his mother, and curses his two sons so that they kill each other. After Oedipus blinds himself, he dies on sacred grounds in the neighborhood of Colonus in Athens, where he is worshipped as a hero and brings benefactions to the city.

The careers of Achilles, Heracles, and Oedipus suggest that the Greek term *heros* differs greatly from our modern understanding of the terms "hero," "ordinary hero," and "heroic." The tales told about these figures also reveal the two strands involved in the study of Greek heroes: the mythic and the cultic. Stories about heroes permeate almost all Greek art forms, whether literary or visual. Heroes play a significant role in traditional oral tales, such as the *Iliad* and the *Odyssey*, which then were recorded in writing. Heroes are often protagonists of tragedies that bear their names, and they make brief appearances in lyric poetry or prose. In the visual arts, heroes are depicted in vase paintings, sculptures, and friezes. They are often prominently displayed on monumental buildings; Heracles's exploits are carved on the temple of Zeus in Olympia and the temple of Hephaestus in the Athenian Agora, where Theseus's exploits are also carved. All of these art forms create a dense mythic network that includes heroes among the gods and goddesses. Yet, unlike their divine counterparts, heroes are inextricably linked to the stories in which they are the main protagonists.

It would be difficult to imagine Achilles without the *Iliad*, or Oedipus without Sophocles's tragedies, *Oedipus Tyrannus* and *Oedipus at Colonus*. Because each work of art describes its heroes in ways particular to its genre, most studies of Greek heroes pay attention to artistic form, particularly literary form. Tragic heroes, for example, are often distinguished from epic heroes, and both are different from the heroes of comedy and romance. Thus the mythic strand in the ancient construction of heroes inevitably requires more attention to literary forms than does the study of gods and goddesses (which instead requires more attention to religious worship and practices). Yet Greek heroes have a cultic aspect too and cannot simply be reduced to aesthetic conceptions.

For example, ancient Greek heroes were often worshipped at their tombs. Oedipus was worshipped at a sacred site in the neighborhood of Colonus in Athens. Heracles had many cult shrines, not only in Greece but also in Egypt. The types of sacrifices offered to heroes differed from those offered to the Olympian gods and goddesses, and in general heroes, or their relics, were believed to confer a divine power and benefactions to the community where they were buried. The Spartans, for example, on the advice of a Delphic oracle, went to considerable effort to find and dig up the bones of Orestes in order to move them to Sparta and thereby reap the rewards of Orestes's support and protection, especially in battle. Although not all Greek heroes had cult shrines, the cultic dimensions of those who did form an important component of their definition and cultural significance in ancient Greece.

In addition to the mythic and cultic strands in the ancient construction of heroes, the scholarly tradition on Greek heroes is so robust, one is almost tempted to consider it a third strand. This scholarly tradition begins with Aristotle, who set out to describe tragic and comic heroes. Yet the most concentrated and fruitful study of Greek heroes is from more recent times. Its origins may be traced to the publication of *Bulfinch's Mythology* (1881) by Thomas Bulfinch (1796–1867) and the first publication of *The Golden Bough: A Study in Magic and Religion* (1890) by James George Frazer (1854–1941). Subsequently, literary scholars, folklorists, anthropologists, linguists, and psychologists (as well as classicists) have studied Greek heroes and have offered varied perspectives that reflect their disciplinary affiliations.

One of the more remarkable features of this rich and diverse scholarly tradition of the nineteenth and first half of the twentieth century is its focus on heroes to the exclusion of heroines. Although the Greeks spent far more time and energy telling stories and carving pictures of heroes (and thus the scholarly preoccupation with heroes reflects Greek interests), Medea, Helen, and Iphigenia are also protagonists of tragedies that bear their names, and they too have cult shrines. The first two full-length studies of Greek heroines as a distinct category were written nearly one hundred years or so after the concentrated study of Greek heroes: Jennifer Larson's *Greek Heroine Cults* (1995) and Deborah Lyons's *Gender and Immortality: Heroines in Ancient Greek Myth and Cult* (1996).

Although the deeds of Greek heroines, like those of Greek heroes, are not exemplary—Medea kills her brother and two sons, and the oft-married Helen is renowned more for her beauty than her actions—they often have a moral aspect. Thus the study of heroines alongside that of heroes presents many interesting challenges and questions. Not only is there is less textual and other evidence about them; it remains an open question whether the many scholarly studies and definitions of Greek heroes might apply to Greek heroines. Are Greek heroines identical to Greek heroes, but for their gender? Or are their deeds and stories sufficiently unique that they do not easily fit into the categories and terms applied to heroes?

The following chapters explore these and other questions about heroes and heroines in Greece and in the ancient Mediterranean, as well as in the scholarly tradition that has sought to define and understand them. Because ancient poetry, especially epic poetry, about heroes and heroines is lengthier and of primary importance for developing an understanding of who an Achilles or an Iphigenia was, greater space is devoted to their tales and less to their explication. Indeed, the vividness and complexity with which Greek artists portray their heroes and heroines make the thousands of years separating our heroes and heroines from their Greek precursors seem not very long at all.

CHAPTER 10

ACHILLES

THE MAKING OF A HERO

Things of a day!

What is a man? What is he not?

A dream of a shade who wanders in Hades.

But when light from Zeus descends,

a shining brightness and sweet life belongs to him.

PINDAR, *PYTHIAN ODE* (8.95–98)

The glory of the divine, which falls upon the figure of the hero,
is strangely combined with the shadow of mortality.

—C. KERENYI, *THE HEROES OF THE GREEKS* (1958)

T he man who would be a hero blazes for a brief moment. He performs an extraordinary act—one that defies the limits set on the lives of ordinary men. He is close to the gods: he may have a divine parent; his talents and beauty may make him godlike in the eyes of men; or he may be beloved of the gods. In all cases, the "shining brightness" that Pindar describes comes from the gods, momentarily scattering the "shadow of mortality" that, because the hero is a human being, has been cast on him from birth. Yet it is ultimately

< **10.1 (OPPOSITE): Heroic banquet.** A hero reclines on a couch and dines while a servant stands nearby. Such reliefs were often used as grave markers for mortals who were worshipped as heroes. Marble relief. Unknown, Greek, eastern Mediterranean, 150–100 BCE. The J. Paul Getty Museum, Malibu, California. *The J. Paul Getty Museum, Villa Collection 96.AA.167: Malibu, California.*

the darkness and not the light that defines the Greek hero. For however close to the gods he may be, the hero must die, often in an untimely, violent, or mysterious way. Only after death can he be immortalized through song or worship at his gravesite, where a community's celebration will ensure his perpetual remembrance.

In this chapter, we see first how each of these factors defines a Greek hero, before turning to a study of hero shrines and hero myths. Four case studies of well-known heroes (Heracles, Oedipus, Theseus, and Achilles) follow. In Chapter 11.1, we pursue the same line of enquiry into the qualities that define heroines.

<table>
<tr><td>**10.1**
HISTORY</td></tr>
</table>

DEFINING GREEK HEROES

A complex network of rituals and stories shapes Greek notions of heroes. Homer uses the word "hero" broadly to describe those battling at Troy. His use of the word, like its English meaning, refers to the main protagonist of a story. Yet many figures who had few or no stories attached to their names were worshipped at gravesites and also called heroes. These heroes may have been of local importance, but no information has survived to identify them. The category of heroes includes such local figures as well as characters from myths, legends (stories that hover between historically plausible and unlikely), and history.

FIVE TRAITS OF GREEK HEROES

Whether described as warriors, athletes, healers, prophets, founders of cities or colonies, lawgivers, generals, politicians, or philanthropists, those described by the Greeks as heroes exhibit most of the following five traits:

(1) **A hero was understood to be a man who had died.** In his *Works and Days*, Hesiod describes "a divine generation of heroic men, called demi-gods (*hemitheoi*)" that dwelled after death on the Islands of the Blessed, an area of Hades resembling Olympus. From this description, some scholars have argued that heroes were originally minor deities, because they escape the dreary eternity in Hades that awaits all men (Chapter 4.1). Yet because Hesiod links these heroes to death and because they were venerated at their gravesites (see subsequently), the word "demigods" suggests that heroes were human beings considered to be near the gods, whether through birth, talent, beauty, deeds, or favoritism.

(2) **Heroes perform extraordinary deeds that may or may not be moral.** Greek heroes perform extraordinary deeds, often of strength and endurance, although these deeds did not always serve the greater good: Achilles waits out most of the Trojan War while his Greek companions die; Oedipus kills his father; Heracles kills his wife and children; Cleomedes kills

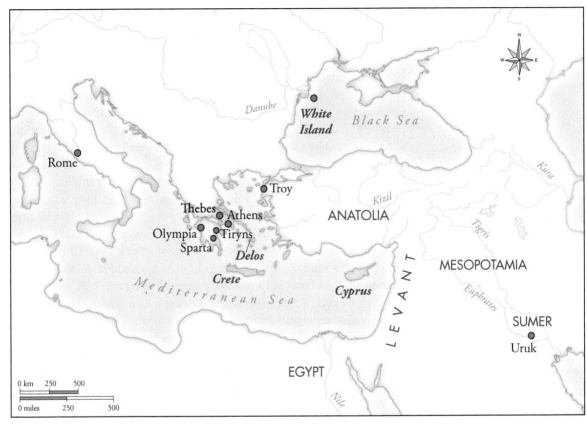

Map 10.1 Achilles and Other Greek Heroes

several schoolchildren. Although historical figures who were recognized as heroes often did benefit their communities, many Greek heroes simply performed deeds that exceeded those of other men.

(3) **Heroes die prematurely, violently, or mysteriously.** The Greeks had a term for someone killed prematurely (*aorus*) and one for someone killed violently (*biaiothanatus*). The existence of these terms suggests that individuals who suffered such deaths were of special concern because their souls might remain angry after death due to their ill treatment in life. Often the mysterious disappearance of the hero's body, regardless of the manner of death, was believed to allow the hero to remain sentient after death. Indeed, heroes escaped the fate of most humans after death, who were unable to see, hear, or observe human activities and spent an eternity wandering in the Underworld (Chapter 4.1). It seems that the living hero's fiery temperament and strength, as well as his release from the fate that befalls all souls in Hades, make him able to assist the living after death and therefore worthy of veneration.

(4) Heroes were worshipped at their gravesites. Belief in the potency of heroes' souls offers one explanation for their worship: even after death they had the power to act on behalf of those who worshipped them or to harm those who did not. Heroes were believed to be as powerful and dangerous in death as they had been in life. If a hero died violently or prematurely, his soul might remain angry after death and might be motivated to harm the living, often by causing famine, plague, infertility, and drought. Thus hero shrines were established to appease the anger of deceased heroes and to harness their vital powers for a community's benefit. The power attributed to the bones of heroes, which could be sought out, fought over, or moved, reinforces the notion that death cannot destroy or weaken a hero's body or soul. Attention to the hero's powers after death may explain why his actions during life, while important, did not need to be moral or ethical. As long as his actions were simply exceptional, such a man could earn recognition as a hero once he had died.

(5) Heroes obtain a form of immortality through song and cult. As we shall see, heroes received sacrifices and dedications in their honor at their gravesites, often at annual festivals, when stories of their lives might be retold. Heroes were celebrated in poetry (such as Homer's epics), which was also recited at festivals. In these ways, the extraordinary deeds of heroes were celebrated and remembered. Heroes, then, managed to escape mortality and live eternally in song and cult, perpetuating the "shining brightness" they shared with the gods.

Plutarch's story of Cleomedes illustrates this five-part definition of heroes (Pausanias 6.9). Cleomedes, an athlete from Astypalaea, experiences an all-too-human rage when he loses a boxing match. After killing his opponent, he returns to his hometown, where in his continued rampage he tears down a school building, killing sixty children. Enraged at his behavior, the Astypalaeans pelt Cleomedes with stones. To escape death, Cleomedes hides in a chest in a temple of Athena. When the Astypalaeans open the chest, however, Cleomedes has vanished. The townspeople consult the Delphic oracle about the meaning of his disappearance. The oracle commands them to worship Cleomedes as a hero because he is "no longer mortal." Thereafter, Cleomedes is worshipped as a hero in the town of Astypalaea.

Like most Greek heroes, Cleomedes performs deeds that are not exemplary but extraordinary (he kills his wrestling opponent and sixty children). Neither a role model nor a moral agent, Cleomedes does not offer a path for other men to follow. His death is mysterious (his body disappears), premature (he is killed in his prime), and violent (he is stoned before he vanishes). His cult, like the cults of all heroes, allows him to achieve immortality through remembrance in song. In these ways, Cleomedes's tale illustrates how hero cults in Greece were part of a religious system in which some men were imagined to retain their vital dynamism after death to protect (or harm) those who worshipped at their shrine. This dynamism or "shining brightness" was not necessarily the light of reason, nor was it in service to "the greater good" or exemplary of moral valor. It was, nonetheless, nearly divine, even beautiful, in its excess—and was honored as such.

HEROES IN CULT

Heroes were worshipped where their bodies were believed to rest. Hero shrines (*heroa*, or *heroön* [singular]) were located at a variety of places: in the center of a community (for example, in its marketplace) or at its boundaries, such as a city gate or walls. Often heroes were worshipped in an open-air space that had been cut off or separated from its surroundings and marked as sacred, sometimes by walls. Within such a space, there may have been any of the following: a mound of dirt of any size indicating a burial, a tomb, a grave-stone, an altar, a small house containing the hero's remains or offerings (also called a *heroön*), a small temple, or a cult statue (Figure 10.2). The gravesites of some heroes lacked elaborate structures or burial markers but were distinguished from other graves by the presence of dedications such as terracotta statues, pots, jewelry, weaponry, or plaques showing males reclining on couches and banqueting. Such plaques suggest the banqueter is "heroized" in

10.2 Model of a hero shrine dedicated to a local ruler in Trysa, Lycia, Anatolia (modern-day Turkey). The shrine's nine-foot walls enclosed monumental tombs and were decorated with limestone reliefs depicting heroes such as Odysseus, Perseus, and Bellerophon. Early fourth century BCE. Kunsthistorisches Museum, Vienna, Austria. *Erich Lessing / Art Resource, NY, ART204768.*

death and now enjoys the sort of luxury that Hesiod suggests surrounds heroes on the Islands of the Blessed (Figure 10.1). In addition to dedications of precious objects, animal sacrifices, food offerings, and annual festivals consisting of mourning, songs, games, and sacrifices took place at hero shrines.

HEROES IN MYTH

Myriad stories and images, in addition to worship at hero shrines, ensured that a hero would be remembered after his death. Considerable written and visual evidence about heroes accumulated over time. Most stories and images describe only a few (sometimes just one) of a hero's adventures. Rarely does any single account describe a hero from birth to death. Thus, heroes' biographies must be culled from written and visual sources that often contradict one another. Classical scholar Fritz Graf offers a useful schema for organizing such sources in his analysis of Medea (Chapter 11.1). He identifies a *vertical* tradition that includes "different versions of the same mythic episode." For example, the story of Odysseus's encounter with the Cyclops appears in Homer's *Odyssey*, in Euripides's play *Cyclops*, and on numerous vases. The story of Jason's quest for the golden fleece is told in Euripides's play *Medea* and in Apollonius of Rhodes's epic *Argonautica*. In these versions, Jason relies on Medea's herbs to put a dragon to sleep so that Jason can safely take its fleece. On one vase, however, the dragon eats and then disgorges Jason (Figure 10.3).

This detail appears in no literary accounts and illustrates how vertical traditions can contradict and enrich each other. All these representations compose a vertical tradition describing one episode. A *horizontal* tradition describes an account created from "different versions [that] yield a running biography of the mythic figure." Most modern books of mythology favor the horizontal tradition, creating cohesive biographies of heroes that smooth out the contradictions in multiple accounts of one episode. Yet such an approach ignores how the genre and date of an ancient work may shape how a hero is depicted. Two literary genres (epic and tragedy) have played an especially important role in shaping how heroes (and heroines) have been understood in antiquity as well as in modern scholarship and arts. Our examination of heroes and heroines in this and subsequent chapters depends largely on those two genres.

Homer's *Iliad* and *Odyssey*, as well as a host of epics that only survive in a collection of mere snippets known as the *Epic Cycle*, committed the deeds of

10.3 Jason is disgorged by the dragon guarding the Golden Fleece as Athena watches. Kylix, from Cerveteri. Douris Painter, fifth century BCE. Museo Gregoriano Etrusco, Vatican Museums, Vatican. *Universal Images Group / Art Resource, NY, ART424807.*

heroes to writing. Epic often emphasizes the splendor of the hero's exploits on the battlefield, in the gymnasium, sailing the seas, or fighting in foreign lands. He is seldom depicted as a stationary figure, content to rule a kingdom or administer a temple. In Homer's *Iliad*, for example, Homer shows Hector returning to Troy and encountering his wife and mother, but Hector will not sit with them. He is compelled to return to the battlefield, where heroes are made. To the epic poets, heroes are dynamic figures defined by their travels, exploits, and actions. They are rarely glimpsed in domestic spaces. There is evidence of heroic qualities in lyric poetry as well. Pindar (522–443 BCE) and the poet Bacchylides (fifth century BCE), who both wrote lyric odes celebrating victorious athletes at the four Panhellenic quadrennial games, often present the athletes they praise in terms similar to those used to describe epic heroes. Tragedians, on the other hand, seldom wrote plays about athletes.

In the Classical Period, epic heroes became the protagonists of Athenian tragedies, the plots of which show them in cities, houses, and communities that impose varied constraints and demands on them. The dramatic conventions of the tragic stage necessitated that heroes' victories on battlefields and against monsters be described (not enacted on stage), and thus these adventures become secondary to relationships between heroes and other men, gods, and family, all of which could be depicted on stage. The tragedians explore how the dynamic and self-motivated men whose courageous exploits were described in epic and lyric poetry could be content with staying at home and cooperating with their fellow citizens. In this way, tragic heroes spoke to the lives of their audiences, who, as citizen-soldiers, fought wars in seasonal campaigns and then returned to the city to live with their wives and govern their cities in coordination with other men. Under the tragedians' scrutiny, Greek heroes are no less majestic than in epic poems, but they confront problems in the more constrained space of the city and the household. Thus each generation of poets imagined Greek heroes differently, which in part explains why any horizontal account of one hero's life is filled with stories that contradict one another and do not create a consistent portrait.

10.4 Heracles, wearing the skin of the Nemean lion, leashes Cerberus. Detail from a red-figure amphora. Andokides Painter, 530–510 BCE. Louvre Museum, Paris, France. © RMN-Grand Palais / Art Resource, NY, ART497632.

The following case studies of four heroes (Heracles, Theseus, Oedipus, and Achilles) combine both horizontal and vertical traditions. A biographical (horizontal) arrangement that follows a hero from birth to death is offered. Literary treatments and visual sources such as vases and temple sculptures that focus on one episode in the hero's life and that have greatly shaped modern understandings of the hero are also included. In addition, brief attention is paid to shrines and festivals attached to the hero. (For case studies of other heroes, see Chapter 12.1.)

HERACLES

Diodorus Siculus (c. first century BCE) writes at the beginning of his summation of Heracles, "I am not unaware that many difficulties beset those who undertake to give an account of the ancient myths, and especially is this true with respect to the myths about Heracles" (4.8.1). Whether viewed collectively or individually, no accounts were quite large enough to embrace either the spectacle of Heracles's many adventures or the magnitude of his suffering.

Heracles is the son of Zeus, although Zeus is not the reason for the large number of myths (and cults) devoted to Heracles. Hera—or, rather, Hera's anger at Zeus's liaison with the mortal woman Alcmene, Heracles's mother—stands behind Heracles's greatness. Disguised as Alcmene's husband, the Theban general Amphitryon, Zeus seduces Alcmene while Amphitryon is away at battle. When Amphitryon returns home, Alcmene becomes pregnant with fraternal twins: Amphitryon's son Iphicles and Zeus's son Heracles. On the day that Heracles is due to be born, Zeus announces that a child born that day and descended from Zeus will be a king among men. But the notoriously jealous Hera had, by then, discovered Zeus's newest infidelity. She not only delays Alcmene's labor but also causes the early birth of another baby, Eurystheus—who is also distantly descended from Zeus. Eurystheus thus fulfills Zeus's prophecy and becomes king of Tiryns—a ruler of men.

THE ESSENTIALS

HERACLES Ἡρακλῆς

PARENTAGE Zeus and Alcmene

OFFSPRING Hyllus (with Deianira), two or four sons (with Megara), and many others

CULT SHRINES Throughout the Mediterranean

After Heracles is born, Hera ruthlessly pursues him. When he is still a baby, she places venomous snakes in his crib. Heracles, in his first feat of strength, effortlessly strangles the snakes with his bare hands. In some accounts, Hera unwillingly or unknowingly nurses Heracles as an infant, thus giving him great strength. (Either the pain unwittingly caused by this unusually strong baby or her realization that she is nursing Heracles causes Hera to push the infant away, thus spilling her milk; this is said to have created the Milky Way.) Hera then instigates the numerous labors Heracles must perform. Driving Heracles mad, Hera causes him to kill his wife, Megara, and their two sons. A Delphic oracle bids him to serve Eurystheus, who then demands that he perform various deeds as a punishment. (Some stories claim Heracles must serve Eurystheus for other crimes.) Twelve such deeds were sculpted on the temple of Zeus in Olympia, and these have become the canonical labors (*athloi*, or *athlos* [singular]) for which Heracles is best known (Figure 10.5). Thereafter, all other trials and journeys of Heracles were called side labors (*parerga*, or *parergon* [singular]).

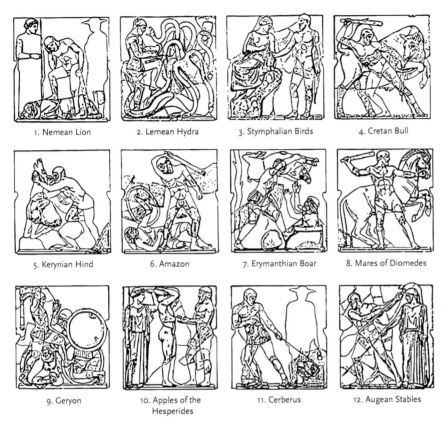

1. Nemean Lion   2. Lemean Hydra   3. Stymphalian Birds   4. Cretan Bull

5. Kerynian Hind   6. Amazon   7. Erymanthian Boar   8. Mares of Diomedes

9. Geryon   10. Apples of the Hesperides   11. Cerberus   12. Augean Stables

10.5 Sketches of metopes depicting Heracles's labors on Zeus's temple in Olympia. Using the surviving pieces of these metopes and a description by Pausanias (5.10.9), the order of the metopes has been reconstructed as follows. (1) Heracles sits, weary from his struggle with the Nemean lion, while Athena watches. Heracles skins the Nemean lion with its own claws, and he is often depicted wearing the lion's skin, which makes his body invulnerable. (2) Heracles kills the Lernaean hydra with the help of Iolaus, who cauterizes its necks to prevent them from growing back. (3) Heracles kills the Stymphalian birds by using castanets manufactured for him by Athena to rouse the birds from their nests. (4) Heracles captures the Cretan bull, bringing it to Marathon, in mainland Greece. (5) Heracles devotes a year to chasing the swift, golden-horned Cerynaean hind that is dear to Artemis. (6) Heracles defeats an Amazon, named Hippolyte, in an attempt to gain possession of her belt. The Amazons were a warlike race of women who dwelled in Scythia, shunned men, and fought on horses using a bow. (7) Heracles displays the Erymanthian boar to Eurystheus, who hides in a pot from fright. (8) Heracles defeats the man-eating, fire-breathing mares of Diomedes. (9) Heracles captures the cattle of Geryon, a three-headed, three-bodied monster who guards them. (10) Heracles obtains golden apples, which are guarded by three females called Hesperides along with a snake. To gain help from Atlas in accomplishing this task, Heracles carries the world that had been resting on Atlas's shoulders. (11) Heracles leads Cerberus, a three-headed dog in the Underworld, to the light of day. (12) Heracles cleans the Augean stables, by rerouting a river through them with Athena's assistance.

By surviving the many trials Hera has imposed, Heracles is allowed to enter Olympus, where he marries Hebe, a goddess whose name means "youth." His access to Olympus makes him unique among Greek heroes. In a curious way, then, Hera's hostility toward Heracles allows him the opportunity to become divine. Indeed, Heracles's name, which means "glory of Hera," indicates that his identity is more bound to this goddess than to Zeus, his father. Without her anger, Heracles would not have set out on his labors. Nor would he have earned his transformation into a god. His worship and renown would not have been nearly as widespread as they were in antiquity; indeed, as both a hero and god, Heracles had more cult shrines than any other hero. Heracles was worshipped throughout the Mediterranean world, from Egypt to Spain and Italy, where the Etruscans and the Romans called him Hercules.

Greek tragedians presented Heracles in rather surprising ways. Each tragedy highlights a particular story about Heracles; none focus on his twelve labors. In Euripides's *Alcestis*, for example, Heracles is rather buffoonish and indulges in wine and food. In the play, Heracles arrives unannounced at the house of Admetus, a longtime friend, and behaves like a gluttonous and boisterous houseguest until he realizes that Admetus is in mourning for his wife, Alcestis. Heracles immediately ceases his carousing in order to wrestle with Thanatus (as the god of death is called in this play) and thereby rescue Alcestis for Admetus. By the end of the play, Heracles has amused the audience as an outsized comic figure but also has redeemed himself as a loyal friend.

In stark contrast, the Heracles of Euripides's tragedy *Heracles Maenomenus*, or *The Madness of Heracles,* is portrayed as a murderer and would-be suicide. The play's title offers a partial explanation of the play's theme. *Maenomenus,* which means "driven mad," refers to an episode when Hera sends two goddesses to drive Heracles insane. The play begins when Heracles returns from his labors and discovers that King Lycus, who hopes to gain control of Thebes in Heracles's absence, is about to kill Heracles's wife, Megara, along with his two sons and his adoptive father, Amphitryon. Heracles slays Lycus, but at the very moment that all seems well, Hera drives Heracles into a maddened state. Enraged, he kills his wife and children. Athena then causes Heracles to fall asleep before he can kill Amphitryon. When Heracles wakes and discovers what he has done, he wants to commit suicide. Theseus, the king of Athens, yet another comrade and friend of Heracles, happens by and persuades Heracles to conquer his shame and grief, and choose to live. Many scholars have interpreted Heracles in *The Madness of Heracles* in terms of contemporary psychology. They view him as a man who, suffering from mental illness most likely caused by his warlike and violent experiences, is unable to adapt to civil society. Euripides offers his Athenian audience a positive view of their city and their king (Theseus) and depicts Heracles as neither a buffoon nor a hero, but a broken man.

Sophocles's play *Trachiniae* (also called *Women of Trachis*) treats the last few hours of Heracles's life. Heracles is now married to Deianira, whom he once saved from the centaur Nessus. While ferrying Deianira across a river on his back, Nessus attempted to rape her; Heracles, coming to Deianira's rescue, shot the centaur with a poisonous arrow. Before dying, Nessus told Deianira that his blood was a love potion. Sophocles's play begins years later, as Deianira awaits Heracles's return (much as Megara did in *Heracles Maenomenus*). When Heracles does appear, he is accompanied by his lover, a young girl named Iole. Jealous, Deianira drenches his clothes with Nessus's blood in an attempt to win back his affections. Yet because this blood has been mixed with the very poison Heracles used to kill the centaur, it too is deadly. Heracles's clothing clings to and tears at his skin. As he endures this grievous pain, he learns that Deianira has poisoned him by mistake and has killed herself in grief at her own misguided actions. As Heracles builds himself a pyre on Mount Oeta, he curses Deianira and demands that his son Hyllus marry Iole, despite Hyllus's protests. Although the audience knows that Heracles ascends to Olympus and lives as a god, this does not render his suffering and unrelenting cruelty toward his wife and child comprehensible or palatable. Sophocles's Heracles acts on his desires and convictions; although he is extraordinary in his actions and suffering, he is a much more troubling than sympathetic figure.

Whether in cults, in mythic vignettes, or on the tragic stage, Heracles defies easy classification. He conquers animals, women, and men alike and sometimes even embodies their traits. Visual depictions of him wearing the Nemean lion's skin, for example, blur the differences between his body and that of the lion, thus suggesting Heracles's affinity with animals (Figure 10.4). Heracles is as much a comic hero as a tragic one. He is a mortal of extraordinary proportions and strength who is nonetheless hunted and continually beaten down by the goddess Hera, and yet, paradoxically, he becomes a god himself.

THESEUS

Theseus is a hero who resembles Heracles, in that they both slay beasts and noxious men and win princesses. Yet Athenian hero shrines, festivals, myths, and tragedies transformed Theseus from a Greek hero into a distinctly Athenian, democratic one. Some myths claim Theseus is the son of Poseidon, the god of the sea, but most myths describe him as the son of King Aegeus of Athens. These myths describe how Aegeus, while traveling through Troezen (an area near Athens), slept with and impregnated Aethra, the daughter of his host, and then left his sandals and sword under a rock. Aegeus instructs Aethra to send the child to him when and if he is strong enough to lift the rock and retrieve the items left there. Once reaching maturity, Theseus succeeds at this task and travels from Troezen to Athens. Along the way he has a series of adventures, comparable to those of Heracles. These were depicted on the Temple of Hephaestus (also called the Hephaesteion) near the Athenian agora, where nine of Heracles's labors were also carved, as well as on the Athenian treasury in Delphi. Both buildings suggest that the Athenians created and canonized a series of adventures for Theseus modeled on Heracles's labors, as well as shaped him into a civic hero who embodied and promoted the greatness of Athens. The exact number of Theseus's deeds was not fixed, as in the case of Heracles; unlike Heracles, most of Theseus's adventures involve defeating bandits and thieves, not animals (Figure 10.6).

After defeating beasts and bandits on his journey, Theseus arrives in Athens and displays both sword and sandal to prove he is the son of King Aegeus. He soon learns that Athens must send seven boys and seven girls to Crete to be sacrificed to the Minotaur, a ransom due because the Athenians lost a war with the Cretans (or, in some myths, in recompense for the murder of King Minos's son in Athens). Theseus agrees to challenge and defeat the Minotaur, freeing Athens of this terrible debt. He volunteers to be one of the seven boys and asks that two (or sometimes seven) boys dress as girls and join him in his attempt to kill the Minotaur. When Theseus arrives on Crete, the princess Ariadne agrees to help him. She gives him a silver thread so that he will be able to leave a path through the labyrinth where the Minotaur lives, finding his way safely back after he kills the monster.

10.6 Adventures of Theseus from Troezen to Athens. Red-figured cup, Athens. Codrus Painter, c. 440–430 BCE. British Museum, London. From the top center and reading to the right, Theseus defeats (1) Cercyon, a wrestler in the Eleusis, who would kill all those he defeated; (2) Procrustes, who would place travelers on a bed and would stretch them, if they were short, or cut off their feet, if they were tall, to make them fit his bed; (3) Sciron, a highway robber renowned for kicking travelers off a cliff and into the sea, where they would be devoured by a large sea turtle; (4) the Marathonian bull, formerly called the Cretan bull because Heracles captured it in Crete and deposited it Marathon; (5) Sinis, a bandit who tied travelers to two pine trees that, when sprung loose, tore them apart; and (6) an enormous sow in Crommyon. In the center of the vase, Theseus kills the Minotaur on Crete. *The Trustees of the British Museum / Art Resource, NY, ART177596.*

After he kills the Minotaur, Theseus, his Athenian companions, and Ariadne set sail to return to Athens, but before they reach their destination Theseus abandons or forgets Ariadne on the island of Naxos (Figure 10.7). In some versions, he also forgets to switch his ship's black sails to white ones as he approaches Athens, in order to signal to his father, King Aegeus, that he has succeeded in his task. Seeing the black sails and thinking Theseus is dead, Aegeus drowns himself in the water near Athens, hence becoming the eponymous hero of the Aegean

Sea. Theseus returns to Athens and rules Athens until his death.

Many Athenian myths credit King Theseus with accomplishments that match historical events critical to the development of Athenian democracy. He was said to have invented coinage as well as the "crane dance," a warlike exercise on Delos; established the cult of Aphrodite Pandemus (Of All the People) in Athens (Chapter 5.1); and expanded the Panathenaic festival in honor of Athena (Chapter 6.1). In these ways, the Athenians made Theseus, although a king in myth, a leader responsible for uniting the populations in and around Athens through shared religious and cultural practices. This unity later enabled the people around Athens to become a democratic polity.

Tragedians often depicted Theseus as a benevolent king of Athens. In *Heracles Maenomenus*, described previously, Theseus appears only in the last scene. He counsels Heracles to not kill himself but instead to return to Athens with him. Theseus's offer of asylum conveys that Athens is hospitable to and capable of sustaining as great a figure as Heracles. Moreover, it is a city characterized by Theseus's reason and hospitality even in the face of irrational violence.

10.7 **Theseus and Ariadne on Naxos.** Detail from a red-figure lekythos (oil flask). Circa , 460 BCE. Museo Nazionale Taranto, Taranto, Italy. *Gianni Dagli Orti / The Art Archive at Art Resource, NY, AA389189.*

In Euripides's *Hippolytus*, a myth about Theseus and Heracles forms the backdrop to the drama's main story, in which Theseus plays an important role. When Theseus accompanies Heracles to the land of the Amazons, he produces a son named Hippolytus with the Amazon Hippolyte and then subsequently marries Phaedra, the sister of Ariadne. At the opening of *Hippolytus*, Phaedra falls in love with Hippolytus, her stepson. When he refuses to accept her love, she hangs herself and writes a note claiming Hippolytus has raped her. Believing Phaedra, Theseus calls on Poseidon to punish Hippolytus. Poseidon's bull confronts those pulling Hippolytus's chariot, causing them to rear and entangle Hippolytus in their reins, fatally injuring him (Figure 8.3, page 339). The play closes with a reconciliation between father and dying son: Theseus realizes Phaedra lied and regrets cursing Hippolytus. Hippolytus forgives his father. The contrast between this scene and the last scene of Sophocles's *Trachiniae* could not be greater. In *Trachiniae*, Heracles exceeds and challenges the human community by virtue of his enduring strength and unyielding passions. He is harsh and places unreasonable demands on his son Hyllus. But Theseus, as a hero of democratic Athens, realizes and seeks to make amends for his mistaken trust in Phaedra and for harming his son. Theseus and Hippolytus embrace at the play's end.

In *Suppliants*, also by Euripides, Theseus agrees to meet the request of some Argive women (the suppliants of the play's title) who beg him for help. On their behalf, Theseus travels to Thebes and uses both rhetorical persuasion and military might to convince the Thebans to release the bodies of the Argive war dead so that the women can bury them. Theseus succeeds and, on receiving the Argive bodies, prepares them for burial himself. This extraordinary gesture characterizes Theseus as a leader who is open to persuasion (the hallmark of democracy), respectful of cultural and religious norms, and militarily strong.

Over time, the Athenians embellished stories about Theseus and made him an Athenian hero who embodied their ideals. At the same time, shrines and festivals in Athens dedicated to Theseus increased. He had at least three hero shrines in Athens. The oldest of these, the Theseion, was believed to contain Theseus's bones. Cimon (510–450 BCE), a great Athenian statesman and general, claimed to have found Theseus's bones on Delos, a strategically and religiously important island in the Aegean Sea, and deposited them in the Theseion. The Pyanopsia was the most important Athenian festival concerning Theseus; during this festival young boys imitated Theseus and his companions when they set out to Crete to destroy the Minotaur. Adapted to demonstrate Theseus's commitment to Athens, rather than simply celebrating his defeat of a beast, the story of the Minotaur was recounted over a festival meal. Combining story and ritual to instruct youth in devotion to Athens, the Pyanopsia taught young boys to imitate Theseus's willingness to serve Athens through military as well as political and rhetorical skill. In the Pyanopsia and on the tragic stage, Theseus provided Athenians with an aspirational image of themselves.

OEDIPUS

The story of Oedipus is known to anyone familiar with Greek mythology, in part because, in modern times, psychoanalyst Sigmund Freud described a developmental stage in young children as the "Oedipus complex" and in part because Aristotle singled out Sophocles's tragedy *Oedipus Tyrannus* for praise in *Poetics*, his essay on tragedy. In addition to *Oedipus Tyrannus* (called *Oedipus Rex* in Latin and *Oedipus the King* in English), Sophocles also wrote *Oedipus at Colonus*, dramatizing later portions of Oedipus's biography, namely, his death and transformation into an Attic hero in the Athenian district of Colonus. It also includes Oedipus's placing of a curse on his two sons that results in their deaths (Sophocles describes the aftermath of their deaths in *Antigone*). We know of at least four cult shrines to Oedipus: at Colonus and the Areopagus in Athens, in Thebes, and at Eteonus in Boeotia. Through the timeless works of Sophocles, the story of Oedipus exemplifies a tragic view of

10.8 Oedipus and the Sphinx. Detail from a red-figure krater. Attributed to the Painter of the Birth of Dionysus. Fifth century BCE. Museo Nazionale Taranto, Taranto, Italy. *Gianni Dagli Orti / The Art Archive at Art Resource, NY, AA389194.*

the world in which the abilities of all people, including wise kings, to know themselves are limited compared to the vast knowledge of the gods.

Sophocles's *Oedipus Tyrannus* depicts a single day in Oedipus's life and one central event: his quest to find the murderer of Laius, the former king of Thebes, and to remove him from the city. The presence of the murderer in Thebes is polluting the land and causing a plague. Throughout the play, Oedipus questions and threatens various Theban citizens in his attempt to find the murderer and to banish him from Thebes. The audience learns through Oedipus's interrogations that, many years earlier, King Laius and Queen Jocasta received an oracle saying their child would kill Laius and marry Jocasta. In an effort to avoid fulfilling the oracle, they ordered a shepherd to abandon their infant son in the hills to die. The shepherd took the child but, rather than letting him die, gave him to the childless king and queen of Corinth. Oedipus also learns that Laius was killed while traveling on the road to Thebes.

THE ESSENTIALS
OEDIPUS Οἰδίπους
PARENTAGE King Laius and Queen Jocasta of Thebes
OFFSPRING Antigone, Ismene, Eteocles, and Polynices
CULT SHRINES Athens, Thebes, and Boeotia

Once Oedipus discovers these facts, he begins to piece them together with events in his own life. Oedipus had once received an oracle predicting that he would kill his father and marry his mother. To avoid fulfilling this prophecy, he left Corinth and those whom he believed were his biological parents. He killed an old man who blocked his passage on a road; solved the riddle of the Sphinx, who was harassing the residents of Thebes (a favorite subject for vase painters, as seen in Figure 10.8); married the Theban queen, Jocasta; became king; and produced four children (Antigone, Ismene, Polynices, and Eteocles). By the play's conclusion, the audience, like the characters on stage, realizes that Oedipus, despite his best intentions and piety, has fulfilled the oracle given to his parents and himself. Horrified, Jocasta kills herself. Oedipus finds her body and blinds himself with the pins from her robe.

Sophocles's Oedipus has become a compelling figure since Sophocles's play was staged in ancient Athens, but not because the plight of Oedipus illustrates the inevitability of fate. Rather, Sophocles's Oedipus is a hero who risks everything to discover the buried truth about Laius's murder and to save his city. His fierce determination, coupled with the extraordinary facts of his life, makes him at once a figure whose fate is frightening to contemplate but who, by Greek standards, is also heroic and worthy of veneration.

In *Oedipus at Colonus*, which takes up the story after the dreadful events of *Oedipus Rex*, Oedipus has been exiled from Thebes (as his presence there was polluting the city). Now an outcast, and blind, he wanders accidentaly into the sacred grove of the Furies in Colonus. Assisted by his daughter (and

10.9 Achilles and his mother, Thetis, in a chariot are approached by worshippers. Fragmentary marble relief. Unknown. 350 BCE. *The J. Paul Getty Museum, 78.AA.264, Malibu, California. Digital image courtesy of the Getty's Open Content Program.*

half-sister) Antigone, who has accompanied him, he pleads for mercy first with the Athenian citizens, who demand that he leave the sacred space he has trespassed, and then with Theseus, the beneficent king of Athens. Oedipus reveals a prophecy he has received: when he dies, his body will bring great blessings on the land where he is buried.

These words of Oedipus reveal the beliefs that motivate hero cults, especially the conviction that a hero's body retains the hero's power even after death. Before Theseus accepts Oedipus into his land, Creon, the king of Thebes, attempts to bring Oedipus back to Thebes so that Thebes will benefit from his body. Polynices, Oedipus's son (and half-brother), also appears and asks Oedipus for succor. But Oedipus considers Polynices an ungrateful child and not only refuses to help him but actually curses him and his brother Eteocles, dooming them to kill each other in battle. The play closes when Oedipus dies and his body disappears in the grove of the Furies. Like Heracles, Oedipus too is implacable and indifferent to his sons. In both instances, one senses that although the Greeks thought heroes could and would help those who worshipped them, heroes were, if angered, equally disposed to cause great harm.

ACHILLES

Just as Oedipus is known primarily through the tragedies of Sophocles, Achilles is known primarily through the *Iliad* of Homer. Achilles is also represented in the *Epic Cycle* (a series of epics surviving only in summaries and fragments), a lost tragedy by Aeschylus, vase paintings, and other brief notices in poetry and prose. These sources, which provide Achilles with a life outside of the *Iliad*, describe his birth, childhood, combats, and death. Achilles had a number of cult shrines. The most important ones were located outside of mainland Greece and around the Black Sea, north of Troy. Of these, the most important was one located on the White Island in the northern section of the Black Sea, where it was believed Thetis, a sea goddess and the mother of Achilles, placed his body before it was cremated. There it was said that Achilles could sometimes be seen or heard singing, and there too Achilles was said to live like an immortal. Although the White Island was a real place, its depictions in myth evoked the Islands of the Blessed, where heroes were imagined to dwell in ease and luxury after death.

Achilles is the son of the sea goddess Thetis, who was destined to produce a son who would be greater than Zeus (Figure 10.9). To avoid this eventuality, Zeus compels her to marry a mortal man, Peleus, to whom she bears Achilles. Thetis attempts to burn off (or, in some versions, boil off) the mortal parts of Achilles in order to make him

THE ESSENTIALS

ACHILLES Ἀχιλλεύς

Parentage King Peleus of the Myrmidons and Thetis (a sea goddess)

OFFSPRING Neoptolemus

CULT SHRINES White Island in the Black Sea

immortal. Because she held him by the heels over either the fire or the boiling cauldron, they became his mortal point of vulnerability. (The idiomatic phrase "Achilles's heel" refers to one's weakness.) Peleus raises Achilles, handing him over to the centaur Chiron to be educated. As a soldier, Achilles (like Heracles and Theseus) encounters an Amazon, whom he fights with and kills (in some versions, he falls in love with this Amazon, whose name is Penthesilia, at the moment of her death). He also kills Memnon, an Ethiopian prince, because Memnon killed Antilochus, one of Achilles's companions. Achilles is killed by Apollo or, in some versions, by Paris, both of whom are archers and shoot Achilles in the heel. None of these stories appear in the *Iliad*, which instead traces the course of Achilles's rage at Troy.

"Anger" (*menis*) is the first word of the *Iliad*. This anger belongs to Achilles, who rails against Agamemnon, one of the commanders of the Greek forces at Troy. Achilles nurses his anger for the first two-thirds of the *Iliad*. Agamemnon confiscates Briseis, a young Trojan girl who is Achilles's war prize, because Achilles has disrespectfully urged Agamemnon to return the young girl Chryseis, also a war prize, to her father. By taking Briseis, Agamemnon both disregards the martial superiority of Achilles and violates his notion of fairness. Enraged, Achilles refuses to help Agamemnon and the Greeks in the battle against the Trojans. Moved by Greek losses, Patroclus, Achilles's comrade (and, perhaps, lover) convinces Achilles to let him wear Achilles's armor and fight the Trojans. When Patroclus is killed by Hector, the bravest son of Priam and the greatest Trojan warrior, Achilles decides to rejoin the battle, even though he knows that if he fights at Troy, he will die.

Achilles first attacks the Trojans near the banks of the river Scamander (Book 21). When he begins to throw their bodies into the river, thus polluting its waters, the river (or the god of the river) becomes angry and begins to raise great waves and chase Achilles. When Achilles accepts that he cannot fight the river, he instead seeks out Hector and kills him. The epic finds its resolution with the abatement of Achilles's anger during his prolonged mourning of Patroclus and the funeral games Achilles conducts in his honor. Achilles then accepts the supplications of Priam, the Trojan king, who asks Achilles to return his son Hector's body. In complying with Priam's request, Achilles fully accepts the reality of his own impending death, as well as the measure and cost of human empathy and love: Achilles, like Hector, will be mourned by his father, whom he will never see again (Book 24). The epic closes with the mourning songs of Hecuba (the Trojan queen and Hector's mother), Andromache (Hector's wife), and Helen (the Spartan queen whose presence in Troy precipitated the war). They lament the life of Hector, who tried and failed to save his city from Achilles's anger. Their words wrap Achilles's grief in their own, transforming the enmity between Greeks and Trojans into a universal sorrow and reminding their listeners that all heroes, however great, must die.

HOMER, FROM THE *ILIAD*

The following excerpts from the *Iliad* describe Achilles as he directs his anger at Agamemnon (and, by extension, the Greeks), attacks the Trojan river Scamander, kills Hector, and finally releases Hector's body. (Line numbers for each excerpt correspond with the numbering for each complete Book.) (Translated by Barry B. Powell.)

⚜
BEFORE YOU READ
⚜

- When Achilles speaks with his mother on the beach, he tells her about the conflict he had with Agamemnon. How does the setting of this scene as well as Achilles's behavior and words characterize him?

- The last scene of Book 1 takes place at a banquet among the gods on Olympus in which a quarrel takes place. Compare this divine quarrel, its consequences and general atmosphere, with the human quarrel and its consequences that Achilles has described to Thetis. How do the differences in these scenes offer a view of the world of heroes in comparison to the world of gods?

- Achilles fights the river Scamander at the height of his battle fury (Book 21). How does this scene characterize Achilles as a hero? Compare Achilles's behavior while fighting the river with his behavior in his encounter with Priam in Book 24. How has he changed?

- How does Achilles fit (or not fit) the description of heroes offered in the first few sections of this chapter?

HOMER, FROM THE *ILIAD* (c. 750 BCE)

FROM BOOK 1

But Achilles burst into tears, and he withdrew
apart from his companions. He sat on the shore beside
the gray sea. He stared over the huge deep.
He raised his arms and prayed to his dear mother:
"Mother, because you bore me to a short life, Olympian   340
Zeus, who thunders on high, ought to have put honor
in my hands. But he has given me no honor at all. For the
son of Atreus, whose rule is wide, has dishonored me.
He has come and taken my girl."

Thus he spoke, tears
streaming down his face. His revered mother heard him   345
as she sat beside her aged father in the depths of the sea.
Swiftly she came forth like a mist from the gray sea. She sat
down before him, as he wept. She took him by the hand
and she spoke his name: "My son, why do you weep?
What sorrow has come to your heart? Tell me, don't hide it,   350
that we both may know."

Then, groaning heavily spoke
Achilles, the fast runner: "You know! Why do I need
to tell the whole story when you already know? We went
to Thebes, the sacred city of Eëtion. We burned it to the ground
and took everything. The sons of the Achaeans then divided
        the loot   355
among themselves. For the son of Atreus they chose
Chryseïs, whose cheeks are beautiful. Chryses then came
to the fast ships of the bronze-shirted Achaeans, a holy man,
a priest of Apollo the far-shooter. He wanted
to free his daughter, and he brought boundless ransom,   360
holding the wreaths of Apollo the far-shooter
around a golden staff. And he begged all the Achaeans, and
above all the two sons of Atreus, the leaders of the people.
All the Achaeans shouted we should respect the holy man
and accept the shining ransom. But Agamemnon, the son   365
of Atreus, did not like this, and he roughly sent the man
away, and he lay on a strong word. Angry, the old man
went off. Apollo heard him as he prayed,
because he was dear to the god, and he sent an evil
shaft against the Argives. The people died like flies.   370
The missiles of the god fell everywhere through the broad
camp of the Achaeans. A knowing prophet explained
the doing of the god who strikes from a long way off.
Straightaway I was first to insist that we appease the god,
but anger seized the son of Atreus. He stood straight up   375
and lay down a threat, which now has come to pass.
The bright-eyed Achaeans are taking Chryseïs in a fast ship
to Chrysê, and they have gifts for the god. As for the other girl,
Briseïs, the heralds have taken her from my tent,
she whom the sons of the Achaeans gave to me.   380
    "But you, if you can, protect your son. Go to
Olympos and beg Zeus, if ever you have pleased him

in word or in something you've done. For I often heard
you boast in my father's halls that you alone
of the gods fended off disaster from the son of Kronos,   385
he of the dark clouds, when the other Olympians
wanted to tie him up—Hera and Poseidon
and Pallas Athena. But you went to him and set him
free from the bonds, having swiftly called to high Olympos
the hundred-hander whom gods call Briareos, but men call   390
Aigaion. He was stronger than his father. He sat
down beside the son of Kronos, glorying in his power.
The blessed gods were frightened of him and did not bind Zeus.
   "Remind him of this incident. Sit by his side.
Seize his knees—to see if he might help the Trojans   395
pen the Achaeans by the prows of their ships, their backs
to the sea. May they die like dogs! Thus may all share
in the wisdom of their chief, and Agamemnon, the wide ruler,
may know that he went insane when he dishonored
the best of the Achaeans."   400

                    Thetis answered him, pouring
down tears: "O my child, why ever did I bear you,
born to sorrow? I wish that you might have stayed
by the ships without weeping, without pain, since your life
is fated to be all too short. As it is, your fate is soon
upon you. You are more wretched than all men.   405
Therefore I bore you, in our halls, to an evil life.
   "I will make your request of Zeus, who delights
in the thunder. I will myself ascend Olympos, clad in snow,
to see if I can persuade him. You stay here, nursing
your anger, beside the swift ships. Don't fight any more.   410
Yesterday Zeus went to Ocean, to the Aethiopians who do
no wrong, to a feast, and all gods went with him. On the twelfth day
he will return to Olympos. Then I shall go to the bronze-tiled
house of Zeus. I will take him by the knees and I think I will
persuade him."   415

          So speaking, she went off. She left Achilles
there in his rage on account of the slim-waisted woman,
whom Agamemnon took away by force, against his will.

*[Omitted: The Greeks return the young girl Chryseis, Agamemnon's war
prize, to her father.]*

When twelve days had passed, all the gods, who live
forever, went in a band to Olympos, with Zeus in the lead.
Thetis did not forget the request of her son. She arose from
the wave of the sea. Early in morning she went up
to heaven and Olympos. She found the son of Kronos,   485
who sees things from far off, sitting apart from the others
on a steep peak of Olympos, which has many ridges. She sat
down near him and took hold of his knees with her left hand,
while with her right she gripped him beneath the chin.
Beseeching, she spoke to Zeus the king, the son of Kronos: 490

   "Zeus, our father, if ever I have helped you among the
immortals either in word or in something I did,
fulfill for me this desire. Give honor to my son
who, more than others, is born to a quick death.
But as it is, now the king of men Agamemnon   495
has not given him honor. He has taken away his prize.
He holds it! But give him honor, O Olympian, counselor Zeus.
Give power to the Trojans until the Achaeans honor my son
and increase his honor." So she spoke.

                 The cloud-gatherer
Zeus said nothing, but sat in silence for a long time.   500
As Thetis had clasped his knees, so now she held him
close, and asked again: "Make me this firm promise,
bow your head to it—or turn me away. You have nothing
to fear, so that I may know how of all the gods I have
the least honor . . ."   505

         Zeus, who assembles the clouds,
was deeply disturbed. He said: "This is a bad
business. You will set me on to quarrel with Hera, who
will anger me with her words of reproach. Even as it is
she is always on my back among the deathless gods, saying
that in the battle I help the Trojans. So leave   510
now or she may notice something! Yes, I'll take care
of this. I'll bring it to pass. Here, let me bow
my head to you so that you will believe me,
for this is the surest sign I give among the immortals—
I will never take it back. It is no illusion. It will always   515
come to pass, whatever I nod my head to."

Then the son of Kronos nodded with his brows,
dark like lapis lazuli, and his immortal locks fell all around
the head of the deathless king. Olympos shook.
    After the two took counsel together in this fashion,   520
they departed, Thetis descending from shining Olympos
into the deep sea, and Zeus went to his house. All the
gods stood up from their seats when he entered. No one
dared to await his coming, but they all stood up.

    So he sat there on his throne, but Hera   525
knew he had made a deal with Thetis of the
silver ankles, the daughter of the Old Man of the Sea.
She spoke to Zeus at once, the son of Kronos,
with mocking words: "Who, my clever fellow,
have you been making deals with? You just love that,   530
to stand apart from me and make judgments about things
that you have decided in secret. Nor do you ever
bother willingly to tell me what you have been up to."

    The father of men and gods said the following:
"Hera, don't hope to know all my thoughts! It will be   535
the worse for you if you do, although I sleep with you.
What you should know, you will know before all other gods
or men. But what I wish to devise apart from
the gods, don't ask about it. Make no inquiries!"

    Hera, with eyes like a cow, the revered one,   540
then said to him: "O most dread son of Kronos!
What a thing you have said! In the past I have never asked
you about your affairs, nor made inquiry, but you
fancied anything you like. But now I greatly
fear in my heart that silver-ankled Thetis has led you   545
astray, the daughter of the Old One of the Sea.
She came this morning and sat beside you and gripped
your knees. I think you promised her that you would give
honor to Achilles, that you would destroy a multitude
beside the ships of the Achaeans."   550

               Zeus, who assembles
the clouds, then replied: "You bitch! You have your ideas,

and nothing gets past you! Nonetheless, there is nothing you can do
about it. You will only drift further from my heart, which will
be the more shivery for you. If this is what I'm thinking,
I must like it. So shut up and sit down! Obey my word,　　　　　555
or all the gods in Olympos will do you no good as I close
in and lay upon you my powerful hands!"

　　　　　　　　　　　So he spoke,
and the cow-eyed revered Hera took fright. In silence
she took her seat, curbing the impulse of her heart.

　　The Olympian gods in the house of Zeus were troubled　　　560
by what had happened, when Hephaistos, known for his craft,
said this, bringing kindness to his dear mother Hera
of the white arms: "Surely this will be a nasty turn,
scarcely to be born, if the two of you quarrel like this
over men who die. You bring squabbling into the midst　　　565
of the gods. There will be no pleasure in the feast, when trouble
has the upper hand. I advise my mother, whom I know to be
sensible in her own right, to be kind to our dear father, so that
he does not tangle with her again and stir up trouble at the feast.

　　Why, what if the Olympian, master of the lightning, wished to blast　　570
us from our seats? For his strength is much the greater.
So—please calm him with gentle words. Then the Olympian
will be kind to us."

　　　　　　　So he spoke, and leaping up he placed
a two-handled cup in his mother's hand, and said to her:
"Courage, my mother! Hang on, though you are irritated,　　　575
or else I may see you beaten with my own eyes.
You are so dear to me, but though grieving you may be unable
to do anything about it. The Olympian is not someone
you want to go up against. Why, I remember the time
that I was eager to save you and he grabbed me by the foot　　　580
and threw me from the divine threshold. I fell all day.
When the sun was setting, I landed on the island of Lemnos,
barely alive. There, after my fall, the Sintian men
quickly cared for me."

　　　　　　　So he spoke, and white-armed
Hera smiled, and, smiling, she took in hand the cup　　　585

from her son. Then Hephaistos, moving from left to right,
poured out wine to all the gods, drawing sweet nectar
from the mixing bowl. An unquenchable laughter
arose among the blessed beings when they saw Hephaistos
puffing along through the palace.   590

                  So they dined all day
until the sun went down. They did not lack for anything
in the equal feast, not the lovely lyre that Apollo
played, and the Muses sang in beautiful response.
But when the bright light of the sun had disappeared,
they went to lie down, each to his own house,   595
where for each one the lame god, famous Hephaistos,
had made a palace with his cunning skill. Zeus,
the Olympian, the master of lightning, mounted his own bed.
There it was always his custom to rest, where sweet
sleep came to him. He went up and fell asleep,   600
and Hera of the golden throne slept beside him.

FROM BOOK 21

              So he spoke, and out of the bank
he pulled his bronze spear, and he left Asteropaios there
lying on the sand after he had taken away his life, and the dark
water lapped around him. The eels and the fishes finished
off Asteropaios, tearing away the fat from his kidneys,
plucking it away as Achilles went his way among the Paeonians,   205
masters of the chariot, who fled along the bands of the swirling
river, because they saw their best man killed in the savage
contendings at the hands and sword of the son of Peleus

Then he killed Thersilochos and Mydon and Astypylos
and Mnesos and Thrasios and Ainios and Ophelestes—   210
and swift Achilles would have killed a lot more except that
the deep-swirling river spoke to him in anger, taking on the form
of a man and speaking from the whirling depths: "O Achilles,
you are strong beyond all other men, and you do evil things
beyond all men. For the gods themselves are always   215
on your side. If the son of Kronos has given it to you
to destroy all the men of Troy, at least drive them
out of my stream and do your dirty work on the plain.

For my lovely streams are filled with dead bodies,
and I can no longer run my waters into the bright sea   220
because it is crammed with corpses that you ruthlessly kill.
So leave off! Astonishment holds me, O leader of the people!"

    Achilles the fast runner then answered him: "So it will be,
O Skamandros, nurtured of Zeus, just as you command.
But I shall not give over killing the Trojans before I have driven   225
them into the city and made trial of Hector in the hand-to-hand.
Either he will destroy me, or I him."

                    So speaking, Achilles
leaped on the Trojans like a power from the spirit world.
And then the deep-swirling river spoke to Apollo: "You
of the silver bow, son of Zeus—Why have you not kept   230
the commandments of the son of Kronos, who strictly ordered
you to stand by the Trojans and to defend them until the late-setting
sun comes forth and casts the deep-soiled earth into shadow?"

    Xanthos spoke and Achilles, famed for his spear, sprang
from the bank and leaped into the middle of the river.   235
But Skamandros rushed upon him with a swelling flood,
and he roused all his streams, stirring them up, and he swept along
the many bodies of the dead that lay thick within his bed,
whom Achilles had killed. These he cast forth onto the dry land,
bellowing like a bull, but the living he saved beneath   240
his beautiful streams, hiding them in the enormous deep eddies.

    A sudden tumultuous wave stood up around Achilles,
and the stream fell over his shield and drove him backward.
He could not stand. He grabbed onto an elm tree with his hands—
shapely, tall—but it fell uprooted and carried away the whole   245
bank with it. The elm stretched over the beautiful streams
with its thick branches, damming the river, falling entirely
into the river. In fear Achilles tried to leap out of the eddy
and to run with his powerful feet over the plain, but the great god
did not let up. He rushed on him with his dark-crested wave   250
so that he might hold back powerful Achilles from his labor,
and ward off destruction from the Trojans. But the son of Peleus
sprang backward as far as a cast spear, like a swooping black eagle,
a hunter who is both the strongest and the swiftest of birds.

Like him, Achilles darted back and on his breast   255
the bronze rang terribly. Swerving, he ran beneath the flood,
but the river flowed just behind him with a great roar.

   As when a man draws off dark water from a spring
to flow beside his plants and garden plots, holding a mattock
in his hands as he clears away obstructions in the channel,   260
and as the water flows all the pebbles beneath are pushed
along and the water murmurs as it glides swiftly down a
slope and outstrips even the man who guides it—even so
the wave of the stream overtook Achilles although he was fleet
of foot: For gods are stronger than men!   265

            For as long
as the good Achilles, the fast runner, tried to make a stand
against the river and to learn if all the gods who hold the broad sky
were putting him to flight, for so long the great wave of the
Zeus-nourished river would strike his shoulders from above,
and he sprang up high with his feet, agonized in spirit.   270
The river ran at his knees with a vicious current, and it
snatched away the ground from his feet.

            The son of Peleus
groaned and looked into the broad heaven: "Father Zeus, why does
not any one of the gods undertake to save me, pitiful as I am now?
If I escape, I should not mind dying later! I do not blame   275
any other of the heavenly gods so much as my mother,
who tricked me with lying words, saying that I would perish
from the fast missiles of Apollo beneath the wall of the heavily armed
Trojans. I wish that Hector had killed me there, the best man
they have. Then a brave man would have been my killer,   280
and a brave man he would have killed. But am I now
destined to die a miserable death, trapped in the great river
like a swine-herder boy swept away as he tries to cross
a water course in the winter?"

          So he spoke, and very quickly
Poseidon and Athena went to him and stood close by,   285
taking on the appearance of men. Holding his hand
in their hands, they made pledges of trust with words.
Among them Poseidon, the shaker of the earth, began to speak:

"Son of Peleus, don't tremble so, nor be so afraid.
We two are your helpers from the gods, and Zeus has given   290
his approval to Pallas Athena and me. It is not your destiny
to die by the river. The river shall soon let up. You will know
it yourself! But we shall give you some good advice,
if you will listen: Do not let your hands rest from the wicked
war before you have penned up the Trojan army   295
behind the famous walls of Ilion—those who get away!
Then get back to the ships, once you have taken Hector's life.
We grant that you gain victory."

FROM BOOK 24

    The aides did not notice great Priam
as he came in. Standing nearby, he took Achilles' knees
in his hands, and Priam kissed the terrible man-killing   465
hands that had taken so many of his sons. As when a painful
madness takes hold of a man and he kills someone
in his homeland, then comes to another people, to the house
of a rich man, and wonder takes hold of those who see him,—
even so Achilles was amazed when he saw godlike Priam.   470
And the others were amazed too and glanced at one another.

    Making supplication, Priam spoke to Achilles:
"Remember your own father, O Achilles like to the gods!
He is old as I am, on the wretched threshold of old age.
Probably those who live around him are wearing him down,   475
and there is no one to ward off ruin and disaster.
But at least he rejoices in his heart when he hears that you
are alive, and he hopes every day that he will see his dear
son returning from Troy. But I have received an evil fate,
because I fathered many sons who were the best in broad   480
Troy, but of them I do not think that any remain.
I had fifty sons when the sons of the Achaeans came, nineteen
from one woman, the others from women in the palace.
Though they were many, the fury of Ares has driven
most of them to their knees. And he who was left   485
to me, who by himself protected the city and those within it—
you have just killed him as he struggled to defend his homeland—
Hector! On his account I have come to the ships of the Achaeans

to ransom him from you. I bring boundless ransom.
So respect the gods, Achilles, and take pity on me,   490
remembering your own father. For I am far more to be pitied
than he—I who did what no man on earth has ever dared
to do—to stretch the hands of my son's killer to my mouth."

    So Priam spoke, and he stirred in Achilles a great urge
to weep for his own father. Taking Priam by the hand   495
he gently pushed the old man away. And so the two men
thought of those who had died. Priam wept copiously for Hector
the killer of men, as he groveled before the feet of Achilles.
And Achilles cried for his own father and now, again, for Patroklos.
Their wailing filled the hut.   500

                But when valiant Achilles
had his fill of wailing, and the desire for it had departed
from his heart and limbs, immediately he rose from his seat.
He raised up the old man with his hand, taking pity on his white
head and his white beard, and he spoke words that went
    like arrows:
"Yes, you wretched man, truly you have suffered many evils   505
in your heart. How did you dare to come alone to the ships
of the Achaeans beneath the eyes of the man who killed your many
fine sons? Your heart must be iron! But come, sit on a chair.
We will let our sufferings lie quiet in our hearts, though burdened
by them. There is nothing to be gained from cold lament.   510
    "For so have the gods spun the thread for wretched
mortals— to live in pain, while they are without care.
Two jars of gifts that he gives are set into the floor of Zeus,
one of evils, the other of good things. To whomever
Zeus who delights in the thunder gives a mixed portion,   515
that man receives now evil, now good. But to the man
to whom he gives only pain, he has made him to be roughly
treated, and ravening hunger drives him over the shining
earth. He walks dishonored by gods and by men.
    "So the gods gave to Peleus wonderful gifts   520
from birth. He exceeded all men in wealth and riches,
and he ruled over the Myrmidons, and the gods gave him
a goddess for a wife, although he is mortal. But to him
the god also gave evil, because in his halls there is no
offspring who will one day rule. He fathered a single child,   525

doomed to an early death. And I will not tend him
when he grows old, for I sit here in Troy very far
from my homeland, bringing misery to you and your children.
    "And yet, old man, we hear that in earlier times
you were rich—all the territory between Lesbos out to sea,   530
the seat of Makar, and inland to Phrygia, and to the boundless
Hellespont. They say that you, old man, surpassed in wealth
and in the number of your sons all those that lived in these lands.
But from the time that the dwellers in heaven brought you
this curse, there is always fighting around your city, and the   535
killing of men. Bear up! Don't be complaining forever in your heart.
It's no use to bemoan your son, for he will never live again,
no matter what you do."

            Then the old man godlike
Priam answered him: "Please don't ask me to sit on a chair,
O Achilles, fostered by Zeus, so long as Hector lies among   540
the ships without the proper care due to the dead. But release
him quickly so that I may see him with my own eyes. Take
the abundant ransom that I have brought you. May you enjoy
these things, and may you come to the land of your fathers,
for from the first you have let me remain alive and behold   545
the light of the sun."

            Then looking angrily from beneath his brows
Achilles the fast runner spoke: "Don't rile me, old man!
I fully intend to let you have Hector. My mother came to me
as a messenger from Zeus, she who bore me, the daughter
of the Old Man of the Sea. And I know full well in my heart,   550
O Priam, nor does it escape me, that some god has led
you to the swift ships of the Achaeans. For no mortal would
dare come to the camp, no, not even one very young. And he
would not escape the notice of the guards, nor would he easily
open the bolts of our gates. Therefore, do not stir more of wrath   555
in me, or perhaps I will *not* spare you within the huts, old man—
even though you are a suppliant—and so transgress the commands
of Zeus."

    Thus Achilles spoke, and the old man
was afraid, and did what he said. Then the son of Peleus sprang
forth from the house like a lion, and he was not alone, for with him   560

followed two of his aides, the warriors Automedon and Alkimos,
whom he honored above all his companions after the dead
Patroklos. They unharnessed the horses and the mules
from the yoke, and they led in the herald, the crier of the old man,
and they set him on a chair. They took down from the well-polished   565
car the boundless ransom for Hector's head. They left two cloaks
and a finely woven shirt so that Achilles could wrap the corpse
and free him to be taken home. Then Achilles summoned
two slave girls to wash the body and anoint it, moving the corpse
to the side so that Priam could not see his son and in his grief   570
be unable to restrain his anger if he saw him, and Achilles'
own heart be then roused to anger so that he killed Priam
against the strict command of Zeus.

                    When the slave girls
had washed the body and anointed it with olive oil, they put
a beautiful cloak and a shirt around him. Achilles himself   575
raised Hector up and placed him on a bier. Together with
his aides, Achilles then lifted him into the polished wagon.

  And then Achilles groaned and called out to his companion
by name: "Don't be angry, Patroklos, if you learn, though you are
in the house of Hades, that I have given up the valiant Hector   580
to his dear father. He brought a proper ransom, and I will
give you as many as is fitting of the things he brought."

  So he spoke, and then glorious Achilles went back into his hut.
He sat on the inlaid chair on the opposite wall from which
he had arisen, and he spoke to Priam: "Your son is given back,   585
old man, just as you requested. He lies on a bier. At dawn
you will see him when you take him from here. Now let us
think of food.
  "For even Niobê with the lovely hair
thought of food. Twelve were her children who perished
in her halls, six daughters and six lusty sons. Apollo killed   590
the boys with his silver bow, for he was angry at Niobê,
and Artemis, who rejoices in arrows, killed the girls.
For Niobê had matched herself with their mother, Leto
with the lovely cheeks. Niobê said that Leto had borne
two children, but she herself had given birth to many. And so   595
Apollo and Artemis, though they were only two, killed all

of Niobê's children. For nine days they lay in their gore, and
there was no one to bury them, because the son of Kronos had turned
the people into stones. But on the tenth day the heavenly gods
buried them, and Niobê bethought herself of food, for she was   600
wasting away with her weeping.

                         "Now somewhere amid
the rocks, in the lonely mountains, on Sipylos, where they say
the beds of goddesses are, the divine nymphs who dance
around the Acheloos river—there, although she is a stone,
she broods over her agonies sent by the gods.   605

                              "So come,
good old man, let us also think of food. Then you can bewail
your dear son, when you have carried him to Ilion. He will
cost you many tears."
                 So Achilles spoke.

10.2 THEORY

THE PLOT OF THE HERO'S STORY

The urban landscape of every Greek city was filled with stories of heroes.
Battles of heroes, such as Heracles or Theseus, against centaurs or Amazons
were a popular motif on sculptural reliefs high on a temple's walls. Many
graves might be distinguished by votive offerings of coins, cups, and jewelry
near a plaque that named and showed a hero banqueting. Additionally, the
adventures of heroes, more than those of gods and goddesses, occupied a
central place in Greek literature, such as epic, tragedy, history, and philosophy. At festivals, choral songs celebrated heroes, and tragedies were often
named after the heroes who served as their protagonists. Not surprisingly,
then, one scholarly response to the large number of stories about Greek
heroes has been to describe and organize them in order to begin the work of
interpretation. To this end, classical scholars have found the work of Vladimir
Propp (1895–1970) and FitzRoy Raglan (Chapter 11.2) particularly useful.

Propp and Raglan generated lists of heroes' adventures that classical
scholars have borrowed to study Greek heroes. Although other approaches are
possible—the religious dimensions of their worship can be studied (Chapter
10.1), or the historical elements of heroes' tales can be used to discover their
importance in a particular place and time, as in the case of Theseus (Chapter 10.1)—the descriptive lists developed by Propp and Raglan have proved especially useful. They have helped scholars distinguish Greek heroes from

heroes in other societies, locate and interpret stories and features unique to a particular Greek hero, link heroes' stories to their social context, and (more recently) compare Greek heroes and heroines. In this chapter, we look at the work of Propp to understand heroes; in Chapter 11, we study Raglan's work and explore its usefulness for studying heroines.

In his book *The Morphology of the Folktale* (1928), Propp studied a small number of Russian fairy tales collected by philologist Alexander Afanasyev (1826–1871). Although "folktale" replaces "fairy tale" in the title of his book, Propp studied only fairy tales, which he, like other scholars, considered a subset of folktales. Whereas both are anonymous oral tales, fairy tales often feature animals, witches, and magical items (Figure 10.10). Because Propp began his scholarly career as a linguist, he aimed to apply a linguistic analysis to fairy tales. That is, he attempted to uncover the "grammar," or hidden rules, that he believed governed how the elements of fairy tales were combined. Through this analysis, he also hoped to show why fairy tales were similar to one another (for example, elements and characters almost always appear in threes—three brothers, three wishes; etc.—but never in twos or fours). Comparison, rather than linguistic reasoning, has informed how other scholars have used Propp's work.

To analyze fairy tales, Propp divided them into the "component parts" of characters and actions. He grouped characters into types: for example, he as-

10.10 Ivan Yakovlevich Bilibin, illustration for the fairy tale "Ivan Tsarevich, the Firebird, and the Gray Wolf" (1902). In this tale, one of the many studied by Vladimir Propp, Ivan, the hero, succeeds in catching the Firebird, winning a princess, and securing a kingdom. In his many journeys into the woods, he meets a talking wolf and several kings, dies and is rejuvenated, and finally outsmarts his two evil older brothers. The story of Ivan has the trappings of many fairy tales (talking animals, deep forests, and three brothers) that most Greek myths about heroes lack. Found in the collection of the Museum of the Goznak, Moscow, Russia. *HIP / Art Resource, NY, AR930934.*

signed the category of "villain" to ogres, evil kings, harmful dragons, and similar malevolent beings. In this way, Propp determined that there are seven broad types of characters, which he called *dramatis personae*, in fairy tales: the hero, the false hero, the princess (or the prize), the villain, the dispatcher, the donor, and the helper. Propp then organized the actions of these seven types into thirty-one broad categories, which he called *functions*. For example, in many fairy tales the hero is given an item that has magical properties, a function Propp described as when "the hero acquires use of a magical agent." Propp also discovered that even though few fairy tales include all thirty-one functions (most have far fewer), the sequence in which the functions appear never varies. This sequence of events—the plot—is one of the most important principles in Propp's analysis. (For a comparable tally of the events in the heroine's tale, see Raglan's list in Chapter 11.2.) The following summary is taken directly from Propp's list in *Morphology of the Folktale*. Some functions are abbreviated, and some vocabulary has been changed for clarity.

1. A family member of the hero departs from home.
2. The hero is warned not to do something.
3. The hero violates this warning.
4. The villain attempts to gain information about his victim.
5. The villain gains information about his victim.
6. The villain attempts to deceive his victim to get his possessions or his person.
7. The victim unknowingly submits to the villain's deception.
8. The villain causes harm to a family member, and/or a family member lacks or wants something.
9. The hero responds to a request or command and departs or is dispatched.
10. A seeker (who is sometimes the hero) decides on an action.
11. The hero departs.
12. The hero is tested to see if he is worthy of help.
13. The hero reacts to the actions of a donor.
14. The hero acquires use of a magical agent.
15. The hero is led to the location of a desired object.
16. The hero and the villain join in combat.
17. The hero is branded.
18. The villain is defeated.
19. The initial lack is resolved.
20. The hero returns.
21. The hero is pursued.
22. The hero is rescued from pursuit.
23. The hero, unrecognized, arrives home or in another country.
24. A false hero presents false claims.
25. A difficult task is presented to the hero.
26. The task is completed.
27. The hero is recognized.
28. The false hero or villain is exposed.
29. The hero is given a new appearance.
30. The villain is punished.
31. The hero ascends the throne.

If Propp's thirty-one functions seem too numerous to be useful, they can be divided into three discrete sections that align with van Gennep's three-part division of initiation rites (Chapters 8.2 and 9.2). These do not appear in Propp's book. Functions 1–11 correspond to van Gennep's first stage (the preliminal period, or separation); functions 12–19 correspond to van Gennep's second stage (the liminal period, or transition/trials); and functions 20–31 correspond to van Gennep's third stage (the postliminal period, or reintegration into society). These striking correspondences suggest that many kinds of storytelling, whether fairy tales, folktales, or myths, share patterns with initiation rites.

In his introduction to Propp's *Morphology*, Alan Dundes acknowledges that Propp did not set out to analyze the content or historical dimensions of fairy tales. Yet he offers some ideas about how Propp's system might be used to explore a wide range of tales and relate them to their social context. For example, Dundes considers the relationship between the structure of a culture's fairy tales and the structure of a culture's "ideal success story." This question offers a starting point for a consideration of the myths of Greek heroes. For example, if all the stories from a culture include a marriage between a man and a woman (function 31 in Propp's list), then the consistent inclusion of this function suggests that marriage is a critical event in the lives of men. Dundes also poses a series of questions about how boys as well as girls might imagine the roles of villains and donors. In so doing, Dundes raises a perplexing question about Propp's analysis that we address in Chapter 11.2: does Propp's list of thirty-one functions apply as well to myths about heroines?

VLADIMIR PROPP, FROM *MORPHOLOGY OF THE FOLKTALE*

BEFORE YOU READ

Propp's list of thirty-one functions has frequently been used to organize and describe myths about Greek heroes.

- Try applying Propp's analysis to myths about Achilles, Heracles, or Theseus. After describing a few Greek heroes in terms of Propp's functions, consider whether certain functions always appear or never appear. What conclusions can you draw from your findings?

- Does using Propp's "measuring stick" allow a mythologist to link stories about Greek heroes to larger cultural or social concepts, such as Greek ideals of masculinity or male citizenship?

- Compare Propp's thirty-one functions to van Gennep's initiatory patterns. How are these two systems for dividing up myths with male protagonists similar? How are they different?

- Do the similarities (or differences) between these two systems lead to you draw conclusions about their usefulness for understanding heroes in ancient Greece?

VLADIMIR PROPP, FROM *MORPHOLOGY OF THE FOLKTALE* (1968, 2010)

THE METHOD AND MATERIAL

Let us first of all attempt to formulate our task. As already stated in the foreword, this work is dedicated to the study of fairy tales. The existence of fairy tales as a special class is assumed as an essential working hypothesis. By "fairy tales" are meant at present those tales classified by Aarne under numbers 300 to 749. This definition is artificial, but the occasion will subsequently arise to give a more precise determination on the basis of resultant conclusions. We are undertaking a comparison of the themes of these tales. For the sake of comparison we shall separate the component parts of fairy tales by special methods; and then, we shall make a comparison of tales according to their components. The result will be a morphology (i.e., a description of the tale according to its component parts and the relationship of these components to each other and to the whole).

What methods can achieve an accurate description of the tale? Let us compare the following events:

1. A tsar gives an eagle to a hero. The eagle carries the hero away to another kingdom.[†]
2. An old man gives Súcenko a horse. The horse carries Súcenko away to another kingdom.
3. A sorcerer gives Iván a little boat. The boat takes Iván to another kingdom.
4. A princess gives Iván a ring. Young men appearing from out of the ring carry Iván away into another kingdom, and so forth.[1]

Both constants and variables are present in the preceding instances. The names of the dramatis personae change (as well as the attributes of each), but neither their actions nor functions change. From this we can draw the inference that a tale often attributes identical actions to various personages. This makes possible the study of the tale *according to the functions of its dramatis personae.*

[†] "*Car' daet udal'cu orla. Orcl unosit udal'ca v inoe carstvo*" (p. 28). Actually, in the tale referred to (old number 104a = new number 171), the hero's future bride, Poljusa, tells her father the tsar that they have a *ptica-kolpalica* (technically a spoonbill, although here it may have meant a white stork), which can carry them to the bright world. For a tale in which the hero flies away on an eagle, see 71a (= new number 128). [Louis A. Wagner]

We shall have to determine to what extent these functions actually represent recurrent constants of the tale. The formulation of all other questions will depend upon the solution of this primary question: how many functions are known to the tale?

Investigation will reveal that the recurrence of functions is astounding. Thus Bába Jagá, Morózko, the bear, the forest spirit, and the mare's head test and reward the stepdaughter. Going further, it is possible to establish that characters of a tale, however varied they may be, often perform the same actions. The actual means of the realization of functions can vary, and as such, it is a variable. Morózko behaves differently than Bába Jagá. But the function, as such, is a constant. The question of *what* a tale's dramatis personae do is an important one for the study of the tale, but the questions of *who* does it and *how* it is done already fall within the province of accessory study. The functions of characters are those components which could replace Veselóvskij's "motifs," or Bédier's "elements." We are aware of the fact that the repetition of functions by various characters was long ago observed in myths and beliefs by historians of religion, but it was not observed by historians of the tale (cf. Wundt and Negelein[2]). Just as the characteristics and functions of deities are transferred from one to another, and, finally, are even carried over to Christian saints, the functions of certain tale personages are likewise transferred to other personages. Running ahead, one may say that the number of functions is extremely small, whereas the number of personages is extremely large. This explains the two-fold quality of a tale: its amazing multiformity, picturesqueness, and color, and on the other hand, its no less striking uniformity, its repetition.

Thus the functions of the dramatis personae are basic components of the tale, and we must first of all extract them. In order to extract the functions we must define them. Definition must proceed from two points of view. First of all, definition should in no case depend on the personage who carries out the function. Definition of a function will most often be given in the form of a noun expressing an action (interdiction, interrogation, flight, etc.). Secondly, an action cannot be defined apart from its place in the course of narration. The meaning which a given function has in the course of action must be considered. For example, if Iván marries a tsar's daughter, this is something entirely different than the marriage of a father to a widow with two daughters. A second example: if, in one instance, a hero receives money from his father in the form of 100 rubles and subsequently buys a wise cat with this money, whereas in a second case, the hero is rewarded with a sum of money for an accomplished act of bravery (at which point the tale ends), we have before us two morphologically different elements—in spite of the identical action (the transference of money) in both cases. Thus, identical acts can have different meanings, and vice versa. *Function is understood as an act of a character, defined from the point of view of its significance for the course of the action.*

The observations cited may be briefly formulated in the following manner:

1. *Functions of characters serve as stable, constant elements in a tale, independent of how and by whom they are fulfilled. They constitute the fundamental components of a tale.*
2. *The number of functions known to the fairy tale is limited.*

If functions are delineated, a second question arises: in what classification and in what sequence are these functions encountered?

A word, first, about sequence. The opinion exists that this sequence is accidental. Veselóvskij writes, "The selection and *order* of tasks and encounters (examples of motifs) already presupposes a certain *freedom.*" Sklóvskij stated this idea in even sharper terms: "It is quite impossible to understand why, in the act of adoption, the *accidental* sequence [Sklóvskij italics] of motifs must be retained. In the testimony of witnesses, it is precisely the sequence of events which is distorted most of all." This reference to the evidence of witnesses is unconvincing. If witnesses distort the sequence of events, their narration is meaningless. The sequence of events has its own laws. The short story too has similar laws, as do organic formations. Theft cannot take place before the door is forced. Insofar as the tale is concerned, it has its own entirely particular and specific laws. The sequence of elements, as we shall see later on, is strictly *uniform.* Freedom within this sequence is restricted by very narrow limits which can be exactly formulated. We thus obtain the third basic thesis of this work, subject to further development and verification:

3. *The sequence of functions is always identical.*

As for groupings, it is necessary to say first of all that by no means do all tales give evidence of all functions. But this in no way changes the law of sequence. The absence of certain functions does not change the order of the rest. We shall dwell on this phenomenon later. For the present we shall deal with groupings in the proper sense of the word. The presentation of the question itself evokes the following assumption: if functions are singled out, then it will be possible to trace those tales which present identical functions. Tales with identical functions can be considered as belonging to one type. On this foundation, an index of types can then be created, based not upon theme features, which are somewhat vague and diffuse, but upon exact structural features. Indeed, this will be possible. If we further compare structural types among themselves, we are led to the following completely unexpected phenomenon: functions cannot be distributed around mutually exclusive axes. This phenomenon, in all its concreteness, will become apparent to us in the succeeding and final chapters of this book. For the time being, it can be interpreted in the following manner: if we designate with the letter A a function encountered everywhere in first position, and similarly designate with the letter B the function which (if it is at all present) *always follows* A, then all functions known to the tale will arrange themselves within a *single* tale, and none will fall out of order, nor will any one exclude or contradict any other. This is, of course, a completely unexpected result. Naturally, we would have expected that where there is a function A, there cannot be certain functions belonging to other tales. Supposedly we would obtain several axes, but only a single axis is obtained for all fairy tales. They are of the same type, while the combinations spoken of previously are subtypes. At first glance, this conclusion may appear absurd or perhaps even wild, yet it can be verified in a most exact manner. Such a typological unity represents a very complex problem on which it will be necessary to dwell further. This phenomenon will raise a whole series of questions.

In this manner, we arrive at the fourth basic thesis of our work:

4. *All fairy tales are of one type in regard to their structure.*

We shall now set about the task of proving, developing, and elaborating these theses in detail. Here it should be recalled that the study of the tale must be carried on strictly deductively, i.e., proceeding from the material at hand to the consequences (and in effect it is so carried on in this work). But the *presentation* may have a reversed order, since it is easier to follow the development if the general bases are known to the reader beforehand.

Before starting the elaboration, however, it is necessary to decide what material can serve as the subject of this study. First glance would seem to indicate that it is necessary to cover all extant material. In fact, this is not so. Since we are studying tales according to the functions of their dramatis personae, the accumulation of material can be suspended as soon as it becomes apparent that the new tales considered present no new functions. Of course, the investigator must look through an enormous amount of reference material. But there is no need to inject the entire body of this material into the study. We have found that 100 tales constitute more than enough material. Having discovered that no new functions can be found, the morphologist can put a stop to his work, and further study will follow different directions (the formation of indices, the complete systemization, historical study). But just because material can be limited in quantity, that does not mean that it can be selected at one's own discretion. It should be dictated from without. We shall use the collection by Afanás'ev, starting the study of tales with No. 50 (according to his plan, this is the first fairy tale of the collection), and finishing it with No. 151.[†] Such a limitation of material will undoubtedly call forth many objections, but it is theoretically justified. To justify it further, it would be necessary to take into account the degree of repetition of tale phenomena. If repetition is great, then one may take a limited amount of material. If repetition is small, this is impossible. The repetition of fundamental components, as we shall see later, exceeds all expectations. Consequently, it is theoretically possible to limit oneself to a small body of material. Practically, this limitation justifies itself by the fact that the inclusion of a great quantity of material would have excessively increased the size of this work. We are not interested in the quantity of material, but in the quality of its analysis. Our working material consists of 100 tales. The rest is reference material, of great interest to the investigator, but lacking a broader interest.

NOTES

1. See Afanás'ev, Nos. 171, 139, 138, 156.
2. W. Wundt, "Mythus und Religion," *Völkerpsychologie*, II Section I; Negelein, *Germanische Mythologie*. Negelein creates an exceptionally apt term, *Depossedierte Gottheiten*.

[†] Tales numbered 50 to 151 refer to enumeration according to the older editions of Afanás'ev. In the new system of enumeration, adopted for the fifth and sixth editions and utilized in this translation (cf. the Preface to the Second Edition, and Appendix V), the correponding numbers are 93 to 270. [Louis A. Wagner]

10.3 COMPARISON

MESOPOTAMIA AND ROME: GILGAMESH AND AENEAS

At the end of the first book of the *Iliad*, Thetis, the sea goddess, cradles her son Achilles's head in her lap and laments the grief that defined his brief life. "Oh my child, why ever did I bear you, born to sorrow? I wish that you might have stayed by the ships without weeping, without pain, since your life is fated to be all too short." Indeed many works other than the *Iliad* represent the death of Achilles in Troy that Thetis laments and predicts. Figure 10.11, for example, shows Ajax, one of Achilles' dear companions, carrying him out of the fray of battle so that he can be buried. In contrast, Homer, in the very first word of the epic, foretells the rage that will propel Achilles and instigate his dispute with King Agamemnon. The tension between Achilles's sorrowful recognition of his brief life and the potent vitality of his anger generates the *Iliad*'s plot. This tension also makes Achilles an heir of Gilgamesh, the hero of the Mesopotamian *Epic of Gilgamesh*, who grieves and rages over the death of his beloved companion, Enkidu. Aeneas, the hero of the Roman poet

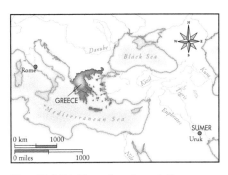

Map 10.2 **Epic Heroes from Sumer to Rome**

Vergil's *Aeneid*, follows in Achilles's wake; he too alternates between sorrow and anger, while duty and the gods motivate his founding of the city of Rome. In this section, we look at how each of these three heroes negotiates grief and anger, thus forming a continuous tradition of epic heroes from Mesopotamia to Rome.

As a distinctly poetic genre, epic conveys stories in ways that shape the character of its central hero. Accordingly, an understanding of Gilgamesh, Achilles, and Aeneas requires an understanding of the four key conventions of the epic genre. First, the scale of epic is expansive. Epics tend to be very

10.11 Ajax carries the dead Achilles. Black-figure amphora. Antimenes Painter, c. 520–510 BCE. *The Walters Art Museum. Baltimore. Walters 48.17.*

10.12 A hero (possibly Gilgamesh) overpowering a lion. Relief from the Palace of Sargon II at Khorsabada. Assyrian, c. 725 BCE. Louvre Museum, Paris, France. © RMN-Grand Palais / Art Resource, NY, ART156553.

long poems, and the actions they describe usually spans years, if not decades. The setting of epic is comparably grand: a battlefield, an entire city, many cities or islands, the ocean or forests, the realm of the gods, the Underworld, or any combination of these. Second, epic is characterized by its content: it usually centers on a war or on a quest (or even both, as in the case of the *Aeneid*). Third, epics are serious in tone, in part as a result of the rhythmic quality of the heroic verses in which they are usually composed. Whereas each verse contains a single thought, strung together they gallop over vast landscapes and punctuate lengthy exchanges of words and violent battles with a steady beat. They capture the hero's dynamism and elevate his story beyond the everyday world of epic's audiences. Finally, the cast of characters in epic is numerous and includes gods, beasts, heroes, men, women, and children.

Not surprisingly, epic protagonists resemble one another. The epic hero is always male, usually has a divine parent, and attempts to make his mark across a broad swathe of time and place. He succeeds in this attempt, but not because he overcomes forces of nature, gods, monsters, or other men, or even because he is superior to those around him in intellect, rhetorical skills, battle prowess, energy, or divine parentage. Paradoxically, the hero succeeds because he loses something essential. His resistance to and acceptance of that loss, set against the expansiveness of the epic, defines his struggle and enables him to become simultaneously wholly human and wholly heroic. As in cults (hero shrines at which heroes were worshipped), the epic hero must be mortal; one of his losses, if not the primary loss, is his confrontation with his own death, even if the epic does not directly portray it. Nowhere is this more apparent than in the figure of Gilgamesh.

GILGAMESH AND THE BURDEN OF MORTALITY

The *Epic of Gilgamesh* tells the story of Gilgamesh, a king of the Sumerian city Uruk (Map 10.2) (Figure 10.12). The earliest written accounts about Gilgamesh are a series of short tales that survive only in fragments and date to around 1800 BCE, almost one thousand years after a historical Sumerian king named Gilgamesh ruled Uruk. Many written and oral stories about Gilgamesh (c. 2800 BCE) continued to circulate over the next few centuries in the ancient Near East. Thus much of the *Epic of Gilgamesh* predates the composition of the *Iliad* and *Odyssey*, and echoes of it can be found in the plots and characters of later Greek and Roman epics. The selections from the *Epic of Gilgamesh* included here are from the standard Babylonian version (seventh century BCE). They highlight the ways in which Gilgamesh rages and grieves over the loss of his companion, struggles in vain against his own mortality, and finally earns heroic glory. His adventures provide an epic pattern for Achilles and Aeneas.

The *Epic of Gilgamesh* begins with a description of the walls of Uruk, which Gilgamesh built, and introduces Gilgamesh as someone "superior to other kings, a warrior lord of great stature, a hero born of Uruk, a goring wild bull" (Tablet I). Gilgamesh is a cruel king whose behavior prompts his people to complain to the gods. In counsel with one another, the gods decide to create a man named Enkidu who is as strong as Gilgamesh. Enkidu, however, is covered in hair, lives in the wilds, and is more animal-like than human. A woman called "the harlot Shamhat" seduces Enkidu, gradually taming him so that he has less kinship with animals and can thrive among human company. Arriving in Uruk, Enkidu stops Gilgamesh from exercising his prerogative as king to spend the night with a newly married bride. After a long wrestling match, they become comrades and engage in a series of exploits during which they kill a sacred animal, "the bull of heaven," dear to the goddess Ishtar. The gods punish them by killing Enkidu (Tablet VIII).

As Gilgamesh grieves inconsolably for Enkidu, he recognizes his own mortality and decides to find a way to be immortal. He sets off to find Utnapishtim, a man who, like Noah in the Hebrew Bible, survived a flood sent by the gods by sheltering in a massive boat along with his family and a selection of animals. Utnapishtim was granted eternal life. Gilgamesh, however, fails the test Utnapishtim sets for him and loses his opportunity to live forever. After this failure, which suggests that no man may escape mortality (Gilgamesh cannot save his own life any more than he could have saved his beloved companion Enkidu), Utnapishtim's wife persuades Utnapishtim to give Gilgamesh a plant that will make him immortal, which a snake steals while Gilgamesh is sleeping. At the close of Tablet XI, where some scholars argue the epic properly concludes, Gilgamesh regrets his loss of the plant and praises the splendor of the walls of Uruk, which will serve to establish his name throughout time. Gilgamesh reconciles himself to the fact that stone may live forever, but a man, however great, must die (Chapter 12.3).

Achilles's trajectory over the course of the *Iliad* parallels Gilgamesh's, but there are significant differences as well. (See Chapter 2.1 on the composition and dates of Homer's epics.) Both epics open with the hero harassing a walled city: Achilles, along with the Greeks, attempts to breach the walls of Troy, whereas Gilgamesh abuses his own population within Uruk's walls. Both heroes refuse to accept the restrictions placed on them by their lofty social positions. Gilgamesh governs his city poorly and mistreats his subjects. Achilles, although a soldier, becomes angry with and defies King Agamemnon, refusing to fight with the Greeks against the Trojans. Whereas Enkidu's death compels Gilgamesh to search for the secret of eternal life, the death of Patroclus compels Achilles to seek revenge by finally joining the battle against the Trojans. Gilgamesh ultimately fails Utnapishtim's test to become immortal. Achilles's fiery battle with the river Scamander is stopped by the gods and thereby defines Achilles as a limited and mortal human rather than an immortal force of nature. When Gilgamesh loses the plant that will make him immortal, he finally realizes that he can only ever be a mortal man. He returns to Uruk and lives within, not outside, its walls, at last ruling his kingdom justly. When Priam, the king of Troy, begs Achilles for the release of his son Hector's body, he summons Achilles to remember his own father, Peleus. Achilles begins to understand his place among the generations of human fathers and sons, and not among gods, rivers, and Trojan enemies. Like Gilgamesh, Achilles becomes fully human while retaining both the glory from the battles he has won and the sorrows from all he has lost. What is perhaps remarkable, as critics have noted, is that Homer follows Achilles's recognition of his mortality with a description of Hector's funeral. Trojan women lament Achilles's enemy Hector, thereby concluding the *Iliad* not with the enmity of the Trojans and Greeks but with female voices singing a lament for all human suffering.

AENEAS AND THE FOUNDING OF ROME

If the *Iliad* begins with rage and ends with sorrow, the *Aeneid* begins with Aeneas's sorrow over the destruction of Troy and ends with him bristling with rage. Vergil (70–19 BCE), the author of the *Aeneid*, has been called the Roman Homer, because he modeled his epic on Homer's *Iliad* and *Odyssey* and his hero Aeneas on Achilles and Odysseus. Yet it is the ways in which the *Aeneid* differs from its Greek models that are significant.

Aeneas appears in the *Iliad* as one of the heroes who fights with the Trojans against the Greeks. The *Aeneid* offers a retrospective account of the fall of Troy, when Aeneas, the son of Anchises and the goddess Venus (the Roman Aphrodite), escapes from the burning city with his father, his son Ascanius, and his city gods but fails to save his wife, Creusa (Figure 10.13). (The courtship of Anchises and Aphrodite is the subject of the Homeric *Hymn* 5 (*To Aphrodite*) in Chapter 5.1.) The *Aeneid* itself, however, begins with Aeneas en route to Italy. His ships are driven off course because of the anger of Juno (the Roman Hera; she is the wife of Jupiter, the Roman Zeus). Whereas Achilles's anger drives the action of the *Iliad*, Juno's anger drives the *Aeneid*. The goddess rages because she is unable to forget that when Paris, the prince of Troy, was asked to choose which of three goddesses was most beautiful (he had to choose between Juno, Venus, and Minerva,

10.13 Aeneas carries his father, Anchises, from Troy. Etruscan terracotta statuette. Fifth century BCE. Museo Nazionale di Villa Giulia, Rome, Italy. *Scala / Ministero per i Beni e le Attività culturali / Art Resource, NY, ART300543.*

the Roman Athena), he chose Venus. In the *Aeneid,* Juno is hostile to the Trojans; it is her rage that generates the epic's plot.

The first six books of Vergil's epic follow Aeneas's journey west to Italy and are modeled on the *Odyssey* (Chapter 12.3), whereas the last six books describe the battles Aeneas wages on Italian soil and are modeled on the *Iliad.* These last six books establish Aeneas as an epic hero in the mold of Achilles. On Aeneas's arrival in Italy, he seeks an alliance with King Latinus of the Latins, and he becomes engaged to Lavinia, Latinus's daughter. Juno causes Amata, Latinus's wife, and Turnus, the king of the Rutulians, who is also a suitor for Lavinia's hand, to resist both a Latin alliance with the Trojans and Lavinia's marriage with Aeneas. When war breaks out between the Trojans and the Rutulians, Aeneas seeks military aid from Evander, king of the Arcadians, and Aeneas agrees to take Pallas, Evander's son, under his protection. The role of Pallas here is similar to that of Patroclus in the *Iliad* or Enkidu in *Gilgamesh*: he is killed in battle by Turnus, and his death provokes Aeneas's wrath. Before his death, the destruction of Troy and the obligation to found Rome burdened Aeneas with sorrow and duty. In the aftermath of Pallas's death, Aeneas's drive to establish Rome becomes wedded to his desire for revenge.

The final scene of the *Aeneid* is modeled on Achilles's confrontation with Hector. When Achilles refuses Hector's pleas to spare him or return his body to the Trojans, Achilles is driven by a desire for revenge, which on the battlefield of Troy is an acceptable and morally neutral motive for his unwavering decision to kill Hector. When Turnus is wounded and begs Aeneas for clemency, however, Aeneas's decision is far more complicated. Anchises has told his son Aeneas that the moral exercise of power demands clemency on the part of the victor toward his defeated enemy. So when Turnus asks to be spared and reminds Aeneas of their fathers (recalling Achilles's encounter with Priam), we might expect Aeneas to yield. But at that moment Aeneas sees the belt that Turnus has stripped as a trophy from Pallas and thinks of the young boy. Enraged, he kills Turnus. The *Aeneid* closes with its hero in a maelstrom of emotions, not with women's laments recounting the destruction of men, as in the *Iliad.* The Roman epic asks its audience to consider how the moral imperative to administer an empire with clemency may not succeed in moderating the excesses of sorrow and anger.

Vergil began composing his epic during the time when Augustus (63 BCE–14 CE) was consolidating his power over Rome. Aeneas stands as a model for both Augustus and the values of the Roman Empire. Vergil even recited some of the first few books for Augustus, who petitioned to read more of the epic as Vergil composed it. And yet Vergil's epic cannot be reduced to state propaganda, in part because the final scene of the *Aeneid* poses a provocative (and still urgent) question: can men (whether mythical, like Aeneas, or historical, like Augustus) who create and govern empires restrain their appetites for revenge and exercise power with reason, duty, and diplomatic rule?

UNKNOWN, FROM THE *EPIC OF GILGAMESH*
&
VERGIL, *AENEID*

One way to understand Gilgamesh, Achilles, and Aeneas is to take into account that their stories are shaped by the epic genre. Each hero faces his own mortality as he navigates seas, battlefields, and his social position. *Note:* Ancient texts often exist only as fragments, frequently illegible or partially worn away or even destroyed. Editors indicate these absences in various ways: barely legible words that have been restored through careful scholarship are placed in brackets, while empty brackets or empty spaces indicate the places where words can't be restored or where the text has been lost. Question marks in parentheses indicate suggested reconstructions. You will encounter many such guesses and absences in the following excerpts from the *Epic of Gilgamesh*. (Translated by Stephanie Dalley.)

Line numbers for the excerpts from *Aeneid* correspond to the full text of each Book. (Translated by Barry B. Powell.)

- How does the hero of each epic express his rage and sorrow?

- Are the actions of these epic heroes extraordinary, moral, or both?

- Use Propp's list of thirty-one functions to describe Gilgamesh, Achilles, and Aeneas. Does Propp's morphology enable meaningful comparisons of these three epic heroes with one another? With Heracles, Oedipus, or Theseus?

- Use van Gennep's three-part division of initiation rituals to divide up the stories of each epic hero. Does van Gennep's scheme illuminate the plights of each hero? Or does his scheme diminish their unique traits and actions?

 ## UNKNOWN, FROM THE *EPIC OF GILGAMESH* (SEVENTH CENTURY BCE)
FROM TABLET I

[Of him who] found out all things, I [shall te]ll the land,	1
[Of him who] experienced everything, [I shall tea]ch the whole.	
He searched (?) lands (?) everywhere.	
He who experienced the whole gained complete wisdom.	
He found out what was secret and uncovered what was hidden,	
He brought back a tale of times before the Flood.	

He had journeyed far and wide, weary and at last resigned.
He engraved all toils on a memorial monument of stone.
He had the wall of Uruk built, the sheepfold
Of holiest Eanna, the pure treasury.   10
See its wall, which is like a copper band,
Survey its battlements, which nobody else can match,
Take the threshold, which is from time immemorial,
Approach Eanna, the home of Ishtar,
Which no future king nor any man will ever match!
Go up on to the wall of Uruk and walk around!
Inspect the foundation platform and scrutinize the brickwork!
Testify that its bricks are baked bricks,
And that the Seven Counsellors must have laid its foundations!
One square mile is city, one square mile is orchards,   20
     one square mile is claypits, as well as the open
      ground of Ishtar's temple.
Three square miles and the open ground comprise Uruk.
Look for the copper tablet-box,
Undo its bronze lock,
Open the door to its secret,
Lift out the lapis lazuli tablet and read it,
The story of that man, Gilgamesh, who went through
     all kinds of sufferings.
He was superior to other kings, a warrior lord of great stature,
A hero born of Uruk, a goring wild bull.
He marches at the front as leader,
He goes behind, the support of his brothers,   30
A strong net, the protection of his men,
The raging flood-wave, which can destroy even a stone wall.
Son of Lugalbanda, Gilgamesh, perfect in strength,
Son of the lofty cow, the wild cow Ninsun.
He is Gilgamesh, perfect in splendour,
Who opened up passes in the mountains,
Who could dig pits even in the mountainside,
Who crossed the ocean, the broad seas, as far as the sunrise.
Who inspected the edges of the world, kept searching for eternal life,
Who reached Ut-napishtim the far-distant, by force.   40
Who restored to their rightful place cult centres (?)
     which the Flood had ruined.
There is nobody among the kings of teeming humanity
Who can compare with him,
Who can say "I am king" beside Gilgamesh.

Gilgamesh (was) named from birth for fame.
Two-thirds of him was divine, and one-third mortal.
Belet-ili designed the shape of his body,
Made his form perfect, [   ]
[   ] was proud [   ]
[   ]   50
[   ]
In Uruk the Sheepfold he would walk about,
Show himself superior, his head held high like a wild bull.
He had no rival, and at his *pukku*
His weapons would rise up, his comrades have to rise up.
The young men of Uruk became dejected in their private
          [quarters (?)].
Gilgamesh would not leave any son alone for his father.
Day and night his [behaviour (?)] was overbearing.
He was the shepherd (?) [   ]   60
He was their shepherd (?) yet [   ]
Powerful, superb, [knowledgeable and expert],
Gilgamesh would not leave [young girls alone],
The daughters of warriors, the brides of young men.
The gods often heard their complaints.
The gods of heaven [ ] the lord of Uruk.
     "Did [Aruru (?)] create such a rampant wild bull?
     Is there no rival? At the *pukku*
     His weapons rise up, his comrades have to rise up.
     Gilgamesh will not leave any son alone for his father.   70
     Day and night his [behaviour (?)] is overbearing.
     He is the shepherd of Uruk the Sheepfold,
     He is their shepherd, yet [   ]
     Powerful, superb, knowledgeable [and expert],
     Gilgamesh will not leave young girls [alone],
     The daughters of warriors, the brides of young men.
     Anu often hears their complaints."
They called upon great Aruru:
     "You, Aruru, you created [mankind (?)]!
     Now create someone for him, to match (?) the ardour (?)   80
          of his energies!
     Let them be regular rivals, and let Uruk be allowed peace!"
When Aruru heard this, she created inside herself the word (?) of Anu.
Aruru washed her hands, pinched off a piece of clay, cast it out into open
          country.
She created a [primitive man], Enkidu the warrior:
          offspring of silence (?), sky-bolt of Ninurta.

His whole body was shaggy with hair, he was
        furnished with tresses like a woman,
His locks of hair grew luxuriant like grain.
He knew neither people nor country; he was dressed as cattle are.
With gazelles he eats vegetation,
With cattle he quenches his thirst at the watering place.
With wild beasts he presses forward for water.   90
A hunter, a brigand,
Came face to face with him beside the watering place.
He saw him on three successive days beside the watering place.
The hunter looked at him, and was dumbstruck to see him.
In perplexity (?) he went back into his house
And was afraid, stayed mute, was silent,
And was ill at ease, his face worried.
[   ] the grief in his innermost being.
His face was like that of a long-distance traveller.
The hunter made his voice heard and spoke, he said   100
        to his father,
    "Father, there was a young man who came
        [from the mountain (?)],
    [On the land] he was strong, he was powerful.
    His strength was very hard, like a sky-bolt of Anu.
    He walks about on the mountain all the time,
    All the time he eats vegetation with cattle,
    All the time he puts his feet in (the water) at the watering place.
    I am too frightened to approach him.
    He kept filling in the pits that I dug [   ],
    He kept pulling out the traps that I laid.
    He kept helping cattle, wild beasts of open   110
        country, to escape my grasp.
    He will not allow me to work [in open country]."

FROM TABLET VIII

When the first light of dawn appeared   1
Gilgamesh said to his friend,
    "Enkidu, my friend, your mother a gazelle,
    And your father a wild donkey sired you,
    Their milk was from onagers; they reared (?) you,
    And cattle made you familiar with all the pastures.
    Enkidu's paths [led to] the Pine Forest.
    They shall weep for you night and day, never fall silent,
    Weep for you, the elders of the broad city, of Uruk the Sheepfold.

The summit will bless (us) after our death,   10
They shall weep for you, the [   ]s of the mountains,
They shall mourn [   ]
[The open country as if it were your father], the field as
if it were your mother.
They shall weep for you, [myrtle (?)], cypress, and pine,
In the midst of which we armed ourselves (?) in our fury.
They shall weep for you, the bear, hyena,
     leopard, tiger, stag, cheetah,
Lion, wild bulls, deer, mountain goat, cattle, and
     other wild beasts of open country.
It shall weep for you, the holy river Ulaya, along
     whose bank
We used to walk so proudly.
It shall weep for you, the pure Euphrates,   20
With whose water in waterskins we used to refresh ourselves.
They shall weep for you, the young men of the
     broad city, of Uruk the Sheepfold,
Who watched the fighting when we struck down the Bull of Heaven.
He shall weep for you, the ploughman at [his plough (?)]
Who extols your name with sweet Alala.
He shall weep for you, [   ] of the
broad city, of Uruk the Sheepfold,
Who will extol your name in the first . . .
He shall weep for you, the shepherd, the herdsman (?),
Who used to make (?) the beer mixture (?) for your mouth.
She shall weep for you, [the wet-nurse (?)]   30
Who used to put butter on your lower parts.
He (?) shall weep for you, the elder (?)
Who used to put ale to your mouth.
She shall weep for you, the harlot [   ]
By whom you were anointed with perfumed oil.
They shall weep for you, [parents]-in-law
Who [comfort (?)] the wife . . . of your loins (?)
They shall weep for you, the young men, [like brothers (?)]
They shall weep for you and tear out (?) their hair over you.
For you, Enkidu, I, (like ?) your mother, your father,   40
Will weep on your (*lit.* his) plains [   ]
Listen to me, young men, listen to me!
Listen to me, elders of Uruk, listen to me!
I myself must weep for Enkidu my friend,

Mourn bitterly, like a wailing woman.
As for the axe at my side, spur to my arm,
The sword in my belt, the shield for my front,
My festival clothes, my manly sash:
Evil [Fate (?)] rose up and robbed me of them.
My friend was the hunted mule, wild ass of the 50
    mountains, leopard of open country.
Enkidu the strong man was the hunted wild ass of
    [the mountains, leopard of open country].
We who met, and scaled the mountain,
Seized the Bull of Heaven and slew it,
Demolished Humbaba the mighty one of the Pine Forest,
Now, what is the sleep that has taken hold of you?
Turn to me, you! You aren't listening to me!
But he cannot lift his head.
I touch his heart, but it does not beat at all.
He covered his friend's face like a daughter-in-law.
He circled over him like an eagle, 60
Like a lioness whose cubs are [trapped] in a pit,
He paced back and forth.
He (?) tore out and spoilt (?) well-curled hair,
He stripped off and threw away finery as if it were taboo.
When the first light of dawn appeared, Gilgamesh
    sent out a shout through the land.
The smith, the [   ], the coppersmith,
the silversmith, the jeweller (were summoned).
He made [a likeness (?)] of his friend, he fashioned
    a statue of his friend.
The four limbs of the friend were [made of   ],
    his chest was of lapis lazuli,
His (?) skin was of gold [   ]

(gap of about 12 lines)

"[I will lay you to rest] on a bed [of loving care] 70
And will let you stay [in a restful dwelling, a dwelling of the left].
Princes of the earth [will kiss your feet].
I will make the people [of Uruk] weep for you, [mourn for you].
[I will fill] the proud people with sorrow for you.
And I myself will neglect my appearance after you(r death)
Clad only in a lionskin, I will roam the open country."

VERGIL, FROM *AENEID* (c. 29–19 BCE)
FROM BOOK 11

Dawn, as time passed, duly rose and left Ocean. Aeneas,
Up before her with the Morning Star, thanks gods for his conquest.
Even though anguish impels him to take time needed to bury
Comrades lost, though his mind is in turmoil because of the slaughter,
He has set high on a mound an immense oak whose limbs he has pruned
     back   5
All the way round and arrayed with the gleaming arms and equipment
Stripped from the ruler Mezentius. He's turning it into a trophy
Honouring you, War's Lord, great Mars, and attaches the fighter's
Blood-drenched plumes, snapped spears, and the corslet, scored by a dozen
Holes gouged through. To what serves as the left hand, he fastens
     the brass-bound   10
Shield, from its "neck," he's suspending the sword in its ivory scabbard.
Seizing his chance—for his captains are all pressing in on him, wildly
Cheering—he rallies his troops as they give him a rousing ovation:
"Men, this achievement is huge. All fear must be banished from now on.
These spoils, my first fruits of the war, have been reaped from a
     proud king!   15
Here is the artwork my hands have created! Behold him, Mezentius!
Now we must march upon one more king and the walls of the Latins.
Ready your weapons! Put war in your souls! Make war what you hope for!
Let's not be caught unawares by delays, and impeded the instant
Heaven nods signs to up standards and march the lads out of
     encampment.   20
No dissent must arise out of fear-fraught inertia and slow us.
  "Let us commit to the earth, as we wait, these friends, these
     unburied
Bodies. In Acheron's depths, that's the only meaningful tribute.
Go!" he said. "Honour these spirits, the pick of the flock, who with their blood
Mothered this new home to life for us all. Give them offerings
     and final   25
Rites. Now our first step should be to have Pallas returned to Evander's
Grief-stricken city. This day, marked black, has removed him and plunged him
Deep in the sourness of death. Yet it found him not lacking in courage."
  Tears fill his eyes as he speaks. He retraces his steps to the dead youth's
Quarters. An old man was guarding the laid-out corpse of the lifeless   30
Pallas. Acoetes had earlier served as Arcadian Evander's
Arms-bearer, then was assigned as companion to his beloved Pallas:
This move he made under auspices boding less happy fulfilment.

Gathered around him were all Pallas' slaves, a good number of Trojan
Men, and, with hair flowing free in the fashion of grief, Trojan women.   35
Once, though, Aeneas presented himself, after passing the high doors,
Beating of breasts started, moaning notes shrilled up to the starry
Skies and the royal marquee re-intoned lamentations of sorrow.
Now's when his eyes get their first glimpse of Pallas: the snow-cold whiteness,
Pillowed head, then the face, the slight chest with the wound an Italian   40
Spear left gaping wide. Tears gush from his eyes as he's speaking:
"Poor lad! Was it upon you that Fortune, who came to us smiling,
Cast evil eye to spite *me*, so that your eyes would never see our realm,
And so you'd never ride home to your father's kingdom in triumph?
This isn't what my departing words to your father Evander   45
Promised for you, when he hugged me as I went away, as he sent me
Off to pursue great power. He feared for us. These were, he cautioned,
Fierce opponents; we'd battle a tough and resilient people.
He, I suspect, is a prisoner, even now, of delusive
Hope. Chances are that he's still making vows, piling gifts upon altars   50
While we are gathered in grief to pay hollow respects to a lifeless
Youth who has no further debt he must pay any god in the heavens.
    "You'll see how cruelly your son died, how you lost what fulfilled you.
Such is our great triumphal return that you've waited and watched for!
Here's how much *my* word is worth! Still, you won't see him come
        back defeated,   55
Scarred by disgraceful wounds. No, Evander, you won't be a father
Wishing death as a curse on a son who's survived. What a mighty
Guardian, Ausonia, you've lost! What a great loss for you too, Iulus."
Ending his tearful lament, he commands them to lift up this piteous
Corpse and dispatches the pick of his whole force, as escort and final   60
Honour guard—men who would join with his father in weeping. A thousand
Troops were but minimal solace indeed for a grief so immensely
Huge, and yet surely the due that was owed to his father, in pity.
    Others, no less fired up, plait switches of oak and arbutus
Withes into wickerwork, weaving a casket and cushioning bier,   65
Raising a couch wattled over with taut-stretched, shadowing branches.
Here, on a farmhand's bedding, they set out their noble young hero
Languid as drooping hyacinth falls, or limp as a violet
Clipped in its flower by a virgin's thumb, but whose shimmering lustre
Lingers, whose perfect form hasn't shrivelled, as yet, though its earthen   70
Mother no longer sustains life's vital strength with her nurture.
Then, bearing matching mantles stiffened with gold and with purple
Dye, comes Aeneas. Sidonian Dido herself, with her once live
Hands had produced them for him, as a pair: her labour of rapture,

Threaded with highlights of fine-spun gold worked into the cross-weave.   75
One of the capes, in his grief, he drapes over the youth, a last tribute
Bridling the hair, now damned to the flames, in a veil of enshroudment.
Many more prizes won in the Laurentine battle he also
Stacks up, and orders the plunder conveyed in a lengthy procession,
Adding some horses, and weapons he's stripped from the enemy's bodies.   80
Then, hands chained behind backs, come the men he is sending for human
Sacrifice, planning to sprinkle the flames with the blood of their slaughter,
Honouring Pallas's ghost. He bids captains convey, with their persons,
Stumps clad in enemy arms, names nailed upon placards as insults.
Wretched Acoetes, enfeebled and robbed of fulfilment in old age,   85
Bruises his chest with his fists, and his nails rip his cheeks as they march him,
Pitching down, hurled prone to the ground the full length of his body.
Then they add chariots, drenched in Rutulian blood, to the march-past.
Aethon, his war-horse, trots past riderless, stripped of its trappings,
Weeping and dampening its cheeks with a flow of magnificent
          teardrops.   90
Some bear his spear and his helmet—just these, for his conqueror, Turnus,
Now has the rest. Then the Teucrians follow, and then the Etruscans,
Full force. Arcadians, weapons reversed, pass in funeral formation.
After the whole of the escort has passed in review and is moving
Onwards, Aeneas remains where he stands and observes, with a
          deep groan: 95
"Fate, with identical horrors of war, calls *us*, from our tears here,
Elsewhere to others. Goodbye for eternity, wonderful Pallas,
Through all eternity, here's my farewell!" That was all. He now headed
Back to the high walls, directing his stride straight into the fortress.

FROM BOOK 12

On and on comes Aeneas, pursuing and raising his spearshaft
Huge as a tree. From his savage heart he taunts him with these words:
"Why dally now at the climax, Turnus, and draw back at *this* point?
We must engage up close and with brute force, not in a foot race!   890
Take any shape, any form that you will, pull in such resources,
Courage or skill, as you have, then pray you can soar to the starry
Heights upon pinions or seal yourself off within earth's hollow chasm."
He shook his head: "It's not words you say in a rage that alarm me,
Raging brute! Gods alarm me, and Jupiter. He is my real foe."   895
Saying no more, he surveys his surroundings and sees a huge boulder
Lying, by chance, on the plain: a huge boulder positioned in old times
Marking the property lines—to prevent a dispute over borders!

Even a dozen hand-picked men of the build earth produces
Now would have trouble just hoisting its great mass up on their shoulders.   900
This hero picks up the rock in his trembling hand, races top speed,
Stretches as high as he can to add torque to its flight at the foeman.
Yet he has no sense he's running, no knowledge he's moving or hoisting
Up in his hand and hurling a boulder of massive proportions.
Knees buckle, blood sets hard in his veins with the cold ice of terror.   905
As for the stone the man threw: it just tumbled through void and through empty
Air, fell short of its length, inflicted a blow upon nothing.

   As in a dream, when languid sleep seals eyes in our night-time
Rest, we're aware, in ourselves, of desperately wanting to reach out
Into some purpose or course; but strength, in the midst of our efforts,   910
Fails us. We feebly slump. Our tongues will not function, our usual
Bodily powers don't support us. No sound, no words find expression.
Such was Turnus's plight. Whatever attempt at heroic
Action he made, the grim goddess frustrated. Conflicting emotions
Whirl through his heart as he stares at Rutulians, stares at the city,   915
Hesitates, frightened, and shakes at the sight of the menacing javelin,
Sees no place to pull back to, no force to deploy on his foeman,
No sign at all of his chariot or of its driver, his sister.
And, as he hesitates still, Aeneas with javelin brandished,
Figures the odds of success with his eyes and, mustering his full strength,   920
Spins off a long-range shot. No boulder propelled from a taut-torqued
Catapult high on a parapet makes such a crack, and no lightning
Leaps with such crackling, thunderous peal. Like a whirling tornado,
Bearing the fury of death, that shaft rips open his corslet's
Rim and the outer edge of his shield's seven layers of protection,   925
Screams through the thick of his thigh. And Turnus, felled by the impact,
Drops to the ground on his knee; and his knee buckles under his hugeness.
Up leaped Rutulians moaning in notes reintoned in the whole hill's
Rippled response, as their voices are echoed around by the high woods.
Low on the ground and on bended knee, he appeals with extended   930
Hand, with an earnest look in his eyes, and declares: "I've deserved this,
Nor am I begging for life. Opportunity's yours; and so use it.
But, if the love of a parent can touch you at all (for you once had
Just such a father, Anchises), I beg you to pity the agèd
Daunus, and give me, or if you prefer, my sightless cadaver,   935
Back to my kin. You've won; the Ausonians have witnessed the vanquished
Reaching his hands out to make his appeal. Now Lavinia's your wife.
Don't press your hate any further." Aeneas, relentless in combat,
Stops; and though rolling his eyes, he holds back his hand from the
      death-stroke.

Slowly but surely, the words take effect. He's begun hesitating,   940
But when a harness catches his gaze, high on Turnus's shoulder,
Gleaming with amulet studs, those pleas have no chance of fulfilment:
Pallas's oh so familiar belt, which Turnus had shouldered
After defeating and killing the boy. It's the mark of a hated
Personal foe. As his eyes drink in these mementoes of savage   945
Pain, these so bitter spoils, Aeneas grows fearsome in anger,
Burning with fire of the Furies. "You, dressed in the spoils of my dearest,
Think that you could escape *me*? Pallas gives you this death-stroke, yes Pallas
    Pallas
Makes you the sacrifice, spills your criminal blood in atonement!"
And, as he speaks, he buries the steel in the heart that confronts him,   950
Boiling with rage. Cold shivers send Turnus' limbs into spasm.
Life flutters off on a groan, under protest, down among shadows.

10.4 RECEPTION

ACHILLES AND WAR POETRY

10.14 *Dying Achilles*. Ernst Gustav Herter, 1884. Achilleion, Corfu, Greece. *Brian Hoffman/Alamy, A1BJ70.*

Dying Achilles (Figure 10.14), at the Achilleion, a palace on the Greek island of Corfu, was commissioned by the Empress Elisabeth of Austria (1837–1898) to commemorate the untimely death (some say suicide) of her son. Later, Kaiser Wilhelm II (1859–1941), the last emperor of Germany and the king of Prussia, who led Germany into the catastrophic World War I, purchased the estate. He moved *Dying Achilles* to make way for a massive bronze sculpture he commissioned, the *Achilles Triumphant* by Johannes G. Götz (1865–1934) (Figure 10.15). Standing more than fourteen feet tall on a pedestal of even greater height and outfitted as a hoplite, Götz's Achilles carries a gold-plated spear and helmet. The inscription on his shield originally read, "To the greatest Greek from the greatest German." Although this inscription has since been removed, both statues remain where the Kaiser placed them.

Both the triumphant and the dying Achilles witnessed the brutal history of war during the last century, as the Achilleion served as a military hospital for the French during World War I and was occupied by German and Italian troops in World War II. In the decades since the wars, the Achilleion has become a museum and diplomatic center. Both statues provide a visual emblem for soldier-poets who have turned to Achilles to understand their experiences at war as well as for noncombatants who have turned to the *Iliad* as a lens through which the trauma and inhuman destruction of modern warfare can be examined. Here we examine three poems written during different conflicts at the beginning, middle, and end of the twentieth century.

During World War I, Achilles was a touchstone by which soldiers, especially British soldiers, tried to make sense of their experiences. Young men at the time—particularly the well-educated young men from wealthier families who were officers in the British military—would have studied Greek and Latin, and the *Iliad* would have been very familiar. Elizabeth Vandiver's study of British poetry from the Great War, *Stand in the Trench, Achilles* (2010), takes its title from a poem by Patrick Shaw-Stewart (1888–1917). Shaw-Stewart wrote his poem when he was on leave from the army in Imbros, an island in the Aegean Sea, where after "three days' peace" he was unexpectedly called back to war. He imagines his return to the trenches as similar to Achilles's return to the fighting at Troy. Yet, instead of looking forward to the glory he will gain, Shaw-Stewart wonders about the purpose of the war, much as Achilles does in the *Iliad* when he complains about the ratio-

10.15 *Achilles Triumphant.* Johannes Götz, 1909. Achilleion, Corfu, Greece. *Brenda Kean/Alamy, CBW920.*

nale of plunging the entire Greek army into a costly war simply to retrieve just one woman, Helen (*Iliad* 1.157–160). Dismayed, Shaw-Stewart asks, "Why must I follow thee?" in reference to Helen.

PATRICK SHAW-STEWART, "I SAW A MAN THIS MORNING" (1915)

> I saw a man this morning
> Who did not wish to die:
> I ask, and cannot answer,
> If otherwise wish I.

Fair broke the day this morning
　　Against the Dardanelles;
The breeze blew soft, the morn's cheeks
　　Were cold as cold sea-shells.

But other shells are waiting
　　Across the Ægean Sea,
Shrapnel and high explosive,
　　Shells and hells for me.

O hell of ships and cities,
　　Hell of men like me,
Fatal second Helen,
　　Why must I follow thee?

Achilles came to Troyland
　　And I to Chersonese:
He turned from wrath to battle,
　　And I from three days' peace.

Was it so hard, Achilles,
　　So very hard to die?
Thou knewest, and I know not—
　　So much the happier I.

I will go back this morning
　　From Imbros over the sea;
Stand in the trench, Achilles,
　　Flame-capped, and shout for me.

Shaw-Stewart recalls Achilles not because he is a model for heroic action, nor even as a soldier who doubts the purpose of war. Rather, he calls on Achilles to help him confront his own death in the trenches. When he asks finally that Achilles stand in the trenches and shout for him, he alludes to the terrifying cry that Achilles directed toward the Trojans with Athena's assistance (*Iliad* 18). In this final image, a distant Achilles seems to offer only a vain hope for comfort and insight.

In a manner similar to Shaw-Stewart, the American poet Randall Jarrell (1914–1965) finds no solace in recalling Achilles. Jarrell's brief poem was written prior to his service during World War II and concerns bombers (fighting planes), about which he would write after he joined the air force.

RANDALL JARRELL, "WHEN ACHILLES FOUGHT AND FELL" (1937)

When Achilles fought and fell,
Joy or pity filled each breast.
When I saw the bomber fall,
My heart felt iron within my breast.

Man looks weak beside the girder—
By the bomb's sight, what is man?
Men have made themselves an image
That does not glass, but judges, man.

Jarrell imagines that those who witnessed Achilles's death experienced the powerful emotions of either "joy or pity." The poet paradoxically feels neither emotion but instead feels "iron" when he writes about witnessing the death from afar of the crew of a crashing airplane. Metal and machinery dominate the next four lines and become a reflection of men's violence against one another. By the poem's end, Achilles is as distant from the poet as from Shaw-Stewart.

Michael Longley (b. 1939), a Northern Irish poet, turned to Achilles to reflect on a ceasefire in 1994 announced during "the Troubles," an Irish term used to describe the conflict in Northern Ireland over whether it should remain part of Great Britain or become part of Ireland. Longley's poem replays the moment when the Greek Achilles and Trojan Priam meet. Shared sorrows unite the two men who were once enemies, as Priam recalls his son and Achilles his father. The final couplet describes Priam's supplication, "which must be done." Priam's gesture encourages reciprocity between the two men and humanizes Achilles. In this way, Longley suggests that an enemy and a war may shape one's identity and one's future more than one's own inclinations.

MICHAEL LONGLEY, "CEASEFIRE" (1995)

I

Put in mind of his own father and moved to tears
Achilles took him by the hand and pushed the old king
Gently away, but Priam curled up at his feet and
Wept with him until their sadness filled the building.

II

Taking Hector's corpse into his own hands Achilles
Made sure it was washed and, for the old king's sake,
Laid out in uniform, ready for Priam to carry
Wrapped like a present home to Troy at daybreak.

III

When they had eaten together, it pleased them both
To stare at each other's beauty as lovers might,
Achilles built like a god, Priam good-looking still
And full of conversation, who earlier had sighed:

IV

"I get down on my knees and do what must be done
And kiss Achilles' hand, the killer of my son."

The *Iliad* and Achilles have not lost their significance for articulating and understanding the tremendous costs to humanity of warfare in this new century. Jonathan Shay (b. 1941), a clinical psychiatrist and medical doctor, argues in *Achilles in Vietnam: Combat Trauma and the Undoing of Character* (1994) that Achilles exhibited the symptoms of a soldier suffering from post-traumatic stress disorder (PTSD). Shay, who treated veterans of the Vietnam War suffering from PTSD, describes the similarities:

> [I was struck by] the similarity of their war experiences to Homer's account of Achilles in the *Iliad*. . . . The thrust of this work is that the epic gives center stage to bitter experiences that actually do arise in war; further, it makes the claim that Homer has seen many things that we in psychiatry have more or less missed. . . . In particular, Homer emphasizes two common events of heavy, continuous combat: betrayal of "what's right" by a commander, and the onset of the berserk state.

In Shay's analysis, Achilles has a "highly developed social morality." But Agamemnon's betrayal of the social value of distributing war prizes fairly, combined with the death of Patroclus, incites Achilles to right these wrongs by doing more wrong. The *Iliad*, according to Shay, is "the tragedy of Achilles' noble character brought to ruin." Shay further explored the connections between Homer's depiction of soldiers and the traumas experienced by modern combatants in *Odysseus in America: Combat Trauma and the Trials of Homecoming* (2002). In both books, Shay has not only alerted veterans and veterans' families to the insight that the *Iliad* might offer about the consequences of war on soldiers; he has also brought the attention of scholars and critics to the uncanny psychological realism of Homer's portraits.

KEY TERMS

Achilles 451

Aeneas 478

Ariadne 446

Cleomedes 438

Colonus 448

Deianira 445

Heracles 442

Heracles's labors 443

Hero cult 439

Hero shrine 439

Hippolytus 447

Hyllus 445

Jocasta 449

Laius 449

Megara 442

Minotaur 446

Oedipus 448

Pyanopsia 448

Sphinx 450

Theseus 445

Thetis 451

FOR FURTHER EXPLORATION

Albersmeier, Sabina (ed.). *Heroes: Mortals and Myths in Ancient Greece.* Baltimore, MD: The Walters Art Museum, 2009. This lavishly illustrated collection of essays provides a well-organized and comprehensive introduction to heroes and heroines in ancient Greece.

Graziosi, Barbara, and Emily Greenwood. *Homer in the Twentieth Century: Between World Literature and the Western Canon.* New York and London: Oxford University Press, 2007. This collection of essays provides a rich sample of how twentieth-century artists have returned to Homer to make sense of war violence. Of particular note is the essay on Christopher Logue's war poetry, which is not discussed here.

King, Katherine Callen. *Ancient Epic.* Malden, MA, and West Sussex, UK: Blackwell-Wiley, 2009. Accessible and comprehensive chapters cover a range of Greek and Roman epics, as well as the *Epic of Gilgamesh.*

Segal, Robert A. (ed.). *Structuralism in Myth: Levi-Strauss, Barthes, Dumezil, and Propp.* New York and London: Routledge, 1996. This collection of essays situates Propp among other theorists of myth who sought to discover patterns in myth. One essay reviews his work.

CHAPTER 11

MEDEA

THE MAKING OF A HEROINE

Men say of us that we live a life free from danger at home while they fight wars. How wrong they are! I would rather stand three times in the battle line than bear one child.

—**EURIPIDES, *MEDEA* (249–251)**

I n Euripides's *Medea*, Medea bemoans the conditions of women's lives in Greece to a surrounding chorus of Corinthian women. She notes that a woman cannot choose her husband and that, no matter the state of her marriage, she must bear her husband's children: a fate, she notes, that is far more dangerous than fighting in a war. Medea's statement is emblematic of the primary tasks of Greek men and women: all male citizens must be soldiers, and all the daughters of citizens must marry and give birth to future citizens. In such a society, the opportunities for men to win glory and distinction through war, athletics, and exploration had no corollary in the lives of their daughters and wives, who ventured from their houses only to the water fountain, market, or temple. It would seem that the activities of men's lives could be magnified, indeed exaggerated, and could provide material for tales about heroes, whereas the daily lives of Greek women would be less inspiring. Yet the Greeks told stories about and worshipped heroines, just as they did heroes.

< **11.1 (OPPOSITE):** Medea kills her son. Red-figure amphora. Ixion Painter. 340–320 BCE. Louvre Museum, Paris, France. *Erich Lessing / Art Resource, NY, ART23396.*

DEFINING HEROINES

In this chapter, we examine cults and myths about heroines, while exploring some of differences between heroes and heroines. We then meet four heroines: Helen, Clytemnestra (with the Furies), Hecuba, and Medea. Along the way, we also consider child and baby heroes, whose stories and cults are in many ways similar to those of heroines.

FIVE TRAITS OF GREEK HEROINES

While the five-point definition of heroes offered in Chapter 10.1 applies to heroines as well as heroes, there are some key differences:

(1) **A heroine was understood to be a woman who had died.** Like heroes, heroines were human beings, not minor deities, and they too were considered to be near the gods, whether through birth, talent, beauty, deeds, or favoritism. However, some women after death were recognized not as heroines but rather as a class of beings between gods and humankind: avenging female spirits associated with the Underworld, not Olympus.

(2) **Heroines perform extraordinary deeds that may or may not be moral.** The extraordinary deeds of heroes usually require them to display great physical strength. In contrast, the extraordinary deeds of heroines often consist of their ability to endure physical or sexual violence. Additionally, the deeds of heroines, more often than the deeds of heroes, tend to have a moral aspect (Chapter 13.1).

(3) **Heroines die prematurely, violently, or mysteriously.** Just as men often died prematurely on the battlefield, many women often died prematurely during childbirth. Stories about heroes and heroines reflect this historical reality. Additionally, in many cases women recognized as heroines had committed suicide (an act of violence directed against the self).

(4) **Heroines were worshipped at their gravesites.** Just as in the case of men, the souls of women who had been killed violently, prematurely, mysteriously, or by suicide were believed to remain sentient after death and to cause famine, plague, infertility, or drought, unless placated by worship in cults. Additionally, the souls of some dead women, if they were not recognized as heroines, were believed to cause the deaths of mothers and infants during childbirth.

(5) **Heroines obtain a form of immortality through song and cult.** Fewer songs have women as their main protagonists, and fewer women were recognized and celebrated as heroines at cult shrines. Additionally, heroines were seldom the sole recipients of worship at such shrines: they were often worshipped along with their fathers, husbands, and sons, although rarely with female members of their family.

Three stories illustrate this five-point definition of heroines. The first story, concerning the young girl Charilla, includes (like the story of Cleomedes, Chapter 10.1) features typical of stories about heroines and heroes. The story of Opheltes introduces the concept of baby heroes, whose tales and shrines resemble those of heroines, whereas the story of Psamathe and her child Linus introduces the concept of the avenging female spirits that often appear in heroines' stories.

Plutarch tells a story about Charilla to explain a ritual during which the king of the people at Delphi slaps a statue with a sandal and then hangs the statue. (Translated by Frank Cole Babbitt.)

PLUTARCH, FROM *GREEK QUESTIONS* 293

A famine following a drought oppressed the Delphians, and they came to the palace of their king with their wives and children and made supplication. The king gave portions of barley and legumes to the more notable citizens, for there was not enough for all. But when an orphaned girl, who was still but a small child, approached him and importuned him, he struck her with his sandal and cast the sandal in her face. But, although the girl was poverty-stricken and without protectors, she was not ignoble in character; and when she had withdrawn, she took off her girdle and hanged herself. As the famine increased and diseases also were added thereto, the prophetic priestess gave an oracle to the king that he must appease Charilla, the maiden who had slain herself. Accordingly, when they had discovered with some difficulty that this was the name of the child who had been struck, they performed a certain sacrificial rite combined with purification, which even now they continue to perform every eight years. For the king sits in state and gives a portion of barley-meal and legumes to everyone, alien and citizen alike, and a doll-like image of Charilla is brought thither. When, accordingly, all have received a portion, the king strikes the image with his sandal. The leader of the Thyiads [female worshippers of Dionysus] picks up the image and bears it to a certain place which is full of chasms; there they tie a rope round the neck of the image and bury it in the place where they buried Charilla after she had hanged herself.

In general outline Charilla's story resembles those told about heroes. Like Cleomedes's deeds, Charilla's suicide is not exemplary. Even if Plutarch praises her character, she is not a role model for other young girls to follow. Like Cleomedes, she dies prematurely and violently (although by her own hand), and her death is mysterious insofar as she is barely known to anyone in Delphi and her identity must be discovered after death. Whereas the Astypalaeans consult an oracle immediately following Cleomedes's mysterious death and thus avoid suffering any harm from his spirit, the Delphians are

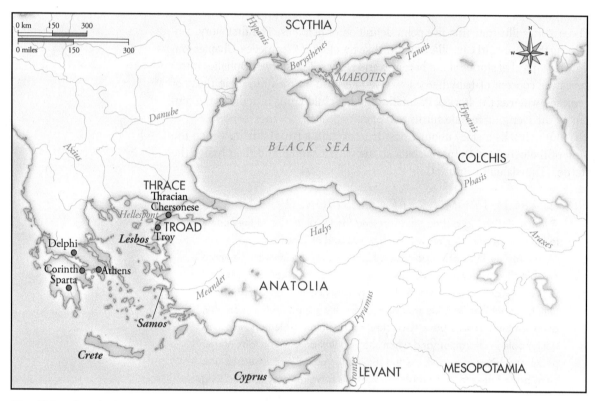

Map 11.1 Medea and Other Heroines

unaware of Charilla's death. Her soul, therefore, has both opportunity and motive to cause famine and drought among the Delphians.

Once the Delphians, after consulting the oracle, begin to worship Charilla as a heroine, she presumably stops harming them. Moreover, the Delphians' burial of Charilla's statue is a symbolic act that is designed to ensure that Charilla's soul is in the Underworld and is less likely to roam and harm them. Like the worship offered to Cleomedes, Charilla's worship ensures her remembrance in the community. By tying a rope around Charilla's statue, the Delphians ritually reenact Charilla's suicide and recall her story, thus perpetuating her memory. In these ways, the story of Charilla illustrates the five-point definition of heroines.

In addition to men and women, babies and young children could also be worshipped as heroes in ancient Greece. Unlike Heracles, who slays snakes when he is an infant, infants and children who become heroes have accomplished no extraordinary feat. Indeed, babies and children have little autonomy or ability to act in the ways that men do. In this regard, baby and child heroes are more like heroines—they have been killed prematurely or violently— and they often appear in the stories and cults of heroines. The young child

Opheltes at Nemea, for example, becomes a child hero. When Hypsipyle, his nurse, leaves him in a field plucking flowers while she fetches water for Amphiaraus and his army, a snake strangles the young child (Figure 11.2). The Nemean games (quadrennial athletic competitions) were established in Opheltes's honor, and the judges of the games were said to have worn black in mourning for the child. Thus the memory of Opheltes was preserved for generations, and his soul, appeased by his continual worship, did not harm the community. Hero shrines to babies may have served a purpose in addition to protection. They provided one way for a community to recognize and lament infants who died at birth or who were abandoned in remote places in the countryside and left to die because of physical ailments or economic necessities.

11.2 Opheltes is strangled by a snake as his nurse, Hypsipyle, watches. Corinthian sarcophagus. Second century CE. Museum of Ancient Corinth, Corinth Greece. *Courtesy of the Ephorate of Antiquities of Corinth.*

In the story of Psamathe, she and her baby son Linus die prematurely and violently and then are worshipped as a heroine and baby hero. In addition, a vengeful female spirit acts on their behalf. Psamathe's story begins when Apollo impregnates her. As is often the case in Greek myths, female consent in sexual encounters is not represented; only the outcomes of such encounters are considered. Fearing the anger of her father, King Crotopus of Argos, Psamathe abandons her baby, Linus, in a forest. The baby is discovered and rescued by a shepherd, who raises Linus among his flock until the child is killed accidentally by King Crotopus's dogs. When the king learns that Psamathe was Linus's mother, he kills her.

To punish the land of Argos for the king's brutality, Apollo sends Poene, an avenging female spirit who "steals" (i.e., kills) newborns. The shepherd who first rescued Linus kills Poene (although it remains unclear how an avenging spirit could be killed). To protect themselves from further revenge for the deaths of Psamathe and Linus, the Argives name one month "Arnius" (Sheep) after the sheep that first saved Linus. They honor Psamathe as a heroine and Linus as a baby hero at a festival during which they slaughter dogs in remembrance of Linus's death and women sing laments for mother and child. The Argives also provide Poene with a gravesite. Inscriptions on her tomb record that she was the avenger of Psamathe and label her a Ker (the plural is Keres). Keres, winged daughters of the goddess Nyx (Night), had associations with the Underworld; they often exacted vengeance on behalf of those who died violently and prematurely (Figure 11.3).

The tale of Psamathe suggests a connection between cults for heroines and cults for infants, as well as the role of avenging female spirits in stories

11.3 Medea rides a chariot given to her by her grandfather, the god Helios. Two winged females variously identified as Poenae (plural of Poene) or Erinyes watch Medea from above. Lucanian red-figure krater, 400 BCE. *Cleveland Museum of Art, OH, USA / Leonard C. Hanna, Jr. Fund / Bridgeman Images, CVL1761945.*

about heroines. It also suggests one of the most important social functions of heroines' cults. Just as a hero cult channels a hero's vitality and strength (which often threatens to spill over into violence) for a community's benefit, a heroine cult recognizes a heroine's reproductive potential (which is often thwarted during the life of the heroine) for a community's benefit.

HEROINES IN CULT

The category of heroines, like the category of heroes, includes mythological, local, legendary, and historical figures who were queens, priestesses, female prophets, poets, colonizers, athletes, and even warriors (such as the Amazons). Their cult shrines were very much like those dedicated to heroes. They could be located within a city (or at its borders) and often included a tomb, a gravestone, an altar, a small temple, dedications, or a cult statue (Chapter 10.1). Yet, unlike heroes, heroines rarely had their own cult shrines and instead shared them with males. In her book *Greek Heroine Cults* (1995), classicist Jennifer Larson describes these figures as "companion" heroines. Often from the mythological realm, companion heroines were worshipped alongside their husbands, sons, and fathers. No doubt, this organization of heroine cults reflected the historical reality of women's lives, which were always circumscribed by their legal male guardians.

One notable example of companion heroines includes Helen who shared a shrine in Sparta with Menelaus. In addition, Alcmene, Heracles's mother, shared a cult shrine with her husband, Amphitryon, in Thebes. Mothers shared shrines with their adult sons, and daughters shared their fathers' shrines. Semele was worshipped alongside her son, the god Dionysus, in three places in Thebes, whereas Hygeia was worshipped alongside her father, Asclepius, the son of Apollo associated with healing. Although almost no stories include Hygeia, whose name means "health," she appears alongside Asclepius in many visual representations, in which she represents the sphere over which he presides (Figure 11.4).

Heroines who were worshipped at shrines without fathers, sons, or husbands—labeled "independent females" by Larson—are few in number. Two Amazons, Antiope and Molpadia, had tombs in Athens and received sacrifices. The mythical prophetess Sibylla had shrines in each of the three locations that claimed to be her birthplace: Marpessos in the Troad, the Ionian town Erythrae, and the island of Samos. Among poets, Corinna (her historicity is doubted) had a tomb in the city of Tanagra, whereas Sappho (ca. 630–570 BCE) was worshipped on the island of Lesbos, her birthplace. Cyniska, a Spartan athlete, won an Olympic victory and had a cult in a grove in Sparta. The number of shrines dedicated to heroines (companion and independent) and babies was small compared to the number of hero shrines. Nonetheless, all of these shrines dotted Greek cities and countryside, making the remarkable lives and deaths of men, women, and children available for contemplation and worship.

HEROINES IN MYTH

As in the case of heroes, there are multiple versions of an adventure attached to a heroine (what Fritz Graf has called the *vertical* tradition) and several different stories from which a number of events can be selected and arranged to create a biography of a heroine's life (the *horizontal* tradition). (These terms are defined in Chapter 10.1). Yet heroines appear with less frequency than heroes in written and visual sources. Thus the material available from a range of sources for studying heroines is sparse.

11.4 Asclepius and his daughter Hygeia (Health) with a snake. Marble funerary relief from the Therme of Salonika. Fifth century BCE. Archaeological Museum, Istanbul, Turkey. *Erich Lessing / Art Resource, NY, ART21941.*

Although heroines make few appearances in epic poetry, they leave a memorable impression. Helen makes cameo appearances in both the *Iliad* and the *Odyssey*, whereas Hecuba and Andromache appear in the *Iliad* and Penelope in the *Odyssey*. All four had at least one heroine cult. More often, however, the epic genre includes women not in the spotlight of narrative action but rather in catalogues (or lists). When Odysseus travels to the Underworld, for example, he lists the women he sees there and describes each in a few lines. In the *Iliad*, Zeus catalogues all the females he found beautiful by way of explaining to Hera that she is far more desirable than any of them. And Hesiod composed the *Catalogue of Women*. Barely noted in epic, the women in these catalogues do not have cult shrines.

In the Classical Period, women were often protagonists in tragedy and comedy. Classical drama, concerned with the just administration and conflicting demands of city and household, allowed for more female characters than did the epic, which dealt primarily with battlefields and distant journeys. Among the Greek tragedians, Euripides was especially interested in the origins of cults. He found women to be an ideal subject for many of his plays. Of his surviving tragedies, Euripides has dedicated and named the greatest number of tragedies after heroines with cult shrines. These include works devoted to Medea, Helen, Andromache, Hecuba, Electra, and Alcestis, and two plays featuring Iphigenia (Chapter 13). His work is especially valuable for considering Greek heroines.

Later Greek artists and writers also took great interest in Greek heroines, as did Latin writers in Rome, who continually reconsidered, adapted, and reworked earlier Greek mythological figures. For this reason, Greek heroines in Roman literature are highlighted in the comparative sections of this chapter and Chapter 13. The following case studies of Helen, Clytemnestra, Hecuba, and Medea provide the biographical sketches, while focusing on tragic treatments and including cult information, to convey Greek conceptions of heroines. (For accounts of other heroines, see Chapter 13.1.)

HELEN

Helen is the offspring of Leda and Zeus (Chapter 3.4) and the sister of Clytemnestra, whose father is Tyndareus, Leda's mortal husband. (In other versions, Helen's mother is the goddess Nemesis, the goddess of revenge.) Her brothers Castor (the son of Tyndareus) and Pollux (the son of Zeus) were called the Dioscuri. The Dioscuri, who are almost always shown on horseback, became the constellation Gemini on their deaths. In some versions of Helen's birth, she alone, or she with her siblings, is hatched from an egg (Figure 11.5). Unlike Clytemnestra, who is fully human, Helen, as the daughter of Zeus, has greater affinities to the divine. In life, her beauty is nearly as great as that of the goddesses, and after she dies, she is said to dwell on the Islands of the Blessed with Menelaus.

THE ESSENTIALS

HELEN Ἑλένη

PARENTAGE Zeus and Queen Leda of Sparta

OFFSPRING Hermione (with Menelaus)

CULT SHRINES Sparta

Helen's miraculous birth is followed by a series of abductions. As a child, she is stolen by the hero Theseus. In some versions, he deposits her with his mother to rear until she reaches marriageable age. Helen's brothers, the Dioscuri, retrieve her from Theseus, whereupon her father Tyndareus then gives her in marriage to the Spartan king Menelaus and asks her many suitors—Hyginus (64 BCE–17 CE), a librarian for the Roman emperor Caesar Augustus, wrote that she had thirty-six suitors—to promise to protect her marriage in the event she should be abducted. Thus, when Paris, the Trojan prince, visits Menelaus and Helen in Sparta and departs with her (whether she was taken against her will or departed voluntarily was a matter of great speculation in antiquity), Menelaus and his brother Agamemnon are easily able to call on the help of many other Greek leaders and kings to sail to Troy and retrieve Helen. In the famous description by the British dramatist Christopher Marlowe (c. 1564–1593), Helen thus becomes "the face that launched a thousand ships." In some accounts, Helen never went to Troy with Paris; rather, a mere phantom in her likeness was at Troy, while Helen herself was in Egypt. In his play *Helen*, Euripides imagines Menelaus showing up in Egypt after the war and departing to Greece alongside Helen.

In most stories, it is Helen (not her phantom) who goes to Troy and lives as Paris's wife during the ten years of war. Once the war ends, she is reunited with Menelaus and returns to Sparta. Homer offers a vision of their life in Sparta after the war amid abundant riches with their two children: Megapenthes, a son, and Hermione, a daughter. Surrounded by precious jewels, regal and beautiful, Helen appears nearly divine. Unlike most Greek women in myth or history, Helen is never confined to her home and never stays in any one place; yet, for the most part, she escapes harm and censure from men. Even after her death, Helen remains married to Menelaus, and they dwell on the Islands of the Blessed in the Underworld. In yet other versions, she joins Achilles on the White Island, where he had a hero shrine and was believed to dwell after death (Chapter 10.1). Both versions of her afterlife stress that she escapes the dreariness of the Underworld.

11.5 The birth of Helen from an egg set on an altar. Red-figure krater. Caivano Painter. 340–330 BCE. National Archaeological Museum of Naples, Naples, Italy. *Scala / Art Resource, NY, ART310015.*

Helen was worshipped with Menelaus in Therapne, near Sparta, at the Menelaion; nearby, her brothers, the Dioscuri, were also worshipped as heroes. Yet Helen was not only worshipped as a companion with these three males. She was worshipped as an independent heroine in both Sparta and Rhodes. There is some suggestion that, in the distant past, Helen had been a goddess; her birth from Nemesis and Zeus may support such a view. Nemesis, the goddess of revenge, was worshipped at Rhamnous, a district near Athens, which thereby allowed the Athenians to claim Helen as their own, and through her to share in the epic past of Homer's world.

CLYTEMNESTRA

Clytemnestra was far less popular in myth and cult than her sister Helen. She married Agamemnon, the brother of Menelaus, with whom she had several children, including Iphigenia, Electra, and Orestes. Clytemnestra is known for one terrible deed: killing her husband Agamemnon and his Trojan concubine Cassandra. Aeschylus's trilogy *Oresteia*, the most well-known treatment of

THE ESSENTIALS
CLYTEMNESTRA Κλυταιμήστρα
PARENTAGE King Tyndareus and Queen Leda of Sparta

OFFSPRING Iphigenia, Electra, and Orestes (with Agamemnon)

CULT SHRINES Sparta

11.6 The ghost of Clytemnestra attempts to rouse the Erinyes. Detail. Apulian red-figure bell-krater. Eumenides Painter. Fourth century BCE. Louvre Museum, Paris, France. Hervé Lewandowski. © RMN-Grand Palais / Art Resource, NY ART150089.

this myth, offers three reasons for her actions: she was angry that Agamemnon took Cassandra as a concubine; she wanted to remain the ruler of Argos, along with Agamemnon's cousin Aegisthus, her lover; or she wanted revenge for Agamemnon's sacrifice of their daughter Iphigenia (Chapter 6.1 and Chapter 13.1). In the second play of the trilogy, her son, Orestes, with the help of Electra, murders Clytemnestra to avenge her murder of Agamemnon. (Sophocles and Euripides also wrote plays about the murder of Clytemnestra by her children, Orestes and Electra.)

In the last play of the trilogy, *Eumenides*, Clytemnestra's ghost rouses the Erinyes, a group of female avenging spirits associated with the Underworld, to pursue Orestes for killing her (Figure 11.6). Imagined as winged, snake-like, and black, the Erinyes are similar to the Keres and are sometimes described as the daughters of Nyx (Night). They are credited in many accounts with the protection of oaths and keeping the order of the cosmos intact. In the *Oresteia*, they agree to hunt down Orestes because he murdered his mother and thereby spilled kindred blood. When Athena exonerates Orestes, the Erinyes are angered and threaten to harm Athens by bringing plague, famines, and infertility. Athena promises that if they relent, they will be worshipped in Athens. They accept her offer and are henceforth worshipped by the Athenians, much in the manner of the heroines.

HECUBA

Hecuba, daughter of a Phrygian king, is the queen of Troy. Married to Priam, the Trojan king, she bears him nineteen sons, including Hector and Paris, as well as many daughters, including Cassandra and Polyxena. In the *Iliad*, she is defined by her anger and her sorrow. When her husband Priam sets out to retrieve Hector's body from Achilles in the Greek camps, she says about Achilles, "If only I could fasten my teeth into the middle of his liver and eat it! Payback for my son" (*Iliad* 24.208–209). In the final book of the *Iliad*, Hecuba's anger over Hector's death modulates into a lament she sings over his body. Later artistic portrayals highlight Hecuba's sorrow

THE ESSENTIALS

HECUBA Ἑκάβη

PARENTAGE King Dymas of Phrygia and Euagora (a nymph)

OFFSPRING Hector, Paris, Cassandra, Polyxena, Polydorus, and many others (with King Priam of Troy)

CULT SHRINES Hellespont and the Troad

as a mother whose many children have died and her rage at the violent manner of their deaths (Figure 11.7).

Euripides's tragedies *Trojan Women* and *Hecuba* portray the fate of Trojan women and children at the hands of the victorious Greeks during the aftermath of the Trojan War. In *Trojan Women*, Hecuba watches as the Greeks select Trojan women (including her daughter Cassandra, and Andromache) to be their concubines and slaves. She tends the body of her grandson Astyanax, the young son of Hector and Andromache, whom the Greeks hurl from the walls of Troy to ensure that no Trojan will grow up to reestablish the defeated city—an unlikely cruelty, given the unlikely possibility. The play ends with Hecuba's demand of Menelaus that he kill Helen, rather than take her back to Greece. Her request fails, and the play closes with Hecuba's attempt to kill herself while Troy burns to the ground and the Greek ships depart from Trojan shores.

11.7 Priam and Hecuba (together, far left) raise their hands as they watch Achilles (wearing a plumed helmet) drag their son Hector's body from his chariot. Athenian black-figure hydria (water jug). c. 520–510 BCE. *Museum of Fine Arts, Boston, Massachusetts, USA / William Francis Warden Fund / Bridgeman Images, BST487715.*

Hecuba's capacity to endure the suffering of her children and grandchildren is more pointed in the tragedy that bears her name. In Euripides's *Hecuba*, Hecuba learns that the Thracian king Polymestor, to whom she had entrusted her son Polydorus for safekeeping during the Trojan War, has killed him, and that the Greeks plan to sacrifice her daughter Polyxena at Achilles's tomb. When both Agamemnon and Odysseus refuse to punish Polymestor or to spare her daughter, Hecuba takes justice—or revenge—into her own hands. She kills Polymestor's two sons and blinds Polymestor. In the final scene, Polymestor foretells her fate: transformed into a maddened dog, Hecuba will hurl herself from the Greek ship on which she sails from Troy to Greece. Her tomb will be known as Cynossema, the Dog's Tomb, a landmark for sailors at the Hellespont. In other versions of her story, Hecuba is stoned to death by Odysseus and his men and is entombed in Sicily, or she is stoned by the Thracians and has a tomb in Thracian Chersonese. She is also said to have a tomb in the Troad.

Hecuba's murder of Polymestor's sons, like Clytemnestra's murder of Agamemnon, has some moral justification. (Cleomedes's murder of sixty children, by contrast, has none.) Because she lives in a world ruled by Greeks who will not pursue justice on behalf of either Hecuba or her children, Hecuba seeks to avenge the murder of her child on her own. But she does not kill the perpetrator of her child's murder; instead, she makes him suffer the very loss he imposed on her. Thus Hecuba becomes a vengeful child killer herself, much like Poene, and also much like Medea, who murders her own children to avenge Jason, their father. The stories of these heroines pose an interesting question: What if women refuse motherhood (or, in the stark terms of myth, actually kill children) once they recognize that a world created by men offers no justice to women or children? In taking up this question, Euripides's *Medea* explores the limitations placed on women in Greek society as well as the establishment of cults to children and women.

MEDEA

Medea is the daughter of King Aeëtes and (depending on the telling) either an Oceanid (sea nymph) named Idyia or the goddess Hecate. Although Hesiod includes a short poem of praise to Hecate, who offers abundance and support to those who worship her (Hesiod's *Theogony*, Chapter 2.1), Hecate is more commonly associated with witchcraft, the Underworld, and ghosts. Through Hecate, from whom Medea is descended and to whom she often prays, Medea too is associated with witchcraft. King Aeëtes is the son of Helios, the sun god; thus Medea has divine ancestry.

THE ESSENTIALS

MEDEA Μήδεια

PARENTAGE King Aeëtes of Colchis and Idyia (an ocean nymph) or Hecate

OFFSPRING Mermerus and Pheres (with Jason) and Medus (with King Aegeus of Athens)

CULT SHRINES Corinth, Corcyra, and Cilicia

Medea's story begins when Jason and the Argonauts (his fellow adventurers on the ship *Argo*; see Chapter 12.1) arrive in Colchis, on the eastern shores of the Black Sea, in order to obtain the Golden Fleece. King Aeëtes demands that Jason perform several deeds to earn the fleece. Without her father's knowledge, Medea helps Jason succeed in all he must do. She gives him magical herbs that protect him from the fire-breathing oxen he must yoke; she advises him to throw a rock into the midst of attacking soldiers so that they fight among themselves; and she gives the dragon who guards the Golden Fleece herbs that put him to sleep. Once Jason grabs the Golden Fleece, Jason and Medea depart hastily from Colchis, taking her brother, Apsyrtus, with them. To distract Aeëtes, who pursues them, she kills Apsyrtus, dismembers him, and throws his body parts in the sea. This act vividly illustrates that women were often viewed as torn between loyalty to their natal family (parents, siblings, and others related to them by blood) and their conjugal family (husband and children)—and thus potentially a threat to both. Collecting his son's body delays Aeëtes and allows Jason and Medea to escape. (The *Argonautica*, a brief epic by Apollonius of Rhodes written during the third century BCE, describes Jason's adventures to and from Colchis and his romance with Medea at Colchis.)

Jason and Medea eventually arrive in Iolcus, where Medea uses her magical herbs once more to Jason's benefit. She chops up a ram and tosses it into a cauldron with herbs that rejuvenate and restore it (Figure 11.8). It leaps out of the cauldron whole and youthful. In some versions, Medea performs this ceremony on Jason's father, who emerges from the cauldron whole and young.

After such a demonstration (whether on a ram or on Jason's father), Medea encourages the daughters of Pelias, Jason's hostile uncle, to perform the same ceremony for Pelias. However, once Pelias's daughters dismember him and fill a cauldron with parts, Medea does not give them the magic herbs, thus making the girls the instrument of their father's gruesome death.

From Iolcus, Medea and Jason flee to Corinth, where they have two sons. After several years in Corinth, Jason decides that he will marry Creusa, the princess of Corinth and daughter of King Creon. Euripides's *Medea* opens on the day that Medea learns that she and her sons are to be exiled so that the marriage of Jason and Creusa can take place without interference from Medea. Before Medea leaves, she gives Creusa a robe and a crown that she has covered in poison. Creusa suffers a terrible death from the poison, as does King Creon when he attempts to rescue his daughter. Medea then performs the deed for which she is most infamous: she kills her two sons, before departing to Athens on Helios's chariot (Figure 11.3).

Euripides's tragedy has so greatly influenced all subsequent treatments of Medea that it has eclipsed accounts that do *not* portray her as the murderer of her sons. In one such version, Medea tries to make her sons immortal by hiding them in Hera's sanctuary (or Hera makes them immortal to reward Medea

11.8 Medea applies magical drugs to a ram in a cauldron. Red-figure hydria. The Copenhagen Painter. c. 470 BCE. © The Trustees of the British Museum / Art Resource, NY ART356672.

for resisting Zeus's sexual overtures). In other accounts, the Corinthian women kill Medea's children when they seek protection in Hera's sanctuary. (Medea is not Greek, and once she is abandoned by Jason, her children would have been considered foreigners.) When a plague strikes Corinth (just as a plague strikes Delphi after the king's ill treatment of Charilla), an oracle advises the Corinthians to establish a cult to Medea's children. Euripides briefly alludes to this cult when Medea says that she will bury her sons in an area sacred to Hera Acraea in Corinth and will establish annual festivals for them (*Medea* 1377).

In Corinth, there was indeed a cult to Medea's children in the sanctuary of Hera Acraea, where their tombs and a statue of a terrifying female called Deima (Terror) were located. Seven boys and seven girls were required to serve Hera Acraea by cutting their hair, donning black robes, and living in the temple for a year. Whereas this yearlong service evokes the structure of adolescent initiation rituals and may very well have served this purpose

(Chapter 8.2), the sanctuary to Hera Acraea was devoted not to adolescents but to young brides and the nurture and care of young children. The statue of Terror, on the other hand, evokes other female avenging spirits like Poene and the Erinyes. Finally, Medea has several cult places in Corcyra and Cilicia, as well as in Corinth (where she is accompanied by her children).

After her death, Medea is said to have married Achilles and to reside with him on the Islands of the Blessed or on the White Island. Like Helen, Medea escapes the dreariness that most mortals meet after death and is established as a heroine in cult and myth. Medea's connection with Achilles alerts us to the fact that, of all the heroines, she most closely resembles Achilles. She shares with him her willingness to commit violence as well as the strength of her anger and her resolve to be honored above all else. Indeed, Euripides's tragedy draws a comparison between Medea and male heroes, provoking the audience to contemplate the dangers of violence, which is praised when exercised by men in Homer's *Iliad* but can lead to terrible consequences off the battlefield, especially within a city or family.

EURIPIDES, FROM *MEDEA*

BEFORE YOU READ

Medea's association with Achilles after death suggests that her anger and powers, while living, were akin to his. Why else imagine them together in death? Euripides not only suggests the ways in which Medea's actions are masculine (at least by Greek standards) but also emphasizes that Medea is a foreigner. She is not Greek, and her ethnic identity distinguishes her from Jason and all the other Greek characters in the play. In the central section of Euripides's play, excerpted here, Medea confronts Jason and then, rather serendipitously, encounters King Aegeus of Athens, from whom she secures asylum for herself once she leaves Corinth. After these two conversations, Medea determines to kill her two sons. (Line numbers in the following excerpt correspond to the full text.) (Translated by James Morwood.)

- Medea and Jason confront each other as though they were litigants in a court case. What are Medea's accusations against Jason? Are her accusations of betrayal justified? If so, what sort of figure does Jason appear to be?
- Jason offers an explanation for why he owes Medea no allegiance or appreciation. What is his explanation? How convincing do you think his explanation might have been to ancient audiences? From your evaluation of his speech, how would you judge his character?
- How does Aegeus's visit spark Medea's decision to kill her sons? Does her decision appear reasonable, moral, or extraordinary?

EURIPIDES, FROM *MEDEA* (431 BCE)

Enter JASON.

JASON. I have noticed many times before, not only now, how harsh passions lead to impossible deeds. After all, if you had borne the decisions of people who are stronger than you with a good grace, it would have been possible for you to stay in this land and in this house. As it is, because you pointlessly insisted on having your say, you will be ban-   450
ished. This doesn't matter to me. As far as I personally am concerned, you can go on for ever saying that Jason is an utter scoundrel. But, as for what you have said against the royal family, you should consider it all gain that you are being punished simply with exile. For my part, when their majesties' passions were roused, I always did my best to calm them and I wanted you to stay. But you would not moderate your foolish behaviour, and always spoke badly of them. And so you will be banished from the land. But nevertheless, even after this, I have not abandoned my friends and have come here because I am thinking   460
about your future, my lady, and how you and the children can avoid being banished without any money—or in want of anything at all. Exile brings many evils in its train. The fact is that, even if you hate me, I could never feel badly towards you.

MEDEA. Vilest of traitors—yes, I can at least call you that, the most cutting insult against a man who is no man—so you have come to us have you, bitterest of enemies to us, to the gods, to me and the whole human race? It is not boldness or courage when one hurts one's friends, then looks them in the face, but the greatest of all human   470
sicknesses, shamelessness. But you have done well to come, since I shall relieve my feelings by denouncing you and you will grieve to hear me.

I shall begin to speak at the beginning. I saved you, as all those Greeks who embarked together on that same ship, the Argo, know, when you were sent to master the fire-breathing bulls with the yoke and to sow the field of death. I killed the dragon which, ever unsleeping,   480
guarded the all-golden fleece, encircling it with many folding coils, and held up for you the beacon of safety. I betrayed my father and my house and came with you—more passionate than wise—to Iolkos under Mount Pelion, and I killed Pelias at the hands of his own children—the most grievous of all ways to die—and destroyed their whole house. And though, vilest of men, you reaped these benefits from me, you betrayed me, and made a new marriage—and this though we have children, since   490
if you had still been without a child, it would have been pardonable for

you to desire this match. No more is there any trusting to oaths, and I am at a loss to understand whether you think that the gods you swore by then no longer rule or that men now live by new standards of what is right—for well you know that you have not kept your oaths to me. Alas for this right hand which you often held, alas for these knees—touched by an evil man in an empty gesture—how we have missed our hopes.

Come now, I shall converse with you as if you were a friend. Yet what benefit can I think I shall receive at your hands?—but converse   500
I shall nevertheless, for questions will show up your vileness still further. Where can I turn now? To my father's house? But I betrayed it, and my fatherland too, when I followed you here. Or to the wretched daughters of Pelias? How warmly they would welcome me in their house—I killed their father! For this is the situation: I have earned the hatred of those dear to me at my home, and have made enemies of those whom I should not have harmed by doing you a favour. In recompense for all this, in the eyes of many women of Greece you have made me happy   510
indeed. What a wonderful husband, what a trustworthy one, I, wretched woman, have in you—if I am to be flung out of the land into exile, bereft of friends, my children and myself all, all alone—a fine reproach to the newly married man, that his children and I who saved you should wander round abegging.

O Zeus, why have you given men clear ways to recognize what gold is counterfeit, but on the body put no stamp by which one should distinguish a bad man?

CHORUS. Passions are fierce and hard to cure when those close to each   520
other join in strife.

JASON. I must, it seems, be no poor speaker, but escape the wearisome storm of your words, lady, like the trusty helmsman of a ship using the topmost edges of his sail. Since you lay too great a stress on gratitude, I consider that it was Aphrodite alone of gods and men who made safe my voyaging. You are a clever woman—but it would be invidious to spell out how Love forced you with his inescapable arrows to save me.   530
But I shan't go into that in too much detail. You helped me and I'm pleased with the result. However by saving me you took more than you gave, as I shall tell you. First of all, you live in the land of Greece in-stead of a barbarian country, you understand the workings of justice and know what it is to live by rule of law and not at the whim of the mighty. All Greeks saw that you were clever and you won a reputation.   540
If you were living at the furthest limits of the earth, no one would have heard of you. I for my part would not want to have gold in my house or to sing a song more beautifully than Orpheus if my good fortune did not become far-famed.

That is what I have to say to you about my labours. After all, it was you who provoked this war of words. As for your reproaches against me over my royal marriage, I shall show you first of all that I am sensible to make this match, as well as demonstrating good sense and in addition proving a powerful friend to you and my children. [*MEDEA makes a gesture of impatience.*] No, keep quiet. When I moved here from the land of Iolkos, dragging with me many hopeless troubles, what happier godsend could I have found than to marry the king's daughter, poor exile that I was. It was not—and this is what really gets under your skin—that I hated sleeping with you, or that I was overwhelmed with desire for my new bride, or that I was eager to outdo our family by having a larger one. I have enough children already and I find no fault with them. My object was—and this is the most important thing—that we should live well and not be in want, for I know that everyone steers well clear of a friend in need—and that I should bring up our children in a manner worthy of my house, and by producing brothers to my children by you, I should place them all on a level footing, unite them into one family and be prosperous. Why should you want more children? And it is in my interests to benefit those alive now by those that are to be born. Surely I have not planned this out badly? You would agree with me if the matter of sex were not provoking you. But you women have sunk so low that, when your sex life is going well, you think that you have everything, but then, if something goes wrong with regard to your bed, you consider the best and happiest circumstances utterly repugnant. The human race should produce children from some other source and a female sex should not exist. Then mankind would be free from every evil.

CHORUS. Jason, what you have said is superficially convincing. But none the less, even if I shall speak against what you think, you seem to me to be acting unjustly by betraying your wife.

MEDEA. Truth to tell, I often view matters differently from many people. In my opinion an unjust man who is a clever speaker incurs the greatest retribution, since if he is confident that his tongue can gloss over injustice cleverly, he has the audacity to stop at nothing. And so he is not so very clever. This is the case with you too. Do not then make a show of generous behaviour towards me with your skilful speaking, for one word will lay you flat. If you had not been a bad man you should have talked me round before making this marriage—not done it without your loved ones' knowledge.

JASON. Yes, I would have had your full backing for this plan, I think, if I'd spoken of the marriage to you—since even now you cannot bring yourself to soften your heart's great rage.

550

560

570

580

590

MEDEA. It wasn't that which stopped you, but your marriage with a barbarian was proving a source of no glory for you as you faced old age.

JASON. Rest assured of this then—it was not for the sake of the woman that I made the royal marriage in which I live now. As I have said already, I wanted to keep you safe and produce royal offspring to be brothers and sisters to our children and thus defend our house.

MEDEA. I hope I never have a wealthy life which brings me sorrow or the kind of happiness which galls my heart.

JASON. You must change your wish, you know, and then you will seem more sensible. You must never see what is to your benefit as distressing to you or think that fortune is against you when it smiles on you.

MEDEA. Go on insulting me. You have your escape route while I shall go in desolate exile from this land.

JASON. You yourself made this choice. You have no one else to blame.

MEDEA. What did I do to deserve it? Was it I who married and betrayed you?

JASON. You uttered unholy curses against the royal family.

MEDEA. Yes, and I am a curse to your house too.

JASON. Enough—I shall not discuss these matters with you any further. But, if you wish to receive any assistance from my resources for the children 610 or yourself in your exile, tell me—for I am ready to give with unstinting hand, and to send tokens of introduction to guest-friends of mine who will treat you well. And you will be foolish to refuse this offer, woman. If you lay aside your rage, you will do better for yourself.

MEDEA. We shall make no use of your guest-friends or accept any favours from you—do not try to give us anything. A bad man's gifts can bring no good.

JASON. Well then, I call the gods to witness that I am willing to give every 620 help to you and the children. But you recoil from what is good for you and in your obstinacy you drive away your friends. This will simply add to your sufferings.

MEDEA. Off with you. As you linger here away from home, desire of the girl you have just married overwhelms you. Go on with your marriage. For perhaps—with god's help it will be said—this will prove the kind of match which will bring you tears.

[JASON goes out.

CHORUS [sings].
> When love comes too violently to men,
> it gives them
> no glory for moral virtue.
> But if Cypris come in moderation,   630
> no other goddess is so delightful.
Never, o mistress, may you anoint with desire
your golden bow's inescapable arrow and shoot it at me.

May temperance befriend me,
the gods' most lovely gift,
and may dread Cypris never madden my heart
with adulterous love   640
and attack me with quarrelsome anger
and insatiate feuding. May she give honour to unions free
    from war
and prove a sharp judge of women's marriages.

O my fatherland, o my home,
may I never be without my city,
trudging on life's difficult path
of helplessness—
the most pitiful of sorrows.
Before that may I have done with this light of life
laid low by death, by death.   650
Of all miseries none is worse
than to lose one's native land.

We have seen this for ourselves. Not as a story
heard from others do I tell it but at first hand.
For, Medea, no city and none of your friends
will pity you as you suffer
the most terrible of sufferings.
If a man cannot unlock a pure heart   660
and respect his friends,
may he perish without reward.
He will never be a friend of mine.

    Enter AEGEUS.

AEGEUS. Medea, greetings. "Greetings," I say, because no one knows a
    better way than this to start a conversation with friends.
MEDEA. And greetings to you too, Aegeus, son of wise Pandion. From where
    have you come to reach this land of Corinth?
AEGEUS. I'm on my way back from the ancient oracle of Phoebus.
MEDEA. Why did you set out to the navel of the earth where the god sings
    his prophecies?
AEGEUS. I wanted to know how I could beget offspring.
MEDEA. By the gods, have you led the whole of your life up till now without   670
    children?
AEGEUS. I am childless by the stroke of some divine power.

MEDEA. Have you a wife or are you unmarried?

AEGEUS. I am not unmarried. I am paired with a wife.

MEDEA. What then did Phoebus say to you about children?

AEGEUS. His words were too clever for a mere man to interpret.

MEDEA. Is it right that I should know the god's response?

AEGEUS. Certainly—for a clever brain is certainly needed.

MEDEA. What was his oracle then? Tell me, if it is right for me to hear.

AEGEUS. Not to unloose the wineskin's hanging foot . . .

MEDEA. Before you do what, or arrive at what land?   680

AEGEUS. Before I come again to the hearth of my fathers.

MEDEA. What do you want that you have sailed to this country?

AEGEUS. There is a man called Pittheus, the king of the land of Trozen.

MEDEA. Yes, as they say, the son of Pelops, a most reverent man.

AEGEUS. I want to impart the oracle of the god to him.

MEDEA. Yes, for he is a clever man and experienced in such matters.

AEGEUS. And he is the dearest to me of all my allies.

MEDEA. I wish you well and hope you meet with all that you desire.

AEGEUS. But why are your eyes so dull and this your skin so wasted?

MEDEA. Aegeus, I have the worst of all husbands.   690

AEGEUS. What are you saying? Tell me clearly what makes you sad.

MEDEA. Jason wrongs me though I did him no harm.

AEGEUS. What has he done? Tell me more clearly.

MEDEA. He has a woman who supplants me as mistress of his house.

AEGEUS. Surely he has not been so brazen as to act in so shameful a way?

MEDEA. Be assured of it—and we, his former friends, are now dishonoured.

AEGEUS. Was he in love or couldn't he bear his relationship with you?

MEDEA. Very much in love—he has proved a traitor to his dear ones.

AEGEUS. So let him go if, as you say, he is a bad man.

MEDEA. He conceived a passion to marry into the royal house.   700

AEGEUS. Who gave her to him? Tell me the whole story.

MEDEA. Creon, who rules over this land of Corinth.

AEGEUS. It is understandable that you are hurt.

MEDEA. It is all over with me. But it is not just that he is leaving me. I am
   being driven out of the country.

AEGEUS. By whom? Now you are telling me of yet another, fresh disaster.

MEDEA. Creon is driving me into exile from the land of Corinth.

AEGEUS. And does Jason consent? I do not approve of this either.

MEDEA. He says he doesn't, yet he is willing to endure it. But I beg you by
   this your beard and your knees—now I am your suppliant—pity, pity me   710
   in my wretchedness and do not look on as I go into desolate exile, but
   receive me in your country at the hearth of your palace. So may your
   desire for children with the gods' help find fulfilment and may you come

to death a happy man. You do not know what a godsend you have found here in me. I shall put an end to your childlessness—through me you will beget children. I know the medicines for this.

AEGEUS. For many reasons, lady, I am eager to grant you this favour, first   720
because of the gods, then of the children whose birth you promise me—for in this matter I am totally at a loss. This is how I see things. If you come to my country, I shall try to protect you as I am in right bound to. However, this much I must state plainly in advance, lady: I shall not be willing to take you from this land. You must leave this country on your own initiative. But if you come to my palace your-self, you will stay there safe from harm and I shall not hand you over to anyone. I want to be without blame in the eyes of my guests and   730
my hosts alike.

MEDEA. Excellent. But if I could have some pledge of this, I should be com-pletely happy with your part in the affair.

AEGEUS. Don't you trust me? If it's not that, what makes you unhappy?

MEDEA. I trust you. But Creon and the house of Pelias hate me. If you are bound to me by oaths, you would not hand me over to them if they tried to take me from the land. But if our compact is simply one of words, not ratified with oaths to the gods, you may perhaps listen to their overtures and become their friend. My situation is weak while they have all the   740
wealth of a royal house.

AEGEUS. You have shown a great deal of caution about the future in what you say. But if you think it a good idea, I do not refuse to do this. It is indeed safer for me to have some pretext to offer your enemies, and your own situation will be the more assured. Name your gods.

MEDEA. Swear by the land of the Earth and the Father of my father, the Sun, and each and every god in addition.

AEGEUS. To do or refuse to do what? Tell me.

MEDEA. Never to cast me out of your land yourself nor, if any of my enemies   750
wishes to take me, to hand me over willingly as long as you live.

AEGEUS. I swear by the Earth and the Sun's bright light and all the gods to abide by the words I hear you utter.

MEDEA. Enough. What are you to suffer if you do not abide by this oath?

AEGEUS. Such fates as befall impious mortals.

MEDEA. Go on your way and good luck go with you. All is well and I shall come to your city as quickly as possible—when I have done what I intend to do and got what I want.

CHORUS [*chants*].
    May Hermes, son of Maia, the god of travel,
    bring you home and may you achieve the purpose   760

you are so eager to gain,
for in my judgement, Aegeus,
you have appeared a noble man.   [AEGEUS *goes out.*

MEDEA. O Zeus and Justice, daughter of Zeus, and light of the Sun, now, my
    friends. I shall win a glorious victory over my enemies. Now I am on the
    way. Now I can hope that my enemies will pay a just price. For this
    man—in that dilemma where we were foundering most—has appeared
    as a haven to save my plans. To him I shall fasten my stern cable by   770
    going to Athens, city of Pallas.
        Now I shall tell you all my plans. Don't expect to receive my words
    with pleasure. I shall send one of my servants to Jason to ask him to
    come to see me. When he arrives I shall speak soft words to him,
    saying that I too think these things are good, that it is well that he has
    made this royal marriage and betrayed me, that all is for the best, all
    has been well thought out. I approve of the marriage he has made to
    the princess by betraying me. And I shall ask him to let my children stay.   780
    Not that I would leave my children in a hostile country for my enemies
    to insult. No, my purpose is to kill the king's daughter with trickery. For
    I shall send them holding gifts in their hands, and bringing them to the
    bride to win repeal from exile from this land—a delicate robe and a
    golden garland. And if she takes these adornments and puts them on
    her flesh, she will die horribly—as will anyone who touches the girl,
    with such drugs shall I anoint the gifts.
        But that is enough of that. I cry out when I think what kind of deed I   790
    must do afterwards. For I shall kill the children, my own ones. Nobody
    is going to take them away from me. My heart steeled to the unholiest
    of deeds, I shall wreak havoc on the whole house of Jason and leave
    the land in flight from the charge of murder, the bloody murder of my
    beloved children.
        Laughter from my enemies is not to be endured, my friends. Come
    what may come! What do I have to gain by living? I have no fatherland,
    no house, no refuge from calamity. It was then that I made my mistake—   800
    when I left my father's house, persuaded by the words of a Greek man
    who with god's help will pay me the penalty. He will never see his sons
    born of me alive again and he will have no son by his newly wed bride,
    since that wretched creature must die a wretched death from my drugs.
        Let no one think of me as weak and submissive, a cipher—but as a
    woman of a very different kind, dangerous to my enemies and good to
    my friends. Such people's lives win the greatest renown.   810
CHORUS. Since you have shared these words with us and I wish both to help
    you and to support men's laws, I forbid you to do this.

MEDEA. There is no other way. I can pardon you for saying this for you do
    not suffer cruelly as I do.

CHORUS. But will you bring yourself to kill the fruit of your womb, lady?

MEDEA. Yes, for this would be the best way to hurt my husband.

CHORUS. But you would become the most miserable of women.

MEDEA. On with it! Until the deed is done, all words are wasted. [to the
    NURSE] But now, go and bring Jason here. I employ you in all matters of   820
    trust. But say nothing of what I have determined on if you care about
    your mistress and are a true woman.

[The NURSE *goes out.*

THE PLOT OF THE HEROINE'S STORY

11.2
THEORY

One approach used by classical scholars to analyze the great number of traditional stories with heroes at their center is to find repeating patterns and then
explain those patterns. In Chapter 10.2, we explored how Vladimir Propp's
work on the repeating patterns in Russian fairy tales might be useful for
studying Greek heroes. This section examines the pattern that FitzRoy
Richard Somerset, the fourth Baron Raglan (1885–1964), found in traditional
tales about heroes in order to consider if it can be adapted to describe and
analyze traditional tales about heroines.

Raglan was interested in the ritual origins of traditional tales about heroes.
In *The Hero: A Study in Tradition, Myth and Drama* (1936), Raglan developed a
list of twenty-two actions in heroic tales in order to demonstrate that traditional
tales about heroes were remarkably similar to one another, no matter their
culture of origin. From this observation, Raglan concluded that tales about
heroes were modeled not on the lives of historical figures but rather on ritual
activities. In other words, traditional tales about heroes were preceded by and
emerged from ritual. Consequently, the heroes described in traditional tales
were originally "ritual personages," not historical figures. Here is Raglan's list
of the twenty-two events in a hero's life from his article "Hero of Tradition":

1. His mother is a royal virgin.
2. His father is a king, and
3. Often a near relative of his mother, but
4. The circumstances of his conception are unusual, and
5. He is also reputed to be the son of a god.
6. At birth an attempt is made, usually by his father, to kill him, but
7. He is spirited away and
8. Reared by foster parents in a far country.
9. We are told nothing of his childhood, but

10. On reaching manhood he returns or goes to his future kingdom.
11. After a victory over the king and/or a giant, dragon, or wild beast,
12. He marries a princess, often the daughter of his predecessor, and
13. Becomes king.
14. For a time he reigns uneventfully and
15. Prescribes laws, but
16. Later he loses favor with the gods and/or his subjects and
17. Is driven from the throne and city.
18. He meets with a mysterious death,
19. Often at the top of a hill.
20. His children, if any, do not succeed him.
21. His body is not buried, but nevertheless
22. He has one or more holy sepulchers.

Although Raglan insists that no single traditional tale describes a specific historical figure, the stories of Greek heroes do have a connection, however distant, to the lives of men (such as kings and warriors) who actually lived in ancient Greece: even if King Theseus is not modeled on a specific king, he shares attributes that would have been assigned to historical kings. Similarly, a hero's fight against a monster may allude to, and indeed exaggerate and distort, the significant portion of men's youth devoted to military training and battle against human enemies. In a similar way, a Greek heroine's struggle against or on behalf of a particular male may allude to (or exaggerate) particular moments in the lives of actual Greek women.

A Greek woman whose male relatives were citizens had to have a male guardian (*kurios*) throughout her life. Her guardianship passed from her father to her husband at the time of marriage. If she became a widow, her guardianship passed to her son or, if she had none, to her father (again) or uncle. At these transitional moments (before marriage and on the occasion of widowhood), a woman would be under the watchful eye of male guardians, in part because her family's offspring and wealth were tied to her actions. In this light, we can discern in tales about heroines a repeating event that may allude to historical conditions of women's lives in Greece, without being a direct record of them. These tales often entertain the possibility of a woman exerting her will and even realizing her desire for a specific partner or a particular course of action at either of these transitional moments.

Antigone's story, for example, vividly demonstrates that the pivotal moment in a heroine's tale often corresponds to the moment when she enters adolescence and chooses to cross the threshold of her father's house. Although Antigone had no cult shrines in her honor, as the daughter of Oedipus and Jocasta she is one of the most familiar figures from ancient Greece, thanks to

Sophocles's tragedies *Oedipus Rex, Oedipus at Colonus,* and *Antigone.* (The first two plays are discussed in Chapter 10.1.)

Sophocles's *Antigone* begins when Antigone determines to bury her brother Polynices, who was killed in the Theban civil war. But Creon, who is the king of Thebes as well as Antigone's uncle and guardian, declares Polynices a traitor and orders his body to remain outside the city walls unburied. Denied a burial, Polynices is thereby also denied the funeral rites that would ensure the preservation of his memory within his family and city as well as the passage of his soul to Hades. Even though Antigone is engaged to Creon's son Haemon, she chooses to defy Creon and bury Polynices, in part out of her love and devotion to her natal family and in part out of respect and piety toward the gods. Antigone confronts Creon in public and insists on pursuing what she argues is a moral course of action (Figure 11.9). In refusing to obey Creon, Antigone elects to forego her marriage and indeed her life.

11.9 Antigone (second from right) is escorted by two guards to Creon (seated). Detail. Red-figure nestoris. Dolon Painter. 380–370 BCE. © *The Trustees of the British Museum / Art Resource, NY, ART497926.*

The transitional moment before marriage is often the narrative center of traditional tales about heroines. At this moment, a heroine may be subjected to male sexual violence, like Psamathe; she may reject a suitor that her father has chosen for her, like Helen; she may choose a suitor without her father's knowledge or permission, like Medea and Ariadne; or she may choose to enter the public world of men, like Antigone, and demand what she believes is justice for a dead relative. In all these instances, the heroine chooses, or is forced, to chart a course both for herself and by herself—often on behalf of, for, or against a man.

Tales about married heroines often focus on the moment when, as widows or as wives who have been separated from their husbands, they must remarry. These heroines often encounter the same kind of trial adolescent heroines face: they must accept or reject a male suitor (who, at this later stage in the women's lives, is usually her husband) or enter the public world of the city in order to pursue an action they have freely chosen. After the Trojan War, for example, Penelope, Clytemnestra, and Helen must decide whether to accept their husbands, whereas the Trojan women (such as Cassandra or Andromache) must accept or reject the Greek soldiers who claim them as their own. After the Trojan War, the Trojan queen Hecuba publicly confronts the Greek generals Odysseus and Agamemnon in an attempt to protect her children. Although her efforts fail and she is transformed into a dog, she escapes from a future as a slave in the household of Odysseus. Thus the historical conditions of women's lives, and particularly the legal necessity of having a male guardian, may explain two moments that constitute dramatic moments in heroines' stories, when questions of power and gender are inextricably connected. Because such moments are repeated in many tales, they may offer one way to find and interpret repeating patterns in the tales of Greek heroines.

BEFORE YOU READ

MARY ANN JEZEWSKI, *FROM* "TRAITS OF THE FEMALE HERO: THE APPLICATION OF RAGLAN'S HERO TRAIT PATTERNING"

Folklorist Mary Ann Jezewski concentrates on Raglan's list of twenty-two actions in traditional tales about heroes, rather than his theories about ritual. Like Raglan, Jezewski studies tales from a number of different cultures. She then adapts Raglan's rubric, providing a modified list of seventeen actions typical in stories about heroines. Unlike Raglan, Jezewski includes evaluative statements such as "she is charming and beautiful" in addition to actions. She does not take into account how the historical conditions of women in Greece (discussed previously) might contribute to the patterns of stories about Greek heroines. Because traditional tales about heroines in ancient Greece have not yet been extensively studied, the question of how to integrate the historical conditions of women's lives, ritual practices, and story patterns remains an ongoing area of scholarly inquiry. The following exercises ask you to incorporate the methods of Propp, Raglan, and Jezewski, collecting and analyzing data to formulate your own conclusions.

- Collect the stories of least ten heroines from ancient Greece. For the purposes of this exercise you may include female characters who do not have cult shrines. Refer to Raglan's list for heroes and formulate a list of no fewer than ten and no more than twenty-two actions. Include as many details as possible from the stories you have collected.

- Do you find any evidence that the historical conditions of men's and women's lives in ancient Greece might account for the patterning you find in these tales?

- Compare your list to Jezewski's list. What are the similarities and differences? How would you explain them?

- In what ways is your list (or Jezewski's) useful for understanding heroines in ancient Greece?

MARY ANN JEZEWSKI, *FROM* "TRAITS OF THE FEMALE HERO: THE APPLICATION OF RAGLAN'S HERO TRAIT PATTERNING" (1984)

Folklorists have recognized that regular patterns exist in the life stories of traditional heroes. VonHahn (1876), Rank (1909) and Raglan (1934) identified hero patterns independently of each other, but the frameworks they devised demonstrate that a similarity of pattern exists in the life stories of selected male heroes of tradition. In an attempt to see whether there is a pattern to the life stories of female heroes as well, and if so whether the pattern is valid cross-culturally, I attempted to apply Raglan's hero traits to the female hero of tradition but found that many of the traits he developed for the male hero did not "fit" the female. Consequently I developed a set of traits that reflect the life story of the female hero. The traits were compiled by investigating the life stories of female heroes in Greek mythology and by extracting certain motifs common to their legends. These were subsequently applied to selected female heroes cross-culturally and in various historical periods.

I define the hero as a person whose life story is passed on by oral tradition and/or written accounts and is remembered for exceptional deeds that have as their basis qualities exemplified in courage, power or magic. The hero may be a character of folktale, legend, myth or history.

The historicity of the hero of tradition has been discussed by various folklorists including Raglan (1936) and Dundes (1980). A major conceptual issue for Raglan was the existence of the traditional hero as a real person. He argued that the traditional hero most likely did not have a basis in history. But Raglan's use of the term myth to categorize the accounts of his heroes' life stories confuses his discussion of the historicity of the traditional hero. He refers to the myth and ritual surrounding the traditional hero when it would be more appropriate to discuss the influence of legend and folktale in patterning the life stories of heroes. Dundes (1980), indeed, states that Raglan's hero narratives are not myths but would be folklorically categorized as folktale or legend. By using legend and folktale in the folkloric sense, as a basis for patterning the life stories of heroes, the existence of the traditional hero as a real person does not present itself as a methodological problem as it did for Raglan and his mythical hero.

If, in fact, the pattern of the life story of a hero who is "real" is similar to the pattern of the traditional hero who has not lived, then the question is raised why these patterns are similar. It may be that the life stories of historical heroes are altered to fit a pattern or that fiction is made to fit life. In any case, a legend develops that encompasses specific motifs to create a life story reflecting appropriate attributes for a hero, attributes which seem to be universal, and which may be reflective of a phenomenon resembling Jung's (1952) "collective unconscious."

The reasons why the patterns exist are elusive and the applicability of a hero pattern cross-culturally is still debated. Nutt (1881) applied vonHahn's hero pattern to Celtic male heroes. Utley (1965) used Raglan's hero traits to "prove" that Abraham Lincoln was a mythical hero. Recently these hero traits have been applied to the life story of Jesus (Dundes 1980). Cook (1965) applied Raglan's hero traits to randomly sampled hero stories from the five major culture areas and concluded that the traits could not be applied cross-culturally outside of the circum-Mediterranean. Each of these authors applied the hero traits only to male heroes.

THE FEMALE HERO

There has been far less research and scholarly emphasis on the female hero than on the male but some recent publications (Coffin 1975, Pearson and Pope 1981, Lefkowitz 1981, Walker 1983) explore the female hero's life story in various ways. A search of the literature failed to expose any research that utilized Raglan's twenty-two elements or any concept of hero trait patterning to study the female hero.

The following is Raglan's trait list: (1934:214)

1. His mother is a royal virgin.
2. His father is a king, and
3. Often a near relative of his mother, but
4. The circumstances of his conception are unusual, and
5. He is also reputed to be the son of a god.
6. At birth an attempt is made, often by his father, to kill him, but
7. He is spirited away, and
8. Reared by foster parents in a far country.
9. We are told nothing of his childhood, but
10. On reaching manhood he returns or goes to his future kingdom.
11. After a victory over the king and/or a giant, dragon, or wild beast,
12. He marries a princess, often the daughter of his predecessor, and
13. Becomes king.
14. For a time he reigns uneventfully, and
15. Prescribes laws, but
16. Later he loses favor with the gods and/or his subjects, and
17. Is driven from the throne and city.

18. He meets with a mysterious death,

19. Often at the top of a hill.

20. His children, if any, do not succeed him.

21. His body is not buried, but nevertheless

22. He has one or more holy sepulchers.

In attempting to use Raglan's trait pattern for the female hero I discovered that the first five of Raglan's traits, those surrounding the hero's parentage and birth, can be found in many legends of female heroes. His traits 6 through 12 are seldom applicable to the female hero, with the exception of trait 9. Traits 13 through 17 need to be revised to apply to the significant events in the legend of female heroes. The death of the female hero seems much less important than the male hero's death by the fact that it is much less frequently emphasized in the legends of female heroes.

Many of the incidents in stories of females in Greek mythology were remarkably similar to each other, just as Raglan had found in his study of the male hero. I compiled eighteen traits that comprise a consistent pattern:

1. Her parents are royal or godlike and

2. They are often related.

3. There is a mystery surrounding her conception and/or birth.

4. Little is known of her childhood.

5. She herself is a ruler or goddess.

6. She is charming and beautiful.

7. She uses men for political purposes.

8. She also controls men in matters of love and sex.

9. She is married and

10. She has a child or children.

11. She has lovers.

12. Her child succeeds her.

13. She does a man's job or deeds.

14. She prescribes law.

15. There are conflicting views of her goodness.

16. Her legend contains the Andromeda theme and.

17. The subsequent resolution of this theme by treacherous means resulting in untimely death or exile, or incarceration, etc.

18. Her death is uneventful and may not be mentioned in her legend.

An explanation of several of the traits is necessary before proceeding to their application. Trait 13 refers to those activities that were deemed the domain of males at the time the female hero lived or her legend was popularized. I found that the female hero's legend revolved around masculine-like deeds she accomplished.

Trait 15 was found to be present in many of the legends of female heroes. The heroes possessed many attributes that were admired by the folk but the female hero's legend also tells of misdeeds (affairs, jealousies, revenges) that are condemned by those recounting the legend.

Trait 16 concerns a particular theme that recurs in the stories of female heroes and probably in those of male heroes—"the Andromeda theme" (Coffin 1975:37). It derives from the classical tale of Perseus. The beautiful Andromeda is tied to a rock as a sacrifice to a monster ravaging her country. Perseus sees Andromeda, falls in love with her, kills the monster, frees her and marries Andromeda. I found the theme repeated in many of the stories presented in this study. The "rescue" may involve the female hero choosing a lover more appropriate to her beauty, intelligence, and social position and being "saved" by this man from a life with one who is not considered a suitable mate for the female hero. In many of the stories of female heroes there is a resolution to the Andromeda theme (trait 17). As Coffin points out, "living happily ever after" is frequently a motif appropriate to characters in marchen but not necessarily to legendary heroes whose complete life stories are recounted. The female hero once "freed" by her rescuer may think twice about spending the rest of her life with him. Her hero looked good to her when he rescued her, but his shine fades after the blood has dried. Legend must resolve this conflict and does so in a variety of ways. The resolution of the Andromeda theme permanently removes the hero and/or her rescuer through treachery, resulting in untimely death or exile, or incarceration.

After developing the traits from stories of female heroes in Greek mythology the life stories of goddesses from around the world; female heroes from ancient Sumer; medieval, 17th, 18th, and 19th century Europe; and dynastic China were reviewed and selected. The incidents of their legends were tabulated and it was found that, indeed, their life stories are similar to those of female heroes in Greek mythology.

11.3 COMPARISON

ROME: MEDEA

Myths about Medea became popular subject matter for carvings on Roman sarcophagi in the second and third century CE, when burial increasingly replaced cremation in the Roman Empire. Battles, hunting scenes, weddings,

11.10 **Medea sarcophagus.** Marble sarcophagus with bas-reliefs. Imperial Roman. Museo Nazionale Romano (Terme di Diocleziano), Rome, Italy. © *Vanni Archive / Art Resource, NY, ART372595.*

abstract floral motifs, and scenes from the life of the deceased—as well as scenes from Greek myths—were among the decorations carved on the sides and lids of Roman sarcophagi. Scholars have puzzled over the significance of these mythological scenes. Were they learned allusions that indicated the deceased had been educated? Did they illustrate the deceased's character? Did they function as consolations for the dead, or for the living?

One sarcophagus that depicts Medea is particularly puzzling (Figure 11.10). On its left, Medea gives her two young sons poisonous gifts to deliver to Creusa. In the center, Creon watches Creusa writhe in suffering from Medea's poisons. In the final scene on the right, Medea is shown contemplating the murder of her sons and in her dragon-drawn chariot.

Some scholars have argued that Medea had become an agent of death to the Romans: in this case, she takes the life of Creusa, who represents the deceased entombed in the sarcophagus. In other interpretations, Medea's departure on her chariot represents the departure of the soul of the deceased. In still other interpretations, by refusing to accept the loss of Jason and causing others to suffer as she grieves, the tale of Medea offers a warning about the dangers of excessive mourning. None of these interpretations have a Greek precedent. Nor do they pertain to Corinthian cults to Medea's children, which to the Romans would have been curiosities from a distant Greek past, if they were known at all.

From this sarcophagus, then, it is clear that the Romans did not merely reproduce Greek myths about Medea. They changed both details and contexts to create new meanings. Roman myths about Medea, therefore, reflect specifically Roman (not Greek) concerns. For the Roman authors Ovid and Seneca, in particular, Medea provided an opportunity to consider the power of art and emotion to transform individuals.

SENECA'S *MEDEA*

Seneca (4 BCE–65 CE) was a Roman political figure, the tutor of Emperor Nero, and the author of essays, letters, and several tragedies, all of which directly discuss or are informed by his Stoic philosophy, by which, Seneca argued,

Map 11.2 Medea in Rome

individuals could find a way to conduct their lives that ensured their happiness. To achieve these goals, they had to seek freedom from poor judgments and distracting emotions, both of which, Stoics believed, were consequences of being ignorant of the divine reason they held to be inherent in the universe. Poor judgments and emotions left individuals easily buffeted by circumstances. The protagonists of Seneca's tragedies, such as Medea, in Seneca's tragedy *Medea*, are often interpreted as suffering because they fail to embody Stoic ideals.

In Seneca's play, Medea first appears as a woman who understands the commitment and devotion that love demands. The American philosopher Martha Nussbaum (b. 1947) suggests that Seneca presents Jason favorably to indicate that Medea has chosen him wisely, and that she loves Jason with a loyalty that she has every reason to expect in return from him. Her love is not unjustified; nor is the emotion of love itself problematic. Rather, Nussbaum argues, from a Stoic perspective Medea has made "a simple mistake about the value of a single man." In overvaluing Jason, Medea is unable to endure his betrayal. This leaves her enslaved to her emotions, not free in the Stoic sense. Thus the high value Medea places on Jason and her love causes her to commit monstrous actions. In a Stoic interpretation of Seneca's tragedy, Medea is less a foreigner or jilted lover, as in Euripides's play, than a representative of every person who has ever been betrayed.

OVID'S *MEDEA*

The Roman poet Ovid (43 BCE–17 CE) wrote about Medea in three different works: a tragedy that has not survived; his epic poem, *Metamorphoses*; and *Heroides*, a collection of letters from mythological women to their lovers, which includes an imagined letter from Medea to Jason (*Heroides* 12). In the *Heroides*, Ovid uses a particular kind of verse, called elegiac meter, to tell familiar stories from a female perspective. Other Roman poets, such as Catullus and Propertius, used elegiac meter to write love poetry characterized by the poet-lover's feelings of longing and despair in the absence of his beloved and his inability to persuade her to love him. Not surprisingly, then, in the *Heroides*, Ovid's Medea is less a powerful sorceress than a jilted lover. She begs Jason (who has already married Creusa, the Corinthian princess) to return to their marriage and their two sons. She recalls their courtship and all she has done for him in order to oblige him, while hinting at her rising anger. The reader knows that Medea will kill Creusa, Creusa's father, and her own sons, but these events are not directly stated or included in Medea's litany of woes. In the *Heroides*, then, Medea is surprisingly subdued. She is not depicted as a woman who revels in her power to seduce men, tame dragons, and commit murder in the name of love.

In Ovid's *Metamorphoses*, on the other hand, Medea is above all else a sorceress. The *Metamorphoses*, which is devoted to "how bodies change," portrays a Medea whose magical abilities suggest her similarity to the poet. Ovid's account of Medea begins in Colchis, but Jason's betrayal is a mere footnote to her actions. Instead, the center of Ovid's account in the *Metamorphoses* is Medea's assistance of Jason when he must complete his tasks in Colchis; her transformation of Aeson, Jason's father, into a young man; and her murder of Pelias. The repetition of the grim scene of Medea dismembering an old man and boiling his body in a cauldron (the first attempt resulting in rejuvenation and the second in death) highlights Medea's ability to change human bodies. Hers is a power similar to that of the gods, who accomplish other transformations Ovid describes. But this ability to cause transformation is also shared by poets such as Ovid. For Ovid's art, like Medea's magic, is capable of describing the transformations the gods accomplish and in this sense is the human counterpart of divine powers over bodies. In Ovid's *Metamorphoses*, then, Ovid implies that his artistry, like Medea's magic, can conquer nature.

OVID, FROM BOOK VII, *METAMORPHOSES*

Ovid describes the action of both Euripides's and Seneca's tragedies—Medea's murder of her sons in Corinth—in a mere five lines (7.390–395). His version of Medea concentrates on Medea's actions prior to her arrival in Corinth. (Translated by A. D. Melville.)

BEFORE YOU READ

- How does the character of Ovid's Medea differ from her character in Euripides's play?

- Compare Medea's strengths, actions, and travels in Ovid's account to Heracles's labors. In what ways is she similar to or different from that male hero? What insights about the character of Medea or female heroines does this comparison offer?

OVID, FROM BOOK VII, *METAMORPHOSES* (c. 1–8 CE)
MEDEA AND AESON

In Thessaly, for their sons' safe return,
The mothers and the aged fathers brought
Gifts to the gods and burnt the high-heaped incense

And the vowed victim with his gilded horns
Was slain; but one was absent from the throng,
Aeson, now near to death, weary and worn
By weight of years. Then said his fond son, Jason:
"Dear wife, to whom I owe my own return,
You who have given me all, whose bounteous favours
Exceeded all my faith—yet, if this thing   10
Your spells can do—for what can they not do?—
Take from my youthful years some part and give
That part to my dear father," and his tears
Fell unrestrained. His love touched his wife's heart—
How different from his!—and she recalled
Her own deserted father far away.
But close she kept her troubled thoughts and answered:
"How vile a crime has fallen from your lips!
So I have power to transfer to another
A period of your life! This Hecate   20
Forbids; not right nor fair is your request.
But more than your request, a greater boon,
I'll aim to give; not with your years I'll dare
The attempt but by my arts, to win again
Your father's years long gone, if but her aid
The three-formed goddess gives and with her presence
Prospers the bold tremendous enterprise."

    Three nights remained before the moon's bright horns
Would meet and form her orb; then when she shone
In fullest radiance and with form complete   30
Gazed down upon the sleeping lands below,
Medea, barefoot, her long robe unfastened,
Her hair upon her shoulders falling loose,
Went forth alone upon her roaming way,
In the deep stillness of the midnight hour.
Now men and birds and beasts in peace profound
Are lapped; no sound comes from the hedge; the leaves
Hang mute and still and all the dewy air
Is silent; nothing stirs; only the stars
Shimmer. Then to the stars she stretched her arms,   40
And thrice she turned about and thrice bedewed
Her locks with water, thrice a wailing cry
She gave, then kneeling on the stony ground,
"O night," she prayed, "Mother of mysteries,
And all ye golden stars who with the moon

Succeed the fires of day, and thou, divine
Three-formèd Hecate, who knowest all
My enterprises and dost fortify
The arts of magic, and thou, kindly Earth,
Who dost for magic potent herbs provide;   50
Ye winds and airs, ye mountains, lakes and streams,
And all ye forest gods and gods of night,
Be with me now! By your enabling power,
At my behest, broad rivers to their source
Flow back, their banks aghast; my magic song
Rouses the quiet, calms the angry seas;
I bring the clouds and make the clouds withdraw,
I call the winds and quell them; by my art
I sunder serpents' throats; the living rocks
And mighty oaks from out their soil I tear;   60
I move the forests, bid the mountains quake,
The deep earth groan and ghosts rise from their tombs.
Thee too, bright Moon, I banish, though thy throes
The clanging bronze assuage; under my spells
Even my grandsire's chariot grows pale
And the dawn pales before my poisons' power.
You at my prayer tempered the flaming breath
Of the dread bulls, you placed upon their necks,
Necks never yoked before, the curving plough;
You turned the warriors, serpent-born, to war   70
Against themselves; you lulled at last to sleep
The guardian that knew not sleep, and sent
Safe to the homes of Greece the golden prize.
Now I have need of essences whose power
Will make age new, bring back the bloom of youth,
The prime years win again. These you will give.
For not in vain the shimmering stars have shone,
Nor stands in vain, by wingèd dragons drawn,
My chariot here." And there the chariot stood,
Sent down from heaven her purpose to fulfil.   80
    She mounted, stroked the harnessed dragons' necks,
Shook the light reins and soared into the sky,
And gazing down beheld, far far below,
Thessalian Tempe; then the serpents' course
She set for regions that she knew of old.
The herbs that Pelion and Ossa bore,
Othrys and Pindus and that loftiest peak,

Olympus, she surveyed, and those that pleased
Some by the roots she culled, some with the curve
Of her bronze blade she cut; many she chose   90
Beside Apidanus' green banks and many
Beside Amphrysus; nor was swift Enipeus
Exempt; Peneus too and the bright stream
Of broad Spercheus and the reedy shores
Of Boebe gave their share, and from Anthedon
She plucked the grass of life, not yet renowned
For that sea-change the Euboean merman found.
    And now nine days had seen her and nine nights
Roaming the world, driving her dragon team,
Then she returned; the dragons, though untouched   100
Save by the wafting odour of those herbs,
Yet sloughed their aged skins of many years.
Before the doors she stopped nor crossed the threshold;
Only the heavens covered her; she shunned
Jason's embrace; then two turf altars built,
The right to Hecate, the left to Youth,
Wreathed with the forest's mystic foliage,
And dug two trenches in the ground beside
And then performed her rites. Plunging a knife
Into a black sheep's throat she drenched the wide   110
Ditches with blood; next from a chalice poured
A stream of wine and from a second chalice
Warm frothing milk and, chanting magic words,
Summoned the deities of earth and prayed
The sad shades' monarch and his stolen bride
That, of their mercy, from old Aeson's frame
They will not haste to steal the breath of life.
    And when in long low-murmured supplications
The deities were appeased, she bade bring out
The old exhausted king, and with a spell   120
Charmed him to deepest sleep and laid his body,
Lifeless it seemed, stretched on a bed of herbs.
Away! she ordered Jason and Away!
The ministrants, and warned that eyes profane
See not her secrets; then with streaming hair,
Ecstatic round the flaming altars moved,
And in the troughs of blood dipped cloven stakes
And lit them dripping at the flames, and thrice

With water, thrice with sulphur, thrice with fire
Purged the pale sleeping body of the king.   130
    Meanwhile within the deep bronze cauldron, white
With bubbling froth, the rich elixir boils.
Roots from the vales of Thessaly and seeds
And flowers she seethes therein and bitter juices,
With gem-stones from the farthest Orient
And sands that Ocean's ebbing waters wash,
And hoar-frost gathered when the moon shines full,
And wings and flesh of owls and the warm guts
Of wolves that change at will to human form.
To them she adds the slender scaly skins   140
Of Libyan water-snakes and then the livers
Of long-living gazelles and eggs and heads
Of ancient crows, nine generations old.
With these and a thousand other nameless things
Her more than mortal purpose she prepared.
Then with a seasoned stick of olive wood
She mixed the whole and stirred it. And behold!
The old dry stick that stirred the bubbling brew
Grew green and suddenly burst into leaf,
And all at once was laden with fat olives;   150
And where the froth flowed over from the pot
And the hot drops spattered the ground beneath,
Fair springtime bloomed again, and everywhere
Flowers of the meadow sprang and pasture sweet.
And seeing this Medea drew her blade
And slit the old king's throat and let the blood
Run out and filled his veins and arteries
With her elixir; and when Aeson drank,
Through wound and lips, at once his hair and beard,
White for long years, regained their raven hue;   160
His wizened pallor, vanquished, fled away
And firm new flesh his sunken wrinkles filled,
And all his limbs were sleek and proud and strong.
Then Aeson woke and marvelled as he saw
His prime restored of forty years before.
    Bacchus had seen from heaven this miracle,
So marvellous, and, learning that his own
Nurses could have their youth restored, obtained
That boon and blessing from the Colchian.

Then, to continue with her witch's tricks,   170
Medea, feigning enmity between
Herself and Jason, fled as suppliant
To Pelias, and there, since weight of years
Burdened the king, his daughters welcomed her.
In a brief while the crafty Colchian
Had won them with a false display of friendship.
She told, among her most deserving feats,
How she had banished Aeson's blighting years,
And, as she dwelt on that, led Pelias' daughters
To hope the like skill might rejuvenate   180
Their father too; and this they begged, and bade
Her name her price, a price unlimited.
She, for a time, was silent and appeared
To hesitate and kept them in suspense
By what seemed weighty thoughts, but in a while,
Giving her promise, "To increase," she said,
"Your confidence, the leader of your flock,
Your oldest sheep, my drugs shall make a lamb."
At once a shaggy ram was brought, a ram
Worn out by untold years, with curving horns   190
Upon his hollow temples. With her knife,
Her knife of Thessaly, Medea slit
His scrawny throat (his scanty blood just smeared
The blade), then in a vat of bronze the witch
Plunged the ram's carcass with her powerful drugs.
They shrank his body, burnt his horns away,
And with his horns his years. Then down inside
The vat was heard a small soft bleating sound;
And in a moment, while they marvelled at
The bleats, out jumped a lamb and skipped away,   200
Frisking to find a mother's milky teat.
The daughters were amazed: her promises
Had proved their truth. They urged her all the more.
   Three times had Phoebus now unyoked his team
When they had plunged in Ebro's sunset stream.
It was the fourth night and the shining stars
Were shimmering as that false enchantress placed
A pot of water on a crackling fire,
Plain water then and herbs that had no power.
And now in sleep like death the old king lay   210

Relaxed and with their king the royal guard,
Sleep given by her magic chants and spells.
The daughters entered at Medea's bidding,
And stood around the bed. "Why wait?" she said,
"Why stand there idle? Draw your swords and drain
His ancient blood, that I with young fresh blood
May fill his empty veins. His age, his life,
Is in your hands. If love and loyalty
Move you at all, unless hope springs in vain,
Do him this service. By those blades of yours   220
Expel old age; plunge in your steel, I say,
And let his sorry fluid flow away!"
    So urged, each in her loving loyalty
Vied in disloyalty, and each, in fear
Of guilt, was guilty. Yet not one of them
Could bear to see her blows. They looked away;
The wounds they gave, those savage wounds, were blind.
The old king, streaming blood, yet raised himself
Upon his elbow; butchered as he was,
He tried to rise from bed. Amid those swords,   230
So many swords, he stretched his pallid arms,
"Daughters, what are you doing? What has armed you,"
He cried, "to kill your father?" Their hearts failed;
Their hands fell. As he spoke again, the witch
Cut short the words and windpipe in his throat
And plunged him, butchered, in the boiling pot.
    Had she not soared away with her winged dragons,
She surely must have paid the price. Aloft,
Over the peak of shady Pelion,
Old Chiron's home, she fled, and over Othrys   240
And those fair uplands that Cerambus' fate
Made famous long ago. (By the nymphs' aid
Wings bore him through the air, and when the earth's
Great mass was whelmed beneath Deucalion's flood,
He escaped unflooded by the sweeping sea.)
She flew past Pitane of Aeolis,
Down on the left, where the long dragon lay,
A shape of stone; past Ida's grove where once
Bacchus had hidden, in a deer's disguise,
The steer his son had stolen; past the tomb   250
Of Paris buried in the shallow sand;
The meadowlands that Maera terrified

With monstrous barks; Eurypylus' fair town
Where wives of Cos wore horns when Hercules
Left with his troops; Rhodes, Phoebus' favourite;
Ialysos where lived the vile Telchines
Whose evil eyes had blighted everything,
Till Jove, in loathing, sank them all beneath
His brother's waves. And then she passed the walls
Of old Carthaea where Alcidamas   260
Would marvel that a gentle dove was given
Birth from his daughter's body. Then she saw
Lake Hyrie and the idyllic vale renowned
When Cycnus suddenly became a swan.
At that boy's bidding Phyllius had brought
Birds and a savage lion that he'd tamed;
Ordered to tame a bull, he tamed that too,
And, angry that his love was spurned so long,
Refused the boy the bull, that last best gift.
Pouting, he cried "You'll wish you'd given it!"   270
And leapt from a high headland. Everyone
Thought he had fallen: he was made a swan
And floated in the air on snowy wings.
But Hyrie, his mother, unaware
That he was saved, in tears dissolved away
And made the lake that keeps her name today.
Nearby is Pleuron, where on fluttering wings
Combe, the child of Ophius, escaped
Her son's assault. And next Medea saw
Calauria's fields, Latona's isle, that knew   280
Her king changed with his consort into birds.
Then on her right Cyllene where Menephron
Like a wild beast would share his mother's bed;
And in the distance she looked back upon
Cephisus weeping for his grandson made
A bloated seal, and on Eumelus' home
Who mourned his son, a denizen of the air.
     At last, borne on her dragons' wings, she reached
Corinth, Pirene's town, where ancient lore
Relates that mortals, when the world was young,   290
Emerged from mushrooms rising after rain.
But when her witch's poison had consumed
The new wife, and the sea on either side
Had seen the royal palace all in flames,

Her wicked sword was drenched in her son's blood;
And, winning thus a mother's vile revenge,
She fled from Jason's sword. Her dragon team,
The Sun-god's dragons, carried her away
To Pallas' citadel, which once had seen   300
Phene, so righteous, and old Periphas
Winging together, and the granddaughter
Of Polypemon floating on new wings.
There Aegeus welcomed her, in that one act
At fault: to be his guest was not enough;
He joined her in the bond of matrimony.

AFRICAN AMERICAN MEDEA

In January 1856, a party of slaves escaped from a Kentucky plantation. The group included a woman named Margaret Garner (also known as Peggy), her husband, Robert Garner, and their four children. The party crossed the frozen Ohio River and sought refuge in safe houses near Cincinnati. About half of the group successfully followed the Underground Railroad to freedom in Canada. The Garner family, however, was trapped by federal officials and slave catchers in the home of Peggy Garner's uncle, a freed slave, who lived near the city. The Garners fought against their attackers. In the course of the fight, Robert shot and wounded one of the marshals attempting to arrest him. Peggy, cornered, killed her two-year-old daughter Mary with a butcher knife. She also attempted to kill her remaining children.

Her trial became a cause célèbre for both defenders of slavery and abolitionists in the decade before the outbreak of the Civil War. Opponents of slavery argued that Peggy had murdered her daughter and planned to kill her other children and herself in order to spare them from a life of slavery. The historical record, however, does not include Peggy Garner's own words about her reasons or intentions. Considerable evidence suggests, moreover, that the child, Mary, was not Robert's but rather that of Peggy's owner. Thus it is possible that Peggy's motivation included an element of revenge.

Almost immediately, Peggy Gardner was compared to Medea, and her story was reinterpreted within the narrative structure of Greek myth. The painter Thomas Satterwhite Noble painted and exhibited the work *Margaret Garner* (1867), which is often referred to as *Modern Medea* (Figure 11.11). The work was part of a series of paintings on the topic of slavery that Noble, the son of a slaveholding family and a veteran of the Confederate army, produced. Noble's portrait, modeled stylistically on French classical paintings, departs

11.11 *Margaret Garner* or *Modern Medea* (1867). Thomas Satterwhite Noble (1835–1904). *From the Collection of the National Underground Railroad Freedom Center.*

from the factual record in portraying three dead children lying between Peggy Garner and her captors. The painting is almost lurid, and certainly sensationalizing. Peggy's expression is angry, while the captors look horrified—but it is left to the viewer to determine if they are horrified by the loss of life or the loss of economic value the dead slave children represented. The painting challenged its audience to consider who was the true monster in this event: Peggy or the slave catchers? The parallels with Medea are similarly suggestive. Were these women driven to infanticide in order to seek revenge, or to spare their children a worse fate—bastard status in Corinth or slavery in the fields of Kentucky? Noble's portrait of Peggy Garner is but one way in which Medea's story challenges us to address difficult social questions in a nuanced, thoughtful way.

Although the association of Peggy Garner's tragic story with the Medea myth seems obvious, it is not, however, simply the fact of infanticide that creates the analogy to Medea. Medea is not the only infanticide in Greek myth. The Theban princess Agave kills her son, Pentheus, in a Dionysian frenzy. After Tereus, the husband of the Athenian princess Procne, rapes Procne's sister Philomela and cuts out her tongue to keep her from telling anyone, Procne avenges the rape by killing the son she shares with Tereus. Yet Procne and Agave, unlike Medea, have not become synonymous with maternal infanticide. What makes Medea different?

The answer lies in Medea's agency and her ethnicity. She alone chooses to kill her children. She is not, like the Greek Agave, overcome with Dionysian passion, to which a modern parallel might be a female infanticide suffering from a profound mental illness. More importantly, Medea is not Greek. To Athenians, the notion of a foreign woman who is free to act on her own volition was frightening. Euripides's play takes for granted that Medea lacks political autonomy in a land different from that of her birth and interrogates how she nonetheless disrupts political dynasties (her murder of Creusa and the king) and destroys families (her own and Jason's future family with Creusa). African American writers of the twentieth and twenty-first centuries, including Countée Cullen, Owen Dodson, and Toni Morrison, have linked Medea's foreign identity to her political oppression and have found in her tragedy a way to explore the status of African Americans in American society. Their works are concerned with situating Medea's motives in the larger social context that she represents.

Countée Cullen (1903–1946) was an American poet associated with the Harlem Renaissance, a flourishing of African American artistic activity centered in the Manhattan neighborhood of Harlem in the 1920s. Cullen, who studied the classics in high school, went on to receive degrees in English from New York University and Harvard. In 1935, he published *The Medea, and Some Other Poems*, a collection that included his verse translation of Euripides's *Medea*. Cullen's *Medea* received mixed reviews. Some white critics wrote patronizingly about the apparent novelty of a black writer taking up a classical author. Black critics, in contrast, questioned whether ancient Greek literature could offer any meaningful insight on the experience of contemporary African Americans. Today, scholars regard Cullen's work as a significant achievement.

Cullen envisioned the role of Medea for the prominent African American actress Rose McClendon (1884–1936). McClendon, unfortunately, died before the play could be performed. In the years since, Cullen's *Medea* has not been widely produced. His choice of a black Medea, nevertheless, invites us to consider the play as (at least in part) a commentary on racial issues, even though Cullen's translation is largely faithful to Euripides's text. Thus, where Euripides explored the differences between Greek and barbarian, Cullen evokes the experience of a black Medea in a white America.

Cullen's *Medea* explores the question of human autonomy and obligation. What gives Medea the right to kill her children? What gives Jason the right to abandon them? Implicit in any defense of Medea or Jason is a claim that their status as parents confers both the ability and the right to dispose of their children as they would any other possession. Cullen, by extending the arc of Euripides's *Medea* both backward and forward in time, resoundingly rejects the claim that any human being, however young, can be owned. Any understanding of human relationships—whether it be the relationship of Medea and Jason as parents in ancient Greece or that of master and slave in America—that depends on concepts of ownership inevitably triggers a brutally destructive and dehumanizing struggle. This struggle is further underscored in Cullen's *Byword for Evil*, an elaboration of his *Medea*, in which he added an introduction and conclusion not found in Euripides. In the final scene of *Byword for Evil*, Jason finds Medea in Athens years after her murder of their sons. There he kills her son, Pandion, who he believes is her child with King Aegeus of Athens. Medea, however, reveals that the child was Jason's. Thus Jason becomes like Medea.

As a director of the theater department at the historically black Howard University, Owen Dodson (1914–1983) played a profound role in shaping the direction of African American theater. Like Cullen, he studied the classics as an undergraduate (in Dodson's case, at Bates College) and mastered traditional verse forms. While still an undergraduate (before his graduation in 1936), Dodson directed a Greek play, Euripides's *Trojan Women*. After college, he studied playwriting at the Yale School of Drama, where he wrote *The Garden of Time* (1939), a treatment of Euripides's *Medea*. Dodson's *The Garden of Time* begins in ancient Greece, but the action shifts to Haiti and Georgia before the Civil War. The characters are transformed along with the settings: Medea becomes Miranda, a Haitian woman, and Jason becomes John, the son of a Georgia plantation owner.

Although African American playwrights have made important contributions to Medea's mythical biography, it is the novelist Toni Morrison (b. 1931) who, in her novel *Beloved* (1987), has perhaps most indelibly traced the connections between Medea and the horrors of American slavery. Morrison has said that although she was aware of the story of Peggy Garner, she chose not to study it extensively. Similarly, whereas Medea's story has shaped the contours of Morrison's work, it would be wrong to reduce the novel to its devastating central action: the murder of a child by her mother.

Beloved describes the fate of Sethe, a former slave who, in attempting to escape from slavery, killed her infant daughter. As a free woman, Sethe lives in a house that is haunted by the ghost of that child. Sethe's relationship with the ghost is so all-consuming that it drives her surviving sons away. "Beloved," the word engraved on the child's tombstone, entered the story, according to Morrison, when the author began to consider who could possibly judge Sethe—who could choose between her suffering and her deeds. It occurred to Morrison that only the child itself would have the moral standing to judge Sethe.

After her mother-in-law dies, Sethe is left with the spirit of Beloved and her surviving daughter, Denver. The African American community treats Sethe with great caution, fearing the pride that led Sethe to kill her daughter. The arrival of Paul D, a former slave from Sweet Home, the plantation where they had lived, upsets the balance of Sethe's home. A struggle ensues between Beloved and Paul D for Sethe's love. In this struggle, Sethe and Paul D must confront the bitterness of their experience of slavery in order to heal. In the end, Beloved leaves, and Paul D returns to Sethe to stay. For Morrison, this theme of remembering is critical to understanding and redeeming the experience of slavery. Morrison dedicated the book to "60 million and more," an allusion both to the millions of Africans and their descendants whose lives were consumed by slavery and to a twofold injunction to her readers. First, Morrison urges us to remember the bitter past lest it be erased by history. But Morrison also suggests that individuals must remember the pain of slavery in order to reconstitute the self that slavery has shattered.

Morrison studied the classics as an undergraduate at Howard University, and scholars have noted her frequent allusion to classical themes in her works. Morrison, however, is also a keen student of the Western literary canon, the Judeo-Christian religious tradition, and the content and culture of African folktales that enslaved Africans brought with them to the Americas. All of these traditions are woven through Morrison's novels. Morrison adapts a Greek mythological frame for Sethe's story but transcends it by embedding the Medea tale into a much more complex meditation on the role of literary and mythic canons as well as memory in history. Writing new Medeas, artists like Cullen, Dodson, and Morrison add to the mythic tradition, deepening and reshaping our understanding of the original story.

KEY TERMS

Agamemnon 504	Erinyes 506	Jason 508
Antigone 520	Hecuba 506	Keres 501
Charilla 499	Helen 504	Medea 508
Clytemnestra 505	Hera Acraea 509	Menelaus 504
Creusa 509	Heroine shrine 502	Poene 501

FOR FURTHER EXPLORATION

Albersmeier, Sabina (ed.). *Heroes: Mortals and Myths in Ancient Greece*. Baltimore, MD: The Walters Art Museum, 2009. This lavishly illustrated collection of essays provides a well-organized and comprehensive introduction to heroes and heroines in ancient Greece.

Clauss, J., and S. I. Johnston (eds.). *Medea: Essays on Medea in Myth, Literature and Philosophy*. Princeton, NJ: Princeton University Press, 1997. This collection of informative essays covers a range of topics on Medea in both Greece and Rome.

Rankine, Patrice. *Ulysses in Black: Ralph Ellison, Classicism, and African American Literature*. Madison, WI: Wisconsin Studies in Classics, 2008. Rankine offers a reading of Countée Cullen and Toni Morrison in a broader consideration of how African American writers have deployed classical myths in their works.

Segal, Robert A. (ed.). *In Quest of the Hero*. Princeton, NJ: Princeton University Press, 1990. Segal offers a brief and lucid introduction to Raglan's work, although he does not consider the topic of heroines.

CHAPTER 12

ODYSSEUS AND QUEST HEROES

Since we are all condemned men and women, with a kind of indefinite reprieve . . . we are immensely interested in survivors, and identify with them in literature, rather more readily than we identify with tragic victims, or even with epic heroes too much contaminated with death. . . . Survivors impress us by their completeness.

—HAROLD BLOOM, *ODYSSEUS/ULYSSES* (1991)

Homer's monumental epics, the *Iliad* and the *Odyssey*, tell the stories of Achilles and Odysseus. Of the two, Odysseus has proved more appealing and accessible to artists and critics (both ancient and modern) than Achilles. Achilles is "too much contaminated with death," in the words of literary critic Harold Bloom. Odysseus, on the other hand, exhibits what Bloom calls a kind of "completeness" that other heroes (including Achilles) lack. The monumental efforts of will and memory required by Odysseus to successfully complete his journey bring his life full circle. He is above all else a survivor, one of the few Greek heroes who returns from the battlefield at Troy and lives to tell the tale. Yet it is Odysseus's long journey, filled with stormy seas, one-eyed giants, witches, and princesses, that has made Odysseus so attractive to generations of readers. His long journey home to Ithaca after the Trojan War makes Odysseus an exemplary quest hero.

< **12.1 (OPPOSITE):** Odysseus listens to the Sirens. Detail from a red-figure stamnos. Siren Painter. Fifth century BCE. British Museum, London, United Kingdom. *Erich Lessing / Art Resource, NY, ART14704.*

12.1
HISTORY

THE HERO'S QUEST

A quest hero is a type of hero known for the adventure he undertakes rather than his remarkable birth or death, a war he has won, or a kingdom he has ruled peacefully. In this chapter, we define the quest hero and describe his key characteristics. We consider the significance of the monsters and other creatures and characters that all quest heroes, including Odysseus, meet on their journeys. Other quest heroes we meet in this chapter include Bellerophon, Jason, and Perseus.

DEFINING A QUEST HERO

A quest hero is one whose primary task is a journey. He is always in motion as he pursues a precious object or person. He comes into conflict with those who try to stop him, and just as often he encounters personages who help him along the way. Because many heroes go on journeys in pursuit of a goal, the distinction between heroes labeled "quest heroes" and other kinds of heroes is one of degree, dependent on the stories told about them. If the written and visual evidence about a hero is primarily devoted to describing a journey he

Map 12.1 Odysseus and Other Quest Heroes

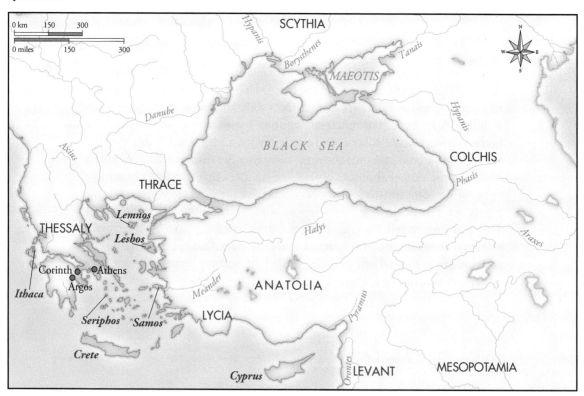

undertakes to obtain an object or achieve a goal, then such a hero is described as a quest hero.

The Anglo-American poet and critic W. H. Auden (1907–1973) distills six factors of a hero's quest that help define this category of heroes. (His essay discussing these factors is included later in this chapter). The six parts are as follows:

1. A "precious Object and/or Person to be found and possessed or married."
2. A long journey, undertaken by the hero.
3. The hero himself.
4. Tests and trials set for the hero that he must overcome.
5. "Guardians of the Object" who test the hero, or who may be "malignant in themselves."
6. Human or animal helpers who offer the hero knowledge, magic, or other assistance that is necessary for his success.

Auden's list can be further understood through the works of Vladimir Propp and FitzRoy Raglan, each of whom listed actions that define the hero's life from birth to death (Chapters 10.2 and 11.2). When the events in the middle sections of Propp's and Raglan's lists (the hero's adventures) dominate the stories told about a hero, then he may best be described as a quest hero. In Raglan's scheme of twenty-two events, for example, events numbered ten through thirteen describe the hero's quest: he journeys to or from his future kingdom, defeats its king and/or a monster, marries a princess, and becomes king.

The heroes in this chapter exemplify quest heroes. Jason, for example, is almost always associated with his journey to Colchis on the Black Sea to obtain the precious object he seeks, namely, the Golden Fleece. He is also associated with the princess he obtains in Colchis, Medea (Chapter 11.1). Similarly, Perseus is best known for his quest to obtain the head of Medusa as well as his rescue of Andromeda, an Ethiopian princess, from a sea monster, whereas Bellerophon is known for his quest for the Chimera. Odysseus, as we shall see, is the prototypical quest hero. Homer's complex and detailed portrait of his character and adventures includes characters who fit into the schemas of both Propp and Raglan, as well as Auden.

All of these heroes encounter characters who impede or assist their journeys. Odysseus is delayed by Polyphemus, the one-eyed giant, whereas Jason and the Argonauts are hindered by the bronze giant Talos. Many of the heroes' helpers (such as Circe, the witch who helps Odysseus, and the Lemnian women who entertain Jason and the Argonauts) are female. Interestingly, these female helpers are not completely benign. If a hero succumbs to their shared desires and remains with any one of them, he will never complete his quest or return home. Indeed, by the end of many heroes' journeys, the categories of "villains" and "helpers"—especially when it comes to female characters—overlap to a surprising degree. Thus these subsidiary characters demonstrate that any single formulaic list is inadequate to fully describe a hero's quest.

Villains and helpers also provide drama and suspense to the hero's quest, sustaining the interest of the poet's audience—after all, what fun would it be to hear about a hero without any adversaries or love interests? Yet, for many modern scholars and critics, the role of villains and helpers in myth and folklore is far more complex and revealing than it would be if they simply added spice to a long narrative.

Villains The villains who populate the quest hero's journey are sometimes not fully human. They may be giants, dragons, or wild beasts, as Raglan suggests, or they may be hybrids (that is, combinations of different creatures: the Chimera is goat, lion, and snake, whereas Medusa is a female with wings). Such beings blur the boundaries that separate human beings from other living creatures. The hero encounters them in caves, under the sea, or on mountaintops, and they act in ways that are socially unacceptable. These wild spaces, and the accompanying wild behavior, suggest that the villain is a creature who lives outside of society's rules, both geographically and morally. Thus quest heroes can be thought of as representing the ideals of their society, whereas the villains these heroes encounter represent characteristics or behaviors that are considered uncivilized or even frightening. Villains, in sum, express ideas about what is not socially acceptable. In Greek myths, these ideas are often linked to ideas about gender.

Both Jason and Odysseus, for example, visit islands whose inhabitants are unknown to them and thus pose great risks to their safety because they are most likely not Greek. In Greek society, a high value was placed on hospitability (*xenia*). Such hospitality involved more than good manners; it was a religious and ethical demand that was overseen by Zeus himself, who was believed to protect both host and guest as they interacted (Chapter 3.1). Hosts were expected to provide food and lodging to guests as well as to help them on their way in exchange for gifts and stories; guests were expected to be courteous and honest. Yet, repeatedly, as we will see, quest heroes (especially Odysseus) encounter hosts on islands far from Greece whose offers of "hospitality" range from the distracting to the downright dangerous. Indeed, on two adventures, hosts (Polyphemus and the Laestrygonians) from whom Odysseus expects succor and food instead kill and eat his comrades.

Helpers If villains are representative of things and behaviors the Greeks found abhorrent, then you might expect the helpers encountered by quest heroes to represent cultural ideals. This would seem to be the case for the princesses encountered by many quest heroes; such characters embody ideal feminine traits and help the hero achieve his goals. For example, Ariadne assists Theseus by giving him a silver string so that he might find his way out of the labyrinth; Medea gives Jason magic potions to help him accomplish his tasks; and Penelope sets up a bow contest between her suitors (who have harassed her in Odysseus's absence) and Odysseus (disguised as a beggar), so that he may defeat the suitors and reclaim both his home and his wife. Yet very rarely does a Greek hero remain with the princess who has helped him. More often, the princess fails to provide the hero with a kingdom (Ariadne), or she turns out to be as dangerous as the villains the hero has encountered (Medea). In Greek heroic quests, then, female helpers are as likely as villains to pose a threat to the hero.

The following synopses of quest heroes treat both the horizontal (biographical) and the vertical (lengthy treatments and multiple, often conflicting, accounts of their exploits) traditions of Perseus, Bellerophon, and Jason. In these case studies, particular attention is paid to the villains and helpers the heroes encounter. Finally, we take a close look at two villains encountered by Odysseus. We consider not only how those villains exemplify Greek suspicions about females and foreigners but also the ways in which Odysseus's encounter with and triumph over each villain demonstrates both the crafty intelligence and the curiously passive nature of his heroism.

PERSEUS

Almost no Greek literary treatments of Perseus's exploits survive. Of the seven tragedies we know of that were devoted to him, only titles and fragments remain. The most comprehensive written source, on which the following is based, is the Roman poet Ovid's *Metamorphoses*.

Perseus is the son of Zeus and Danaë; his grandfather, Acrisius, is the king of Argos. Having received a Delphic oracle that his grandson would kill him and usurp his throne, Acrisius imprisons Danaë in a room. But Zeus appears to her in the form of a shower of gold and impregnates her. When Perseus is born from this union and Acrisius overhears the baby crying, he locks both Danaë and the child in a large trunk and sets it out to sea, as putting them to death directly would incur the wrath of the gods. The trunk floats close to the island of Seriphos, where it is hauled out of the sea in a fisherman's net. Dictys, the brother of Polydectes, the king of Seriphos, welcomes and shelters Danaë and her child. But Danaë's freedom is short-lived; Polydectes, rebuffed as a suitor by Danaë, imprisons her in his house and sends Perseus to the Temple of Athena, where he spends his youth. (In other versions, Danaë and Perseus live out the next few years in Dictys's hut.)

Perseus's quest is inaugurated when he reaches adulthood. In most stories about Perseus,

THE ESSENTIALS

PERSEUS Περσεύς

PARENTAGE Zeus and Danaë

OFFSPRING Seven sons and two daughters (with Andromeda)

CULT SHRINES Athens, Seriphos, and Argos

12.2 **Perseus chases a monstrous Medusa.** Black-figure kyathos. Theseus Painter. 510–500 BCE. *J. Paul Getty Museum, Malibu, California, 86.AE.146. Digital image courtesy of the Getty's Open Content Program.*

Polydectes asks him to retrieve the head of Medusa as a way to dispense with the young man so that he might marry Danaë. Medusa, along with her two sisters, is a Gorgon. They are daughters of Phorcys, a sea deity, and Ceto, a sea creature. Of the three Gorgons, Medusa alone is mortal and is especially dangerous to mortal men: if a man looks at her, he will become immobilized and turn to stone.

Medusa as Villain Medusa is usually depicted as winged, wearing a short tunic and boots. Although her face is especially terrifying, with its grimacing mouth, protruding tongue, bulging eyes, and animal-like nose, Medusa is most familiar for the poisonous snakes she has instead of hair. In the known representations of Medusa and her sisters, they are most frequently depicted facing the viewer in a frightening manner (as anyone who looked at her directly was said to be turned to stone). Medusa is also often shown running from Perseus, attempting in vain to escape a gruesome decapitation at his hands (Figure 12.2).

In order to find Medusa and her sisters, Perseus must first locate three nymphs who will give him weapons to accomplish his task. He first visits the three Graeae (Gray Ones), also called Phorcydes, who are sisters of the Gorgons. Collectively, the Graeae have one eye and one tooth, which they share among themselves. Perseus snatches the tooth and the eye, promising their return in exchange for information about the location of the three nymphs. When Perseus reaches the nymphs, they give him winged sandals that enable him to fly, a bag in which to hide Medusa's head from view, and a cap of Hades that has the power to make its wearer invisible. (In other versions, Hermes, Athena, and Hephaestus are sometimes credited with giving Perseus these gifts, as well as a sickle and a mirror, which Perseus uses to decapitate Medusa while avoiding looking directly at her.) Perseus succeeds in finding the Gorgons and then decapitates Medusa, stowing her head safely in his bag (Figure 12.3).

During Perseus's return to Seriphos, he flies over Libya, where drops of Medusa's blood seep from the bag and produce a vast number of poisonous snakes. He also encounters the Titan Atlas, who threatens Perseus and thus provokes him to reveal Medusa's head. One glimpse of the head immediately immobilizes Atlas, turning him into a large mountain. In Ethiopia, Perseus finds the princess Andromeda tied to a rock and left to be devoured by a sea monster. Andromeda's punishment was demanded by the Nereids (sea nymphs), who were angry at her mother Cassiopeia for bragging that Andromeda was more beautiful than they. Cepheus, Andromeda's father, promises Perseus that he may marry his daughter if he saves her but then plots with Andromeda's actual betrothed, Phineus, to kill Perseus so that Phineus might still marry her. In other versions, Cepheus honors his promise, but Phineus and a troop of men attempt to kidnap Andromeda during the celebration of her wedding to Perseus. Perseus uses Medusa's head as weapon, turning Phineus and his men to stone, and then marries Andromeda. With her, he sires seven sons and two daughters.

After these Ethiopian adventures, Perseus and Andromeda return to Seriphos to release Danaë from Polydectes. Perseus shows Polydeuctes Medusa's head, turning the treacherous king into stone, and establishes the faithful Dictys as the new king of Seriphos. Finally, Acrisius learns of the survival of both Danaë and Perseus. Although the accounts vary, Perseus engages in an athletic contest attended by Acrisius. He hurls a disc that accidentally hits Acrisius, killing him. In this way, the Delphic oracle predicting that Acrisius would be killed by his grandson is fulfilled.

There is almost no mention of Perseus's death in ancient sources. Pausanias (a Greek author living under the Roman Empire) reports that Perseus was worshipped at cult sites in Athens and Seriphos, as well as in Argos, where Medusa's head was said to be buried. Near Medusa's head was also the grave of Gorgophon (Gorgon-Slayer), the daughter of Perseus, about whom almost nothing is known, other than Pausanias's claim that she was the first woman to remarry after the death of her husband rather than remain a widow as was the custom (2.21.7).

Medusa and the Feminine In addition to written accounts, many arresting visual images of Perseus and Medusa survive, suggesting ways to interpret their encounter. Although, as we have seen, Medusa is best known in her depictions as a winged monster with a fanged grin and snaky hair (Figure 12.2), she is also occasionally depicted as a beautiful winged maiden, whose sleeping posture emphasizes her vulnerability to Perseus's attack (Figure 12.3). Several ancient authors, including Pausanias and Ovid, present Medusa as a beautiful and fully human young woman. (Ovid even reports that Medusa had

12.3 Perseus beheads sleeping Medusa. Detail from a red-figure pelike. Polygnotus. 450 BCE. *Image copyright © The Metropolitan Museum of Art. Image source: Art Resource, NY, ART500333.*

especially lovely hair.) When Poseidon sexually violates her in Athena's temple, Athena punishes Medusa for defiling her temple. To modern sensibilities, it would seem that Poseidon should have been punished by Athena for raping Medusa. But ancient notions of crime and responsibility work rather differently. (Compare, for example, Artemis's treatment of Callisto, who was raped by Zeus; see Chapter 8.1.) As punishment for defiling her temple, Athena turns Medusa's hair into snakes. Rather than attracting men, Medusa now could only frighten them away (*Metamorphoses* 4.770). What could these two very different views of Medusa—a lovely young woman and a primordial monster—suggest about her meaning?

Two additional details from the stories of Perseus's decapitation of Medusa offer insight into this question. First, when Perseus decapitates her, Medusa gives birth to Chrysaor, a mortal male, and Pegasus, a winged horse, from her neck. Although frequently described in written sources, the birth of Medusa's offspring (the result of her rape by Poseidon in Athena's temple) is rarely shown in surviving visual sources. A sarcophagus from Cyprus is an exception (Figure 12.4). It shows how Chrysaor and Pegasus struggle to free themselves from her neck. Medusa seems to reach her arms up to pull them out. A dog quietly watches; Perseus placidly walks away. This startling scene emphasizes that Medusa is not only mortal but also a mother. Second, when Medusa is decapitated, she or her sisters were said to wail so beautifully that Athena invents a flute to imitate their songs.

Medusa's gruesome death, therefore, brings both beautiful music and the magical winged horse Pegasus into the world. In her qualities as both a female and a villain, Medusa is similar to the dangerously seductive female creatures Odysseus encounters on his journey, such as the Sirens (who delay men on their shores with their beautiful songs) or Scylla (who is also a beautiful daughter of Phorcys and Ceto, like the Gorgons, and is punished by a goddess). To the list of dangers that female creatures pose to quest heroes Medusa adds fecundity. Whereas Danaë gives birth to Perseus (who ultimately costs Acrisius his life), Medusa, though dead, gives birth to Chrysaor, Pegasus, poisonous snakes, and flute music. Her bewitching, beautiful, appalling head retains its creative powers, but they transform men into stone. The stories of Medusa suggest that female powers include procreation, magic, and art—alluring properties that threaten to transform men and their world in ways they cannot fully control.

12.4 Medusa, Perseus, and the birth of Chrysaor and Pegasus. Limestone sarcophagus. 475–460 BCE. *Image copyright © The Metropolitan Museum of Art. Image source: Art Resource, NY, ART500334.*

BELLEROPHON

Bellerophon is best known for his taming of the winged horse Pegasus and his defeat of the Chimera. Bellerophon's father was Glaucus, the Corinthian king (some accounts make the god Poseidon his father), and his mother was the queen, Eurymede. After killing a noble man (in some accounts he slays his own brother), he is exiled to the land of Proteus. Proteus, the brother of Acrisius (Perseus's grandfather), ruled Argos or Tiryns. When Bellerophon rejects the love of Stheneboia (or Anteia), the wife of Proteus, she claims that he tried to rape her. Not wanting to kill Bellerophon, Proteus sends him to his wife's father, King Iobates in Lycia, with a letter that (unbeknownst to Bellerophon)

THE ESSENTIALS

BELLEROPHON Βελλεροφῶν

PARENTAGE Poseidon and Eurynome, Queen of Corinth and wife of King Glaucus

OFFSPRING Hippolochus, Isander, and Laodamia (with Philonoe)

CULT SHRINES Corinth

explains Bellerophon's offense and asks Iobates to kill him. Iobates, like Proteus, does not want to anger the gods by slaying a man who entered his land as a friend, so he sends Bellerophon to kill the Chimera, believing that he will not survive.

The Chimera was a hybrid female monster. Her head was that of a lion and could breathe fire, a goat's head protruded from her back, and a snake's head was at the tip of her tail (Figure 12.5). With the help of Pegasus, Bellerophon succeeds in killing the Chimera. King Iobates then sends Bellerophon out to battle the Solymoi, a warlike race of Lycians, and the Amazons. When Bellerophon succeeds in these battles too, King Iobates sends some of his men to ambush Bellerophon. But Bellerophon fends off their challenge as well. At this point, King Iobates stops trying to kill him and offers his daughter Philonoe in marriage.

There are few myths about Bellerophon. In one of the best known, he tries to reach Olympus while riding Pegasus. Bellerophon's quest to reach Olympus is an affront to the gods, for whom Olympus is reserved. To fend off Bellerophon's assault on the divine realm of the heavens and to punish him for his effrontery, Zeus sends a gadfly to sting Pegasus, who throws Bellerophon off his back. Bellerophon falls to earth and is rendered limp or blind. Pausanias reports that Bellerophon had a cult site in Corinth (2.2.4). Although Bellerophon's adventures are relatively few in comparison to those of Odysseus or Perseus, his taming of Pegasus and his victory over the monster Chimera make them especially memorable.

12.5 Bellerophon and Pegasus confront the Chimera. Spartan black-figure kylix. Boreads Painter. 565 BCE. *J. Paul Getty Museum, Malibu, California, 85.AE.121. Digital image courtesy of the Getty's Open Content Program.*

JASON

Jason's quest intersects with Medea's myths (Chapter 11.1). Although Medea plays a significant role in the stories attached to his name and is responsible for his demise, there is far more to his life than his ultimately tragic relationship with her.

Jason's father was Aeson, the founder of a city (also called Aeson) in Thessaly. Aeson's brother (Jason's uncle) was Pelias. Aeson and Pelias shared a mother named Tyro, but whereas Pelias's father was the god Poseidon, Aeson's father was the mortal Cretheus. Thus Jason, unlike many heroes, has no divine parents or grandparents, although he is favored by Hera and helped by Athena. Like many heroes, he is raised away from his homeland—in this case, by the centaur Chiron in the mountainous regions of Thessaly. His return to his family precipitates his immediate departure. As Pelias, Jason's uncle, is making a sacrifice to his father, Poseidon, Jason turns up wearing only one sandal. Because Pelias had received an oracle telling him to beware of a man wearing one sandal, Pelias sends Jason on a quest that he believes Jason will not survive. He demands that Jason recover the Golden Fleece, which is guarded by a never-sleeping dragon in Colchis, on the Black Sea. In some versions, Pelias claims that Jason must obtain the Golden Fleece to justify his future kingship of the region.

Jason sets out from Iolcus on the *Argo*, a ship constructed by a man named Argus with the help of Athena. Because wood from prophetic oak trees was used in the ship's construction, the *Argo* has the ability to speak. As in the expedition to Troy (Chapter 10.1), illustrious men from all over Greece agree to sail with Jason, forming a band of sailors called the Argonauts. They have a series of adventures before arriving in Colchis (Map 12.2). The Argonauts travel to the island of Lemnos (in the northern Aegean Sea), where Hypsipyle, the queen, rules the Lemnian women, who have killed their husbands for being unfaithful. There, Jason fathers two sons with Hypsipyle, and the Argonauts have children with the other Lemnian women. Traveling further north into the Propontis Sea, they land on the shores of Mysia, north of the Troad, and are well received by Cyzicus, king of the Doliones. However, after their friendly departure, a high wind blows the Argonauts back to land during the night. The Doliones, not recognizing the Argonauts in the dark, begin fighting with them, and Jason accidently kills King Cyzicus. They flee and eventually land in Thrace, where the Argonauts encounter Phineus, a blind king who is starving to death because harpies (birds with female heads resembling the Sirens) steal his food. In exchange for killing the harpies, Jason receives directions from Phineus to Colchis. Phineus also gives Jason

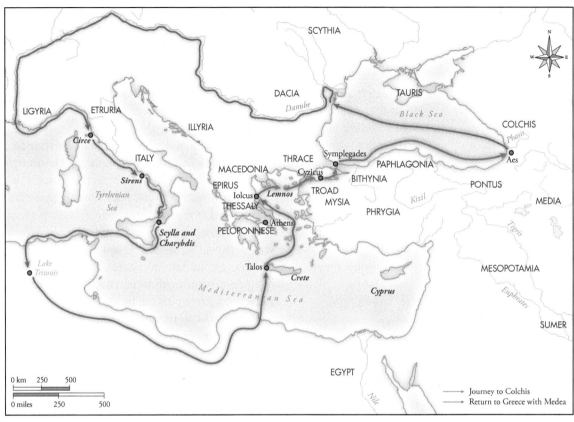

Map 12.2 The Voyages of Jason, the Argonauts, and Medea. Although some of these sites (such as Iolcus) actually existed, many other places are mythical. Their locations are speculative; this map reflects the conjectures of scholars and commentators over the centuries.

advice on how to defeat the treacherous Symplegades Rocks on his way to Colchis, which would otherwise have crushed the *Argo*.

Once Jason arrives on Colchis, he learns that King Aeëtes has possession of the Golden Fleece and will not part with it. King Aeëtes demands that Jason perform three tasks: he must tame and yoke fire-breathing oxen and plough a field with them; he must plant the teeth of a dragon and then defeat the soldiers, called Spartoi, who immediately spring up from such teeth; and, finally, he must defeat the dragon who guards the Golden Fleece. Jason accomplishes all of these tasks because Medea, the princess of Colchis and daughter of Aeëtes, provides him with drugs to protect him from the fire of the oxen, drugs to make the dragon sleep, and a ruse to make the Spartoi fight one another rather than attack Jason.

Once Jason obtains the Golden Fleece, he, the Argonauts, and Medea (accompanied by her younger brother Apsyrtus) flee from Colchis. [Interestingly, Jason had cult shrines in and around Colchis (Strabo 1.2.39).] On their way home to Greece, Medea dismembers Apsyrtus and throws his body parts into the ocean for King Aeëtes to collect and bury—a tactic they adopt to delay Aeëtes from catching them. Jason and the Argonauts, now with Medea, go on to yet another series of adventures.

Jason and Medea encounter three figures whom Odysseus also meets on his return to Ithaca. They first meet with Circe, who absolves them of the pollution they sustained by killing Apsyrtus. They next sail by the Sirens and avoid listening to their dangerous songs. Finally they pass by the six-headed monster Scylla and the whirlpool Charybdis. When the Argonauts are stranded on a sandbank in Libya, they prepare to die, until three nymphs visit Jason and advise that the Argonauts carry the *Argo* for twelve days until they reach Lake Tritonis. There, a shallow channel leading back to the sea allows them to continue their journey. Sailing northward, the Argonauts defeat Talos, a giant made of bronze who hurls rocks at passing ships to keep them away from Crete. This giant had one vein between his neck and ankle, which was attached by only one nail. (In this single but fatal weakness, he resembles the giant Cyclops whom Odysseus encounters, who has only one eye.) Driven insane by Medea's drugs, Talos removes this nail so that all his ichor (divine blood) pours out of him, draining him of life (Figure 12.6).

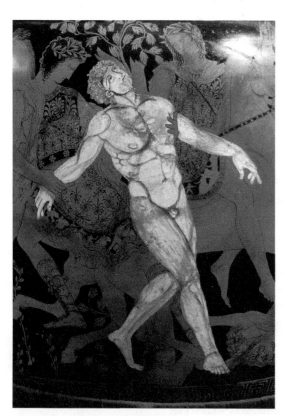

12.6 The death of Talos (detail). Detail from a red-figure Attic krater. 420–390 BCE. Museo Archeologico Nazionale Jatta Archaeological, Ruvo Di Puglia, Italy. *Scala / Art Resource, NY, ART88902.*

Many of these adventures appear in the *Argonautica* by Apollonius of Rhodes (third century BCE), a Hellenistic poet, Homeric scholar, and librarian who served in the Library of Alexandria in Egypt. (Map 12.2 is based on this account.) Apollonius, however, devotes more verses to describing Medea's growing love for Jason. Indeed, the stories concerning Medea seem to eclipse Jason's quest because Medea has a boldness and ferocity that Jason often lacks.

In her exploits with Jason in Greece, Medea develops in stature from a subservient female helper to a female hero who stands alongside Jason. On arriving in Iolcus, Medea restores the youth and vitality of Jason's father Aeson with her sorcery, dismembering him and placing his limbs in a cauldron with magical potions. Aeson emerges from the cauldron alive, whole, and young again. When the daughters of Pelias (Jason's uncle, who sent him on the quest for the Golden Fleece) witness Medea's resurrection of Aeson—in some versions, Medea rejuvenates a sheep (Figure 11.8, p. 509)—they ask her to give them her magic so that they might similarly restore their father, Pelias, to vitality. But when they dismember Pelias and throw his limbs in a pot, Medea refuses the promised magic, and he dies. Thus Medea destroys Jason's tormenter. From Iolcus, Jason and Medea arrive in Corinth. They marry and have two sons, and Medea takes on the role of princess. As we have seen (Chapter 11.1), their relationship takes a ghastly turn when Jason attempts to win yet another princess: Creusa (Ovid names her Glauce), whose father is Creon.

As quest heroes often defeat villains to win a princess and kingdom, at this point in the intertwined adventures of Jason and Medea, Medea shifts from being the princess of a distant and foreign (non-Greek) kingdom to being a villain. Jason must defeat Medea so that he can marry the princess Creusa. Medea, however, will not be easily subdued, and she eventually thwarts his heroic quest. She kills Creusa and Creon as well as her two sons by Jason, before departing on a chariot drawn by dragons belonging to Helios, her grandfather. She then goes to Athens, where she has secured refuge for herself with King Aegeus. To the degree that Medea becomes a villain that Jason must remove from his path to win a princess and kingdom, she embodies and expresses the overlapping of categories among females, foreigners, and villains in the quests of Greek heroes.

ODYSSEUS

In the *Iliad*, Odysseus is often contrasted with Achilles, who shines as the best of the Greek warriors. This is most apparent in the embassy to Achilles's tent (*Iliad* Book 9). When the Trojans are nearing the Greek ships and many Greek warriors have been injured, Agamemnon realizes how desperately the Greeks need Achilles to rejoin their ranks. He sends Odysseus, who is recognized as the most eloquent and diplomatic Greek warrior, to lead an embassy to Achilles's tent in order to offer him gifts and persuade him to return to battle (Chapter 10.1). Odysseus is accompanied by several Greeks, including Ajax, whose brief and direct speech Achilles praises (Figure 12.7). To Odysseus, who reports the long list of gifts that Agamemnon has promised to give to Achilles if he returns to battle, Achilles responds, "I hate that man like the gates of Hades' house who conceals one thing in his heart, but says another" (9.305–307). Achilles implies here that Odysseus is deceitful, that his eloquence is misleading and his words do not express his true thoughts and intentions. Intransigent and rash, Achilles is too young and too emotional to negotiate with Odysseus.

It is true that, for his part, Odysseus chooses his words carefully and most certainly "conceals in his heart" many of his thoughts and feelings. Restrained, eminently practical, eloquent, and intelligent, Odysseus thinks before speaking and acting. These abilities, often described as

THE ESSENTIALS

ODYSSEUS Ὀδυσσεύς

PARENTAGE King Laertes and Anticleia of Ithaca

OFFSPRING Telemachus (with Penelope)

CULT SHRINES Ithaca

12.7 Achilles (sitting) welcomes Odysseus, followed by Ajax. Red-figure Attic skyphos. Macron. Circa 480 BCE. Louvre Museum, Paris, France. © RMN-Grand Palais / Art Resource, NY, ART150157.

"passive heroics," and his cunning intelligence (described subsequently) allow Odysseus to survive not only the battle at Troy but also the long journey home, during which both his cunning and his rhetorical skills help him to resist dangerous seductions and to triumph over villains.

Like other heroes, Odysseus has a divine lineage. Zeus is a distant ancestor of Odysseus's father, Laertes, whereas Anticleia, his mother, is the daughter of Autolycus, the son of Hermes. Autolycus names the boy Odysseus, a word that comes from the Greek verb *odussasthai*, "to be angry with" or "to cause suffering." (In Latin, his name is Ulixes, whereas in English it is Ulysses.) Autolycus explains that he has suffered at the hands of men and women (although he does not specify how), and he therefore asks that his grandson's name commemorate his own life as well as Odysseus's maternal heritage. Odysseus's name becomes prophetic, as he becomes a man who will both suffer and cause others to suffer during his life.

Cunning Intelligence and Passive Heroics Odysseus's cleverness or cunning intelligence (*metis*), the trait for which Athena is known (Chapter 6.1), has earned him the epithets "very clever" (*polumetis*) and "very tricky" (*polutropos*) in Homer. As a descendant of Hermes, Odysseus has been labeled a trickster hero as well as a quest hero. He is endlessly resourceful and talented in the manner of both Athena and Hermes. Like Hermes, he is a shapeshifter, a master of disguise who escapes the detection of nearly everyone he meets. And like his patron goddess, Athena, he is a man of many crafts and talents: a shipbuilder, a farmer, an athlete, and a warrior. Endowed with such talents and fortunate in his divine benefactors, Odysseus is a hero equipped to survive in any setting.

In stories not included in Homer's *Odyssey*, Odysseus is always plotting and tricking others to ensure his survival. When Menelaus first asks Odysseus to fight with him at Troy, Odysseus (who does not want to leave Ithaca) pretends to be insane, until the princely soldier Palamedes places Telemachus, Odysseus's son, in danger and Odysseus saves him, thus revealing his sanity. With his trickery exposed, Odysseus agrees to go to Troy and then seeks to gather the best Greek warriors. When Thetis dresses her son Achilles as a girl so that the Greeks will depart for Troy without him, Odysseus lays weaponry and jewelry before a group of girls among whom Achilles is hiding. When Achilles reaches for the weapons and not the jewelry, he reveals his true identity—just as Odysseus did in response to Palamedes's trick. In both tales, Odysseus engages in trickery and acts both against and on behalf of his fellow Greeks. Moreover, it is Odysseus's trickery, not Achilles's bravery, that wins the Trojan War. Odysseus devises a large wooden horse in which Greek soldiers hide. Once it is wheeled behind the Trojan walls, the Greeks leave their cover and conquer the city, sealing both the fate of Troy and Odysseus's reputation for cunning intelligence.

Odysseus's cunning intelligence—often expressed in his rhetorical eloquence, which easily slips into deceitfulness, and his political acumen, which betrays his self-interest—defines his character in tragedies. Sophocles's tragedy *Ajax* begins after Odysseus, speaking more artfully than Ajax, has persuaded the Greeks to give him Achilles's arms. Whereas Ajax believes that, as the better warrior, he deserves the weapons, Odysseus claims that his clever device of the Trojan Horse has secured the victory of the Greeks over Troy. Odysseus's persuasive rhetoric leads to his acquisition of Achilles's arms and to Ajax's decision to kill himself after failing in an attempt to seek revenge on the Greeks. Odysseus then mediates a dispute about whether Ajax should be buried as a traitor (because of his attack on the Greek encampment) or as a soldier. Odysseus speaks with a skill and compassion that the other characters lack, arguing that Ajax should be buried with honors.

In Sophocles's play *Philoctetes*, Odysseus is a self-serving mentor to Neoptolemus, the son of Achilles; he counsels Neoptolemus that gaining one's objective outweighs all other considerations, including ethical ones. In the tragedies of Euripides, Odysseus appears both as a cutthroat politician (*Iphigenia at Aulis*) and as a man who must balance his moral inclinations against the necessities of the situation in which he finds himself (*Hecuba*). In these ways, tragedians explored the ambiguity of Odysseus's cunning intelligence in order to address the complex demands made on male Athenian citizens in both their public and private lives.

In addition to depictions of his cunning intelligence, Odysseus is also described as "passive" by some modern scholars because of his willingness to maneuver around hardship, to lie in ambush, and to keep silent about all that is in his heart and mind. Odysseus certainly does not lack physical strength, and he deploys it in feats of active heroics. But he also excels in the quieter but no less essential skills of planning, thinking, and keeping still. In his emblematic encounter with the Sirens, Odysseus plans strategically to defend his crew against their enchantments while allowing him to listen to and learn from their songs without succumbing to the dangers they present. He gives bees' wax to his men to plug their ears and has himself tied to his ship's mast so that he will not abandon both boat and crew while in thrall to the Sirens' songs. Rather than try to fight and destroy the Sirens, he ensures that he will be physically *incapable* of taking any action. The episode with the Sirens is also just one of many in which Odysseus contrives to satisfy his insatiable desire to acquire knowledge, a desire that is noted in the poem's opening lines, where Odysseus is described as learning the minds and cities of men (Figure 12.1). As Odysseus sails the high seas and encounters two especially memorable villains, the giant Polyphemus and the female monster Scylla, we come to appreciate the ambiguous nature of Odysseus's many talents.

Polyphemus, the Cyclops Homer describes the confrontation between the crafty Odysseus and the lumbering, one-eyed giant Polyphemus in rich detail (Figure 12.10). Indeed, Polyphemus and his fellow Cyclopes are represented by Homer as prone to rely on physical force because of their large size. At first glance, the story of Odysseus's battle against Polyphemus is similar to Jason's encounter with Talos or the biblical narrative of David and Goliath, in which intelligence triumphs over brute strength. But, rather quickly, the tale of Odysseus and Polyphemus becomes more complicated than a simple confrontation between brains and brawn.

Polyphemus is one of several Cyclopes (the plural of Cyclops) who dwell on one of the islands that Odysseus and his crew visit. Odysseus judges the Cyclopes to be lawless and arrogant because they do not pursue the activities that, by Greek standards, make a society civilized. He observes that the island's harbor is well suited to protect ships and that its verdant and rich land would support agriculture. But, he notes, the fields are uncultivated, and the harbor has no ships; nor are there public spaces marked for gatherings. Odysseus surmises that the island's inhabitants do not engage in agricultural work or seafaring. In addition, the lack of public gathering spaces suggests that those who live on the islands do not engage in the kind of conversation that leads to self-government or the cultural enterprises and social organizations that are the hallmarks of Greek civilization. Indeed, from this observation he deduces that each Cyclops establishes rules over his family, while being indifferent to his neighbors. Through these descriptions of the Cyclopes' society, we see how this encounter with a villain conveys not just an element typical of heroes' tales but cultural information as well.

Odysseus's actions in the cave of a Cyclops are as much a clash of cultures as a fight of brains against brawn. Odysseus and his men enter a cave that is well ordered and brimming with food, giving evidence of its owner's successful animal husbandry. There are baskets of cheese and buckets of milk, and well-built enclosures separating healthy lambs and baby goats from adult sheep and goats. Although Odysseus and his men admire the organization of the provisions, they do not hesitate to help themselves—uninvited—to all the food they want. Once sated, Odysseus's men beg him to leave the cave with as much as cheese and animals as they can get safely to their ships. But Odysseus is not persuaded by their pleas, for he wants to meet the cave's owner in the hopes that he might offer Odysseus gifts in addition to food—a typical practice among Greek guests and host.

When the cave's owner, a Cyclops named Polyphemus, enters, surprised and angry to see that uninvited strangers have feasted on his food, he asks if they are pirates: that is, if they are uncivilized thieves. (The reader is tempted to make a similar assumption.) But after the Cyclops eats some of Odysseus's men in revenge for Odysseus' violation of his cave, he loses the sympathy of the reader, showing himself to be cruel and frightening. Odysseus, on the other hand, takes the opportunity to demonstrate once again his cleverness. He tricks the Cyclops into getting drunk and then blinds him by driving a burning stake through the sleeping giant's eye, thereby creating the opportunity for him and his men to escape by clinging to the wool under the bellies of Polyphemus's sheep as they are let out to pasture.

Odysseus, it must be said, appears less than purely heroic in this episode, and Polyphemus seems not altogether wicked. When the blinded Polyphemus addresses his prized ram, who seems to be walking with great difficulty, he gently pets the animal and wonders if he is sorrowing for his master's ill fortune. Polyphemus doesn't realize that the ram is walking slowly because Odysseus is clinging to its wooly underside, using the poor animal to sneak past the Cyclops to freedom (Figure 12.8). Polyphemus appears compassionate, even empathetic, toward his animals. Appreciating Polyphemus's tenderness in this simple exchange with his ram encourages an alternative view of him, and of Odysseus.

Many scholars, observing these details in Homer's text, argue that Odysseus's forays into foreign lands can be interpreted as representing Greek colonizing efforts in the Mediterranean. In this view, the Cyclopes are similar to people who defended their property and families from Greek colonizers, and whose languages and customs were different from (and therefore viewed as inferior to) the Greeks. Seen in this light, the blundering and simple Polyphemus may represent Greek fears about non-Greeks, whereas Odysseus represents the cunning and bravery of the colonizing Greeks. As we have seen, the quest hero is almost always seen to represent cultural norms (in this case, Odysseus is the civilized and civilizing colonizer), whereas the villainous monsters the hero encounters reflect the exaggerated defects of those who are imagined to be outside of those norms (Polyphemus is a deformed, dangerous, and barbaric foreigner).

Scylla Odysseus's encounter with the female monster Scylla offers an interesting contrast to his encounter with Polyphemus. Scylla is part human, part fish, and part dog (Figure 12.9). She lives in a cave on

12.8 Odysseus escapes from Polyphemus's cave. Athenian black-figure column krater. 550–500 BCE. *The J. Paul Getty Museum, Malibu, California. Villa Collection 96.AE.303.*

12.9 Scylla. Terracotta plaque. Fifth century BCE. Louvre Museum, Paris, France. © RMN-Grand Palais / Art Resource, NY, ART427580.

cliff opposite Charybdis, a female whirlpool that swallows ships whole. (Jason, the Argonauts, and Medea also encountered Scylla and Charybdis [Map 12.2].) Because the dogs that grow from Scylla's groin eat human beings, Odysseus and his crew are in great jeopardy when they must sail between Scylla and Charybdis.

Although Odysseus tries to rally the courage of his men when he reminds them of their triumph over Polyphemus, Scylla still manages to capture and devour six of the sailors. And, in some ways, Scylla is even more savage than Polyphemus, who at least was a skillful farmer and manager of livestock. Further removed from human society than Polyphemus, Scylla creates chaos on Odysseus's ship, overwhelming the hero with mind-numbing terror and causing him to flail wildly and ineffectively with his sword. To a seafaring people like the Greeks, Scylla may have also embodied the restless energies of the open seas, where sailors are far from any visible port and prey to the fearsome appetites of unseen and unknown sea monsters.

This terror of the open seas and its creatures and the anarchic confusion Scylla represents through her hybrid body are of a specifically female nature. To some scholars, the dangers she presents are an extreme manifestation of the dangers that all female creatures present to Odysseus. Throughout the *Odyssey*, the hero and his crew are threatened by delay and even destruction at the whims of such beings (Map 12.3). For example, the beautiful nymph Calypso delays Odysseus for years on her faraway island with promises of immortality, whereas on another island the skillful sorceress Circe offers him a life of indulgence and pleasure. The sirens seduce him with their songs of praise, and the king's daughter Nausicaa holds out the promise that he will become king of Phaeacia if he marries her. Each of these beautiful females tempts Odysseus with different versions of a charmed life, and all (at least at first) seem quite different from Scylla. But, just like Scylla, all of them would keep Odysseus with them on remote islands, indefinitely delaying Odysseus from completing his quest and returning to his own wife on Ithaca. Whereas Scylla is the most negative version of this idea, she is different from the others by degrees, not in kind.

Even Penelope, the faithful wife of Odysseus, threatens to delay the hero from completing his quest. Homer describes Odysseus and Penelope as likeminded. They have the same strengths: they are patient and clever, and they are restrained in their speech. The matrimonial harmony demonstrated by Odysseus and Penelope at the end of Book 23 of the *Odyssey* is seldom represented in tales of quest heroes. The encounter of Penelope and Odysseus is told by the flickering lamplight of their private, late-night conversations, and the reader is lulled into

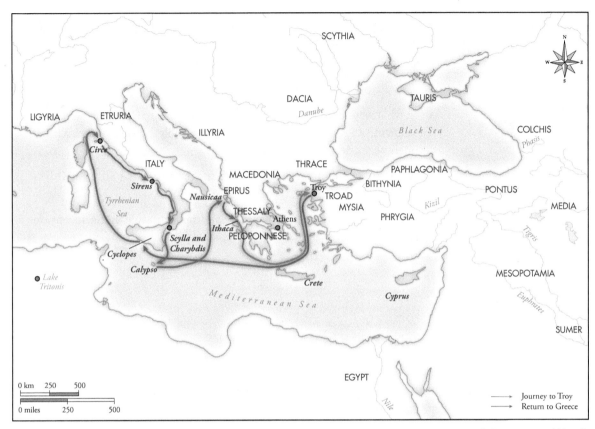

Map 12.3 The Odyssey. Although some of these sites (such as Ithaca) actually existed, many other places are mythical. Their locations are speculative; this map reflects the conjectures of scholars and commentators over the centuries.

believing that Odysseus's quest has ended with their reunion. But after Odysseus tells Penelope about his adventures, he informs her that he must leave home again in search of a land where no one has heard of Poseidon, in order to establish the worship of Poseidon in a new place and thereby appease the god. Thus, at the epic's close, Penelope, like all the women and female creatures that have come before her, must not delay Odysseus from his quest.

HOMER, FROM THE *ODYSSEY*

ʬ
BEFORE YOU READ
ʬ

Homer's *Odyssey* traces the voyage of Odysseus from Troy to Ithaca, where the second half of the *Odyssey* takes place (Books 13–24). On Ithaca, Odysseus disguises himself as a beggar to test the loyalties of his family, servants, and townsmen. He defeats the suitors who have depleted the resources of his house and recovers both his loyal wife Penelope and his kingdom. The following reading selections focus on two key adventures of

**BEFORE YOU READ
CONTINUED**

Odysseus long before he arrives home: his visit to Circe's palace (Book 10) and his journey to the Underworld (Book 11). (Line numbers for each excerpt correspond with the numbering for each complete Book.) (Translated by Barry B. Powell.)

- In what ways does Odysseus's encounter with Circe (spelled "Kirkê" in the following translation) differ from or resemble his encounter with Polyphemus (as described previously)?

- What sorts of dangers do female creatures like Circe pose for Odysseus and his men?

- How and why does eating play such an important role in the adventures of Odysseus and his men?

HOMER, FROM THE *ODYSSEY* (c. 750 bce)
FROM BOOK 10

"In a low place they found
the house of Kirkê, made of polished stone, in an open meadow.
There were wolves around it from the mountains, and lions
whom Kirkê had herself enchanted by giving them potions.
They did not rush up to the men, but waving their
long tails fawned about them. It was just as when   200
hounds will fawn about their master when he returns
from feasting, knowing he will bring them tidbits
to appease their hunger—so did these lions and wolves
of mighty paws cringe around them.

"The men were terrified
beholding what seemed terrible monsters. They stood   205
outside the doors of Kirkê, a goddess with beautiful
hair. They heard Kirkê sing within in a lovely
voice as she went back and forth before a great loom,
immortal, weaving a delightful, shining design
to please the gods.   210

"Polites spoke first, a natural
leader, whom I loved before all others, and trusted most:

'My friends, someone sings as she goes back and forth before
a wondrous loom, making the floor echo all around.
It is either some goddess or a woman. But let us make
ourselves known.'   215

       "So he spoke, and they all called out
to her. Promptly she came forth and flung open the shining
doors. She invited them in. In their ignorance they all
obeyed, except for Eurylochos, who suspected a trap.

   "She gave them seats on lovely couches and chairs.
She mixed up a drink of Pramnian wine and cheese   220
and barley and bright honey, pouring in dangerous potions
so that they might forget their native land. When she
had served them, and they had drunk, she struck them
with her wand, then penned them up in her sties.
They now had the heads of swine, and a pig's snort   225
and bristles and shape, but their minds remained the same
as before. They wailed as they were penned up, but Kirkê
threw them acorns, both sweet and bitter, and the fruit
of the dogwood, the food that pigs, slithering in slime,
so love to eat.   230

      "Eurylochos came back quickly
to the swift black ship, to tell what happened
to his companions and what was their intolerable fate.
But at first he could not speak a word, though he wished to,
so overcome with grief was he in his great heart.
His eyes filled with tears and he gave forth   235
a deep sigh. Then when all of us questioned him,
amazed, at last he told of the doom of his comrades:
'We went through the forest, noble Odysseus, just
as you ordered. We found the house of Kirkê,
in a low place made of polished stone, in an open   240
meadow. There, someone was going back and forth before
a great loom, singing sweetly, either goddess or woman.
They all called out to her. Promptly she came forth
and flung open the shining doors. She invited them in.
In their ignorance all of them agreed, but I alone   245
remained outside, suspecting a trap. Then they
vanished all together, and not one of them appeared
again, though I sat there for a long time and watched.'

"So he spoke, and I cast my silver-studded sword
around my shoulders, huge, made of bronze, and I shouldered   250
my bow too. I urged him to lead the way.
But he seized my knees and begged me, wailing, and spoke
words that went like arrows: 'Don't make me go there again,
you who are nurtured by Zeus, but leave me here!
For I doubt that you yourself will return, nor will   255
you bring back any of our comrades. But let us who
remain swiftly flee. There is still chance for escape!'

"So he spoke, but I answered him: 'Eurylochos,
you stay here beside the hollow black ship, eating and drinking.
I shall go alone, for go I must.'   260

"So speaking
I went up from the ship and away from the sea. But as
I journeyed through the sacred forest to the great house
of Kirkê, a connoisseur of drugs, Hermes of the golden
staff met me in the form of a youth who is just getting
his beard, in the comeliest time of life. He took   265
my hand and he said to me: 'Where are you going,
unhappy man, traveling alone through the hills,
knowing nothing of the country? For Kirkê has
penned-up your companions behind thick bars,
and turned them all into pigs! Do you plan on letting   270
them go? I'm telling you that you yourself will not return,
but will remain there in their company. But come,
I will free you from danger—I will save you. Here, take
this powerful herb and go to Kirkê's house. It will ward
off the evil day from you.   275

"'Now let me tell you
the deceptions that the goddess Kirkê has in store.
She will make a potion for you, and mix drugs
with your food. But she will not be able to enchant
you because of the herb that I will give you. I will
tell you the whole story. When Kirkê strikes you   280
with her long wand, then you must draw your sword
from your thigh and rush at Kirkê as if you wished
to kill her. She, in fear, will then urge that you sleep
together. Don't refuse the goddess's bed, if you wish
to free your companions and entertain yourself. But first   285
force her to swear a great oath to the blessed gods

that she will plot no further evil against you. Otherwise,
when your clothes are off, she will unman you.'

   "So speaking, Argeïphontes drew the herb from the ground
and gave it to me, showing me what it looked like.   290
At the root it was black, but its flower was like milk. 'The gods
call this *moly*. It is difficult for mortals to dig,
but there is nothing the gods cannot do.' Then Hermes
went off to high Olympos through the wooded island,
and I went on to the house of Kirkê, my brain boiling   295
with thoughts.

        "I stood before the doors of the goddess
with beautiful hair. Standing there, I cried out, and the goddess
heard my voice. Promptly she opened the shining doors
and invited me in, and I followed, disturbed in my mind.
She suggested I sit on a lovely chair with silver rivets,   300
finely made, with a footstool attached. She prepared
a potion for me in a golden goblet, bidding me drink it.
But she placed drugs within it, wishing me ill.

   "She gave it, and I drank it, but was still not enchanted,
so she struck me with her wand and said, 'Go now to the sty!   305
Lie with your companions!'

        "So she spoke. I drew
my sword from my thigh and rushed on Kirkê as if
I wished to kill her. But she with a loud cry
ducked beneath the sword and seized my knees,
and wailing spoke words that flew like arrows: 310
'Who are you? Where is your city? Who are your parents?
I can't believe that you drank my potion and yet
were not entranced. No other has withstood this drug,
once he has drunk it and it has passed the barrier of his teeth.
The mind in your breast cannot be enchanted! Surely   315
you are the trickster Odysseus. Argeïphontes of the golden
staff always said you would come, returning from Troy
in your swift, black ship. But come, put away your sword
in your scabbard. Let us go to my bed, there to mingle
in love. Let us learn, lying together, to trust one another.'   320

   "So she spoke, and I answered her in turn.
'Kirkê, how can you think that I would be gentle

with you, who in your halls have turned my men
into pigs? You would keep me here, bidding me
with deceitful thoughts to go to your room and there   325
to have sex with you. But when I am naked you would
unman me! I don't think I want to bed with you until
you swear, goddess, a great oath that you will not plan
further evil against me.' That's what I said, and right away
she swore as I asked. And when she had sworn,   330
then we went to her bed and I mingled with the very
lovely Kirkê.

"Meanwhile the four servants busied
themselves in the house, where they did all the housework.
They were children of the springs and the forests
and holy rivers that flow to the sea. One of them   335
spread purple cloth on the chairs, and beneath the cloth
white linen. Another set up tables of silver in front
of the chairs and placed golden baskets upon them. A third
mixed honeyed wine in a silver bowl, and set out
golden cups. The fourth drew water and lit a   340
fire beneath a large tripod, and warmed the water.
When the water had boiled in the brilliant bronze, she sat
me in a tub and bathed me from the great tripod,
mixing the water so that it was just right. She poured
it over my head and shoulders until she had taken   345
all the dispiriting weariness from my limbs. And when
she had bathed me, and rubbed rich oil in my skin,
she cast a shirt and a beautiful cloak over my shoulders.
She brought me into the hall and sat me down in a chair
with silver studs, wonderfully made, and a footstool   350
was fixed beneath it. A servant brought in a beautiful,
golden vase, and poured water over my hands into
a silver basin for me to wash. Beside the basin
she set up a shining table, and on it, the bashful
servant placed bread and all kinds of meats, making   355
free use of what she had on hand. She urged me to eat,
but I was not at ease in my mind. I sat with other thoughts,
as I considered the evil that might come.

"When Kirkê saw me
sitting but not eating, in deep sorrow, she stood beside me
and spoke words that flew like arrows: 'Why do you sit,   360

Odysseus, as if you were dumb, eating out your heart?
Nor do you touch your food or drink. Do you suspect
some other deceit? But you should not be afraid,
for I have sworn to you a mighty oath.'

                   "So she spoke,
and I answered: 'Kirkê, what sort of man, if he did   365
his duty, would dare to partake of food or drink before
he had freed his companions and beheld them before
his eyes? But come, if you urge me with true good will
to drink and eat, let them go, let me see my trusty
companions with my own eyes.'   370

               "So I spoke, and Kirkê stalked
from the chamber, holding her wand in her hand. She opened
the door to the sty and drove them out. They were like
nine-year-old porkers. As they stood around her, she went
among them and anointed each with another charm.
The bristles fell from their limbs that earlier a harmful   375
charm of Queen Kirkê had caused to grow. They were men
again, but younger than before, and more handsome, and taller.
They recognized me, and clung each one to my hands.
A passionate sobbing took hold of them, and a tremendous
sound reverberated throughout the hall. Even the goddess took pity.   380

  "She came near to me and spoke: 'Son of Laërtes, nurtured
by Zeus, much-devising Odysseus, go now to your swift ship
and the shore of the sea. First of all, drag your ship onto the shore,
and conceal your possessions and your weapons in a cave.
Then come back, and bring all your trusty companions.'   385

  "So she spoke. I was content with her advice. I went
to the ship and the shore of the sea. I found my trusty
companions wailing piteously around the swift ship, warm
tears poring down their cheeks. Even as calves, lying in a field,
jump up and prance around their mothers as they come   390
in a herd into the yard, having grazed their fill—for the pens
no longer hold the calves, but mooing constantly
they run about their mothers—even so did those men
crowd around me when they saw me, weeping copiously.
It seemed as if we had reached our native land, and the city   395
itself of rugged Ithaca where we were born and raised.

"With a hearty cry they spoke to me words that went like
arrows: 'Seeing you return, you who are nurtured by Zeus, we are glad
as if we had returned to Ithaca, our native land. But come,
tell us of the fate of our other companions.' So they spoke.   400

"I answered with gentle words: 'First of all, drag the ship
up onto the land, and place our possessions, and our armor,
in a cave. Then let us all hurry up to Kirkê's holy house
where you may see your companions both eating and drinking.
They have everlasting store!'   405

"So I spoke. At once they obeyed
my words. Eurylochos alone held back my companions and spoke
to them words that went like arrows: 'What? Are you crazy?
Where are you going? Are you in love with death? You would go
to the house of Kirkê, who will change you to pigs or wolves
or lions that you might be forced to guard her house? Just what   410
Cyclops did when our companions went to his fold,
and this *brave* Odysseus followed with them! He killed them
with his reckless behavior.'

"So he spoke. I weighed in my mind
whether I should draw my sword from my strong thigh
and cut off his head, rolling it on the ground, though he was   415
a close relation, my brother-in-law. But my companions
held me back with sweet words, saying: 'You who are
nurtured by Zeus, we will leave him behind, if you order it,
to remain beside the ship and guard it. Lead us to the holy halls
of Kirkê.'   420

"So saying, they went up from the ship and the sea.
Nor did Eurylochos remain beside the hollow ship,
but he followed along, unnerved by my savage rebuke.

"In the meanwhile, Kirkê kindly had bathed my other
companions and anointed them with rich oil, and cast shirts
and fleecy cloaks about their shoulders. We found them feasting   425
away in Kirkê's halls. When they saw and recognized one
another, face to face, the men burst out crying, and the hall
rang with their sobs.

"Standing near me, the beautiful goddess
said: 'No need for all this weeping any longer. I know

the great sorrows you have suffered on the briny deep, and how　430
many pains cruel men have shown you on land. But come,
eat and drink! Let your spirits rise, as they were when
you first left your native land, rugged Ithaca. As it is,
you are feckless, discouraged, thinking always of the hardship
of travel. It's hard to be happy when you have endured so much.'　435

　"So she spoke, and we did as she suggested.
Then we remained there all of our days for a full year eating
the abundant meats and drinking the delicious wine.
But when a year had passed, and the seasons turned
as the months passed along, and the long days came to an end,　440
then my trusty companions called me out, and they said:
'Odysseus, you are behaving strangely! We must think
of our native land, and whether destiny grants that we be
saved, and whether we will return to our high-roofed homes
in the land of our fathers.'　445

　　　"So they spoke, and my proud
heart agreed. We sat all day long until the sun went down,
dining on endless flesh and sweet wine. And when the sun went
down and the darkness came on, they took their rest throughout
the shadowy halls.

　　　"But I went up to Kirkê's very beautiful bed
and beseeched her, clinging to her knees, and the goddess　450
heard my voice. I spoke words that went like arrows:
'O Kirkê, complete the promise that you made for me,
to send me home. My spirit is anxious to be gone,
and the spirit of my companions too, whose grief breaks
my heart as they surround me, mourning whenever　455
you are somewhere else.'

　　　"So I spoke, and the beautiful goddess
answered me: 'Zeus-nourished son of Laertes, resourceful
Odysseus, don't remain longer in my house if you are unwilling.
But first you must complete another journey—to go
to the house of Hades and dread Persephone, to ask　460
for a prophecy from the breath-soul of Theban Tiresias,
the blind prophet, whose mind remains unimpaired.
To him even in death Persephone has granted reason,
that he alone maintains his understanding. But the others
flit about like shadows.'"　465

"When the holy Persephone
had scattered the breath-souls of the women here and there,
up came that of Agamemnon, the son of Atreus, groaning.
The breath-souls of all those who died and met their fate   365
in the house of Aigisthos were gathered around him.
Agamemnon right away knew who I was, after
he had drunk the black blood. He complained shrilly,
pouring down hot tears, throwing out his hands toward me,
longing to embrace me. But there was no lasting strength   370
or vitality, such as once dwelled in his supple limbs.

"I wept when I saw him and took pity in my heart,
and spoke to him words that went like arrows: 'Most glorious
son of Atreus, king of men, Agamemnon, what fate
of grievous death overcame you? Did Poseidon overcome you,   375
raising up the dreadful blast of savage winds among
your ships? Or did enemy men do you harm on the dry
land as you cut out their cattle or their beautiful
flocks of sheep, or fought for a city, or for women?'

"So I spoke, and he answered me at once: 'O son   380
of Laërtes, of the line of Zeus, resourceful Odysseus—
it was not Poseidon who overcame me, raising up the dreadful
blast of savage winds among my ships, nor enemy
men who harmed me on the dry land, but Aigisthos
contrived my death and fate and killed me with the help   385
of my accursed wife. He invited me to his house and gave
me a meal, as you kill an ox at the manger. So I died
a wretched death, and my companions died in numbers
around me, like pigs with white teeth who are slaughtered
in the house of a rich and powerful man at a wedding feast,   390
or a potluck, or a thriving symposium. You've witnessed the death
of many men, either in single combat or in the strong press of battle,
but in your heart you would have pitied the sight of those things—
how we lay in the hall across the mixing-bowl and the tables
filled with food, and the whole floor was drenched in blood.   395

"'But the most pitiful cry I heard came from Kassandra,
the daughter of Priam, whom the treacherous Klytaimnestra killed
next to me. I raised my hands, then beat them on the ground,

dying with a sword through my chest. But the bitch turned away,
and although I was headed to the house of Hades, she would   400
not stoop to close my eyes nor to close my mouth! There
is nothing more shameless, more bitchlike, than a woman
who takes into her heart acts such as that woman devised—
a monstrous deed, she who murdered her wedded husband.
I thought I'd return welcomed by my children and slaves,   405
but she, knowing extraordinary wickedness, poured shame
on herself and on all women who shall come later, even on those
who do good deeds!'

"So he spoke, but I answered: 'Yes, yes,
certainly Zeus with the loud voice has cursed the seed of Atreus
from the beginning through the plots of women. Many of us   410
perished for Helen's sake, and Klytaimnestra fashioned
a plot against you when you were away.'

"So I spoke,
and he answered at once: 'And for this reason, be not
too trusting of even *your* wife! Don't tell her everything
that you know! Tell her some things and leave the rest unsaid.   415
But I don't think you will be murdered by your wife—
she is too discreet and carries only good thoughts in her heart,
this daughter of Ikarios, the wise Penelope. We left
her just a young bride when we went to war. She had
a babe at her breasts, just a little tyke, who now must be   420
counted among the number of men. How happy he will be
when his father, coming home, sees him, and he will greet
his father as is the custom! My own wife did not
allow me to feast my eyes on my son. She killed me
before that.   425

"'And I will tell you something else,
and please consider it: Secretly, and not in the open, put your
boat ashore in the land of your fathers! For you can no longer
trust any woman. But come, tell me this and report it
accurately, whether you have heard that my son Orestes is alive
in Orchomenos or in sandy Pylos, or even with Menelaos   430
in broad Sparta. For Orestes has not yet died on the earth.'

"So he spoke, but I answered: 'Son of Atreus,
why do you ask me these things? I don't know the truth of it,

whether he is alive or dead. It is an ill thing to speak words
as empty as the wind.'   435

"And so the two of us stood there exchanging
lamentations and pouring down warm tears. Then came
the breath-soul of Achilles, the son of Peleus, and of the good
Patroklos, and of Antilochos, and of Ajax, the best in form
and stature of all the Danaäns after Achilles, the good son of Peleus.

"The breath-soul of Achilles, the fast runner, recognized me,   440
and, groaning, he spoke words that went like arrows: 'Son of Laërtes,
of the line of Zeus, resourceful Odysseus—poor thing! How will
you top this plan for audacity? How have you dared to come
down to the house of Hades where the speechless dead live,
phantoms of men whose labors are done?'   445

"So he spoke,
but I answered him: 'O Achilles, son of Peleus, by far
the mightiest of the Achaeans, I came here out of need
for Tiresias, to see if he had advice about how I might come
home again to craggy Ithaca. I have not yet come to Achaea,
nor walked on my own land—always I'm surrounded   450
by misfortune. But Achilles, no man in earlier times or in those
that came later is more fortunate than you. When you were alive
we honored you like the gods, and now that you are here, you rule
among the dead. Therefore do not be sad that you are dead,
O Achilles.'   455

"So I spoke, and he answered me at once:
'Don't sing praise to me about death, my fine Odysseus!
If I could live on the earth, I would be happy to serve as a hired
hand to some other, even to some man without a plot of land,
one who has little to live on, than to be king among all the dead
who have perished. But come, tell me of my good son,   460
whether he followed me to the war and became a leader or not.
Tell me of my father Peleus, if you know anything,
whether he still holds honor among the many Myrmidons,
or whether men deprive him of honor throughout Hellas
and Phthia because old age has taken possession   465
of his hands and feet. For I am not there to bear him aid
beneath the rays of the sun in such strength as I had
when at broad Troy I killed the best of their people,

defending the Argives. If in such strength I might come
even for a short time to the house of my father, I would   470
give pain to those who do him violence and deny him honor—
reason to hate my strength and my invincible hands!'

   "So he spoke, and I answered: 'Yes, I know nothing of Peleus,
but I'll tell you everything I know about Neoptolemos, your son,
just as you ask. I brought him in a hollow well-balanced   475
ship from Skyros to the Achaeans who wear fancy shin guards.
Whenever we took council about the city of Troy, he always
spoke first. His words were on the mark. Only godlike Nestor
and I surpassed him. But when we fought with bronze
on the plain of the Trojans, he did not remain in the mass   480
of men, not in the throng, but he ran forth to the front,
yielding to none in his power. He killed many men
in dread battle. I could never tell them all nor give their
names, so many people did he kill defending the Argives.
But what a warrior was that son of Telephos whom he slew   485
with the bronze, I mean Eurypylos! And many of that man's
companions, the Keteians, were killed because of gifts desired
by a woman! Eurypylos was the best-looking man I ever saw,
after the good Memnon.

       "When we, the captains of the Argives,
were about to go down into the horse that Epeios made,   490
and I was given command over all, both to open and close the door
of our strongly built ambush, then the other leaders and rulers
of the Danaäns wiped away their tears and their limbs trembled
beneath them. I never saw your son with my own eyes
either turning pale in his beautiful skin nor wiping   495
away a tear from his cheeks. He constantly begged
me to let him go out of the horse. He kept handling the hilt
of his sword and his spear heavy with bronze. He wanted
to lay waste the Trojans. And when we sacked the steep city
of Priam, after taking his share, a noble reward, he went up   500
into his ship unharmed, not struck with the sharp spear
nor wounded in the hand-to-hand, such as often happens in war.
For Ares rages in confusion.'

       "So I spoke, and the breath-soul
of Achilles, grandson of Aiakos the fast runner, went off,
taking long strides across the field of asphodel, thrilled   505

> because I said his son was preeminent. Other breath-souls
> of the dead and gone now stood in a crowd. Each asked
> about what was important to them."

12.2
THEORY

THE QUEST HERO

One of the most widely known and beloved poems about Homer's *Odyssey* is "Ithaca" by the Greek poet Constantine P. Cavafy (1863–1893). Here is the first stanza (translated by Daniel Mendelsohn):

 ### C. P. CAVAFY, *FROM* "ITHACA" (1911)

> As you set out on the way to Ithaca
> hope that the road is a long one,
> filled with adventures, filled with discoveries.
> The Laestrygonians and the Cyclopes,
> Poseidon in his anger: do not fear them,
> you won't find such things on your way
> so long as your thoughts remain lofty, and a choice
> emotion touches your spirit and your body.
> The Laestrygonians and the Cyclopes,
> savage Poseidon; you won't encounter them
> unless you stow them away inside your soul,
> unless your soul sets them up before you.

At first glance, it may seem like rather odd advice to encourage the reader to hope for a long journey: after all, Odysseus suffered over the course of his journey precisely because it was so long. Yet it gradually becomes clear that the poet sees the journey of Odysseus as a metaphor for life itself. He urges the reader to live life as though it were a long and rich adventure. The only monsters one would meet on such an adventure, the poet suggests, are those within—those which a reader might "carry . . . within your soul." In other words, Odysseus's journey (indeed, every hero's journey) is an extended metaphor for every person's life, and every person's life is shaped by his or her desires and fears, as well as the encounters shared along the way. These two notions—that the hero's journey is a metaphor for every person's life and that inner worlds meaningfully intersect with outer experiences on such journeys—explains the timeless universality of the hero's quest. This understanding is fundamental to the interpretations of the hero's quest to which we now turn.

JOSEPH CAMPBELL'S MONOMYTH

The American mythologist Joseph Campbell (1904–1987) adapted the work of many scholars to understand why a similar plot structure of the hero's journey was found in myths, folktales, and literature from around the world. Campbell delineated the hero's journey in a series of events similar to Raglan's scheme. Campbell also compared the hero's journey to initiation rituals as defined by van Gennep (Chapter 8.2). Campbell argued that the hero, like the initiate, sets out on a voyage away from home (the separation/preliminal stage), encounters adversaries and undergoes trials (the trials/liminal stage), and then returns home fundamentally changed by (and frequently wiser for) the experience (the reintegration/postliminal stage).

Because heroes' stories following this basic plot occur in societies from all different places and all different times, Campbell labeled the hero's journey a "monomyth." In *The Hero with a Thousand Faces* (1949), Campbell describes the monomyth in the following way: "A hero ventures forth from the world of common day into a region of supernatural wonder: fabulous forces are there encountered and a decisive victory is won: the hero comes back from this mysterious adventure with the power to bestow boons on his fellow man." Campbell explained the appeal of quest heroes and their stories by arguing that we are all heroes of our own lives. That is, according to Campbell, the life of every person follows the plot of the quest hero.

Campbell was also interested in the villains and the helpers that a hero meets on his journey. Although these subsidiary characters remain on the margins of a hero's quest, they nonetheless occupy an important role in understanding something fundamental about quest heroes. Villains and helpers may reveal flaws in a hero's character, if he is imagined from their perspective. More importantly, it is in the encounters with villains and helpers that the hero's internal desires and fears collide with his external world.

Campbell relied on the work of the Swiss psychiatrist and psychotherapist Carl Jung (1875–1961) to understand how the hero's engagement with helpers and villains corresponds to a psychological process that transpires below the threshold of consciousness (Chapter 7.2). Campbell, following Jung, argued that

12.10 Polyphemus. Terracotta head from Smyrna, Turkey. Fourth century BCE. Louvre Museum, Paris, France. *Erich Lessing / Art Resource, NY, ART63124.*

the hero happens on villains and helpers in his environment who interest him and who are important to his quest because they resonate with hidden aspects of his personality. This mingling of inner and outer worlds in the encounters the hero makes on his quest is similar to the process Cavafy describes: "you won't encounter them / unless you stow them away within your soul."

Ultimately, for Campbell, the hero's journey is the story of how an individual integrates his dream world with his waking life. Because the plot of the hero's quest never varies, and because the hero's journey represents the collision of the hero's unconscious with his conscious, the hero's quest seems filled with great meaning. Even when everything goes terribly wrong on the hero's quest, it somehow feels necessary and unavoidable.

SUBJECTIVE EXPERIENCE AND THE EXTERNAL LANDSCAPE

In "The Quest Hero," poet and literary critic W. H. Auden (1907–1973) offers a definition of quest heroes that, although less schematic than that of Raglan or Campbell and less anthropological than that of van Gennep, still shares some common traits with those conceptions. Auden emphasizes how the hero's quest, no matter how outlandish, represents the internal realities not of the hero (as Campbell suggested) but rather of the readers of the hero's adventures. Auden wryly observes that, despite the popularity of quest heroes, the audiences for such stories rarely embark on quests for adventure themselves. In other words, the hero's quest (with its voyages, monsters, princesses, etc.) does not correspond to the *objective* facts of most people's lives.

If the hero's quest seems somehow familiar, even sensible, no matter how fantastic or imaginary, this is because the hero's quest resonates with the reader's *subjective* experience. The quest hero's journey, Auden argues, reflects how individuals, especially the readers who thrill to these stories, experience their own lives. Heroes and regular people alike move through time, encounter various characters who are felt to be either harmful or helpful, accomplish their goals, and satisfy their desires. Whereas some of these accomplishments may seem fleeting, others are deeply significant in the establishment of one's identity.

Perhaps most importantly, the landscape the hero traverses and the characters he meets are not just in distant land but also very near. These exploits acquire meaning because they represent and respond to desires, fears, and hopes that not only lie at the hero's heart but are also reflected deep in the reader's subconscious. After offering a six-part definition of the hero's quest, Auden asks, "Does not each of these elements correspond to an aspect of our subjective experience of life?" For Auden, the villains and helpers encountered by the quest hero evoke subjective experiences shared by all readers.

W. H. AUDEN, *FROM* "THE QUEST HERO"

Review Auden's six-part definition of the quest hero.

- Compare Auden's six-point list to Propp's and Raglan's lists. Of the three, which do you think is most useful for studying Greek heroes? Of the three, which do you think is most useful for studying contemporary action figures? Explain your answers.

- What sorts of insights do a psychological approach to (Auden), a ritual approach to (van Gennep), and a formal description of (Propp) quest heroes offer?

- In what ways does Odysseus's encounter with Circe fulfill Odysseus's psychological as well as practical needs? To what needs and desires of male readers or female readers might such a fantastical journey correspond?

W. H. AUDEN, *FROM* "THE QUEST HERO" (1961)

To look for a lost collar button is not a true Quest: to go in quest means to look for something of which one has, as yet, no experience; one can imagine what it will be like but whether one's picture is true or false will be known only when one has found it.

Animals, therefore, do not go on quests. They hunt for food or drink or a mate, but the object of their search is determined by what they already are and its purpose is to restore a disturbed equilibrium; they have no choice in the matter.

But man is a history-making creature for whom the future is always open; human "nature" is a nature continually in quest of itself, obliged at every moment to transcend what it was a moment before. For man the present is not real but valuable. He can neither repeat the past exactly—every moment is unique—nor leave it behind—at every moment he adds to and thereby modifies all that has previously happened to him.

Hence the impossibility of expressing his kind of existence in a single image. If one concentrates upon his ever open future, the natural image is of a road stretching ahead into unexplored country, but if one concentrates upon his unforgettable past, then the natural image is of a city, which is built in every style of architecture and in which the physically dead are as active citizens as the living. The only characteristic common to both images is a sense of purpose; a road, even if its destination is invisible, runs in a certain direction; a city is built to endure and be a home.

The animals who really live in the present have neither roads nor cities and do not miss them. They are at home in the wilderness and, at most, if they are social, set up camps for a generation. But man requires both. The image of a city with no roads leading from it suggests a prison; the image of a road that starts from nowhere in particular suggests, not a true road, but an animal spoor.

A similar difficulty arises if one tries to describe simultaneously our experience of our own lives and our experience of the lives of others. Subjectively, I am a unique ego set over against a self; my body, desires, feelings, and thoughts seem distinct from the *I* that is aware of them. But I cannot know the Ego of another person directly, only his self, which is not unique but comparable with the selves of others, including my own. Thus, if I am a good observer and a good mimic, it is conceivable that I could imitate another so accurately as to deceive his best friends, but it would still be I imitating him; I can never know what it would feel like to be someone else. The social relation of my Ego to my Self is of a fundamentally different kind from all my other social relations to persons or things.

Again, I am conscious of myself as becoming, of every moment being new, whether or not I show any outward sign of change, but in others I can only perceive the passage of time when it manifests itself objectively; So-and-so looks older or fatter or behaves differently from the way he used to behave. Further, though we all know that all men must die, dying is not an experience that we can share; I cannot take part in the deaths of others nor they in mine.

Lastly, my subjective experience of living is one of having continually to make a choice between given alternatives, and it is this experience of doubt and temptation that seems more important and memorable to me than the actions I take when I have made my choice. But when I observe others, I cannot see them making choices; I can only see their actions; compared with myself, others seem at once less free and more stable in character, good or bad.

The Quest is one of the oldest, hardiest, and most popular of all literary genres. In some instances it may be founded on historical fact—the Quest of the Golden Fleece may have its origin in the search of seafaring traders for amber—and certain themes, like the theme of the enchanted cruel Princess whose heart can be melted only by the predestined lover, may be distorted recollections of religious rites, but the persistent appeal of the Quest as a literary form is due, I believe, to its validity as a symbolic description of our subjective personal experience of existence as historical.

As a typical example of the traditional Quest, let us look at the tale in the Grimm collection called "The Waters of Life." A King has fallen sick. Each of his three sons sets out in turn to find and bring back the water of life which will restore him to health. The motive of the two elder sons is not love of their father but the hope of reward; only the youngest really cares about his father as a person. All three encounter a dwarf who asks them where they are going. The first two rudely refuse to answer and are punished by the dwarf, who imprisons them in a ravine. The youngest answers courteously and truthfully, and the dwarf not only directs him to the castle where the Fountain of the Waters of Life is situated but also gives him a magic wand to open the castle gate and two loaves of bread to appease the lions who guard the Fountain. Furthermore, the dwarf warns him that he must leave before the clock strikes twelve or he will find himself imprisoned. Following these instructions and using the magic gifts, the youngest brother obtains the Water of Life, meets a beautiful Princess who promises to marry him if he will return in a year, and carries away with him a magic sword which can slay whole armies and a magic loaf of bread which will never come to an end. However, he almost fails because, forgetting the dwarf's advice, he lies down on a bed and falls asleep, awakening only just in time as the clock is striking twelve; the closing door takes a piece off his heel.

On his way home he meets the dwarf again and learns what has happened to his brothers; at his entreaty the dwarf reluctantly releases them, warning him that they have evil hearts.

The three brothers continue their homeward journey and, thanks to the sword and the loaf, the youngest is able to deliver three kingdoms from war and famine. The last stretch is by sea. While the hero is asleep, his older brothers steal the Water of Life from his bottle and substitute seawater. When they arrive home, their sick father tries the water offered by the youngest and, naturally, is made worse; then the older brothers offer him the water they have stolen and cure him.

In consequence the King believes their allegation that the youngest was trying to poison him and orders his huntsman to take the hero into the forest and shoot him in secret. When it comes to the point, however, the huntsman cannot bring himself to do this, and the hero remains in hiding in the forest.

Presently wagons of gold and jewels begin arriving at the palace for the hero, gifts from the grateful kings whose lands he had delivered from war and famine, and his father becomes convinced of his innocence. Meanwhile the Princess, in preparation for her wedding, has built a golden road to her castle and given orders that only he who comes riding straight along it shall be admitted.

Again the two elder brothers attempt to cheat the hero by going to woo her themselves, but, when they come to the golden road, they are afraid of spoiling it; one rides to the left of it, one to the right, and both are refused admission to the castle. When the hero comes to the road he is so preoccupied with thinking about the Princess that he does not notice that it is made of gold and rides straight up it. He is admitted, weds the Princess, returns home with her, and is reconciled to his father. The two wicked brothers put to sea, never to be heard of again, and all ends happily.

The essential elements in this typical Quest story are six:

1. A precious Object and/or Person to be found and possessed or married.
2. A long journey to find it, for its whereabouts are not originally known to the seekers.
3. A hero. The precious Object cannot be found by anybody, but only by the one person who possesses the right qualities of breeding or character.
4. A Test or series of Tests by which the unworthy are screened out, and the hero revealed.
5. The Guardians of the Object who must be overcome before it can be won. They may be simply a further test of the hero's *arete*, or they may be malignant in themselves.
6. The Helpers who with their knowledge and magical powers assist the hero and but for whom he would never succeed. They may appear in human or in animal form.

Does not each of these elements correspond to an aspect of our subjective experience of life?

1. Many of my actions are purposive; the *telos* toward which they are directed may be a short-term one, like trying to write a sentence which shall express my present thoughts accurately, or a lifelong one, the search to find true happiness or authenticity of being, to become what I wish or God intends me to become. What more natural image for such a *telos* than a beautiful Princess or the Waters of Life?
2. I am conscious of time as a continuous irreversible process of change. Translated into spatial terms, this process becomes, natu-rally enough, a journey.

3. I am conscious of myself as unique—my goal is for me only—and as confronting an unknown future—I cannot be certain in advance whether I shall succeed or fail in achieving my goal. The sense of uniqueness produces the image of the unique hero; the sense of uncertainty, the images of the unsuccessful rivals.

4. I am conscious of contradictory forces in myself, some of which I judge to be good and others evil, which are continually trying to sway my will this way or that. The existence of these forces is given. I can choose to yield to a desire or to resist it, but I cannot by choice desire or not desire.

Any image of this experience must be dualistic, a contest between two sides, friends and enemies.

On the other hand, the Quest provides no image of our objective experience of social life. If I exclude my own feelings and try to look at the world as if I were the lens of a camera, I observe that the vast majority of people have to earn their living in a fixed place, and that journeys are confined to people on holiday or with independent means. I observe that, though there may be some wars which can be called just, there are none in which one side is absolutely good and the other absolutely evil, though it is all too common for both sides to persuade themselves that this is so. As for struggles between man and the forces of nature or wild beasts, I can see that nature is unaware of being destructive and that, though there are animals which attack men out of hunger or fear, no animal does so out of malice.

In many versions of the Quest, both ancient and modern, the winning or recovery of the Precious Object is for the common good of the society to which the hero belongs. Even when the goal of his quest is marriage, it is not any girl he is after but a Princess. Their personal happiness is incidental to the happiness of the City; now the Kingdom will be well governed, and there will soon be an heir.

But there are other versions in which success is of importance only to the individual who achieves it. The Holy Grail, for example, will never again become visible to all men; only the exceptionally noble and chaste can be allowed to see it.

Again, there are two types of Quest Hero. One resembles the hero of Epic; his superior *arete* is manifest to all. Jason, for example, is instantly recognizable as the kind of man who can win the Golden Fleece if anybody can. The other type, so common in fairy tales, is the hero whose *arete* is concealed. The youngest son, the weakest, the least clever, the one whom everybody would judge as least likely to succeed, turns out to be the hero when his manifest betters have failed. He owes his success, not to his own powers, but to the fairies, magicians, and animals who help him, and he is able to enlist their help because, unlike his betters, he is humble enough to take advice, and kind enough to give assistance to strangers who, like himself, appear to be nobody in particular.

12.3 COMPARISON

MESOPOTAMIA AND ROME: GILGAMESH AND AENEAS

In her 1953 book *The Sword from the Rock: An Investigation into the Origins of Epic Literature and the Development of the Hero*, classical scholar Gertrude Rachel Levy writes, "[Heroes] navigate the waters of death to learn their destiny from an ancestor or prophet, as Gilgamesh, Odysseus and Aeneas did. If they find what they seek, they are likely to lose it again." Aeneas, the hero of the Roman epic *Aeneid*, and Gilgamesh, the hero of the Mesopotamian *Epic of Gilgamesh*, share affinities not only with Achilles in the *Iliad* (Chapter 10.3) but also with the Odysseus of the *Odyssey*. Like Odysseus, who travels to Hades in Book 11 of the *Odyssey*, both Gilgamesh and Aeneas travel to the Underworld in order to gain knowledge from an ancestor or guide. A journey to the Underworld is a common feature in heroes' quests; the Greek word *katabasis*, which translates as "descent," is used in English to describe this particular kind of adventure. In this section, we consider the distinctions and similarities among the journeys to the Underworld of Gilgamesh, Aeneas, and Odysseus.

12.11 Odyssey greets Teresias, rising from the ground, in the Underworld. Detail from red-figure calyx krater. Dolon Painter. 380 BCE. *Bibliotheque Nationale, Paris France. Erich Lessing / Art Resource, NY, ART13902.*

GILGAMESH AND THE WATERS OF DEATH

During the course of the *Epic of Gilgamesh*, Gilgamesh goes on two long quests. On the first quest, he and his beloved companion Enkidu set out to conquer the monster Humbaba and steal the cedar trees he guards. They successfully defeat the fierce, fire-breathing monster and decapitate him. On their return to the city of Uruk, Gilgamesh refuses the seductions of the goddess Ishtar, who, enraged by his rejection, sends the bull of heaven against the two heroes. They succeed in defeating this monster, but Ishtar demands that Enkidu die as a punishment for the bull's death (Chapter 10.3). His death compels Gilgamesh to contemplate his own death (Tablets II–VI). Gilgamesh mourns Enkidu, building a statue in his honor and promising that the whole city of Uruk will lament him (Tablet VIII). Nonetheless Gilgamesh remains inconsolable and wonders, "Shall I die too? Am I not like Enkidu? . . . I am afraid of Death, and so I roam open country" (Tablet IX). Gilgamesh then embarks on a second quest to understand and possibly escape his own mortality.

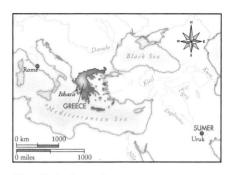

Map 12.4 Odysseus from Mesopotamia to Rome

Wearing only a lion skin, his matted hair indicating that he has shrugged off the trappings of civilization, Gilgamesh leaves Uruk. He travels through a mountain pass of complete darkness until he reaches an earthly paradise where "spiky bushes were visible, blossoming with gemstones." There he meets Siduri, "the alewife, who lives by the sea." She instructs him to find a ferryman in order to pass over the waters of death, where he meets with Utnapishtim, a man who has survived a global flood and has, along with his wife, been granted eternal life. Utnapishtim explains to Gilgamesh that "death is inevitable at some time" and that Gilgamesh is fortunate because "a throne has been set down for [him]." In other words, Utnapishtim urges Gilgamesh to accept his mortality and enjoy his fortunate birth in this life as a king.

Gilgamesh's grief and fear are not appeased by this advice, however, and so Utnapishtim sets Gilgamesh a test to see if he is worthy of gaining the eternal life he so desires: Gilgamesh must stay awake for six days and seven nights. But, exhausted from his journey, Gilgamesh falls immediately to sleep. To keep track of how long he sleeps, Utnapishtim's wife bakes a loaf of bread each day. When Gilgamesh awakes and sees the number of loaves she has baked, he realizes he has failed the test.

To compensate him for his failed attempt to gain eternal life, Utnapishtim tells Gilgamesh about a plant at the bottom of the sea that, should Gilgamesh find it, will grant him eternal life. Gilgamesh again travels across waters. He finds the plant, but it is stolen by a snake. Gilgamesh finally accepts that he cannot escape mortality. He returns to Uruk and rules his kingdom wisely, without the violence and indifference that characterized his kingship before his relationship with Enkidu and his visit with Utnapishtim. For Gilgamesh, his kingdom is a consolation, although it is not the goal for which he embarked on his quest. Gilgamesh accepts Utnapishtim's explanation of mortality and his advice not to scorn the small portion of living that the gods have granted him.

ODYSSEUS IN THE UNDERWORLD

The *Epic of Gilgamesh* predates Homer's *Odyssey* and *Iliad* by several centuries, and each Greek hero is modeled to some degree on Gilgamesh. Just as the motif of Achilles's grief over the loss of Patroclus recalls the sorrow of

Gilgamesh at the death of Enkidu, the journey of Odysseus to the Underworld is, in broad outline, similar to Gilgamesh's journey through the waters of death. Yet Gilgamesh seeks immortality, whereas Odysseus travels to the Underworld in order to learn from Tiresias how he might return home to Ithaca (Book 11) (Figure 12.11). His journey does not bring him existential insight about the finitude of human existence, nor is it especially solitary or grim. Rather, Odysseus's visit to the Underworld is a largely social enterprise, consisting of a series of engaging conversations. It is fueled by Odysseus's curiosity not only about how to get home to Ithaca (the reason for his visit) but also about the larger human community: those he left behind in Ithaca and Troy, as well as those communities of which he was never a part. Odysseus speaks with the spirit of his mother, Anticleia, who tells him what has happened in Ithaca during his absence. He talks to a number of women, whom he did not know while they were alive, who describe their experiences while their husbands were at war. Odysseus's conversations with them once again demonstrate that knowledge is as desirable to him as material goods and reveal his empathetic intelligence.

Odysseus also converses with the ghosts of his companions at Troy. They tell him about their travails on their sea voyages back to Greece and, more importantly, what happened to them once they reached their cities and families. These stories complete the tales of the heroes that began in Troy and were recounted in the *Iliad*. Through them, Odysseus's past takes on a new and more somber aspect. He realizes that most of his companions have died, and he will not meet them in life again even if he manages to return to Greece. Thus, through his encounter with his companions in the Underworld, Odysseus realizes his past as an Iliadic hero has come to end.

Odysseus's time in the Underworld, then, is very different from the time spent by Gilgamesh. It allows Odysseus to survey his past at Troy, to understand Penelope's time without him, and to anticipate his future in Ithaca. In contrast, when Gilgamesh traverses the waters of death, he comes away with an understanding of life's finitude. Although he does not relinquish his grief for Enkidu, he is able at last to place Enkidu's death and his own within a framework of human generations and human achievements bounded by city walls and communities. Gilgamesh chooses to return to Uruk and rule as king, although this is a consolation for the immortality he could not gain; he did not desire to be king, nor was becoming a king the reason he set out on his quest. Odysseus, on the other hand, chooses Ithaca, his kingship, swineherds, loyal dogs, his wife, and his son, with gleeful relish. His conversations in the gloomy halls of the Underworld promise the warmth of the fires in his own halls in Ithaca and spur him to continue homeward to achieve his heart's desire.

AENEAS IN AVERNUS

In Vergil's *Aeneid*, Aeneas, like Odysseus, travels west from Troy. Vergil very deliberately took Odysseus's journey as the model for Aeneas's travels. Yet the formal similarities between these journeys are dwarfed by their differences. Aeneas narrates the tales of his journey to Dido and the Carthaginians, just as Odysseus narrated his adventures to the Phaeacians. Although Aeneas travels to a few of the same places as Odysseus, he meets far fewer fantastical characters. Instead, most of Aeneas's adventures culminate in the acquisition of an oracle through which he increasingly develops a sense of the mission imposed on him from the gods: to found Rome with his band of surviving Trojans.

The process of developing an understanding of his quest continues when Aeneas goes to the Underworld (called Avernus). He is guided not by his own curiosity and desire but by the Cumaean Sibyl, a priestess. Aeneas's journey is explicitly didactic because he learns about the ancestors and history of the new land and its people where he will found Rome. As one of the last places he visits before establishing his new kingdom, Aeneas's trip to the Underworld succeeds in transforming him into Rome's founder.

VERGIL, FROM *AENEID*
&
UNKNOWN, FROM THE *EPIC OF GILGAMESH*

BEFORE YOU READ

Whether leaving Troy or founding Rome, Aeneas, unlike Gilgamesh and Odysseus, is always in the company of others. This fact distinguishes Aeneas from Gilgamesh and Odysseus. It suggests that Aeneas's quest is different from theirs because, rather than representing an attempt to ensure his own immortality and fame, the efforts of Aeneas are directed toward other people. Exploring similarities and differences among these three heroes can lead to greater insight about each one of them. *Note*: Ancient texts often exist only as fragments, frequently illegible or partially worn away or even destroyed. Editors indicate these absences in various ways: barely legible words that have been restored through careful scholarship are placed in brackets, while empty brackets or empty spaces indicate the places where words can't be restored or where the text has been lost. Question marks in parentheses indicate suggested reconstructions. You will encounter many such guesses and absences in the following excerpts from the *Epic of Gilgamesh*. (Translated by Stephanie Dalley.)

Line numbers for the excerpts from *Aeneid* correspond to the full text of each Book. (Translated by Frederick Ahl.)

- Aeneas's and Odysseus's journeys to the Underworld are more similar to each other than to Gilgamesh's. What are some of the similarities? What is their significance?

- What does each hero learn or accomplish on his journey to the Underworld that he could not learn or do in the land of the living?

VERGIL, FROM *AENEID*
FROM BOOK 6

Father Anchises, deep in a hollow valley of greenness,
Was, as it chanced, making careful review of the souls in
        confinement   680
Who, in time, would ascend to the light. He was holding a census,
Counting up all his descendants, the grandsons he doted on, weighing
Fates and fortunes of men, strength of character, power of body.
But, when he noticed Aeneas approach, reaching out across meadows,
He too opened his arms, reached both hands eagerly forward.   685
Tears were now flooding his cheeks, words poured from his mouth
       in a torrent:
"Have you at last really come? Did righteous love for your father
Conquer the rough road here as I thought it would! Son, can I really
Gaze at your face, hear the voice that I know, and be able to answer?
This thought I nurtured live in my mind, I was sure it would
       happen,   690
While I was counting the days. And my anxious hopes didn't fool me!
I have you now! I've heard of the lands, the extent of the seaways
You, dear son, have traversed. What a beating you've taken from
       danger!
Oh, how I worried that Libya's powers might harm you in some way!"
He, in reply, said: "Father, your sad image, rising before me   695
Time and again compelled me to push to this boundary's threshold.
Anchors are down in Etruscan waters. We've made it! So, father,
Give me your hand! Give it, don't pull away as I hug and
       embrace you!"
Waves of tears washed over his checks as he spoke in frustration:
Three attempts made to encircle his father's neck with his
       outstretched   700
Arms yielded three utter failures. The image eluded his grasping
Hands like the puff of a breeze, as a dream flits away from a dreamer.

Through this, Aeneas observes in a nearby vale, a secluded
Grove with its green-leafed canopy rustling over the woodlands,
And river Lethe too, flowing on past dwellings of calmness.   705
Peoples and nations, too many to count, seethe all around, swarming
Much as, on summer's serene, warm days, honey bees in the meadows
Settle on so many species of flowers, pour over the lilies'
Whiteness. The countryside's live with the hum of their buzzing.

Shocked by this sudden sight, unaware of its meaning, Aeneas   710
Asks for some answers: what river might this be which flows over
    yonder,
Who are the people who've crowded the banks in a giant formation.
Father Anchises replies: "They're souls that are due second bodies:
So fate rules, and they're drinking now from the waters of Lethe,
Draughts that will free them of care and ensure long years of
    oblivion.   715
    "These are the souls, my family's line I've been wanting for ages
Just to parade in your presence, to set in your mind, name and
    number,
So you can, now you've found Italy, share my delight more
    profoundly."
"Father, must I then suppose some souls of ineffable lightness
Soar, once again, to the sky just for reincarnation in clumsy   720
Bodies? What terrible passion for daylight possesses the poor things?"
"Son, I will not hold *you* in suspense," Anchises commences.
"I'll tell you now." He proceeds to reveal every detail in order:
    "First, you must grasp that the heaven and earth and the sea's
        liquid flatness,
Also the gleaming sphere of the moon, constellations, the huge sun   725
Feed on internal Energy. Mind, which suffuses these cosmic
Limbs, pervades the vast body and keeps the mass vital. This
    mixture
Generates life within humans and beasts, flying creatures, and also
Monsters Ocean spawns below marbled plains on its surface.
Fire endows them with force, and the source of the seeds for
    that fire   730
Is, though it's slowed and restricted by noxious bodies, the heavens.
Earth-made flesh, limbs slouching to death, dull much of its vital
Force, causing people to fear and desire, suffer pain, and feel pleasure,
Fail to see open skies in their prisons of darkness and blindness.
Even when life has departed, along with their last glimpse of
    daylight,   735
Not all traces of evil are gone from these pitiful creatures,
Not all bodily maladies leave. Of necessity, many
Harden and grow, become deeply ingrained in mysterious manners.
Therefore the souls are both punished and cleansed, and they pay off
    the hanging
Balance of crimes in the past. Some are stretched, hung up to the
    empty   740

Breezes, while others are cleansed of their ingrained crime by
    immersion
Deep in a giant whirlpool, or burned from within by a fire.
Each of us suffers his ghostly pain. When it's over, we're sent out,
All through Elysium's breadth. Just a few of us stay in the Blessèd
Fields. When the circle of time is complete, some day in the
    future,   745
Purged of the last trace of crime ingrained, they are left with ethereal
Power of perception, the fire of its clear breath, pure and untainted.
    "God summons all these souls, when they've rolled time's wheel
        for a thousand
Years, to convene in a mass at the Lethe, Oblivion's waters,
So, with their memories wholly erased, they can walk beneath
    heaven's   750
Dome yet again and begin to desire to go back into bodies."

Finished, Anchises propelled both Aeneas and, with him, the Sibyl
Into the midst of the seething and noisy assemblage, and
    clambered
High on a mound from whose top he could plainly distinguish
    the faces
Passing in long lines before him and note their identities clearly.   755
    "Come now: I'll set out in words the whole sequence of glory that
        follows
Dardan sons in the future: illustrious spirits, descendants,
Souls that remain to be born of Italian peoples and go forth
Bearing our name. And I'll teach you what *your* fateful destiny offers.
    "That man, you see him, the youth who now leans on an as yet
        unblooded   760
Spear, is allotted the next place in line: he's the first who'll be rising
Up to the bright sky's breezes. His blood will be partly Italian:
Silvius—'Woodsman,' an Alban name. He's your posthumous
    offspring,
Child of advanced old age. So your wife, Lavinia, will rear him,
Too late for you, in the woods, to be king and the father of more
    kings.   765
Our descendants, through him, will long be the masters of Alba.
    "Procas is next, over there, he's the glory of Troy and its people,
Then Capys, Numitor too, and the man who'll give *your* name
        revival:
Silvius Aeneas, as righteous in life as he's valiant in warfare,

He'll be king among kings, if he ever becomes king of Alba.   770
Fine young men! Take a look! What a great show of strength they
    can proffer,
Shading their brows with the Citizens' Oak for their rescue of others.
"These men will found Nomentum for you, Gabii and Fidenae.
These men will place Collatia's fortress high on the hilltops,
Also Pometia and Castrum Inui, Bola and Cora.   775
They will exist in the future as names; now they're lands, but they're
    nameless.
    "Next, Mars' son will join the parade as his grandfather's comrade:
Romulus born of a mother, herself of Assaracus' bloodline:
Ilia. See how this man has twin crests crowning his helmet,
And how the father himself now marks him with *his* stamp of
    godhood?   780
    "Here's the man under whose auspices famous Rome will encompass
Earth's full extent with her power; and in courage will rival Olympus!
One city's circuit of walls will embrace seven citadel summits,
Well fulfilled in her offspring of men, as is mighty Cybele,
Who, in her turreted crown, rides a chariot drawn through the
    Phrygian   785
Cities, the radiant mother of gods who embraces a hundred
Grandchildren: all live in heaven, each claiming the sky as a birthright.
    "Marshal your eyes' twin gaze this way now! Look at this people,
Look at your Romans! For Caesar is here, all Iulus' descendants,
Marching towards their places beneath sky's arching expanses.   790
Here's the man you've heard promised to you so often, he's here now:
Caesar Augustus, born of a god, who will one day establish
All through the farmlands of Latium once, long ago, ruled by Saturn,
Ages of Gold. He'll extend Roman power beyond far Garamantes,
East beyond India too, to a land that lies under no mapped stars,   795
Outside the paths of the year and the sun, where sky-bearing Atlas
Spins on his shoulders the blaze of the star-studded orb of the heavens.
Caspian kingdoms already await his arrival, and shudder,
As does Maeotia's land, at the gods' oracular warnings.
Nile's seven mouths to the sea now riot in turmoil of terror.   800
Not even Hercules crossed so much of the earth in his travels,
What if he shot down a bronze-hoofed doe, if he tamed Erymanthus'
Forested woodlands, what if he terrified Lerna with arrows?
Conqueror Bacchus' journey was shorter when guiding his chariot's
Tigress team from the summit of Nysa with reins made of ivy.   805
So, do we still hesitate to extend our strength by our manhood?"

UNKNOWN, FROM THE *EPIC OF GILGAMESH* (SEVENTH CENTURY BCE)

FROM TABLET X

Ur-shanabi spoke to him, to Gilgamesh,   1
   "Why are your cheeks wasted, your face dejected,
   Your heart so wretched, your appearance worn
      out,
   And grief in your innermost being?
   Your face is like that of a long-distance traveller.
   Your face is weathered by cold and heat [   ]
   Clad only in a lionskin, you roam open country."
Gilgamesh spoke to him, to Ur-shanabi the
      boatman,
   "How could my cheeks not be wasted, nor my
      face dejected,
   Nor my heart wretched, nor my appearance worn   10
      out,
   Nor grief in my innermost being,
   Nor my face like that of a long-distance traveller,
   Nor my face weathered by wind and heat [   ]
   Nor roaming open country clad only in a
      lionskin?
   My friend was the hunted mule, wild ass of the
      mountain, leopard of open country,
   Enkidu my friend was the hunted mule, wild ass
      of the mountain, leopard of open country.
   We who met, and scaled the mountain,
   Seized the Bull of Heaven and slew it,
   Demolished Humbaba who dwelt in the Pine
      Forest,
   Killed lions in the passes of the mountains,   20
   My friend whom I love so much, who
      experienced every hardship with me,
   Enkidu my friend whom I love so much, who
      experienced every hardship with me—
   The fate of mortals conquered him!
   For six days and seven nights I wept over him: I
      did not allow him to be buried
   Until a worm fell out of his nose.
   I was frightened and [   ].
   I am afraid of Death, and so I roam open country.

The words of my friend weigh upon me.
I roam open country for long distances; the words
    of Enkidu my friend weigh upon me.
I roam open country on long journeys.   30
How, O how could I stay silent, how, O how
    could I keep quiet?
My friend whom I love has turned to clay:
    Enkidu my friend whom I love has turned to
    clay.
Am I not like him? Must I lie down too,
Never to rise, ever again?"
Gilgamesh spoke to him, to Ur-shanabi the boatman,
    "Now, Ur-shanabi, which is the way to
    Ut-napishtim?
Give me directions (?), whatever they are; give
    me directions (?).
If it is possible, I shall cross the sea;
If it is impossible, I shall roam open country
    again."

[Omitted: Ur-shanabi instructs Gilgamesh to build a boat that Gilgamesh can then use to cross the water to visit Ut-napishtim. Gilgamesh
reaches Ut-napishtim and then tells him about Enkidu.]

[Ut-napishtim spoke to him, to Gilgamesh],   40
    ["Why are your cheeks wasted, your face
        dejected],
    [Your heart so wretched, your appearance worn
        out],
    [And grief in your innermost being]?
    [Your face is like that of a long-distance
        traveller].
    [Your face is weathered by cold and heat . . .]
    [Clad only in a lionskin you roam open
        country].
[Gilgamesh spoke to him, to Ut-napishtim],
    ["How would my cheeks not be wasted, nor my
        face dejected],
    [Nor my heart wretched, nor] my appearance
        [worn out],
    [Nor grief in] my innermost being,   50

[Nor] my face like [that of a long-distance
        traveller],
[Nor] my face [weathered by cold and heat . . .]
[Nor] roaming open country [clad only in a
        lionskin]?
My friend was the hunted mule, wild ass of the
        mountain, leopard of open country,
Enkidu my friend was the hunted mule, wild ass
        of the mountain, leopard of open country.
We who met and scaled the mountain,
Seized the Bull of Heaven and slew it,
Demolished Humbaba who dwelt in the Pine
        Forest,
Killed lions in the passes of the mountains,
My friend whom I love so much, who   60
        experienced every hardship with me,
Enkidu my friend whom I love so much, who
        experienced every hardship with me—
The fate of mortals conquered him! For six days
        and seven nights I wept over him,
I did not allow him to be buried
Until a worm fell out of his nose.
I was frightened [   ]. I am afraid of
        Death, [and so I roam open country].
I roam open country for long distances;
The words of my friend weigh upon me.
The words of Enkidu my friend weigh upon me.
I roam the open country on long journeys.
How, O how could I stay silent, how, O how   70
        could I keep quiet?
My friend whom I love has turned to clay:
Enkidu my friend whom I love has turned to
        clay.
Am I not like him? Must I lie down too,
Never to rise, ever again?"
Gilgamesh spoke to him, to Ut-napishtim,
    "So I thought I would go to see Ut-napishtim the
        far-distant, of whom people speak.
    I searched, went through all countries,
    Passed through and through difficult
        lands,

And crossed to and fro all seas.
My face never had enough of sweet sleep,   80
My fibre was filled with grief.
I made myself over-anxious by lack of sleep.
What did I gain from my toils?
I did not make a good impression (?) on the
    alewife, for my clothes were finished.
I killed a bear, hyena, lion, leopard, tiger, deer,
    mountain goat, cattle, and other wild beasts of
    open country.
I ate meat from them, I spread out their skins.
Let her door be bolted against grief with pitch and
    bitumen!
Because of me, games are spoiled [   ],
My own misfortunes (?) have reduced me to
    misery (?)."
Ut-napishtim spoke to him, to Gilgamesh,   90
    "Why do you prolong grief, Gilgamesh?
Since [the gods made you] from the flesh of gods
    and mankind,
Since [the gods] made you like your father and
    mother,
[Death is inevitable (?)] at some time, both for
    Gilgamesh and for a fool,
But a throne is set down [for you (?)] in the
    assembly [   ]."

AFRICAN AMERICAN ODYSSEUS

Odysseus, as we have seen, is both a quest hero and a trickster figure. By relying on his wits, he is able to overcome all manner of challenges, whether in the form of one-eyed giants, seductive females, roaring oceans, his fellow sailors' mutinous or foolish behaviors, or his own predilection for gluttony. Yet Odysseus is also a man of sorrows, burdened by a lifetime of losses and suffering. His constant movement, numerous adventures, and complex sorrows make him a versatile figure, one that has engaged ancient and modern imaginations alike far more often than the brave Achilles and the enduring Heracles.

This section examines the works of two African American artists: "The Odyssey of Big Boy," a poem by Sterling A. Brown (1901–1989), and *Their Eyes Were Watching God*, a novel by Zora Neale Hurston (1891–1960). Both of these works allude to the story of Odysseus and are informed by African American experiences.

Artists of African descent who are part of the African diaspora have found both Medea and Odysseus particularly compelling figures for articulating their experiences. The African diaspora refers to the movement of people from Africa to other parts of the world, whether during the Atlantic slave trade or as a result of more recent wars and genocide. For artists of African descent who live outside of Africa, the story of Medea has provided one way to represent an African American woman with no legal rights who must rear her children in a society so unjust that infanticide can be understood as an act of love, however desperate (Chapter 11.3). Homer's *Odyssey*, on the other hand, has offered a way to describe a life-threatening journey across hostile waters from Africa. To a man (or a woman) who must leave home, Odysseus, as a clever strategist, offers ways to survive in hostile lands; and, as the singer of his own tales, he offers a vision of how art can turn suffering into an act of defiance and beauty.

Toni Morrison, whose own profound engagement with the Medea myth we explored in Chapter 11.4, addresses the Ulysses theme and hints at the reasons for its prevalence in the literature of African American artists in a conversation about her novels with Richard Stepto. Morrison observed the following:

> The big scene is the traveling Ulysses scene, for black men. They are moving. Trains—you hear those men talk about trains as though they were their first lover—the names of the trains, the times of the trains. And boy, you know they spread their seed all over the world. They are really moving! Perhaps it's because they don't have a land, they don't have dominion. You can trace that historically, and one never knows what would have been the case if we'd never been tampered with at all. But that going from town to town or place to place or looking out and over and beyond and changing and so on. . . . It is the Ulysses theme, the leaving home.

Morrison refers to two events that have created and shaped African American culture. For African Americans, the first historical event that deprived men (and women) of African descent of land and dominion was the Atlantic slave trade, or the Middle Passage (1500—1800s), during which millions of Africans were sold into slavery and transported across the Atlantic to the Americas. The second event was the Great Migration (1910–1970), an exodus of nearly six million black people from the American south to cities in the north and the

12.12 *The Sirens' Song (1977)*. Collage of various papers with paint and graphite in the series Black Odysseus. Romare Bearden (1911–1988). Smithsonian Institute, Washington, DC. *The Sirens' Song ©Romare Bearden Foundation/Licensed by VAGA, New York, NY. Courtesy of DC Moore Gallery, New York.*

west, where industrial jobs were available and where there were no Jim Crow laws that institutionalized racism. These events provide the historical context for the quests of Sterling A. Brown's protagonist, Big Boy, and Zora Neale Hurston's protagonist, Janie, for which "A Black Odyssey," a series of collages by Romare Bearden (1911–1988) provides a visual parallel.

Bearden was born in North Carolina and worked for decades in Harlem in New York City before moving to the Caribbean island of St. Martin. His monumental series "A Black Odyssey" recalls the landscape of Africa, African American figures from the American south, and the vibrant colors of the Caribbean. Bearden recasts Homer's epic: Poseidon is an African god of water, for example; Circe is a conjure woman (an African woman who has great powers from her practice of voodoo) and Odysseus is an African American hero who has made any number of journeys, from Africa to the Americas and from the

American south to the north. Bearden's series demonstrates that both the *Odyssey* and the lives of African men have universal elements (Figure 12.12).

Sterling A. Brown was a professor at Howard University, a literary critic, a scholar of African American folklore, and a poet. His poem "Odyssey of Big Boy" is narrated by Calvin "Big Boy" Davis, a raconteur and guitar player; Brown studied Davis's songs as part of his lifelong interest in African American folktales.

Brown imagines Davis as the poet-narrator of "Odyssey of Big Boy." The poet-narrator recounts his journey through the American south in search of work in a southern African American vernacular. Although Davis, unlike many of the black men to whom Morrison refers, is not a lover of trains, his story is bracketed by two historical figures associated with the railroads. The poem begins with the story of Casey Jones (1863–1900), a railroad engineer who died trying to stop the train he was driving from crashing, and ends with the story of John Henry, a legendary African American steel driver who worked for the railroads, hammering steel into rocks in order to make holes for dynamite. Like the sea in the *Odyssey*, trains are both a means of travel and a cause of death in "Odyssey of Big Boy"; as Davis says, "Train done caught me on de trestle." Davis also mentions Stagolee (Lee Shelton), who was convicted of killing a man who knocked off his hat, and Jazzbo (Jazzbo Brown), a legendary delta blues musician, both of whom are the subject of numerous songs and folktales.

 ### STERLING A. BROWN, "ODYSSEY OF BIG BOY" (1932)

> Lemme be wid Casey Jones,
>   Lemme be wid Stagolee,
> Lemme be wid such like men
>   When Death takes hol' on me,
>   When Death takes hol' on me. . . .
>
> Done skinned as a boy in Kentucky hills,
>   Druv steel dere as a man,
> Done stripped tobacco in Virginia fiel's
>   Alongst de River Dan,
>   Alongst de River Dan;
>
> Done mined de coal in West Virginia,
>   Liked dat job jes' fine,
> Till a load o' slate curved roun' my head,
>   Won't work in no mo' mine,
>   Won't work in no mo' mine;

Done shocked de corn in Marylan',
   In Georgia done cut cane,
Done planted rice in South Caline,
    But won't do dat again,
      Do dat no mo' again.

Been roustabout in Memphis,
   Dockhand in Baltimore,
Done smashed up freight on Norfolk wharves,
    A fust class stevedore,
      A fust class stevedore. . . .

Done slung hash yonder in de North
   On de ole Fall River Line,
Done busted suds in li'l New York,
    Which ain't no work o' mine—
      Lawd, ain't no work o' mine.

Done worked and loafed on such like jobs,
   Seen what dey is to see,
Done had my time wid a pint on my hip
    An' a sweet gal on my knee,
      Sweet mommer on my knee:

Had stovepipe blond in Macon,
   Yaller gal in Marylan',
In Richmond had a choklit brown,
    Called me huh monkey man—
      Huh big fool monkey man.

Had two fair browns in Arkansaw
   And three in Tennessee,
Had Creole gal in New Orleans,
    Sho Gawd did two time me—
      Lawd two time, fo' time me—

But best gal what I evah had
   Done put it over dem,
A gal in Southwest Washington
    At Four'n half and M—
      Four'n half and M. . . .

Done took my livin' as it came,
　　Done grabbed my joy, done risked my life;
Train done caught me on de trestle,
　　Man done caught me wid his wife,
　　　His doggone purty wife. . . .

I done had my women,
　　I done had my fun;
Cain't do much complainin'
　　When my jag is done,
　　　Lawd, Lawd, my jag is done.

An' all dat Big Boy axes
　　When time comes fo' to go,
Lemme be wid John Henry, steel drivin' man,
　　Lemme be wid old Jazzbo,
　　　Lemme be wid ole Jazzbo. . . .

Davis's first-person account of his life is not nostalgic: he does not pine for home like Odysseus. Rather than the precious objects (like the Golden Fleece) that Jason must find, or the Chimera that Bellerophon pursues, Davis's odyssey is in quest of employment. Moreover, Davis does not rescue a princess, as Perseus rescues Andromeda. Instead, Davis recounts his lovers, each beautiful and each associated more or less with a particular place. These vignettes capture how he has improvised his life, taking and creating possibilities of work and love where he found them. Through these, the poet-narrator conveys a versatility and energy that unifies his varied experiences. By the poem's conclusion, the reader appreciates the poet's bravado and determination to forge a meaningful life.

Davis imagines himself among the legendary men of folklore, who have attained immortality through remembrance in song. Like Odysseus, who gives order to and sings of his own adventures in the *Odyssey* (Books 9–12) and assures their place in memory by returning home and recounting them to friends and family, so too does Davis ensure his immortality through song. Additionally, by insisting that one can compose a life that is rooted not in place but rather in action and style, Brown offers a parable of profound relevance for African Americans who were forcibly deprived of land and dominion. The imaginary adventures of Calvin "Big Boy" Davis also suggest how anyone who feels unmoored in our contemporary, globalized world can weave together the strands of fractured work histories, fragmented families, and far-flung travels to create a composite life lived with the courage and panache worthy of an epic tale.

The protagonist of Zora Neale Hurston's 1937 novel, *Their Eyes Were Watching God*, is Janie Crawford. Janie has been hailed as one the most defiant and powerful female characters in American literature; at first glance, her tale might seem to fit better in a chapter devoted to heroines. Yet Janie has been repeatedly compared to Odysseus because she too embarks on a quest, over the course of which she survives three violent marriages, a flood of biblical proportions, and a conviction for murder. Like Odysseus, she is a shape-shifter who escapes easy categorization: she has both white and black ancestors and at different times has both masculine and feminine traits. Indeed, some critics have suggested that Janie is a composite of Odysseus and Penelope.

Janie Crawford is also akin to Odysseus (and Calvin "Big Boy" Davis in "Odyssey of Big Boy") because of the novel's framing structure: Janie narrates her adventures to her friend Phoeby. Her tale, like Davis's song, ends back where it begins, with triumphant storytelling about a life filled with travels directed by work, loves, and sorrows. Hurston herself led a life worthy of an *Odyssey*. A professionally trained anthropologist as well as an acclaimed novelist and short-story writer, Hurston conducted fieldwork in America, Haiti, and Honduras. She worked to conserve the folktales as well as the vernacular of African American southern culture through her writings.

Their Eyes Were Watching God opens with Janie and Phoeby sitting together on the porch late one evening. Janie begins with her origin story. Her grandmother, Nanny, raises Janie and arranges for her to be married at an early age to a much older man who lives on a desolate farm. Janie's husband expects her to be as much a farm laborer as a wife. When Nanny dies, Janie abandons her husband to run off with Joe Starks, who promises her respectability and freedom from farm work in the town of Eatonville, Florida. Starks purchases a store and expects Janie to become his storekeeper. Soon, Stark's store seems to Janie as limiting as her first husband's rural farm. Moreover, Starks will not let Janie attend town events or even speak publicly when he becomes mayor. At home, he becomes abusive. When Starks eventually dies, Janie inherits the store and continues to work there until Vergible "Tea Cake" Woods, a man several years her junior, arrives in town. They fall in love and depart for the Florida Everglades.

In some respects, Tea Cake shares the negative qualities of Janie's first two husbands. He is abusive: he beats Janie and even steals her money to throw a large party that he will not let her attend. Yet Tea Cake is also different from the other husbands. Tea Cake and Janie have a fully realized sexual relationship and share a camaraderie absent from Janie's other marriages. Additionally, they have a degree of parity with each other—for example, they work together in the fields.

Janie and Tea Cake's relative harmony is irrevocably changed when the Okeechobee Hurricane (which really happened, in 1928) floods the

Everglades. Trying to escape the rising waters, Janie and Tea Cake are attacked by a rabid dog. Tea Cake rushes to save Janie and is bitten, contracting rabies. Janie is eventually forced to shoot the increasingly maddened Tea Cake when he attempts to kill her. Tried and exonerated for Tea Cake's murder, Janie returns to Eatonville. The final scene picks up where the first scene left off: Janie recounting the tale of her life to Phoeby, her friend in Eatonville.

Hurston's novel echoes the *Odyssey* in two key ways: one structural and one symbolic. Although Janie is the narrator of her stories, Hurston chooses nonetheless to tell her story in third person throughout most of the novel. Hurston blurs the line between omnipresent narrator and protagonist, just as Homer does by assigning a portion of direct narration to Odysseus (Books 9–12). In both instances, the trickster-protagonists of these quests slip in and out of the role of narrator and character. Second, Hurston's novel begins and ends with an allusion to a journey by sea and to Odysseus. The novel opens with the image of ships on the horizon, symbolizing the possibility that a man's dreams may never be fulfilled. Hurston writes: "Ships at a distance have every man's wish on board. For some them come in with the tide. For others they sail forever on the horizon, never out of sight, never landing." At the end of *Their Eyes Were Watching God*, Janie reflects on her life and evokes the sea.

ZORA NEALE HURSTON, FROM *THEIR EYES WERE WATCHING GOD* (1937)

> Then Tea Cake came prancing around her where she was . . . Tea Cake, with the sun for a shawl. Of course he wasn't dead. He could never be dead until she herself had finished feeling and thinking. The kiss of his memory made pictures of love and light against the wall. Here was peace. She pulled in the horizon like a great fish net. Pulled it from around the waist of the world and draped it over her shoulder. So much of life in its meshes! She called her soul to come and see.

As Janie climbs the stairs to sleep, she laments that she no longer can wrap herself in Tea Cake's sun-filled shawl. Instead, she "calls her soul" to wonder at the dusk-filled fishing net she has loaded with her experiences from her journey. Like Odysseus, who returns to Ithaca with tales of his adventures, Janie brings back stories that nourish the soul.

Hurston notes at the beginning of *Their Eyes Were Watching God* that "the dream is the truth." Homer (or Odysseus) might say, "The myth is the truth." Odysseus, Big Boy Davis, and Janie share an essential trait that distinguishes them from other quest heroes and heroines: they are the narrators of their own tales of survival. They each possess the ability not simply to travel beyond the horizon but to make sense of that experience, to make it authentic and true, so that it becomes part of the enduring, universal world of myth and folklore.

Key Terms

Andromeda 545
Bellerophon 551
Chimera 551
Danaë 547
Dictys 547

Golden Fleece 552
Gorgon 548
Jason 552
Medusa 548
Odysseus 555

Penelope 560
Perseus 547
Polyphemus 558
Scylla 559
Sirens 550

For Further Exploration

Brann, Eva. *Homeric Moments: Clues to Delight in Reading the Odyssey and the Iliad.* Philadelphia: Paul Dry Books, 2002. Brann offers a collection of lively short chapters on key moments in the *Odyssey* and the *Iliad.*

Foley, John Miles (ed.). *A Companion to Ancient Epic.* Malden, MA, and Oxford: Wiley-Blackwell, 2005. This collection of recent essays offers a comprehensive and panoramic view of the range of scholarly approaches to ancient epics.

Hall, Edith. *The Return of Ulysses: A Cultural History of Homer's Odyssey.* Baltimore, MD: The Johns Hopkins University Press, 2008. In this model study of how reception studies can illuminate classical texts, Hall looks at how artists, working in a variety of mediums, respond to various episodes in the *Odyssey.*

Schweizer, Bernard, and Robert A. Segal (eds.). *Critical Insights: The Hero's Quest.* Ipswich, MA: Salem Press, 2013. Segal's introduction, as well as the essays that follow, offers a number of clear definitions and examples of quest heroes.

CHAPTER 13

IPHIGENIA AND QUEST HEROINES

It is certainly true that the male hero from Homer to Hemingway often demonstrates his heroic power by killing and dominating others; but it is not accurate to assume that this macho heroic ideal is the archetypal heroic pattern. An exploration of the heroic journeys of women—and of men who are relatively powerless because of class or race—makes clear that the archetypal hero masters the world by understanding it, not by dominating, controlling or owning the world or other people.

—CAROL PEARSON AND KATHERINE POPE, *THE FEMALE HERO IN AMERICAN AND BRITISH LITERATURE* (1981)

To find quest heroines in ancient Greek myth is itself a kind of quest. As we have seen, among ancient Greek citizens, the lives of women were controlled by their male guardians (whether father, husband, son, or uncle), who decided when and whom they would marry and where they would live. Although women were not confined to their houses and had access to markets, temples, and communal water fountains, they did not sail the seas, tend flocks in uninhabited wild spaces, or participate in military campaigns as men did. In sum, their opportunities for journeys that could be reimagined as heroic were few, even if poets and artists were not limited by historical reality. Not surprisingly, then, there are few surviving stories of heroines whose adventures would qualify as quests: journeying over vast distances and

< **13.1 (OPPOSITE):** **Iphigenia in Tauris.** Fresco from the House of L. Caecilio Giocondo in Pompeii. First century CE. Museo Archeologico Nazionale, Naples, Italy. *Erich Lessing / Art Resource, NY, ART71656.*

overcoming tremendous challenges while encountering helpers and villains along the way. For this reason, trying to locate women in the literature of ancient Greece who might qualify as quest heroines yields few examples. A new approach is needed.

THE HEROINE'S QUEST

This chapter does not look for female counterparts to quest heroes. Instead, following the ideas proposed by scholars Carol Pearson and Katherine Pope in *The Female Hero in American and British Literature* (1981), we argue that in ancient Greece heroines were often described as attempting to understand, rather than conquer, the world. These mythical women were depicted as pursuing moral goals that serve, rather than dominate, those around them. In this respect, the fictional heroines described by the Greeks (especially in the genre of tragedy) resemble more familiar historical figures recognized as heroes because of their actions on behalf of their community, such as the Spartan general Brasidas, whom the Amphipolitans honored as a hero for his protection of their city during the Peloponnesian War (Thucydides 5.11), and (much later) Christian martyrs and saints. In exploring this resemblance, this chapter highlights the importance of stories about heroines in evolving conceptions of heroic behavior from Homer to the first few centuries of the Common Era. From this perspective we revisit heroines we met in earlier chapters, such as Medea, Clytemnestra, and Hecuba, and we meet Antigone for the first time. We also look closely at the story of Iphigenia, who exemplifies the heroine as a moral figure.

CHANGING DEFINITIONS OF HEROES AND HEROINES IN ANCIENT GREECE

Greek heroes and heroines, as described in the previous three chapters, were celebrated in both song and cult because they were believed to still be active and powerful even after death. Death is the common factor that unites the stories of all heroes and heroines and is required for their elevated status. Yet, beyond this common requirement, there was considerable variation among heroes and heroines. They could be fictional characters, such as the kings, queens, and warriors of Homer's epics. They could exist somewhere on the spectrum between fictional and historical characters, such as founders of colonies, philosophers, poets, and prophets. And they could be entirely historical figures for whom considerable documentary evidence exists, such as generals, warriors, athletes, philanthropists, or benefactors of their communities.

It is this last category that is most intriguing in terms of the recognition of "heroes" in Greek culture. During the fourth century BCE, there was an increase in the worshipping of these historical figures—usually male—as heroes at their tombs. This practice of reverence of dead heroes (and, to a lesser extent, heroines) at their place of entombment continued in a modified form in the worship of Christian martyrs and saints during the first few centuries of the Common Era. Stories of heroines came to play an important role in this process, as the following brief survey indicates.

Heroes in the Classical Period and in Tragedy

Beginning in the sixth century BCE, historical figures were increasingly recognized as heroes. In Athens, for example, the male lovers Harmodius and Aristogeiton became heroes because they killed the Athenian tyrant Hipparchus during a Panathenaic festival (514 BCE). This act was considered a foundational moment in the establishment of Athenian democracy, even though Hippias, the brother of Hipparchus, became the next tyrant and remained so for several more years (510 BCE). Harmodius and Aristogeiton were praised as tyrannicides (tyrant slayers) and liberators. Statues of the two men were commissioned with public funds and were placed in the Athenian agora, and songs praising them for securing "equal rights under the law" (*isonomia*) for all Athenian citizens were performed in private and

13.2 Harmodius and Aristogeiton, the tyrant slayers. Roman copy. Museo Archeologico Nazionale, Naples, Italy. *Alfredo Dagli Orti / The Art Archive at Art Resource, NY, AA356070.*

public settings (Figure 13.2). Yearly sacrifices were offered to the tyrannicides, and they gradually gained the status of heroes. Indeed, so valued were the tyrannicides by the Athenians that when their statues were stolen by the invading Persians (480 BCE), they were immediately replaced. And when, centuries later, Alexander the Great found the original stolen statues in the Persian court in Susa, he returned them to Greece (330 BCE).

The statues, songs, and worship of the tyrannicides were a form of social memory or popular history. By these means, a historically important event that enshrined patriotic values was widely circulated and preserved in Athens. The tyrannicides, following the pattern set by mythological heroes, committed a daring act of physical courage and died shortly afterward. Similarly, the Greek soldiers who died during the Persian Wars received honors that were nearly identical to those given to heroes; some scholars argue that they actually entered the ranks of heroes. These include, most famously, the soldiers from the Battle of Marathon (490 BCE) and those from the Battle of Plataea

(479 BCE). But here a difference between heroes of myth and historical figures such as the tyrannicides and the war dead can be detected: the tyrannicides and the war dead were understood to have died for a cause that the state and its members recognized as necessary as well as morally good, whereas many mythological heroes often act on their own behalf and for their own glory.

As historical figures acting on behalf of their communities were increasingly treated as heroes, fictional heroes from myth were depicted in tragedies in a manner that was less laudatory and more critical. Heroes on the tragic stage were not shown accomplishing the heroic deeds that earned them their fame and recognition in earlier written and visual descriptions. Instead, the very traits that earned them heroic status were shown to have exacted a terrible toll on them and those around them (Chapter 10.1). Euripides, for example, shows Heracles after his labors have been accomplished, when in a maddened state he kills his wife and children. Sophocles, too, shows us an Ajax who slaughters sheep in a fit of rage before killing himself. And Agamemnon is murdered by his wife, Clytemnestra, in Aeschylus's trilogy, the *Oresteia*.

In contrast, Theseus was often presented on the tragic stage (including Sophocles's *Oedipus at Colonus* and Euripides's *Suppliants*) as an exemplary king of Athens who embodies the most noble values of Athenian justice and democracy, especially its welcoming stance toward foreigners and its willingness to help suppliants. Yet these plays do not depict the adventures of Theseus that made him a hero in the first place, such as defeating the Minotaur or killing the numerous bandits and thieves he encountered on his journey from Troezen to Athens. In other words, on the tragic stage, male heroes (except for Theseus) are shown in a singularly unflattering light: isolated, following their own inclinations, and both suffering and causing others to suffer.

Heroines in the Classical Period and in Tragedy Although almost no female historical figures were recognized as heroines during the Classical Period, as there were few opportunities for women to demonstrate courage on the battlefield or political acumen in the agora, female characters appeared with great frequency on the tragic stage. Several of these women were worshipped as heroines. The prevalence of female characters in tragedy has provoked much scholarly interest. Why would a society that greatly limited the economic, political, and social autonomy of women nonetheless create female protagonists in tragedies?

One answer to this question concerns the role of tragedy in relation to epic. Although the tragedians borrowed figures from the world of mythology (especially Homer), they offered "updated" versions of these heroes that showcased their relevance to fifth- and fourth-century-BCE audiences. Epic, for example, emphasized individual heroic valor but no longer commanded the attention of the Athenian soldiers in the audience, who fought together in

Map 13.1 Iphigenia and Other Quest Heroines

phalanxes and alternated in quick succession between their wartime lives on military campaigns and periods of peacetime activities among their families. Tragedy showed these heroes returning to their cities and families, an experience that soldiers in the audience shared. Thus tragedians highlighted how earlier forms of poetry that celebrated the exploits of individual heroes were inadequate to address contemporary concerns through plot.

A tragedy set in the home rather than on the battlefield required female characters—wives, mothers, daughters, sisters, widows, and prospective brides—who paraded across the tragic stage in order to tell stories that were not part of the epic tradition. (It is important to remember that no women actually acted on the Greek stage. All roles, including those of female characters, were played by men.) Female characters on the tragic stage were given their own stories, and they acted in ways seldom seen in epic. Not only did these characters not subordinate themselves to the male characters; they were often critical of the status quo as articulated by the powerful male characters. Female characters allowed tragedians to include multiple perspectives, presenting a world at once more complex and more intimate than the epic world of war and travel. These performances integrated contemporary concerns into old stories.

Tragedians used female characters not only to express a way of thinking and being in the present world but also to criticize the world of the playwright and his audience, daring to address broad social concerns. Tragic heroines, such as Iphigenia or Clytemnestra, often pointed out the fault lines in the world beyond the tragic stage. They exposed the contradictory demands placed on individuals, whether male or female, by family, religious practices, and service to the state. Tragic heroines often acted publicly and against the wishes of their legal guardians (or other powerful male figures) to address a moral, religious, or social wrong. The motives of tragic heroines include preservation of their families, proper worship of the gods, and the benefit of the larger social good, rather than (as is frequently the case with tragic heroes) their own benefit.

Although their actions did not require physical strength, they often required intelligence, planning, courage, and fortitude. Even when their actions had harmful consequences, tragic heroines were almost always presented as acting in reaction to insupportable demands made of them or as motivated by their concern for others. Tragic heroines were rarely motivated by self-preservation. Some tragic heroines, like Antigone, risked their lives or, like Iphigenia, willingly gave up their lives to escape a world in which the values they uphold have no meaning. Thus tragic heroines offered alternative views of the status quo: they pointed out the excesses of male violence in war or its aftermath and advocated for the interests of children and the household even against (or in defiance of) the interests of the state.

In serving all these functions, tragic heroines reflected (or, perhaps, contributed to) a change in the broader category of historical figures whose achievements were recognized as heroic and who were revered as heroines and heroes. On the tragic stage, it was a single *human* action motivated by *human* impulses, rather than noble birth or slaying a monster, that defined tragic heroes and heroines. Tragic heroines, in particular, were defined by the moral quality of that singular action. In a similar fashion, historical figures, both male and female, were increasingly granted heroic stature as a result of actions undertaken for the greater good of the community. Gradually, the epically heroic actions and frequently supernatural adventures of an Achilles or Heracles receded into a distant and mythic past.

THE NEW HEROINE (AND THE NEW HERO)

In *New Heroes in Antiquity: From Achilles to Antinoos* (2010), classicist Christopher Jones (b. 1940) uses the term "new heroes" to describe historical figures worshipped as heroes for their social and civic acts. Aratus of Sicyon, for example, was less successful as a military general than as a diplomat: in the latter role he secured his city's welfare and peace through negotiations and diplomacy (late third century BCE). He was honored in a hero shrine, called the Arateion, during two festivals. The families of new heroes such as Aratus promoted their heroic status and powers by building elaborate hero shrines decorated with reliefs that showed their deceased family member banqueting in the afterlife. These not only imitated earlier hero reliefs that depicted heroes at banquets but also cultivated the hopeful belief that these new heroes would be as beneficent after death as they were in life. In this way, families furthered their own social and political ambitions. Jones argues that social factors such as these transformed historical figures into new heroes. To his study we add the heroines of tragedy.

Tragic heroines played a role in the transition from mythic heroes to new heroes (historical men and women who benefited their cities). In this chapter, we refer to heroines, tragic or otherwise, as new heroines to indicate that they acted in public to benefit others or to address a social, religious, or moral wrong. Their frequent appearance in tragedies during the Classical Period corresponds with the rise of the new hero. Together, new heroes and new heroines began to change the broader category of heroes and heroines. The following section looks at heroines discussed in Chapter 11 to fill out the category of the new heroine as well as to demonstrate that almost all female characters on the tragic stage, however unlikely, fit into this category.

At first glance, it makes no sense to describe Clytemnestra, Medea, or Hecuba as new heroines. They certainly do not seem to act on behalf of or out of concern for others, much less out of love, nor are their actions undertaken in the service of addressing wrongs. Each of these women is a particularly brutal murderer. Clytemnestra kills Agamemnon and his concubine Cassandra and attempts to kill her son, Orestes. Medea kills her own two sons, and Hecuba kills two young sons of Polymestor before blinding him. The acts of these three women are, without a doubt, both cruel and violent by ancient and modern standards alike.

Yet each of these women acts on behalf of a person or principle that has been violated or betrayed. Clytemnestra acts in part to punish Agamemnon for the murder of their daughter Iphigenia. The fact that the Furies, who by avenging those who spill kindred blood promote and protect family loyalty above any bonds of marriage or state, assist Clytemnestra suggests that her murder of Agamemnon rightly serves this principle (Figure 11.6, p. 506). Medea acts to spare her sons the difficult fate of ethnic outcasts and orphans in a world hostile to both. Hecuba, too, acts to avenge the death of her son Polydorus. Thus, even though the actions of Clytemnestra, Medea, and Hecuba are not depicted on the Greek stage as acceptable or justified, they are motivated by equally violent and unjustified wrongs. For this reason, these three female characters can be considered new heroines, although their inclusion in this category is worthy of further consideration and is given its due in the next section of this chapter.

Some female characters fit more easily (or, at least, palatably) into the category of the new heroine because their actions are not violent. Antigone, the heroine of Sophocles's tragedy *Antigone*, seeks to bury her brother, who was killed in a struggle for control of Thebes. For Antigone as well as the tragedy's audience, to leave a corpse unburied and without the proper funeral rites was a terrible punishment. Antigone sees it as her duty as kin to give her brother a decent burial, even if the state (personified by King Creon, her uncle) forbids it. She risks being caught in defiance of the king (who is also a senior male family member) to serve what she believes are larger moral imperatives. When Creon condemns her to be buried alive in a cave and left to die of starvation, Antigone chooses instead to hang herself. Although the limited scope of Antigone's choices is typical for heroines, it does not diminish the dignity and moral commitment behind her actions.

Similarly, Polyxena, the Trojan daughter of Hecuba and Priam, chooses the manner in which she will die. In Euripides's *Hecuba*, the Greeks resolve to sacrifice Polyxena, Hecuba's daughter, on the tomb of Achilles. This act, even though Euripides sets it in the distant heroic past of Homer, is nonetheless against custom, as the Greeks did not practice human sacrifice. In this way, Euripides characterizes the victorious Greeks at Troy as prone to excessively violent acts because of their own boastful pride, which would have been shocking to contemporary Greek audiences. When Polyxena chooses not to resist and willingly offers herself to the sword, her actions are in stark contrast to those of the Greeks. In this way, Euripides uses the innocence of Polyxena to accentuate the abandonment of custom and morality by the war-mongering Greeks, just as Sophocles uses the suicide of Antigone to highlight Creon's abuse of power. Although Polyxena's acts lacks the moral stature of Antigone's defiance of Creon, both tragic heroines, along with Clytemnestra, Medea, and Hecuba, confront and defy male power to pursue a course of action that they believe is justified and moral. In this sense, they are all new heroines. So too is Iphigenia, in the two plays by Euripides that bear her name.

IPHIGENIA IN AULIS AND AMONG THE TAURIANS

Before Euripides composed his two plays *Iphigenia in Aulis* (405 BCE) and *Iphigenia among the Taurians* (414 BCE; often titled *Iphigenia in Tauris*), Iphigenia was well-known from many myths, including Aeschylus's *Oresteia*, which recounts her sacrifice at Aulis. She was also revered in ritual, including her worship at Artemis's sanctuary in Brauron (Chapter 8.1). In his plays, Euripides was most likely expressing his reactions to the Sicilian expedition at the end of the Peloponnesian War (415 BCE), a controversial military campaign that eventually ended in defeat for Athens because of poor leadership and lack of a clear purpose. *Iphigenia in Aulis* expresses despair over the military failures of generals, a justified critique of Athens' leaders before and during the Sicilian expedition, whereas *Iphigenia among the Taurians*, written during or immediately after the Sicilian expedition, expresses a desire to return to Greece from afar, a desire likely shared by the Athenians on the failed military campaign to Sicily.

In each play, Iphigenia acts heroically on behalf of her principles as well as those she loves. *Iphigenia in Aulis* explores her choice to die with dignity, a choice similar to that faced by Polyxena. As the play begins, Iphigenia's father, Agamemnon, and the armada he leads with his brother, Menelaus, have been unable to sail to Troy from Aulis because of the calm weather and lack of wind. Agamemnon learns from the seer Calchas that Artemis demands the sacrifice of Iphigenia in exchange for the release of winds favorable to sailing. When Agamemnon decides to sacrifice his daughter to the goddess, he writes to his wife, Clytemnestra, asking that she send Iphigenia to Aulis under the deceitful pretense that their daughter will marry the illustrious warrior Achilles. Shortly after Iphigenia and Clytemnestra

13.3 Artemis saves Iphigenia at the altar. "Diana of Versailles," Roman marble copy after the original from the end of the fourth century to the early third century BCE. *Artemis and Ifigenia, IN 0482. Courtesy of Ny Carsberg Glyptotek.*

arrive at the camp, they learn the true reason why Iphigenia has been summoned. No amount of pleading or reasoning will dissuade Agamemnon from sacrificing his daughter; he is under threat of mutiny by the restless troops, who have learned of the reason for Iphigenia's presence at the camp. With few options before her, Iphigenia chooses to go to the altar willingly. As she walks before the troops to her death, her calm demeanor offers a contrast to Agamemnon's vacillations; her bridal gown contrasts with the military attire of the males surrounding her; and her youth and idealism make her an emblem of untarnished devotion to the state (and obedience to her father) that stands out in a military encampment swarming with corruption, foolhardy ambition, and bloodlust.

Iphigenia in Aulis was revised in antiquity and has two endings. In the first ending, Iphigenia walks to the altar and presumably is slaughtered. In the second, which may have been added at a later date, a messenger reports that Iphigenia vanished and a deer appeared in her place at the altar (Chapter 8.1). Iphigenia's rescue in this alternative

THE ESSENTIALS

IPHIGENIA Ἰφιγένεια

PARENTAGE King Agamemnon and Clytemnestra of Argos

OFFSPRING None

CULT SHRINES Brauron

ending is depicted—and explained—in the heavily damaged sculptural group shown here (Figure 13.3): Artemis herself lifts Iphigenia from the altar and places a deer in her stead. This later ending creates a segue to *Iphigenia among the Taurians*, in which Iphigenia serves as a priestess to Artemis (Map 13.1), where Thoas, the king of the Taurians, demands that she oversee the sacrifice of any Greek sailor who might land on his shores. *Iphigenia among the Taurians* opens with the arrival of Iphigenia's brother, Orestes, and his friend Pylades, who have been commanded by a Delphic oracle to return the statue of Artemis in Tauris to Greece. Through a series of signs and letters, Iphigenia and Orestes eventually recognize each other and plot an escape from Tauris. Iphigenia is the architect of their plans, and through her clever lies and machinations they succeed in fooling Thoas and leaving Tauris.

Iphigenia among the Taurians has little of the solemnity of *Iphigenia in Aulis*. The restoration of family, rather than its destruction, closes the play, as brother and sister sail home together. Yet, in both plays, Iphigenia acts on principle. In *Iphigenia in Aulis*, she chooses to die with dignity on behalf of Greece, her father's military success, and the will of the goddess. In *Iphigenia among the Taurians*, she acts on behalf of her brother and family. In both plays, bravery in the service of selfless devotion to a community or ideal is emphasized. In this way, Euripides offered criticism of Athens's military and political positions.

Many other tragedians depicted female characters not merely as subordinate helpers or adversaries (as in earlier epics) but as protagonists in their own rights. Despite being powerless within the family and social structures depicted by the tragedians, these new heroines embodied a willingness to act on behalf of others, often for a greater good. Although the new heroes defined by Jones were historical individuals rather than fictional characters, because these new heroines often suffered or died as a consequence of their actions, their stories had a poignancy and power that the historical evidence for new heroes might seem to lack. The influence of these new heroines can be traced in the female characters in later romance novels from antiquity as well as emerging stories about early Christian martyrs and saints, as we shall see later in this chapter.

BEFORE YOU READ

EURIPIDES, FROM *IPHIGENIA AMONG THE TAURIANS*

This play has been called a tragicomedy or a romantic comedy because it contains plot devices associated with those genres, such as mistaken identities, exciting escapes, and happy endings. The play has three distinct parts: first, a description of the non-Greek setting and characters; next, the touching recognition scene between Iphigenia and her brother, Orestes; and, finally, the exciting escape and salvation that conclude the play. Each of these parts is infused with a longing for Greece and for the reunification of family and the spirit of friendship. *Iphigenia among the Taurians* exemplifies the fundamental motivation of many new heroines: devotion to others and to a greater good beyond one's own reputation and well-being. Indeed, this play reverses the action of Iphigenia's sacrifice at Aulis, in which Agamemnon chooses fame and fortune over familial bonds when he sacrifices Iphigenia. Here, in stark contrast, Iphigenia risks all to save her brother and his friend Pylades from being sacrificed. She succeeds where Agamemnon failed and thereby preserves her family and herself. The opening act of the play takes place in the front of the temple of Artemis and offers a portrait of Iphigenia, Orestes, and Artemis. In so doing, it offers an example of a heroine and hero who differ from their epic predecessors. (Line numbers in the following excerpt correspond to the full text.) (Translated by James Morwood.)

- Iphigenia and Orestes describe their past and in so doing recall myths introduced in earlier chapters as well as display their current crisis and their personalities. How would you describe each character? Compare Iphigenia to Medea and Orestes to Achilles: How are they similar or different? Are they heroic in the manner of a Medea or an Achilles?

- How is Artemis characterized in this play? Is her portrayal here consistent with her portrayal in the myths and rituals described in Chapter 8? How do you account for the similarities and difference you observe?

- A herdsman describes his capture of Orestes at great length. How does Euripides use this tale to characterize Orestes, Pylades, Greeks, and Taurians?

- Compare the definition of new heroines presented here with the definition of heroines offered in Chapter 11.1. Which definition best suits Iphigenia in this play? Which definition best suits Medea, Clytemnestra, and Hecuba?

EURIPIDES, FROM *IPHIGENIA AMONG THE TAURIANS* (c. 412 BCE)

IPHIGENIA. Pelops, the son of Tantalus, arrived with his swift mares at Pisa and married the daughter of Oenomaus. She bore Atreus to him. And Atreus' sons were Menelaus and Agamemnon. I am Agamemnon's daughter Iphigenia, the child of Clytemnestra whose father was

Tyndareus. My father slaughtered me, or so he thought, in sacrifice to Artemis for Helen's sake in the famous bays of Aulis beside the eddies which Euripus whirls round and round with frequent gusts of wind as it ruffles the dark-blue sea. For it was there that King Agamemnon assembled a Greek sea-force of a thousand ships, wishing to win the crown of glorious victory over Troy for the Achaeans and to do Menelaus the favour of avenging the outrage to Helen's marriage.

However, he could get no winds and that made sailing impossible. Faced with this crisis, he resorted to divination from burnt offerings, and Calchas spoke these words: "O Agamemnon, commander of this army of Greece, you shall not unmoor your ships from the land before Artemis receives your girl Iphigenia as her slaughtered victim. For you vowed that you would sacrifice to the goddess of the moon the most beautiful thing that the year produced. Well, Clytemnestra your wife bore a child in the house"—said Calchas, applying the title of most beautiful to me—"which you must sacrifice."

And in a scheme instigated by Odysseus, they said that I was to marry Achilles and took me away from my mother. I, poor girl, came to Aulis. They lifted me up above the altar and were on the point of killing me with the sword. But Artemis stole me away and gave the Achaeans a deer in my place. She sent me through the bright air and brought me to live in this land of the Taurians where Thoas rules, a barbarian among barbarians. He got this name thanks to his speed, for he runs as if his swift feet are wings. She made me her priestess in this temple. In that office, by the customs in which the goddess rejoices, I begin the holy rites of her festival. Only its name is fair: I keep silent about the rest in fear of the goddess [for by the city's ancient custom I sacrifice any Greek man who puts to shore in this land.] I begin the ritual of his slaughter [but the unspeakable deed is for others to perform inside this temple of the goddess].

I shall tell to the air the strange visions which the night time brought me, and see if that brings any healing. In my sleep I seemed to have escaped from this land and to be living in Argos and sleeping in the middle of my girls in our maiden quarters. An earthquake shook the surface of the ground. I ran out, and as I stood outside I seemed to see the cornice tumbling from on high and the whole roof thrown down in ruin from its topmost column. Only one supporting pillar of my father's house was left standing—so it appeared in my dream—and from its capital it let fall locks of golden hair and spoke with a human voice. Then I, in due observance of this art of killing strangers that I practise, sprinkled it with water as a victim doomed to death, weeping as I did so.

For this is how I interpret my dream. Orestes is dead—he was the victim that I sprinkled in preparation for sacrifice. The pillars of a house are its male children, and those on whom my holy water falls are killed. [And I cannot apply my dream to any other relatives, for Strophius had no son on my death-day.] 60

So now I wish to pour libations for my brother, separated though we are,—that at least I can do—in company with my handmaidens, the Greek women whom the king gave to me. But for some reason they are not here yet. I shall go inside this temple of the goddess where I live.

IPHIGENIA goes into the temple. ORESTES and PYLADES enter.

ORESTES. Take care, watch out that there's nobody on the path.

PYLADES. I am keeping my eyes open and looking around everywhere.

ORESTES. Pylades, do you think that this is the goddess's dwelling to which we steered our ship over the sea from Argos? 70

PYLADES. I do, Orestes, and you must think so too.

ORESTES. And this is the altar where drips Greek blood?

PYLADES. Its coping is certainly red with blood.

ORESTES. And do you see the heads hung up under the coping?

PYLADES. Yes, these are the trophies of foreigners that they have killed. But we must stay on our guard and look around us everywhere.

ORESTES. O Phoebus, into what new snare have you led me now by your oracle, after I have avenged my father's blood by killing my mother? Troop upon troop of Furies drove me as I fled, an outcast from my 80 land, and I have completed many a race as I doubled back on my track. So I came to you and asked how I could find an end of spinning madness, an end to the troubles which I endured as I wandered Greece. You told me to go to the shores of the Taurian land where Artemis your sister has her altars, and to take the image of the goddess which they say fell from the sky here into this temple. And after I had taken it, whether by stratagem or good luck, and braved all the 90 danger, I should give it to the land of the Athenians. (As for the sequel, nothing further was said.) That done, I could breathe again after my labours.

In obedience to your orders I have come here to an unknown, inhospitable land. And I ask you, Pylades—for you have shouldered this labour with me—what should we do? For you see the lofty walls which encircle the temple. Shall we climb up ladders? How could we avoid being seen? Or should we use crowbars to break open the bronze doors though we know nothing about their bolts? But if we plan to enter 100 by the doors and are caught opening them, we shall be killed. No, rather than die, let us flee on the ship on which we sailed here.

PYLADES. To run away is intolerable, and we are not accustomed to behave in that manner. We must not hold the oracle of the god in dishonour. Let us slip off from the temple and hide ourselves in the caves which the dark sea swills with its waters—at a distance from our ship in case anyone spots our vessel and tells the king, and then we are seized by force.

But when the eye of gloomy night has come, we must summon up the   110
courage to take the carved image from the temple with all the cunning we can bring to the task. Look there—where there is space between the triglyphs to let ourselves down. Brave men do not flinch from ordeals but cowards never amount to anything. We have not rowed so far on our voyage only to turn back from our goal.

ORESTES. Your advice is good and I must follow it. We must find some place where the two of us can hide ourselves without being seen. I shall not be to blame for the failure of the god's oracle. We must not flinch. For   120
the young, there is no excuse for shirking a task, however hard.

[Omitted: After Orestes and Pylades depart, Iphigenia and the Chorus come on stage and bemoan their exile from Greece. Iphigenia then explains (again) how she came to be priestess of Artemis in the land of the Taurians.]

IPHIGENIA (*sings*). From the start the spirit that pursues me has been a spirit of bad fortune—
from that marriage night when my father untied my mother's girdle.
From the start, those goddesses, the Fates presiding at my birth,
tightened the thread of destiny round my childhood and made it bite.
The unhappy daughter of Leda   210
gave birth to me, the first-born child of the marriage,
and brought me up, but I was promised by a vow,
destined to be slaughtered in a grim sacrifice,
the outrage committed on me by my father.
The Greeks set me down from a horse-drawn chariot
on the sands of Aulis,
a bride—o sorrow! I was no bride—
for the son of the daughter of Nereus—alas!
But now I dwell a stranger
in a barren land by an inhospitable sea.
I have no husband, no child, no city, no friend—   220
yet I was wooed by Greeks.
I sing no song to Hera, the goddess of Argos,

I do not embroider with my shuttle
on the soft-voiced loom
an image of Athenian Pallas
and the Titans,
but I stain the altars as, to the hideous music of their screams,
I send blood-boltered strangers to their doom.
Pitiful are the cries they pour forth
and pitiful the tears they shed.   230
And now I have forgotten all that,
and I weep for my brother who has died in Argos.
I left him still a baby,
still young, still a child
in his mother's arms and at her breast,
Orestes, heir to the sceptre of Argos.

CHORUS. But look, here is a herdsman who has come from the
sea shore to tell us some news.

Enter HERDSMAN.

HERDSMAN. Daughter of Agamemnon and Clytemnestra, listen to the strange
events which I shall report to you.
IPHIGENIA. What is there so alarming about your news?   240
HERDSMAN. Two young men have rowed safely through the dark-blue Clash-
ing Rocks and come to our land—a welcome sacrifice to slaughter to
the goddess Artemis. Lose no time in preparing the holy water and the
first offerings.
IPHIGENIA. Where are they from? What country's clothes do the strangers
wear?
HERDSMAN. They are Greeks. That is the one thing I know, nothing more.
IPHIGENIA. Can't you tell me the strangers' names? Didn't you hear them?
HERDSMAN. One of them called the other Pylades.
IPHIGENIA. And what was the name of the stranger's companion?   250
HERDSMAN. No one knows this. We didn't hear.
IPHIGENIA. Where did you see them? And where did you meet and capture them?
HERDSMAN. By the shore of our inhospitable sea where the waves break.
IPHIGENIA. Tell me, what have herdsmen to do with the sea?
HERDSMAN. We went there to wash our cattle in the sea water.
IPHIGENIA. To return to my previous question, how did you capture them—by
what stratagem? I would like to know this. [It is strange that no Greeks
have come here until now. The altar of the goddess has not yet been
dyed with streams of Greek blood.]

HERDSMAN. When we were driving our cattle from their woodland pastures   260
to the sea which flows out through the Clashing Rocks, there was a
broken cliff, hollowed out by the constant erosion of the rolling waves,
where the purple-fishers shelter. There one of us herdsmen saw two
young fellows and he crept back to us on tiptoe. "Don't you see them?"
he said. "These are gods sitting here." And one of our number, a pious
man, held up his hands and looked at them and prayed: "O son of the
sea-goddess Leucothea, lord Palaemon, guardian of ships, be gracious   270
to us. Is it the two Dioscuri who sit on the shore, or are they the darlings
of Nereus who fathered the noble company of fifty dancing Nereids?"

But someone else, an irreverent man with a rash, anarchic spirit,
laughed at his prayers. He said that they were shipwrecked sailors sitting in the cleft in fear of our custom, for they must have heard that we
sacrifice strangers here. He seemed to most of us to be talking sense,   280
and we thought it a good idea to hunt down sacrificial victims for the
goddess in accordance with our local rites.

Meanwhile one of the strangers left the rock cleft, and stood there
jerking his head violently up and down. He groaned aloud as his hands
shook and he rushed about in a frenzy of madness. And he shouted like
a hunter: "Pylades, do you see this one? Can you not see how that one,
a she-dragon from Hell, wants to kill me and turns her weapons, the
fearful vipers of her hair, against me? This one nearby wings her way
breathing fire and murder, holding my mother in her arms, now a massive stone, so that she can throw her on me. O horror! She will kill me.   290
Where can I take refuge?"

We could see no such forms as he described, but he misinterpreted
the lowing of cattle and the barking of dogs as the similar sounds which
they say the Furies make. Thinking he was going to die, we cowered
together in fright and sat there silently. Then he drew his sword in his
hand and, rushing into the middle of the heifers like a lion, struck them
with his blade, plunging it into their flanks and ribs—he believed that he
was keeping off the goddesses, the Furies, in this way—until the sea
bloomed red with blood.   300

Meanwhile each one of us, as we saw our cattle falling to the ground
amid this carnage, began to arm ourselves and blew on spiral shells to
summon the local inhabitants. For we thought that herdsmen would be
no match for the strangers who were fit, well-built and young. Soon a
large number of us had gathered. The stranger's pulse of madness was
stilled and he fell down, his chin dripping with foam. And when we saw
that he had collapsed so conveniently, everybody energetically threw   310
weapons and struck blows. But the second stranger wiped off the foam
from his friend's face and protected his body by screening it with the

sturdy material of his cloak. He was dodging the missiles which threatened to hit him and looking after his dear friend with dutiful attention.
The stranger then regained consciousness and, leaping up from where
he lay, he realized that a surge of enemies was rolling against them and
that imminent danger stared them in the face. He cried out in anguish.
However, we didn't slacken our efforts as we pelted them with stones
and pressed hard on them from every direction.

At this moment we heard that terrible cry to arms: "Pylades, we shall   320
die. See that we die with honour. Draw your sword in your hand and
follow me!" When we saw both of our enemies brandishing their swords,
we all ran to take refuge in the woods on the cliffs. But every time that
some of us fled, the others would move to the attack and hurl missiles at
our enemies. However, if the strangers drove them back, those who had
just now been giving way began to pelt the enemy in their turn. But it
was incredible. Though missiles were flying from innumerable hands, no
one had the good fortune to hit the victims destined for the goddess. It
was with difficulty that we managed to overpower them and it was not   330
through any courage on our part that we did so. What happened was
that we surrounded them and knocked the swords out of their hands with
stones, and they sank to their knees in utter exhaustion.

We took them to the king of this land. When he saw them he sent
them with all speed to you for lustral purification and sacrifice. You
have often prayed for such strangers as victims, maiden, and if you kill
strangers like this, Greece will make atonement for your death and pay
the penalty for your slaughter at Aulis.

CHORUS. You have told an amazing tale about this madman, whoever he is,   340
who has come from the land of Greece to this inhospitable sea.

IPHIGENIA. Well then. You go off and bring the strangers while we shall see
that the holy rites here are duly prepared.

A PARADIGM FOR THE NEW HEROINE

13.2
THEORY

In her book *Adventures with Iphigenia in Tauris: A Cultural History of Euripides'
Black Sea Tragedy* (2013), the classicist Edith Hall (b. 1959) defines Iphigenia
as a quest heroine by modifying W. H. Auden's analysis of quest heroes
(Chapter 12.2). According to Hall, there are six imperatives that a quest heroine in ancient Greece must fulfill. The quest heroine must

I. Be the protagonist of a story that does *not* revolve around "romance, sex,
marriage, or parenthood"

2. Travel far
3. Have a relationship with a god or goddess
4. Have moral and intellectual authority
5. Be courageous and lead others
6. Be a role model for others

Although Hall notes that Iphigenia fits this pattern quite well, she acknowledges that almost no other heroines in ancient Greece do. Thus any attempt to locate and define quest heroines in a manner akin to quest heroes and to limit the sort of love that motivates heroines is too restrictive to create a category of Greek heroines. It is, however, worth noting that Hall's definition of quest heroines shares one trait with the definition of new heroines described in the previous section—namely, an emphasis on the heroine's connection and duty to loved ones.

In *Psyche as Hero: Female Heroism and Fictional Form*, feminist scholar Lee R. Edwards surveys female protagonists in both ancient and modern novels to develop a working definition of heroines that also emphasizes how love and connection (whether romantic, filial, civic, or religious) motivate heroines to act. Edwards's definition of female heroes or heroines (she uses these terms interchangeably) aligns with and further elaborates on the definition of new heroines offered earlier in this chapter. Although she finds that many of the heroines she studies do indeed go on quests, Edwards is less interested in defining heroines by their journeys over land and water, by those who help or harm them, or even by their goals. Thus Edwards bypasses the descriptive analyses of heroes of the works of Vladimir Propp, FitzRoy Raglan (Chapters 10.2 and 11.2), and W. H. Auden (Chapter 12.2). Instead, Edwards defines heroines by combining ideas from the anthropological works of Arnold van Gennep (Chapter 8.2) and Victor Turner (Chapter 9.2) with literary analysis.

The first heroine in Edwards's study is from the Roman novel *The Golden Ass*, by Apuleius (125–180 CE). Apuleius tells the story of Lucius, who accidently turns himself into an ass when he steals some magic from a witch. As an ass, he overhears the story of Amor (also called Cupid) and Psyche. This story within a story forms the basis of Edwards's study. The following exploration of Edwards's ideas also begins with Apuleius's tale of Amor and Psyche.

APULEIUS'S TALE OF AMOR AND PSYCHE

Psyche is the youngest and most beautiful of a king's three daughters. She is so famous for her beauty that people flock to the king's palace to see her, and in this way she inadvertently provokes the jealousy of the goddess Venus (the Roman name for Aphrodite). Venus commissions her son Amor (Roman for Eros) to punish Psyche by shooting her with one of his arrows and causing her to fall in love with a lowly man. Just before Amor's arrival, Psyche is already wretched because her fame and beauty paradoxically leave her isolated from all around her. Seeing Psyche grow weak and sad, the king sends ambassadors to the Delphic oracle to learn which, if any, of the gods is angry with her. He receives a most unwelcome response to his question: the oracle commands the king to send Psyche alone to a mountaintop, where a serpent will steal her away and make her his bride.

Dressed in black and accompanied as if for a wedding—or a funeral—by her family and people from her town, Psyche sets out for the mountain. When her family and townspeople depart and leave her, Psyche is gently carried by winds to a forest, where she comes on a palace fashioned from ivory, gold, silver, and precious stones. When Psyche enters the palace, she finds a table set with food and is served a meal by invisible servants who serenade her with harp and song. When she goes to bed that evening, she is visited by Amor, who does not reveal his identity, instead presenting himself as the palace's owner and her husband. He warns her never to look on him. They spend the night together, and he departs before sunrise (Figure 13.4).

Psyche and her mysterious husband continue in this manner for quite some time until she becomes very lonely and asks her husband if her two sisters might visit her. Although he warns her of their possible ill intentions, Psyche insists. When the sisters visit and see how rich and fortunate Psyche is, they become envious; when she tells them she is pregnant, they convince Psyche that her husband will eat her and her child. Out of envy rather than concern for her welfare,

13.4 Amor and Psyche embrace. Terracotta statuette from Myrina. First century BCE. *Museum of Fine Arts, Boston, Massachusetts, USA / Bridgeman Images, BST1762526.*

they advise Psyche to light a lamp at night to see the true form of her husband, and to bring a razor to kill him. Persuaded by the wisdom of their plan, Psyche does as instructed. However, once she lights her lamp, she sees that her husband is a beautiful young man with wings—none other than Amor himself, who had fallen in love with her when he was commissioned by his mother to shoot her with an arrow. As Psyche stares at Amor, some oil falls from her lamp on his skin, burning and waking him. Realizing she had violated her promise not to look at him during the night, Amor immediately leaves the palace.

Psyche, even more in love with Amor than ever, sets out to find him and win him back. She travels over a great distance to the dwelling of Venus, where Amor is recovering from the wounds Psyche inflicted. Even more dangerously,

Venus is now angry with as well as jealous of Psyche. Venus demands that Psyche complete four tasks to win back Amor. Her first task is to separate a pile of tiny mixed seeds, a task Psyche accomplishes with the assistance of friendly ants. For her second task, Psyche must collect wool from fierce sheep who pasture by a river. Some friendly reeds advise her to wait until the sheep pass under a nearby tree whose branches will rub across their backs, thereby gathering wool for her. For her third task, Psyche must retrieve water from the river Styx as it flows down a sharp cliff. An eagle, seeing her plight, grasps her pitcher and fills it for her. Finally, Psyche must take a box to Proserpina (Roman for Persephone) in the Underworld and ask her to fill it with beauty for Venus. On the journey there and back, Psyche must be careful not to allow herself to become distracted by the pleas for help from those who have died.

Psyche accomplishes all that she was commanded, yet once she is no longer in the Underworld, she cannot resist opening the box of beauty. The box, however, was filled not with beauty but with eternal sleep, which pours over Psyche. Psyche would have remained asleep forever had Amor not set out to find her. He collects and returns sleep to its box and gently pricks Psyche with one of his arrows to wake her. In order to avoid his mother's jealousy and anger, Amor appeals to Jupiter (Roman for Zeus), who agrees to make Psyche immortal. In Olympus, Psyche gives birth to Joy, her daughter by Amor.

Psyche, like Iphigenia in Euripides's *Iphigenia among the Taurians*, goes on a quest that resembles the quests of many Greek heroes. Psyche must leave her palace, go alone on a perilous journey, overcome obstacles with the assistance of helpers, and obtain precious objects. Like Heracles, who cleans the Augean stables with Athena's help, Psyche separates seeds with the help of ants. Like Jason, who must retrieve the Golden Fleece, guarded by a fierce dragon, she must get wool from dangerous rams. Like all Greek heroes, she too travels to the Underworld in order to retrieve something precious. Her story easily fits into the lists of Propp and Raglan. Yet Edwards, as we will see, offers an interpretation of Psyche as a heroine that does not rely on Propp or Raglan and that also differs from the two strands of interpretation that have dominated the scholarship about this tale.

Apuleius's tale has inspired two interpretative traditions that depend on whether Amor and Psyche's love is treated as human or divine. The familiar European fairy tales "Beauty and the Beast" and "Sleeping Beauty" share similar plot devices and suggest a reading of Amor and Psyche's love as ultimately human: a young girl far from home, a wicked or jealous older woman, a mysterious lover, and a sleeping potion. In "Beauty and the Beast," the innocent girl is loved and attended by a "beast" whose true identity and form is only revealed once their mutual love develops and, after perilous trials, is declared. The beast reveals himself to be a human being, albeit one who has been transformed by malevolent magic into an animal body; he is redeemed by the love of a woman who proves herself both chaste and brave, capable of transforming him from beast to a man.

Early Christians, however, treated the love between Psyche and Amor as divine. Because *psyche* is the Greek word for "soul," and Amor is a divinity whose name (in Latin) means "love," the tale was understood as an allegory for how the soul (Psyche) seeks and, through work and hardship, gains divine love (Amor) and blissful (as exemplified by the creation of Joy) eternal life. But in Edwards's reading, the love shared by Amor and Psyche is distinctly human and has a social dimension. In her view, the love described by Apuleius is not divine so much as a moral and deeply human motivation that makes action heroic and inspires individuals to act on behalf of others.

DEFINING THE NEW HEROINE IN ANTHROPOLOGY AND LITERATURE

Edwards develops her definition of heroines from the work of Arnold van Gennep (Chapter 8.2) and Victor Turner (Chapter 9.2). You will recall that van Gennep identified three stages of initiation rituals: separation (the actions that separate initiates geographically, symbolically, and psychologically from their current status or identity); trials (the experiences and events that initiates must undergo in order to achieve or enter into a new status); and reintegration (the events that reintroduce initiates with their new identity to society). Turner, who was influenced by van Gennep's work, was especially interested in the second stage of initiation rituals. He labeled initiates during the second stage "liminars" or "threshold people" because, whereas they no longer have the status they had prior to the ritual, they are not yet recognized by society in their new status. They are, in Turner's words, "betwixt and between," standing on the threshold between two identities.

Turner expanded the category of ritual liminars or threshold people to include people who, although not initiates, nonetheless occupy a "betwixt and between" position. For example, students in college are often adults but have not yet earned the necessary credentials to enter careers in their field. Similarly, individuals experiencing a life-threatening illness are removed from daily routines and full participation in their communities. All of these individuals fall outside of their respective societies in some way. Yet their outsider status is temporary, and they may at some point re-enter society as full-fledged members. Their liminality is often characterized not simply as outside social norms but as "lowly" by social standards (often liminars are poor and powerless). Nonetheless, their liminality will end. However much they challenge the ideas, values, and ways of the society at whose edges they hover, most usually seek to and succeed in returning to society's folds.

"Marginals," on the other hand, live on the edges of society but will never occupy its center. They exist outside of society's structures in a permanent way. Members of a religious order, for example, may spend their lives living in relative poverty and rejecting the trappings of society. Turner, who witnessed the countercultural movements of the twentieth century, considered members of those movements (such as the hippies of the 1960s) as marginals. For them to become full-fledged members of a society, the values and priorities of society itself would have to change.

Using this anthropological framework, Edwards defines heroes as liminars (those temporarily outside of society) but heroines as marginals (those permanently outside of society). Women in patriarchal societies, she observed, will never be granted the same political, legal, social, and economic privileges or access to resources enjoyed by men. Because heroines are never going to gain positions of power, particularly if "power" in a culture depends on military accomplishment, heroines are especially suited to "challenge the belief that society must rest on war and conquest." Moreover, heroines are better suited to the task of finding strength in love and connection to others, rather than in opposition to or conquest of others.

As Edwards points out, the ability of heroines to seek knowledge and power through love and connection is not limited to females, even if it is a modality most easily understood by women and other individuals who are outside of the systems of power, whether liminars or marginals. Thus Edwards's analysis of heroines provides a way to consider and evaluate heroes as well. Like those of Pearson and Pope (see Chapter 13.1), Edwards's heroines provide role models for all people because they offer a mode of action that depends not on physical strength but rather on moral and ethical reasoning, ideals that transcend the "macho heroic ideal" and are available to everyone. Edwards's understanding of heroines expands the definition of new heroines, suggesting its universality for men and women in the past as well as the present.

BEFORE YOU READ

LEE R. EDWARDS, FROM *PSYCHE AS HERO: FEMALE HEROISM AND FICTIONAL FORM*

In this excerpt, Edwards defines liminars and marginals before considering Apuleius's tale of Amor and Psyche.

- How does Edwards define heroes? How and why are they liminars?

- Edwards claims that Psyche "represents not femininity but heroism." What sort of heroism does Psyche represent?

- Edwards argues that Psyche's marriage to Amor at the tale's conclusion does not reinstate female subordination to the male. Edwards calls it "a sign of triumph, not capitulation." Why is Psyche's marriage triumphant in Edwards's view?

- If Psyche is a marginal, has she succeeded in rearranging society to accommodate different values than those that were dominant before her quest?

LEE R. EDWARDS, FROM *PSYCHE AS HERO: FEMALE HEROISM AND FICTIONAL FORM* (1984)

Dreaming, we are heroes. Waking, we invent them. Conscious, unable to recreate the universe according to the patterns of desire, we require heroes to redeem a fallen world. Seductive figures, bold and daring, heroes promise power to the weak, glamour to the dull, and liberty to the oppressed. Their thoughts and actions cut channels into custom's rock. They cross borders, advance into new territory, inspire revolt. Dreamers' agents, necessary fictions, heroes enact our sleeping visions in the world, in daylight. We dream our heroes. In exchange, our heroes alter us.

Dreams are improvisations, private theatricals, unpredictable and fragmentary. Heroism, however, is a public drama, produced by a collective imagination, directed by a common will. Its narrative is formal, even stylized. Its principals have principles in common: each is unique, all are analogous. Heroes resemble one another in behavior, inner makeup, and relationship to their surroundings. Yet, the specific details of heroic narratives—the actions they record, the heroes they depict—vary, like the content of our dreams, and reflect, as dreams do, a particular confluence of circumstance and psyche. Incarnations of abstract ideals and ineffable desires, heroes have no necessary attributes. They play a role, but cannot be typecast. Sex, class, status, occupation have great historical and social resonance, but not inherent meaning. A culture's heroes reflect a culture's values. Where values clash, heroic types conflict.

Western culture, for example, has represented heroes typically as military leaders: commanding, conquering, and above all, male. Erect before us, such figures are the Picts' perpetual descendants, woad-dyed warriors hoping that the spectacle of their naked physical magnificence will awe their enemies into submission. Sacking Troy, seeking the Grail, dying at the Alamo, in Flanders' fields, or on the Cross, their costumes change; their character remains. Even Christ, oddly peaceful in this company, must be remembered as the bringer of a sword; the crucifixion of God's son, not a carpenter's surprise, is the apotheosis of noblesse oblige. Within this context—patriarchal, hostile, preoccupied with rank—the woman hero is an image of antithesis. Different from the male—her sex her sign—she threatens his authority and that of the system he sustains. This is so not because of what men and women really are, if such imponderables are ever fully knowable, but because of the positions assigned to men and women in every society our culture has devised. Leading a fugitive existence, her presence overlooked, her identity obscured, the woman hero is an emblem of patriarchal instability and insecurity. From her perspective, all social contracts have been bargained in bad faith and must be renegotiated. History, she reminds us, has buried the Picts.

. . . .

Feminism, in recent years, has provoked an interest in women heroes, but such figures have a lengthy history. Indeed, the Greek myth of Amor and Psyche, retold by Apuleius in the second-century narrative, *The Golden Ass,* provides a classic example of the female heroic paradigm. The story of the love between a mortal woman and a male god, of Psyche's passionate yearning for Amor, of Amor's evasions and manipulations, and Venus' jealousy of both the beautiful maiden and her own son, emphasizes a quest that fuses power's needs with love's.

Its surface is romantic, but Psyche's character, her deeds, her relationships with the surrounding world—natural, social, and supernatural—are typically heroic. Her beauty is both curse and blessing, a sign of social value and a stigma that thrusts her from society. Men worship her but will not marry her. Women are jealous. Her parents are unable to protect her from the oracle's prediction that she faces immediate extinction. Gods, both Amor and his mother, persecute and torment her. Separated from parents, family, friends, and finally from Amor, Psyche suffers a progressive isolation; it ends only when her successful completion of seemingly impossible tasks restores the lovers to each other. Mediating between an alien nature and an equally frightening, if more familiar culture, she sorts the disordered seeds of Ceres, captures the sun's rams' golden fleece, contains life's rushing waters in an urn. Contending against death, she pays her coins to Charon, throws sops to Cerberus, and resists pity for those who would trap her in the underworld, as Aeneas resists Dido's supplications and Henry V leaves Falstaff in the dust. With some supernatural assistance, Psyche twice defies the gods, first when she uncovers Amor's true identity, a second time when she takes for herself a prize designed for Venus. Like Prometheus, she steals immortal secrets for humanity. The marriage with which the tale concludes is a sign of triumph, not capitulation. Psyche's deeds have deified her, transformed Amor, fertilized life on earth, altered Olympus' eternal ethic. The promise of a new order, metaphysical as well as physical, is celebrated and continued in the birth of a daughter, not a son. Patriarchy's heir has been displaced.

Psyche's heroism, like all heroism, involves both doing and knowing. The pattern of the tale parallels the growth of consciousness. Each material advance marks an increase in psychic range, an apprehension of what was formerly forbidden and inaccessible. The possibility of the woman hero is contingent only on recognizing the aspirations of consciousness as human attributes; it is the absence of this understanding that has kept Psyche and her heroic daughters so long in shadow. For if heroism is defined in terms of external action alone and heroic actions are confined to displays of unusual physical strength, military prowess, or social or political power, then physiology or a culture that limits women's capacities in these areas thereby excludes women from heroic roles. But if action is important primarily for what it tells us about knowledge, then any action—fighting dragons, seeking grails, stealing fleece, reforming love—is potentially heroic. Heroism thus read and understood is a human necessity, capable of being represented equally by either sex.

Apuleius' tale is significant for being a myth of heroic questing and internal growth that concentrates on the possibilities of *human* development and change. In contrast to most myths the patriarchy has retained, "Amor and Psyche" resolutely makes the main representative vehicle a woman who represents not femininity but heroism. When, near the tale's end, Psyche defies Venus and discovers the secrets hidden by Persephone, her treatment violates mythological convention. Unlike Eve or Pandora, Psyche is neither punished nor reviled. She is not cited as the source of sin and human woe; instead she is hailed as a goddess, adored as the font and source of pleasure and delight. Psyche's immersion in the archetypal patterns of heroic action supports a reading of heroism as an asexual or omnisexual archetype and suggests that heroic actions may be culturally atypical. Psyche's labors and those of Hercules are analogous and equal expressions of heroic possibilities. Like the deeds of Achilles, Ulysses, Jason, and Ahab, Psyche's actions resonate for all of us, men and women alike. And as Psyche is—marrying, not murdering; offering pleasure instead of pain; transforming the world rather than subduing it—so might we all wish to be.

The goal of the quest in this tale is love: an expression and an alteration of the possibilities of individual relationship. Such love is born, the narrative's conclusion demonstrates, only when the encounter is reciprocal. Amor and Psyche both participate. The bond between them consciously acknowledges what was formerly unconscious or repressed. For Amor, just as for Psyche, the prospect of intimacy means separation from the mother and an end to childhood's idyll. The tale is at pains to show that we are each—male and female, mortal virgin and great god of love—our mother's frightened child, potentially both her extension and her rival. In entering into a relationship with Psyche, Amor is disobedient to Venus. Psyche's encounter with the power of eroticism occurs in a supposed paradise of love. A torrid, shadowed, and subterranean place that exists only at night, it is the creation of Amor's desire, the expression of his insecurity. Having been displaced by Psyche from this self-protective darkness, he returns for solace to his mother's perfumed bedroom. There, wounded, passive, helpless, infantalized, he is imprisoned for most of the tale. In thrall to Venus and to his own fears and misapprehensions, he is rescued by Psyche when she makes him rescue her from Persephone's spell. Gazing on divine mysteries, Psyche chances death, learns the gods' secrets, empowers another, and lives. Bringing her treasure, as the hero must, from a dream's darkness into daylight, she successfully concludes her quest in a transforming act of love. At the tale's end, she and Amor again embrace. No longer caught in a deathly marriage where the first plunge into sexuality must be a fatal fall, the lovers now accept the risks attendant on self-revelation and the dispossession of old authorities by a new system of valuation that Psyche has created.

All heroism, in fact, appeals to love, makes love its end, relies on faith where knowledge is impossible. Even *The Iliad,* memorialized by Simone Weil as a "poem of force," concludes not with the spectacle of Hector's bloody body being dragged around the fallen city but with Achilles and Priam joined in prayer, reconciled, if only for a moment. Love, in this sense, is neither romantic nor sexual. A social rather than a private impulse, it seeks expression in a public form and brings about a change from an old idea of community to a new ideal, one Victor Turner calls "communitas." This term conveys a vision of community in its spiritual rather than its administrative or geographic sense. Communitas is "spontaneous, immediate, concrete . . . as opposed to the norm-governed, institutionalized abstract nature of social structure" (*RP,* p. 114). The participants in this relationship confront one another directly and create a "model of society as homogeneous and unstructured" (*RP,* p. 119). Communitas is the state brought to birth by Psyche's transformation of self and society, her union with Amor, and the offspring their relationship produces. Amor's hostility toward communitas—an expression of love freely given between individuals loosed from socially or divinely imposed restraints—reflects the extent to which

Psyche's quest raises a living heroism against the dead hand of ritual. Heroic power is inseparable from the love the hero expresses and inspires.

It is this connection between love and power, so often glossed over in narratives and interpretations of male heroism, that is the central structure of "Amor and Psyche." Psyche's child, always in utero referred to as a son, is born a girl and named Pleasure. The change is startling. Heroines typically have sons, hostages to patriarchy, signs that their marriages have been retreats and that they have been incorporated again into an unchanged world. But Pleasure—sensuous, unmanly, feminine—is love's product, a vital expression of communitas. Where instinct and intellect are fused, Pleasure is born. In a culture that sees love as expressive primarily of sexuality alone and as contained only in relationships that reinforce social and economic hierarchies, the need to liberate eros from this hidden bondage can best be perceived and represented by figures who are truly marginal to society, as women have been rendered marginal in patriarchal culture. Nonetheless, this quest is the prototype of all heroic action.

ROME: THECLA

Thecla was a young woman who lived in Iconium (modern day Turkey) during the second century CE. From a wealthy family, she was preparing to marry an equally wealthy young man named Thamyris when she happened to hear the apostle Paul (5–67 CE) preach about Jesus. Like many a Greek heroine, just before her wedding Thecla refused to follow the path set for her. She rejected Thamyris in favor of entering the public sphere to live a celibate life and to travel throughout the Mediterranean, spreading the teachings of Jesus. Thecla managed twice to escape being martyred. She lived a long life and died uneventfully.

Both ancient and modern scholars debate the historicity of Thecla. Some think she did not exist at all, and that all the stories about her are forgeries. Others argue that, although her stories may not be factually accurate, they nonetheless approximate the life of second-century Christian women who devoted themselves to celibacy and to preaching about Jesus. As the patron saint of Tarragona in Spain and at the center of many scholarly and Christian debates, Thecla seems far removed from mythological figures such as Medea or Antigone. Yet intriguing lines of continuity may be traced from the new heroines and heroes of Greece to the stories of Christian saints. In this section, we compare early Christian martyrs and saints to new heroines.

Map 13.2 Thecla from Iconium to Rome

SAINTS AND MARTYRS IN EARLY CHRISTIAN COMMUNITIES

There are striking similarities between the worship of Greek heroes and heroines beginning in the Greek Iron Age (1150 BCE), which evolved in the Classical Age (490–323 BCE) to include new heroes, and the Christian cults of saints and martyrs, which began in the first century CE in the Roman Empire. Christians who were martyred by the Romans as well as those who pursued virtuous deeds and asceticism (i.e., refused marriage and wealth in favor of spiritual pursuits) during the first to fourth centuries CE were sometimes worshipped by fellow believers after their death. Holy persons (usually ascetics) were believed to be able to perform miracles while living, as were martyrs during the period shortly before their execution. After death, their miraculous powers were believed to remain in their bodies. They were worshipped and petitioned at their tombs, and annual celebrations on the day of their martyrdom were observed.

Although martyrs and holy persons were venerated at their tombs in ways similar to Greek heroes and heroines, there were nonetheless important differences. Greek heroes and heroines were powerful in their own rights, not because they were believed to be in communion with other deceased heroes or heroines or gods. Moreover, Greek heroes and heroines were imagined to be close to or under the earth, near their tombs. They were thought to be neither in the heavens or Olympus nor in close proximity to the gods.

Christian holy persons and martyrs, on the other hand, were believed to be in heaven—even if their corpses (or parts of their corpses, known as relics) were occasionally believed to work miracles. Additionally, whereas the bodies of heroes and heroines might be sought and moved from one tomb to another because their powers were believed to inhere in their corpses, their actual physical remains were not revered or handled. In contrast, Christian holy persons and martyrs, once they had died, were believed to be in communion with one another, to be intimate with God, and to reside in the heavens. Their decaying bodies and clothes were lovingly dug up and touched and very often divided so that they could be shared among several places, where they might attract attention and serve as a conduit to God.

One such early martyr was the bishop of Smyrna, Saint Polycarp. In 156 CE Polycarp was brutally tortured and burned at the stake for his refusal to revere the emperor of Rome. In a written account by members of his church, they describe how "we took up the bones, which are more valuable than precious stones and finer than refined gold, and laid them in a suitable

place, where the Lord will permit us to gather ourselves together as we are able, in gladness and joy,
and celebrate the birthday of his martyrdom." In
later centuries, the repositories of the relics often
became centers of Christian worship. Polycarp, for
example, is the patron saint of Naupactus in western
Greece, where his right arm is kept as a relic at the
Holy Monastery of Panagia Ambelakiotissa.

In sum, Greek heroes and heroines were remembered and celebrated as they were when they were
alive: powerful, beautiful, and even frightening.
Christian saints and martyrs were remembered and
celebrated for their suffering in adherence to their
faith; their decaying bodies were venerated because
they recalled the transience of earthly life even as
they promised communion with eternal life.

As the veneration of martyrs and holy persons
became ever more important to Christian communities, control of their tombs became a social and spiritual concern to the early Christian church as it tried
to consolidate its worshippers and doctrines into one
system (fourth to sixth centuries CE). Here, too, we
see a difference from earlier Greek practices. A hero
or heroine's worship at a shrine rose in popularity or
faded into obscurity along with the fortunes of its
local community. No central religious authority or
organization sought to codify or control it. The cults
of martyrs and saints, however, increasingly became

13.5 Thecla with two wild beasts. Terracotta ampulla (flask). Sixth to seventh century CE. Louvre Museum, Paris, France. © RMN-Grand Palais / Art Resource, NY, ART167305.

sites of contestation among local elites and bishops, who saw them as sources
of influence and spiritual authority (and, for the less scrupulous, opportunities for profit, especially as believers made pilgrimages to visit tombs and
relics).

NEW HEROINES AND MARTYRS

Although the preceding section describes some of the differences between
the more general category of Greek heroes and heroines and Christian martyrs (Chapters 10.1 and 11.1), the intriguing similarities between Christian
martyrs and new heroines are worthy of consideration.

The word "martyr" comes from the Greek word meaning "to witness."
Martyrs served as witnesses to their beliefs during their deaths, which were,
from the beginning, elaborate public spectacles. Nero, the first Roman emperor to order the execution of Christians, arranged for such exotic torments

as for them to be covered with pitch and used as torches or draped in animals skins and torn apart by dogs (64 CE); Thecla herself, as we shall see, was set upon by (and ultimately saved from) lions, bears, seals, and bulls (Figure 13.5). (The Roman historian Tacitus suggests that Nero wanted to distract the Romans from a six-day fire that burned through Rome and that most suspected Nero himself had started [*Annals* 15.44].) During the next three centuries, the Roman officials who ordered the executions of Christians most often said the Christian refusal to worship the Roman emperor as a god posed a threat to the Roman Empire (as in the case of Saint Polycarp). The manner of martyrs' deaths was always public and cruel, even if the methods were not as elaborate as Nero's, and increasingly placed the daily struggles of their early Christian communities to worship Jesus in a larger perspective. Far from discouraging their beliefs, the spectacle of martyrdom galvanized the fledgling community's resolve to resist Roman persecution.

Paradoxically, martyrs became empowered by their public deaths, not unlike new heroines. The passive suffering of martyrs, their "passion" (as in the Christian sense of the "passion of Christ"), neither was an act of violence nor incited violence. Yet, because they could not be compelled to cooperate with the Romans or act against their Christian beliefs, the deaths of martyrs both limited and criticized the powers of the Roman state. Thus, martyrs pursued a form of self-determination within very limited opportunities for action. Although only a few new heroines, like Iphigenia, Polyxena, or Antigone, "chose" to die in a manner akin to Christian martyrs, their actions nonetheless were a form of self-determination and a critique of their society, because their decision to act in public challenged normative rules. The account of Thecla, a Christian woman who escaped martyrdom twice, highlights the similarities between her (and, by extension, other early Christian martyrs) and Greek new heroines.

THECLA AS A CHRISTIAN HEROINE

The life of Thecla is known to us through two texts: "The Acts of Paul and Thecla," from the apocryphal New Testament (stories omitted from the New Testament but including the same characters and plots), and an anonymous fifth-century-CE compilation of stories called the *Life and Miracles of Thecla*. Stories about Thecla's life very likely derive from oral stories told at her tomb as described by Egeria, a Christian woman from Gallacea (modern Galicia, Spain) who made a pilgrimage to Jerusalem in the late fourth century CE. Egeria kept a diary of her experiences for a spiritual community of women in Spain, whom she addresses in her writing. In the following passage, Egeria describes her visit to the tomb of Thecla in Seleucia on her return (translated by M. L. McClure and C. L. Feltoe).

EGERIA, FROM *THE TRAVELS OF EGERIA* (c. 483 CE)

Thence I entered the borders of Hisauria and stayed in a city called Coricus, and on the third day I arrived at a city which is called Seleucia in Hisauria; on my arrival I went to the bishop, a truly holy man, formerly a monk, and in that city I saw a very beautiful church. And as the distance thence to saint Thecla, which is situated outside the city on a low eminence, was about fifteen hundred paces, I chose rather to go there in order to make the stay that I intended. There is nothing at the holy church in that place except numberless cells of men and of women. I found there a very dear friend of mine, to whose manner of life all in the East bore testimony, a holy deaconess named Marthana, whom I had known at Jerusalem, whither she had come for the sake of prayer; she was ruling over the cells of *apotactitae* [Christians who renounce all possessions] and virgins. And when she had seen me, how can I describe the extent of her joy or of mine? But to return to the matter in hand: there are very many cells on the hill and in the midst of it a great wall which encloses the church containing the very beautiful memorial. The wall was built to guard the church because of the Hisauri, who are very malicious and who frequently commit acts of robbery, to prevent them from making an attempt on the monastery which is established there. When I had arrived in the Name of God, prayer was made at the memorial, and the whole of the acts of saint Thecla having been read, I gave endless thanks to Christ our God, who deigned to fulfil my desires in all things, unworthy and undeserving as I am. Then, after a stay of two days, when I had seen the holy monks and *apotactitae* who were there, both men and women, and when I had prayed and made my communion, I returned to Tarsus and to my journey.

Egeria says that she both prayed and "read the whole of the acts of saint Thecla," which most likely refers to "The Acts of Paul and Thecla" (included at the end of this section). Egeria's diary suggests that Thecla's story, like those of many martyrs, was told repeatedly at her tomb and was carried home by pilgrims, who likely shaped and embroidered on the story as it was retold. In this light, it is not surprising that saints' tales came to resemble early romances, in which both hero and heroine go on a quest to find their true love, often surviving harrowing adventures filled with fellow travelers, helpers, or villains. Whereas a martyr's true love is Jesus, with whom spiritual unity is sought, similarities can be traced between the tales of Greek new heroines and those of Christian saints and martyrs.

BEFORE YOU READ

UNKNOWN, *FROM* "THE ACTS OF PAUL AND THECLA"

Thecla's story as reported in "The Acts of Paul and Thecla" has many affinities with early tales of romance heroines (such as Amor and Psyche) and the Greek stories of new heroines. Thecla takes decisive action at the time of her marriage. She has a series of adventures as she pursues her goal: not a human lover, but a divine one. She places herself in the public sphere on behalf of others as well as her divine love, and her acts offer a critique of Roman society. Like Iphigenia and Polyxena, when sent to die, Thecla does not cower but instead meets her death willingly and with dignity in order to demonstrate her unshakeable commitment to her beliefs. Although her options are limited, she nonetheless chooses how to act and in so doing becomes a "witness" to her beliefs. In sum, whether through narrative patterns or motives, female Christian martyrs resemble both the new heroines of Greek tragedy and the heroines of ancient romances. (Translated by J. K. Elliott.)

- In what ways (other than those already mentioned) does Thecla resemble Greek heroines whom you have already encountered?

- Thecla is sent to the arena to be martyred twice. She survives thanks to the intervention of other females (a lioness and a patroness). To what degree is femaleness associated with Christian piety and kindness?

- Antigone acts on behalf of her (biological) family against the state. Thecla, on the other hand, acts against her family's (specifically her mother's) wishes. How do Thecla's actions redefine her notion of family? How might they serve to define a notion of family among early Christian communities?

UNKNOWN, *FROM* "THE ACTS OF PAUL AND THECLA" (SECOND CENTURY CE)

(2) ACTS OF PAUL: ACTS OF PAUL AND THECLA 7–43

7. And while Paul was speaking in the midst of the church in the house of Onesiphorus a certain virgin named Thecla, the daughter of Theoclia, betrothed to a man named Thamyris, was sitting at the window close by and listened day and night to the discourse of virginity, as proclaimed by Paul. And she did not look away from the window, but was led on by faith, rejoicing exceedingly. And when she saw many women and virgins going in to Paul she also had an eager desire to be

deemed worthy to stand in Paul's presence and hear the word of Christ. For she had not yet seen Paul in person, but only heard his word.

8. As she did not move from the window her mother sent to Thamyris. And he came gladly as if already receiving her in marriage. And Thamyris said to Theoclia, "Where, then, is my Thecla that I may see her?" And Theoclia answered, "I have a strange story to tell you, Thamyris. For three days and three nights Thecla does not rise from the window either to eat or to drink; but looking earnestly as if upon some pleasant sight she is devoted to a foreigner teaching deceitful and artful discourses, so that I wonder how a virgin of her great modesty exposes herself to such extreme discomfort.

9. "Thamyris, this man will overturn the city of the Iconians and your Thecla too; for all the women and the young men go in to him to be taught by him. He says one must fear only one God and live in chastity. Moreover, my daughter, clinging to the window like a spider, lays hold of what is said by him with a strange eagerness and fearful emotion. For the virgin looks eagerly at what is said by him and has been captivated. But go near and speak to her, for she is betrothed to you."

10. And Thamyris greeted her with a kiss, but at the same time being afraid of her overpowering emotion said, "Thecla, my betrothed, why do you sit thus? And what sort of feeling holds you distracted? Come back to your Thamyris and be ashamed." Moreover, her mother said the same, "Why do you sit thus looking down, my child, and answering nothing, like a sick woman?" And those who were in the house wept bitterly, Thamyris for the loss of a wife, Theoclia for that of a child, and the maidservants for that of a mistress. And there was a great outpouring of lamentation in the house. And while these things were going on Thecla did not turn away but kept attending to the word of Paul.

11. And Thamyris, jumping up, went into the street, and watched all who went in to Paul and came out. And he saw two men bitterly quarrelling with each other and he said to them, "Men, who are you and tell me who is this man among you, leading astray the souls of young men and deceiving virgins so that they should not marry but remain as they are? I promise you money enough if you tell me about him, for I am the chief man of this city."

12. And Demas and Hermogenes said to him, "Who he is we do not know. But he deprives the husbands of wives and maidens of husbands, saying, 'There is for you no resurrection unless you remain chaste and do not pollute the flesh.'"

13. And Thamyris said to them, "Come into my house and refresh yourselves." And they went to a sumptuous supper and much wine and

great wealth and a splendid table. And Thamyris made them drink, for   50
he loved Thecla and wished to take her as wife. And during the supper
Thamyris said, "Men, tell me what is his teaching that I also may know
it, for I am greatly distressed about Thecla, because she so loves the
stranger and I am prevented from marrying."

14. And Demas and Hermogenes said, "Bring him before the Governor Castellius because he persuades the multitude to embrace the new
teaching of the Christians, and he will destroy him and you shall have
Thecla as your wife. And we shall teach you about the resurrection which
he says is to come, that it has already taken place in the children and that
we rise again, after having come to the knowledge of the true God."   60

15. And when Thamyris heard these things he rose up early in the
morning and, filled with jealousy and anger, went into the house of
Onesiphorus with rulers and officers and a great crowd with batons and
said to Paul, "You have deceived the city of the Iconians and especially
my betrothed bride so that she will not have me! Let us go to the governor Castellius!" And the whole crowd cried, "Away with the sorcerer for
he has misled all our wives!," and the multitude was also incited.

16. And Thamyris standing before the tribunal said with a great   70
shout, "O proconsul, this man—we do not know where he comes from—
makes virgins averse to marriage. Let him say before you why he
teaches thus." But Demas and Hermogenes said to Thamyris, "Say that
he is a Christian and he will die at once." But the governor kept his resolve and called Paul, saying, "Who are you and what do you teach?
For they bring no small accusation against you."

17. And Paul, lifting up his voice, said, "If I today must tell any of
my teachings then listen, O proconsul. The living God, the God of vengeance, the jealous God, the God who has need of nothing, who seeks
the salvation of men, has sent me that I may rescue them from corrup-   80
tion and uncleanness and from all pleasure, and from death, that they
may sin no more. On this account God sent his Son whose gospel I
preach and teach, that in him men have hope, who alone has had
compassion upon a world led astray, that men may be no longer under
judgement but may have faith and fear of God and knowledge of honesty and love of truth. If then I teach the things revealed to me by God
what harm do I do, O proconsul?" When the governor heard this he
ordered Paul to be bound and sent to prison until he had time to hear
him more attentively.

18. And Thecla, by night, took off her bracelets and gave them to   90
the gatekeeper; and when the door was opened to her she went into
the prison. To the jailer she gave a silver mirror and was thus enabled
to go in to Paul and, sitting at his feet, she heard the great deeds of

God. And Paul was afraid of nothing, but trusted in God. And her faith also increased and she kissed his bonds.

19. And when Thecla was sought for by her family and Thamyris they were hunting through the streets as if she had been lost. One of the gatekeeper's fellow slaves informed them that she had gone out by night. And they examined the gatekeeper who said to them, "She has gone to the foreigner in the prison." And they went and found her, so to   100 say, chained to him by affection. And having gone out from there they incited the people and informed the governor what had happened.

20. And he ordered Paul to be brought before the tribunal, but Thecla was riveted to the place where Paul had sat whilst in prison. And the governor ordered her also to be brought to the tribunal, and she came with an exceedingly great joy. And when Paul had been led forth the crowd vehemently cried out, "He is a sorcerer. Away with him!" But the governor gladly heard Paul speak about the holy works of Christ. And having taken counsel, he summoned Thecla and said, "Why do   110 you not marry Thamyris, according to the law of the Iconians?" But she stood looking earnestly at Paul. And when she gave no answer Theoclia, her mother, cried out saying, "Burn the wicked one; burn her who will not marry in the midst of the theatre, that all the women who have been taught by this man may be afraid."

21. And the governor was greatly moved, and after scourging Paul he cast him out of the city. But Thecla he condemned to be burned. And immediately the governor arose and went away to the theatre. And the whole multitude went out to witness the spectacle. But as a lamb in the wilderness looks around for the shepherd, so Thecla kept   120 searching for Paul. And having looked into the crowd she saw the Lord sitting in the likeness of Paul and said, "As if I were unable to endure, Paul has come to look after me." And she gazed upon him with great earnestness, but he went up into heaven.

22. And the boys and girls brought wood and straw in order that Thecla might be burned. And when she came in naked the governor wept and admired the power that was in her. And the executioners arranged the wood and told her to go up on the pile. And having made the sign of the cross she went up on the pile. And they lighted the fire. And though a great fire was blazing it did not touch her. For God,   130 having compassion upon her, made an underground rumbling, and a cloud full of water and hail overshadowed the theatre from above, and all its contents were poured out so that many were in danger of death. And the fire was put out and Thecla saved.

23. And Paul was fasting with Onesiphorus and his wife and his children in a new tomb on the way which led from Iconium to Daphne.

And after many days had been spent in fasting the children said to Paul, "We are hungry." And they had nothing with which to buy bread, for Onesiphorus had left the things of this world and followed Paul with all his house. And Paul, having taken off his cloak, said, "Go, my child, 140 sell this and buy some loaves and bring them." And when the child was buying them he saw Thecla their neighbour and was astonished and said, "Thecla, where are you going?" And she said, "I have been saved from the fire and am following Paul." And the child said, "Come, I shall take you to him; for he has been mourning for you and praying and fasting six days already."

24. And when she had come to the tomb Paul was kneeling and praying, "Father of Christ, let not the fire touch Thecla but stand by her, for she is yours"; she, standing behind him, cried out, "O Father who made the heaven and the earth, the Father of your beloved Son Jesus 150 Christ, I praise you that you have saved me from the fire that I may see Paul again." And Paul, rising up, saw her and said, "O God, who knows the heart, Father of our Lord Jesus Christ, I praise you because you have speedily heard my prayer."

25. And there was great love in the tomb as Paul and Onesiphorus and the others all rejoiced. And they had five loaves and vegetables and water, and they rejoiced in the holy works of Christ. And Thecla said to Paul, "I will cut my hair off and I shall follow you wherever you go." But he said, "Times are evil and you are beautiful. I am afraid lest another temptation come upon you worse than the first and that you do 160 not withstand it but become mad after men." And Thecla said, "Only give me the seal in Christ, and no temptation shall touch me." And Paul said, "Thecla, be patient; you shall receive the water."

26. And Paul sent away Onesiphorus and all his family to Iconium and went into Antioch, taking Thecla with him. And as soon as they had arrived a certain Syrian, Alexander by name, an influential citizen of Antioch, seeing Thecla, became enamoured of her and tried to bribe Paul with gifts and presents. But Paul said, "I know not the woman of whom you speak, nor is she mine." But he, being of great power, embraced her in the street. But she would not endure it and looked about 170 for Paul. And she cried out bitterly, saying, "Do not force the stranger; do not force the servant of God. I am one of the chief persons of the Iconians and because I would not marry Thamyris I have been cast out of the city." And taking hold of Alexander, she tore his cloak and pulled off his crown and made him a laughing-stock.

27. And he, although loving her, nevertheless felt ashamed of what had happened and led her before the governor; and as she confessed that she had done these things he condemned her to the wild

beasts. The women of the city cried out before the tribunal, "Evil judgement! impious judgement!" And Thecla asked the governor that she might remain pure until she was to fight with the wild beasts. And a rich woman named Queen Tryphaena, whose daughter was dead, took her under her protection and had her for a consolation. 180

28. And when the beasts were exhibited they bound her to a fierce lioness, and Queen Tryphaena followed her. And the lioness, with Thecla sitting upon her, licked her feet; and all the multitude was astonished. And the charge on her inscription was "Sacrilegious." And the women and children cried out again and again, "O God, outrageous things take place in this city." And after the exhibition Tryphaena received her again. For her dead daughter Falconilla had said to her in a dream, "Mother, receive this stranger, the forsaken Thecla, in my place, that she may pray for me and I may come to the place of the just." 190

29. And when, after the exhibition, Tryphaena had received her she was grieved because Thecla had to fight on the following day with the wild beasts, but on the other hand she loved her dearly like her daughter Falconilla and said, "Thecla, my second child, come, pray for my child that she may live in eternity, for this I saw in my sleep." And without hesitation she lifted up her voice and said, "My God, Son of the Most High, who are in heaven, grant her wish that her daughter 200 Falconilla may live in eternity." And when Thecla had spoken Tryphaena grieved very much, considering that such beauty was to be thrown to the wild beasts.

30. And when it was dawn Alexander came to her, for it was he who arranged the exhibition of wild beasts, and said, "The governor has taken his seat and the crowd is clamouring for us; get ready, I will take her to fight with the wild beasts." And Tryphaena put him to flight with a loud cry, saying, "A second mourning for my Falconilla has come upon my house, and there is no one to help, neither child for she is dead, nor kinsman for I am a widow. God of Thecla, my child, help 210 Thecla."

31. And the governor sent soldiers to bring Thecla. Tryphaena did not leave her but took her by the hand and led her away saying, "My daughter Falconilla I took away to the tomb, but you, Thecla, I take to fight the wild beasts." And Thecla wept bitterly and sighed to the Lord, "O Lord God, in whom I trust, to whom I have fled for refuge, who did deliver me from the fire, reward Tryphaena who has had compassion on your servant and because she kept me pure."

32. And there arose a tumult: the wild beasts roared, the people and the women sitting together were crying, some saying, "Away with 220 the sacrilegious person!," others saying, "O that the city would be

destroyed on account of this iniquity! Kill us all, proconsul; miserable spectacle, evil judgement!"

33. And Thecla, having been taken from the hands of Tryphaena, was stripped and received a girdle and was thrown into the arena. And lions and bears were let loose upon her. And a fierce lioness ran up and lay down at her feet. And the multitude of the women cried aloud. And a bear ran upon her, but the lioness went to meet it and tore the bear to pieces. And again a lion that had been trained to fight against men, which belonged to Alexander, ran upon her. And the lioness, en-   230
countering the lion, was killed along with it. And the women cried the more since the lioness, her protector, was dead.

34. Then they sent in many beasts as she was standing and stretching forth her hands and praying. And when she had finished her prayer she turned around and saw a large pit full of water and said, "Now it is time to wash myself." And she threw herself in saying, "In the name of Jesus Christ I baptize myself on my last day." When the women and the multitude saw it they wept and said, "Do not throw yourself into the water!"; even the governor shed tears because the seals were to devour such beauty. She then threw herself into the water in the name   240
of Jesus Christ, but the seals, having seen a flash of lightning, floated dead on the surface. And there was round her a cloud of fire so that the beasts could neither touch her nor could she be seen naked.

35. But the women lamented when other and fiercer animals were let loose; some threw petals, others nard, others cassia, others amomum, so that there was an abundance of perfumes. And all the wild beasts were hypnotized and did not touch her. And Alexander said to the governor, "I have some terrible bulls to which we will bind her." And the governor consented grudgingly, "Do what you will." And they bound her by the feet between the bulls and put red-hot irons under their gen-   250
itals so that they, being rendered more furious, might kill her. They rushed forward but the burning flame around her consumed the ropes, and she was as if she had not been bound.

36. And Tryphaena fainted standing beside the arena, so that the servants said, "Queen Tryphaena is dead." And the governor put a stop to the games and the whole city was in dismay. And Alexander fell down at the feet of the governor and cried, "Have mercy upon me and upon the city and set the woman free, lest the city also be destroyed. For if Caesar hear of these things he will possibly destroy the city along with us because his kinswoman, Queen Tryphaena, has died at the theatre gate."   260

37. And the governor summoned Thecla out of the midst of the beasts and said to her, "Who are you? And what is there about you that not one of the wild beasts touched you?" She answered, "I am a

servant of the living God and, as to what there is about me, I have believed in the son of God in whom he is well pleased; that is why not one of the beasts touched me. For he alone is the goal of salvation and the basis of immortal life. For he is a refuge to the tempest-tossed, a solace to the afflicted, a shelter to the despairing; in brief, whoever does not believe in him shall not live but be dead forever."   270

38. When the governor heard these things he ordered garments to be brought and to be put on her. And she said, "He who clothed me when I was naked among the beasts will in the day of judgement clothe me with salvation." And taking the garments she put them on.

And the governor immediately issued an edict saying, "I release to you the pious Thecla, the servant of God." And the women shouted aloud and with one voice praised God, "One is the God, who saved Thecla," so that the whole city was shaken by their voices.

39. And Tryphaena, having received the good news, went with the multitude to meet Thecla. After embracing her she said, "Now I   280 believe that the dead are raised! Now I believe that my child lives. Come inside and all that is mine I shall assign to you." And Thecla went in with her and rested eight days, instructing her in the word of God, so that many of the maidservants believed. And there was great joy in the house.

40. And Thecla longed for Paul and sought him, looking in every direction. And she was told that he was in Myra. And wearing a mantle that she had altered so as to make a man's cloak, she came with a band of young men and maidens to Myra, where she found Paul speaking the word of God and went to him. And he was astonished at seeing   290 her and her companions, thinking that some new temptation was coming upon her. And perceiving this, she said to him, "I have received baptism, O Paul; for he who worked with you for the gospel has worked with me also for baptism."

41. And Paul, taking her, led her to the house of Hermias and heard everything from her, so that he greatly wondered and those who heard were strengthened and prayed for Tryphaena. And Thecla rose up and said to Paul, "I am going to Iconium." Paul answered, "Go, and teach the word of God." And Tryphaena sent her much clothing and gold so that she could leave many things to Paul for the service of the poor.   300

42. And coming to Iconium she went into the house of Onesiphorus and fell upon the place where Paul had sat and taught the word of God, and she cried and said, "My God and God of this house where the light shone upon me, Jesus Christ, Son of God, my help in prison, my help before the governors, my help in the fire, my help among the wild beasts, you alone are God and to you be glory for ever. Amen."

43. And she found Thamyris dead but her mother alive. And calling her mother she said, "Theoclia, my mother, can you believe that the Lord lives in heaven? For if you desire wealth the Lord will give it to you through me; or if you desire your child, behold, I am standing beside you."

And having thus testified, she went to Seleucia and enlightened many by the word of God; then she rested in a glorious sleep.

13.4 RECEPTION
TEN YEARS OF IPHIGENIA IN NEW YORK CITY

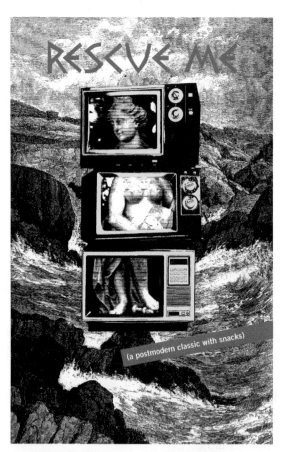

13.6 Playbill from the premier of Michi Barall's Rescue Me. http://www.broadwayworld.com/off-off-broadway/article/MaYi-Theatre-Company-Presents-RESCUE-ME-by-Michi-Barall-20100322#.U6nE6Rnt214. ©Another Limited Rebellion, Courtesy of the Ma Yi Theater Company.

Over the centuries, Euripides's two plays about Iphigenia have been received and interpreted by scholars and artists alike. *Iphigenia in Aulis*, the more grave and tragic of the two, has proved more popular and is frequently restaged during times of war. In such productions, Agamemnon's self-serving rhetoric contrasts with Iphigenia's innocent nobility and reveals how a militaristic society shapes and corrupts human relations. *Iphigenia among the Taurians*, on the other hand, with its adventures, harrowing escapes, and happy endings, has attracted less attention. Its themes are not immediately apparent; its tone is lighter, and Iphigenia's machinations provoke less interest than her decision to die in *Iphigenia in Aulis*.

Despite differences in plot and tone, Euripides's two plays share one feature that makes any modern interest in them seem rather remarkable: they both concern human sacrifice. In *Iphigenia in Aulis* Agamemnon chooses to sacrifice his daughter Iphigenia; in *Iphigenia among the Taurians* Iphigenia prepares the Greeks to be sacrificed—a service she is compelled to perform for Thoas, king of the Taurians. How, we might wonder, can a story about human sacrifice be adapted to discuss contemporary issues?

This section looks at two plays that use human sacrifice as a key metaphor or plot device. Both premiered in New York City during the same decade (1999–2010) and are distinguished by their wildly inventive use of collage, videos, pop music, food, and much more to render these plays thoroughly contemporary. Charles L. Mee's *Iphigenia 2.0* adapts *Iphigenia at Aulis*, and *Rescue Me: A Postmodern Classic with Snacks* by Michi Barall (who is married to Charles L. Mee) adapts *Iphigenia among the Taurians*. Like Euripides's plays, these modern adaptations vary in tone and intensity as they present (and in one case completely ignore) Iphigenia's status as a heroine. Taken together, they make a compelling case for how the apparitions of heroes and heroines of Greek myth on stage continue to offer audiences a way to examine their own lives.

CHARLES L. MEE'S *IPHIGENIA 2.0*

In the introduction to his website, the (Re)making Project, where all his plays are published, Charles L. Mee (b. 1938) writes, "Please feel free to take the texts from this website . . . cut them up, rearrange them, rewrite them, throw things out . . . and then please put your own name to the work that results." Mee has frequently remade (or, as he might say, "stolen") Euripides's plays. Using the original characters and stories as a starting point, Mee remakes the tragedies by layering in videos, songs, and images.

Mee's technique has been variously described as collage, mash-up, and pastiche. His *Iphigenia 2.0* is typical of this mode of composition. Although Mee closely follows Euripides's plot, he adds a barrage of modern references and veers between parody, comedy, and tragedy. In both Euripides's and Mee's versions, Agamemnon lies to Iphigenia, telling her that Achilles wants to marry her in Aulis before the troops depart to Troy. When she arrives at Aulis with her mother, Clytemnestra, Agamemnon's lie is soon discovered. Clytemnestra tries to get Achilles to save her daughter, but it becomes clear that the only possible resolution is for Iphigenia to be slaughtered. Faced with her inevitable sacrifice, Iphigenia chooses to go willingly to her death, preserving her dignity and self-assertion while revealing the treachery and barbarity of the Greeks.

In Mee's play, this plotline is preserved but for the fact that the troops, not Artemis, demand Iphigenia's death. Of the four soldiers on stage, who represent the army, one tells Agamemnon, "The prospect of death in war is certain for some, and so they ask for you to be the first to accept this certainty." The absurdity and cruelty of their demand matches that of Artemis in Euripides's version (the Greeks, as we have seen, never thought of their gods as particularly kind or rational). Their demand introduces the question of moral fitness for leadership in times of war, a question whose urgency increases when Menelaus reads a catalogue of war atrocities and Agamemnon frets about his decision to lie to and kill Iphigenia. The soldiers' cavalier attitudes as they strut and dance in anticipation of Iphigenia's murder displays how costly the absence of moral leadership—here in the figures of Agamemnon and Menelaus—can be.

The soldiers' antics and blithe attitudes are matched by those of the bridesmaids who accompany Iphigenia to Aulis. They tell tales of bachelorette parties that feature hot tubs and male strippers. Although their stories lack the violence and horror of Menelaus's war stories, they are equally hollow. As the stage fills with ever more stories in colloquial idioms (the soldiers demand, among other things, Oreo cookies and the *New York Times*) and seemingly mindless action (during Iphigenia's wedding, the soldiers and bridesmaids dance together), this hollowness becomes palpable. Reviewing a 2007 production of the play for *New York* magazine, theater critic Jeremy McCarter compared this mash-up to a history lesson with "all the weird stuff that crossed your mind during class" and considers that this "frenetic collage actually does a pretty apt job of capturing our overexposed, ADHD-riddled society."

In Mee's rendering, Iphigenia's consent to be sacrificed is presented as a desire to escape such a crass and shallow society. Her moral clarity offers a startling relief from the pettiness, fear, and vanity of her father, Agamemnon, and her uncle Menelaus, who spend much of the play bickering with each other about who is less or more worthy to lead the Greek troops. At this pivotal moment, Mee's script presents one of the central ambiguities of Euripides's play: Is Iphigenia deluded by the values of the militaristic culture her father espouses, or is she able to see a way out of the emptiness that surrounds her through her decision to die? In this way, Mee asks his own audience to consider whether Iphigenia is a heroine for our times.

MICHI BARALL'S *RESCUE ME: A POSTMODERN CLASSIC WITH SNACKS*

Michi Barall (b. 1970) has also turned to Euripides to create a heroine for contemporary times. In her adaptation of *Iphigenia among the Taurians* (2010) (Figure 13.6), Iphigenia announces, "I'm 34, I'm single and I hate my job. I'm probably too old to have kids." As in Euripides's play, Iphigenia is stuck in Tauris, preparing Greek visitors for sacrifice at the behest of King Thoas and the goddess Artemis. But in Barall's play, Iphigenia works in an immigration agency. She carries file folders and has two assistants, Sandra and Lydia, who are charged with checking IDs. As Iphigenia explains, "If you're Greek, you will be detained and executed. It's policy. You will be sacrificed to the goddess Artemis." Because Iphigenia has escaped being sacrificed by her father in Greece and because Tauris offers her refuge, Iphigenia carries out its cruel and arbitrary policy against Greeks. While working, Iphigenia is obsessed with learning about the scandals and activities of the Greek elite, such as her family members, in the news. Her obsession with gossip marks her as both modern and shallow.

Barall's Artemis has both ancient and modern attributes. She is an amalgam of divinity and bureaucracy as well as a dramaturge (someone who helps a theatre company develop plays for performance). She shows maps on a video and explains to the audience where the land of the Taurians is located. She also argues with Iphigenia about lighting and staging. In this fashion, Barall's play shatters theatrical conventions by making the audience aware that they are watching a play. Perhaps the most notable example of breaking the separation between the world of the play and the audience is when Artemis and Iphigenia call on a classical scholar to explain the mythological background of the play while the audience is offered snacks. A question-and-answer session, hosted by nationally and even internationally recognized classical scholars, follows. Thus the mash-up of ancient and modern elements (Artemis watches telenovelas; Thoas dresses and sings like Elvis Presley; Sandra and Lydia drink Diet Coke and take migraine medication) and the breaking of theatrical illusion make Barall's play "postmodern."

Barall's play also asks the audience to consider whether or not there is an unbridgeable gap between Euripides's play about human sacrifice and the present. She suggests that immigration policies separating families and denying refuge to those whose lives are threatened are a form, however indirect, of human sacrifice. Her Iphigenia is a globe-trotting immigrant heroine who for a time resists being shaped by the inhumane demands of those who surround her but ultimately succumbs.

KEY TERMS

Amor 620
Antigone 610
Iphigenia among the
   Taurians 610

Iphigenia in Aulis 610
Psyche 620

Thecla 629
Tyrannicides 605

FOR FURTHER EXPLORATION

Cooper, K. *Band of Angels: The Forgotten World of Early Christian Women.* New York: Overlook Press, 2013. Cooper's chapter on Thecla provides a compelling interpretation of her in the context of her contemporaries.

Edwards, L. R. *Psyche as Hero: Female Heroism and Fictional Form.* Middleton, CT: Wesleyan University Press, 1984. Although Edwards does not address ancient heroines, other than Psyche, her various analyses of fictional heroines offer ways to think about Greek heroines.

Hall, E. *Adventures with Iphigenia in Tauris: A Cultural History of Euripides' Black Sea Tragedy.* Oxford: Oxford University Press, 2012. Hall offers a brief analysis of Iphigenia as a quest heroine followed by a broad survey of how Euripides's play *Iphigenia among the Taurians* has inspired artists over the centuries.

Jones, C. P. *New Heroes in Antiquity: From Achilles to Antinoos.* Cambridge, MA: Harvard University Press, 2010. This brief book comprehensively surveys the worship of heroes (although not heroines) and considers the continuity between them and Christian saints and martyrs.

SELECT BIBLIOGRAPHY

CHAPTER 1: CLASSICAL MYTHS AND CONTEMPORARY QUESTIONS

Bascom, William. "The Forms of Folklore: Prose Narratives." *Journal of American Folklore* 78 (1965): 3–20.

Cline, Eric H., and M. W. Graham. *Ancient Empires: From Mesopotamia to the Rise of Islam*. Cambridge: Cambridge University Press, 2011.

Coupe, Laurence. *Myth*. London and New York: Routledge, 1997.

Csapo, Eric. *Theories of Mythology*. Malden, MA, and Oxford: Wiley-Blackwell, 2005.

Cupitt, Donald. *The World to Come*. London: SCM Press, 1982.

Doty, William G. *Mythography: The Study of Myths and Rituals*. Tuscaloosa and London: University Alabama Press, 2000.

Gardner, Jane. *Roman Myths*. Austin: University of Texas Press, 1993.

Graf, Fritz. *Greek Mythology: An Introduction*. Translated by Thomas Marier. Baltimore, MD: The Johns Hopkins University Press, 1996.

Holland, Glen. *Gods of the Desert: Religions of the Ancient Near East*. Lanham, MD: Rowman & Littlefield, 2010.

Midgley, M. *The Myths We Live By*. London and New York: Routledge, 2004.

Snell, Daniel C. *Religions of the Ancient Near East*. Cambridge: Cambridge University Press, 2011.

Van de Mieroop, Marc. *A History of the Ancient Near East ca. 3000–323 BC*. Malden, MA, and Oxford: Blackwell 2007.

CHAPTER 2: CREATION

2.1 HISTORY: A GREEK CREATION STORY

Buxton, R. (ed.). *From Myth to Reason? Studies in the Development of Greek Thought*. Oxford: Oxford University Press, 1999.

Clay, Jenny Strauss. *Hesiod's Cosmos*. Cambridge: Cambridge University Press, 2009.

Cline, Eric H. *1177 BC: The Year Civilization Collapsed*. Princeton, NJ: Princeton University Press, 2014.

Dickinson, Oliver. *The Aegean from Bronze Age to Iron Age*. London and New York: Routledge Press, 2006.

Edwards, Anthony T. *Hesiod's Ascra*. Berkeley and Los Angeles: University of California Press, 2004.

Hall, Jonathan. *A History of the Archaic Greek World: ca. 1200–479 BCE*. Malden, MA, and Oxford: Wiley-Blackwell, 2006.

Lamberton, Robert. *Hesiod*. New Haven, CT: Yale University Press, 1988.

Pomeroy, S. B., et al. *Ancient Greece: A Political, Social, and Cultural History*. 3rd ed. Oxford: Oxford University Press, 2001.

Scott, Michael. *Delphi and Olympia: The Spatial Politics of Panhellenism in the Archaic and Classical Periods*. Cambridge: Cambridge University Press, 2010.

Sproul, Barbara C. *Primal Myths: Creation Myths around the World*. New York: Harper One, 1979.

Thomas, Carol G., and Craig Conant. *Citadel to City-State*. Bloomington and Indianapolis: Indiana University Press, 1999.

2.2 THEORY: THE SOCIAL WORLD SHAPES MYTH

Doty, William G. *Mythography: The Study of Myths and Ritual*. Tuscaloosa and London: University of Alabama Press, 2001.

Strenski, Ivan (ed.). *Malinowski and the Work of Myth*. Princeton, NJ: Princeton University Press, 1992.

2.3 COMPARISON: LEVANT: CREATION STORIES

Alter, Robert. *The Art of Biblical Narrative*. New York: Basic Books, 1981.

Bremmer, Jan. *Greek Religion and Culture, the Bible and the Ancient Near East*. Leiden, the Netherlands: Brill, 2008.

Burkert, Walter. *Babylon, Memphis, Persepolis: Eastern Contexts of Greek Culture*. Cambridge, MA: Harvard University Press, 2004.

———. *The Orientalizing Revolution: Near Eastern Influence on Greek Culture in the Early Archaic Age*. Translated by Margaret Pinder. Cambridge, MA: Harvard University Press: 1998.

Campbell, Antony F., and Mark O'Brien. *Sources of the Pentateuch: Texts, Introductions, Annotations*. Minneapolis, MN: Augsburg Fortress Press, 1993.

Harrison, Jane Ellen. *Mythology*. New York: Harcourt Brace, 1924.

Niditch, Susan. *Chaos to Cosmos: Studies in Biblical Patterns of Creation*. Chico, CA: Scholars Press, 1985.

Puhvel, Jaan. *Comparative Mythology*. Baltimore, MD: The Johns Hopkins University Press, 1989.

2.4 RECEPTION: TITANS IN MODERN ART

Bremmer, Jan N. "Remember the Titans!" In: *The Fall of Angels*. Edited by Christopher Auffarth and Loren T. Stuckenbruck, pp. 35–61. Leiden, the Netherlands: Brill, 2004.

Okrent, Daniel. *The Great Fortune: The Epic of Rockefeller Center*. New York: Penguin Books, 2004.

Roussel, Christine. *The Art of Rockefeller Center*. New York: W.W. Norton, 2005.

CHAPTER 3: **ZEUS AND HERA**

3.1 HISTORY: ORDER AND REBELLION

Cook, A. B. *Zeus: A Study in Ancient Religion.* Cambridge: Cambridge University Press, 1914.

Deacy, Susan, and Karen F. Pierce (eds.). *Rape in Antiquity: Sexual Violence in the Greek and Roman Worlds.* London: The Classical Press of Wales, 1997.

Dowden, K. *Zeus.* New York and London: Routledge, 2006.

Farnell, Lewis Richard. *The Cults of the Greek States.* Vol. 1. Oxford: Oxford University Press, 1896.

Kampen, N. B. (ed.). *Sexuality in Ancient Art.* Cambridge: Cambridge University Press, 1996.

Kerenyi, C. *Zeus and Hera: Archetypal Image of Father, Husband and Wife.* Princeton, NJ: Princeton University Press, 1975.

Lalonde, G. V. *Horos Dios: An Athenian Shrine and Cult of Zeus.* Leiden, the Netherlands, and Boston: Brill Academic, 2006.

Langdon, M. K. *A Sanctuary of Zeus on Mount Hymettus.* Princeton, NJ: American School of Classical Studies, 1976.

Larson, J. *Ancient Greek Cults: A Guide.* New York and London: Routledge, 2007.

Lefkowitz, Mary R. "'Predatory' Goddesses." *Hesperia* 71:4 (2002): 325–344.

Lloyd-Jones, P. H. J. *The Justice of Zeus.* Berkeley and Los Angeles: University of California Press, 1971.

Munn, M. *The Mother of the Gods, Athens and the Tyranny of Asia: A Study in the Sovereignty in Ancient Religion.* Berkeley and Los Angeles: The University of California Press, 2006.

O'Brien, Joan V. *The Transformation of Hera: A Study of Ritual, Hero, and the Goddess in the Iliad.* Lanham, MD: Rowman & Littlefield, 1993.

Omitowoju, Rosanna. *Rape and the Politics of Consent in Classical Athens.* Cambridge: Cambridge University Press, 2002.

Yasumura, Norika. *Challenges to the Power of Zeus in Early Greek Poetry.* London: Bristol Classical Press, 2011.

3.2 THEORY: UNIVERSAL QUESTIONS SHAPE MYTH

Doniger, Wendy. *The Implied Spider: Politics and Theology in Myth.* New York: Columbia University Press, 1998.

Doniger, Wendy, and Laurie Patton (eds.). *Myth and Method.* Charlottesville and London: University Press of Virginia, 1996.

O'Flaherty Doniger, Wendy. *Other Peoples' Myths: The Cave of Echoes.* New York and London: Macmillan, 1988.

3.3 COMPARISON: LEVANT: FLOOD STORIES

Burkert, W. *Babylon, Memphis, Persepolis: Eastern Contexts of Greek Culture.* Cambridge, MA, and London: Harvard University Press, 2004.

Campbell, A. F. and M. A. O'Brien. *Sources of the Pentateuch: Texts, Introductions, Annotations.* Minneapolis: Fortress Press, 1993.

Cohn, Norman. *Noah's Flood: The Genesis Story in Western Thought.* New Haven, CT, and London: Yale University Press, 1999.

Dalley, S. *Myths from Mesopotamia: Creation, the Flood, Gilgamesh and Others.* Oxford and New York: Oxford University Press, 1993.

Davies, P. R., and J. Rogerson. *The Old Testament World.* 2nd ed. Louisville, KY: Westminster John Know Press, 2005.

Frymer-Kensky, T. "The Atrahasis Epic and Its Significance for Our Understanding of *Genesis* 1–9." *The Biblical Archaeologist* 40 (1977): 147–155.

Noth, M. *A History of Pentateuchal Traditions.* Translated by Bernhard W. Anderson. Englewood Cliffs, NJ: Prentice-Hall Inc., 1972 (1948).

Rabin, E. *Understanding the Hebrew Bible: A Reader's Guide.* Jersey City, NJ: KTAV Publishing House, 2006.

Shaviv, Samuel. "The Polytheistic Origins of the Biblical Flood Narrative." *Vetus Testamentum* 54 (2004): 527–548.

Smith, M. S. *God in Translation: Cross-Cultural Recognition of Deities in the Biblical World.* Tubingen, Germany: Mohr Siebeck, 2008.

West, S. "Prometheus Orientalized." *Museum Helveticum* 51 (1994): 129–149.

3.4 RECEPTION: LEDA AND THE SWAN
IN MODERNIST POETRY

Cullingford, Elizabeth Butler. *Gender and History in Yeats' Love Poetry.* Cambridge: Cambridge University Press, 1993.

Davidson Reid, Jane. "Leda, Twice Assaulted." *Journal of Aesthetics and Art Criticism* 11:4 (June 1953): 378–382.

Elliott, Bridget. "The 'Strength of the Weak' as Portrayed by Marie Laurencin." In: *On Your Left: The New Historical Materialism, Genders 24*, pp. 69–109. New York: New York University Press, 1996.

Feder, Lillian. *Ancient Myth in Modern Poetry.* Princeton, NJ: Princeton University Press, 1971.

H.D. (Hilda Doolittle). *Collected Poems, 1912–1944.* New York: New Directions, 1983.

Neigh, Janet. "Reading from the Drop: Poetics of Identification and Yeats' 'Leda and the Swan.'" *Journal of Modern Literature* (2006): 145–160.

Sword, Helen. "Leda and the Modernists." *PMLA* 107 (1992): 305–318.

CHAPTER 4: **DEMETER AND HADES**

4.1 HISTORY: LIFE AND DEATH

Bremmer, Jan N. *The Early Greek Concept of the Soul.* Princeton, NJ: Princeton University Press, 1983.

Farnell, Richard. *The Cults of the Greek States.* Vol. 3. Oxford: Clarendon Press, 1896–1909.

Foley, Helene P. *The Homeric Hymn to Demeter: Translation, Commentary, and Interpretative Essays.* Princeton, NJ: Princeton University Press, 1993.

Garland, Robert. *The Greek Way of Death.* Ithaca, NY: Cornell University Press, 2001 (1995).

Parca, Maryline, and Angeliki Tzanetou (eds.). *Finding Persephone: Women's Rituals in the Ancient Mediterranean.* Bloomington: Indiana University Press, 2007.

Richardson, N. J. *The Homeric Hymn to Demeter.* Oxford: Oxford University Press, 1979.

Sourvinou-Inwood, Christiane. *"Reading" Greek Death: To the End of the Classical Period.* Oxford: Clarendon Press, 1995.

4.2 THEORY: MYTHS REINFORCE SOCIAL NORMS

Blundell, Sue. *Women in Ancient Greece.* Cambridge, MA: Harvard University Press, 1995.

Foley, Helene P. "A Question of Origins: Goddess Cults Greek and Modern." In: *Women, Gender, Religion: A Reader.* Edited by E. A. Castelli. 193–215. New York: Palgrave, 2001.

Goff, Barbara. *Citizen Bacchae: Women's Ritual Practice in Ancient Greece.* Berkeley and Los Angeles: California University Press, 2004.

Hawley, Richard, and Barbara May Levick. *Women in Antiquity: New Assessments.* London and New York: Routledge Press, 1995.

Parca, Maryline, and Angeliki Tzanetou (eds.). *Finding Persephone: Women's Rituals in the Ancient Mediterranean.* Bloomington: Indiana University Press, 2007.

4.3 COMPARISON: MESOPOTAMIA: A SUMERIAN MOTHER GODDESS

Bottéro, Jean. *Religion in Ancient Mesopotamia.* Translated by Teresa Lavender Fagan. Chicago: University of Chicago Press, 2001.

Jacobsen, Thorkild (trans.). *The Harps that Once . . . Sumerian Poetry in Translation.* New Haven, CT: Yale University Press, 1987.

Jacobsen, Thorkild. *The Treasures of Darkness: A History of Mesopotamian Religion.* New Haven, CT: Yale University Press, 1978.

Kramer, Samuel Noah. *Sumerian Mythology.* Philadelphia: University of Pennsylvania Press, 1998.

Penglase, Charles. *Greek Myths and Mesopotamia: Parallels and Influence in the Homeric Hymns and Hesiod.* New York and London: Routledge Press, 1994.

4.4 RECEPTION: PERSEPHONE IN CONTEMPORARY WOMEN'S POETRY

Dove, Rita Frances. *Mother Love.* New York: Norton, 1995.

Gluck, Louise. *Averno.* New York: Farrar, Straus and Giroux, 2006.

House, Veronica. *Medea's Chorus: Myth and Women's Poetry since 1950.* New York: Peter Lang, 2014.

Lifshin, Lyn. *Persephone.* Los Angeles, CA: Red Hen Press, 2008.

Townsend, Alison. *Persephone in America.* Carbondale: Southern Illinois Press, 2009.

Zucker, Rachel. *Eating in the Underworld.* Middletown, CT: Wesleyan University Press, 2003.

CHAPTER 5: **APHRODITE, HEPHAESTUS, AND ARES**

5.1 HISTORY: LOVE AND STRIFE

Breitenberger, Barbara. *Aphrodite and Eros: The Development of Erotic Mythology in Early Greek Poetry and Culture.* New York and London: Routledge, 2007.

Budin, Stephanie Lynn. *The Myth of Sacred Prostitution in Antiquity.* Cambridge: Cambridge University Press, 2008.

Crudden, Michael (trans.). *The Homeric Hymns.* Oxford: Oxford University Press, 2001.

Cyrino, Monica S. *Aphrodite.* New York and London: Routledge, 2010.

Farnell, Richard. *The Cults of the Greek States.* Vol. 2. Oxford: Clarendon Press, 1896–1909.

Kondoleon, Christine, et al. *Aphrodite and the Gods of Love.* Boston and New York: MFA, 2011.

Larson, Jennifer. *Ancient Greek Cults.* New York and London: Routledge Press, 2007.

Ludwig, Paul W. *Eros and Polis: Desire and Community in Greek Political Theory.* Cambridge: Cambridge University Press, 2002.

Oliver, James H. *Demokratia, the Gods and the Free World.* New York: Arno Press, 1979.

Smith, Amy C., and S. Pickup (eds.). *Brill's Companion to Aphrodite.* Leiden, the Netherlands: Brill, 2010.

Rosenzweig, Rachel. *Worshipping Aphrodite: Art and Cult in Classical Athens.* Ann Arbor: University of Michigan Press, 2004.

5.2 THEORY: MYTHS CHALLENGE SOCIAL NORMS

Ortner, Sherry. *Making Gender: The Politics and Erotics of Culture.* Boston: Beacon Press, 1996.

Winkler, John J. *The Constraints of Desire: The Anthropology of Sex and Gender in Ancient Greece.* New York and London: Routledge Press, 1990.

5.3 COMPARISON: MESOPOTAMIA: ISHTAR

Bolger, Diane, and Nancy Serwint. *Engendering Aphrodite: Women and Society in Ancient Cyprus.* Boston: American Schools of Oriental Research, 2002.

Budin, Stephanie Lynn. *The Origin of Aphrodite.* Bethesda, MD: CDL, 2003.

Dalley, Stephanie (trans.). "The Descent of Ishtar to the Underworld." In: *Myths from Mesopotamia.* Translated by Stephanie Dalley. Oxford: Oxford University, 1998.

Faulkner, Andrew. *The Homeric Hymn to Aphrodite: Introduction, Text, and Commentary.* Oxford: Oxford University Press, 2008.

Goodison, Lucy, and Christine Morris. *Ancient Goddesses: The Myths and the Evidence.* Madison: University of Wisconsin Press and British Museum Press, 1999.

Karageorghis, Jacqueline. *Kypris: The Aphrodite of Cyprus: Ancient Sources and Archaeological Evidence.* Nicosia, Cyprus: A. G. Leventis Foundation, 2005.

5.4 RECEPTION: PYGMALION IN HOLLYWOOD

Cukor, George (director). *My Fair Lady.* CBS Warner, 1964.

Gillespie, Craig (director). *Lars and the Real Girl.* MGM and Sidney Kimmel Entertainment, 2007.

James, Paula. *Ovid's Myth of Pygmalion on Screen: In Pursuit of the Perfect Woman.* London and New York: Bloomsbury Academic, 2011.

Marshall, Garry (director). *Pretty Woman.* Buena Vista/Touchstone, 1990.

CHAPTER 6: **ATHENA AND POSEIDON**

6.1 HISTORY: WISDOM AND WAR

Barber, E. J. W. "The Peplos of Athena." In: *Goddess and Polis: The Panathenaic Festival.* Edited by Jennifer Neils, pp. 103–118. Princeton, NJ: Princeton University Press, 1992.

Deacy, Susan. *Athena.* New York and London: Routledge, 2008.

Deacy, Susan, and Alexandra Villing (eds.). *Athena in the Classical World.* Leiden, the Netherlands: Brill, 2001.

Detienne, Marcel, and Jean-Pierre Vernant. *Cunning Intelligence in Greek Culture and Society.* Translated by Janet Lloyd. Chicago: Chicago University Press, 1974.

Farnell, Lewis Richard. *The Cults of the Greek States.* Vol. 1. Oxford: Clarendon Press, 1896.

Larson, Jennifer. *Ancient Greek Cults: A Guide.* New York and London: Routledge, 2007.

Loraux, Nicole. *Born of the Earth: Myth and Politics in Athens.* Translated by Selina Stewart. Ithaca, NY: Cornell University Press, 2000.

———. *The Children of the Athena.* Translated by Caroline Levine. Princeton, NJ: Princeton University Press, 1994.

Neils, Jennifer (ed.). *Worshipping Athena.* Wisconsin: University of Wisconsin Press, 1996.

Otto, Walter F. *The Homeric Gods: The Spiritual Significance of Greek Religion.* Translated by Moses Hadas. London: Thames and Hudson, 1954.

Thompson, Wesley. "Weaving: A Man's Work." *Classical World* 75 (1982): 217–222.

6.2 THEORY: THE MIND STRUCTURES MYTH IN OPPOSITIONS

Leach, Edmund R. *Claude Lévi-Strauss.* Chicago: University of Chicago Press, 1970.

Lévi-Strauss, Claude. *Myth and Meaning: Cracking the Code of Culture.* New York: Schocken Books, 1995.

———. "The Structural Study of Myth." *Journal of American Folklore* 68 (1955): 428–444.

Segal, Erich R. (ed.). *Structuralism in Myth: Levi-Strauss, Barthes, Dumezil, and Propp.* London and New York: Routledge, 1996.

Zeitlin, Froma. "The Dynamics of Misogyny: Myth and Mythmaking in the *Oresteia.*" *Arethusa* 2 (1978): 149–181.

6.3 COMPARISON: EGYPT: NEITH

Assman, Jan. *The Search for God in Ancient Egypt.* Translated by David Lorton. Ithaca, NY: Cornell University Press, 2001.

Austin, M. M. *Greece and Egypt in the Archaic Age.* Cambridge: Cambridge University Press, 1970.

Baines, John. "Egyptian Myth and Discourse: Myths, Gods, and the Early Written and Iconographic Record." *Journal of Near Eastern Studies* 50 (1991): 81–105.

Bernal, Martin. *Black Athena: The Afro-Asiatic Roots of Classical Civilization.* Vols. 1–3. New Brunswick, New Jersey: University of Rutgers Press, 1991–2006.

Boardman, John. *The Greeks Overseas.* New York and London: Thames and Hudson, 1999.

Hart, George. *Egyptian Myths.* Austin: University of Texas Press, 1990.

Lesko, Barbara S. *The Great Goddesses of Egypt.* Norman, University of Oklahoma Press, 1999.

Lloyd, Alan B. *Herodotus Book II: Introduction.* Leiden, the Netherlands: Brill, 1975.

McClain, Brett. "Cosmogony (Late to Ptolemaic and Roman Periods)." In: *UCLA Encyclopedia of Egyptology,* 1(1). Edited by Willeke Wendrich. UCLA: Department of Near Eastern Languages and Cultures, nelc_uee_7976. Los Angeles, CA, 2011. Retrieved from: https://escholarship.org/uc/item/8tf3j2qq, July 1, 2015.

Traunecker, Claude. *The Gods of Egypt.* Translated by David Lorton. Ithaca, NY: Cornell University Press, 2001.

Van Binsbergen, Wim M. J. (ed.). *Black Athena Comes of Age: Towards a Constructive Re-Assessment.* Berlin: LIT Verlag, 2011.

6.4 RECEPTION: ATHENA AS A POLITICAL ALLEGORY

Florman, Lisa. "Gustav Klimt and the Precedent of Ancient Greece." *The Art Bulletin* 72 (1990): 310–326.

Harden, J. David. "Liberty Caps and Liberty Trees." *Past & Present* 146 (1995): 66–102.

Korshak, Yvonne. "The Liberty Cap as a Revolutionary Symbol in America and France." *Smithsonian Studies in American Art* 1 (1987): 52–69.

Lazarus, Emma. *The Poems of Emma Lazarus.* New York: Houghton, Mifflin, 1888.

Marom, Daniel. "Who Is the 'Mother of Exiles'? An Inquiry into the Jewish Aspects of Emma Lazarus' 'The New Colossus.'" *Prooftexts* 20 (2000): 231–261.

Warner, Marina. *Monuments and Maidens: The Allegory of the Female Form.* Berkeley and Los Angeles: University of California Press, 1985.

CHAPTER 7: HERMES AND HESTIA

7.1 HISTORY: FROM HERMS TO HERMES

Athanassakis, Apostolos. "From the Phallic Cairn to Shepherd God and Divine Herald." *Eranos* 87 (1989): 33–49.

Brown, Norman Oliver. *Hermes the Thief.* Madison: University of Wisconsin Press, 1947.

Burkert, Walter. *Greek Religion.* Translated by John Raffan. Cambridge, MA: Harvard University Press, 1985.

Clay, Jenny Strauss. *Politics of Olympus: Form and Meaning in the Major Homeric Hymns.* Bristol, UK: Bristol Classical Press, 2006.

Farnell, Lewis Richard. *The Cults of the Greek States.* Vol. 5. Oxford: Oxford University Press, 1909.

Johnston, Sarah Iles. "Myth, Festival and Poet: The 'Homeric Hymn to Hermes' and Its Performative Context." *CP* 97 (2002): 109–132.

Johnston, Richard W., and David Mulroy. "The Hymn to Hermes and the Athenian Altar of the Twelve Gods." *CW* 103 (2009): 3–16.

Larson, Jennifer. *Ancient Greek Cults: A Guide.* London and New York: Routledge Press, 2007.

Marinatos, Nanno. "Striding across Boundaries: Hermes and Aphrodite." In: *Initiation in Ancient Greek Rituals and Narratives.* Edited by David B. Dodd and Christopher A. Faraone, pp. 130–152. New York and London: Routledge Press, 2003.

Osborne, Robin. "The Erection and Mutilation of the Hermai." *PCPhS* 211, n.s. 31 (1985): 47–73.

Otto, Walter F. *The Homeric Gods: The Spiritual Significance of Greek Religion.* Translated by Moses Hadas. London: Thames and Hudson, 1954.

Quinn, Josephine Crawley. "Herms, Kouroi, and the Political Anatomy of Athens." *Greece and Rome* 54 (2007): 82–102.

Vernant, Jean-Pierre. *Myth and Thought among the Greeks.* Translated by Janet Lloyd and Jeff Fort. Cambridge, MA: Zone Books, 1983.

Versnel, Hank S. *Coping with the Gods: Wayward Readings in Greek Theology.* Leiden, the Netherlands: Brill Academic, 2011.

7.2 THEORY: THE MIND STRUCTURES MYTH IN ARCHETYPES

Brown, Norman Oliver. *Hermes the Thief.* Madison: University of Wisconsin Press, 1947.

Doxey, Denise M. S.v. "Thoth." In: *The Oxford Encyclopedia of Ancient Egypt.* Edited by Donald B. Redford. Oxford: Oxford University Press, 2001, 2005.

Gates, Henry Louis. *The Signifying Monkey: A Theory of African-American Literary Criticism.* Oxford: Oxford University Press, 1989.

Hall, Calvin S., and Vernon J. Nordby. *A Primer of Jungian Psychology.* New York: Plume, 1973.

Hynes, William J., and William G. Doty (eds.). *Mythical Trickster Figures: Contours, Contexts and Criticisms.* Tuscaloosa and London: University of Alabama Press, 1993.

Jung, Carl Gustav. *The Archetypes and the Collective Unconscious.* Translated by R. F. C. Hull. Princeton, NJ: Princeton University Press, 1981.

Radin, Paul. *The Trickster: A Study in American Indian Mythology.* New York: Schocken Books, 1976 (1956).

Reesman, Jeanne Campbell (ed.). *Trickster Lives: Culture and Myth in American Fiction.* Athens: University of Georgia Press, 2001.

Segal, Robert A. *Jung on Mythology.* Princeton, NJ: Princeton University Press, 1998.

7.3 COMPARISON: EGYPT: THOTH

Bleeker, Claas Jonco. *Hathor and Thoth: Two Key Figures of the Ancient Egyptian Religion.* Leiden, the Netherlands: Brill Academic, 1973.

Boylan, Patrick. *Thoth, the Hermes of Egypt.* Oxford: Oxford University Press, 1922.

Fowden, Garth. *The Egyptian Hermes: A Historical Approach to the Late Pagan Mind.* Princeton, NJ: Princeton University Press, 1993.

Richter, Daniel S. "Plutarch on Isis and Osiris: Text, Cult, and Cultural Appropriation." *TAPHa* 131 (2001): 191–216.

Stadler, Martin A. "Thoth." In: *UCLA Encyclopedia of Egyptology,* 1(1). Edited by Willeke Wendrich. UCLA: Department of Near Eastern Languages and Cultures. nelc_uee_8802. Los Angeles CA, 2012. Retrieved from: https://escholarship.org/uc/item/2xj8c3qg. July 1, 2015.

Versnel, Hank S. "Mercurius amongst the 'Magni Dei.'" *Mnemosyne* 27:2 (1974): 144–151.

7.4 RECEPTION: HERMAPHRODITUS IN PRE-RAPHAELITE ART

Ajootian, Aileen. "Monstrum or Daimon: Hermaphrodites in Ancient Art and Culture." In: *Greece & Gender.* Edited by B. Berggreen and Nanno Marinatos, pp. 93–108. Athens: The Norwegian Institute at Athens, 1995.

———. "The Only Happy Couple: Hermaphrodites and Gender." In: *Naked Truths: Women, Sexuality and Gender in Classical Art and Archaeology.* Edited by Ann Olga Koloski-Ostrow and Claire L. Lyons, pp. 220–242. London and New York: Routledge, 1997.

Bermúdez, José Luis. "The Concept of Decadence." In: *Art and Morality*. Edited by José Luis Bermúdez and Sebastian Gardner. 111–130. London and New York: Routledge Press, 2003.

Brisson, Luc. *Sexual Ambivalence: Androgyny and Hermaphroditism in Graeco-Roman Antiquity*. Translated by Janet Lloyd. Berkeley and Los Angeles: University of California Press, 2002.

Bullen, J. B. *The Pre-Raphaelite Body: Fear and Desire in Painting, Poetry, and Criticism*. Oxford: Oxford University Press, 1998.

Cooper, Emmanuel. *The Sexual Perspective: Homosexuality and Art in the Last 100 Years in the West*. New York and London: Routledge Press, 2008.

Delcourt, Marie. *Hermaphrodite: Myths and Rites of the Bisexual Figure in Classical Antiquity*. Translated by Jennifer Nicholson. London: Studio Books, 1961.

Lupack, Barbara Tepa. *Illustrating Camelot*. Rochester, NY: Boydell & Brewer, 2008.

Ostermark-Johansen, Lene. "Between the Medusa and Pygmalion." *Victorian Literature and Culture* 38 (2010): 21–37.

Pacteau, Francette. "The Impossible Referent: Representations of the Androgyne." In: *Formations of Fantasy*. Edited by Victor Burgin, James Donald, and Caplan Kaplan, pp. 62–84. London and New York: Routledge, 1986.

Pease, Allison. "Questionable Figures: Swinburne's *Poems and Ballads*." *Victorian Poetry* 35:1 (1997): 43–56.

Seagroatt, Heather. "Swinburne Separates the Men from the Girls: Sensationalism in *Poems and Ballads*." *Victorian Literature and Culture* 30:1 (2002): 41–59.

Swinburne, Algernon Charles. "Hermaphroditus." In: *Poems and Ballads & Atalanta in Calydon*. Edited by Kenneth Haynes, pp. 65–66. London: Penguin Books, 2000.

CHAPTER 8: **ARTEMIS AND APOLLO**

8.1 HISTORY: FROM ADOLESCENCE TO ADULTHOOD

Calame, Claude. *Choruses of Young Women in Ancient Greece: Their Morphology, Religious Role and Social Function*. Translated by Derek Collins and Jane Orion. Lanham, MD: Rowman & Littlefield, 1997.

Cole, Susan Guettel. "The Social Function of Rituals of Maturation: The Koureion and the Arkteia." *ZPE* 55 (1984): 233–244.

Detienne, Marcel. "Forgetting Delphi between Apollo and Dionysus." *Classical Philology* 96 (2001): 147–158.

Dowden, Ken. *Death and the Maiden: Girls' Initiation Rites in Greek Mythology*. London and New York: Routledge, 1989.

Faraone, Christopher A. "Playing the Bear and the Fawn for Artemis: Female Initiation or Substitute Sacrifice?" In: *Initiation in Ancient Greek Rituals and Narratives*. Edited by David B. Dodd and Christopher A. Faraone, pp. 43–68. London and New York: Routledge, 2003.

Farnell, Lewis Richard. *The Cults of the Greek States*. Vol. 4. Oxford: Oxford University Press, 1907.

Fischer-Hansen, Tobias, and Birte Poulsen. *From Artemis to Diana: The Goddess of Man and Beast*. Copenhagen: Museum Tusculanum Press, 2009.

Graf, Fritz. *Apollo*. London and New York: Routledge, 2009.

Larson, Jennifer. *Ancient Greek Cults: A Guide*. London and New York: Routledge, 2007.

Lloyd-Jones, Hugh. "Artemis and Iphigenia." *JHS* 103 (1983): 87–102.

Newton, Michael. *Savage Girls and Wild Boys: A History of Feral Children*. New York: St. Martin's Press, 2003.

Otto, Walter F. *The Homeric Gods: The Spiritual Significance of Greek Religion*. Translated by Moses Hadas. London: Thames and Hudson.

Perlman, Paula. "Acting the She-Bear for Artemis." *Arethusa* 22 (1989): 111–134.

Pettersson, Michael. *Cults of Apollo at Sparta: The Hyakinthia, the Gymnopaidai and the Karneia*. Stockholm: Svenska Institutet I Athen, 1992.

Sourvinou-Inwood, Christiane. *Studies in Girls' Transitions: Aspects of the Arkteia and Age Representation in Attic Iconography*. Athens: Kardamitsa, 1988.

Steel, Karl. "With the World, or Bound to Face the Sky: The Postures of the Wolf-Child of Hesse." In: *Animal, Vegetable, and Mineral: Ethics and Objects*. Edited by Jeffrey Jerome Cohen, pp. 9–34. Washington, DC: Oliphaunt Books, 2012.

Vernant, Jean-Pierre. *Mortals and Immortals: Collected Essays*. Edited by Froma I. Zeitlin. Princeton, NJ: Princeton University Press, 1991.

8.2 THEORY: MYTH, RITUALS, AND INITIATIONS

Burkert, Walter. *Home Necans: The Anthropology of Ancient Greek Ritual and Myth*. Berkeley and Los Angeles: University of California Press, 1983.

Deflem, Matheieu. "Ritual, Anti-Structure, and Religion: A Discussion of Victor Turner's Processual Symbolic Analysis." *Journal for the Scientific Study of Religion* 30 (1991): 1–25.

Doty, William G. *Mythography: The Study of Myths and Rituals*. Tuscaloosa and London: The University of Alabama Press, 2000.

Graf, Fritz. "Initiation: A Concept with a Troubled History." In: *Initiation in Ancient Greek Rituals and Narratives*. Edited by David B. Dodd and Christopher A. Faraone, pp. 3–24. London and New York: Routledge, 2003.

Lincoln, Bruce. *Emerging from the Chrysalis: Studies in Rituals of Women's Initiation*. Cambridge, MA: Harvard University Press, 1981.

Van Gennep, Arnold. *Rites of Passage*. Translated by Monica B. Vizedon and Garielle L. Caffee. Chicago: University of Chicago Press, 1960.

8.3 COMPARISON: ANATOLIA AND ROME: CYBELE

Brenk, Frederick E. "Artemis of Ephesos: An Avant Garde Goddess." *Kernos* 11 (1998): 157–171.

Brown, Edwin L. "In Search of Anatolian Apollo." *Hesperia Supplements* 33 (2004): 243–257.

Collins, Billie Jean. "Hero, Field Master, King: Animal Mastery in Hittite Texts and Iconography." In: *The Master of Animals in Old World Iconography*. Edited by Derek B. Counts and Bettina Arnold, pp. 59–74. Budapest: Archaeolingua Alapitvany, 2010.

Collins, Billie Jean, Mary R. Bachvarova, and Ian C. Rutherford (eds.). *Anatolian Interfaces: Hittites, Greeks and Their Neighbours*. Oxford: Oxbow, 2010.

Dietrich, B. C. "Late Bronze Age Troy: Religious Contacts with the West: Common Functions and Background." *Historia: Zeitschrift fur Alte Geschichte* 29 (1980): 498–503.

———. "Some Evidence from Cyprus of Apolline Cult in the Bronze Age." *Rheinisches Museum fur Philologie* 121 (1978): 1–18.

Guterbock, Hans G. "Troy in Hittite Texts? Wilusa, Ahhiyaya and Hittite History." In: *Troy and the Trojan War: A Symposium Held at Bryn Mawr College, October 1984*. Edited by Machteld J. Mellink, pp. 33–44. Bryn Mawr, PA: Bryn Mawr College, 1986.

Koester, Helmut (ed.). *Ephesos Metropolis of Asia: An Interdisciplinary Approach to Its Archaeology, Religion, and Culture*. Valley Forge, PA: Trinity Press International, 1995.

LiDonnici, Lynn R. "The Images of Artemis Ephesia and Greco-Roman Worship: A Reconsideration." *Harvard Theological Review* 85 (1992): 389–415.

Payne, Annick. "Lycia—Crossroads of Greek and Hittite Traditions?" In: *Papers on Ancient Literatures: Greece, Rome and the Near East*. Edited by E. Cingano and L. Milano, pp. 471–488. Padova: S.A.R.G.O.N, 2008.

Rogers, Guy M. *The Sacred Identity of Ephesus: Foundation Myths of a Roman City*. New York and London: Routledge, 1991.

Roller, Lynn E. *In Search of God the Mother: The Cult of Anatolian Cybele*. Berkeley, Los Angeles, and London: University of California Press, 1999.

Solomon, Jon (ed.). *Apollo: Origins and Influence*. Tucson and Arizona: University of Arizona Press, 1994.

West, Martin L. *The East Face of Helicon: West Asiatic Elements in Greek Poetry and Myth*. Oxford: Clarendon Press, 1999.

8.4 RECEPTION: ACTAEON AND DAPHNE IN CONTEMPORARY POETRY

Brown, Sarah Annes. *Ovid: Myth and Metamorphosis*. London: Bristol Classical Press, 2005.

Fowler, Rowena. "'This Tart Fable': Daphne and Apollo in Modern Women's Poetry." In: *Laughing with Medusa: Classical Myth and Feminist Thought*. Edited by Vanda Zajko and Miriam Leonard, pp. 381–398. Oxford: Oxford University Press, 2008.

Heath, John. *Actaeon: The Unmannerly Intruder: The Myth and Its Meaning in Classical Literature*. New York: Peter Lang, 1992.

Warner, Marina. *Fantastic Metamorphoses, Other Worlds: Ways of Telling the Self*. Oxford: Oxford University Press, 2002.

CHAPTER 9: DIONYSUS

9.1 HISTORY: ENCOUNTERING DIONYSUS

Bernabe, Alberto, M. Herrero de Jauregui, A. I. Jimenez San Cristobal, and R. Hernandez Martin (eds.). *Redefining Dionysus*. Berlin and Boston: De Guyter, 2013.

Bremmer, Jan. "Greek Maenadism Reconsidered." *ZPE* 55 (1984): 267–286.

Burkert, Walter. *Ancient Mystery Cults*. Cambridge, MA: Harvard University Press, 1987.

Carpenter, Thomas H., and C. Faraone (eds.). *Masks of Dionysus*. Ithaca, NY: Cornell University Press, 1993.

Detienne, Marcel. *Dionysus Slain*. Translated by Mireille Mullner and Leonard Muellner. Baltimore, MD: Johns Hopkins Press, 1979.

Heinrichs, Albert. "Changing Dionysiac Identities." In: *Jewish and Christian Self-Definition 3: Self-Definition in the Graeco-Roman World*. Edited by Ben F. Meyer and E. P. Sanders, pp. 137–160. London: SCM Press, 1982.

———. "Greek Maenadism from Olympias to Messalina." *HSCP* 82 (1978): 121–160.

———. "Loss of Self, Suffering, Violence: The Modern View of Dionysus from Nietzsche to Girard." *HSCP* 88 (1984): 205–240.

Kraemer, Ross S. "Ecstasy and Possession: The Attraction of Women to the Cult of Dionysus." *HThR* 72 (1979): 55–80.

McGinty, Park. *Interpretation and Dionysus*. The Hague, the Netherlands: Mouton, 1978.

Meyer, Marvin W. (ed.). *The Ancient Mysteries: A Sourcebook of Sacred Texts*. Philadelphia: University of Pennsylvania Press, 1999.

Otto, Walter F. *Dionysus: Myth and Cult*. Translated by Robert B. Palmer. Dallas, TX: Spring, 1993 (1965).

Schlesier, Renate (ed.). *A Different God? Dionysus and Ancient Polytheism*. Berlin and Boston: De Guyter, 2011.

Seaford, Richard. *Dionysos*. London and New York: Routledge, 2006.

Zeitlin, Froma I. "Playing the Other: Theater, Theatricality and the Feminine in Greek Drama." *Representations* 11 (1985): 63–94.

9.2 THEORY: INITIATIONS AND INVERSIONS

Babcock, Barbara A., and Macaloon, John J. "Commemorative Essay: Victor W. Turner (1920–1983)." *Semiotica* 65 (1987): 1–28.

Edsjo, Dag Oistein. "To Lock Up Eleusis: A Question of Liminal Space." *Numen* 47 (2000): 351–386.

Hoffmann, Richard J. "Ritual License and the Cult of Dionysus." *Athenaeum* 77 (1989): 91–115.

Turner, Victor. *The Anthropology of Performance.* New York: PAJ, 1986.

———. "Betwixt and Between: The Liminal Period in Rites of Passage." In: *Forest of Symbols.* Edited by Victor Turner. 93–111 Ithaca, NY: Cornell University Press, 1967.

———. *The Ritual Process: Structure and Anti-Structure.* Ithaca, NY: Cornell University Press, 1968.

9.3 COMPARISON: ANATOLIA AND ROME: CYBELE AND ATTIS

Bogh, Birgitte. "The Phrygian Background of Kybele." *Numen* 54 (2007): 304–339.

Bremmer, Jan N. "Attis: A Greek God in Anatolian Pessinous and Catullan Rome." *Mnemosyne* 57 (2004): 534–573.

Lancelotti, Maria Grazia. *Attis between Myth and History: King, Priest and God.* Leiden, the Netherlands: Brill 2002.

Roller, Lynn E. *In Search of God the Mother: The Cult of Anatolian Cybele.* Berkeley: University of California Press, 1999.

Roscoe, Will. "Priests of the Goddess: Gender Transgression in Ancient Religion." *History of Religions* 35 (1996): 195–230.

9.4 RECEPTION: DIONYSUS AS A GOD OF THE 1960S

Aviram, Amittai F. "Postmodern Gay Dionysus: Dr. Frank N. Furter." *Journal of Popular Culture* 26:3 (2004): 183–192.

Boe, John. "Don't Dream It, Be It: *The Rocky Horror Picture Show* as Dionysian Revel." *The San Francisco Jung Institute Library Journal* 4 (1983): 63–65.

Brecht, Stefan. "'Dionysus in 69' from Euripides' 'The Bacchae,'" *The Drama Review TDR* 13:3 (1969): 156–168.

De Palma, Brian. *Dionysus in 69.* 1970. In: *Hemispheric Institute Digital Video Library,* New York University. Permalink: http://hdl.handle.net/2333.1/mcvdncsq, July 1, 2015.

Hall, Edith, F. MacIntosh, and A. Wrigley (eds.). *Dionysus since 69: Greek Tragedy at the Dawn of the Third Millennium.* Oxford: Oxford University Press, 2005.

Reverman, Martin. "The Appeal of Dystopia: Latching onto Greek Drama in the Twentieth Century." *Arion* 3s, 16:1 (2008): 97–118.

Soyinka, Wole. *The Bacchae of Euripides: A Communion Rite.* New York: W.W. Norton, 2004 (1973).

Wetmore, Kevin J. *The Athenian Sun in an African Sky.* Jefferson, NC: McFarland, 2002.

Zeitlin, Froma I. "Re-Reading Dionysos in the Theater." In: *A Different God? Dionysos and Ancient Polytheism.* Edited by Renate Schlesier, pp. 535–554. Berlin: De Gruyter, 2011.

CHAPTER 10: **ACHILLES: THE MAKING OF A HERO**

10.1 HISTORY: DEFINING GREEK HEROES

Albersmeier, Sabina (ed.). *Heroes: Mortals and Myths and in Ancient Greece.* Baltimore, MD: The Walters Art Museum, 2009.

Antonaccio, Carla M. *An Archaeology of Ancestors: Tomb Cult and Hero Cult in Early Greece.* Lanham, MD: Rowman and Littlefield, 1994.

Burgess, J. S. *The Death and Afterlife of Achilles.* Baltimore, MD: The Johns Hopkins University Press, 2009.

Edmunds, L. "The Cults and Legend of Oedipus." *Harvard Studies in Classical Philology* 85 (1981): 221–238.

Foley, J. M. (ed.). *A Companion to Ancient Epic.* Malden, MA, and Oxford: Blackwell, 2005.

Graf, F. "Medea, the Enchantress from Afar: Remarks on a Well-Known Myth." In: *Medea.* Edited by James J. Clauss and Sarah Iles Johnston, pp. 21–43. Princeton, NJ: Princeton University Press, 1997.

Levy, G. R. *The Sword from the Rock: An Investigation into the Origins of Epic Literature and the Development of the Hero.* London: Faber and Faber, 1953.

Nagy, G. *The Ancient Greek Hero in 24 Hours.* Cambridge, MA, and London: Belknap Press of Harvard University, 2013.

———. *The Best of the Achaeans: Concepts of the Hero in Archaic Greek Poetry.* Rev. ed. Baltimore, MD: The Johns Hopkins University Press, 1999.

Price, T. H. "Hero Cult and Homer." *Zeitschrift fur Alte Geschichte* 22 (1973): 129–144.

Stafford, Emma. *Herakles.* New York and London: Routledge, 2012.

Visser, Margaret. "Worship Your Enemy: Aspects of the Cult of Heroes in Ancient Greece." *The Harvard Theological Review* 75 (1982): 403–428.

Walker, Henry J. *Theseus and Athens.* Oxford: Oxford University Press, 1995.

Whitley, James. "The Monuments that Stood before Marathon: Tomb Cult and Hero Cult in Archaic Athens." *American Journal of Archaeology* 98 (1994): 213–230.

10.2 THEORY: THE PLOT OF THE HERO'S STORY

Dundes, Alan. "Binary Opposition in Myth: The Propp/Levi-Strauss Debate in Retrospect." *Western Folklore* 56 (1997): 39–50.

Propp, V. *Theory and History of Folklore.* Translated by A. Y. Martin and R. P. Martin. Edited with an introduction and notes by Anatoly Liberman. Minneapolis: University of Minnesota Press, 1984.

Segal, Robert A. (ed.). *Structuralism in Myth: Levi-Strauss, Barthes, Dumezil, and Propp.* New York and London: Routledge, 1996.

10.3 COMPARISON: MESOPOTAMIA AND ROME: GILGAMESH AND AENEAS

Feldman, Louis H. "Homer and the Near East: The Rise of the Greek Genius." *The Biblical Archaeologist* 59 (1996): 13–21.

Foley, J. M. (ed.). *A Companion to Ancient Epic.* Malden, MA, and Oxford: Blackwell, 2005.

Foster, B. R. (trans. and ed.). *The Epic of Gilgamesh.* New York and London: W.W. Norton, 2001.

Green, Thomas. "The Norms of Epic." *Comparative Literature* 13 (1961): 193–207.

Harris, William V. *Restraining Rage: The Ideology of Anger Control in Classical Antiquity.* Cambridge, MA: Harvard University Press, 2001.

King, Katherine Callen. *Ancient Epic.* Malden, MA, and West Sussex, UK: Blackwell-Wiley, 2009.

Konstan, David. "The Passion of Achilles and Aeneas: Translating Greece into Rome." *Electronic Antiquity* 14 (2010): 7–22.

Levy, G. R. *The Sword from the Rock: An Investigation into the Origins of Epic Literature and the Development of the Hero.* London: Faber and Faber, 1953.

Van Wees, Hans. *Status Warriors: War, Violence and Society in Homer and History.* Amsterdam: J C Gieben, 1992.

Westenholz, J. G. "Heroes of Akkad." *Journal of the American Oriental Society* 103 (1983): 327–336.

10.4 RECEPTION: ACHILLES AND WAR POETRY

Graziosi, Barbara, and Emily Greenwood. *Homer in the Twentieth Century: Between World Literature and the Western Canon.* New York and London: Oxford University Press, 2007.

Jarrell, Randall. *The Complete Poems*, pp. 425–426. New York: Farrar, Straus and Giroux, 1981.

Longley, Michael. *The Ghost Orchid.* Winston-Salem NC: Wake Forest University Press, 1995.

Shay, Jonathan. *Achilles in Vietnam: Combat Trauma and the Undoing of Character.* New York: Simon and Schuster, 1994.

———. *Odysseus in America: Combat Trauma and the Trials of Homecoming.* New York: Scribner, 2002.

Vandiver, E. *Stand in the Trench, Achilles: Classical Receptions in British Poetry of the Great War.* New York and London: Oxford University Press, 2010.

CHAPTER 11: MEDEA: THE MAKING OF A HEROINE

11.1 HISTORY: DEFINING HEROINES

Albersmeier, Sabina (ed.). *Heroes: Mortals and Myths in Ancient Greece.* Baltimore, MD: The Walters Art Museum, 2009.

Clauss, J., and S. I. Johnston (ed.). *Medea: Essays on Medea in Myth, Literature and Philosophy.* Princeton, NJ: Princeton University Press, 1997.

Corti, L. *The Myth of Medea and the Murder of Children.* Westport, CT: 1998.

Griffiths, E. *Medea.* London and New York: Routledge, 2006.

Holland, L. L. "Last Act in Corinth: The Burial of Medea's Children (E. *Med.* 1378–83)." *Classical Journal* 103 (2008): 407–430.

Johnston, S. I. *Restless Dead: Encounters between the Living and the Dead in Ancient Greece.* Berkeley: University of California Press, 1999.

Larson, J. *Greek Heroine Cults.* Madison: University of Wisconsin Press, 1995.

Lyons, D. *Gender and Immortality: Heroines in Ancient Greek Myth and Cult.* Princeton, NJ: Princeton University Press, 1997.

Pache, Corinne O. *Baby Heroes and Child Heroes in Ancient Greece.* Urbana and Chicago: University of Illinois Press, 2004.

11.2 THEORY: THE PLOT OF THE HEROINE'S STORY

Segal, Robert A. (ed.). *In Quest of the Hero.* Princeton, NJ: Princeton University Press, 1990.

Somerset, FitzRoy Richard (Baron Raglan). "The Hero of Tradition." *Folklore* 45 (1934): 212–231.

11.3 COMPARISON: ROME: MEDEA

Benton, Cindy. "Bringing the Other to Stage: Seneca's Medea and the Anxieties of Imperialism." *Arethusa* 36 (2003): 271–284.

Clauss, J., and S. I. Johnston (ed.). *Medea: Essays on Medea in Myth, Literature and Philosophy.* Princeton, NJ: Princeton University Press, 1997.

Costa, C. D. N. (ed.). *Seneca: Medea.* Oxford: Clarendon Press, 1973.

Fyfe, H. "An Analysis of Seneca's Medea." In: *Seneca Tragicus: Ramus Essays on Senecan Drama.* Edited by A. J. Boyle, pp. 77–93. Berwick, Australia: Aureal, 1983.

Gessert, Genevieve. "Myth as Consolatio: Medea on Roman Sarcophagi." *Greece and Rome*, 2nd ser. 51 (2004): 217–249.

Guastella, Gianni. "Virgo, Coniunx, Mater: The Wrath of Seneca's Medea." *Classical Antiquity* 20 (2001): 197–220.

Nussbaum, Martha C. *The Therapy of Desire.* Princeton, NJ: Princeton University Press, 1996.

Pavlock, Barbara. *The Image of the Poet in Ovid's Metamorphoses.* Madison: University of Wisconsin Press, 2009.

11.4 RECEPTION: AFRICAN AMERICAN MEDEA

Corti, Lillian. "Countée Cullen's Medea." *African American Review* 32 (1998): 621–634.

Furth, Leslie. "'The Modern Medea' and Race Matters: Thomas Satterwhite Noble's 'Margaret Garner.'" *American Art* 12 (1998): 36–57.

Hatch, James V. *Sorrow Is the Only Faithful One: The Life of Owen Dodson.* Urbana: University of Illinois Press, 1995.

Hyman, Rebecca. "Medea of Suburbia: Andrea Yates, Maternal Infanticide, and the Insanity Defense." *Women's Studies Quarterly* 32 (2004): 192–210.

McElduff, Siobhán. "Epilogue: The Multiple Medeas of the Middle Ages." *Ramus* 41 (2012): 190–205.

Rankine, Patrice. *Ulysses in Black: Ralph Ellison, Classicism, and African American Literature.* Madison: Wisconsin Studies in Classics, 2008.

Reinhardt, Mark. "Who Speaks for Margaret Garner? Slavery, Silence, and the Politics of Ventriloquism." *Critical Inquiry* 29 (2002): 81–119.

Walters, Tracey L. *African American Literature and the Classicist Tradition: Black Women Writers from Wheatley to Morrison.* New York: Palgrave Macmillan, 2007.

Weisenberger, Steven. *Modern Medea: A Family Story of Slavery and Child-Murder from the Old South.* New York: Hill and Wang, 1999.

CHAPTER 12: ODYSSEUS AND QUEST HEROES

12.1 HISTORY: THE HERO'S QUEST

Bloom, Harold (ed.). *Odysseus/Ulysses.* New York and Philadelphia, PA: Chelsea House, 1991.

Brann, Eva. *Homeric Moments: Clues to Delight in Reading the Odyssey and the Iliad.* Philadelphia: Paul Dry Books, 2002.

Cohen, Beth (ed.). *The Distaff Side: Representing Females in Homer's Odyssey.* Oxford: Oxford University Press, 1995.

Cook, Erwin. "'Active' and 'Passive' Heroics in the *Odyssey*." *The Classical World* 93 (1999): 149–167.

Dougherty, Carol. *The Raft of Odysseus.* Oxford, Oxford University Press, 2001.

Finkelberg, Margalit. "Odysseus and the Genus Hero." *Greece and Rome*, 2nd ser. 42 (1995): 1–14.

Hogan, Patrick Holm. "The Epilogue of Suffering: Heroism, Empathy, Ethics." *Substance* 30 (2001): 119–143.

Said, Suzanne. *Homer and the Odyssey.* Oxford, Oxford University Press, 2011.

Schein, Seth L. (ed.). *Reading the Odyssey: Selected Interpretative Essays.* Princeton, NJ: Princeton University Press, 1995.

Van Nortwick, Thomas. *The Unknown Odysseus: Alternative Worlds in Homer's Odyssey.* Ann Arbor: University of Michigan Press, 2008.

12.2 THEORY: THE QUEST HERO

Campbell, J. *The Hero with a Thousand Faces.* Novato, CA: New World Library, 2008.

Crane, Gregory. "The *Odyssey* and the Conventions of the Heroic Quest." *Classical Antiquity* 6 (1987): 11–37.

Schweizer, Bernard, and Robert A. Segal (eds.). *Critical Insights: The Hero's Quest.* Ipswich, MA: Salem Press, 2013.

12.3 COMPARISON: MESOPOTAMIA AND ROME:
GILGAMESH AND AENEAS

Foley, John Miles (ed.). *A Companion to Ancient Epic.* Malden, MA, and Oxford: Wiley-Blackwell, 2005.

King, Katherine Callen. *Ancient Epic.* Malden, MA, and West Sussex, UK: Blackwell-Wiley, 2009.

Levy, G. R. *The Sword from the Rock: An Investigation into the Origins of Epic Literature and the Development of the Hero.* London: Farber and Farber, 1953.

12.4 RECEPTION: AFRICAN AMERICAN ODYSSEUS

Gabbin, Joanne V. *Sterling A. Brown: Building the Black Aesthetic Tradition.* Charlottesville and London: University of Virginia Press, 1994 (1985).

Hall, Edith. *The Return of Ulysses: A Cultural History of Homer's Odyssey.* Baltimore, MD: The Johns Hopkins University Press, 2008.

Hurston, Zora Neale. *Jonah's Gourd Vine; Mules and Men; Their Eyes Were Watching God.* New York: Quality Paperback Books, 1990.

Lock, Helen. "Zora Neale Hurston and the African American Odyssey." *Southern Cross Review* 77 (2011), online e-review.

Lupton, Mary Jane. "Zora Neale Hurston and the Survival of the Female." *The Southern Literary Journal* 15 (1982): 45–54.

McConnell, Justine. *Black Odysseys: The Homeric Odyssey in African Diaspora since 1939.* Oxford: Oxford University Press, 2013.

Miller, Shawn E. "'Some Other Way to Try': From Defiance to Creative Submission in *Their Eyes Were Watching*." *The Southern Literary Journal* 37 (2004): 74–95.

Morrison, Toni. *Conversations with Toni Morrison.* Edited by Danille Taylor-Guthrie, p. 26. Jackson: University Press of Mississippi, 1994.

O'Meally, Robert G. *Romare Bearden: A Black Odyssey.* New York: DC Moore Gallery, 2009.

Rankine, Patrice D. *Ulysses in Black: Ralph Ellison, Classicism, and African American Literature.* Madison: University of Wisconsin Press, 2006.

Rowell, Charles H. "'Let Me Be with Ole Jazzbo': An Interview with Sterling A. Brown." *Callaloo* 14 (1991): 795–815.

Sanders, Mark A. "Sterling A. Brown and the Afro-Modern Moment." *African American Review* 31 (1997): 393–397.

Tidwell, John Edgar, and Steven C. Tracy (eds.). *After Winter: The Art and Life of Sterling A. Brown.* Oxford: Oxford University Press, 2009.

CHAPTER 13: IPHIGENIA AND QUEST HEROINES

13.1 HISTORY: THE HEROINE'S QUEST

Alcock, S. E. "Tomb Cult and the Post-Classical Polis." *American Journal of Archaeology* 95 (1991): 447–467.

Brown, P. *The Cult of the Saints: Its Rise and Function in Late Christianity.* Chicago: University of Chicago Press, 1981.

Covington, C. "In Search of the Heroine." *Journal of Analytic Psychology* 34 (1989): 243–254.

Hall, E. *Adventures with Iphigenia in Tauris: A Cultural History of Euripides' Black Sea Tragedy.* Oxford: Oxford University Press, 2012.

Jones, C. P. *New Heroes in Antiquity: From Achilles to Antinoos.* Cambridge, MA: Harvard University Press, 2010.

Pearson, C., and Katherine Pope. *The Female Hero in American and British Literature.* New York and London: R.R. Bowker, 1981.

13.2 THEORY: A PARADIGM FOR THE NEW HEROINE

Byrne, Mark Levon. "Heroes and Jungians." *The San Francisco Jung Institute Library Journal* 18 (2000): 13–37.

Edwards, L. R. "The Labors of Psyche: Toward a Theory of Female Heroism." *Critical Inquiry* 6 (1979): 33–49.

————. *Psyche as Hero: Female Heroism and Fictional Form.* Middleton, CT: Wesleyan University Press, 1984.

13.3 COMPARISON: ROME: THECLA

Cooper, K. *Band of Angels: The Forgotten World of Early Christian Women.* New York: Overlook Press, 2013.

————. *The Virgin and the Bride: Idealized Womanhood in Late Antiquity.* Cambridge, MA: Harvard University Press, 1996.

Dunn, S. "The Female Martyr and the Politics of Death: An Examination of the Martyr Discourses of Vibia Perpetua and Wafa Idris." *Journal of the American Academy of Religion* 78 (2010): 202–225.

Elliott, J. K. *The Apocryphal Jesus: Legends of the Early Church.* Oxford: Oxford University Press, 1996.

Johnson, S. F. *The Life and Miracles of Thekla: A Literary Study.* Washington, DC: The Center for Hellenic Studies, 2006.

Kraemer, Ross Shepard. *Unreliable Witness: Religion, Gender, and History in the Greco-Roman Mediterranean.* Oxford: Oxford University Press, 2011.

Matthews, S. "Thinking of Thecla: Issues in Feminist Historiography." *Journal of Feminist Studies in Religion* 17 (2001): 39–55.

McClure, M. L., and **C. L. Feltoe** (ed. and trans.). *The Pilgrimage of Egeria.* New York: Macmillan, 1919.

Tilley, M. A. "Scripture as an Element of Social Control: Two Martyr Stories of Christian North Africa." *The Harvard Theological Review* 83 (1990): 383–397.

13.4 RECEPTION: TEN YEARS OF IPHIGENIA IN NEW YORK CITY

Bacalzo, D. "Iphigenia 2.0." *Theater Mania,* August 24, 2007.

Barall, M. *Rescue Me* (Premiere). Directed by Loy Arcena, starring Jennifer Ikeda as Iphigenia. Ohio Theater, New York, the Ma-Yi Theater Company. 2010.

Blankenship, M. "Get the Goddess a Coke." *TDF Stages,* April 2010.

Brantley, B. "The Face of Evil, All Peaches and Cream." *New York Times,* June 25, 1999.

Donovan, D. "Rescue Me." *Curtain Up: The Internet Theater Magazine of Reviews, Features, Annotated Listings,* April 2010.

Foley, H. P. *Imagining Greek Tragedy on the American Stage.* Berkeley and Los Angeles: University of California Press, 2012.

Hall, E. *Adventures with Iphigenia in Tauris: A Cultural History of Euripides' Black Sea Tragedy.* Oxford: Oxford University Press, 2012.

McCarter, J. "Sing, O Mash-Up." *New York Magazine,* September 10, 2007.

Mee, C. L. *Iphigenia 2.0* (Premiere). Directed by Tina Landau, starring Louisa Krause as Iphigenia. Signature Theater Company at the Peter Norton Space. 2007.

————. *The (Re)making Project.* http://www.charlesmee.org/about.shtml. July, 1, 2015.

Mee, Erin. "Shattered and Fucked Up and Full of Wreckage: The Words and Works of Charles L. Mee." *The Drama Review* 46 (2002): 83–104.

Sutton, B. "Greek Tragedy Gets a Heroic Rescue." *The L Magazine,* April 12, 2010.

Synder, D. "Rescue Me: Michi Barall Riffs on a Greek Myth—with Snacks for the Audience!" *New York Time Out,* April 6, 2010.

Zinoman, J. "Way before Lindsay and Britney, Chaos Swirled around Iphigenia." *New York Times,* August 27, 2007.

TEXT CREDITS

219: *The Homeric Hymns*, Michael Crudden, trans. Oxford University Press, 2009. By permission of Oxford University Press.

228: Copyright © 1990 from *The Constraints of Desire: the Anthropology of Sex and Gender in Ancient Greece*, John J. Winkler. Reproduced by permission of Taylor and Francis Group, LLC, a division of Informa plc.

237: Dalley, Stephanie. *Myths from Mesopotamia: Creation, The Flood, Gilgamesh, and Others*, Oxford University Press, 2009. By permission of Oxford University Press.

CHAPTER 6: **ATHENA AND POSEIDON**

247: Aeschylus, "Eumenides," *Aeschylus, The Oresteia*. Translated by Alan Shapiro and Peter Burian, Oxford University Press 2004. By permission of Oxford University Press USA.

260: Aeschylus, *The Oresteia*, Alan Shapiro and Peter Burian, trans. Oxford University Press, 2004. By permission of Oxford University Press.

269: From *Aeschylus: The Oresteia*, 2/e by Simon Goldhill. Copyright © 1992, 2004 Cambridge University Press. Reprinted with permission of Cambridge University Press.

276: Clagett, Marshall, ed. and trans. *Ancient Egyptian Science: A Source Book. Vol. 1, Part 2, Knowledge and Order*. Philadelphia: American Philosophical Society, 1989. Reprinted with permission.

281: Lazarus, Emma. "The New Colossus." *The Poems of Emma Lazarus*. New York: Houghton, Mifflin and Company.

CHAPTER 7: **HERMES AND HESTIA**

285: Excerpts from HOMERIC GODS by Walter F. Otto, translated by Moses Hadas, translation copyright © 1954 by Moses Hadas, renewed 1982 by Elizabeth Hadas. Used by permission of Pantheon Books, an imprint of the Knopf Doubleday Publishing Group, a division of Penguin Random House LLC. All rights reserved.

296: *The Homeric Hymns*, Michael Crudden, trans. Oxford University Press, 2009. By permission of Oxford University Press.

313: Excerpt from "Hermes Slips the Trap" from TRICKSTER MAKES THIS WORLD: MISCHIEF, MYTH AND ART by Lewis Hyde. Copyright © 1998 by Lewis Hyde. Reprinted by permission of Farrar Straus and Giroux, LLC.

324: Republished with permission from University of California Press. Lichtheim, Miriam, ed., *Ancient Egyptian Literature: The New Kingdom*. Copyright © 2006 University of California Press. Permission conveyed through Copyright Clearance Center, Inc.

326: Plato, *Phaedrus*, Robin Waterfield, trans. Oxford University Press, 2009. By permission of Oxford University Press.

328: Swinburne, Algernon Charles. "Hermaphroditus." *Poems and Ballads & Atalanta in Calydon*. Ed. Kenneth Haynes. London: Penguin Books, 2000.

CHAPTER 8: **ARTEMIS AND APOLLO**

335: From *Animal, Vegetable, Mineral: Ethics and Objects*, edited and translations by Jeffrey Jerome Cohen, Oliphaunt Books, an imprint of Punctum Books. Licenced under Creative Commons Licence 4.0 International, https://creativecommons.org/licenses/by-nc-sa/4.0/

349: *The Homeric Hymns*, Michael Crudden, trans. Oxford University Press, 2009. By permission of Oxford University Press.

358: *The Homeric Hymns*, Michael Crudden, trans. Oxford University Press, 2009. By permission of Oxford University Press.

363: Ken Dowden and Niall Livingstone, eds. *A Companion to Greek Mythology*, Copyright © Wiley-Blackwell, 2014.

374: Trzaskoma, Stephen M. (translator). *Two novels from Ancient Greece: Chariton's Callirhoe and Xenophon of Ephesos' An Ephesian Story: Anthia and Habrocomes*. Copyright © 2010 by Hackett Publishing Company Inc. Reprinted by permission of Hackett Publishing Company, Inc. All rights reserved.

381: A.E. Stallings. "Daphne" from *Archaic Smile*, 1999 University of Evansville Press.

382: Heaney, Seamus. "Actaeon." Patience Agbabi et al. (Ed.). *Metamorphosis: Poems Inspired by Titian*. London UK: National Gallery Company Ltd. © Estate of Seamus Heaney and reprinted by permission of the Estate and Faber and Faber Ltd.

383: Copyright © Don Paterson 2012. Reproduced by permission of the author c/o Rogers, Coleridge & White Ltd., 20 Powis Mews, London W11 1JN.

CHAPTER 9: **DIONYSUS**

387: Euripides, 'Bacchae', *Euripides Bacchae and Other Plays*, Translated by James Morwood. *Oxford World Classics*, 2008. By permission of Oxford University Press.

401: Euripides, *Euripides' Bacchae and Other Plays: Iphigenia among the Taurians; Bacchae; Iphigenia at Aulis; Rhesus*, James Morwood and Edith Hall, trans. Oxford University Press, 2008. By permission of Oxford University Press.

410: *The Homeric Hymns*, Michael Crudden, trans. Oxford University Press, 2009. By permission of Oxford University Press.

414: Csapo, Eric. "Riding the Phallus for Dionysus: Iconology, Ritual, and Gender-Role De/Construction," *Phoenix* 51, No. 3/4 (Autumn/Winter 1997): 253-295. Reprinted by permission of the author.

421: Catullus, *The Poems of Catullus*, Guy Lee, trans. Oxford University Press, 2009. By permission of Oxford University Press

CHAPTER 10: ACHILLES: THE MAKING OF A HERO

435: Pindar, *Pythian* 8.95 – 98. Translated by Lisa Maurizio.

435: Kerenyi, C. *The Heroes of the Greeks*. London: Thames and Hudson, 1981. Page 3.

453: Homer. *Iliad*, Barry B. Powell, trans. Oxford University Press, 2013. By permission of Oxford University Press.

470: MORPHOLOGY OF THE FOLKTALE, Second Edition, by Vladimir Propp, translated by Laurence Scott, Revised and Edited with a Preface by Louis A. Wagner, Copyright © 1968. Published University of Texas Press.

480: Dalley, Stephanie. *Myths from Mesopotamia: Creation, The Flood, Gilgamesh, and Others*, Oxford University Press, 2009. By permission of Oxford University Press.

486: Vergil, *Aeneid*, Frederick Ahl, trans. Oxford World Classics, 2008 reprint. Oxford University Press, 2008. By permission of Oxford University Press.

491: Shaw-Stewart, Patrick. "I Saw A Man This Morning." Vandiver, E. *Stand in the Trench, Achilles: Classical Receptions in British Poetry of the Great War*. New York and London: Oxford University Press, 2010.

493: "When Achilles Fought and Fell" from THE COMPLETE POEMS by Randall Jarrell. Copyright © 1969, renewed 1997 by Mary von S. Jarrell. Reprinted by permission of Farrar, Straus and Giroux, LLC.

493: From COLLECTED POEMS by Michael Longley. Published by Jonathan Cape. Reprinted by permission of The Random House Group Limited. AND, From *The Ghost Orchid* by Michael Longley, published in the US by Wake Forest University Press © 1994. "Ceasefire" was most recently published in *Collected Poems* in 2007.

CHAPTER 11: MEDEA: THE MAKING OF A HEROINE

497: Euripides, "Medea," *Euripides Medea and Other Plays*, Translated by James Morwood. *Oxford World Classics*, 2008. By permission of Oxford University Press.

499: Plutarch. *Moralia*. with an English Translation by Frank Cole Babbitt. Cambridge, MA. Harvard University Press. London. William Heinemann Ltd. 1936. volume 4. (section 293).

511: Euripides, *Medea and Other Plays by Euripides,* James Morwood, trans. Oxford University Press, 2009. By permission of Oxford University Press.

523: Reprinted with permission from *New York Folklore*, 10.2 (Fall/Winter 1984). Jezewski, Mary Ann, "Traits of the Female Hero: The Application of Raglan's Hero Trait Patterning."

529: Ovid, *Metamorphoses*, A.D. Melville, trans. Oxford University Press, 2009. By permission of Oxford University Press.

CHAPTER 12: ODYSSEUS AND QUEST HEROES

543: Harold Bloom, "Introduction" in *Odysseus/Ulysses*. New York and Philadelphia: Chelsea House Publishers, 1991. Pages 1–2.

562: Homer, *The Odyssey*, Barry Powell, trans. Oxford University Press, 2014. By permission of Oxford University Press.

574: "Ithaca" from C.P. CAVAFY: COLLECTED POEMS by C.P. Cavafy, translated by Daniel Mendelsohn, introduction, notes and commentary, and translation copyright ©2009 by Daniel Mendelsohn. Used by permission of Alfred A. Knopf, an imprint of the Knopf Doubleday Publishing Group, a division of Penguin Random House LLC. All rights reserved.

577: Auden, W.H. "The Quest Hero," *The Texas Quarterly* 4 (1961), pp. 81–93. Published by University of Texas Press. Reprinted with permission.

586: Vergil, *Aeneid*, Frederick Ahl, trans. Oxford World Classics, 2008 reprint. Oxford University Press, 2008. By permission of Oxford University Press.

590: Dalley, Stephanie. *Myths from Mesopotamia: Creation, The Flood, Gilgamesh, and Others*, Oxford University Press, 2009. By permission of Oxford University Press.

596: "The Odyssey of Big Boy," from THE COLLECTED POEMS OF STERLING A. BROWN, edited by MICHAEL S. HARPER. Copyright © 1980 by Sterling A. Brown. Reprinted by permission of the Estate of Sterling A. Brown.

600: Hurston, Zora Neale. from *Their Eyes Were Watching God* (1937).

CHAPTER 13: IPHIGENIA AND QUEST HEROINES

603: Carol Pearson and Katherine Pope, *The Female Hero in American and British Literature*, RR Bowker LLC, 1981. Reprinted with permission.

613: Euripides, *Euripides' Bacchae and Other Plays: Iphigenia among the Taurians; Bacchae; Iphigenia at*

Aulis; Rhesus, James Morwood and Edith Hall, trans. Oxford University Press, 2008. By permission of Oxford University Press.

625: Excerpts from *Psyche as Hero: Female Heroism and Fictional Form* by Edward R. Lee © 2000 published by Wesleyan University Press. Used by permission.

633: McClure, M.L. and C. L. Feltoe, ed. and trans. *The Pilgrimage of Egeria.* London: Society for Promoting Christian Knowledge, New York: Macmillan Co. 1919.

634: Elliott, J.K. *The Apocryphal Jesus: Legends of the Early Church,* Oxford University Press, 2008. By permission of Oxford University Press.

ART CREDITS

CHAPTER 1: CLASSICAL MYTHS AND CONTEMPORARY QUESTIONS

1.1: Erich Lessing/Art Resource, NY, ART200190.
1.2: Image copyright © The Metropolitan Museum of Art. Image source: Art Resource, NY, ART378594.
1.3: bpk, Berlin/Vorderasiatisches Museum, Staatliche Museen Berlin/Olaf M. Tessner/Art Resource, NY, ART478723.
1.4: Timothy McCarthy/Art Resource, NY, ART165537.
1.5: "The Realm of the Shades" ©Romare Bearden Foundation/Licensed by VAGA, New York, NY. Courtesy of DC Moore Gallery, New York.

CHAPTER 2: CREATION

2.1: Erich Lessing/Art Resource, NY, ART74681.
2.2: © RMN-Grand Palais/Art Resource, NY, ART154717.
2.3B: © Florin Stana/Shutterstock, 194965928.
2.4: Gianni Dagli Orti/The Art Archive at Art Resource, NY, AA379724.
2.5B: © f8grapher/Shutterstock, 138597086.
2.6: Alinari/Art Resource, NY, ART129980.
2.7: Staatliche Antikensammlungen und Glyptothek München. Photograph by Renate Kühling. S80 Beazley Archive number: 213977.
2.8: The J. Paul Getty Museum, Villa Collection, Malibu, California, 86.AE.169.
2.9: Staatliche Antikensammlungen und Glyptothek München. Photograph by Renate Kühling, 596.
2.10: Ashmolean Museum/The Art Archive at Art Resource, NY, AA566705.
2.11: Image copyright © The Metropolitan Museum of Art. Image source: Art Resource, NY, ART500336.
2.12: The New York Public Library/Art Resource, NY, ART497620.
2.13: Melvyn Longhurst/Alamy, E6RE48.
2.14: imageBROKER/Alamy, CY0A65.

CHAPTER 3: ZEUS AND HERA

3.1: Gianni Dagli Orti/The Art Archive at Art Resource, NY, AA389426.
3.2: © Vanni Archive/Art Resource, NY, ART382686.
3.3: bpk, Berlin /Antikensammlung, Staatliche Museen, Berlin, Germany /Ingrid Geske/Art Resource, NY, ART358210.
3.4: Scala/Ministero per i Beni e le Attività culturali/Art Resource, NY, ART407274.
3.5: Gianni Dagli Orti/The Art Archive at Art Resource, NY, AA389421.
3.6: Yale University Art Gallery/Art Resource, NY, ART325369.
3.7: Erich Lessing/Art Resource, NY, ART105413.
3.8: Nimatallah/Art Resource, NY, ART85617.
3.9: Erich Lessing/Art Resource, NY, ART204850.
3.10: Erich Lessing/Art Resource, NY, ART200891.
3.11: Erich Lessing/Art Resource, NY, ART21449.
3.13: © BnF, Dist. RMN-Grand Palais/Art Resource, NY, ART488780.
3.14: The Philadelphia Museum of Art/Art Resource, NY, ART318651. © Fondation Foujita/Artists Rights Society (ARS), New York/ADAGP, Paris 2015.

CHAPTER 4: DEMETER AND HADES

4.1: The J. Paul Getty Museum, Villa Collection, Malibu, California. 86.AE.680. The Theoi Project: Greek Mythology. Website © 2000-2011 Aaron Atsma
4.2: Erich Lessing/Art Resource, NY, ART200836.
4.3: bpk, Berlin/Antikensammlung, Staatliche Museum, Berlin /Johannes Laurentius/Art Resource, NY, ART 301136.
4.4: bpk, Berlin/Antikensammlung, Staatliche Museum, Berlin/Johannes Laurentius/Art Resource, NY, ART 301171.
4.5: © RMN-Grand Palais/Art Resource, NY, ART 147733.
4.6: Alfredo Dagli Orti/The Art Archive at Art Resource, NY, AA356430.
4.7: bpk, Berlin/Antikensammlung, Staatliche Museum, Berlin/Johannes Laurentius/Art Resource, NY, ART450592.
4.8: HIP/Art Resource, NY, AR9146068.
4.9: Nimatallah/Art Resource, NY, ART18.
4.10: bpk, Berlin /Vorderasiatisches Museum, Staatliche Museen, Berlin, Germany/Olaf M.Teßmern/Art Resource, NY, ART497597.
4.11: Janet Gorzegno.

CHAPTER 5: APHRODITE, HEPHAESTUS, AND ARES

5.1: RISD Museum, Museum Appropriation Fund 25.089.
5.2: Erich Lessing/Art Resource, NY, ART58590.
5.3: Gianni Dagli Orti/The Art Archive at Art Resource, NY, AA393928.
5.4: Museum of Fine Arts, Boston, Massachusetts, USA/ Francis Bartlett Donation/Bridgeman Images, BST487717.

CHAPTER 6: **ATHENA AND POSEIDON**

CHAPTER 7: **HERMES AND HESTIA**

CHAPTER 8: **ARTEMIS AND APOLLO**

CHAPTER 9: **DIONYSUS**

GLOSSARY/INDEX